Who Lies Wins

A novel based on actual judgments in Britain's family court

Parental alienation arising from disputed hearings in family-court is a devastating problem affecting millions of families around the world. Much as we addressed domestic violence several decades ago, we treat parental alienation as a domestic issue rather than what it is; a problem affecting communities, school systems, police and court systems, mental-health and financial institutions, and crucially, legislative bodies. Our social, cultural and legal systems sanction and even promote parental alienation at the expense of our children's wellbeing. Malicious Mother syndrome is now a recognized condition, causing child abuse, often at a developmental stage that will leave a lifelong mark on the child of a disputed family-law judgment. This calamitous situation grows progressively worse while legislation exists to encourage and incentivize members of family-law to profit from the easy money family-court offers avaricious, amoral members of family-law to litigate. We all agree that financially motivated litigation is never in the child's best interests and always benefits the family-law members, yet no checks and boundaries exist to prevent the abuse of children by inappropriately qualified '*judges*' being played by greed motivated members, almost always reflecting gender prejudice in the process.

Who Lies Wins *is based on an actual case in Britain's family court that took place in April 2015. A disputed hearing brought by one parent, a practicing member of family-law, who followed an ambush separation by removing the four-year-old child from his home, concealing the new address and blackmailing the other parent for visitation. Opposing the heartbroken parent's family-court application for visitation by transparent abuse of legal process, and then bringing a malicious claim for 'beneficial entitlement' based on blackmail in the absence of any evidence. The story includes detailed correspondence from the case revealing the sordid underbelly of deceit enabled by arcane British family-law legislation. A process where many members, unrestrained by the ethical code published by the Solicitors Regulation Authority, or even the basic ethical standards of humanity, profit handsomely by creating and exploiting the misery of children. A legal system with no working appeals process and no accountability for members thanks to the protection offered to them by contempt laws.*

"Who lies wins" is a work of fiction. Names, characters, places, and incidents either exist solely as a product of the author's imagination or are used fictitiously. Although its form is that of an autobiography, it is more than that. Space and time, fact and fiction have been arranged to suit the flow of the story. Current statutes from British family-law are referenced and this information is freely available via the Law Society's web site and the internet. The published views from CAFCASS, including that '*100% of cases disputed in family court involve parental alienation and child abuse*' are considered public domain. Without limiting the rights under copyright reserved above, no part of this publication may be reproduced, stored or introduced into a retrieval system, or transmitted, in any form or by any means (electronic, mechanical, photocopying, recording or otherwise) without the prior written permission of the publisher of this book.

ISBN: 9781688766013

Dedication

This book is dedicated to my son who would still be with me
but for corrupt family-law members and the
deafening silence from Britain's ministry of justice.

The picture you drew of your family for fathers day, 2013. The last thing you ever gave me.
That's Mummy, Daddy, Evan, your brother, beautiful Maria looking down and William your dog.

ACKNOWLEDGMENTS

"We live in an age where lawyers destroy justice." Michael Ellner

"Thieves walking in broad daylight." David Byrne

"This is a shameful past, in which a prevailing culture of secrecy and self-protection led to unnecessary suffering for many victims and their families." Fact

"Children deserve to know the truth. No parent should be protected by any law concealing their child harming actions from the affected child." Fact

"The epidemic of family-court child-abuse must change. End cronyism. End protection for dishonest incompetent members by arcane contempt legislation. Make family-law member miscreants accountable where judgments harm children. Remove child-based decisions from the criminal arena that is a court room; and from a criminal legal process designed for trained prosecutors to harass murderers and rapists in a 'beyond all reasonable doubt' adaptation allowing for opinion-based judgments representing considerable doubt. Separating parents are not criminals. Respect the rights of the child to see both parents and not become embroiled in the Malicious Mother syndrome that so frequently accompanies and prospers from this criminal approach in adversarial court hearings. End the gender discrimination favoring Mothers as primary carers by default. Stop the child-abusing rot that grows in British family-law." Anonymous

"MotherFu#kers" Snoop Dog

CONTENTS

Foreword

Breaking up is hard to do, but when there are children involved, breaking up is something else. Parental separation affects one third of children in the UK. More than 30% of British children are left at the mercy of separating parents reaching agreement that is child centric. For those children who are not that fortunate, whose separating parents choose to place material benefit above their child's best interests and choosing to litigate, the family-court service gets to pass judgment for their future. Sadly, this is the same family court service where the CEO of CAFCASS, Anthony Douglas, has observed that "*100% of the children involved in disputed cases are subject to parental alienation and child abuse*." That number is approximately 10,000 children per annum in the UK.

Details of Family court judgments and the abuse they visit on children remain largely secretive. An unapproachable unpleasant taboo subject protected by its own anonymity-assuring legal statutes. To date, I have not found one single prosecution against a member of family-law in an area where it is clear hundreds of thousands of children have been abused. It remains the case that an accomplished family-law solicitor working in London can expect £500 (plus VAT at 20%) per hour. A good barrister mining that same family-court seam can expect £10,000 a day.

WHO LIES WINS is based on an actual story from family court about a child we shall call Sam and details how a number of miscreant members of family law conspired to place Sam's interests below their own remuneration, breaking their own laws in the process.
Paid to prey
  they disobey
    the laws they choose
      for child abuse
  Sam's story raises critical issues regarding the state of British family-courts regard for children's rights during parental separation. We examine the sustainability of the current process; with Judges sitting in court rooms applying arcane adversarial legal principles, historically established to prosecute hardened criminals, like murderers where children become victims of judgments predicated on criminal law. At its very heart, family law determining matters relating to a child's interests cannot proceed in this type of adversarial court-based system. There is a better way and it's not hard to understand. Parents, vulnerable at the time of family breakdown, find their visitation opportunities dependent on a process of financial demand that includes cross examination by aggressively trained, slick money-motivated legal professionals skilled at winning maximum amounts in courts operating without sensitivity or even basic regard, for children's rights to see both parents. Fueling animosity between parents in these cases where the advice from family-law itself is to "*avoid increasing animosity between parents because it is 'never in the child's best interests*".

Guidance that is overridden in 100% of disputed cases in the interests of making rewarding punitive judgments against one parent for the benefit of the other. A process that invariably ends up harming the child. Abusing the child's rights to see both parents without being drawn into the hostility that acrimonious litigation represents. We continue to allow a court system where an unregulated judge can place monetary reward for one parent above the child's right to see the losing parent, without needing to take into account an appeals process. Because we allow family court judges to make un-appealable judgments. And when this reality is disclosed in pursuit of a principle called justice, even the top level of law firm will not act in pursuit of justice without first receiving extortionate payment. It is routine practice that a family court judge can make a judgment based exclusively on opinion, absent of both any evidence or any experiential familiarity with the particular subject matter guiding that opinion. In the current British family law system, any family court judge can make an opinionated, evidence free judgment that is un-appealable, conveniently sidestepping the checks and balances we expect in a fair and transparent judiciary. As a consequence of which, children's lives are effectively ruined while members of family law all get paid. Family court, on a good day for members of family-law, is a child abusing scam, by analogy, like taking candy from a baby.

This story focuses specifically on one deputy district court family-judge, whom we shall call Cecelia Flaherty, who made an un-appealable judgment that blighted the life of child, seemingly beyond repair, flaunting the regulatory guidelines in place for this process with reckless abandon, before braggadiciously repairing for 'champagne and fun' on social media, using her name and position for self-aggrandizement. Cecelia Flaherty was a last-minute switch judge, whose judgment was determined before the court doors opened, leading to costs consequences for one parent, who did not choose to break up the family unit and was the primary-carer for the child, measured in the millions; and the end of a young boy's life with that parent. For good measure, this judgment by Judge Flaherty awarded costs against the losing parent, the defendant. Over £500,000 of legal charges rewarding the litigant parent who chose to break up the family (romancing his sexually irresistible fitness instructor) and pursue damages for doing so, including obstructing visitation as a lever for financial benefit, all costs for bringing the claim to court; along with 8% interest until payment. Co incidentally, the winning litigant parent who chose to sue in family-court instead of allowing the child to see both his parents, is a member of family law. As is the switch judge, Cecelia Flaherty, whose means motive and opportunity in the judgment are clear along with the consequences of that judgment, written six years later with the benefit of hindsight.

It is common guidance from the regulatory body for Judges in family court that; '*punitive judgments fuel animosity between parents. Causing increased animosity harms the child's relationship with both parents.*' Knowing that and still persisting with acrimony generating judgments that are demonstrably wrong, is willful child abuse. Unless we apply child-centric reform to family-law we will look back in 25 years-as complicit in enabling a system that abuses the children it is intended to protect. This reform will not come from within family-law. It would be counter intuitive for family-law to remove itself. The momentum for change must come from government action, representing the will of the people.

My experience of family-law has been very similar to blind-siding violent rape. The product of extreme deliberate aggressive malice. It left the emotional scars of forceful vicious rape and not a gender specific rape, as you will read later in the book in the letter from the ministry of justice confirming how family courts do not favor by gender. By their account, the Ministry of Justice write in 2019 that even a woman, as is the case in this story, can experience the worst of prejudice without having concern for any prejudice by gender by family-court judges trusted to make appeal-free judgments. Although many Fathers claim family-law discriminates in favor of the Mother, we have Malicious Mother Syndrome as a researched condition to back up this common experience from victims of family-court, we must accept the ministry of justice determination that judges do not discriminate in favor of the Mothers. It is just coincidence that no one is researching malicious Father syndrome. When it comes to feeling raped by family court, there is no gender discrimination. Of course you need only ask the last 1,000 victims of Britain's family court to see how right the MOJ is. Almost exactly 50% of men won the child? No gender discrimination.

The biggest challenge in writing this gender-neutral book about that life changing attack has been believing these events actually happened. And reliving the bitter injustice of a child abusing process of larceny the consequence of which is:

That I no longer see my son. Removed from my life by deceit and blackmail.

That my son has lost the largest part of his childhood with me that can never be replaced.

That I can no longer live in my home in my home country as a result of a family court judgment.

That I no longer have my primary source of income, a business built up over 30 years of work and investment. Not even 1%.

That no one has gone to jail for the conduct you will read about including but not limited to; Corruption, deceit, larceny, perjury, child-abuse, fiduciary failures, insurance fraud, abuse of office and serial breaches of the Solicitors Regulation Authority ethical code.

That there is no avenue towards bringing the miscreants to accountability because the Ministry of Justice operate a blind-eye denial system that has been working for decades.

It sounds too implausibly far-fetched to be a work of fiction. For this reason I apologize in advance for the long-windedness of the read ahead. I could not just summarize the past 6 years in a brief recollection of *what, where, when and how.* With a dash of means, a mash of motive and a splash of opportunity.

Along with my apology for the time this book will take you to absorb, I offer the assurance that the letters I have chosen to include in this 'whistleblowing' context form but a mere iceberg tip of the volume of legal correspondence that came at me from the members of family-law. The lengthy disclosures serve to measure the extent of the fight I put up for my sons benefit, to alert those responsible for the sanctity of law in the United Kingdom of irregularity. I hope the ends in this case justify the means and I thank you for your time investment in reading. It will have been worth both of our whiles if it leads to improved opportunities for children at the mercy of family law.

Essentially what lies ahead forms three sections.

The **first** will establish my life and personal growth experience prior to any involvement with family law. To establish whether my life experience prepared me to be a good parent, with a value system worth passing on to a child; or not.

The **second** is the ten-year period in which I was a partner in family-law. The inner workings of Family law in Surrey and in London. Living with my solicitor partner, who I housed as a trainee solicitor unable to make ends meet on £35K PA when we met, until he left, on fathers-day, as a millionaire owner of his own law firm.

And the **third**, the meat and vegetables of the story, deals with the six years since fathers-day 2013. And that is where you will need to set aside some free time to follow the legal arguments that make family law, statistically by number, the greatest danger to children in the UK. Sir Jimmy Savile may be gone but young children involved in disputed hearings still have family court judges to contend with.

The spoiler alert is; you will see how only significant legislative amendments will fix a system that ruins the lives of millions around the world, those former colonies whose legislation is based on the British model of family-law. Who take their lead from British law.

We can change the future for ten thousand British children whose lives are blighted by family-court judgments every year. And following on from that, hundreds of thousands more world-wide just by removing the veil of secrecy protecting family-law members and applying common sense decisions in legislation protecting children's rights. To stop production at the misery factory that is family-court.

British family-court is a broken system where opportunists ruin lives in the shadows, safe in knowing their contempt laws continue protecting their entitlement as members of family law in a model that is the same all over the world with only very few exceptions.

1   Where do I begin

The timeline. From Johannesburg to Thameside.   1985 up to 2003

Commonly there is a binary explanation for everything and personalities are no exception. Some people are motivated by doing good for others. And some are selfish. For some greed is paramount. For others the gift is in the giving. Essentially, everything comes down to one of two possibilities. The eternal struggle between light and dark. Let's start this story there.

Philotimia is a Greek word for a concept that is common in the character of every traditionally raised Greek. In Greek culture, you either have philotimia, or you do not. Literally philotimia translates between *'friend of honor'* and *'love of honor'*. In practice, philotimia is acting for the highest good in awareness of kindness and honor. For traditionally raised Greeks, philotimia is considered to be the highest of all virtues, setting the standards for family and social living; based on apportioning an ethical measure to all decisions in pursuit of the highest good. In its simplest form, the term means "doing good"; taking actions that reflect exemplary behavior and demonstrate the personality and the manner in which one was raised. *Philotimia* to a Greek is essentially a way of life. I know no other culture where such value is attached to the simple act of kindness. I think of it as placing the pursuit of truthfulness as paramount. A belief which places dishonesty at the base of all that is worst in human nature. That is the constant element through this story. The struggle between one version of honesty and the value of dishonesty in a process where the measure of truth resides with one person's opinion, free from any accountability checks.

As Professor Boole's binary logic makes clear. You either are or you are not. It is all down to one of two possibilities. You are either honest or you are not. A fact untouched by the opinion of a dishonest person. Of course, not all Greeks manifest philotimia as anyone watching the annual Athens derby between Olympiakos and Panathinaikos will attest. But equally as any visitor to Greece will also know, many Greeks are the kindest, warmest most hospitable generous people imaginable. A country of 10 million who took in 2.5 million Syrian refugees following the religious Civil war there.

I think of myself a Greek first and a take pride in my familiarity and relationship with philotimia. Growing up in a Greek home in Johannesburg through the seventies I was indoctrinated with this idea that above all, the measure of my success would be to demonstrate philotimia. It made sense to me from the beginning of my awareness. After all, what could be more important than kindness and learning enough to know how to do the right thing. It left me with an advanced sense of the value in justice. And the dangers attached to injustice. And why silence in the face of injustice is not an option. Binary conclusion? Justice, representing the highest good, is crucial. Injustice cannot be allowed to stand.

Learning how to learn was my first lesson.

I felt that after an early start in this process I had learned something valuable and when I became aware of the value in my learning process; I wanted to share what I have learned. What I took away from my Greek childhood and study of Greek culture was that philotimia runs through the Greek DNA. In my case, it was emphasized above all else from my earliest awareness of action and consequence and has all of my life made me aware that philotimia drives my life choices. The truth has always been at the fore of my quest for knowledge. Certainly it made a career in music – making people happy – a good choice. Initially my work would be pleasing people. Like any performing musician. A pleaser. The reward is in the giving. The truth is obvious in the moment. You play as best you can and people react spontaneously, usually with joyful applause. Happier for being a part of the experience than they would have been otherwise. A simple truth. So let's start this story on the basis that I was raised as a Greek, in a middle class South African experience where there was some trauma arising from profound loss at age ten, providing an early opportunity to learn about the meaning of life and its possibilities outside of the cocoon of a stable family unit, but with a firm awareness and appreciation for philotimia.

The consequences embracing the value in this philotimia, developing into a lifestyle based on pursuing my own truth, beginning with understanding happiness as the product of making others happy. A choice that has been both rewarding; in that I have never wavered from helping those I was able to help which has earned me considerable goodwill and gratitude both personally and socially. But, remembering Boole again, for every upside there is a downside. What was never made clear in my Greek kindness-based upbringing is that helping and harming are often the same thing. Where there is a kindness motivated yen there is inevitably a thieving yin waiting to pounce. I made it to the age of 45 before I learned just how wretched the consequences of helping the wrong person can be. And at that point I had a four-year-old child at the center of my world, the focus of all that I had learned. In terms of the want factor any negotiator identifies in winning an adversarial negotiation, I had one great weakness. I loved my child enormously and would do anything to provide for his best interests. Exactly as you would expect from a loving parent who chose to have a child later in life, twenty years after the first, and raise the child as a stay home parent.

Here is the timeline of my story.

1965. I was born Greek, but grew up in South Africa. I am fluent in Greek. It is the language of my intuitive education. The programming in my DNA. I learned about religion through Greek orthodoxy. My dreams were in Greek throughout my childhood. English is the language of my schooling, my education and my life experience.

1975. I experienced profound loss when one parent died suddenly and the other disappeared in a fog of depression. I was ten and learned to raise myself. And found the bright side in the early experience giving me a head start on developing critical thought.

1985 I left South Africa and I moved to London. Both to escape the unkind barbaric political climate in South Africa as well as to pursue my ambitions to live with freedom-of-speech and opportunity, with like-minded people in the Europe of my ancestors. Where I could learn and share my truth without fear of censure. I arrived at

Heathrow with my boyfriend from South Africa, Paul Smith. We planned our escape together. We had £3,000 between us and the address of Pauline, a friend of a friend, who lived in a village in Surrey we had both never heard of, called Weybridge. Pauline rented us a room for £50 per week providing an entry to a lovely bohemian lifestyle and the opportunity to find a lifestyle that suited our ethical aspirations. Pauline, who was some 20 years older than us, and loved to tell stories of the wonderful 60's Kings Road she grew up in; where she met Jimi Hendrix, and Mick Jagger, would frequently walk around nude. As if it was the most natural thing in the world. Which of course it is. Pauline was the best of a liberal English woman. Truthful. Compassionate and kind, funny and encouraging. My first new Age friend who modelled a way of living I had never even read about and provided a welcome landing place for our new life in England. As a new immigrant in a foreign country I recognized Pauline's approach as philotimia. English style.

Paul and I emigrated to the UK to escape the nastiness of South Africa's unsophisticated social order and through the tremendous good fortune that so frequently accompanies diligent work, found many wonderful kind people who appeared at just the right time, who made the transition easy. I had no idea where I was but it still felt like home. And I knew where I wasn't. Starting again in England in 1985 with a Greek passport, the benefits of being young and attractive, with boundless reserves of energy, a soft South African accent and a repertoire of original songs, a guitar and a reasonably professional demo tape was exciting rather than frightening. I was fortunate to find work, from the first week post arrival, as a musician, in studios and performing live in a solo show with guitar and voice. Just as long as I explained my accent was Greek and not South African. At that time racist prejudice against white South Africans ran strong. But I hit the ground running. I was booked for sessions in my first week and did my first paid gig 5 nights after arriving in the UK. Buffers wine bar in Weybridge paid me £25. The crowd had a blast and after that first memorable night I was very quickly as busy as I could be. For considerably more money.

1986 is next. The year I married Paul and bought my first property. Some six Months after arriving at Heathrow with everything I owned in a bag I could carry, on a rainy summers day I married the 'boy next door' from South Africa, Paul Smith, my boyfriend since the age of 16, when he was 18. My best friend and a very sexy young man. I had a Greek passport. He had a South African passport. England did not welcome South African passports. Greece was a half-member of the EU then and the passport provided EU rights of residence. A spousal visa was the sole possibility for Paul to remain in the UK. Although we had not planned to marry so young, or actually, ever, six months had passed and his visa was to expire. The Boolean conclusion was; either we stayed together, married, or he would have to return to South Africa. File that decision under philotimia. And I liked Paul. We did much of our growing up together. He didn't want to go back. I knew how he felt. It may be that time revealed we were not suited as marriage partners but we were then trustworthy loyal friends and very much in love in a way that made our aspirational and ethical differences seem less important.

We were married on a rainy day. The sky was yellow. The Earth was grey.
Signed the papers and we drove away.

Just like the song. He bought me a ring that morning from a Weybridge jewelry shop. We had two witnesses, one was my guitar tech, who took photos on my 35 mm Pentax camera. When the film was developed, it turned out that it had been exposed to light. Not one photo was saved. A dark omen. Not one photo of that auspicious occasion? But in my memory Paul did look great. And there was a lot of love between us that day. We drank champagne all night and ate a fine meal at the Casa Romana and went to sleep happy. Things only began to turn the following morning when he told his father. We spent our first months in the UK living in Pauline's house in Radnor Road. I knew no one in the UK when we arrived. Literally. My first circle of friends was the audience at my gigs.

Then one moment arrived that was to change my fortunes. I had the phone number of a friend of a friend from Yeoville. Manfred Liebowitz, who as Manfred Mann enjoyed a lot of success in the UK as a pop artist with many hit songs, starting in the sixties with many hit songs like 'Doo wah diddy' and 'Pretty Flamingo'. Manfred had a working studio, the Workhouse, and when I phoned his number, by the end of our conversation he had invited me to visit, for an audition. That same day. *"There's no time like the present"* he said. I drove up to the Elephant and Castle, using the A to Z handbook that was the GPS of its day, and found myself in his fabulous studio drinking coffee and chatting about my hopes and dreams. Kindly, Manfred offered helpful advice. Two weeks days after arriving with next to nothing and knowing no one, I was working full-time as a gigging entertainer and soon after that as a recording studio writer/producer. Earning money. Making most excellent new friends. Phew.

Paul, like me had dropped out of University. He wanted to work with horses. He loved horses, but struggling to get established in a new Country in 1985 in his early twenties was not an easy time for him. Reflecting on that time, clearly we married too young and in the face of conflicting pressures from two disapproving parents. His Catholic father, Petrus, made no secret of his disapproval of the Greek neighbor. I had never met anyone who disliked me as openly as his dad. A horrible man. On one occasion he threatened me with his big handgun. I ran for my life convinced his intention was to end it. Deluded and dishonest in that peculiarly Catholic deviant way. Driven by hatred and resentments and disregard for common courtesy. He would go on to win many enemies. My Greek orthodox parent was similarly disapproving of Paul. And from us kids, the feelings were returned with interest in both directions. Looking back to 1985, I can say both of us were unfortunate to have such unpleasant thoughtless, religious parents wishing such black harm on our teenage love. But whatever differences we had, Paul wanted to live in England as much as I did and I was his friend. For a time we were united by the nasty parental disapproval but the fact is we never overcame the obstacles of living together in that place and time and finding our authentic selves together. I kept my head down working as much as I could in my music world. He did the same in his developing interest in child psychology. And although we didn't initially know the extent of how far, we grew in very different directions. For some years we had a great time together. As much fun as teenage lovers emigrating and marrying young could ever expect to have; before the differences between horsey interests and music became conversational challenges. Subjects of mutual interest became harder to find when we sat down to talk. Finding time to talk became a subject of mutual disinterest.

The other significant timeline event from **1986** was buying my first home. 28 Thameside. The freehold and the leasehold for Apartment B. One of three Leasehold apartments attached to the freehold. 28 Thameside was a traditional Victorian terrace three level family home, converted into three leasehold flats in 1985. The one we bought was the nicest of the three, the middle floor flat. With a spectacular picture postcard view of verdant Thames Riverbank. One I would never tire of in the 29 years I lived there, watching the Thames roll past my window on its way to the City.

1989 was a big year. We had a son. A beautiful son, named Evan, after my father. In the Greek Orthodox tradition. Under enormous parental pressure on both sides we went through the christening ritual. I apologized to Evan on the day. And many times since. Is there any more abusive ritual process than baptism into a toxic belief system for a child not yet able to say Fuck off?

Now I had a mortgage and a child to ensure I had very little time to mope around. I was busy day and night, possessed with that enormous youthful energy available in the twenties. And I felt very much at home in the music world, meeting many great musicians. Despite the stressors on my failing marriage, I loved my new home from the get go. I was more at home there on day one than I ever was in my years in South Africa. With my guitar and one-woman musical show, I was by now booked on average six nights a week; in wine bars and pubs around London, where I had a following that was much like a support group. By day I was producing recordings in my studio. Soon that was six days a week. Soon that was £250 a day flat rate for my time. Whatever money I made I put into upgrading my studio. I had ears, a good sense of timing, some writing skills and a pleasing can do attitude with sound design. People paying me for this skillset was simply fabulous. I was all engrossed in this joyful pursuit.

Paul's divorce announcement came on a Saturday afternoon. We were walking the towpath on one of my rare days off. When he blurted it out.

Divorce.

But I had a gig that night, so there was no opportunity to cry, or fall to pieces after 6 PM. I had to load the car with my gear and drive around 70 minutes to North London for my show. Happy and smiling and playing my heart out to 400 people in Islington's premier Music pub. I didn't even think of Paul or his announcement once during the gig. I had to be focused on putting on the best show I could. Or I could not have started with 'Good evening ladies and gentlemen'. I rocked, as was essential in that gig at that time. I sang my heart out to 400 friends. And what better therapy is there than that, I can now reflect. "When in doubt, sing." After the gig I packed up and then it hit me on the drive back. Paul wouldn't be there when I got home. My first night in England without him.

Evan was two when we divorced. We did the best we could to co-parent. I learned a bit about family-law. There were tensions when Paul remarried very quickly and started a new family, placing a high demand on Evan's exclusive attention with a new step-parent. We were fortunate to have a tremendously helpful social worker to mediate. There was tension. There was some animosity. But when I reflect, we both learned to put the child above our grievances and personal disappointments with each other's decisions. After his swift marriage, in a relationship which began before our divorce, our friendship was beyond salvage and we seldom spoke again. However, and it is crucial to the outcome, we learned to speak only about our son. Any matters not directly related to the raising of our son were off limits. And that worked fabulously.

Evan grew to be a remarkable young man. In his thirtieth year at time of writing. Our great parenting moment was to agree to only ever talk about our son. And we only ever talked about him and what was best for him. No lawyers were involved. Our mutual disappointments with each other were buried underneath the hope we would be better parents to our son than married partners. No litigation to stir up animosity. No members of family-law were paid to interfere with our decision to agree on what was best for our child. Making the smoothest path out of the ruin of a broken family for a young child meant he never once heard us argue or raise voices. No money that went into his private education went instead to family law. Which his younger brother, Sam, can one day consider in the context of where the half million pounds family-lawyers billed me in fees to stop him being with me might have better been spent.

1992 was when the decree nisi arrived. After Paul left I stayed in the matrimonial home. I had paid the mortgage from the outset, so I kept that on, and as soon as I could, I paid him his half and put the sole title into my name. There was a family court hearing, but it was not hotly disputed. We did the best we could to agree visitation for Evan, receiving advice from the social worker who advised the court. And arriving at our own conclusion that we both wanted the best for our son. Our divorce cost around £10,000 in total. Good value was my lesson to never marry and not have more children.

1992 – 1997.   And after divorce time passed as it does, so inconspicuously. The Thatcher government whose economic policies brought me so close to ruin with the high interest rates on my property loan, lost the election and the new lot lowered interest rates and I turned a corner professionally and personally. I stopped doing live gigs for cash, partly because my voice burned out badly from the endless hours of shouting tirelessly in smoke filled rooms. I started a record label where I worked exclusively on projects signed to my label giving me an interest in the copyrights. I did many music recording sessions. I was lucky enough to have some great friends in music. I loved making musical recordings. It was an art form I felt rewarded me in many ways beyond simple payment. I felt at home in a studio setting. Making recordings has been my thing since I first connected two cassette players together to record four tracks.

After the divorce I had my first encounter in family law when Paul remarried and wanted more of Evan than was fair. Evan was not yet four. This first encounter with family law left me with one stand out experience: The role of the social worker. Very different to my second experience of family law 21 years later. But this was 1992.

Social workers would examine the child's best interests and had some authority to affect the decisions on visitation. Evan was the sweetest three-year-old who adored me in a way no one had before. I struggled at letting him go away from me. It felt wrong. Intuitively it was an affront to let my baby go. But there you have it. The child has the right to see both parents. Having an articulate properly trained social worker to work in a therapy context to assist me made all the difference. When couples separate with a young child involved, invariably the child's prospects for visitation will be affected in direct proportion to the animosity between the parents. Because the parents are separating the likelihood for animosity is high. Having an independent professional third party in the form of a social worker empowered to report to the Court and guide the visitation decisions was effective. The quality of that person, representing that vital role for a child is critical. This I learned is because the role is not a highly paid one. The individuals fulfilling this role are motivated by wanting to do what's best for the child and not what's going to enrich them. It is a reference to my 'Philotimia' view and the Boolean – one of two types of people.

In that first experience with British Family law, the social worker's input made all the difference. The child's future was not determined solely by an adversarial win or lose court judgment fought between opposing lawyers. Instead a seasoned professional motivated entirely by the child's best interests had a major say in the outcome of the court's decision and the child's future. I look back on the visitation we agreed and see that it worked out as well as it could. Largely because the talks about the child and the feuding parents took place outside of family court. A court room is no place to decide a child's future between traumatized parents better served by sympathy than aggressive cross examination.

There is no escaping the reality that a broken family affects a child's prospects.

Shortly after that, and the social worker thing was in 1992, the government changed the system. Budget changes led to CAFCASS to represent the children's interests. Apparently, because the cost of the social worker service I had seen and been so impressed by was deemed too expensive. CAFCASS would have consequences. Paying low level low trained staff to make decisions way above their pay grade. What if it's true. Pay peanuts you get monkeys? Monkeys to make decisions in court rooms that turn a child's future into the flip of a bent coin.

The empty sorrow I felt when Evan left for parental visits was traumatic. That is not an admission of guilt of any 'mental infirmity'. It is a simple fact. Any parent who is forced to let their child leave their care, into the custody of an individual who is generally, at that time of separation, hated, will understand. That first night when his room was empty is burned into my memory with the residue that I would never make the same mistake again. Being a part of a broken family. Bringing a child into the world to be a part of a broken family. Not something I would risk doing again. I took away the firm impression that one should never have a child if that child is to grow up in a broken family. What a sorrowful burden for a young person to process. The two people he loves and relies on hate each other.

Just no.

Never.

The song that most resonated with me at the time was called "I never will marry." The album I listened to most was "Torch" by Carly Simon. I learned a great version of Hoagy Carmichael's *"I get along without you very well"*.

Meanwhile the clock kept turning. I worked my way through 12-hour days until the decade turned to the nineties. Thatcher went in 1990, and in 1997 Labour won by a record margin of discontent with Tories. The Blair years began. I was by now in my thirties. I had started a record label and invested in a commercial recording studio where I kept an office and dealt with my own publishing from the commercial work I had done, as well as signing talented friends and minding their rights for a very modest 10%. This alternate income source had enabled me to cut back on gigs and commercial recording sessions. I was excited by the business learning curve, negotiating contracts and distribution rights, and finding that I actually enjoyed the mental challenge of making good business decisions. I learned well and that led to some reward. My musical earnings rose significantly. I got luckier the harder I worked at having fun. A successful publishing company started paying me top dollar for consulting on music publishing. With all my other commitments, on the weekends I wasn't with Evan, I would do ten days straight of 16-hour days. Although I can't really call it work, because I loved what I did. Meeting many of the great talents in the UK and making many recordings I could only have dreamed of making when I was a kid growing up in South Africa, listening to records made by the kind of musician I had now become.

With the increased earnings, came the opportunity to invest. In 1993 I bought the second of the three leases in my home at 28 Thameside. The second of the three leases attached to my freehold title, 28C Thameside. This was the apartment above 28B, a two-bed property, also with a spectacular Thames view and after an intense period of renovation, again requiring every last penny I could raise from a work schedule of ridiculous hours a day, an amount in six figures, which was more than the purchase price of the lease, I moved upstairs into 28C and began renting 28B out at 'top dollar'.

I had become a landlord.

I immediately found a comfort zone in being a good landlord. I enjoyed housing people and providing tenants with a pleasant place to live. This was a good fit for my philotimia. I especially enjoyed having, for the first time, regular dependable monthly income. The closest I ever came to a salary job.

By the end of the nineties I was well on the way to thinking more like a fully formed adult. Growing up with frugality had taught me the value of shrewd investment. My mortgage on 28B was paid off, I had no mortgage on 28C and approaching my mid-thirties at this stage, I was for the first time, free from the weight of financial pressure that accompanied my ownership of 28 Thameside from the outset. Property prices had risen in the cycle they do in London and my reality was; I was living in gratitude for the freedom I now had to choose my work projects. My royalties from copyrights I had made over the past ten years added up to a meaningful amount paid every quarter. I had achieved my goal of passive income replacing the need to perform gigs daily.

Evan, my beautiful son was growing beautifully. He was by now at boarding school. A weekly boarder at a private school where he was showing signs of academic promise. I loved our weekend time together. I wished I could have spent more time with him although I was grateful for the time we had. I was painfully aware of how much of his life with me was lost in the back and forth of a broken family. The roller coaster between the joy of his return and the veil of tears I would drive through to deliver him back to his father. Every sorrowful goodbye reminded me that I would never repeat that process with another child. Although his dad went on to have two more children quickly, I determined never to take that risk again. Another child from a broken family is the last thing this over populated Earth needs.

That became a deal breaker for several of my relationships in the nineties. At that age marriage and children is a driving call. I wanted neither. (I get along without marriage very well.) Looking back, I was coping better than well, after the hiccup of divorce and the financial burden of home ownership in a high-interest rate down-market. Being single, self-accountable, running a business and successfully developing a property portfolio that generated more income than it cost and all the while trying (and I think, succeeding) to be a loving responsible parent. And having fun with it all.

I had the three most effective anti-depressants working for me even though I didn't know it at the time. Cigarette smoking was the first, earning good money was the second. And reciprocated love for my beautiful son was the third. Only later when I had to learn about coping with depression and chronic anxiety, I reflected that nothing works better than smoking cigarettes and making what feels like a lot of money. By this time, my early thirties, acquiring the third and last lease for my freehold ownership of 28 Thameside was my goal. The third lease was the apartment below the two refurbished apartments above. A small ground floor one bed flat which had never been refurbished, owned by an elderly man, who I looked after as first responder for the council 'age concern' program. Derek was a real character responsible for creating the career of David Essex, including a favorite song of mine 'Rock On'. Often Derek would knock on the ceiling when I was songwriting upstairs and call me down. "*That one's a hit*" he would assure me. Once the dust settled on his departure, I would own all three properties attached to the freehold.

When I bought the freehold title to my property in 1986, I knew that once I had I acquired all three leaseholds I could maximize the value of the property by extending and refurbishing. It was, with the advice of my Financial Advisor, my fifteen-year plan to accumulate the means to buy the other two leasehold apartments so I would own the entire building. And it was about fifteen years before I was able to take on the building work. Once I had title to all three leases tied to the freehold I planned to upgrade the entire building from top to bottom. New roof. New everything. And extend the footprint outwards and downwards to add another thousand-square foot of habitable space.

For some years since the late 90's I had been friendly with successful local property developer, Cliff, who became an excellent tutor in this area of my interest, encouraging my ideas for enlarging the entire building and refurbishing in a high-quality approach to finishing the interiors, to attract high quality tenants. Cliff had bought and developed many properties, possibly 100 by his account, and I recognized in him a tremendous gift for increasing the value of South West London real estate. I found his passion for property development mirrored mine for music. And I shared music moments with him as he shared property stories with me. My goal was to have three rental units, with, eventually, no mortgage. My pension years income. I completed my costs projection and determined, with Cliffs helpful input, I would need a budget of £500,000 to achieve my goal. Following this expenditure, I would then have 3 desirable rental properties and my longer-term goal was to then look for a property to build from scratch for myself. Incorporating all I had learned from property development. Aspects I required included easy access to central London. With some land and room for a separate studio. And a self-contained residential annex in the garden where I could have my father, Evan, live out his old age, when he was no longer able to look after himself in South Africa.

At this time in the Blair years, property prices were soaring. Prices per square foot were more than double when I first bought the freehold of 28 Thameside. In foreign exchange, one pound was around $2. The economy was booming. All of Europe seemed to be buying CD's from small independent labels in the UK. My label was moving thousands of CD's every month at top price. With good steady income I had a good feeling that investing the proceeds in real estate was going to work out well. Aside from generating income from my properties, I enjoyed land-lording and many of my tenants through the years became good friends. Occasionally I was even able to help people by housing them and looking after them through a hard time in a manner very much at odds with commercial interest and very much in line with providing kindness that I found added value to my self-esteem. I never shirked from helping wherever I could. On occasions I gave record deals to people simply on the basis that I could when nobody else would.

On one occasion, in the nineties, I housed a retired Irish Catholic gentleman who was drinking himself to death from a broken heart for two years without receiving any rental. Instead of evicting him, when he was unable to pay rent, but still able to go to the pub every night), on many occasions I would prepare a meal and take it up to him. I didn't want him to get ill and I saw that he was not eating. He was so sad. And such a dignified drunk in that uniquely Irish Catholic way. How could I not offer help when I could afford to. Possibly not the best example of my entrepreneurial capitalist land-lording skills. '*Are you crazy*' said my father when I told him it was two years since the last rent. '*You work so hard to get it and then you give it away.*' I remember, and it makes me smile, that when my Catholic alcoholic tenant was two years in arrears, he would still knock on my door on Friday nights and ask if he could 'borrow' a twenty to go to the pub.

'*Of course you can*'. I didn't see a deficient tenant frauding me on rent and loans that would never be repaid. I saw a man broken by love, hanging onto a past that depended on denial and the kindness of others. He believed the Lord would provide. How ironic that it was an atheist who stepped up. In return I learned from him. His relationship with alcohol provided me with an insight into Ireland. As he told me in one of our lovely long chats in his flat, "*God invented alcohol so that the Irish wouldn't rule the world.*" I was fortunate to be able to afford to offer kindness on that level. I felt grateful. Two years of free housing with food and drink money thrown in. And this to a Catholic?

2000.   The year I gave up my big addiction. Cigarettes. A landmark year in my life. My symbolic midpoint. I had just broken up with yet another lovely partner who wanted the marriage and children I did not. I took stock of all I had done and all I had not. My achievements and my failures. I did my personal accounting and my greatest deficit was allowing the Cigarette companies to continue profiting from keeping me addicted. Even despite my numerous determined efforts to quit. I started smoking at 18 in South Africa when I was introduced to my first cigarette. I was hooked from the first inhale. My body chemistry made me a perfect patsy for that drug chemistry. Cigarettes became my mood stabilizing crutch during that period of my life. I was a natural born smoker from that first rush of chemicals from the lungs to the brain. Nothing calmed me more than the cigarette hit and so, soon after realizing I was addicted and all that came with knowing for the first time the humiliation of addiction, I determined to give up. I was not in control. What was this powerful force over me? Abstinence lasted two weeks. I learned how true Mark Twain's observation is. "*Giving up is easy. I have done it hundreds of times.*"

I would go on to give up many times. But invariably, that one puff would suck me back in. I loved to smoke. It kept my mood balanced. If I did not smoke, I became anxious. Although I did not know it at the time, the anti-depressant qualities in cigarettes were just the right balance for my own predisposition to serotonin irregularity. My improved financial circumstances by this time, arriving at this more mindful adult zone in life's seven stages, at 35, gave me the opportunity to make important choices with more clarity as well as having more means at my disposal. My own little mid-life crisis gave me the opportunity for a life reboot.

What if I became a professional non-smoker?

I set out to reinvent myself as a mindful, responsible adult. Being the best person I could be. Putting away those childish things, like harmful addiction. What if I stopped pleasing others at my own expense. What if I got to know myself better. What if I stopped pursuing money through work and worked only for the highest good. Evan was in his first year of University. He was a tremendous encouragement to me during his weekends and holiday visits. He knew about the extent of my addiction and I was motivated by the thought that he would be proud of my achievement once I overcame this addiction. I was grateful to have the means, with good passive income, in a financially stable place where I felt able to take a year, or two if necessary, off; to become a fulltime professional non-smoker. I found myself in the weeks approaching my big birthday with a new awareness and it all came together on my birthday. That was day one of my new life as a non-smoker.

I had help. One person in particular. My Irish 'Anam Kara' came visiting daily to motivate and encourage me in my one day at a time plan. The closest thing one can compare to an angelic visitation. And in a synchronous twist that spoke of karmic kindness, someone from Ireland. Effectively, I retired from anything that had a deadline attached. I budgeted my life for the next two years without the need to work for anything other than my new job. At the same time, In the back of my mind I was developing a novel. I thought I might be a Paperback writer. But then came 2001.

2001 was the year of the fire.

By this time, as the millennium drew to a close, for the first time I felt I had unlearned the restrictive lessons of my upbringing, moving past the disappointment of my personal failures, my divorce, my cigarette addiction, my fear of failing at musical performance, my fears of the unknown ahead as a single person, and was by now waking up every morning excited by my diary free lifestyle, wondering what each new day held in store for me. I had learned to hold myself in high esteem. I had no appointments. No deadlines. Life was a great gift and I would relish every moment I had available to me. I was playing tennis to a high level and meeting with interesting, inspiring friends while markedly excluding any negative thinkers from my circle of influence.

Post-divorce I had had a good few love affairs, but my most recent break up was the most traumatic. Eric Jarvis was my longest-term serious partner, at two years, during which time we had discussed children and decided on a trial run at responsible parenting with a dog. So, when we split, because he wanted marriage and children and I remained committed to not bringing another child into a world where being from a broken family is a possibility, I ended up with the product of our trial run at confirming the extent of my aversion to having a second child. A little black and silver schnauzer named William. Who was the best dog in the world. Ever.

Who had just become the child of a broken family. William was to experience the withdrawals from cigarette smoking with me, when his coughing fits prompted a vet visit, where it was established his exposure to passive smoke was the cause of his lung issues. We were inseparable. Even in our tobacco addiction. Eric went on to marry and have the child he wanted. We never spoke again, although I did e mail him when William died with that news.

Just around the time when I was first able to 'stop and smell the roses' without waking daily as that beast of burden struggling under financial-pressure, I recognized the extent of my undiagnosed PTSD from my South African experience. Especially being left at age ten after one parent died by the other disappearing into depression and leaving me to find my own way. Having to grow up very fast. Now I had no excuse for putting off the work to unravel the effects of PTSD. Having quit smoking also meant I had quit the anti-depressant chemicals that had been moderating my mood whilst a smoker. Now I had to address the root cause of this weight. Early life trauma. And the variety of disappointments relating to the inhumanity of the world I grew up in. Having foregone the bliss of ignorance and religion, I was far too aware of humanities greed related cruelty and exploitation to not feel the pain. And now, at last, in my two year-off period of total focus on putting myself first, I was finally benefitting from the wonders of therapy, when another great life experience arrived.

The year was 2001.

One minute I had a home that wasn't on fire and an hour later, I didn't.

It was a Friday night. At around 9pm I had finished the dinner I prepared for my date that evening, grilled Monkfish and Greek salad, and with my friend, Agi, was sofa bound, watching a movie on my huge big Sony Trinitron TV. My thirtieth birthday present to myself after a particularly meaty PRS royalty check. It was huge, taking up a big part of the room with its deep projector style display. In mid movie, out of nowhere we both heard a loud clunk. Like a pane of thick glass cracking.

William the dog started barking. What was that sinister sound? I paused the movie on my VHS cassette player and went to investigate, but was unable to locate the source. Disturbed from our movie progress and with William (the young schnauzer) showing some anxiety following this noisy interruption I decided to take William for a wee walk round the block and stop for a glass of wine at the Kings Head. (Where William had many friends waiting to see him on his nightly rounds.) We were gone for less than an hour. Upon our return, I saw a small crowd was gathered outside my home looking up.

"There's a fire" my tenants in 28C reported to me.

I found out later that the loud clunk we heard was the original Bakelite switch, a material commonly used as a circuit breaker when the house was wired for electricity in the 20's, cracked under the overload of too many electric appliances. Electric wiring of the twenties having no foresight into how many appliances a household 80 years later would run. The Bakelite switch overheated and cracked. The circuit to the fuse-board was broken, the fuse didn't trip for this reason. The wiring under the floorboards super-heated. And eventually that raised the temperature to a level that caused the floorboards to combust. A few hours later, after the fire brigade finished their foamy wet work, my home was a blackened stinky ruin from which almost nothing survived. My top of range Taylor guitar, bought in Los Angeles just months before for $9,000, was black dust, identifiable only by the strings attached to what remained of the tuning pegs. Everything I owned was incinerated. All of my mementoes of memories transformed to dust, replaced in one flash by the one in progress. The cleanser that is fire. When I left my house that day the total inventory of my material possessions was: My car, the clothes I wore, my dog William, but not his lead. My handbag, my wallet and its contents, cards and about £200 in cash. And one old Greek Orthodox icon that mysteriously survived the flames.

As a responsible freeholder and property owner with a good IFA guiding my building insurance through the years, I was fully covered for this type of claim. I had after all owned the property for 16 years by this time and had full buildings and contents covered, adjusted annually as advised by my broker, contents allowing for new acquisitions and buildings considering inflation and increasing costs of building.

I was immediately rehoused under the policy cover while my home was repaired, in a like-for-like similar accommodation and the lost rental from the upper flat, 28C, was paid by Insurers in full. The Insurer was the AXA. And the service was exactly as you would hope at a time like that. Kudos to the AXA. That's what you pay Insurance for. I moved into my new rental housing two days after the fire. Life carried on while my property was restored to its pre-incident condition and some 8 months after the fire all repairs were complete. The upper two levels, 28B and 28C were entirely rebuilt, re-plumbed and rewired, redecorated and refurnished. I moved back into my home, which was now two brand-new apartments, 28B on the first floor and 28C on the second. I lived in 28C, while I rented the larger one, 28B for 'top dollar'. I enjoyed living in 28C. The top floor flat, with a slanted ceiling and a picture postcard window view looking down across the Thames. It had a different energy to the flat below, 28B. Which had also been my marital home, so moving out had the appeal of a new location.

And here we are then in **2003**.
I had finally bought the third lease of my freehold property, 28A, the one-bedroom ground floor flat and the least valuable one in the property because unlike the other two, was undeveloped in any way since it was built in 1896. I now owned all three leases as well as the freehold. The property development plan that began in 1986 when I bought the freehold and the first lease, 28B, could finally come to fruition. This bottom floor flat, 28A, was not modernized after the fire and still had the old-style Bakelite linked electrics and lathe and wattle walls and ceilings. It was a blank canvas for developing with nothing worth keeping. Not even the walls. I was in a position to develop this 2,000-foot area over two levels exactly as I chose, which was a great opportunity to stamp my own design choices on an historic building. I thought of it as an art project.

To bring the story in line with the time in my personal circumstances, in summary, by the start of the new millennium I was, for the first time in my life since starting paid work, enjoying some freedom from financial pressure. I had achieved a degree of financial independence that meant I could choose how to spend my time, with no need to accept any work on offer just to pay the bills. And now I was planning to develop my property asset to a significant up value. Being single as I approached forty was a great deal less troubling for the fact that I was feeling happy. The shadow 'fear of failure' that drives every musician one way or the other, was gone. I had by now sold, or been a remunerated part of CD sales in excess of 2 million. I didn't feel the need to prove anything to anyone. I no longer was defined by being "as good as my last gig." I was healthy, fit, and had any number of possibilities for date nights. My discrimination in avoiding dating clingy whackos was serving me well. I had membership to a walking-distance tennis club, with clay courts, for good quality social introductions and daily tennis outings. And best of all, my lovely William for company. A joy that cannot be understated. William was a soul dog who loved me unconditionally. I had Evan back from boarding school on alternate weekends, sharing his progress through academia and relying on my input in a most rewarding way for me.

Many times I thought of Eric, my lost love. My ex, who bought William with me, and who made the decision to leave William with me when we parted. I learned a lot about separation and the best interests of the child in our parting. Even though William was technically not a child. He was loved by two parents equally. And each had half a right to him. Technically, when we separated and did the accounting on who gets what, bearing in mind dogs are chattels and Eric owned 50% of William, he could have raised a claim. Instead he considered what was best for William. Eric put Williams needs first, leaving him with me because it was after all Williams home. And although William loved us both, William did have that special bond with me. That much was clear. From the dog's point of view, leaving him with his preferred choice was the right choice. I thought then that this type of decision should always be made with the child's best interests to the fore. Yes, William was a dog, but same difference. When parents separate, what is best for the child?

By 2001, two years after Eric left, past my mid-thirties and one year after I quit smoking, I was doing pretty well personally and professionally. I could choose what I wanted to do and who I wanted to do it with. And what I wanted to do was write books, to share what I had learned, and enjoy making music for the creative fun of it. To pursue my bliss, in a Joseph Campbell style. Which included finding happiness by making others happy. I had enjoyed several committed relationships post-divorce, with mostly well-chosen appropriate romantic partners. The qualities that attracted me most were intelligence and kindness. Mostly my relationships in that decade were with younger partners that lasted no more than 12 months. I required monogamy and enjoyed being in a relationship, but never saw the need to marry anyone. Usually this would lead to discontent with my partner of the time starting around the 12-month mark. A conversation would follow involving long-term planning, highlighting marriage and children, and we would both move on.

I already had one beautiful child and was surprised at how often I was approached to have another. I was not to be drawn to the prospect of having another child. The lessons of a broken family were well learned. But I was all too aware that everyone had the right to enjoy parenthood and would happily end my relationship to enable this for my partner. I had no acrimonious break ups, and crucially, I had former partners who remained loyal friends long after we were no longer intimate. My longest relationship was between 1998 and 2000. Almost two years. Eric, who I thought I would grow old with.

I thought I adored Eric.

And then the subject of children came up. Children and the biological clock. I had done everything young in my life. I finished school young. I started University young. (17) I emigrated young. I bought my first home young. And I had some earning success young. But I never had the urge to be with child again. I had my full of parenting interest met by Evan, at that time a weekly boarder, with me on alternate weekends. Providing a great reward for my parenting time with him in mirroring critical thought that was both intelligent and kind. In the matter of having a child in my late thirties, there were many compelling reasons not to. Subconsciously I was not optimistic about prospects for any new arrival into a cold cold world. I lacked confidence that the stupid's in our number of homo sapiens, the 50% + who believe in blind faith and the headlong rush into environmental destruction in the name of profits for their unprincipled greed, would not succeed in my lifetime. After all, George 'the village idiot' Bush had been elected to lead the world's most powerful, nuclear army, under direct orders from God. I was not overly optimistic about winning prospects for the right side in the battle between the greedy and the compassionate. The light and the dark. Consciously, I was all too aware of the consequences for a child in a broken family. That was the driver in my reluctance to have a child with Eric. Eric knew that and he wasn't having any of it. He wanted marriage and children. He was very clear on what he wanted in life and in love. In the course of convincing me, our compromise was a trial run with a dog. Eric and I bought a Black and Silver miniature Schnauzer together. We chose the type of dog we would like to raise together. Through the kennel club we located a registered breeder. And 8 weeks after a litter were born on 1 April 1998, we headed to Godalming to have a look. We knew there was litter of eight puppies. Two were pure black, three were Black and Silver and the rest were salt and pepper. I noticed there were only seven puppies in the group around the mother.

"I thought there were eight pups".

"Oh yes. That one. He's always off on his own looking around."

And sure enough, on the other side of the garden this tiny little dog was snuffling around, curiously. Not needing the mother like the rest of the litter. Off on his own making inquiries. Sniffing around with a swagger that made plain, this was the independent thinker in the group. That was it. Perfect match between beauty and intelligence. We took him there and then. The owner warned that pups will cry a bit when separated from their mother. Not that dog. From the get go he was filled with joy and embracing every new smell with joyful interest. So brave he was that we named him after William Wallace, the brave Scott. His appetite for life was already fully developed when we met. 14 months later we separated because Eric wanted children and I did not. Not even one. I already had one. We had a mature conversation where we both set out our respective positions. When we separated the matter of Williams custody was faced. Eric decided that William would be happier with me. There was no conflict. No financial settlement. No acrimonious litigation. Just a sit-down dinner meeting, awkward though it was, and an agreement based on what was for the best. I knew Eric loved William like a child but Eric went off to work in an office every day. I went off to work in Studios where William was not only always welcome, he was welcomed as a celebrity. After that sad but dignified separation, in which I look back to this day with a lasting deep affection for how it is possible for two people who love each other to separate without causing the other harm, I had a benchmark set for how adults can love and separate without allowing greed to turn to hate that harms the child. Eric's wise choice worked out great for William and me.

2 The meet cute. Valentine's day, 2003
How when and why I romanced Nico Krasnopovich

During the years leading up to Valentines night 2003, one constant in my lifestyle living in a quaint picture postcard English village on the river Thames was the Kings Head pub; located about halfway down Thameside Road. At that stage of my life, no longer a gigging musician working nights, almost every night at around ten pm I would go for my evening constitutional at the local pub, almost always meeting my local pub buddy, Alan, there. This process began with an evening walk for William of Thameside, the black and silver Schnauzer about whom not enough can be said. Typically it would be a ten-minute walk, often in rain, with an umbrella, where William enjoyed his evening business outing before we made our way to the pub almost invariably arriving at the same moment as Allan, my longest running regular drinking buddy and my oldest friend in the village. Literally. (He was 35 years older than me.) I was tremendously fond of Allan. A giant compassionate intellect. The kind of friend you cherish for a lifetime.

Other locals in the pub in those heady days leading out of the nineties and into the new millennium, the ten o clock crowd, who timed their pub arrival for ten pm every night included Nigel the gardener, who looked after my home gardening requirements with his roundly calloused Irish hands and his 30 year old Land Rover, his beautiful partner Martina the fashion designer, Jake, the huge ex con, with H A T E and L O V E tattooed on his knuckles. Who *'Did the crime and did the time'* and wrote moving poetry about it. Jake always stood when I came into the pub. And greeted me with a bow. Jake did 16 years for armed robbery. He explained it as *"I was 18. I was foolish. I had just arrived from Poland and I knew no better."*

Then there was my next-door neighbor, Adrian, something of a legend in Thameside for his flower-show business, his connections with royalty, and his destructive alcohol addiction. Who taught me well in the matter of helping and harming. Adrian was a desperately alcoholic former advertising executive, whose French wife Sylvie would buzz on my door at 3 am on more than one occasion, waking me with her soft French accent saying *"Andrea. Please elp."* After which I would buzz her in and use warm water-soaked cotton wool to clean the blood off her bruised face following another of his drunken marital slugfests. He of the bulky 6.2" frame, she a petite 5.1". Drink assisted domestic violence at its most virulent. I would make up the spare bed for her, and go back to sleep.

She would always be gone when I woke up, always leaving a note that read *"Thank you so much. You saved my life. Love Sylvie."* An elegant Parisienne who could have done so much better than Adrian. I felt awful for her. I sat her down with a cup of tea and talked to her in my best life coach feminist voice. She knew she had to leave the relationship.

How I tried to help him overcome his destructive addiction. He knew how hard I was trying and perhaps that is why one day he rang my door bell. I showed him in. His body language was slumped over.

"I want help. I have found a rehab that will work for me. I am ready to make the change. I know one drink is too many and a thousand is not enough."

"How can I help Adrian?"

"I need a thousand pounds for the treatment. There is no admittance without the payment."

He was so compelling. He had all the details of the program. The names and backgrounds of the key therapists. Adrian was so clearly determined to win this time. Of course I gave him £1,000, twenty brand new fifties in an envelope, which I sealed and wrote *"Treatment"* on the cover, along with all the motivational words of encouragement and support you can imagine. He left me with the cash envelope firmly placed in his inside jacket pocket, headed directly for the train station and the start of his new life as a former alcoholic. I gave him a firm hug as he left. Willing him forward to his new self. I had shared the best of my own story in overcoming addiction. He had paid attention. He had showed me he remembered the lessons I had shared and was ready to take own his own Mark Twain moment. I felt good about my role, making sure that I watched him turn into the train station and the journey to a new life. A few hours later I went to the store with William, which took me past the Albion pub, where I saw a familiar face propping up the bar. I confronted him. "Adrian"? He was so toasted I don't think he even remembered our meeting just two hours before. As is my way with life's lessons I told him *"after this we can never speak again."* And we never did. Adrian lost everything because of his alcoholism and some years later died a pauper's death in an assisted living council facility.

When Sylvie finally left 29 Thameside, fleeing one step ahead of what may well have been the final drunken punch, to return to her family home in Paris, she left her collection of seventeenth century French art, which Adrian sold for drink money. She left Neddie, her perfectly groomed Yorkie. Which must have broken her heart still further. I looked after Neddie too for a while, after he was found wondering on the towpath as an abandoned emaciated filth covered mess. Rescuing the wounded and despairing being a great privilege I have been fortunate enough to enjoy more than once. It has been a repeating pattern in my life and to an extent I was not properly aware of this pattern until the consequences became clear to me.

Sometimes helping helps. Sometimes it does not.

I couldn't help Adrian. My help harmed him. I could help Neddie. And Sylvie. Who know where the line lies.

A good deed seldom goes unpunished.

A line I might have used as a title for this story.

In any event, this is one of many stories from 'the Pub', where the still beating heart of the Thameside generations preceding mine beat loudest. Where the ghost of our forebears on the barstools whispered suggestively of the *'pint you shouldn't have.'*

It was a happy period of my life, living in this 600-year-old village of Thameside. It was a real English village atmosphere even though, by train, Waterloo station was just 30 minutes away. Stuff was happening in Thameside. People were nice. And the clique of articulate locals, in which I was the only non-British born honorary member, met most nights in the pub. As a cultural bonding place, I know of nothing comparable to the English local pub. I maintain the absence of psychiatrists and therapists in the UK at that time was down to the value of people talking to each other over a drink. Pub culture as was for many hundreds of years went into cardiac arrest when smoking was banned. Ironically enough, the ban on smoking was catastrophic for the traditional English Pub business. Pubs went bust left right and center and the land was bought by so called yuppie property developers turning them to overpriced apartments for first time buyers on the soaring London property market. The survivors became Gastro pubs with bathrooms often frequented by cocaine users. Only a thin skeleton of the pubs that prospered before the tobacco ban survive to this day. In my local, coincidentally, one of the survivors of the tobacco ban and still with the character of the great British local's pub, I knew everyone. Certainly the reason for its survival was the locals frequenting it daily. I had a valued circle of friends and enjoyed evening walks to the pub with William as a sweet part of every day that made living alone not lonely at all. 'It takes a village' in so many ways. I think back to that time in my life as a unique experience. Being part of a small English village where everyone knew everyone. Where the culture of British integrity still existed and abounded. And kindness was a popular currency. Even amongst the criminals, who for some reason harking back to the days of highwaymen, made up a noticeable sector of the Thameside community. Part of the quaint English character was the inherent racism. In my early years visiting the local, the number of times my soft South African accent attracted bitter drunken comments of '*Why don't you back home*' gave me a good opportunity to educate racists. Eventually even the local lawyer who felt validated by his British superiority learned to not mess with a Greek on the grounds of racial superiority. I played my part in confronting and assisting the social conduct of racists, recognizing that the very construct of racism was born in England and bred into every successive post slavery generation, most probably in pubs just like the one I enjoyed frequenting.

Then, for me and my life, the clock clicked onto 14 February, 2003. Valentine's day. What if I had decided to go on a date that night, instead of opting to walk William to the Pub? I had thought about it. I knew my regular pub buddy Allan would not be in before ten, but William wanted to go out. And so off I went, ten minutes before eight. Out of my usual schedule. Floating into the unknown in a sliding door moment I would love to revisit with a time machine and wonder how much I might do differently.

Certainly my judgment was badly off that fateful night.

The pub was already full when I arrived around 8'ish with William. My usual crew, Allan and the regulars, were not there yet. This was an entirely different crowd. Much younger. Fewer locals. Looking around I saw Mandy the flautist, another of my lengthy local friendships which began in the Kings Head, who was in a group with a curiously attractive geeky bespectacled young man who caught my eye. Literally because he was staring at me. Nico Krasnopovich, who appeared to be gawping at me as if dumbstruck. I went over to say hello. Mandy introduced us. "*Nico is a lawyer*" she explained, leading to a firm handshake. They were the same age and had gone to the same junior school. Thameside locals, both considerably younger than me. We talked. There was a distinct frisson of sexual interest from the nervy young man which I recognized and was intrigued by. Flirty innuendos fizzled past in that peculiarly British way. Hardly cradle snatching from my perspective, and on that night, in that place, I was curiously interested in a romantic gesture. I wondered if this was love at first sight but dismissed the notion. After the pub closed I invited a small group including Mandy and Nico back to my home, a five-minute walk from the pub, for a late-night night-cap. Here I was on Valentines night, looking at a somewhat nerdy bespectacled young man with high cheekbones, an awkward smile and a determined interest. Although I knew he was younger than me, I guessed about a decade, I wasn't thinking marriage and children. I don't know what I was thinking, it just kind of evolved out of unlikeliness. I think it was the way he kept staring at me. A spark was lit. Again the thought crossed my mind. Is this love at first sight, or just the pub Merlot? His lack of confidence was intriguing. All things considered; we were an unlikely pair. Age. Height. Interests. Income. Social circles. Come to think of it, there is not one thing that I can remember as being a reason we should be together. Just sheer blind confluence of alcohol and warm temperature on Valentines night. And his affection for William, who failed to guard me, by returning Nico's interest.

Soon after we went for our first date in a restaurant in Esher. I paid. Nico seemed smart and very interested. And respectful. Quietly spoken and engagingly naive. Someone who evidently deserved to be better off than they were. By the bottom of the second bottle of wine our relationship was up and running. I hadn't asked his age yet. It was implicit in arranging our date that he would be uncomfortable in such an expensive restaurant so I made plain that it would be my treat. And that precedent would follow for many years. I liked that he was open about that. Up front. He had no disposable income. I had plenty. Something about him I liked, perhaps as Chris Andiotis (my Greek family friend and sometime business-advisor who visited frequently from South Africa) observed when he first met Nico shortly after I had, "*He sounds just like Eric.*" He observed that their accents were similar. He said "*Are you sure it's not a rebound relationship from the Eric?*". Only with hindsight Chris.

That was March 2003. Our relationship had begun.

Krasnopovich Vs Leandros as it would become ten years later in family-court. A lengthy dinner with Asian fusion starters, ample wine and lots of talk. Life, love, the universe, British family-law careers, past mistakes, successes and future ambitions. A trawl through the been-there done-that list. And I guess, although we had met before, that was technically our first date so it was 'love at first sight.' The 'your place or mine' conversation was not an option. I saw where he lived, and as a footnote, in the time we were together, I never stayed one single night at his place. A modest small flat above a fish and chip shop in a rough location. Rough in every way that spoke of low-income and the smell of overused frying oil. His home was literally on the other side of the tracks to my entire life. The surrounding geography was economic hardship. Although he owned a flat and a car, both were entry level examples, in which there was no equity. I felt bad for him. Later that first night at my place after a roof down ride in my BMW convertible, overlooking the Thames in the picturesque village of Thameside he commented on the experience in a way that is easily reviewed in hindsight.

"*Wow your house is amazing.*"

Reading as I write, I am bemused at how obvious it was from the outset. It took him ten years but I am convinced that process of '*what's yours I want for mine*' began that first night. He saw a lifestyle he had never experienced close up and determined to get it. Initially by marriage and when that failed, by a legal device you will read about in due course called '*Beneficial Entitlement.*'

From that first night I knew it was something very different to my feelings with previous romances, like Eric. Not that there was no chemistry of the type associated with sexual-interest. But absent was heart racing thrill I associated with the various facets of romance driven passion; the mutual reward that comes from caring for the other more than yourself in that most intimate of exchanges. This was something unfamiliar to me or I would have recognized it sooner. I liked him. I had feelings for him. I was interested in learning more about him. But intuitively I recognized something was off in that department. And my way of processing was, unfortunately, found my recidivism to that Greek upbringing. Philotimia. I would place helpful kindness above the thrill of the chase. Later I would understand his comments about sexual abuse as a child made a great deal of sense.

Less than four weeks after our first date I agreed that Nico should move into my home. I thought I was inviting him although with hindsight, subsequent events make plain a different intention. It may well have been love at first sight; him falling in love with my house. Nico was then, in 2003, a young trainee solicitor still struggling to find his feet. At 38, I was considerably older which is for some reason more acceptable and workable when the older partner is the man. On paper, as a couple, I knew it was an improbably high risk but he seemed so determined and for me it had been awhile since I had a live-in lover. Nico made a fuss of William, who responded favorably, so that swung it. I trusted Williams judgment. Perhaps a little more than one should when considering the limitations of a dog's brain. Mostly though, I think it was an age thing. Over thirty-five and single, we are programmed to raise the value of having a life partner. There is that age where it is simply the right time to partner up and the next person who walks into the room is the one for no better reason. We discussed the pros and cons of our cohabitation in advance. By that stage, since my divorce in 1992 I had invited several previous boyfriends to live in my home. I had the space. And it was a nice place by any standards. It felt good to share it with someone. Since Paul (my husband) left, in fact I had housed, maybe seven boyfriends, the longest relationship in cohabitation being Eric, and that was a two-years. I had never had problems with boyfriends leaving. My choices had been above-average good. I have generally been fortunate in my choice of partners, post-divorce.

Evidently so, because every separation was as close to amicable as the word implies. I ran through all seven in the course of writing this paragraph and can say, every one, if asked would agree, the word amicable is not inappropriate in the context of our separating. I had no idea then that Nico would be so very different. Many reasons for housing Nico made sense to me, mostly, because Nico was struggling financially. A young man with historical debts and with limited job advancement prospects. He was working as a junior lawyer in the family-law office of Surrey firm MWT Solicitors, for a boss he despised with every reference to her. Christa Small he described to me en route to our first meeting as *"A fat, arrogant South African legal dinosaur with the dress sense of a Palestinian refugee."*

Nico felt Christa was holding him back by using him as menial labor. Allocating him the dogs-body work and taking all the high-net-worth meaty cases for herself. His average divorce billing came out at less than ten percent of hers. Christa was the head of department. He wanted what she had, her hourly rate, her billable hours, that high net-worth work so badly I felt his burning passion for it.

When we met in 2003, Nico was earning some £35,000 a year in his entry level position in family law with a hefty 90% mortgage on his flat in Hounslow, an entry level starter home he managed to pay for by renting the second room to his sister, Dog. Yes, that's not a typo. He called his sister Dog. I never came to terms with why they called each other dog, yet that was their reality at every meeting. *"Alwhyte Dog?"* More significant for my concern was his serious debt. Moving in with me would enable him to rent his flat for income. Step one in helping him away from the poverty consciousness underpinning his every decision. I was made aware of the scale of his problems by the disclosure that he was still paying off his student loan and living on credit card debt each month as he would run out of money by the third week after payday. Bearing in mind that nuisance Greek philotimia motivation, it seemed easy for me to help this younger person with a leg up economically. Not just helping financially, but also as it was clear to me where the gaps in his communication skill set lay, guiding his personal growth. I thought, quite rightly, that it would be easy for me to make a big difference in his life. And helping is, as I learned ten years later, my great weakness. Because Nico was unable to make it to months end before running out of money completely, I was able to help with small loans. A thousand here, two thousand there. He drove a worn-out Suzuki car that was not safe. I helped him get a better car. Small amounts for me, at key times, made a big difference for him. In the guise of help, I very quickly identified the twin priorities in his life being to get out of debt and make some inroads on his career. Get him to experience the financial independence that enables real life choices. Smarten up appearance.

Speak with more authority.

Stop projecting under confidence.

Stop saying 'Uhm' before every new sentence.

Start being your authentic self.

Find your passion and pursue it to the best of your effort.

Stop saying, 'if I had'.

Stop blaming others.

Buy some smart suits.

Smile more.

Exude confidence.

Make the person you're talking too feel they are the most special person you have ever met.

I thought he was worth helping. In his personality I saw the potential for a sharp intellect held back by a self-doubt and a maudlin anxious vulnerability. An as yet unexplored capacity for diligent critical thought. Nico suffered from frequent anxiety attacks, starting the first night he moved in with me. This was another area I felt able to help with, both through my own experience in this regard, and my subsequent work in this mental illness. Although he disclosed he had had benefitted from sessions with a therapist on this issue, I could see there was still work to be done. Nico Krasnopovich ticked many boxes in the areas where I felt most able to offer life changing help. Krasnopovich, as he shall henceforth be referred to, smoked when we met and was exploring the options of having a tattoo. I was by now nearly two years clean of smoking and had become severely allergic to the smell of smoke. Smoking around me was a no brainer choice if he wished to continue a romance with me. On our first date night, sitting by my fireside, he asked *"Do you mind if I smoke?"*

"You can smoke as much as you want, you just can't do it here".

Helping and harming are often the same thing. I knew this at the time and became aware of some alpha male resentment towards being told what to do, with repeated reminders of how uncomfortable he felt at not being able to enjoy even one cigarette after his dinner. But if there was one early bright red warning sign, it came in the form of his binge drinking. During the working-week he avoided alcohol entirely although

I usually enjoyed a few glasses of wine with dinner and thought it strange that Nico would not drink with me, except on Friday and Saturdays, when he drank excessively and became a different person. From early on it became apparent that he would undergo a personality change after even one glass of white wine. Unrecognizable from his sober persona. In the Jekyll and Hyde transformation he would become this nasty, scabrous embittered angry person. Different to the extent I had concerns over a schizophrenic origin. Very quickly that became another condition in our relationship.

"No more white wine. It makes you a different person. Not someone I could be with."

He agreed right away. Aware that there was an issue with white wine. Curiously other alcohol was fine. Only white wine affected him in this way. I just found it curious that he knew this about white wine before I made it a condition, yet did nothing about it until I made it a condition Whether Krasnopovich had any reservations about any of my lifestyle habits was not made clear at the time. I don't think so, other than a mild resentment at being made to choose between smoking, drinking white wine, having a tattoo, *'a small one on my shoulder'* and properly addressing the underlying cause of his anxiety attacks by way of therapy. Aside from helping in the areas where my superior age and experience made it easy, the timing for me was right to share my life with someone. A life-partner. Something about that stage in my life, between 35 and 40, made the idea of settling down with one person especially appealing. Both the information I had gleaned in my journey to that age as well as the degree of financial independence I had achieved placed me in a position to find my purpose in offering help. It was for myself also the 'last chance saloon', in case I decided to bring a child into the world although that would have been a subconscious motivation as it was clearly not in my plan at the outset. Materially I could house him at no cost while he rented his apartment and with my experience in small business I could quite easily see how best to guide his career choices towards increased income. While sharing my experience in 'self-help' towards enabling and up-lifting him personally and professionally. Again, the Greek DNA might be to blame for this unreserved generosity in which the reward comes from the giving. Before I understood the full extent of how 'a good turn seldom goes unpunished' I had a rent-free house guest happily occupying all of my attention in analyzing and advising on his career choices. And accepting four figure loans with affectionate thanks. After moving in with me in a cost-free agreement that would last for the next two years Krasnopovich rented out his apartment, soon achieving £800pm. Despite the basic math's of £800 pm for ten years because he was living with me for free, he would later launch a financial claim against me, claiming he suffered to his 'detriment' through being with me. Ten years at say £9,000 per annum. That is some £90,000 a judge determined did not warrant mitigating his claim for detriment in any way? But, more about his family-court claim later.

While Nico was enjoying free housing with me, I was happy to invite him to travel to many of my favorite destinations. Which involved foreign travel on a scale he had not encountered before. As he had no money and I wouldn't have travelled alone it was my pleasure to show him a world he had never seen before. This included many trips, around the UK and abroad. I took Nico to Havana, where he got to walk down the Malecon to the Nacional Hotel for dinner at Bugsy Siegal's table, the actual location where Organized Crime was birthed. We watched cigar rollers in the Partagas factory, met the actual cigar roller who made Churchills cigars for twenty years, and drank

Mojitos in the Bacardi building. One especially generous invitation I made to Nico involved my interest in Bob Marley. Nico accompanied me on my bucket list visit to 9 Mile, in Jamaica, to the one room shack where Cedella Booker, a 16-year-old impregnated by a 42-year-old Englishman, Norval Marley, raised Robert Nesta Marley, who would go on to live an extraordinarily full-life before dying of cancer aged 36. Marley's body was returned to his birth home, to a mausoleum built next to the one room shack in 9 Mile with three things; his Gibson 'special' guitar, a Bible and a large spliff. Nico got to hear the Bob Marley story told with the visual of this reality as a prop. I hired a driver to take us to Bob Marley's house in Hope Road, in Kingston, formerly the home of Chris Blackwell, whose record label Island Records launched Bob Marley and the Wailers in the 70's. Where Bob lived after he made his first real money with his first big seller '*No Woman no cry*' and bought the Hope road house from Chris Blackwell. It is where he wrote and recorded many of his most important songs. Nico got to stand in the exact spot where the shooter who shot 'Tuff Gong' stood, firing down into the kitchen where Bob sat. He got to enjoy the full Bob Marley story in the exact location where it began and ended. Between the extreme poverty and the violence of Trenchtown.

And for good measure, because Nico found the roads in Jamaica frightening and was dreading the bumpy drive back to Montego Bay from Ocho Rios, I flew Nico in a private plane back to Montego Bay airport, to connect directly with the flight back to London. A touch of rock star living. He loved it. So did I. And as I had a good income, the cost was no problem either. It was nice for me as a musician to share this insight into Bob Marley's life with my non-musical boyfriend and the opportunities for fun that spending a little money on educational travel enabled.

On average we travelled four times a year to my favorite destinations. All of which Nico enjoyed without offering, or being asked for, any financial contribution for the first 5 years, by which time he was in a better financial position and able to offer half of the costs in the travels. Which I accepted.

Years later when it came to 'financial accounting' in his money grabbing litigation against me, no value was attached to any of those 'gifts'. A notable moment in the annals of gratitude as a concept. Showing gratitude is a measure of growth. The absence of gratitude is the mark of something else. Perhaps the weight of this as an offense against courtesy is heavier in Greek culture where the lexicon makes descriptive provision for people who do not understand or value gratitude.

During Krasnopovich's Court hearing following his claim of 'beneficial entitlement' against me, he claimed he had suffered detriment as a result of being with me. Which he used to justify what would later amount to his flat-out theft of multiple millions from me. Everything I owned was not enough for him. He had suffered detriment you see.

He successfully convinced last minute switch Judge Flaherty that he was entitled to ownership of my home because I had '*promised him we would be 50/50 like husband and wife*', absent of one single shred of supporting evidence. When considering the travel and education element alone, not just its cost, but its benefit on his professional development as a lawyer attracting high net worth clients, it is especially difficult to not think of him as the worst kind of ingrate.

Devious. Deceitful. Dishonest. Triple D. Then there's the fourth. Detriment.

During the first three years of his life with me, Krasnopovich continued working under Christa, head of the family law department at MWT. Christa Small is a Durban born lawyer who gave Krasnopovich his first trainee solicitor job in family-law, training him from a start of nothing, in a mentoring role as his boss in family-law. Business mentoring that was met not with the gratitude one might expect in this type of relationship, but instead an endless array of mocking criticisms for her brusque South African ways. Krasnopovich shared with me that after passing the bar, scraping through with a low grade, he struggled to find any work. So he falsified his results and the first person he sent this modified resume too was Christa, who offered him a job, albeit at an entry level wage. A win win in its way. Each day's summary of his working day which formed the conversation during our dinners together would include heated reference towards Christa's faults. '*The dinosaur of family law*' being his go-to comment to more than one guest at our home enquiring after Christa. Her wardrobe was the butt of many of his jokes. *"She showed up in the most hideous coat I can only assume she found in the Epsom charity shop"*. Initially Christa was his role model in forming his own take on the ethics of family law. And upon reflection Christa was a dinosaur of family law. Her mentors lesson for her eager apprentice being, in one sentence;

"You practice what you preach as a divorce lawyer. You fight to get the most you can for your client. That's your job."

That sums up Krasnopovich's legal training in one sentence. And that includes consideration for children's well-being. The more billable hours you put in the more likely you are to reach your annual target and the closer you get to the success that defines a member of British family law. The most valuable element at your disposal in winning for your client is the want for visitation on the opposite side. That's where your negotiating position has the most leverage. Child access. That's the key to a winning financial settlement. It is a simple formula to build a career in family law on. In ten years of seeing this relationship between the mentor, Christa, and the mentee, Krasnopovich, close up, I never once heard one single reference in the context of a child case to the child's best interests. That is a commonality amongst all of the most successful beneficiary members of family law who I met over the course of those ten years as a partner in family-law. The top lawyers are there to win money. The system is structured as it is to enable the top lawyers to earn by making money in this way. And while family law operates as an adversarial process between two sets of law firms it will continue alienating parents and abusing children for no more than one certainty. Enrichment of the entitled members of family law. They know it and they love it. Easy money. Dinosaur laws so easy to manipulate by even the simple minded willing to put in long hours.

3 The freehold transfer

Getting Insurance after the fire is expensive. The family solicitor has a good idea for cheaper Insurance

Shortly after Krasnopovich moved in with me in June 2003, my buildings insurance came up for renewal. As freeholder and leaseholder I was responsible for the Buildings Insurance on the house and the contents insurance of the leases. A process I had completed without difficulty for the previous 16 years with the assistance of Ken Quinton, of Firndowne Insurance. Ken was a reference from my financial advisor Larry Chester, which, as was the case with so much of Larry's advice, was working out well. In 2001, just weeks before the Saudi led attack of 911 in the USA, in a curious event that was one of several curious events to befall me in my time at Thameside, my house caught fire. The cause was a failed Bakelite switch dating back to the original electrical installation, which was, unsurprisingly for a house built in 1896, unable to cope with the increasing demands placed on the electrical circuit with the advent of so many more electrical devices drawing on power than existed when the first electrical installation was put in place. The electronic circuitry is common problem with older Victorian homes, and one of the essentials to approach when developing these properties. The wiring went in during the 1920's, when the electrical demands did not foresee the multitude of appliances that would follow. The developer who did the conversion in 1985 of the three-level house into three separate flats cut a corner there and used the existing old wiring. He simply added a fuse box for each flat to connect to the Electric supplier. On this night in 2001 the original 1920's Bakelite switch located under the floorboards in the middle flat blew and that broke the electrical circuit to the fuse box. With no fuse to cut the circuit, the wires under the first-floor floorboards overheated, reached a red-hot glow and then combusted. The upper two levels fire-balled in a process that incinerated almost everything I owned. Imagine that. Losing almost everything you own.

After the fire I had the liberating experience of being homeless and free of all possessions. I very quickly understood "You don't own your possessions. They own you." William's bedding and toys were now black dust. I had car keys and a car, my wallet, but very little else as I drove away that night with William. Not even a toothbrush or one single item of clothing. William was as carefree as ever. He didn't notice that he owned nothing at all. He was just happy to be with me. Real love is not like a material possession. What a feeling that was and what a uniquely helpful life experience. Free from the burden of ownership, but with what mattered most, my true and loyal companion by my side. It felt like a freedom party. A lesson in values and priorities and gratitude. The emancipation of Andrea from material chains. An experience no words could adequately describe. The instinct being to see the event as bad news, while the actuality was, it felt like a tremendous gift. A joyous occasion. I owned nothing more than I needed at that moment.

Ken Quinton my Insurance broker was my first port of call after the fire and, being properly insured, as I have been since becoming a property owner since 1986, I was immediately rehoused. The broker contacted the Insurer, the AXA, and within hours a loss adjuster was appointed, and during the first conversation with the broker, the rehousing was agreed. Ken told me to locate a suitable property, similar in location and size to what I had. I contacted an agent and he set up four viewings that very afternoon, based on like-for-like properties. The policy cover I have always had, for buildings and contents provides for 'like for like' housing.

I was living then in 28B Thameside, a two-bed flat in the middle slab of the terrace. And renting out the one above 28C. From the available choices of like-for-like accommodation presented by the agent, I chose a cute little two bed cottage at £2,000pm in West End, near Esher, close to long parkland walks for William. William and I moved in that same evening and the first purchase in my new set of material possessions was a super luxurious bed for William. It was a sweet time, nine months living in rental property, owning nothing, and approaching the assembly of new possessions with some care. I learned if something is worth owning, it should be the very best of that particular item. Experiencing the 'rebirth after fire' turned what might have been a bad thing into a beautiful opportunity for reinvention. Realizing the extent to which possessions own you. And weighty cost of responsibility attached to maintaining ownership. I approached refurnishing my life with caution. My first purchase was excellent quality bedding from Bentall's. The AXA Insurance repaired my burned house. To its pre-incident condition. Ken Quinton oversaw the whole process in the least stressful way for me. And about 9 Months after the incident, works to Thameside were complete. Two levels, 28B and 28C were completely rebuilt, rewired and plumbed, and furnished to a luxury standard. I terminated the rehousing lease in 2002 and returned to Thameside, moving into the completely rebuilt top flat, 28C and immediately found a good quality tenant for 28B at top dollar. William loved being back home. Taking up his station on the sofa arm which gave him a direct sight of the River outside. He could keep an eye on the towpath between his personal inspection walks. Nothing would escape his vigilant eye. Anyone approaching the house would be identified by his specific bark reserved for this purpose, appearing shortly before the door bell ringing. Not long after my return to Thameside and my two brand-new apartments, I met Krasnopovich. And just a few months after he moved into my home the reinsurance notice arrived from the Insurance broker.

"Bad news" Ken said. *"Because the fire claim exceeded £50,000, the AXA are not prepared to reinsure. And I am having a hard time finding anyone else."*

I ticked the box of a name who had claimed more than the red flag trigger amount for regular cover. The property in my name was now assessed as a high risk. Blighted for Insurance purposes. I had to answer the question *"Have you claimed more than £50,000 in the past five years."* Answer yes and the system kicks you out. I tried calling other insurers myself, and every-one was the same. The £50,000 question.

"Have you claimed more than £50,000 in the past five years?"

Ken Quinton called to discuss the options. Insurers had to, by law, provide cover for one year following the claim, but that year had passed and now they were declining cover. For the 2003- 2004 period. My only option, Ken explained, was to pay a specialist insurer a high premium reflecting the high risk. And in four years-time, I would be able to go back to the AXA.

As fortune would have it this conversation was in place when Krasnopovich returned from work one evening and as is the way with these things, it became the theme du jour over dinner that night, the outcome of which was his professional advice;

"Put the freehold in my name. I will apply for Insurance and answer no to the question, "have you claimed recently", which will be true, and let me insure the house, until the claim history has expired, after which I simply transfer the title back to you. I want to help in some small way for all you have done for me." The title was the freehold to my home and responsible for providing Buildings Insurance for my home, which is divided into three leaseholds covered by this policy. Although in itself the freehold has only a nominal value. (I paid £1,500 for it) its main function is to ensure the three leases are protected with Buildings cover. And take care of the maintenance for all communal parts. The value in the property is in the long leases, not the freehold. Ken Quinton's lowest quote for the 'high risk' cover was in the region of £2,800 however Krasnopovich returned after a brief period of internet enquiry to say he found a policy at £400 PA. Ironically the underwriter was the AXA. My first thought was, it can't be legal. And so, as always when facing a financial decision relating to my property, I consulted my IFA, Larry Chester, the second professional person I met when arriving in the UK in 1985. (The first was my accountant to this day.) Every financial decision I made ever since moving to the UK was guided by Larry. Including the Insurance of my property. The meet with Larry over this 'freehold transfer for Insurance' was memorable. He was adamant that this advice from Krasnopovich was effectively Insurance fraud and that I not pursue it.

"I can't advise you to do this. You will be misleading Insurers with a lie. Basically. Its Insurance fraud"

It was also the first time Larry heard about Krasnopovich moving in with me. Larry was immediately, protectively suspicious of Krasnopovich and his motives. And made his suspicions clear. I left that meeting having decided to decline Krasnopovich's offer and go ahead with the expensive policy from Ken. In an awkward conversation later that day when Krasnopovich returned from work I explained Larry's concerns.

"We won't be able to have you as the named policy holder. Larry says it's not legal. It would be misleading Insurance and tantamount to fraud."

His reply was firm. *"He's not a lawyer. I am. This is completely legal."*

I listened. And allowed him to convince me. Technically Krasnopovich may have been right. In law the devil is in the detail. As a lawyer he knew answering 'No' to the £50,000 question was not a lie. But. And the But is obvious. The following day I went for a second meet to revisit the subject with Larry, referring him to Krasnopovich's comment. The meeting did not go well. *"I cannot be associated with this decision. You know what my position is. You are on your own with this. Just make sure that if you do it you get him to sign a trust agreement to give your Freehold back when the five years have passed."*

Larry's last word to me when I confirmed I was going to accept Krasnopovichs' advice was *"You're making a mistake."* Fortunately though, because he was concerned about the legality, Larry kept detailed memos of that period. A paper trail that would prove extremely helpful in the court case. Larry was the first witness to step forward after Krasnopovich's lying claim was served on me and I saw that Krasnopovich claimed that he 'absolutely owned' the freehold. It was his title.

I called Larry Chester as soon as I saw that claim. He assured me he had the original letter he sent following our meeting in 2003, as well as memos of our two meets and his advice. "*I will gladly be a witness if this goes to court*" he assured me. His notes included the agreement to transfer the title with a written declaration of trust providing for its return 'upon demand'. A useful insurance for me if he was going to pursue his lying claim. A reputable Independent financial adviser with a paper trail showing beyond any doubt exactly why the freehold went into Krasnopovichs' name. presented this idea so confidently there was some appeal for me in paying £400 pa instead of £2,800 pa. And I agreed. I transferred the Freehold into his name enabling him to take out the buildings insurance policy at the lower rate, which I then paid in full, as usual. I thought of his part in this as some form of repayment for the loans I had given him, that were never repaid. Here was something he could do for me by way of repayment. At the same time, acting on Larry's advice, I had a lawyer prepare a simple 'Declaration of trust'. Which in summary is a document confirming he held the title in Trust for me and would return the title to me upon request. Simple. In this way late in 2003, Krasnopovich came to own the Freehold of my home, in a Trust agreement which made him the Lessor and me the Lessee. My name on the titles of the long leases remained unchanged. All that did change is Krasnopovich became the named party on the Insurance cover. And his name went to the Land registry as the Freeholder. With that done, he signed a new Insurance policy with the AXA, declaring that he had not claimed over £50,000 in the past five years. And agreed the same level of cover I had had before exactly as I required of him. I paid the cost for the year in advance directly to the broker. Buildings and contents. Exactly as I had done previously. And since.

For whatever reason, the AXA did not cross reference the property with the name on the policy. I pointed out that they were likely to do that, I mean, it makes sense, but Krasnopovich told me they would not and he was right. He knew at that time; they went by the name of the Insured party and not by the property address. He had checked with a property lawyer at his firm, he confirmed to me. His legal advice to me was good. I closed the matter by thinking it would only be 4 years, one year had already passed, and my name would be clear for buildings insurance and we would simply reverse the procedure. Krasnopovich would transfer the title back at the Land registry, at no cost to me, and no one would ever know.

And as 2003 came to a close, that was that. My freehold was in his name. And the house had insurance cover with the AXA at the lower rate. He was the trustee Lessor, and each year that followed, he would follow my instruction to renew cover, which I would then pay in full.

4 The break up and make up 2008

"she wants to fuck you". Drunken text messages from members of family law

After some five years together, since Valentine's day 2003, Krasnopovich's progress up the work and social ladder was modest if consistent. I applied my best efforts to impact on his career positively. One example was to stop him going umm after every third word. *"Pay me a pound for every time you say Umm."* Soon he could complete a whole phrase with measured timing and without ums and ahs. I didn't actually take any of the hundreds of pounds he would have owed in this process.

The dinner table conversation every night for the first year was entirely about him. Revisiting events of his day and then interpreting his reaction and offering suggestions on alternatives.

When less is more.

When to turn on charm, timing.

And to discriminate.

Notice what shoes they wear.

Get rid of time wasters quickly. Don't waste one moment.

And crucially, recognize that this is a great opportunity you have to influence the lives of children. That is the highest aspiration for this gig. It is what attracted me to helping him in this way. Recognizing that in family law, members have a unique opportunity to impact on the lives of children. Sort out warring parents to find the best outcome for the children. Use the power of your position to manipulate them through strength of will towards agreeing the best case for the children. That is the highest purpose of this job and where you will find the most significant return. The first few years rewarded me with some gratitude that made prudence, most notably a co-habitation agreement seem unnecessary. Our finances never co-mingled and all the leaseholds were in my name. 28B since 1986. For the first two years he lived entirely off my generosity and aside of making no contribution to the costs of his lifestyle living with me, he benefitted from numerous loans of small amounts near months end to tide him through. £1,000 here, £2,000 there. (On multiple occasions.) Gratefully acknowledged with a *'thank you honey xxx'* email. (Of which 3 were admitted as evidence in court totaling £7,000). With the considerable financial gap between us so transparently clear, it never occurred to me to have a cohabitation agreement drawn up. Or to draft loan terms for the loans I was making, albeit I didn't really expect to be repaid until Krasnopovich was financially able to do so without difficulty. And I knew that would take some time at the rate he was progressing. I was just pleased to be able to make such a profound impact on someone's life in which the signs of progress were so clearly evident.

Until:

Time moved forward and by 2007 it was clear on an intuitive level that our relationship had peaked and was headed in a downward direction that experience informed me spelled only one outcome. I would identify the turning point as the Month his salary increase in the family department at MWT reached a point where he was not wholly reliant on me for financial support. His growing discontent in our living arrangement became palpable. Most noticeably around his irritation with Evans visits.

Evan was then a 20-year-old hard working student, at University of West Sussex, with a penchant for playing computer games with the headphones on when visiting. Perhaps a conflict of interest reared its head with Krasnopovich. There is always the potential for attention rivalry in a relationship featuring a child from the past. When Eric and I separated he gave me a very helpful list of reasons why. At number two was. "*I will never be the number one love of your life. That is Evan.*"

I thought about that for many years after and he was right. I put a great deal of my life and attention into Evan. And all of my love. Time and attention that never went to Eric. Just a simple fact of dynamics surrounding relationships where one side has a child. While, in our case making matters worse, the other wants a child but sees no prospect of that happening. It was an issue for Eric that I barely noticed because whenever Evan arrived home, I was so thrilled to be with him. Eric noticed and never understood why I loved another child so much but did not want to have a child with him. I still don't know the answer to that. I just wasn't ready to have a child. After seeing the horrible mess of a broken family, I would never want to risk putting a child through that. The only upside memory brings from that experience is my enduring interest in family law. All that I saw and learned from that period of seeing the madness that consumes separating partners arguing over a child who becomes no more than leverage for money. It is a unique level of madness that should have its own name. No one hates more viciously than a parent using their child to win some sense of victory over a former lover.

Meanwhile, back in 2008 by now, as my relationship with Nico was winding down, there were multiple signs it was along the same lines as Eric's leaving. He resented the fact that I had a child and he did not and I would not have one with him. Or get married. In material terms, my estate, at that time was a net amount of over £2 million. I didn't actually work this out. I had not, up until that moment, ever considered attaching a numerical value to my worth. It was Nico, during a walk down the towpath who casually mentioned "*Do you know your net worth is over two million*". I didn't think much of it at the time, but again with hindsight? What a curious thing for a boyfriend to say. I had no idea how much I was worth. How did he?

Why did he?

My net worth, whatever it would be many years later, at the time of calculation, including the three leases and the freehold, was to be Evan's inheritance. I had a will to this effect.

Generally, despite being at the end of another relationship I thought would have continued, I was at a good stage of life, reflecting the long work hours and good business decisions of the past 25 years. I had a passive income stream that meant I could choose how I spent each day for the rest of my life. That is to say, at the time I met Krasnopovich and invited him into my life, that is where I was. And since then the market had gone up. Despite Krasnopovich's numerous entreaties; and he proposed many times through the years, marriage was not in my sights, even though I did want to please him. Too many warning signs, attached to the unhappiness I saw at the core of his being. That thing I had tried so hard to fix was not a complete job. Community of property, me marrying him would have been contrary to my growing awareness that his interest in me was money first, romance second. The misinterpreted 'bad boy' thing that interested me in the same way as a rehabilitation officer with an empty schedule, showed me a link between his inner discontent and his understanding of gratitude. He focused on what he did not have rather than being grateful for what he did. My impression that I could see much of what he needed to learn made those qualities in him attractive to my interests as a helper and healer. That was the positioning between us. A teacher maybe.

But not as a wife.

I think all my other relationships reflect the same balance. I am attracted to the idea of being kind and helpful to my partners. And post separation I think it is true to observe that all look back on their time with me in a positive way. I have confirmed this to some extent with the majority of my exes. But after five years with Nico, despite small successes seeing an end to the anxiety attacks and the poor decision making with drink and drugs and sleeping with married women which was the extent of his dating experience before me, the absence of sincere honest affection and the imbalance between gratitude and presumption – devaluing qualitative generosity by taking-for-granted, presented me with a discontent that heralded an imminent end to the relationship. The absence of basic honesty was real. Something observed by several of my friends who would later disclose to me their disappointment at seeing I started dating Krasnopovich. Days would go by and I would realize he had not on one single occasion made my day better. As I always tried with everyone I met. And as I believed I had modeled for him. He just didn't care about anything but his own work progress.

Hmmmm. Hindsight.

Krasnopovich's ongoing obsessive commitment to prioritizing work above all else and seeing people primarily as potential clients masked a deeper denial of living in his own reality. Ironically he would conversationally refer to the shortcomings in the 'work life balance' of his work mates when so clearly his own was askew. Now, after 5 years the graph of progress between the X of his improvement from the personality issues blighting his personal growth and the Y of my feeling of reward at helping him grow into the person he wanted to be was firmly headed away from its zenith. A straight line downwards. This was slow dancing in a burning room but at least one of us knew where the fire escape was. I recognized the signs. Matters came to a head one night in October 2008. The previous year had seen a marked increase in late nights out which he explained as 'Networking'. With potential clients, as this is how you grow your client base in Divorce law. Often he would return stinking drunk on the last train to Thameside. I never looked for lipstick on his collar but that's because I am above that sort of suspicion. I have never known jealousy as anything more than a base emotion which I got past after my first relationship. If you don't trust your love and allow jealousy to contaminate your feelings, the worst will always follow. I don't do jealousy. I was however increasingly concerned that despite his enthusiastic explanations of how the meetings were working out, he would not drink on most nights with me, while on his networking nights, he would; Invariably coming home sloshed, reeking of alcohol. Staggering.

In 2008, as these events occurred we were living in a rental property following a flood at my Thameside home. While remedial works were being completed in my home, the Insurance cover provided a like-for-like rehousing. Which was a pleasant three bed apartment ten minutes-walk from the building works at my home. Works projected to last for 9 months. After one of Krasnopovich's networking nights in the City, when he arrived back shortly before midnight, I was already in bed. As usual he would text me regularly and I knew when he was on the train from Waterloo. That night he walked into the bedroom, wobbly on his feet, reeking of alcohol, and kissed me hello with a sloppy '*Hi honey, I'm home*'. I felt physically revolted. He was texting when he got home, his phone still in his hand. He put the phone on the bedside table while he stumbled to the bathroom. While he was out of the room the phone beeped as a text message came in and, by reflex, I looked to see who it was. He had been out with a Barrister friend to Chambers at 1 Hare Court. Where lawyers and barristers 'network' and get pissed. The new text in a long list of texts they must have been exchanging on the train ride was from his barrister mate Alfie Geadah and was just one line.

"She wants to fuck you".

I had a heart racing moment when for the first time I realized all was not as it seemed with Nico Krasnopovich. I decided to say nothing, leave the phone and feign sleep. There was no advantage to be gained by confrontation. I knew then that our relationship was over. Not just because of the text, whatever innocent explanation could be attached to its context, but because of how the text made me feel at that time and place in my life and his life. I did not want to be a party to suspicions and jealousy. That I felt these searing pangs of this base-energy was in itself my official notice the relationship was over. I felt that it was almost as if he had provoked that reaction in me by his drunken sloppy conduct and leaving the phone right next to me when such an incendiary message appeared. Later, in conjecture, I wondered if it was done on purpose. Such was the extent of my distrust. The next day I called my dear friend, a wonderfully intuitive therapist who knew all about Nico and me, Luisa Hay, and arranged to meet her for a talk. We walked for hours through the forest near her home in the outskirts of Bournemouth and talked. I disclosed the text I had seen, its effect on me and my interpretation of how I felt. By the end of the walk, after hours of exploring every possibility and every sign, it was clear that on every level, the best way forward for both of us was to separate with all haste. The highest good, we concluded, was that he pursue his goals. His career, and the marriage with children and a picket fence suburban house, so clearly to the fore of his current wish list. And I continue my own journey and meet the right partner if that was to be. I had a long hug with Luisa, who has been like a mother from another planet to me and left assured that I had arrived at a thoughtful and mindful best-case decision. I felt good. I had done everything for the highest good and was confident that I was soon to begin a new chapter in my life, away from servicing Nico's needs. With my mind firmly made up I arranged to meet him after work the same night at the Kings Head, which he only reluctantly agreed to.

"Do we have to honey; I have a splitting headache from last night".

We met in the Kings Head where he arrived directly from the train at the same time as I arrived from home. He saw me, gave me a 'hi honey' kiss on the cheek, and headed straight for a vague friend standing alone at the bar; Fannie, an unfortunately overweight unattractive local pub lass from Glasgow whose hostile Catholic ways I found desperately unattractive. Something Nico knew and was quite transparently using as a shield to stay away from talking to me. Knowing I would not want to join any conversation with Fannie involved. He bought her a drink while I looked on bemused. He simply ignored my presence and kept on talking tirelessly to Fannie, who, perhaps unwittingly, provided him with the opportunity to avoid any private conversation with me. I expect because he most likely had seen the 'sex' text the night before and had some idea that I had seen it. And for that reason, because he knew where the conversation was headed, he was spending what was clearly the absolute minimum amount of time possible with me. Avoiding the inevitable. I became increasingly annoyed standing in the pub with an empty wine glass while he chatted away gaily with Fannie. When it was clear that he was not going to join me for a private conversation, I decided the pub was not going to be the place to have that talk and so I proposed we drink up and head home. He declined. Emphatically. *"I'm enjoying talking to Fannie. Come on Honey, stay for one more."* The atmosphere became even more awkward.

"I'm leaving then, stay as long as you want. See you later."

I left and headed up Thames road towards the rental property to start packing. Literally. The works on repairing my home from the flood of 2008 were nearing completion and one room on the ground floor was basically habitable. As I walked the five minutes down Thames road back to the rental, I formulated my relocation plan. I intended calling my handy man John B first thing, and having a bed put in that newly carpeted room and 'camping' there until the building works completed. The kitchen and bathroom on that level were just weeks from being complete and at that time there was a working shower and toilet. For Krasnopovich, there would be three months left on the lease for the rental property and that would be enough time for him to find his next port of call. His own flat in Hounslow was coming up for lease renewal so it would be easy for him to just move back to where he was when we met, 5 years before. The details of separation were all worked out in my head. I had more or less completed all the small aspects of our separation. By the time I opened the front door my decision was made. I was going to pack and leave. Hopefully before he got back from his drinking session with Fannie. Simple. No need for any big upset. We just went in different directions. No harm done. But I had only just begun packing when he arrived back from the pub. Obviously after seeing me leave he had decided to check in, coming straight over in an affected embrace saying *"Aw honey are you cross with me"*.

I was by this stage past conversation and continued packing an overnight bag, at which point he saw what I was doing and realized events had moved on beyond his control. I don't remember the exact final words, but the net effect was, I would leave to spend the night in a hotel and return the following day while he was out at work to fetch my things. So it wouldn't be necessary to have any dramatic final farewell. I reminded him the term left on the lease at the rental would give him three months to decide whether he wanted to go back to his flat or move closer to town perhaps? He didn't say anything. Not a word. Just stared at me, disbelieving. I think at that time, in his heart, on some level, he was quite relieved that the break up was so well managed. With no disruption to his work schedule. I left that night without any drama, just my overnight bag on my shoulder, my laptop in its case, and a *"bye"* as I clicked the door closed behind me. William was at my side throughout. He seemed to intuit what was happening, as usual with that dog. He stayed close to my ankles while I packed and was just inches away as we walked out. Walking reassuringly close on his virtual lead. Guarding my aura closely. Or so he seemed to think. Giving Krasnopovich a simmering glare as he followed me out. I walked towards Thameside Road with William skipping and bounding around the sidewalks he knew so well for the ten-minute walk, which took me past Jo's house, my friend and neighbor on Thameside.

The lights were still on. She was still up watching TV and what are friends for if not a surprise late night visit at a time like this. After a friendly chat about events and a few beers with Jo and her husband Tom, I spent the night in their guest room. Both Jo and Tom expressed relief that I had left Krasnopovich.

'*You are worth so much better*'.

In the days that followed I learned this was a consensus amongst my long-term friends. That night I let William sleep on the bed with me. I placed him gingerly at the foot of the bed and he settled right in. He was over the moon. Lying very still in case I changed my mind. He knew sleeping on the bed was a very rare special occasion. He seemed to radiate happiness. Great sleep hygiene for me.

The following morning bright and early I called my handyman John B, who arrived soon after to help me. I had a bed installed on the ground floor at Thameside and arrived midmorning at the rental with Johns Van to empty out my belongings from there. I left linen for Krasnopovich to not have to worry about that. Before I left I had John help me and we cleaned the place, bathroom and kitchen. I explained the new arrangement to the Land Lady. I would honor the rest of the lease for Krasnopovich to remain at the rental. Krasnopovich would have almost three months to arrange his next accommodations, most probably moving back to his flat.

And by the end of the day, that was that. After five years, I was lying alone in my comfortable bed in a clean freshly prepared bedroom. With a new duvet and new bed linens. My first night back in my home in Thameside alone in a freshly painted room in a building site felt like a great new beginning. Like a weight had lifted. I didn't play any music. Just enjoyed the silence. I lay back breathing deeply. Expelling with each breath all the bad memories of Krasnopovich and his anxieties. Untangling my roots with him, one by one. Letting him go. Breathing my way back to my-self. Visualizing the untangling so effectively I could feel the dirt falling off the roots as they untangled and separated. I felt excitement building at all that lay ahead. All the possibilities available to me. Travel came to mind. Soon as the house works were finished I would take a long trip. America. Maybe drive the West coast from South to North. Fly to San Diego, rent a convertible and just drive until I felt like stopping. Head for Seattle. Better still, perhaps get a big Motorbike. A cruiser, like a Harley. Ride that coast highway. From San Diego up to Seattle. Stopping in Quinton Tarantino Motels on the way. With that last thought in a clear head leaving a warming glow of good feeling, I slept soundly for the first time in a year. Deep restorative sleep. By the time I awoke I felt a shift. My philotimia was for once directed at myself and not someone else. I felt good. Not sorrowful, as I was for months after Eric left. Then, there was a sense of lost love but that was swamped in the realization that this was unmistakably the best decision. It felt right on every level, including for Krasnopovich's interests. He so wanted marriage and children. Now he could pursue that without me holding him back. That day passed in a joyful bubble and the next night was better still. Weeks passed with no word between us and I very quickly settled back into my old ways. I started playing guitar for hours each day, writing thousands of words for a short story project. Playing tennis almost every day for two hours. Cooking dinner for my elderly neighbor, Peter Knightley. I actually enjoyed being his first responder and carer. He was such a bright spirit and so imbued with unconditional good intentions. It felt a little like coming out of a coma. Alive to putting my own interests to the fore. I didn't call Krasnopovich and he didn't call me. The only remaining issue between us was the return of the freehold following completion of the current Insurance claim. I figured that could wait. No pressing urgency. The Building reinsurance, which was the sole driver for addressing the freehold matter, was six months away. He was still a practicing lawyer and I did not imagine he would jeopardize that by doing anything stupid like spoil the Insurance claim that was in his name. About a month passed as I settled into my single life in my home, a two-level ground floor apartment, which was by this time almost completely redone following the flood. With hundreds of thousands of pounds of fixtures and fittings exactly where I had chosen to put them. The money I had worked hard to earn being put to good use.

And then the siding doors moment happened; my phone rang and I saw Nico's name on caller ID. No way was I going to answer. The phone rang on. I decided to answer only when I thought he might be in trouble. This could be an urgent call for help? Kindness. Gets you every time. But I was confident that I was very much done with his dishonesty and reassured that separation was best for both and felt confident this would come across clearly in any conversation. I would be extremely cautious about offering any help whatsoever. Nico started by thanking me for answering. Perceptive as ever.

"*I wonder if you would give me five minutes. Just a quick chat.*"

It was around 6.30 and would have been the time he usually arrived home from work, on the evenings when he wasn't 'Networking.' In what hindsight reveals as a moment of imperceptive weakness I agreed.

"*Five minutes. That's fine.*"

If only we had time travel to turn sliding doors. Just say no; "*sorry, I'm busy*" and hang up. He arrived at my door looking good. He had clearly made an effort. He launched into a highly charged speech before the door had even closed behind him. Within two minutes the talk was punctuated with tears.

This was a man who could not go forward in life without me.

He expressed his overwhelming desire to have a child with me and was effusive with his complimentary references to my qualities as a parent.

He said '*I love you and I can't imagine living without* you' delivered with the same tears I would recognize later in one of his Court appearances, when lying to last-minute switch judge Flaherty.

"*You are the most amazing person I have ever met. You have the most brilliant mind. I will never meet anyone as advanced as you. I will do anything to make you happy. I know what it takes and I will make it happen. I know I fucked up. But I also know exactly why. Let me explain.*"

What followed was a ten-minute speech. An immaculately prepared and presented, pleading argument, possibly the most compelling performance of his life as a professional liar. Nico Krasnopovich was going to lay 'all his cards on the table.' He asked me to enter into a dialogue with him towards a carefully structured agreement to partner up, not to marry him, which he explained he now understood was off the table, but to make a parental agreement to have a child together. Whereby, from my part:

I would agree to have a child with him and take care of raising the child. I would be the stay home mother able to paint a picture of an ideal human I wanted to see on this blank canvas of a new life, who, given our good DNA, would likely be a remarkable human being. I could train him, or her, in tennis from an early age. Maybe a future Wimbledon champion. We would have the means to take coaching all the way. This child would have the best of everything and especially affection. If I would agree to support his business growth, financially and with my business input, he was sure that he could rise to the highest earning levels in family law. Maybe even starting his own firm. Whatever happened next, he would be certain to provide all the expenses to give that child every opportunity and ensure I would be there to raise him without any distractions in the shape of having to earn income. He would provide. Perhaps though, I would assist applying my entrepreneurial skills towards establishing a successful new business in order that this would fund the child's needs. I would be the parent raising the child to my set of values, which he professed to admire above anyone he had met before. He returned to his theme with regularity, unafraid of repetition.

"You are by far the most advanced person I have ever met. Your ethical standards will translate perfectly to being a mother at this stage in your life it's the one thing you haven't done. You missed out on being there full time with Evan. Look at how you are with Evan. And imagine having a completely fresh canvas with no limit to the colors and brushes necessary to create a masterpiece of humanity.

Together we can collaborate on raising a child with all the privileges of our generation, in terms of dedication as well as opportunity, to be someone who could change the world for the better. Imagine the best of both of us in a child. How amazing would that be. And you know I will always have your back in being the best parent you can be."

He reiterated the extent to which I would be able to take on this authors role free of any liability in the costs of raising the child and was assured, repeatedly, following my reference to Evans experience. That there was no possibility of ever revisiting the broken family situation that affected Evan.

"You know how strongly I feel about broken families. I couldn't take the chance of bringing a child into a broken family."

"That will never happen. I give you my word. I want to be a parent. And I want to be a parent with you. I want you to have the full experience of being a mother all the time. Not just the way it was with Evan. I am committing to this with my heart and soul. It is my promise to you."

"To be clear. If there is any prospect of bringing another child into a broken family, you have no business going any further. You will need to convince me beyond all doubt that this is the case."

"I swear on my life. On everything that I hold dear. That will never happen. You have my word."

And from his part Krasnopovich agreed to undertake all of the child's expenses. *"I will draw up a business plan and show you. I will be able to pay the costs of a child without imposing on you. You can look at raising the child full-time without any financial pressure."*

He would commit to boosting his career to make enough to retire young so we could all travel as a family. I would stay home to raise the child, whilst assisting his business from home. We discussed what this would involve; editing legal letters for him, and guiding him to start his own law firm. *"With your experience in small business and my experience with family law, we can start a law firm we can own 100% of. That will pay for the best schooling and life opportunities for our child."*

Being a stay home mom there all the time with the child free from the burden of financial pressure was the carrot he dangled to convince me. I finally felt ready to have a child and in this tearfully emotive display I recognized his enthusiasm for this prospect was sincere. I did know enough about his family law experience to see how setting up a firm could be possible and despite his weaknesses as a person, I knew he had an eye for opportunity that married up well with making money out of family law. Having agreed in principle to consider taking this talk forward, I raised with him the specifics of the costs involved, having the firm impression that he had no idea. I had the experience of actual costs in raising a child in private education. Evan, at that time 20, was privately educated from the age of 3. Primarily my concern once the hurdle of the broken family had been crossed was cost. I was comfortable in my life at that stage and had learned a great deal about parenthood through my 20-year-old son. I asked Krasnopovich what he thought it would cost to raise a child 'with all opportunities". "Let's start from there. I will draft a business plan for all the costs for the first 18 years of a child's life, including private schooling. As well as how I plan to increase my earnings." And with that he kissed me, and I let myself go with the moment. The seed of the idea that I would have a child was planted. My concerns that I would have to increase my earning to pay for a child in my fifties and sixties, assuaged. Our new relationship would be based on bringing a child into the world and each playing a role in making a happy balanced life for that child. But first, the specifics had to be written down and agreed.

Krasnopovich asked to stay the night but I declined. "*Let's not rush this. It's vital we have every aspect understood and agreed before we go forward. Until then, stay at the rental and I will meet you for dinner tomorrow.*"

In the days and weeks that followed we met every night, starting with Krasnopovich presenting draft one of his business plan in which he identified the costs of a child in the first four years as zero.

We were not off to a good start.

Zero? FFS. Our age difference appeared far greater then than at any previous moment. But gradually we added flesh to the bones of the agreement. We addressed the reasons for our break up. He recognized that he had fallen short in terms of the relationship but that was not because he didn't love me, rather that he was so upset at the direction we were going, not getting married and having a child as I was approaching my forties, with a clock ticking on that possibility. His exact words were "*I can get over not being married yet, but I can't keep waiting for a child with you. And I do not see myself never experiencing fatherhood. I can see so clearly that we would raise an amazing child. I am truly sorry for the way I hid my head in the sand over my feelings. I should have been more open and direct with you.*"

The reasons for his seeming disrespect and late-night drunken returns from his overly abundant networking nights out, which would now be reined in, was all because he was upset at our relationship not going to the next level. I never mentioned the 'She wants to fuck you' text. Neither did he. For weeks we worked on drafting a written agreement. He learned that in fact babies do cost something in the first four years. And in the background, the idea that I had this opportunity to experience parenthood at this later stage in life was generating its own momentum. Our 18-year plan included buying a joint property in 5 years. He would qualify for a large mortgage after the formation of a new business, with two years accounts. By then I would have no mortgage on my three flats. Which would be rented at a premium to provide a steady passive income for me to pay my half of the new home and he would be earning big from his new firm, enabling him to pay his half of the mortgage. I went as far as agreeing that when we got to this point, we could marry. He seemed ecstatic over the developing agreement. We both identified the type of property we would like. Details of size, garden space, a separate annex for use as a studio. A granny flat for Evan in the event that he needed looking after in his final years. All achievable in a good area for schools in the £2.5 million price range. All of which was set out in numbers on a spread sheet. During this time I met with Larry (my IFA) and went over the 18-year plan. Filling in the blanks on the loans that would be necessary, what that would cost and how best to channel the income from my rentals for tax efficiency. Larry generated mortgage quotes for both the proposed matrimonial home as well as separate loans for rental property possibilities. Documents which, in the Flaherty hearing, would be useful in showing that we planned to buy a home together. Not stay in my home as a 'matrimonial home' as Krasnopovich would go on to claim. A great deal of consideration and effort went into dotting the i's and crossing the t's in Nico and Andrea's parental plan before we finally signed off on an agreement. Had we not reached this agreement to reconcile in November 2008, we would not have had a child and in all likely-hood he would have met and married someone else and had the children he was obsessed with having. Although I agreed to this 18-year plan, subject to the specific clauses I required, I did not agree marry Nico. He asked more than once *"Why don't we get married and make that commitment together?"*

The truthful answer is, although I had hoped for change, Krasnopovich is habitually dishonest. His 'bad boy' thing was attractive on a casual sex basis at the start. Then his vulnerability played on my helper instinct. But ultimately, his business is based on lying and to his credit, he is right up there with the best of them. The traditional ethical concern for 'as you sow you reap' or 'do unto others as you would have them do to you' is absent. It is all about billable hours. Whatever it takes. It's not lying, in his mind. It's an interpretation of truth that excludes elements whilst repeating others for effect. Effective legal lying is an acquired skill. Selective emphasis and compensatory selective omission. Krasnopovich went from basic amateur lying skills rewarding him with just £35K annually when we met, to a millionaire when he left. The growth in his income runs parallel to his development as a skilled confident liar.

My part in this is real. I coached him towards winning cases although, to be clear, my motivation was always to win in order to be able to help children. That's is for me the great irony in how this story has played out. I learned a great deal from my first experience of parenthood with Evan. I saw my role in a family-law-family as guiding Nico towards seeing the real prize in this occupation is using your power to ensure that children get the best deal possible.

Where we went wrong is when he humored me by seemingly agreeing.

Sadly though. As subsequent events make all too clear, Krasnopovich's interest is net worth first. Children's best interests never more than leverage to service that interest. In the matter of all that advice and guidance I gave, as with the money generosity, I feel duped. His dishonesty took many forms. Throughout our relationship he repeatedly asked for loans, many of which were never paid back in a dishonest fashion, requiring a prompt from myself, leading to an email that went *"Oh, sorry honey, I forgot I promised x ....."*.

I recognized in him a fundamental inherent dishonesty, just as his equity partners at MWT did when they expelled him in disgrace for the same reason. It is unusual to hear of an equity partner being expelled for dishonesty. In a 'clear your desk right now' moment. Escorted out of the building on the spot. Krasnopovich experienced that because, he was then and is still, fundamentally, intrinsically dishonest. He has that ability to present ridiculous lies with a straight face as if he believes, that we see trending in Politics.

The last thing I will say of that reconciliation is this. When considering his proposal I made plain to him that I had overcome depression. That I had a history of depression, since the loss of my family unit aged ten. Made worse by my unpleasant experience with the South African security police. And that all of my subsequent life choices were based on avoiding triggers for that unwelcome condition. I believe he filed that information away for this fathers-day ambush moment. Knowing exactly how best to create a family-law label of 'mental infirmity'. It is true that I had no symptoms of depression for decades, until that traumatic experience on fathers-day. Described by one therapist to me as 'a crucifixion.' Executed without any ethical reservation by an individual prepared to go that extra mile to create a winning position for a blackmail demand.

He understood what I was disclosing to him and assured me that 'my aim is true.' Five years later he engineered the fathers-day mafia hit and set into motion the events that followed.

5 The parenting agreement
The last thing the world needs is another child from a broken family. Convince me that will never happen

At the heart of the breakdown of our relationship in 2008 was the matter of having children. Krasnopovich wanted to. I did not. Children cost a lot. Financially and emotionally. The world was overpopulated. I already had a son, 19 at that time. My beautiful John, recently headed off to Uni to learn about brain function. I was all too aware that Krasnopovich had no idea of the emotional side of parenting. In his work training as a lawyer in family law, children are chattels, valued by their parent's net worth. He seemed to me to be the least paternal person I had met. I was genuinely surprised that he wanted a child at all. It appeared more as a conscious social decision than an instinctive one. The product of nurture in a schooling that projected marriage to a good little wife with 2.4 children and an Aga in the kitchen and a man cave and a Porsche SUV. I was still in my 20's when my marriage ended and I learned first-hand the reality of a broken family as a parent, to add to my child's eye view of the same experience of profound loss from when I was ten. From both sides, the unknown is optimisms best friend. But now, as a fully formed adult living in awareness of my authentic self, with the benefit of twenty-years of experience raising one child in a broken family I knew the disadvantages of broken family parenting and I knew in all certainty that this was not a process I would ever revisit. This was a trigger to my depression. I had explained it as "Depression is a luxury I cannot afford." In all our conversations on the child subject the isolated point was this; I was not interested in risking the possibility of a broken family. A concern that remained alongside my reservations about Krasnopovich's development as a person in the absence of the traditional paternal instincts. I imagined that if all it ever said on my memorial was *"She never knowingly brought a child into a broken family"* I would consider that a life well lived. I still thought there was much personal growth ahead for Krasnopovich before that level of commitment for fatherhood could be entered into.

Could I have been more-clear?

To say I labored this point exhaustively is a fair estimation. My position regarding motherhood began with *"I am not interested in any possibility that involves a child growing up in a broken family."*

How abundant his reassurances were. He stuck at 2 children for a time and eventually it came to one. One child to enjoy the best of everything. Possibly even to play at Wimbledon in 20 years-time. The thought of coaching my son in tennis was a shrewd aspect of Krasnopovich's presentation of how much I would enjoy having a child. Knowing my appetite for the game. Krasnopovich was persuasive and he identified possibly the only reason I would have another child in light of all the reasons why I shouldn't at this late age for parenthood. Raising Evan was a shared business. I was not there the whole time. I was working long days and nights. I missed his first steps. I missed chunks of his development as is the way with co-parenting in a broken family.   Krasnopovich presented a picture of me raising a child, being there all the time. Without the financial pressures accompanying raising a child. This took the form of two pillars of argument.

The first being financial, the second emotional.

The financial side was an in-depth assurance that we would prioritize his legal career to ensure the costs of the child would be met in this way. The business plan part of the parenting agreement Krasnopovich drew up for the proposed child had to detail costs of raising a child, because I knew from experience what they really involve, whilst it was plain that he did not. His business plan began with costs for the first 4 years as 'zero'. Believing that the costs of a child only start with schooling. Some revision followed and eventually we arrived at a realistic budget. This would accommodate a live-in nanny to assist with Sam as I would need some time each day for my business interests. Land-lording, book writing, music composition and legal letter writing for Nico. He would pay the cost of the nanny from the legal business. I would work from home and have the opportunity to enjoy his second pillar of argument. The emotional side of raising a child myself, being there all the time for all the stages and getting to raise my own child. A 100% parent.

And as the plan progressed so did my interest in parenthood. This opportunity to be an older parent had some growing appeal. My final opportunity to raise a child with the resources and the time while still able to look forward to being there for a 21st birthday. And it came to that one decision. Krasnopovich wanted to have children and at that age, the clock was ticking. If we were to be together, I could not deny him the opportunity to experience fatherhood. It was either, separate and let him find someone else to have a child with, or come up with a workable agreement to have a child together. As is often the case in my communication, a song lyric formed the header to the subject.

"If you can't feed a baby. Then don't have a baby." Michael Jackson wrote.

I understood the emotional needs in feeding a baby. The final word in the decision was; *'I am not interested in having a baby in a broken family. If we are going to do this it will not be to bring another child into a broken family.'*

Only after exhausting his best efforts to convince me did I accept his assurance that we would put all other considerations to one side in our joint commitment to ensuring this proposed child would not end up as another statistic of a broken family.

A firm physical contact, deep eye presentation of; *"that will never happen"* followed. And it didn't until four years after Sam was born and a new set of interests nullified all previous agreements and commitments in Krasnopovich's legal brain. None more than the arrival of financial independence. Not only seeing a £350,000 gross income in year one of the new law firm, but more significantly, knowing that was just the start of the earnings curve in the business plan. He had his first taste of big money and he loved it. More than anything. What a temptation. Your now captain of the world. With the power of money promising so much more money. You deserve whatever you want. Surely that's how reward works?

It seemed the lessons of our break up (in 2008) were well learned on his side. His discontent and late-night absences explained by his heartbreak at not being able to have a child with his love. Missing out on that huge life experience. It took about 5 weeks after that 'fateful' night when he showed up at my door, to complete a detailed 18-year plan. To have a child and raise him. And find great schools for him and pay for it all. In many ways we made a good team. He is smart, with a good memory for detail and crucially, willing to say anything without getting distracted by small details, like truthfulness. There was a productive yin and yang symmetry in our relationship. I felt I offered the ethical anchor to ensure his ability to lie without blinking an eyelid would ensure he would not cross any lines where children were involved. We were very much a gardener and a flower in the analogy.

The perfect union is between a gardener and a flower. Two gardeners sometimes works. Two flowers never will.

And this is borne out by the fact that for almost all of the time we were together Krasnopovich would refer ethical decisions in his work to me, often inviting me to write the draft letters both for MWT clients and even more so with the new firm, Krasnopovich McDonald LLP. Over the few weeks that this parenting agreement took to complete, we remained living apart, he in in the rental property while I stayed in the hastily prepared room at my building site home in Thameside. We signed off the agreement in principle some ten months before May 2009, when I gave birth to Sam. The pregnancy was a happy time, in which my belief that the womb baby responds to sounds meant a great deal of Bach piano music was played a great deal. I had previously spent a year making an album of Bach music and that album is the soundtrack to Sam's growth in utero. My experience of musical composition recognizes Bach as a uniquely influential musical source. I would often play guitar parts during the pregnancy, on several of the many collectible guitars then in my collection which produced beautiful resonant sounds. Occasionally met by kicking in the womb. Kick kick sounded to me like '*Yes I like that one. Play it again*'. My happy audience of one getting off to an early start. Feeling the vibration of beautiful elevated music on a superior quality stringed instrument resonating right to his little fetus ears. Womb dancing to the sound of Bach. Ana Vidovic was another great player of Bach whose sounds the young fetus enjoyed and who was in fact the player I had on in the background during Sam's entry to planet Earth. Sam was born to the sound of music. Good music. Bach was his musical midwife in the delivery. I remember *Ode to Joy* was playing when the midwife passed Sam into my arms and I saw him for the first time.

My beautiful Sam. Love at first sight. From his first breath.

Although Christa at MWT had given Krasnopovich his first position in family law, effectively giving him the career he now had, along with showing him the ethical steps to take towards becoming a rainmaker, prioritizing billable hours to high net worth clients, after Sam was born Nico's growing ambition made him bitter that Christa was obstructing his progress. He began routinely bad-mouthing Christa, routinely bad mouthing her to prospective clients enquiring about Christa while at the same time accepting social invitations to Christa's home, where he would be sweetness and light. Hmmm. I saw a side of Krasnopovich that worried me. If he lied with such a straight face to Christa, his mentor and work confidante, then ……. …….. There was a red flag but I was not paying attention. We had a firm agreement in which I was totally committed. And I had Sam. The center of my world. As soon as possible, with the goal of leaving Christa's shadow, Krasnopovich moved from her office to take over as head of the newly vacant position in MWT's Surbiton office. It was a good career move. And had a salary rise to go with it. By now he was up to £60,000 PA. Gross.

6 William's stroke and Krasnopovich's expulsion

William of Thameside and my goodbye with the greatest schnauzer never to be expelled by his law firm partners for lying

After moving to the MWT Surbiton office, free from his resentment arising from Christa's boorish South African dominance and being in a catchment area with many high net worth clients, head-of-department Krasnopovich was enjoying some success at work. Up and running as a player in the family-law game. By this time we had discussed the idea of leaving MWT and setting up a new law firm and early diligence towards this end was underway. With this salary increase, I raised the suggestion that he might start paying towards housing costs at Thameside. He did the math for me and determined he could afford to pay £500 a month. He was earning £800 monthly from renting his own flat, but he explained that he still had to pay the mortgage on that. My average cost for living expenses (excluding mortgage) was £2,500 monthly so £500 was helpful. And for the first time, Krasnopovich was free of debt and financially confident enough to be able to contribute to his cost of living with me. The start of big change came in 2011 when Christa very suddenly and unexpectedly left MWT, where she was the well-established head of the family law department. She had been approached with a much better offer from a City firm looking to start a family department, to exploit this growing market. Christa had approached Krasnopovich, to effectively poach him from MWT for an increased salary at the new City firm. I discussed the merits of this move at length with Krasnopovich and in the course of the pros and cons debate, the mechanics and advantages of setting up a local law firm became increasingly clear. More money and more control. And crucially, not under Christa, with whom Nico appeared to have a schizophrenic relationship, bad mouthing her at every opportunity and then calling her for friendly advice without a second thought. Thameside was a good area not over served by family law firms as was the case in Surbiton. Krasnopovich had some 180 open files at MWT, divorces underway, many of which would mature into court hearings over the next year, which is when the payment would come in for the divorce lawyer. (Eventually this client base would translate directly into £180,000 for the new firm's first year accounts.) The big billing in a family law department being the court hearings and the time intensive demands of securing a financial settlement and child visitation. Clearly, a settlement uncontested would mean little or no revenue for the divorce lawyer. That is not the sort of work divorce lawyers get rich from. Often Krasnopovich would report to me over dinner that he had billed ten hours that day at his then rate of £350 per hour, for MWT. (Plus VAT.) I would sometimes wonder how that worked when he had only been at work for eight hours. But from what I saw of family law in the ten years of living with a member, this overcharge is not uncommon. People getting divorced (or separated) are at their most vulnerable and it's not difficult to run up the bill dramatically. What are they going to do about it at that point? Their lowest ebb in life being the client demographic.

It was also clear that his salary was no more than 20% of the total he invoiced for the firm. Much of the balance going towards the annual distributions made to the equity partners. He talked about becoming an equity partner the way a 350-pound American talks about Hamburgers. The dynamic of that time in my happy home was; a young child growing up in a joy filled buzzing musical atmosphere with art and activity, a good piano, a proper drum kit, numerous guitars around, his own ukulele and his own nanny, Sally, 18, who entertained him when I needed to get some work done. I was fairly indifferent about the nanny's contribution as I had Sam around all the time. I never left home to go to work. I effectively retired from any session work, and focused my work interest on writing a book. I had always wanted to write a novel and now I had the opportunity, in a process which would take place in my studio at home in the room located next to the living room where the door was always open for Sam to come in for a play whenever he tired of Sally. Something that happened several times daily during the working hours. Often these visits would lead to a musical moment, like playing drums together or playing piano and showing him a scale. He was close to mastering the major scale with his left hand. In C. Do re mi fa so la ti do. Whatever I was doing at the time his curly golden locks appeared bouncing through the studio door, would go to one side and he would have my full attention. He would always have a question ready to start his visit with. *"Mummy, where do clouds come from?"* Krasnopovich would get back at 6.15 most week days, the networking evenings now reduced to an average once a week. Usually he would spend some play time with Sam and me before his bedtime, after which we would enjoy the evening meal I prepared daily and catch up on the day's events. In percentage terms, as we had planned and agreed, I was there all the time for Sam and Krasnopovich made sure to allow 10% of his time to be with Sam. Most days.

As his work at MWT progressed the time came for a decision on equity partnership. The bottom line was, although Krasnopovich intended leaving MWT, it made financial sense to invest in equity partnership for the bigger payout on departure, and, crucially, he would own his own files. Important when considering what was being planned with setting up a new law firm and taking the files. As an employee taking the files would be theft. As a partner, the lines were more blurred. Partners own their own files. Starting a new law firm without any clients would have been a very different prospect to taking a guaranteed £180,000 to help the first year along.

He calculated the cost of buying in equity at MWT and found he had just over a forty-thousand-pound shortfall. Another young lawyer at MWT, Serena, was made partner at the same time and we marked the occasion with a celebratory meal with Serena and her husband, who worked as a fireman. During conversation at that dinner I learned Serena was taking out a loan to finance her buy-in equity, which would cost her just 5% in interest. Later Krasnopovich raised the matter with me. He had most of the equity buy in sum in savings, but was a little short. *"£40,000 would do it."* Krasnopovich didn't want to take out a loan because of the expense. *"Isn't it a waste of 5% honey."* When he asked me for forty thousand pounds for this purpose I transferred the money to his account the following day. It made sense to help my son's parent in his business. After all, his success was our success. Obviously, being inappropriately filtered for dishonest business by the lens of kindness that is my outlook, and unable to imagine my trusted partner as dishonest, I did not draft a letter of agreement for the loan. Or even think of putting it in writing. Nor would I need to. The bank statement transfer of £40,900 (It turned out he needed £900 more to make up the full amount) is the record. The gift was the interest on the money. Not the money itself. Very clearly understood. *"I only need the money until the end of the year. My first partners disbursement is in December and that will more than cover the loan amount."*

I knew from Krasnopovich's figures the cash-flow of the MWT business and how much the partner distributions at the year-end would be. Krasnopovich assuring me in this way that his pay-out would be far in excess of the loan amount and that he would repay the loan in full then. I filed it in my brain as a loan coming back inside of 12 months. At worst. And moved on. Again, with hindsight, when December came and went and January too, I should have flagged the absence of any payment and connected it to that promise, but the restrospectomer does not enable us to reset time or sensibility. As the clock ticked ever forward in a busy and rewarding business time in my life I simply forgot about the equity loan. I had developed an interest in trading shares in my portfolio with some £250,000 coming and going, up and down on occasions as much as 40%, and because that was very much an up cycle with some big sell profits, I simply didn't notice a £40,900 shortfall. I suppose Krasnopovich must have convinced himself that the money was a gift. Although, who can tell. The pillar of his truth always stood on shaky Nico-centric ground. The matter of the £40,000 only came back to my attention later the following year in a dinner conversation where I was recalling my annual progress in stock trading.

After all the ups and down, and that was a year when I had lost money on BP following the Deepwater Horizon leak, I had closed that year with a 7% growth on my capitol, the value of my portfolio, excluding the dividends paid in that year, which I thought was pretty good. I mentioned it in our toast at dinner that night. Krasnopovich replied to this news by announcing he was making 11% on his portfolio.

"What portfolio is that? You have a portfolio and you haven't paid back the equity loan?"

What followed was a full-bodied apology for forgetting he meant to pay it back with the first partners disbursement and the reassurance that he would get onto it. Days later, without any notice, a transfer of £10,000 appeared in my bank account with the reference *'Equity Loan repay'* with an email note confirming *"I have transferred £10K. how much do I owe you again?"*.

"Thanks for the ten K. The balance is £30,900." I replied, in an email that was admitted in the court hearing. Six Months later, another transfer for £5,000 went through. And then another £2,000. Bank reference. *'Equity loan repay'*. Clearly he was begrudging having to pay back the equity loan. Reinventing the agreement based on his promise to repay the full amount with the first partners disbursement. Eventually, years later, in April 2013, two months before his fathers-day announcement, out of the blue a payment for £13,000 appeared in my account, which brought his total repayment of the loan up to exactly £30,000. That payment had a different bank reference. *'Final payment equity loan'*. No reference to the emails and reminders that the total was £40,900. No mention of anything in conversation. Eventually, as delicately as I could, mentioned *"By the way, that final equity loan payment you sent. Its £10 grand off the principle."* His reaction was to ignore me. I didn't push it. I was then blissed out on my Sam time and took a sanguine view of –

whatever. It's only ten grand. To date that £10,900 remains un paid despite written reminders and bank statements from the period documenting the amounts involved. In addition to this, there were numerous occasions, 3 in which I have email reminders which were shared with Clam for the April 2015 hearing, where Krasnopovich would need a few thousand pounds to meet his monthly targets. This pattern of free loans not ever repaid only ever went in one direction. Clearly it is relevant that from the very beginning of our relationship, money was asked for and given. A pattern. A balance between generosity and gratitude that never found an equal footing.

This seems the right time to mention the diamond ring. A story involving Aristotle Onassis, Christie's, and a world leading Gemologist. Sometime in 2009, with a baby approaching, Krasnopovich asked me for a ring. He had a thing for rings. And declared he had always wanted a proper man's diamond ring. 'Just a nice stone on a simple ring.' A compromise for not getting married before the child. A 'proper' diamond. He specified, with a suggestive grin. That seemed fair. I have no interest in jewelry and consider all diamonds blood diamonds, but as a sign of commitment to our co-parenting agreement I decided to treat him to his request. Cutting the long story short, about the world-famous gemologist and the Christies auction with King Constantine, I treated him to a ring following the Christies Onassis' jewelry auction that cost £16,000. It suited him. His commitment ring. He was so grateful to accept it. He kissed me repeatedly. "*Thank you honey. That's so amazing.*" Such gratitude. He wore it every day. I added it to the house contents policy cover.

Early in 2012 the plans to leave MWT and set up the new business advanced. Having set up several small businesses in my past, I drafted the original business plan for Nico with cash-flow projections based on his answers to the relevant questions. We made a good team in this way. He was efficient and punctual with an eye for opportunity. This came in the form of flying close to the 'articles of partnership'. Basically, poaching staff from MWT, which is a breach of conduct offence by a regulated member of the Law Society. In this case, being one of many, Caroline McDonald, who was a top fee earner for MWT property department was approached. I thought it was a sensible idea to take a partner to share the costs of the business. And Caroline McDonald looked to me like the best option, smart and generating real impressive numbers. They were paying her £80,000 a year and she was generating over half a million in turnover. With just one secretary's wage to tale off the gross amount. In our first meeting Caroline indicated that she could realistically achieve a million in turnover with just one secretary and adding one para legal. She would require three networked office spaces. We had several dinner meets discussing options for her to join Krasnopovich in the new business and how the partnership would be structured. It would be called 'Krasnopovich McDonald LLP. Family law and Property law work well together. The business model is that each would contribute to the operating costs of the business, hardware and software, rental and leasing, Insurance and services, with each keeping 100% of their department billing. The cash-flow projection, based on the input Krasnopovich provided me with for a spreadsheet, was that in year one the family department would generate £350,000, rising to £500,000 in year two, and with recruitment of 2 'rainmaker' junior lawyers 3yq, £750,000 in year three. The design of the office which I sketched out placed computer points and power outlets in the correct position to allow for the growth over three years. Although initially only four people would start up, (Two lawyers plus their secretaries) there were ten connected spaces with power and IT ports spaced appropriately to accommodate the coming growth. Krasnopovich was concerned that MWT would find out that Caroline was leaving to join him. That would have had serious consequences. Although Caroline's Property department at Krasnopovich McDonald was separate to Krasnopovich's family department, in the Court proceedings that followed in a necessary financial disclosure, I saw that in 2014, year one, where she had claimed she could make £1 million in turnover, Caroline generated £1.1 Million, working with one secretary and one legal assistant. Small wonder that MWT were pissed off when they learned that Krasnopovich was poaching her. Very nice career uplift for Caroline, from the £80K salary at MWT less than two years before. Although on the night of the launch for Krasnopovich McDonald, Caroline proposed a toast to me by way of thanks with the words "*We wouldn't be here without you*" I never saw any gratitude for my impact on her life. Caroline and Steve, the father of her child, who lived together in a similar arrangement to myself and Krasnopovich. Steve also owned the home in his sole name and raised the child as the home person. Caroline had disclosed to Krasnopovich they appeared to be having some relationship difficulties, asking for advice on how best to separate. Now that Caroline was making good money Krasnopovich's firm advice, which he shared with me, was that Caroline should get rid of her partner before he would have a claim on her new-found wealth.

Krasnopovich guided this separation to the best of his ability, ironically enough, in light of what happened not long after, discussing every aspect of what Caroline was disclosing about Steve, her daughter's father with me. But when it came to the execution of Krasnopovich's advice, Caroline didn't succeed and the last I heard they were still together. His approach to her proposals for separation being more or less "*Fuck off if you want but I am keeping the child.*"

I think Krasnopovich learned from this experience that it is best to make sure the separation lays the outgoing partner low so they will not be able to keep the child.

Ambush and shock work best for this purpose. Helps explain why he chose fathers-day to take my child. And the 'no mediation' approach to irrevocable separation, immediately. Then say the parent is depressed and mentally infirm. And tell CAFCASS the child might not be safe alone with that parent. All you need is a doctor confirming the parent is depressed. And a judge who you know will agree to whatever you ask.

Two events conspired leading up to Krasnopovich's expulsion from MWT ahead of the planned departure. The plan was to first set up the new office, effectively in secret. He would resign from MWT, accusing them of poor treatment, following the advice of Christa, and by engaging the services of a high-powered Employment lawyer costing some £500 ph., Dave Marshall, who would make heavy handed accusations of unfair conduct against MWT. This tactic, attack being the best defense, would shorten the necessary notice period for a partner withdrawing from the partnership. Usually notice for leaving equity partnership is a period of 6 months, put in place to prevent partners leaving with maturing files that have high value. And allowing the partnership to allocate the clients of the outgoing partner internally.   In Krasnopovich's case there were at least 160 client files coming due in the next six months, and the value of these he estimated for my cash flow projection as 'approaching £200,000'. This income from his MWT clients would underpin cashflow for the first year in the new business. That meant getting the files out and the client list from MWT was a priority. The client files exist on the firm's server, managed by a professional IT director, accessed through a secure connection by the partners, involving passwords and records of all traffic in and out. The challenge was to remove the entire database of client details as well as the library of legal documents needed to operate a family law practice. Client agreements. And so on. All the standard documents you need in a law firm. Getting them past the IT guy at MWT and the safeguards preventing digital theft from their Server without a trace proved to be no real challenge at all. Nico went in with a 64gig flash drive and simply copied the entire client database onto it. Discretely. Weeks before the expulsion day all the files and client notes were transferred to my computer, along with a full set of legal documents, client agreement forms and such, from MWT, which would simply have the words MWT replaced with Krasnopovich McDonald and provide a ready to go solution for the new business. Having this entire library of legal documents for a Family Law business for free cannot be overstated. Certainly the web site could not have been completed to that level without access to all that legal terminology. Thank heavens for the Find Replace function. *Find* MWT LLP. *Replace.* Krasnopovich McDonald LLP.

After identifying and visiting four possible premises for the new firm, we, being myself, Krasnopovich and Caroline, agreed on a location in Thameside. The central location was ideal for the conveniences of Thameside. The office was a former language school, divided over two levels. The lower being allocated for Caroline and the upper for Krasnopovich. Property and family. The initial lease was for three years, with the business plan allowing for the purchase of a building and moving after three years. The premises were a mess. Evidently nothing was worth keeping if this was to be presented as a happening law firm. In a very short space of time, little more than one month, I transformed the space into ready to go legal offices, replacing almost everything inside. Carpets over three levels of staircase, 18 new radiators, new front door. New stair railings. Using the trades I had on speed dial for my properties, I had all floor carpets replaced, new toilet and boiler installed, and the wiring for the electronic requirements of the new office put in place, with certification. I would typically be there on site for hours daily. Paying for the works, much of it in cash as is the way with the trades, and making sure things happened fast. I have been paying trades for work for over twenty years of land-lording and have a good network of reliable professionals, without which this conversion into offices would not have happened in the way that it did. High quality work, done well and quickly at a fair price. I bought the computer server (Dell) and recruited an IT specialist to install the legal software and manage the secured network accounts. I set up logistics for workspace communications ports to allow for the staff growth, starting with two for each office, and allowing for a further one for Caroline and five for Krasnopovich. Five suitably powered PC desktops came in from PC World, and laptops for the two partners, all of which I configured with email accounts and the appropriate software. (Microsoft Office licenses and later the specific legal accounting software package installed by the company.) All of which went on my Amex card. During this set up period, I do not recall seeing either Krasnopovich or McDonald visit the new law firm premises once during working hours. They were putting in the hours at MWT. I worked alone on the office set up. Simply put, I scheduled the works, chose and purchased all the necessary hardware and printed materials, provided an on-site supervisory presence and paid all the bills. Put phone contracts in place, Internet connection. Chose and collected mobile phones for the partners. Registered the .com and .co.uk domain names for the business and built a designer website, that would have been billed at £10,000 had it been charged for. Caroline's notice period was easy, because she was not a partner and simply had to work three months-notice while remaining coy about her reasons for leaving. Krasnopovich's departure became complicated when just ten days before the date agreed between Patrick Ruert, then managing partner of MWT and Krasnopovich's advisor's, employment law specialist Dave Marshall and Christa Small, were called into an emergency partners meeting. What could be so serious that Patrick Ruert would call this extraordinary meeting? It was made clear in an email to Krasnopovich that a serious conduct offense had occurred. Krasnopovich indicated to me his concern that they may have found out about Caroline leaving to join him in the new firm. The memo circulated amongst the other partners was that there were grave concerns over Krasnopovich's conduct as a partner and all partners who were available on short notice to attend this extraordinary meeting should do so. Serena, who was made equity partner at the same time as Krasnopovich, didn't attend but did send in a strongly worded condemnation of Krasnopovich's character. *"Krasnopovich is deceitful and dishonest"* she wrote. Her proxy vote was for expulsion. '*Wow. I thought they were friends'* according to Krasnopovich.

It was a tense time. The new office was not ready. And a great deal was riding on keeping the client base loyal to Krasnopovich. The day before the MWT partners meeting calls and emails flew between Krasnopovich, Dave Marshall, the employment lawyer and Christa, who took a great interest in advising Krasnopovich, seemingly unaware of the way Krasnopovich spoke about her in professional situations. I attended the emergency meeting with Krasnopovich in Surbiton, in the MWT boardroom, instead of his employment lawyer. Why me and not his employment lawyer? He told his lawyer I knew the matter better and would be better placed to speak in his defense. Which I think was correct. I was up for it. At my argumentative best. I felt confident. I was going to stand up for my partner against these horrible people saying such nasty things. I was ready to be Suzie from the Larry David Show. When the time came to address the assembled partners I think I did a convincing job of pointing out the futility of expelling him just a week before his notice period with all the bad feeling that would generate when just letting it play out made so much more sense. However in that boardroom that day it was clear they were beyond angry at Krasnopovich. I very quickly formed the view that they knew something I did not. It didn't make sense otherwise, based on the facts as I knew them. Managing Partner Patrick Ruert chaired the meet. In no time at all they called a vote and the outcome was immediate expulsion from the partnership for dishonesty. I reflect on that meeting by saying, all present were all extremely hostile without exception and I concluded early on, they knew something that Krasnopovich had not shared with me. Darn. Hindsight is a bitch. Krasnopovich hardly said a word throughout. Leaving the talking up to me. From beginning to end, the show of hands vote, no more than one hour had passed. Krasnopovich was escorted to his desk to clear his things and hand over his keys, while I pulled the car up front to help him carry his box of possessions out of the Surbiton office for the last time. I was alarmed by what I saw at that hearing.

There was a disconnect between what Krasnopovich had told me and what Patrick Ruert and the partners were saying. Another flag turned red only by hindsight. Still. He could depend on my blind loyalty and he did.

M E M O R A N D U M
To: All Sites
From: Patrick Ruert
Date: 20th March 2012

re: Nico Krasnopovich

Nico Krasnopovich has been expelled from the partnership with immediate effect. Serena Denning and Jacky Roach will be primarily responsible for dealing with his workload and any queries from clients which would otherwise be addressed to Krasnopovich should be directed to either of them.

Regards
Patrick Ruert
Managing Partner

After the MWT expulsion we drove straight back to my home where I set up a workstation for Krasnopovich in the dining area. It was around 2pm when we arrived home. The new office for the law firm would not be ready for another week, even though my guys were working day and night to complete. And there was not a moment to be lost in contacting the clients following the unexpected expulsion. Krasnopovich was on the phone within ten minutes of arriving back at Thameside. With a battle-plan. MWT took Krasnopovich's mobile phone line as a first priority following the expulsion meeting and all incoming calls to his number were going to one of the partners advising the caller that Krasnopovich had left and a new partner would be available to take over their matter. I checked that by calling the number when we got home, anticipating that MWT would do exactly that. The person who answered Krasnopovich's phone was Brandon Bennigton. One of the partners. By good fortune and even more, by intelligent design, I had already arranged two mobile phone contracts with new Blackberry's for both partners and so there was a new mobile number as well as a new landline for the business available right away.

The first order of our business was to compile an email mailshot of all the clients involved. Essential that they had Krasnopovichs' number. Good thing we already had the client database. Many hundreds of emails went out with a letter I drafted and perfected announcing the move to a new firm in Thameside, more equipped to provide a better personal service. And after completing the mailshot, Krasnopovich started a round of phone calling each one for a personal reassurance. Nina, Sam's nanny, was asked to work late seeing Sam to bed that night while we both worked till late on contacting every single client. This would not have been possible without the foresight to remove a copy of the client database from MWT in readiness for this very moment.

There was also a website ready to go. Along with professional photos in black and white of the partners, shot specifically for the website. I copied the website design after seeing Dave Marshalls firms page. Which was the coolest LLP website I had seen at that time. Along with my record label designer, Vincent Van Arl, I had completed the website to a high standard in a short space of time. I registered three domain names (Krasnopovich McDonald.co.uk, Krasnopovich McDonald.com and NicoKrasnopovich.com) all hosted on my existing server contract, all of which were in my name and paid for by my business Thames Recordings Ltd. So on that day all the moving parts were all in place. All it took was for me to activate the index page to make the site visible online on www.KrasnopovichMcDonald.com and www.KrasnopovichMcDonald.co.uk. The website was online and looking good with all the contact details, including the new office address, an hour after we arrived back from the expulsion meeting. On the same day that Krasnopovich was expelled from MWT, before we went to sleep very late that night, about 180 clients had all received a phone call and an email, with a designer letterhead, showing a new professionally designed working website with a business address and phone numbers all presenting a confidence assuring impression that Krasnopovich was leaving MWT to start his own firm to provide a better service for the clients. Obviously all the costs in every aspect of establishing Krasnopovich McDonald LLP were paid by myself. I had both partners come to the house for a professional photo shoot resulting in a series of shots for the website.

Slightly interesting in the context of the website is that his friend Alfie Geadah, of the late night drunken "*she wants to fuck you*" texts, provided a testimonial which I had used as a reference on the web page, as did another barrister, Simon Hazelwood, who would represent him in the litigation against me. Seems strange that I asked Nico for recommendations to include and Simon Hazelwood was the first to volunteer. The next time I heard his name he was cross examining me on Krasnopovich's behalf, starting every sentence with "*I put it to you you are lying Miss Lee.*" He was lying then. Simply put, Simon is not an honest man. He made a sensible career choice with family-law, where lying is a valued quality for a barrister.

Then there's the matter of the photo copyright infringement.

I have been taking photos all of my life. I have owned many good camera's and at that time had a Canon with several quality lenses. I uploaded many of my photos to a professional photo library, including pictures licensed for library use by photo agencies including Getty, Pond5 and Adobe. Tranches of these copyright pictures were published on a closed access Private Flickr account, accessible only through a legal click-to-agree portal specifying the terms and conditions of use for copyright content. To be clear. They agreed legal terms and condition governing the use of the pictures. I pointed this out as soon as I saw in the disclosure bundle that there were twenty color pictures lifted from my library. Interestingly enough the twenty photos Hazelwood included in his presentation to Flaherty, my copyright pictures from Flickr, were, apparently, not protected by copyright law because family law courts are not bound to respect international copyright law. This is the explanation I was given by British family law. Even if the pictures have nothing to do with the safety of the child, as is the case here, family lawyers are somehow indemnified from prosecution arising from deliberate copyright theft. Does that sound like a reasonable authority to grant a family-court judge? Absent of any connection to a child's welfare or interests, family court members can breach copyright law. Either that is true, or there will be an investigation and accountability for a number of breaches of copyright law.

And in the final reference to the LLP website and registration of all to do with that in my name and legal ownership, when Krasnopovich left he requested I transfer the ownership of the website domain names and the physical hosting of the web sites to him. I consulted with my friend Chris Andiotis, who is a successful businessman and also Sam's godfather, for which reason he has been a frequent advisor in my business. In that conversation I was all too aware that I held a powerful negotiating tool should any dispute arise with Krasnopovich. The registration of the domain names meant I could control the online presence of the business as I saw fit. For example. I could have demanded a sum of money for my work in the business. Along with a confirmation that there would be no further litigation of any sort. I could have used it to demand repayment of the balance owing on the Equity loan for the MWT Partnership? I could have said "*Unless you return Sam within 24 hours I am going to post a new front page on the business web site saying you have stolen my son.*" All titles for the web presence were in my name. All content was owned by myself. All web presence was hosted on my (Thames Recordings Ltd) server. And the owner of the hosting server was a business friend of mine for over 20 years. My Credit Card merchant account was used for card payments to the business. Many clients paid by credit card. Those funds were in my account, awaiting transfer to the firms account. It made perfect sense in the separation of assets, such as our small level of personal co-mingling was, to transfer my title on his domains at the same time as his name on my Freehold title. My position, as advised by Chris Andiotis, was "*I will transfer your business title as soon as you transfer my Freehold title back to me. I will take advice from Chris and come back to you on how to complete the transfer. I will not make any demands on you for this transfer, beyond the reciprocal title transfer.*"

In my talk with Chris we discussed the transfer of the two titles. Focusing specifically on the value in not increasing animosity because it is harmful to the child's best interests. Krasnopovich at that time had not yet begun any litigation. I believed he would come to his senses soon enough and see that Sam should be with me.

"*Don't hardball him. Just agree that you give him his title, he gives you yours. That's the end of it. I will talk to him and tell him the same thing. He knows how important you are for Sam. He won't risk fucking that up.*"

Chris emphasized tirelessly that the most important thing was not to get into acrimonious litigation and to put the child's best interests to the fore. Acting as our mediator, he had a series of conversations with Krasnopovich to the same effect. The content of which would form a part of his witness evidence at the Flaherty hearing. Chris represented me in negotiations with Krasnopovich before I hired a member of family-law. His conversations and emails made clear that the freehold transfer was linked to the Web domain name transfer. Evidenced in writing and as a part of his evidence in person. These emails and conversations would provide the court with an independent, credible rebuttal of Krasnopovich's entire claim. Simply put. Chris and his evidence ended Krasnopovichs claim prospects. Krasnopovich knew that. Because the Insurance was paid for the year and the renewal was still a few months away, I requested that Krasnopovich date the transfer of my Freehold title to the same date as the Insurance renewal. I would take out the renewal policy and the title transfer would be effective from that date. Ensuring uninterrupted cover. I would instruct a solicitor to prepare the title transfer document for the land registry and that would be that. The web domain titles though were subject to a more urgent pressure. They controlled not just the ownership of the domain, but the admin and hosting for the web page. Which would need ongoing regular updates that I was certainly not going to do. And so, after agreeing with Chris that he would transfer my title back in time for the insurance renewal, that same day Chris called to tell me to authorize my web hosting company to transfer all titles to Krasnopovich. And to migrate the website files to the new server that Krasnopovich had found for this purpose. I paid my web guys charge for this function and that same day the web domains were put in his name and the business website was transferred seamlessly to the new server, containing all the same content, originally lifted off the MWT website page and including the copyright profile photos of Krasnopovich and McDonald which I still owned. I did exactly as was agreed. I was not looking at legal options to leverage my control of his business titles. Just concluding the separation that Krasnopovich had demanded as quickly as possible and with the minimal acrimony. My sole interest was my son. Next would be his part of that agreement, transferring my freehold title back to me. Guess how that worked out?

Just hours after his expulsion from MWT a new website was online with a professional logo (designed by Vincent, my record label designer and a top-level art professional, at my brief and paid for by myself). With professional art direction, the paint color of the interior of the offices was matched to the sand tone of the logo. I bought paint mixed to match that color precisely and paid my house painter, who had painted my properties for the past 15 years, to paint the new premises. A top-level paint job as usual from Gareth. The presentation aspect of the new business was tip top. For this reason, when Krasnopovich was expelled, instead of losing all the clients he had with MWT, the net result of that day's work and the preparation that went into it, is that the accounts for the new firm one year later showed that 95% of the clients poached from MWT moved with Krasnopovich. The new firm could not have succeeded without the client's that he brought from MWT. The business plan relied on that income. People half way through the lowest ebb in their lives do not want to start again with someone new. A factor even second-rate divorce lawyers readily exploit. Over £180,000 was the amount that showed up in the new firms accounts from the clients poached from MWT client database.

That year, 2012 to 2013 seemed to have things going on course. Sam had a new nanny, Nina, who was just fantastic with him and a joy to have around. A kind young Polish girl, worldly wise at 21. Always smiling and radiating positivity. They looked so good together, a beautiful pair, both outwardly and inward. Manes of curly hair. Radiating joyfulness. I do not recall one single outing where the three of us were anything less than radiant with joy. I had some time to myself to spend on business, all of which was going well.

Happy times for Sam. And for me.

I spent my days working on my book project, writing emails for the business, managing my stock portfolio with occasional buys and sells, managing musical copyrights that needed occasional contracts, writing music when the impulse moved me, and being an efficient land lord. All possible because my trust in Nina was such that I knew Sam would be having a great time with her. I had an open-door office, so it was clear to Sam from the outset that if he wanted to see me, he could always come in. And he did. Always arriving at the door with the patient courtesy he had been taught, waiting for me to finish what I was doing before looking over to him, where he would ask his question of the day. He had learned to think about this before he came in. So we always got off to a good start for each visit. We enjoyed hours of quality time every day in my studio office, usually playing musical instruments. From age three he had an immediate and mesmeric interest in Michael Jackson. I would sit him at the drum kit and play the hits loud on my Studio monitors as he drummed along. Sam had his own drum kit. A professional level kit made by Roland. He had a few drumming favorites. 'Back in Black', 'Beat it' and 'Jump' topped his drumming list. Learning the words and singing along while he smacked away at the snare and hi hat. Not yet able to reach the bass drum pedal, which I would play for him while he sat on my lap, very occasionally whacking me on the head with a drumstick overenthusiastically stretched for a cymbal.

Drumming was going well.

I bought Sam a fantastic top of range Yamaha Piano to grow up with a Piano in the house, as I had, in Evan's Johannesburg home. Every day I would see that he had some Piano time. He experienced sitting at a piano making sounds on black and white keys from the age of two onwards. He was making connections. Musical development was visibly growing 'Do reh mi fah so la ti do'.

Piano was going well.

William the dog was an ever present in all of our lives, having welcomed Sam into his home and taken to protecting him. William was to have his near fatal stroke in June of 2012, which I see now was a turning point in that model of what seemed to be a perfect life.

"Are you going to have him put down" Krasnopovich announced angrily when woken one night by William falling on the floor upstairs. After his stroke, William couldn't stand. His nails would scratch on the wooden floor followed by a thud as he would fall over. "*I'm in court later I need to sleep"* he hissed.

This selfish insensitivity was upsetting to me. Worse though than wanting me to kill my dog, was that to everyone who asked, he loved William to bits. There was in that experience an insight into a layer of deceit and capacity to present himself quite honestly in whatever the position required, that put me on notice.

Williams stroke started one evening, around 7, with Krasnopovich calling me from my office in the next-door room.

"*Somethings wrong with William.*" I rushed into the lounge. He was in a convulsive fit. I picked him up and tried to calm him. Hugging him. He spasmed quite violently and then lost consciousness. I drove straight to the Vets, just ten minutes away. Amos, my South African vet friend and William's vet from day one was waiting. He examined William and his face made no secret of the prognosis.

"It's a fifty-fifty if he will come out of the coma at all. And if he does, he will never have full function again. The kindest thing is to put him to sleep now. But it's up to you. He is older than the average life span for his breed. 14 is a good innings for a Schnauzer. He could still have some quality of life. But it will be hard work even in the best-case scenario." Of course I couldn't have William killed while there was a 1% chance of him living on. This was the most special dog in my life and my companion through so many great adventures. For as long as there was any chance of him coming out of the coma, I would keep the opportunity alive. Amos suggested I take him home as there was no point leaving him there unconscious. At least if he never did wake up, I would have the chance to say goodbye. That awful night when I brought him back from the vet, he did wake up. A little. He was semi unconscious and it was unclear whether he would survive till morning. Nico had gone to bed, he had court the next day, and I sat up most of the night in my studio with William on my lap. Stroking him and transmitting loving energy. Imagining that I was healing him with my love and positivity. I spoke to him and reached an agreement. He was 14. If he committed to making 15, I would let him go. But first he had to get well and get back to his work walking the towpath. I told him this and he understood as dogs do. My decision was to support him, as he had me through hard times and let nature decide when it was time. The determining factor would be his ability to enjoy food. When he was no longer able to eat, I would let him go. Until then, he was to be indulged with every passing moment. I closed this agreement with William, and left him in his studio bed while I went for a nap as the sun was coming up. Later that day when Krasnopovich returned from work, I told him my decision. He disagreed. He was disgusted by Williams infirmity. "*He will mess the house. The chances of him ever walking again are negligible. The vet's advice was right.*"

The distance between us became a new challenge. For the first three months of his rehabilitation, when he was unable to walk, with his head fixed at a 33-degree angle to the right, I would support his weight and walk him, including as was obviously necessary, for his toilet breaks. Supporting his weight by holding him under his chest to allow him to move his feet without him having to support any real weight until gradually he built up his strength and learned to walk again. First by dragging his rear legs, and then slowly, learning to move all four legs in unison without falling over. He was a fighter, committed to trying. Instead of our normal morning walks down the towpath, we did our rehab. I carried him to the towpath, and put him down. He would try walk. And fall. And I would support him until he could take a step on his own. Then release him. He would take a step or two and fall. And so it went day after day. After several week's he began to improve and eventually would go on to walk again without support, but at that time, when he disturbed Krasnopovich's sleep, he was still falling over when he tried to get to the rear door to wee. And the sound of him dragging his heels on the wooden floor as he tried to get up after the thumping sound of his fall carried through to downstairs. Most times, when I heard him falling over in the night, I would go upstairs and help him outside to do his business. Krasnopovich became increasing resentful of this bent-out-of-shape dog making noise in the night. Upsetting his sleep when he had important work to do. William did honor our agreement. He made it to his fifteenth birthday on 1 April 2013. By then he was walking, albeit stiffly, and was enjoying his food. He could walk about a mile down the towpath and look like he was engaged. Sniffing, weeing, although he couldn't stand and wee as he used to. He adapted, and wee'd like a bitch, standing with rear legs akimbo. His head was much straighter, angled at about 10 degrees to the right. And his back was still hunched at an awkward angle. But in the main, he could walk on the towpath and do his business. Sam was a great part of his rehabilitation, showing him love and playing his part in the physical therapy. William could give and receive loving attention. When my Californian dog lover friends Bobby and Midge visited, shortly before the end, he recognized them as friends and showed great pleasure in their attention. They are two great dog lovers who have dog friends all over the world. William had many friends in the human world. A really special dog with a huge personality.

Being my intuit and energy mirror, William reacted badly to events of fathers-day and Sam's departure. His anxiety rose as mine did. My sleeplessness affected him. He felt my pain. He was looking for Sam, with his glazed over milky eyes which by now saw very little more than shadows. He went stumbling round the house, following his nose. He could smell Sam. But where was he? I knew he was looking for Sam. But no Sam was to be found. William looked confused. William's health declined at the same pace as mine. Just 7 days later, on the 23rd of June, I put his meal out in his bowl. Always, for 15 years, food time was the most exciting part of his day. His body clock went on food time. Through the years at five-to-five every evening he would come up to me in my studio and tap my leg. Five o' clock dinner. You could set your watch by his timing.

This day though, it was all over.

He looked heartbroken as I was. When he got to the bowl, he could barely raise his head over the edge, his neck crocked at a 30-degree angle to the right in a form of paralyses. Perhaps he had had another stroke. Eventually, with great determination that must have come from a distant memory he got his head over the plate edge and his face fell into the food. He couldn't move. Or move his mouth. I picked him up. He looked at me through glazed eyes, which could barely see anymore and told me it was time. From then on I never put him down. I called John B to accompany me to the Vet. I couldn't trust myself to say goodbye and drive. John B came straight over and we drove to the Vets, me holding William on my lap and stroking him whilst tears rolled down my cheeks onto his stiff head. The vet, Amos, was as efficient as you might expect from an Onderstepoort graduate.

I made it into the death room, still holding William while the vet prepared the injection, looking into his eyes which by now were milky and drained of the sparkle that once lit up his perfect Schnauzer coloring. He could barely move, his body hard and stiff. And then as the needle approached I simply could not contain the overwhelming heaving gasps and tearful anguish. I handed John B the dying William and he saw it through till the last breath while I ran outside the surgery and sobbed uncontrollably. I cried streaming tears for what seemed like hours. John drove me home. Everyone should have a friend like John B.

All the sorrow of the past tumultuous week came out in the first tears I cried since fathers-day which made up in quantity for what they lacked in timing. In trying to find a positive from this I thought of how much like a Country music song my life had become.

My man done left me (Do da da dum) for a younger bride
Took away my boy, (Do da da dum) my joy and my pride
He took all of my money, (Do da da dum) took it in his stride
Then my boys' great big heart broke, and he be my dog - he just up and died.

That humorous approach didn't work out as well as I had hoped. I was sad for a long time. I am still sad about losing William and not being able to process that loss with Sam. Every 1st of April, his birthday, I raise a glass to my boy.

William of Thameside. Who made it past his fifteenth year just as we agreed.

7   Dinner party one week before fathers-day, 2013
Calm right before the storm

The turn of the year from Christmas 2012 to early 2013 was a typical London winter season with a firmly established routine for a four-year-old. Alarm wake up at 7, getting Sam ready for his morning at The Lansbury nursery. Getting Sam dressed and breakfasted before dropping him at the Lansbury. Krasnopovich would head to the bus stop for the short ride to his office and I would usually head out to a coffee shop with William for a coffee with Jo and Tom and then onwards for a writing session in a coffee shop. Most days I would collect Sam from the Lansbury and we would have a period of three or four hours together alone before Krasnopovich returned from work. Usually around 6.30 pm.

After he started nursery at the Lansbury, we let Nina go, although with much regret from me and from Sam. We loved Nina like part of the family. But Nico paid her wage and he felt it was more than we could afford. Whenever I arrived to collect him from the Lansbury, invariably when he saw me coming, he would run and jump into my arms.

"Mummy. My Mummy."

He loved being with me and was expressive about it. The short drive home from the Lansbury was accompanied by his choice of music. For many week's it was the acapella version of 'Beat it'. Other Michael favorites were 'The way you make me feel', 'Jump', 'Back in Black' and 'Human Nature.' Usually we would pull up in front of the house before the song had ended, which would require sitting in the car until the end of the song, before rushing into the house to take on the next adventure. Joyfulness was the lifeblood of every day.

On 8th June 2013, eight days before fathers-day, as was often the case in my home, Chris Andiotis came to visit for dinner. And in town that Month were two friends visiting London from Laguna Beach, who were invited. Nicole Brown, a former South African singer and her friend, the charismatic Tammie Davis. Chris and Sam had a great relationship, as you would expect from a conscientious godfather, and on every visit Chris would spoil him with a gift. On most occasions after the marriage Chris was accompanied by his wife Maria, Sam's *'favorite girl in the world, beautiful Maria,'* but on this trip Chris was in town for a week on business, travelling alone. No Maria excitement for Sam. As usual I prepared the dinner. A roasted joint of beef bought from my friendly butcher Dale Peters, a purveyor of splendid quality meat products, served medium rare, en jus, with Greek style roasted potatoes and abundant steamed broccoli. We had a super evening of chat, with good food and wine. Sam came up to say goodnight, with a hug for everyone. A happy, balanced, polite, beautiful four-year-old. The guests all called the following day to thank me. Chris would later say of that night.

"It was incredible. You wouldn't have known anything was wrong. He was exactly as normal."

The same comment came back from Nicole Brown when she learned of Krasnopovich's decision.

"I am stunned beyond belief. He looked the picture of happiness. And so did you. I felt quite jealous at how you all looked so happy. I have never seen anything like this. It goes way beyond acting. That really was a man looking as happy as any man could be."

And he did appear exactly as normal. There was no indication that the dark discontent that was surely festering inside was in fact dark discontent festering inside. However, with hindsight, the past three months had seen some significant landmark moments that I simply under-valued. The first was the end of the accounting year for the new business Krasnopovich McDonald. Krasnopovich had reached and exceeded the business plan cash-flow target for the first year of £350,000. A stunning achievement. He was at that time 39. Just ten years after we had met, when he was earning £35,000 PA while paying off student loans and struggling from pay-check to pay-check, relying on loans in between, he was finally on the road to financial independence. The first time in his life when he had seen six figures in his bank account. A uniquely empowering experience for someone so motivated by money. The net calculation after tax and expenses was he earned £250,000. Around that time, early 2013, Krasnopovich started to lose weight. His weight went from around 80 kg to 65 kg. Which was very noticeable. Not that he was fat, but since Sam's birth he had put on maybe ten kilos. His goal was to get back to his weight at 18, which was 65 kilos. He had signed on for personal training at the gym close to his work, where he would go at every opportunity. I encouraged it, as I did with everything Krasnopovich had an interest in pursuing.

What I failed to consider fully though was how the increasingly frequent gym sessions coincided with significant weight loss, and as Stevie Wonder might have observed

'Far more frequently your wearing perfume, with you say no special place to go'. In Krasnopovich's case, this special place was the gym. The fitness classes were usually in his lunch hour break, but increasingly he would go after work, arriving home later than usual. Something Sam noticed as well. From an average of 10% of his parental time, his time with Sam lessened appreciably. He asked me to vary the dinner menu to exclude carbs and red meat.

Whilst the nanny Nina had been a great success, since the day Sam first saw her, and for the two and a half years she had been a joyful part of our lives, whom Sam loved tremendously, Krasnopovich started to take against her. Seemingly an irrational resentment that others were enjoying such quality time with his son whilst he was at work. What I may have missed then is how much he resented me for the very special relationship I had with Sam. Schizophrenically confusing admiration with resentment is how one therapist would later explain it to me. My special time with Sam was only possible, to his way of thinking, because he was out working and I got to have all the quality time. And all the fun. What didn't help this insecurity, and was most likely a trigger point followed his arrival home, late one day from a fitness class, to find me and Sam engaged in a game. He opened the door and entered the lounge theatrically spreading his arms to announce.

"Sam my baby. Daddy's home."

To which Sam replied after a dismissive glance, with an unmistakably calculated tone

"Go away daddy" before returning his focus to our game.

This started a trend of rejection that went on for weeks. Sam simply didn't want to see his father. Eventually Nina and myself working separately and together, convinced Sam that this was not nice for daddy but he was then a determined 4-year-old who knew what he wanted and what he did not. And for a period of some three weeks, Krasnopovich would come home to this nightly ritual of;

"Go away daddy".
"Sam, poor daddy, that's not nice. Give daddy a hug."

Hindsight shows, children have reliable instincts that we often lose with the passage of time.

8 The fathers-day mafia hit, 16 June, 2013
How Sam was removed from my home

16 June 2013 was a Sunday. It was fathers-day. Our day was to begin with breakfast at Steve's Café, where Sam looked forward to seeing Jo and Tom, as was his regular Sunday arrangement. After carb loading at breakfast I was competing in a club tennis tournament at the Lansbury starting at 11 am. Krasnopovich would bring Sam to watch the end of my match, also providing an opportunity for Sam to have a half hour in the children's play area at the Lansbury. After going home to shower and change we were due for lunch at three at Krasnopovich's sisters' home in Worcester Park. Dog, as he called her, although her name was Mary. The first half of the day went to plan. I had helped Sam prepare a Father's Day card for Nico. He was four and at that stage of development couldn't be expected to know an occasion such as fathers-day without prompting. I made sure he had the card made with a 'Happy Father's Day' message. "To the best Daddy in the World.' I asked him to draw a picture of his family for the card, which he did, adding "Beautiful Maria" and William the dog to himself and his mum and dad. His family of five. Nico seemed indifferent to the gift, which I thought deflated Sam's enthusiasm for the effort, although with hindsight I now know why.

I hid my disappointment over his reception of this very good effort by Sam and set off to play my tennis match, in the course of which I twisted my Achilles tendon rather painfully, hobbled to the sideline and called time on the match. Retired hurt. I phoned Krasnopovich with this news and he came earlier than expected to fetch me from the club. I iced my inflamed tendon for ten minutes and took an anti-inflammatory after which I went for a soak in the tub to assist my damaged tendon.

While I was soaking in the tub he came to call me for the lunch at his sisters. Much as drinking white wine produced a nasty reaction in Krasnopovich which opened a window to a different personality, the company of his sister would make him, as well as her, go onto a routine that would last the duration of their meeting. A deeply unattractive teenager-like 'chav' condition involving Gangsta Black accents and racial profanity. The two siblings would go back in time to some pact they made in their teens, when they addressed each other as "Dog" in the style of the gangsta rap artists of that period. Almost every conversational start would end with some black-culture hipster reference to Niggahs. Or, the more PC, Nyga. *"Yo dog. How's my nyga."* It is fair to say that I would not under ordinary circumstances ever socialize in any way with the younger Krasnopovich daughter, Dog, and found every occasion in which the siblings met up to go through their anchoring sequence of 'Awight Dog' a trial to the spirit. One which I generally endured with good grace, however on this day, with the pain from my inflamed Achilles and with a high degree of tension emanating from Krasnopovich after the failure to properly acknowledge Sam's splendid effort at making a Fathers-day card, I could not face another sibling lunch in Dog's very small house in Worcester park. Where I had real concerns over Sam's exposure to Dog's child, slightly younger than Sam, who modelled a behavioral deficit I found at odds with Sam's best interests developmentally.

I said *"Would you mind terribly if I sit this one out, walking is an issue, I could do with putting my feet up for a few hours."*

Krasnopovich glared at me wordlessly before sweeping out of the bathroom, leaving without even sending Sam downstairs to say goodbye. That struck me as weird as I heard the door slam from upstairs to mark their departure.

Little was I to know then that I would never see Sam again in my home.

Upon reflection, that last moment in which we were a family of three was when Sam handed Krasnopovich his Fathers-day card, in the café over morning breakfast. I spent the afternoon watching tennis on TV and resting my inflamed tendon on ice. Krasnopovich got back around 6 pm, passing straight by the living room to Sam's bedroom, explain to me later that Sam already had his dinner and was tired out so he had put him straight to bed. Without bringing him in to say goodnight to me?

Strange.

After coming upstairs, Krasnopovich had a new face on, looking closer to relaxed and friendly. He smiled and asked *"Would you like to go out for a drink"*. I was surprised.

"What about Sam, we'll need a babysitter."

"I have already called Jo and Tom and they are on their way."

They arrived around that time, looking a little confused. It was unusual that he should ask them to babysit at such late notice. My first thought was. Great he has seen how nasty he has been all day and this is the fathers-day make up. We walked down the tow path to the Kings Head. Along the way we passed a rose garden, with roses in full bloom and I asked him to stop, to take a picture of him in this beautiful light. I was reminded that this was the location where I have him his £16,000 ring, although I thought better than to remind him of it. We arrived at the pub, I ordered two large vodka tonics. We sat down. He began without any introduction.

"I want to separate. I have outgrown you and I no longer find you attractive."

This was delivered in a hard way. Not that there is a polite way to say those words, but this was un-mistakably harsh, done with maximum prejudice. Not simply the content of the words, but the tone of the delivery. Those were eyes brimming with hatred that had just switched on when I sat down with the drinks. Like an actor going into character. It was not a face I had ever seen on Nico Krasnopovich before. I felt eviscerated. As If I had sat down and someone had just leaned forward to thrust a jagged edge blade six inches into my stomach before turning it 360 degrees. All the while, keeping steady eye contact. I was momentarily lost for words. The first thing I could think of was;

"We have a child. We have to try therapy or work something out."

"No. My mind is made up. There is no point in discussing it. No point in therapy. We will separate as soon as the logistics are in place."

He then looked me in the eye and said *"how do you feel."*

I could not believe the deep hatred I saw in that look but there it was.

Unmistakable.

This was a back-alley ambush. A sneak attack. Someone had taken away the lovely vulnerable amenable father of my four-year-old, and in his place was this hate filled fount of furious bitter malice. I said nothing more, my reaction being 'get out of here.' I stood up to leave. No further conversation was possible. I had no words to say so we walked back in silence. We arrived back at Thameside where Jo and Tom waited and I told them

"*Nico wants to leave me and Sam.*"

An incredibly awkward period followed where Jo tried to talk to Krasnopovich, before he quickly excused himself and went downstairs. Jo and Tom stayed with me for an hour, as stunned as I was, before they left and I decided to go for a walk. No way did I want to go anywhere near Nico. I walked and kept walking, mile after mile down the towpath past, past Bray and onwards. Eventually the ache in my legs told me to turn around and I walked back towards Thameside, watching the sun rise over the Thames along the way. By the time I reached home it was after 8 am and Krasnopovich had left for work and dropped Sam at the Lansbury Nursery. The house was empty. I took a deep breath and started on my list of calls. The people in my inner circle of trust. I called my father, Chris Andiotis, Vincent, and Luisa Hay and then arranged to go for a walk with Jo, my neighbor. I tried calling Ruth, Krasnopovich's mother, however she was not answering my call. That was disappointing. By the end of that day it was clear to me that Krasnopovich was indeed determined to separate and that he obvious option of discussing reconciliation was evidently off the table. Chris was the first, but not the last to point out '*no one leaves a happy home unless there is someone else.*' The consensus between my instinctive reaction and those closest to me was that this was an enormous betrayal in which the shock of the moment placed on hold the practical matters that would now become necessary. It was immediately clear to me that at 48 years of age, I was not going to revisit the family-court nonsense I had already experienced once, knowing what I knew about family law as a partner for 10 years. I was now forced by circumstance to review the parental arrangement from 2008 which led to the family of three that was now at an end. My first thought was that our parental agreement remained unchanged by his new ambitions. His decision though would require adjustments. In a flood of realization during that first day, I visited all the untruths and deceptions that Krasnopovich had visited upon not only me, but Sam as well.

The first and most critical survival instinct at that point was to separate physically. I could not be in the same space as Krasnopovich. Before I had pause to clear my head and decide what to do next, he had collected Sam from nursery and both were gone. Krasnopovich moved to his mother's home with Sam. Initially I thought that Sam's Granny, Ruth, would be a good custodian for a few days until her deviant son came to his senses and agreed to some relationship counselling, or, if he was determined to separate, agree to mediation to agree reasonable visitation for him after Sam came back home. I wrote to Nico by email the next day. My first attempt to agree custodial arrangements for Sam. I would be available to raise Sam as agreed. Nothing had changed in my commitment to raising my child. I would not be involved in any legal visitation arguments, conceding that he was the professional in family-law and in a position to abuse legislation as he saw fit. I pleaded to his parental side to recognize what was best for Sam. Sam should stay with me in his home and his father could have him whenever suited. I would work with him to be sure he had Sam for the maximum amount of time available, bearing in mind his long work hours and availability to be with Sam. I realized while writing that first letter the extent of my failure in allowing Sam to be removed from my home. And the inference behind how Nico had played it, with the mafia hit approach, to get Sam out and under his sole control. What a clever member of family-law. Keeping all the balls in his court. His mother Ruth, the granny, would not take my calls. I realized quickly, she was siding with her son. Who knows what he had told her to involve her in what now looked increasingly like child kidnap. I had not seen Sam since our breakfast on fathers-day and the sense of loss had grown in a straight line since then. I was crying inside for him over what I knew was about to unfold. Although by this time I had not actually cried at all. I was still in what I think of as stunned shock. The full extent of what lay ahead for Sam was immediately clear to me and that broke my heart. I had seen that particular type of madness that grows between former lovers who turn on each other. Vindicating their decision to part by turning bad feeling into pure bitter hatred. I felt I had seen in his eyes at that fathers-day meeting, that same hatred I recognized as irredeemable. A look I knew with all certainty did not bode well for a best-case outcome. The manner of his announcement and the process that followed, taking the child out of his family home, told its own story. All the lies Krasnopovich had told, going right back to our first date, started filtering through my happy-denial lens. Initially, in those first few weeks I had to depend on a degree of denial. Surely the intuition of the parent would rise above the training of the lawyer. But denial was not going to affect reality. Every paternal memory I turned to for reassurance mirrored back at me the obvious. From the very beginning, you got played.

It was all a sham; the love promises, the written assurances, the 18 year-plan for the child's education. This was never love. This was always no more than a cynical avaricious opportunist seizing the moment. As Terry Britten said *'What's love got to do with it.'* With hindsight, I had no sorrow over feelings of being 'dumped', There was no emotional reaction relating to a lowered self-esteem. I have always been attractive to the opposite sex. Perhaps, quite wrongly, I feel that I am likeable and that is why I have been so fortunate in my life with so many beautiful talented, kind romantic partners. My trauma in this experience began with the picture of Sam's future. What would become of him left to Krasnopovich's devices. I knew even before I had formulated the words to articulate it that Krasnopovich's absent parenting instinct and commitment to a career in which clients are chattels, would lead to him claiming sole ownership of Sam and negotiating for monetary gain. It was his training and he was nothing if not predictable. As a divorce lawyer he would associate a value to his time and in the absence of the marriage certificate he had tried so hard to achieve without success, the next best hook to the payday he saw me as, was Sam. More specifically, my want factor to be with Sam. I experienced a horrible flash of awareness of all that I had chosen to overlook.

During that first week of processing I knew that I had made a tremendous mistake in letting him take Sam out of my home. A mistake because I had recognized early on, but not acted as I should, by calling police and demanding the child be returned. Why didn't I call the police? I regret that now. I see in hindsight I was afraid. Baiting the family law bear with a police call would be an invitation for vengeance that would end in family court. My choice was reason and what's best for the child. Wrong choice as I now accept. Because I assumed that his concern for the child's best interest would know that this child needed to be with me for his wellness. Removing a child from this ideal home environment with his caring loving parent and using that child's want factor in seeing his mother as a negotiating lever for financial benefit just couldn't happen. That much felt clear to me, no matter how flawed I knew he was as a person I could not imagine anyone would do that, least of all someone working in family law who knew the damage acrimony between parents does to children.

Surely?

It took me a few days longer than sensible to realize how wrong I was. Completely wrong. I had been played with the mafia hit on father's day. Executed with maximum prejudice to flatten my usual inner strength and give him the opportunity to relocate the child legally. By the time I realized his game plan and relocated myself in the present it was too late. He had by then moved out of his Mother's and into a rental property. He then flatly refused to provide me with the address. Baiting me to instruct a family lawyer and start up expensive litigation. Sam had been moved out of my home and now for the rebuilding to start, the new relationship with Sam had to go through Krasnopovich like a prison warden. He held all the cards. He would ensure there would never be unfettered contact between my son and me unless a key proviso was first met. Before I could see Sam in these constrained circumstances where my intuitive position was to take him home with me, knowing he is my son, who I have been with for his entire life and who relies on me for his developing thought process I had to contextualize for Sam an explanation for the end of his innocent years and the prospects that lay ahead for the child of a broken family in which mummy was disempowered. No longer able to explain things that made sense to a four-year-old. No longer able to say 'everything will be alright' with conviction. Especially as I knew by then that Krasnopovich was in freefall, without an ethical compass to guide him. With a legal training to excise compassion from his parental instincts. Transposing his parental instincts through the filter of a legal training into a battle, with a winner and loser. In which he had clearly executed a premediated abduction of the child for no higher purpose than to ransom him back in exchange for money. While freeing himself from any commitment, to pursue his lustful attraction to his (married) fitness instructor.

Trust cannot be overvalued as a co-parenting requirement and once the separation was announced as it was, an ambush betrayal as the first move in his carefully structured borderline illegal series of strikes in which access to the child was the most powerful card. I faced a brick wall. On one side I had to locate the child and go and fetch him. As I knew he wanted. On the other, I knew I was being gamed and had to be careful not to fall foul of a legal process he played with such thoughtless confidence.

I felt very much as if I had been mugged with this fathers-day mafia hit. And that it was done deliberately so that Krasnopovich could extract the child from my control whilst I was knocked down from the blow. And that is precisely what happened. He made the separation as nasty as possible to deliver the most effective trauma, in the educated hope that it would have a disabling effect on my reaction.

He had asked many curious questions about my depression history, especially as a 10-year-old having to look after myself. Fathers-day. A Sunday night. He knew my Mother had died on a Sunday. My dog Heidi had died on a Sunday. This was a day I was physically injured from the tennis slip, limiting my mobility, meaning I was in actual real pain as well. Immaculate timing, fit for purpose. Later when I had top level legal advice, it read:

"The mistake she made was letting him remove the child from her home."

A mistake I do accept I made, which was more of an unforced error, willed upon me by someone who knew exactly what they were doing. But for that mistake alone, family law cannot be excused any liability for what followed.

9 Laptops and suspicions
Finding the facts and listening to smart friends

In the first week after fathers-day I showed careful consideration over who I shared my story with. Reliable sage advice is crucially important if the best decisions are to follow. Jo and Tom, already knew. They were who Krasnopovich called on fathers-day to babysit. The first person I called when I was lucid and ready the following morning was my father. His advice would be important. He immediately declared that "*I knew he was rubbish. Where is Sam. Why did you let him take him away?*"

My second call was to Chris Andiotis in South Africa. Sam's godfather, my street-smart big-brother business advisor and friend. He said.

"*I can't believe it. I was there just a week ago and he looked as happy as can be. There's something going on. It makes no sense. No one breaks up happy home unless they are seeing someone. Fuck this is awful news for Sam.*"

I spent almost all of the day on the phone to the people I trusted most. I called Luisa Hay. My new age friend. Vincent, my artist friend and twenty-year confidante in creative thinking. And later, allowing for the time difference in California, Philip, whose calm reassurance was a most welcome voice in my head, reminding me of who I am and would be again. Phillip was just great at listening and giving very short conclusions. All of which centered on getting Sam back without delay.

That night I arranged to meet one of my closest friends and confidantes from the Kings Head for a 'private chat'. Allan, my then 75-year-old neighbor and drinking buddy over a twenty-year period living in Thameside, a man who is a wonderfully wise and widely respected intellect. He knew Krasnopovich as well as anybody and had been a guest at many of our dinner parties, as we had been at his. I am not alone in knowing this special gift for sage advice Alan represents to his close circle of friends.

Allan heard me through without interruption and before he had said a word there were tears running down his cheeks. He got it. This was not your normal separation. He was the first to observe "*It sounds like a Father's Day mafia hit*". (Writers credit.) Soon after, Allan's conversation turned to Chris Andiotis' observation that in situations such as this it is likely there is a new romantic interest, or to paraphrase Chris "*There is only one reason someone breaks up happy home.*"

That conversation with Allan led to the conclusion it is better to know than not to know and as he promised he would, the following morning Allan provided me with the number of a Private Investigator who used to work for Kroll. Find out exactly what you are dealing with before you act. I thought this was good advice at a time I was very aware that I should only listen to the smartest minds I knew at a time like this where my own thinking was impaired by this ever-present cloak of melancholy. I was extremely careful about who I trusted as confidantes. I felt fortunate to have a friend like Allan, who cared for me and gave my matter his full attention.

"He is going to war with you. First up, get the facts. Find out why is he doing this and why now? And why has he taken Sam? I am afraid it looks to me like he is going to act like a lawyer, not a father."

A Private Detective. Very glamorous it sounded, in its own way and although my first thought was 'this is going to be expensive' I knew the value of receiving advice gratefully. A case of not being pound wise and penny foolish. I called the 'PI' and with Allan as my introduction reference, outlined my situation. The PI agreed to meet me the same day at the local cricket club, Thameside cricket club, in the coffee bar. Our meeting lasted twenty minutes. He outlined the menu of technological possibilities for recording mobile phone calls and text messages. And the costs per hour of surveillance. My brief to him was simply to establish details of any romantic interest, as much for my peace of mind in moving on as anything else. We agreed a flat fee which he assured me was a favor price, because of his enormous respect for Allan. He would allocate time over one week to establish whether or not there was substance to my suspicions about the fitness Instructor. I supplied him with Krasnopovich's work address, email, and mobile phone number along with the details I had of the Fitness instructor. I clarified whether there was any prospect of illegality in his appointment and he assured me there was not.

Within five days I was summoned for a meeting at the cricket ground coffee shop for my client update. He confirmed to me Nico was "fixated" on his fitness Instructor, fourteen years his junior. That they were meeting for dinner that same night. They had met for dinner the previous night. He showed me a photo taken the previous night. Nico with a physically attractive young thing gazing into each-other's eyes at a table for two in a restaurant. And another, walking out, hand in hand. He provided me a flash drive. *"There is a recording on here between the two of them made over their dinner last night and here is the transcript."* He handed me a two-page document, and another two-page document of with time and place as the column headers. *"This is all the text messages they have exchanged and the details of each meeting in the past week. The fitness instructor is married. Krasnopovich is pressuring her to leave her husband. He has offered to do her divorce for free. He has offered her his professional services to speed up the divorce."*

One text from Krasnopovich read;
"It will cost you nothing. You will be divorced in less than 6 weeks and I will be single."

My detective's impression was that the romantic relationship was driven more by his side than hers and appeared to be his obsession. He confirmed that this single father was out every one of the past five nights while Sam was left at home with a babysitter. His mother, Sarah Krasnopovich. 70. Most curiously he told me that it was surprising how easy his job had been. Almost as if Nico wanted to be found out.

"Either that or he is pretty dumb."

He told me that the girlfriend had pictures of them together on her social media despite the fact that she was still married. Included in the documents was a text exchange from Krasnopovich encouraging her to divorce 'so they could be together' because now he had shown he was serious she should allow him to handle her divorce immediately.

"Just unusual" was the detective's conclusion.

"It's possible he wants you to have this information. It's possible he has become foolish with lust for this girl. He wouldn't be the first. He'll wake up in a few months

and realize what he's lost. Or maybe he is using this girl to make you angry. That is possible. Trying to get some kind of reaction from you."

My take away after reading the facts made clear that Krasnopovich had planned this departure for some time. He text messaged regularly with his secretary, who was evidently also his confidante in matters of romance. Those messages made plain that he had been setting up the 'move' for some time. Which returned me to thinking about the great deceit. Why didn't he say something if he was so unhappy? I concluded it was quite simply a case of; he came into a lot of money with the new business. Saw the potential for a new life, and decided, as captain of the world, he could have whatever he wanted, so off he went. To claim his kingdom.

"Poor man want to be rich. Rich man want to be king." Sam's role in all of this was collateral. To make sure Andrea pays up. Because his £350,00 gross income was a taste of winning and he wanted more. He evidently valued my interest in having Sam at £100,000. I remembered just weeks prior to fathers-day before when we were in La Manga for a week at a tennis academy, a few flags I missed. When we got to La Manga in May of 2013, Krasnopovich used my Mac Laptop to log onto his work emails. When we travelled he did not take his laptop with, preferring the convenience of using mine for his work. I have had a top of range mac laptop since Steve Jobs first launched the first Mac laptop and have always offered its use to Nico when we travelled. Daily during our La Manga trip, at some point in each day, Krasnopovich would ask if he could use my laptop to check his emails. On one of those occasions he did not log out of his account as he was usually very careful to do, leaving his private email account open on the page where I couldn't help but notice a personal email signed off with an X. That doesn't look like a work mail?

I asked him *"who is writing to you in such a friendly way."*

Especially as, while we were on holiday we had agreed he would not feed his compulsive work addiction and spend time with Sam and me.

"Oh that".

He paused long enough for hindsight to remind me was suspicious. *"That's my fitness Instructor. She doesn't want me to get out of shape while I am away so she is sending me a workout routine to do here."*

Really?

The second point of interest with that laptop and Krasnopovich's use of it was in recruiting Belinda Rostock from MWT, his former firm, who expelled him for dishonesty. Belinda was a younger lawyer, 3 years qualified and establishing a good reputation at MWT where she worked in the family law department for the past two years. Krasnopovich identified her as a valuable recruitment target for the new partnership LLP, Krasnopovich McDonald, a rainmaker, as is the commonly used term for self-starters in legal employment. A series of wooing emails flowed, including a generous increase in her salary with MWT. Because Krasnopovich didn't want a paper trail linked to Belinda's work email, as this type of poaching recruitment was in breach of the articles of partnership at MWT which still affected him and which he knew could be used against him in any adversarial situation, he used my laptop for all that super-confidential correspondence. With his own private yahoo email account set up for this purpose, as an alternative to using his MWT email that went through the MWT server and could be accessed by his partners at the Firm. The entire correspondence between Belinda Rostock, Krasnopovich, and then Caroline McDonald agreeing the formal offer for Rostock to leave MWT and join them, existed in a folder on my Mac, named Krasnopovich McDonald. Some twenty-five emails in total. If MWT's managing partner was to get hold of those emails, the consequences for Krasnopovich could have been severe.

Jumping forward to August of 2013.

My home was burgled. I arrived home from a brief outing, returning to continue a letter I had begun on my laptop, located on the lounge desk in front of the fireplace. Where I liked to sit cross legged on the rug for my writing work. I sat down to begin and had the surreal experience of reaching out to start typing when I noticed something was wrong. The laptop wasn't there. What? But I had only been gone for 90 minutes. I had driven my car for a service to the Mercedes guy within walking distance, and walked back from the garage. I looked around in case I had forgotten taking the laptop into my office. Not there. I looked for the case which was exactly where it always lived. The power supply was there. On the writing desk next to where the laptop had stood was an unsealed envelope with £150 written large on the front. It contained three fifty-pound notes for my handyman John B to collect for recent house work. Strange that an envelope with cash was still there if burglars had been in the house. In fact, after a thorough examination, of obvious valuable items, nothing was missing except the laptop.

My first thought was "*all the information on the Belinda Rostock thing, as well as the PI report about the fitness Instructor girlfriend is on that laptop. As well as all my notes from Clam about his efforts to secure Sam's address and all my files on the visitation application.*"

At that point, maybe thirty-five minutes after arriving back and searching for the laptop, I called the police. Within twenty minutes a SOCO arrived. A new term to me, Scene of Crime Officer. The forensic guy who establishes the facts. The SOCO established there was no forced entry and in a process of elimination asked who else might have had keys. I hadn't thought of that. Nico had been gone for some two months by this time and when he moved his stuff out I had asked him to leave his key on the dining room table. Which he had done. As far as I knew, he only had two Yale keys for the two doors he needed to get into 28A, the ground floor flat. After the SOCO finished his report a detective inspector from Surrey Police arrived. They conferred and identified two suspects. Krasnopovich and his fitness Instructor girlfriend. A weight of circumstantial evidence but no actual forensic evidence. As the officer told me "*It seems clear only one person has a motive here. There is no sign of forced entry. He is a lawyer so it's unlikely he will have kept the laptop. Unless we can trick one of them into a confession, laptop, we will not have a case if they simply deny all knowledge. But we will try a surprise interview and see if one of them trips up. We will go unannounced to his office and see if he shows any signs of guilt. Take it from there.*"

Both Krasnopovich and his fitness Instructor were interviewed that same day by Police. Both denied any knowledge. The following day the officer reported back to me that this meant their case was at a dead end. "*Between you and me, it's pretty clear what has happened, but this guy is not an idiot. Even if we get a search warrant for his home, he will have made sure there is nothing to find.*"

His leaving advice was to claim it on the Insurance. He gave me the investigation report with the reference necessary for the Insurance claim. Later still an officer from Surrey Police arrived, a Trauma counseling officer, trained to offer victim support following burglary. I was impressed. A high standard of police support. It was traumatic. Someone came into my home and stole my laptop which contained important, possibly vital life changing information. I enjoyed the hour-long chat with the Police therapist. Very helpful I had no doubt that someone with a key had come in after seeing me leave with the car and removed the laptop. Who would have a motive for that? There were many more items of greater value. The most valuable item in the laptop was the data. Who would have a motive for that? Means motive and opportunity is how detectives work. One person had all three.

I proceeded with an Insurance claim for the burglary. The contents Insurance in August 2013 was in Krasnopovich's name. The contents policy provided for this type of theft, which had a police incident report. The value of the laptop claim was £1,800. Krasnopovich, the names policy holder never claimed for the theft, or if he did, never gave me the money. Do I believe a member of family-law orchestrated a burglary, possibly imposing on his adventurous athletic young girlfriend to take a key he provided and tell her where to go and what to look for, knowing when I would be out, to steal a laptop containing documents that might lead to his disbarment? Whatever, the net outcome is I lost £1,800 of Mac. I had paid for insurance cover. The policy holder was Krasnopovich. The police provided a report for Insurers. The Insurer was the AXA. In my story, this is a common theme:

1) Andrea pays for Insurance policy
2) Named policy holder is Krasnopovich
3) AXA is Insurer
4) An incident occurs requiring Insurance cover
5) No payment ever reaches Andrea

Shortly after fathers-day, little more than one week, I received an email letter from Krasnopovich requesting my proposals for how to finalize separating our joint assets. This was after he had been allowed free access to 28A the first Saturday after his departure, along with his removals van, to take whatever he wanted. I thought the wording in his email was curiously suspicious. We had no co-mingled finances so it was a straightforward prospect. He referred to the specifics of our joint assets. We shared a car. A five-year old Mercedes. That and a TV and a sofa which we had purchased jointly. He had £16,000 in the form of a diamond ring I had given him which he said was a '*gift not to be accounted for*' and that was excluded from his list of things to be divided, his total demand in 'jointly owned assets' being well below the value of the ring. Chris had told me to leave the ring out of any accounting as per this extract from an email from Chris:

"That's small change. Just call it a gift. Focus on Sam. Just agree to split the jointly owned stuff 50/50. Value the car and give him half. Or give him the car and let him pay you half of what he thinks it's worth. If you need a car, I will get you one. Not a problem. Let him keep the ring. Big deal. Make sure you get Sam back fast. He is the only thing that matters here. Don't let time pass before you have him."

And that is the tone I took from the outset. I just agreed with whatever he wanted to return to my home with movers and take 'his stuff'. He asked if I would leave the house while he was there. I agreed. I requested that after he was done, he should leave his keys behind. I did not take any security measures with any of my valuable items even though I knew he was going to be alone in the property and was by now, not my friend. The only area I locked was my studio, which contained my Mac server with all my private and work-related documents. The fact is, I had far more on my mind than worrying he might take any of my valuables. I wanted my son back. My approach was to not be adversarial in any way. He would see the importance of not separating a child from his parent. After that Saturday move out, where he took whatever he wanted to with unlimited time and manpower to take whatever he wanted to, he sent me a list with headers, asking that I fill in my proposals.

This is my reply to Krasnopovich's Separation list:

---

2 July, 2013

Car. Glasses guide valuation with the remedial works done is at best case £10K. Will pay you half. £5K. Or you take the car and give me £5K.

Flat possessions. Almost everything here was paid for by me, including all beds and almost every furnishing. All appliances I paid 100% of. Anything that's yours you took with your movers when you moved out.
All that remains are two recent purchases made 50/50. The TV and the sofa. Second hand valuation on the sofa is £300. The TV, which is wall mounted, with no stand available should it be moved, as I didn't keep its stand when it was wall mounted. Sold as is will fetch second hand no more than £300. I will offer £1,000 in total towards both items, or that you can take the sofa and TV and pay me £1,000.

Title deed. 28 Thameside. You advised me to transfer it to your name in 2003 for the advantage in house insurance quotes. I did so in trust that once the 5-year Insurance blight on my name for the fire damage had expired, you would transfer it back. The 5-year claims limit has long expired and I have formally requested the return of the title deed. Don't try and sell it back to me. Please return it as soon as the insurance renewal arrives and put that back in my name. I transferred your Domain names when you requested.

House Insurance. Is arranged through your broker in your name. It falls due in October. I will reinsure in my name as soon as possible and will trust that you are ethically bound by your profession not to vindictively cancel the policy and expose me to a position of being uninsured. As soon as I have Insurance in place I will let you know and we can transfer the title back to my name.

Domain name and web site transfer. I have transferred admin to your appointed IT guy for nicoKrasnopovich.com, KrasnopovichMcDonald.co.uk and Krasnopovich McDonald.com. I now have no control over any of the Business assets in my name. I paid Kim to migrate the KM website to the new server on the same day you asked for it. I expect transfer of my Freehold title as soon as insurance renewal falls due as you agreed.

Last month house accounts. Decide whatever you feel appropriate. I have paid out over 10K for May/ June. Including all your La Manga costs. I will attach the list of costs, including your business costs on my card. Pay whatever amount you decide is fair.

Amex. The Work card is in my name which is for your sole use at the firm. Please arrange to open a new Amex account in your own name. Let me know when this is done for me to close my account without inconveniencing you. Currently there is over £5,600 of your work costs on my card. Please pay it off. Obviously I am the sole named account holder and yours is a second card on my account which has a facility to go to £100,000. It's not appropriate that you keep using this card

The ring. The commitment ring I bought for you. I am sure you will never wear again for reasons that are more than obvious and would appreciate its return. Or consider its £16,000K value in full and final settlement and leave the car and the TV and sofa. And return my son.

With no reply in within two weeks, I sent this letter to Krasnopovich.

---

15 July, 2013

Nico,

I am writing further to my separation list proposals which you have not replied to.

I feel a sword of Damocles in your holding the freehold title over my head, which I have requested you return. This is not helpful in any way for either of us. We agreed a list of items to complete separation and get on with the custody aspect. I transferred title to your business domains. You agreed to transfer the freehold title. I did as I promised. You have not replied to my reminders for the freehold transfer giving cause for suspicion. What is the problem?

Please agree in writing the freehold transfer details for insurance renewal and let's be done with it. All that has happened since fathers-day has been your choice, not mine. I did not give up on my family.

You have already cleaned out the house of all but the TV and sofa. You had open access and unlimited time to remove anything you wanted to.

The half value of the car? Why not consider as a thank you for my efforts in setting up your web presence – or your new front door – or your carpet choice and installation. Or setting up 4 Castello Street. Or seeing you through the Patrick Suert expulsion meeting. Whatever. Consider your flat and all the work I put into helping you manage tenancies – arrange cleaners – arranging painting and decorating and window treatments - your new front door there - checking new tenants in and so on. Reading meters for tenant turnarounds. You had all the rent from your flat without ever thanking me for my input. I sponsored your living expenses completely for two years when you were broke and you had the income from renting your property.
I have not interfered with any of the articles that I controlled in trust for you – like your web domain names – your web site – your work files stored here at my expense

– your access to take whatever you wanted from the house. And have responded immediately to your every request since you left without once taking an adversarial position.

The only thing that matters now is making the best for Sam. I know Chris has called you with the same advice. It appears vindictive and provocatively malicious that you are ignoring my request for something you know is wrong. Please confirm in writing you will transfer the freehold back on the Insurance renewal date without further delay.

I want my son back. You are making financial demands seemingly conditional to seeing my son. For heavens sakes. You are talking about a total value of just a few thousand pounds which I am not even arguing over while in the background my son is desperate to see me and me to see him while you argue about small change? Money has nothing to do with me wanting my son. Do not go there. Enter into a mediated arrangement for the 50/50 time we can each restructure for having Sam. If you are not prepared to return him to his home immediately and trust we can agree his time with you once you have settled down.

I hope to hear from you soon.

Andrea

And that letter met a reply. A **without prejudice** email demand for £100,000 in full and final settlement for what he described as Sam's housing. Copied verbatim from his Yahoo account email to me. Complete with his usual disregard for spell check.

To Andrea Lee
From Nico Krasnopovich

WITHOUT PREJUDICE

18 July, 2013

Subject: Visiation

Andrea,

I need £100,000 to rehouse Sam. If you can't pay it in a lump sum, I will agree to ten monthly payments. I will accept your written confirmation for visitation arrangements.

Nico

By that time, around one months after Father's Day, Krasnopovich had moved to a rental near Thameside. I did not have the address. I emailed requesting the address. He simply ignored my email request. I texted a second request. He ignored that. I emailed a third request. Same outcome. That had a damaging effect on my already traumatized condition. Not knowing where my 4-year-old was fomented a new anxiety in me that once activated has never fully disappeared. And what to do next? My reality was I did not know where my son was. My last correspondence with Krasnopovich was a demand for £100,000, making plain that visitation would only follow this agreement. And yet, I felt that the clear connection between payment of a six-figure sum and visitation with my child was simply wrong. It was no less than blackmail. Once again I turned to my smartest friends for advice. Unanimously the consensus was use a family law solicitor to make the request in writing. He will not be able to ignore a solicitor's letter. I delayed appointing a solicitor as long as I could. I knew all too well how family court works and his role as a paid-up member with his own law firm. Especially I knew how he operates as a family law member and did not take the measure of sending him a legal letter lightly. I simply had no alternative because I wanted to know where my son was and I was becoming desperately anxious that he would continue obstructing visitation unless I gave him £100,000. That is the point where I appointed a family-law solicitor, to find out where Krasnopovich was housing Sam and later, after 13 weeks passed with awful toxic letters from Krasnopovich changing arrangements at the last minute and making sure that for 13 weeks in a row, despite my best efforts, Sam was unable to see me and I was unable to see him, to make an application in family court for visitation.

Krasnopovich's position was entrenched. "£100,000 or you will not see him".

My last attempt to write before taking legal advice was a long heartfelt letter that Chris advised me not to send. *"You are writing too father. But Nico is thinking like a lawyer. There is no upside letting him know how much he has hurt you. He sees your weakness. There is no emotional side for him. It's just money."*

I felt it was worth trying on the basis that I didn't want to look back and say I had not tried everything in my power to do what's best for Sam. And at the very least to have a contemporaneous record of what happened.

Here is the letter sent before any lawyers were instructed. 4 July 2013:

Nico.

I am putting my thoughts to paper for the purpose of a record of events, largely for Sam's sake, should he ever need to know what happened to us on fathers-day.

Sam historically.
Sam has just turned four. When he was born, we put everything into raising a happy and beautiful boy in a stable family unit in which you played your part and I played mine. We agreed the securing presence would be that I stayed home and I was there constantly every time Sam needed something. I played my part as his mother and primary carer and you yours as his father, and in the context of Sam's educational expenses only, the primary breadwinner. I provided the home for him and the day to day living expenses. I spent all of his waking hours with him. You averaged at most 10%. As we agreed would be the case, I was there for him all the time. I changed my

working position to become a full-time writer very much with this in mind. Being home to attend Sam's needs. As we discussed exhaustively in our parental agreement.

You went to work and came home each day to find a perfectly adjusted well balanced boy. I spent hours in every single day with Sam, always there for him in the next room and he had the experience of mummy and daddy fully in his life even though you were working a long five-day week.

After one-year Nina started helping with Sam. As we had agreed, you paid the costs of the nanny. You moved forward at work and I continued staying at home, seeing Sam for hours during the course of each day where he only had to call for me as I was in the next room. Something he did a lot as you would expect from a young child. You understand all too well how close the relationship between Sam and myself has been. He has a good foundation in piano, guitar and drums. We have exactly the close bond that was agreed as my part when we agreed to have a child. And you convinced me that there was no possibility of my ever revisiting the broken family scenario.

Your work progress.

I remained a daily constant with Sam whilst committing to the partnership with you and supporting your work progress to the best of my ability and business acumen. Often in time terms this would include hours each day in reviewing your work correspondence, editing your letters, and giving opinions and discussing tactical decisions on matters in which you needed a sounding board.

When you were offered MWT equity partnership in 2009 I went through the decision on whether you should accept it in the first case, and then when you did, financing it with some 40K from my investment account. Worth noting that you paid it back very slowly, long after you had funds to invest in ISA's of your own, it took many years to repay, and to date it is still not fully repaid. And although you know I paid interest of over a thousand pounds during that term in making the funds available to you, I never asked for that cost reimbursed nor did you offer. It was an investment in our future. I supported you financially as well as emotionally and practically. And tactically. It is sad to reflect that you loaned money with the promise of repayment, which never followed. When it came time to leave MWT with the strategy for leaving early and formulating a best way forward in keeping all your work files for transfer to the new business, I was with you and in consultation for many hours of each day. It became as much a part of my life as yours, leaving little or no time for me to attend my writing targets, which were less important in the context of necessity to get you out of MWT and into the new business. It is not inaccurate to say I lived and breathed that entire episode with you all the way.

I took you too the partners disciplinary meeting when they expelled you and how many hours did we spend discussing Patrick Suert and his unpleasant approach to your exit. The talks with Christa and David the employment lawyer. When you were called in by the Partners, you chose me to accompany you over your lawyer, because you told him "Andrea will do a better job. She knows more about it."

The priority in my life was twofold. Being there for Sam and being there to help you. Even down to having well considered meals ready every night. As a consequence my time and attention in pursuing my own career lessened accordingly. Something I accepted on the basis that we were a team, working well together with the long-term objective of raising a child in a stable family. Everything I did was with the best intentions for the family. Specifically. My son. Of course you know all too well the nature of the parenting agreement we both committed to.

Starting Krasnopovich McDonald
By April of 2011, you were in the process of exiting MWT and we were working on setting up your new practice. I have folders on my computer reminding me of the amount of work I put into enabling the business start-up. From the original draft of the business plan, to the final one used for the bank. The To do list – all of which when I look at it now – was excellently done, reflective of my own experience in setting up small businesses, as well as executed with totally diligent attention. With the benefit of looking back at that business plan and cost projections one year later, I observe it was spot on the money. That was a job extremely well done. We made a great partnership. With one observation.

All the money went in one direction. From me to you. 100% of all expenditure between us flows in one direction. There is no record of one single deposit from your account to mine by way of loan. There are many going in the other direction.

Setting up the office for the new business in one month while you were still working notice at MWT was all down to me. Transforming a disused old English school into a trendy law firm was almost 100% my effort, done with my network of contacts in the building trades, as well as on my credit card. All my own work ambitions were firmly put on hold in your time of need to get you up and running as a high earner. I felt very much a part of the business. It was almost like our second child. I did not expect repayment. It was done as we agreed to provide for our son.

My daily routine then was being there for Sam's needs, helping you in the business, and with the time in between working on my book and looking after my business affairs. In that order of priority.

Sam in the last year.
As you became more immersed in the business, you spent more time in meetings and the occasions when you were late increased. Sam went through phases in reaction to this.
  *For weeks he would greet your arrival with '**go away daddy**'.*
  I made it my goal to coach him out of doing that, explaining that 'daddy has to go to work to make money so you can go to a nice school' and similar variations that would prepare him for your return in the best way possible so he would be happy and excited to enjoy those few hours of quality time you had with him each evening.

The time I spent with Sam in our family was the most complete experience of my life. I have played no role better than that of Sam's parent. I love Sam and Sam loves me. That you would seek to use this loving relationship between mother and child to extract money from me beggar's belief.

Following the arrival of Sam I believed the balance of our relationship was in our agreement that you invest time in the high earning work and I spend more time at home for him. Your work being more likely to generate private school fees than mine for this purpose. It is the agreement we made when reconciling in 2008. Detailed in our parental agreement along with your unswerving reassurance that you would 'Not bring another child into a broken family.' I thought this was working well, albeit that you were often out late and with ever lessening explanations. Your 'networking meetings' became increasingly frequent and, on many occasions,, I would have to put him to bed explaining that he could sleep in our bed until daddy came home, on many occasions after ten pm.

I believed in the context of our mutual interests that this was working well, both for Sam's wellbeing as well as for your business progress. And for encouraging the bond between you and your son. That my own work was affected as a consequence was of concern to me, but tempered by the thought that I was at least succeeding with my first priorities. I had no suspicions that your long working hours might have been breeding a pattern of discontent.

As Sam approached his 4th year, we changed his pattern, preparing him for school, letting the nanny go, increasing his nursery time. We visited all the school options for him, and we jointly picked the school we decided on for him.

Written into our parental agreement was that you would underwrite the school costs from the business and that was one balancing aspect of my declining earning and your increasing earnings, arising from our parenting arrangement. It may be that you have changed direction in romance, but you cannot undo this agreement.

Fathers-day, 16 June, 2013.
Our plan that day was breakfast with Jo at the cafe, my tennis tournament at the Lansbury, where you would drop me off, and then return with Sam to watch the second match while he had a play on the Lansbury swings, and then lunch at your sisters for 3. I went to tennis and was injured in the first set leading to me leaving early. You came to collect me and I was in the bath recovering, when you said 'time to go to my sisters' and in a moment of despair at the prospect given my sore mood from tennis and the painfully boring prospect of lunch in Worcester Park, I asked if I could not go. 'I just can't face it. Please can I miss this one'. You left without saying anything. With a black face. Yes, it is true that I found socializing with your sister difficult. She is not the smartest kettle on the stove top as you have observed on more than one occasion. Hindsight shows that had I come with to your sisters for Father's Day lunch, you would not have made that call to the babysitter to set up events of that evening. You called a babysitter and when you arrived back from your sisters, asked me for a drink. I believed you wanted to make up for not doing anything nice earlier in the day, which I had found strange.

I was quite excited by the prospect of having a drink and some dinner with you. On the walk there through the rose garden I remarked how lucky we are to live in such a beauty filled place. There was no inkling of anything untoward from you even then. You posed, smiling for a photo in the rose garden.

In the bar we sat down, I brought over two Vodka tonics and you made your announcement

'I want to end the relationship. I have outgrown you. I no longer find you attractive'.

When I asked you if we could try to work things out you flatly refused. Instead, you asked me how I felt. I told you I was devastated. That was an understatement. I felt like I had been stabbed in the stomach with a barbed blade. That this came out of the blue is an understatement. We left the Kings Arms while I was numb with shock. I was still dazed when we got home, where Jo and Tom waited. They were shocked beyond belief, especially by the way you had asked them to babysit knowing what you were going to do, without any inkling of what you were doing when you asked them to babysit. They thought it was psychotic behavior, which of course it is. We all learned something new about you on fathers-day.

I didn't sleep that night, or the next. I was unable to properly process what appeared to me to be unreal. I have not seen Sam since you left for lunch at your sisters on fathers-day. The consequences for me not seeing him have been devastating. Imagine what it must be like for him? I can't imagine you can.

The period before fathers-day
After ten years in our relationship, less one bad month in 2008, I thought we were progressing toward our goals. We agreed to have a child and raise him. Sam was clearly blossoming. You were clearly blossoming at work and I felt my contribution to both was the defining measure of my own success. All the reasons I agreed to when we decided and agreed to have a child followed a natural order. I did my bit and I thought you were doing yours. Sam was simply the perfect child. I was besotted with him. And he showed me unconditional love all the time.

Our life had no obvious indicator of discontent. There was never one occasion since I invited you to live in my home that I did not express joy at seeing you. From the moment I met you I have shown you love, kindness and mindful generosity. My life was planned around you and the child we agreed to have together. I know that in recent weeks you appeared unusually stressed and restless. I thought that was work related stress with the reemergence of the Trotter complaint and the run-in over the partnership accounts with Caroline. I had no indication and no way of knowing it was because you were nurturing deep and bitter discontent.

We had a dinner party with Chris just one week before fathers-day. Everything that night appeared as the picture of a happy family. Tammie and Nikki both said the same. What a picture of a perfect family with such a beautiful baby.

Richard Nastase said to me 'every time I came into the house I saw a warm happy family. This has totally blindsided me.'

Jo had not an inkling that anything was amiss and we have coffee with her every morning? Had I known something was troubling you to the point of abandoning your family I would certainly have discussed it with her, or she would surely have sensed something was seriously wrong. She didn't. You concealed your need to break up completely and with unbelievable skill.

Why would you do that?

It took a week to clear the muck of your deceit but the facts are glaring. On the surface, right up until fathers-day, you gave everyone and including myself the impression that all was progressing well, outside of the normal pressures of work. Is there any other way you could have got Sam out of the house, away from me and under your access control?

We had calendar dates booked in directly after fathers-day. The following Thursday, four days later, on 20 June we were booked for the parents evening at Sam's new school. We had David and Nicolette's wedding booked for Friday 28th, June. You even confirmed the menu dinner options for me in the RSVP email. That is pretty fucked up deceit. We had the alternate day collection for Sam's new school arranged, with every detail of the new school requirements considered and agreed. We had a diary of travel planned this year, including three weeks in California. Phillip was expecting us, with a diarized schedule. We had a future in progress involving a young child and a parental agreement. There was no warning to me that you were going to break up our family with no opportunity to discuss it. As Chris has said on more than one occasion, there is only ever one reason a man breaks up a happy family home. Although in your case I think the money was an added factor.

Contact in a broken family.

I accept that we will not be able to co-parent in the traditional alternate weekend model that involves remaining a presence in each other's lives. I have no confidence in your integrity and believe you are fundamentally intrinsically dishonest. You will not stop at anything to get your way in any situation, including abusing Sam's best interests. I am clear that your actions in choosing fathers-day to create the opportunity to remove the child from me and all that goes with the events of that day is indistinguishable from the conduct of a child abuser. Using a legal training to contrive a separation in which you use the child as collateral to extract a six-figure sum from me. I do not see how you will find an entirely new and convincing version of yourself worthy of basic respect, with which I can enter into a functional agreement for co-parenting.

My proposal that we alternate school term and holiday is based on the principal that we are both his parents and should have equal roles in his upbringing. This way Sam gets to spend approximately the same amount of time with each parent.

You are committed to your work. Obsessively so. You will not spend more than 10% of your daily time with Sam. And he is worth so much more than the ethics you model as a family lawyer. We can agree holiday times at your convenience. Between ourselves. In writing. Put Sam's best interests first and work out a realistic schedule between your time for work and your time to spend with your son. Do not make it necessary for me to run up a legal bill to see my son.

My understanding of what happened

On fathers-day there was one trigger. When I declined going to your sisters for lunch. You were angry and that anger led you to the decision to act there and then. It seems *to me you were committed to having sex with your fitness instructor and made up what you chose to believe to get out of your relationship. Your anger management failed you and the temptation to follow temptation outweighed your parental commitment. You saw an opportunity on a Sunday that was also a special family day. Had I not been injured in tennis and missed that lunch you would not have called the Jo to be babysitter and made your separation announcement. And you would not have been photographed out for a candlelit dinner with your (married) fitness instructor not long after leaving.*

Sam's broken family prospects
For your father's-day Sam drew a picture of his family. Mummy, Daddy, Evan, William and Maria. Today his family has no William, no Evan, no Maria and no Mummy. This is something I would have done anything to avoid. You already know my position with regard to broken family parenting and despite your assurances that convinced me to have a child with you, Sam is now what we swore would never happen. The product of a broken family. That commitment we made to raise him as a family was ended unilaterally. You can explain it to him in whatever way you see fit, but the reality is you ended his innocent life on an anger driven whim because I never came to lunch with your sister, and although you refer to longstanding underlying discontent, you never disclosed as much as 'we need to talk.' You made no effort to discuss any alternative to dishonoring your promise to raise a child with me.

Clearly, you saw the accounts in April. The end of year one of the big money move. And you saw then that you had achieved the £350K target. You took the product of our best efforts together, setting up a firm that followed my guidance and support from concept to execution and when you saw the money, you reneged on your word and made it all about you. You have placed money above all else. Less than two months after seeing your first big payday, you were out the door, straight into the arms of a younger model. Instead of agreeing a school payment plan for Sam and getting on with your new life, you took him and ransomed him back to me for a six-figure sum. Attack is the best form of defense?

Sam's residential parent
I would like you to agree that that I continue to raise Sam in his home. We can discuss the amounts of time with each parent. I propose with me in term time and you see him on holidays. In which I will agree to whatever times and dates you choose to suit your convenience. I can continue dedicating my time to the role of his primary carer and I am quite capable of providing the same stable loving family home he knew with or without your support on the school fees. I will be able to keep him in his same familiar bedroom and be the same full-time parent attending his every need. He would continue to have me there all of the time and see you as much as before, the convenient 10% of your time, during his holiday. In all likelihood this arrangement will give you more time with Sam than his is accustomed to. I will ensure he has a Skype and can talk to you whenever you want. Every night if you choose.

I can continue raising Sam in a way that your career and your current interests do not allow. It will certainly assist you in enjoying your new-found freedom and enable you to pursue your new relationship without the need for babysitters.

Keeping hold of him as you are doing whilst still working long hours at the firm means you will continue paying people to look after him while you work and I know in all certainty, your commitment to the work buzz is likely to see you spend more time in the office, not less. Sam's life with you will be spent mostly being looked after by others. In this holiday scenario you can have him for lengthy periods during school holidays – possibly using a locum – to spend pure undistracted quality time with him.

Sam loves me in a different way to you. I am his mirror. You know I am strong in many ways as a centered parent and as events have shown, less likely to give up on his best interests than you are. Your time with him, uninterrupted by work would give you both a better relationship. Where he does not tell you to "Go away" in despair at your late arrivals when work invariably comes first.

The financial arrangement
There is not much to agree. We are not married. We have no comingled finances. No bank accounts, no loans. You have use of my Amex for the business (Which you owe £5,6k this month.) You can pay that off and take out a new Amex in your own name from the following monthly cycle. There were two legal titles to transfer. Your domain names in my name have already been transferred to you as agreed, and my freehold title which you will transfer when Insurance comes due. I will not come after you for any money. I expect you to honor the parental agreement for school fees paid by the firm. I hope you will attach a value to a one-off payment for my input to the firm and leave that to your conscience. My focus is solely what's best for Sam.

Conclusion
As partners we have been complimentary. We are both intelligent and articulate enough to have been able to work through your relationship ending concerns and, even had we then agreed that the relationship was over, I would have had the closure of knowing why and that I had applied my best efforts toward keeping Sam in a stable family unit. As I committed to in making a parenting agreement with you in 2008. That I had worked tirelessly at supporting you in your business growth as an adjunct to prioritizing and providing daily loving care for Sam, placing my own selfish interests to one side, discarding me as you have and applying financial conditions to Sam being with me is devastating. I would have done anything to preserve Sam's stability and I will always deeply regret that irrespective of your ambitions and discontent the value you attached to Sam's relationship with me was not enough to warrant engaging in a dialogue over salvaging the relationship or directing it to a workably amicable conclusion no matter how much you felt I had become unattractive to you. Or how attractive you found your fitness instructor. Perhaps it would have been more honest to say 'I have outgrown your net worth.' Or even "now that I am financially independent I can choose to be alpha male and I choose to have sex with a much younger fitter partner instead."

It is clear that you ambushed me with this break up demand, out of the blue, knowing it was the only way you could remove the child from his home and that you did it for the leverage it gives you to pursue a financial demand.

Frankly, I am disgusted by your dishonesty. £100,000 or I can't see my son? Eventually, Sam will know this. You are flying fast and loose in the face of right and wrong. How much money is your son's life with his parent worth?

Andrea

By early August the tone had descended to exchanges of 'Without Prejudice', after the Instruction of David Clam, my solicitor member of family law. My neighbor and friend Jo had been trying to arrange a weekend visit for Sam, using emails and texts with Krasnopovich. However after three weeks and 100 emails, Jo had recused herself from being intermediary, after feeling 'burned by the toxic correspondence' going between Krasnopovich and myself. Which turned inflexibly on "Give me the £100,000 or there will be no visit." For the record, he never responded to my request for the Amex card settlement – leaving a balance £5,672.12 at the point when I decided to just pay it off and have his signing power cancelled. He never paid the £10,900 shortfall on the equity loan. And the £16,000 of jewelry I had given him was never acknowledged. That is about £36,000 just in gifts and card payments I overlooked to remove any adversarial possibility. I wanted to see Sam free of any encumbrance by his deviant parent. I could not have presented a more agreeable, generous approach to assuring him I was not coming after him for maintenance or a share of the business we started together in an agreement. But the response was a binary option. Pay me £100,000 and have Sam. Do not and you never will. And my expensive member of family-law, David Clam was reliably assuring me that Krasnopovich was never going to place the child's interests above his material greed. "*I know him all too well. I am afraid your optimism is unrealistic.*"

Without Prejudice.
2 August, 2013.

Nico.

Jo is no longer prepared to facilitate contact with Sam and for this reason I am writing to arrange the alternative intermediary for contact arrangements. You never replied to my letter of 29 June or addressed any of the contents and this is in part why Jo has withdrawn. She is affected by your 'Toxic Correspondence'. Do you even read what you write? Are you aware of how toxic your word choices are and the consequences for a young child of these choices?

Following Jo's withdrawal from the role of intermediary I will agree an alternative for contact with Sam in someone you know and trust. I will relay the next date when the arrangements are in place. I note here that the only way I can reach Sam is through you. And that is not right. You are trained as a family lawyer. You know that it is not right to withhold the child's address from his mother. I believe I could call the SRA about this and you would be told to provide the address without delay.

Although I had already made the connection between the emails and the frequency of your fitness classes, following legal advice I engaged the services of a private detective which confirms the full extent of your sexual interest in another and understand the reason why you were so unwilling to even talk about counselling before breaking up your family. Whilst living a lie with me and operating such a convincing deceit that no one around us, especially myself, had any inkling that you were harboring your relationship ending intention, clearly has had an adverse effect on our prospects for collaborating in the future.

The outcome of paying an investigator has been helpful and insightful for my understanding of what happened when reviewing the itemized details of your not so clandestine sexually motivated relationship with your fitness instructor. I am forwarding a few excerpts from the document I was given which includes text messages you sent to your secretary, which you will recognize were sent in the week after you left:

"Just annoying as she so hot and the chemistry is amazing!"

"The babe and I have had a long talk and we all sorted. Breakdown in communication basically. It was quite funny, we were having a very loud and animated conversation in the gym!"

"God I am in so much trouble with this girl, need to be careful… Anyway, we have two weeks away from each other so that might put things into perspective a bit for me, or just make me more lust driven than I already am!!!"

I see from the photos that she is extremely fit. It is kind of you to pressure her into divorcing her husband Tomasz by offering your divorce services for free. Her Facebook page featuring your pictures so openly demonstrates a reassuring mutual commitment. I guess you never mentioned to her that you were in a relationship with a four-year-old son involved. Either that, or she doesn't care, which bodes well for Sam's step-mum prospects. The second aspect of our communication going forward relates to your legal demands, threatening me with the enormously confident weight of your legal prowess. It is no less than blackmail. I wonder what the SRA would say about your blackmailing efforts to conceal my son from me and trade visitation for a six-figure sum?   In my letter of 29 June, I offered you the opportunity to reach a settlement between ourselves without recourse to legal process. You made it impossible for me to communicate directly towards an amicable settlement and as a result all correspondence relating to the financial conclusion between us will now follow my solicitor's advice, which you are all too aware will cost me. Accounting issues that need to be addressed:

My laptop which you used in La Manga still has the emails to Belinda Rostock from when you attempted to recruit her from MWT in March, 2013, Caroline's correspondence with you on poaching staff from MWT with four detailed mails about "the need for secrecy" and how aware you both are of the risk that MWT will find out.

You reference the specific consequences if Patrick Suert finds out you and Caroline are poaching staff from MWT. Those emails make plain that you have breached your articles of Partnership with MWT. And again, the SRA would most likely consider this a breach of ethical conduct by yourself. You have basically ripped them off, £180,000 in client fees alone. And used me as your accomplice in doing so. With regard to Sam's school; you have made it impossible for me to participate in Sam's schooling as a result of telling Clock to pursue me for the school costs. That is not what we agreed. It is simply wrong to make an agreement to have a child and agree how their education will be funded and then about-face and demand money from me instead. It is both blackmail, breach of an agreement, abuse of a child, and unsavory.

You know the priority I placed on Sam's education. Access to Sam will of necessity now have to be decided through family-court. That is an awful decision you have made that can never be confused with acting in the child's best interests. It should not have been this way. All of this is your choice. You are making decisions as an avaricious lawyer, not as a loving responsible father. You are abusing your own child. Building walls that can never be breached. Finally, it is of practical importance that with regard to the freehold, you are on notice that as the freeholder you have a duty of care to maintain the buildings insurance. I am advised that any failure to do so or to transfer the freehold without notice, affecting the building insurance, will place liability for any claim on yourself. I propose the transfer of the freehold title back to my name dated the week of the 19th November, 2013. The date of the Insurance renewal. I have paid the costs up until then for the current policy cover. I will take out policy cover in advance of the renewal date. I will instruct my lawyer to complete the paperwork to reduce this to no more than a signature for you. Until then please be advised that you remain responsible for all the obligations of the freeholder including the insurance. I followed your legal advice to transfer the title to your name and trust you will not seek to benefit from that advice, or use it to cause me harm. You are bound by the provisions of the trust agreement to honor your fiduciary responsibilities.

I will reply to your latest financial demand once my solicitor returns from holiday next week. There is no need to reply to this letter.

Andrea

10 PTSD, depression, the Priory and Cafcass
Is it safe to take medical advice and see a therapist when you are a parent?

This is the chapter on depression. Because often separation causes depression. That time in life, when separating with children involved, often results in a level of depression so profound it should be given its own classification. It leads to a vulnerability leaving the affected some distance from rational responsible decision making. A condition smart divorce lawyers identify and target. How else would people of ordinary means cough up more money than they have in their pensions towards legal fees relating to their children's visitation? Family court usually involves people who are depressed being interrogated in a system that is designed for criminals. My point is that family law needs to allow for the fact that an adversarial arena is not the appropriate setting for a depressed person to make decisions that will affect a child's life.

Historically depression is understood as a vague science. As a mental illness.

Many who are bi-polar do not even know it. Many are not bi-polar and believe they are. Many treat depression as a weakness, with a 'man up' approach. Medical advances in the past 70 years enable others to take anti depressant's and hope for the best. Some learn to treat their depression and progress. Others never recover. Multi-national pharmaceutical companies do multi-billion-dollar annual business in drugs for depression and related maladies. I believe we all have a relationship and experience of depression. And an opinion on how to understand it and treat it. The smarter we are the more likely it is we will be affected by depression. The dumber and more satisfied we are with the bliss of ignorance, the less predisposed we become to the depression that follows knowing and caring. Often the trigger for depression is a stress incident. That is now widely recognized as a condition called PTSD.

Post-Traumatic Stress Disorder (PTSD) is an **anxiety disorder** that can develop after experiencing or witnessing a traumatic event.

In conventional psychology we read; "Dopamine is a chemical (neurotransmitter) that is used by the nerves to send "messages." When a nerve releases dopamine it crosses a very small gap called a synapse and then attaches to a dopamine receptor on the next nerve. When dopamine levels are depleted in the brain the nerve impulses, or "messages," cannot be transmitted properly and can impair brain functions: behavior, mood, cognition, attention, learning, movement, and sleep."

I have experienced several traumatic incidents giving rise to depression, starting with the breakup of my family unit, the death of one parent and the disappearance of the other into a cloud of depression lasting many years, when I was ten. Profound loss at a time before therapy and counselling at a sensitive developmental stage. Later I was traumatically held by the Apartheid police, placed in a staring contest with my own mortality. That left a traumatic effect. I had neither therapy nor medication. But I did have cigarettes and whatever anxiety-causing chemical imbalance may have been present in my brain was no match for the greatest mood modifier available over the counter. As an anti-depressant, smoking is unbeatable. In a life-defining process involving hard work I overcame depression and functioned at a high level. I had never talked about depression and mental illness before family law used it as a discriminatory label against me. But here we are, it was. I was profiled by last minute switch judge Flaherty as mentally infirm and judged accordingly. Despite the reality that I had a number of medical professionals attesting to my mental health, the judge was able to simply dismiss medical doctors' reports in my matter on a whim. And the purpose of that whim was to use a medical condition against my sons' best interests. To enable her to pass off her opinion as a legal judgment, no matter how far from the professional assessment it was. The doctor's determination was irrelevant in her court, because she simply declared it so. This forms an important aspect of how we regulate family law. On two levels. One is obviously, profiling a mental illness is wrong. And second, is it our right to represent ourselves in Court? If someone is unwell, should the proceedings be delayed until they are well enough to attend in 'sound body and mind.' Especially if the time period referred to is as brief as one Month? To be present in sound mind and body when a judge rules on our lives? A judge placed in this position of enormous power, with a child's future depending on their competence. Operating within a limited checks and boundaries on their ability as 'fit for purpose' judges of children's futures. Can a maliciously motivated, ethically bankrupt elderly woman operating on a foundation of prejudicial stereotyping that categorizes depression as a mental illness discounting one parent from any involvement with their child, awarding maximum costs against one parent, also be an appropriate family court deputy district judge? And if the answer is, "they can't", then where is the accountability process for this level of child abuser acting as an officer of the court and getting away with it. Making judgments targeting mental illness without even a basic insight into the medical condition relating to depression. To contextualize the extent of Judge Flaherty's use of my 'mental infirmity' to rubber stamp her own predetermined judgment by profiling me as mentally infirm at every opportunity, here is my own disclosure. You decide whether it was appropriate for Flaherty to label me as mentally frail' and whether this form of profiling properly represents the impartiality we expect from a member of the judiciary. Or, whether pursuing this prosecution of someone on the grounds of 'mental infirmity' to end a child's relationship with his parent, is in fact, bang to rights, child abuse by a family-court judge. Is this last-minute switch judge Flaherty, fit for purpose, as a family-court judge? Or, was she right in her conduct, ensuring my son no longer has one parent in his life.

It is my view, in a general sense, that we all deal with depression to some degree. As sentient beings our capacity to react sensitively to traumatic events can manifest as depression. "I guess that's why they call it the Blues" because everybody hurts sometimes. Feeling depressed is a normal part of growing up. There is a scientifically quantifiable correlation between higher intelligence and education to diagnosable depression. And that is not surprising. There is much to be depressed about. The more you learn about the ways of the world, the death of our planet through the greed of the empowered elite, the more depressing it is. Those content with blind faith and the asking of no-questions in a life without curiosity, cannot experience the sorrow that learning of horrible things brings. Ignorance is bliss for them. There is no thoughtful bedrock for depressions mold to find purchase. The more we learn about humankind's awful ethical abuses, the harder it becomes to 'stay on the sunny side.' Our history of mass killing and child abuses and the endless persecution of the weak by the strong in our might-is-right evolution where half the world live in extreme life-blighting poverty is, to all but the totally insensitive, depressing. It is the converse of the saying 'ignorance is bliss'. Knowledge is often an enabler of depressing information processing. It is how we deal with the wrongs in life that balances depression and degree of function. This is an integral stage in the journey to self-awareness.

I had never taken any medications for depression or PTSD, anxiety or insomnia prior to June 2013, apart from cigarette smoking, which I learned is the most power anti-depressant available. That cocktail of some 100 chemicals the manufacturers incorporate into cigarettes boost dopamine. (Whilst making the user brand addicted at the same time.) It was only after I gave up smoking at 34 that I properly identified the gloominess associated with the chemical imbalance underpinning depression. That would have been, by my own diagnosis, dopamine deficiency, caused by actual physiologic changes in the brain. A medical condition, just like any other, with a cause and a cure. A chemical imbalance. Not a lack of mental fortitude. Or cowardly submission. I read up on the subject, consulted with medical friends, and the outcome of my learning led me to make lifestyle and dietary changes to increase dopamine levels, increase serotonin rich dietary elements and promote a positive outlook to 'cure' feelings of depression. I took a holistic view to treating the symptoms of depression with lifestyle adjustments. After giving up smoking, I spent the next two years occupied fully by living a healthy lifestyle, exercising, playing tennis most days, eating well, lots of Brazil nuts and other serotonin rich foods, and using light, visiting sun regularly for Vitamin D. And by discriminating relentlessly; only interacting with kind intelligent uplifting people wherever that was possible. I managed that by setting aside time to do nothing else except focus on one job description.

Non-smoker.

And it worked. I had no symptoms of depression. I was productive and enthusiastic and energetic.

I have some history with undiagnosed PTSD and depression. After my first encounter with profound loss when I was ten, I began the learning curve of how to overcome depression by analyzing myself, benefiting from the wisdom of books and friends, and diagnosing myself as a high functioning depressive, with some remarkable skills, replacing melancholic sorrow with energetic curious joyfulness in the quest for knowledge. Music was my medicine. Whenever I felt the incoming sense of dread, I would sing. And breathe. I recognized depression as a luxury I could not afford. And recognized the shadow of sorrow approaching as a reason to shine the light of my most enthusiastic effort in finding joy. Positivity through kindness became my mantra. *"The meaning of life is to be happy. The way to be happy is by making others so."* Alternatively, Eric Idles words resonated. *"Always look on the bright side of life."*

Being a musician made me a pleaser by nurture as well as nature. Nothing uplifted me more than seeing a positive outcome follow my helping others less fortunate with whatever I was able to offer by way of helpful considered kindness. After a good gig, leaving a room filled with happy smiling people, I felt a glow of positivity that would see me through to the next gig. At least that was the case for the first ten years of my new life. For me growing up in South Africa and being so close to the offensive behavior typified by the racist Christian superiority so many embraced with indifference as normal and legislated accordingly, was traumatic. Of course I did not think of it that way at the time. That would come much later, during therapy sessions at the Priory. We do not always identify the most traumatic events until viewed in retrospect.

Growing up, every time I saw this awful Christian White supremacy at work I felt, to some extent, traumatized. I was far too thin skinned to ever make a good South African. And far too thoughtful to ever make a proper God believer, in any of the multiple exclusive options. As I grew through my teens, the more I saw of South African culture, the sadder I became. It was an immense challenge to adjust to finding the appropriate way to speak to Black folk. Many of whom could not cope with being treated kindly and might well misinterpret it as an opportunity to behave offensively. For me, it was a hopeless no-win situation. I was fortunate though in having had opportunities to help wherever possible and I found great comfort in doing that, but on many occasions I was totally incapable of meaningful help and I have learned these unresolved stressors, being disempowered from helping when witness to injustice, leaves a thin layer of memory somewhere near the subconscious. And when these moments of outrage reach a collective mass threshold, and a pin prick of sorrow pierces the holding membrane, something unpleasant happens to one's joyfulness. All kinds of past sorrows leak out. Intermingling in a gushing stream of melancholy that can become overwhelming. But in my early life, I had the stability to cope. I had my own room and a loving cook to make my every meal. With four dogs for my lessons in trust and a library filled with books for my access to knowledge. And a piano, and music. And safe space for long walks. What I missed in loving human interaction I compensated for by enjoying the contents of more than one library. Information is strength, I heard early on, and that was true for my developing confidence. I had never even heard of SSRI's (Selective Serotonin re-uptake Inhibitors) and I doubt they existed then in South African medicine. You just got on with it. Or you offed yourself, as several of my contemporaries did. Three in one year of high school.

By 2003, when I met Krasnopovich, my mental health issues with depression that began at age ten had benefitted from a considerable amount of work and therapy and learning and I considered myself to be at pretty advanced state of wellness. I had absorbed many of the lessons that turn negatives to positives and lived in gratitude and kindness. I had enjoyed many beautiful relationships since the divorce from Paul Smith and had the ongoing unconditional love of a beautiful Black and silver schnauzer, William, who came into my life in 1998. Becoming a parent helped a great deal. Evan was by now in his teens and a weekly boarder at a top English school. He visited each parent on alternate weekends. I kept his room in my home at Thameside as if he was there all the time. My awful addiction to cigarettes was finally vanquished and possibly for the first time in my life, I felt I had achieved a level of personal growth from knowing the height of the hurdles I had overcome. The stressors giving rise to depressive imbalance were largely under new management. I had grown from student to teacher. Or at least, learning by teaching. I was earning well, doing what I loved. Living a healthy life. Sleeping well. Helping people around me. My home was in good repair, after the fire (2001) led to a rebuild, it was like new. Attracting fine tenants at top dollar rents. Property prices had doubled since I bought into the London market. And with the royalties coming in from the albums I had produced or written, to supplement the rental income, I had for the first time in my life the opportunity to explore life choices free of financial pressure. I had survived the fire, navigated the bumps in the road, beaten the addiction and was walking in fields of green. Literally. Verdant England, where I lived on the bank of the Thames, surrounded by wavy, fertile, sun drenched fields of seasonally affected golden green. Mostly my choices by this stage involved pursuing my bliss. Helping by sharing my life lessons and my skill set. Giving back some of the good fortune I had enjoyed. I felt grown up for the first time. Free from the constant fear of failure and the poverty consciousness of growing up as I had done, with no resources of my own, and relying on making a living by playing music as an independent musician in a notoriously underpaid and unreliable income source. Free from the subconscious horror dreamscapes from my South African experience. Of violence and suppression and planet threatening ethical corruption.

Achieving some financial independence was possibly the biggest step in my anti-depression therapy. Learning that few single causes help defeat depressive impulses more than material success. Having enough income to not have to wake every morning worrying about paying bills gave me the opportunity to focus all my energy on my own wellness. And self-awareness. And that work was paying off.

I was feeling happy. *Pretty pretty happy.* I had seen Larry David on TV and realized I was not alone in this world of functional creative anxiety.

And then came the enormous life-changing shock of that fathers-day mafia hit.

Like a cricket bat cover drive to the side of the head, having a concussive effect on my positivity. Fracturing the border of cohesive padding that had each trauma recessed, processed and packed in just the right position. It seemed all the work I had done to be well and balanced and confident in my self-esteem was undone in one cacophonous moment. All the gloom I had dealt with and banished from my process returned in one gushing tsunami of all-encompassing drenching despair.

"But we have a child. This is not the deal we made."

Soon after the traumatic theft on fathers-day, into that big area once occupied by restorative sleep came a flood of odium-spiked memories of previous anxiety. Once that dam wall regulating the flow of my thought processes was ruptured, there was just no stopping the lava flow of despair. Foul, rank reminders of past horrors. What point all that work towards success if it can be removed by one slice of the betrayer's blade. The moment I lived in had slipped between its place in past and future. My dependent child was not there. The person I had trusted with my life had betrayed that trust.

Where was my son?

The center of my world was missing, the foundation of my very existence, my love, was stolen and like a sky diver at 25,000 feet, emotionally I went into free fall. With no higher purpose than to find a rip cord before I hit the ground. One breath at a time. After about 6 days of struggle, sleepless nights and unhealthy weight loss because I couldn't eat anything, I followed friendly advice to seek medical help. That medical advice led to prescription medication and medical reports which, in the course of this litigation were seized on as an opportunity for Clock / Krasnopovich to target my *mental illness*. An opportunity last-minute switch judge Flaherty would grasp like *manna from heaven* for her purposes. (Actual words used by the barrister in the proceedings that followed.)

The doctor identified my condition as 'chronic depression.'

In the Flaherty hearing you will read in her own words the extent to which she took that diagnosis and profiled me as *mentally infirm*. This profiling happened and it is my intention to record it here because, it was so very wrong and unacceptable on so many levels. Bringing the credibility of family-court into disrepute as this judge has done. At the very least it is my intention to disclose the extent to which Flaherty targeted a medical condition to turn to her convenient prejudice and for this reason I am disclosing background in a personal matter which should not at any point have been allowed as admissible evidence in a claim for beneficial entitlement. Nor seized upon as a target for punitive action, including the abuse of a child. But my mental health was identified by Flaherty as the single most determining factor, used cynically and deceitfully to affect a family court judgment that ended my son's relationship with his parent. I say this profiling conduct is not what family law judges are empowered to represent and that accountability must follow to prevent reoccurrence of same. Cecelia Flaherty, the last-minute switch judge, has a case to answer. If not to legal accounting, because no family court judge is ever brought to account no matter how egregiously disingenuous their offense, then to herself. As a human knowing the consequences of her actions. This includes child abuse, prejudicial profiling, presenting amateur psychological speculation as a legal argument. And creating a precedent in which other children can be abused by family-court judgments. Cecelia Flaherty is a judge not-fit for purpose. I have no doubt Cecelia knows I am of good character and a fine parent. My charitable work alone for the Marie Curie Cancer foundation and other cancer related support groups is not secret. For 12 years I did an annual fundraiser. On one occasion raising £10,000 for cancer treatment that saved someone's life. Twice, for 4 years with my downstairs neighbor, and then for 5 years with the second, I was first responder for the Councils 'help the aged' in home care program, available 24/7 to show up as first responder. That was a daily responsibility which I undertook with enthusiasm and diligence, on more than one occasion showing up to assist and attend following a fall, ten minutes before the ambulance arrived. On any level, there is no way anyone who knows me, or anyone making even a cursory examination of my stature as a person imagines my level of depression might represent a danger to my son. It was only used as a blade to effect an injury to my prospects of defending the claim in family-court. In legal obfuscation to enable the abuse of a child for nothing more than financial benefit awarded by one member of family law to another. A deceit contrived and employed by two awful liars playing family-court for a fat payday, without regard for the harm this might visit upon a four-year-old child.

The second professional meeting I had after arriving in the UK in 1985 was with my financial advisor to this day, Larry Chester, whose office was and remains in Weybridge. Several times each year we would meet and discuss my options. My first professional meet in the month I arrived in England, was with my accountant, who told me I should take advice from an IFA as I was starting my new life of ambition in

London and his recommendation was that Larry would make a great fit as my Financial Advisor. From the first year I arrived, with a growing income from my session work, he would guide me to the prudent financial position. In one of our first chats he helped me think about a fifteen-year plan. I worked steadily and earned steadily and my finances reflected this. By 2003, seventeen years after I bought the building and first leasehold of my home, 16 years after my 15 year financial planning called for it, I was ready to buy the last of the three leases, the leasehold to 28A, the ground floor flat, and secure financing through Larry to invest in turning the all three flats into top quality rental properties. I spent a fun 18 months in developing my home, in a refurb costing almost £500,000. After which time my property was valued above £2 million. This was around the time I met Nico Krasnopovich, the young and awkward lawyer working along the poverty line at MWT, one of the largest Law Firms in Surrey. He moved into my home in 2003. After 2 years of contributing nothing to living expenses while a beneficial guest in my home, who accepted considerable financial assistance in ending his debts, and enjoying some four foreign holidays a year at my expense, his income in 2005 had improved to the point that he felt able to make a monthly contribution of £500 towards household expenses. At that time, 2005, when I moved downstairs to 28A, my monthly fixed expenses averaged £2,500pm, excluding my mortgage. The annual gas bill alone in that property was on average £600pm. My mortgage payment at that time was £2,600 pm. To be clear, £500pm was simply a token payment. Krasnopovich continued to be heavily subsidized at my expense.

For clarity, in relation to the finding of Judge Flaherty in the claim of beneficial entitlement by Krasnopovich and Clock, at no time was Krasnopovich ever named on any mortgage, nor even involved in any of the talks on the refinancing or cost of the building works I undertook two years after he moved in. In relation to the ownership, financing and objectives regarding my property, no one would know more and have a more significant documentary trail than Larry Chester. For anyone tasked with making a decision on the facts of the ownership of my properties, the very matter before the court of Cecelia Flaherty, who better to provide independent evidential insight into the claims of ownership than the financial advisor who brokered all my loans for the property loan and advised on the plan for development and subsequent rental.

Larry for this obvious reason would be an important witness, the most relevant witness, should anyone be interested in reliably establishing the facts about my home and my intentions regarding my properties. After we moved downstairs to my newly refurbished designer flat in 2005, time passed in a well-ordered privileged lifestyle. Krasnopovich went off to work every day, returning at 7 most days for his dinner bought and prepared by myself. While I made music albums, wrote songs and ran my publishing company and studio business and collected rents. And then enjoyed ending my working day by preparing a high-quality meal for us to enjoy. Krasnopovich kept working long hours at family law, eventually escaping the clutches of his junior role assisting his mentor, Krista, whom he resented with a furious anger between each period of seeking her advice. He transferred as head of department to the Surbiton office, where he became even more work obsessed than before. And the cracks that were leaking dishonesty became a river.

In 2008 I broke up with Krasnopovich. He was a mess. We were done. My work there had gone as far as it could.

Then, with great skill and considerable deceit, over a period of one month he successfully convinced me to make up and overrode my grave concerns over his honesty by entering into a carefully worded parental agreement providing the detail of a child we would raise together. He made promises of reformation. Detailed agreements on future conduct that addressed all of my multiple concerns over his suitability as a parent and we planned raising a child together. Less than a year later Sam arrived and for the duration of the relationship with Sam I felt balanced and, dare I say it, contentedly happy, throughout the five years from when we agreed to have a child until the day he left with the child. Once I had committed to the relationship with Krasnopovich and having a child, that was it. I left no room for doubts.

My time with Sam was the happiest period of my life. Bar nothing. From the moment he woke up until the moment he fell asleep, my joy at being a part of his life and having him in mine was immeasurable. My sunshine, made me happy when skies were grey. He was so happy around me. The mirror of my joy. And then, one month after Sam's fourth birthday, came fathers-day. All the previous instances of PTSD that I had overcome and all the lessons I had learned in this process wove into one horrifying new awareness. The truth that was the foundation for my life turned out to be a pane of glass that had shattered into a million pieces. Nothing was the same. I knew exactly what was going to happen next and it broke my heart. I couldn't sleep, couldn't eat, and couldn't think about anything but the broken pieces of the life that should have been for Sam. And for what? Uncontainable lust for a fit younger person, his fitness instructor, and love of the big paycheck reflecting the new firms first year's success. £350,000 for one year. The processing time, from the moment Krasnopovich played his separation hand until I knew what the years ahead held in store, I would say spanned no more than one minute. Bright clear reality dawned like a crashing wave. Having experienced separation and acrimony with Evans dad when I had the energy of a 25-year-old to look forward into the unknown, all my unspoken doubts about Krasnopovich and his character exploded into a fireball of clarity. This was a liar and a betrayer. Rotten to the core, who would stop at nothing to get his way. To win his idea of victory at any cost. I knew the character having played an instrumental role in enabling him to become the family lawyer he was over the previous ten years. All of which meant there could be no best-case scenario in agreeing a separation based on the best interests of anyone other than himself. Even though, as events showed, it took me longer than it should have to fully accept that this was the case, which I attribute to not understanding how low it was possible for a human to go when the love and life of a 4-year-old child is in play. The manner of his announcement; the fundamental deceit in not disclosing his 'dissatisfaction' for the purpose of addressing any concerns and his timing of fathers-day as the occasion to tell me, followed by his firm assurance that 'there is no prospect of mediation' all fused into a 60 second medley of fizzing dot joining.

All the pieces of the past fell into place with the present and revealed the future.

My first thought was "Everything he ever said was a lie. What does that mean for our agreement to have a child?" In the days following the shock of his fathers-day declaration, my close friends from a few doors down, 23 Thameside, Jo and Tom looked after me like real friends do. They were in shock themselves. After a week of walking and talking and watching, Jo told me that I was not looking well and determinedly suggested I go for medical help. She told me about a friend of hers from work who had used anti-depressants during a painful break up and swore they saved his life. I had never used anti-depressants before. I am historically anti big pharma.

(Passionately so.) I have never taken pharmaceutical product other than occasional anti biotics and even then, only when it was a real medical necessity. Headache pills and such were a no no for me. We discussed anti-depressants and initially I was not interested. Jo eventually convinced me to take medical advice from my GP. She wrote a personal note to Dr. Simon and off I went on my bicycle for that first meeting at his surgery where I was diagnosed with chronic depression and prescribed SSRI's. (Selective Serotonin uptake re-inhibitors) which essentially boost the amount of serotonin in the brain leading eventually, for some, to a more cheerful outlook. I would go on to learn a great deal about chemicals and brain function in psycho pharm. My first prescription was the first line the NHS use. Citalopram. My doctor, Adam Simon was insightful and informative. Answered all my questions well and advised me that going onto SSRI's would involve a period of 2 – 4 weeks in which things might get worse. Which proved to be the case. But then, almost imperceptibly, for me, Citalopram showed some benefits. I became less anxious and more able to focus on positives. Not the same calming effect of cigarettes, but a feeling, quite possibly a placebo effect, that my next breath was not likely to be my last. Of course the SSRI medication was only treating the symptom, not the cause. The cause was. I wanted my son. I was traumatized by the persistent obstruction of my efforts to have him with me, and soon after, the awful injustice of being blackmailed by a member of family law who I knew was using my love for my child as the leverage for a financial demand. Knowing how that would trigger my depression. Acting with deliberate malice to target a medical condition he was aware of and had elected to use from the moment he set up the ambush moment on fathers-day to achieve his targets as a winner in family-court.

Later, in California I was referred to Dr. Mark Zetin as a leading specialist in Psycho Pharm. From Dr. Zetin I learned more about the differing approaches to anti-depressant medications in US medicine. It is a complex subject with a world of science behind differing view-points. I know more about the subject now than I ever would have wished for. The cause of my depression is not seeing my son. The remedy is, seeing my son. That this condition in my case is in no way a threat to the child's well-being is a matter of record from every doctor since my first GP, Dr. Simon. My Priory therapist wrote as much to the court. Dr. Zetin wrote in a letter to Flaherty's court and of course as every single person who knows me knows, any implication that my being depressed poses a risk to my son is nonsense.

I love my son and am offended on many levels that members of family court would knowingly profile the very condition they caused as the reason for denying my son visitation with me while profiling me as 'mentally infirm' in a court judgment entirely at odds with professional medical diagnosis, based instead on the opinion of one woman. Last minute switch Judge Flaherty. I expect there are hundreds of thousands of separated parents around the world who will identify with this. Unsubstantiated and untrue accusations of being unfit used to win obstruction of visitation and for financial benefit of the lying parent. The most cynical child abuse imaginable. Lying to obstruct visitation.

The same previous abstinence is true of sleep medication. Before fathers-day 2013, I had never used any sleep medication. (Apart from red wine and occasionally beer.) As I had not slept for virtually 6 days straight after the shock of father's-day I was prescribed the first of what would become a long series of different sleep medications, benzodiazepines which would work for a while before I would develop tolerance to that particular brand and have to move onto another. From the outset of advice on sleep, Dr. Simon pointed out the guiding principle. Getting good sleep is the first priority in achieving wellness. That is when the brain repairs itself. Lack of sleep gives rise to all manner of related problems. "*It is like having a broken leg. Nothing else matters until you get that leg fixed. If you have to take medication to get good sleep then so be it.*" Sleeplessness became a real threat to my health. Most days I would stay awake until midnight, take my sleeping pill and try to sleep, waking at 2am in a state of high anxiety. Fortunately, I have learned a great deal about sleep hygiene, including many sessions with a leading California sleep doctor, as a result of which I now get as much sleep as I need most of the time. But that was a long journey.

After Krasnopovich left with Sam I found myself unable to return to my bedroom as it required walking past Sam's room. So I slept upstairs, on the sofa. On average, with the sleep meds I had then, I slept 2 or 3 hours a night, waking around 2 am. Wide awake. High heart rate, Sweaty and anxious. Alone and worrying about my son. With the same tension I would imagine accompanies a mother watching a child drowning, being held back by chains from jumping into a rescue. Most nights I would then make a hot chocolate in a travel mug and set off on my bicycle in the darkness, down the Thames towpath than ran past my home, pedaling away until the sun rose and then turning back, to get to the Café in time for breakfast with Jo and Tom. I could not have been more fortunate in terms of cycling opportunities. My home on the Thames opened onto a towpath, historically where the horses would walk dragging barges, hence the name Tow path. Even in darkness with just moonlight, the straight and level path was easily accessible and my night vision more than adequate to see me through until the dawn broke. A single lane width level lane, often just a sandy path with occasional Locks surrounded by black top, which runs on for miles and miles. A flat, safe, deserted path, ideal for a long cycle meditation. Another fortunate reference is that this event happened in June, mid-summer. I can't imagine having gone through this challenge in dark, wet winter.

I found great comfort in cycling the tow path in moonlight. Generally it was warm enough for me to cycle in a t shirt and sweat shirt. 2013 was a hot summer. I would ride with music on my headphones, using my high-quality studio AKG's which provided a full sonic experience when connected to my iPhone, which I would load with appropriate music. I went through a few albums at the time that really resonated, none more so than the Tedeschi Trucks album "Made up Mind". Susan Tedeschi's voice of such emotive sorrow, blending so harmoniously with the way Derek Trucks plays that SG Slide. His 'weapon of mass emotion.' Of course, as is the way with musical stamping I can now never listen to that album ever again. Tedeschi Trucks though go down on my list of the most effective medications that helped me through a hard time.

Music helps knowing others have survived similar sorrow. Cycling down the towpath for ten miles at 3 in morning with a hot chocolate to line my acid stomach, listening to loud soulful musicians on studio quality headphones provided me with a way to get through the night for those first few months.

In the first few months I struggled with eating. I had no appetite for any food. I lost 10 kilograms before September. I felt it was a case of one breath at a time.

Although I have enjoyed a coffee or two daily for many years, I was unable to drink coffee at all in those early months. Coffee potentiated my constant anxiety that did not recede at any time. I quite literally could not get Sam out of my mind for even a few moments respite.

How was he

Where was he

Had he finished his broccoli

What song was he enjoying listening to?

Where was my goodnight cuddle?

What must he be thinking has happened?

An all-consuming, whirlpool riptide of anxiety from which there was no way out. I found occasional respite in retail therapy, justifying the expense of a top of range Specialized bicycle for my four-hour rides.

At that time in my life, cycling was the best therapy imaginable. The best for that cycle of my sorrow. Aerobic exercise was my way of pedaling to wellness.

11 My first two sights of Sam
Weeks after father's-day, Sam. 4 years old, found his way back to the house and called for me

One of Krasnopovich's first nasty decisions in parental alienation and child abuse found its consequence one day in July. Less than one month after fathers-day.   Sam was at nursery at the Lansbury. I considered showing up and taking him with me. But again, as with failing to call the police, I did not want to poke the family law bear. My decision was still to reach an agreement between the two parents that served the child's best interests. And I knew if I collected him from the Lansbury, I would meet the full fury of Krasnopovich and family court. I did not want to bump into Sam while this uncertainty meant I had no way of reassuring him or explain to him what was going on and so I decided to stay away from my tennis club until the custody matter was resolved. I knew all too well what would happen if he saw me at the club.

"*I want to come home with you mummy*" is what I knew he would say. And then what?

Of course I can look back now in retrospect knowing I should have just picked him up and brought him home. And let Krasnopovich do his legal worst. But at the time I was mindful of not putting Sam in the middle of this blackmailing nastiness. I wanted the visitation to be agreed by Krasnopovich without animosity. I believed he would soon realize Sam was best off with me full time. The Lansbury was my tennis club and also the location of Sam's pre-school. I played tennis there almost every day and at one time won the top-level Open League. My tennis buddies there were the best of friends. The manager of the Lansbury, Richard Nastase is another friend I have been able to assist in another instance of the philotimia that has accompanied my life. In 2012 Richards houseboat caught fire and sank and he found himself suddenly homeless. I had a self-contained studio annex on my property which was at that time vacant. When I heard the news of the fire affecting his boat, I phoned Richard, who was standing looking at the water 12 feet above where his blackened home lay on the river bed. Good timing for me to offer him a no cost place to live until he was able to repair his living arrangements, which would turn out to be some 18 months. Sam, was two and a half at that time, and became very close with Richard, who had a song he would sing for Sam's enthusiastic enjoyment. Sam would call him 'Jack Frost.' (Because the first time he appeared out of the snow from the garden annex he looked like he was coming out of the ice.) Richard, myself and Sam went on to form '*The World-Famous Band*', which gave Sam the opportunity to be a lead singer and Ukulele basher. Richard was then like a fourth member of our family. I would call him in to join us for dinner many nights of each week. It was Richard who called me that day in July to say that Krasnopovich had phoned the Lansbury Nursery staff to put them on notice not to let Sam leave with me. As the Club manager, he was informed by the Nursery manager.

"I want to let you know that Nico has called the nursery head to say If you show up to collect Sam, they are on notice to not let you take him". This from the family-lawyer to the nursery manager. I thanked Richard and thought about what had just happened. That call was unnecessary on the face of it. It was provocative, putting my social network, the club where I played tennis, where many of my closest friends were, on notice that I was a potential kidnapper and putting it out that the Father, the family lawyer, had concerns over the safety of his child from the other parent. One parent could not be trusted to collect her own son from nursery? Sending a message that Sam's mother was unfit. A tactical move that gave me pause to consider that this man was truly acting from a place of deep darkness. The very next day, while I was still processing that decision by Krasnopovich, whilst sitting at the dining room table working on my laptop, I heard a shout from outside. Loud. Almost a scream. A child's voice.

"Mummy. Mummy."

I went to the side window to peep out, from the shadows. There was a group of kids from the Lansbury walking past my home on the way to the club. Sam was standing there right in front shouting at the house. He had managed to distance himself behind the group of some fifteen kids walking past. He shouted again. At the top of his lungs.

"Mummy. Mummy."

He didn't see me. I simply dissolved into tears. The teacher led him away. She was of course on notice from Krasnopovich. I closed the curtains and cried for hours. Unspeakable sadness. I knew then that Krasnopovich was thinking ahead to litigation. Creating his paper trail. And not concerned that Sam would have to experience standing outside his home shouting '*Mummy. Mummy*' before being ushered off by a forewarned teacher. This happened in July of 2013. Sam was just four. He had not seen me for many weeks. His father's demand for £100,000 was in effect. Even after this four-year-old child managed to step away from the group being led by the teacher, right outside the home he was taken away from weeks before, and cried out for his Mother with the best of his ability – he still had to face the disappointment of that moment. As crushing a disappointment for us both as it was a triumph for Krasnopovich and the members of family-law. My GP, Dr. Simon, who it may be said is a throwback to the days when the NHS was the pride of Britain, kept an eye on me following his first prescription. In a follow-up meeting he did the usual examination; blood pressure, questions on reactions to the meds, and specifically, my sleep. Or more accurately, my extreme insomnia. He focused on the trauma caused by not seeing my son and recommended I get therapy. Grief counselling, to help cope with the sorrow. He pointed out that while therapy was something he could prescribe on the NHS, being underfunded and crippled by delays to all but essential medical care, by the time the NHS appointment came up I would no longer need it and so he asked if I had the means to pay for therapy myself. Something he urged me to do without delay. It was good advice and I acted on it. Unfortunately, later in the book you will read Flaherty's dismissive comments about this doctor, as well as the other medical professionals in my story. For this reason, I will disclose some background on the medical help I have received.

I know the founder of the Priory socially. His wife, Chrissie, who is Eric Clapton's therapist, was at that time a regular at my coffee mornings in Thameside. A half hour chat with Chrissie led to an initial series of ten one-hour appointments with a leading psychotherapist, a specialist in grief counselling, at the Priory, in Barnes, just a ten-minute drive away. The Priory is a bit special as a medical facility. It is a sizeable, lovely white building standing in green landscaped English gardens, like a manor house of wellness, a short skip up the A3 from Thameside. Just driving there and parking, looking out at that white and green clean space helped me feel uplifted. These weekly sessions benefitted me greatly. Helping me focus on myself and my decisions regarding my son's best interests. These visits coincided with the period in which I was trying to have Sam spend weekends with me, but was experiencing horrifically cynical obstruction by Krasnopovich. It helped to have a therapist to talk to each week about both Krasnopovich's actions as well as the likely effect on the child. My goal was to arrive at the best way to look after Sam. Receiving advice from a skilled professional was invaluable. I can reflect on my experience of the Priory as only extremely positive, with benefits continuing to this day. Speaking to smart well-educated professionals is one positive action anyone can take during a struggle and I was fortunate to have this supportive opportunity with the top level of professional. And yet, for seeking help and for seeing a therapist, Judge Flaherty labelled me as mentally infirm and used this label to punish me to the full extent of her ability, knowingly ending my parenting relationship with my son. As you will see in her judgment, with recurrent references returning to this theme. The number of times they refer to '*But you were at the Priory at this time*' as if only drug addicts go there when they can't cope with their addictions. Her default position on my conduct was "*but we all know you are mentally infirm.*"

Her evidence? I saw a therapist at the Priory. Where most of my time was spent learning the child psychology aspects affecting my four-year-old to enable me to make the most informed decisions.

My first visit with Sam happened after about 4 weeks and came about because of Philip. Philip was once married to my deceased cousin, Stephanie, who I was very close with. As a result of that relationship, Philip has been a confidante in my life for many years. He had also hosted Krasnopovich with me in his California home on the occasions when we visited California, most recently during the pregnancy in 2009 when we spent a month in California, considering the possibility of buying there and moving to raise Sam in California. I had moved £50,000 over at an exchange rate of 2-1, with a view to finding a bargain following the crash of 2008.

Philip and his then wife Stephanie had flown to South Africa to meet Sam when he was 6 months old, on the occasion of Chris Andiotis' wedding to Maria. They were both besotted with Sam and called from California to speak with him weekly on Skype. Stephanie would call him 'Big S.'

"*How is Big S.*"

Philip adored Sam from the get go and Sam responded. He knew who he liked and he was raised on Skype calls. They sent him gifts and he loved Skype chatting with them. Philip was one of the first people in my inner circle who I called after fathers-day with my 'sad news'. From the outset his concern was Sam's well-being. His immediate reaction was alarm that I had allowed Krasnopovich to remove Sam from my home. So much so that he flew over from California within weeks of hearing the fathers-day news, to meet with Krasnopovich, to speak to his old friend, giving me the assurance that he would "*Make sure you see Sam. That is the most important thing*".

Hoping to succeed where the lawyer had so far failed, Philip felt his friendly relationship with Krasnopovich would be helpful in negotiating and settling the visitation issue without delay and so it proved to be. On a Friday afternoon, two days after Philip's arrival, Krasnopovich agreed to drop Sam off with Jo and Tom, who would bring him to meet me in the Park at a familiar location where we had walked a great deal throughout his life. Philip accompanied me and was there at the arranged time when Jo brought Sam over. They pulled up and when he saw me he ran and leapt into my arms.

"*My Mummy.*"

We hugged each other for what seemed like five minutes. I tried but failed to prevent tears flowing from both eyes. Eventually I put him down and we went for a walk hand in hand, saying nothing, as I couldn't speak without crying. As we walked in silence, Sam started to sing. We had been learning songs to sing for some years. I would pick a song and we would learn it together. 'Old Macdonald' was the most recent song we had been learning together and that's what he started singing then. In a clear voice. Projecting.

'*Old Macdonald had a farm. Ee I e e I . Oh......*'

Trying through song to communicate with me. At one point he looked earnestly into my tearfully red eyes, holding onto both of my hands, the sorrow shining from his eyes and said

"*I remember everything.*"

The meeting lasted one hour during which time I cried for about 55 minutes and for hours after. It wasn't intentional. I simply could not prevent the tears. Sam said "*Mummy why are your eyes red?*"

When the time came for Jo to drive him back to his father, I gave him a last hug and my baseball cap. He looked stunned to be leaving. Intuitively it was simply wrong on every level. He wanted to come home with me as if awakening from a bad dream. It was simply awful and clear to all present that this amount of sorrow could not be visited on either of us again. Work would have to happen to make things better. I was clear in my mind at that time that all I had to do is call Krasnopovich and say "*You win. You can have your £100,000.*" With hindsight, I wish I had, although then again, his character is such I believe he would have found another layer of demand to drive home his advantage before allowing Sam to be with me.

After that first meet I had a debrief with Philip and Jo and took away from the experience that whatever happened next I had to establish regular scheduled visits with Sam by any means necessary, even if it meant going to court. The subject of the £100,000 blackmail met a mixed reaction. Philip agreed that it was wrong to give into that demand because he had no legal right to withhold my son from me and that if I gave in on that demand, it would not end there.

Chris on the other hand, in our daily conversations with him in South Africa, said "*He is a lawyer. There are no ethics there. He has told me, unless you give him the money you will not see Sam. I think you should just raise a mortgage and pay him to leave you and Sam alone. I think he will do that. He doesn't have time for Sam anyhow. The way he is talking about you tells me he plans to challenge your fitness in court. Because you went to see a therapist. You cannot trust him one inch. You are underestimating how good he is at lying in court."*

During this time I also considered the advice of the Priory Therapist, who explained that in disputed proceedings where parents hate each other and nothing can be relied on for the children, one constant is the Post. She emphasized that there was a possibility this would go to court and whatever that involved, I should keep up a form of regular communication with my son while legal animosity meant the other parent could not be relied on to make good decisions for the child's well-being. We determined that I would send cards, hand written with drawings on them if possible, on a weekly basis. My drawing skills are at best, limited, but I approached this challenge with enthusiasm. I went with Jo to an Art supply shop and bought drawing materials for this purpose, and from that week forward, every week I sent a card with a drawing. The original "Letters to Sam." Six years later I am still sending letters to Sam. *'Children love getting things in the post.'* It's something they can rely on as parents can't interfere with post. And in disputed proceedings, as appeared would be the case here, the importance of sending regular letters, I agreed with my therapist, was uppermost.

I had no direct communication with Krasnopovich after the first few email exchanges. His emails to me were 'Without prejudice' and so clearly written from an adversarial legal standpoint that I could see no benefit in dealing directly with him on anything to do with Sam. I blocked him from my e mail account, requiring that he go through the intermediary for any contact with me. That was Jo, Sam's unofficial secular godmother. He was friendly with Jo and she was the obvious choice for this sensitive role. My thinking was; knowing someone else was reading what he was writing would make him less inclined to present blackmail threats. He had made his financial demand and that was that. No money, no kid. And that never changed.

Jo was a good choice for intermediary being my neighbor of 25 years and a friend whom I met with for coffee almost every morning for as long as there have been coffee shops on Thames Road. Our twenty-minute start-to-the-day coffee meets in Bridge road over a 15-year period. On many of the mornings whilst Krasnopovich lived with me, he was included in these coffee breakfasts. Sam had been visiting Jo at Steve's Café every Saturday morning at 8 for almost all of his life. They had a good relationship. Sam loved Jo and Tom. (Her husband, the artist.) Sam couldn't wait for his meets on Saturday. He would check *"what day is it today"*.
"It's Saturday".
"Yay. We are seeing Jo and Tom today?"
Through Jo I sent my first written request to have Sam overnight that coming weekend. This was about one month after fathers-day. The visitation proposal was to collect Sam on a Saturday morning, returning him on a Sunday evening. Written up in a formal way as I had learned in my previous experience of visitation agreements in Evan's case. How could he say no to that? Sam would be as distraught as I was. Surely it was the only sensible and responsible thing to do. Agree just one night to get the ball rolling. And we could go from there. The first visit was arranged and it looked like all was going to happen. I prepared his room and planned the activities we would do together during the available time.

Guitar playing. Piano playing. Drum whacking with a Michael Jackson song loud on the studio speakers. Kicking a soccer ball in the park. Making a fresh juice in the kitchen together with the super dooper Oscar juicer that he enjoyed loading, before a sit-down dinner and watching the latest Disney movie on TV together on the sofa. Bath time with new ducky (Krasnopovich had taken ducky with when he left.) New ducky was identical. And the next morning going for breakfast at Steve's Café, as we did every weekend for most of his life, with Jo and Tom.

On the Thursday afternoon before Sam's first visit, Krasnopovich cancelled our weekend visit, by email to Jo. He demanded a string of reassurances. Presented in a way that made it impossible to comply within the time, even had I been agreeable to giving in to his transparently controlling, ridiculous demands. His list included photos of the bedroom where Sam would be sleeping. He demanded a signed, legally binding assurance that I would not discuss anything about the separation with Sam.

"You cannot talk to him about anything to do with the relationship breakdown. I will need that undertaking signed and returned before I drop him off."

"He must phone me at 7 pm on Saturday to say goodnight. If he does not I will drive straight over and collect him."

A list of conditions which placed the visitation terms entirely within his control in a way that made it clear, he was not going to allow unfettered visitation for Sam to see me. I knew that his emails were no more than a legal maneuvering to show he had responded to the request for visitation, however, I knew he was not going to allow it, just as he had promised me, until he received his demands.

£100,000. Money first. See boy later.

His letter with its onerous conditions could not in any way be confused with a Father who was looking to encourage visitation between his son and his son's mother. It was always a factor in my thinking that I had to believe he was encouraging visitation because he knew it was best for Sam. I never believed any of the various legal assurances relating to visitation orders because I knew that the only reason he would ever allow Sam to be with me is if he supported '*unfettered* visitation'. It was as clear as daylight from the outset that he used visitation as his negotiating strength in controlling whatever demands he felt he could impose on me. Not for one second did I see any sight of a parent concerned by what the child wanted.

Soon after he left Thameside, after the tentative emails about a 'Financial settlement' and after making sure I had transferred the domain name titles for the Law firm held in my name as well as his web site held on my server account, he wrote to me, a *Without Prejudice* letter, in which he made a financial demand, a six-figure cash sum, of £100,000, ostensibly for rehousing Sam and himself. After that payment was made I was assured he wanted nothing more than for Sam to be with me '*as much as he wants to be'*. Just not before the payment was made.

There was no mention of any 'Beneficial Entitlement' and no mention of any interest in 28B, my middle flat. Or indeed any reference to any 'promise of marriage and being 50/50 like we were married.' That would come later; only after he retained Tim Clock to represent him. When I retained a family law solicitor to pursue the address of where Sam was, because without the address I couldn't even send a letter, Krasnopovich retaliated by announcing he had retained a lawyer too. One I was assured by my solicitor, David Clam, had '*an awful reputation as a City lawyer driven by litigation above all else. This is a guy who does not look to settle. I am very much concerned that Nico has chosen this approach.*' Who was Tim Clock and why did a family law professional, Krasnopovich, one with his own law firm, need to hire a cut-throat city family lawyer with a reputation as an aggressive adversarial litigator to help trade visitation with Sam? Why would a parent, a family law member with his own law firm, professing to want what's best for the child, retain a cut-throat city lawyer to negotiate visitation in a separation where he had no interest in my property title, or mortgages and no intermingled finances? I had been careful to ensure our business affairs were always kept separate. No joint bank accounts. In fact, he did not know any detail of my stock trading portfolio, or my mortgage commitments. Or even, the monthly bills I covered in living the lifestyle that we did. I was in no doubt that he cancelled that first visit because his financial demand had not been met, not because he had any realistic concerns over where Sam would sleep or that he would not survive being away from him one whole night without calling at 7 pm. Or that he really thought a gagging order on anything to do with his conduct getting back to Sam could ever really be effective. It could not have been a clearer instruction.

You will not see him until you pay.

I had made my position clear regarding payment in a reply to his demand email. We were not married. Our finances were never intermingled. He had his flat, and received all the rent from that since I housed him, free for the first two years. That was, by simple calculation of his rental income from that property at some £800 a month, for ten years, around £90,000. My house was mine, bought in 1986, when he was 12. He had not contributed one penny to either the works to the house or the mortgage payment. He was not named on any mortgage and it was abundantly clear from the wills we made in 2010, that he knew he was not named as an owner. Nor that he had any expectation to be named on the title. He only had the freehold in his name because of the Insurance matter. And he was legally obligated to return it. Certainly, claiming to own it and use it to drive a claim against me made him liable for breach of the fiduciary responsibilities inherent in the ownership if the title. I had no concerns that he might make a financial claim against my property given the extent to which I had supported his residence there with little or no contribution from himself. In terms of his residence in my property in the event of my death, our agreement was that he could live on in 28A, for as long as he chose to be in residence, but that the title would go to Sam and Evan equally. My two heirs.

He had the business, the law firm generating for him over £250,000 net after tax at that time, with a significant growth potential which I had invested in for no other reason than that it would provide for Sam's future. An integral part of our parenting agreement. My reply to his demands, reflecting the considered advice I had received confirming my own view, was that he chose to leave (I did not mention the fact he chose to leave to pursue his lust for his married fitness instructor) and should do so without claiming from me. And in turn I would not claim from him putting to one side I had a valid claim for a share of the business we set up in a written parental agreement related to having a child together in the first place. I would not vary the parental agreement. Nor should he.

He had more than enough money to pursue his dreams, in no small measure thanks to me, and he should now put the child's best interests to the fore and not start litigation. I was clear that I would support Sam entirely if he stayed with me full time in which case I would not come after Krasnopovich for any maintenance. I did expect that he would pay Sam's school fee's as that agreement between us could not be unilaterally discarded. The most important consideration was who would be best for bringing up Sam now that Krasnopovich's actions, taking the child away and housing him without giving me the address and asking me for £100,000 before he would allow visitation made clear no co-parenting option was available.

My intention was to wait until he came to realize that Sam wanted to be with me and that obstructing this simply for money would reveal itself as poor decision making with real consequences, not the least of which would be the effect on his own relationship with Sam. I had no doubt that I was the best option for raising Sam, having already raised him for the first 4 years of his life, in which Krasnopovich spent at most 10% of his day with him. In fact, very little would change for Sam other than Krasnopovich would not be sleeping in the house and would see him on weekends. Krasnopovich was so preoccupied with his work that, if the first four years were anything to go by, seeing his son for an hour in the morning and, on most nights, an hour or two before sleep was the most the child could look forward to. Krasnopovich went out for networking meets as a matter of course. At least one night a week, meaning on those nights Sam would not see him at all. I was with him all day, all the time. I had shifted my work life priorities to be available for this exclusive purpose. And, as an older parent, with considerable life experience including a twenty-year-old son, I was a dedicated and patient parent with identifiable skills in terms of parenting. In an objective debate on what would be in Sam's best interests I have no doubt that he would have been better off with me. In percentage terms, I was there all of his life. Krasnopovich averaged 10% of his time with his son. A child centric decision-making process on what would be best for Sam post separation could never have arrived at the judgment of last-minute switch Judge Flaherty.

After the first visitation cancelation Jo tried to set up our meet for the following weekend. A string of emails and more conditions followed. All very reasonably worded by Krasnopovich expressing his various concerns in this amended list of reasons to deny access. Simply put, every passing week Krasnopovich kept alive the possibility of a visit each week until the Thursday evening, when he would introduce a new element to prevent the visitation. Unmistakably this was *"Pay me the money and you get to see him."* Unmistakably his last-minute cancelation was timed to cause maximum upset. The sleazy lawyer tactic of issuing demands at the very last minute on a Friday afternoon. After three weeks and many emails, Jo reported to me that she could not continue in the role of intermediary. The toxic correspondence from Krasnopovich was breaking her heart. She had never seen this level of malice filled wording regarding a child. She described *'seeing Sam used as a Football'* in his game of greed as too much. Jo requested that I ask someone else to liaise with Krasnopovich. Jo, Sam's godmother and advocate since birth, was done. Heartbroken. Recusing herself as an act of self-preservation. That's how extreme the letters from Krasnopovich and Clock were. A nice sensible intelligent considerate professional person, a friend and a mother, had to withdraw from any dealings, even though she clearly loved Sam dearly. *"All he had to do was agree to let Sam see his mother for a weekend, but he wrote a book of reasons why it wouldn't be possible. Each reason more implausible than the last. All the while Sam is dying to see you and he knows it. I just can't understand the mindset behind this diseased thinking. I am afraid this toxic logic is making me feel quite ill."*

After Jo the second intermediary was Celia Silver. Married to my friend the accomplished guitar playing dentist and soulful man who is a double for the Monk character from US TV, Tony Silver. Celia was a great choice as intermediary. She knew Krasnopovich as a dinner guest in her home from many dining occasions prior to the separation. Celia was also relatively neutral as I was more of a friend to her husband who was also my dentist, and Krasnopovich hers. Celia is also one of the nicest most ethically balanced people imaginable, a mother of two grown children. Both lovely balanced human beings. Here was a clear opportunity to have an unpaid intermediary provide visitation details for Sam to be with me every weekend from the get go. Celia lived close by.

All Krasnopovich needed to agree was 1.) a drop off time at Celia's home and 2.) a collection time.

There really was nothing more to it than that. Sam would be staying in his own bedroom in my house. There was no issue on any planet including his or family-law, that I represented any kind of risk or danger to my son. The contrary is a fact. My son was desperate to see me as was I to see him.

Celia took on the arrangement with some enthusiasm. *"I am sure I'll get Nico to agree. Who wouldn't want to see Sam with you?"* She gave me a big reassuring hug. And yet, the same process followed, right from the first week of Celia's time as intermediary. E mails arranging visitation between Celia and Krasnopovich. Arrangements made. More Emails exchanged. Cancelations followed, usually on a Thursday evening, but increasingly on a Friday afternoon, at 5.30. The words Toxic correspondence came up increasingly. Celia became increasingly disenchanted. And uncomfortable with Krasnopovich's tone of writing. *"You warned me about what Jo said and I couldn't imagine how anyone could get so offended by emails. But now I understand. This is truly toxic. What is the matter with him?"*

Week ten saw a little twist. That week I was invited to bring Sam to join manager of Crystal Palace, Ian Holloway, in his box for the Palace vs Sunderland home game at Selhurst Park. I met Ian, who very kindly agreed to offer this opportunity knowing that *"only a crazy person would refuse to allow a boy to have this introduction to the beautiful game"*.

Sam was by that time four and a half and I thought arranging to take him to his first football game as the special guest of a premier league manager would offer Krasnopovich an opportunity to backdown from his *'pay the money first and then you can see the child'* position, and put the child best interests first. Sam had two years of Sunday football under his belt. He knew about kicking a ball and what football meant. He was absolutely old enough to enjoy being at a football match for the first time. For any boy the chance to be introduced to the beautiful game in this way, with the manager of the team in a home stadium, Selhurst park, watching from the managers box was, I thought, something so clearly fine that even a member of family-law driven by a focused monetary agenda would put aside the traditionally low ethics associated with family law members and consider, even if just for this one occasion, the child's best interests. Should I let my son go see a football match with his Mother? Let's see what my lawyer thinks.

I was enthusiastically optimistic right up until 5 on Friday. Timing is especially important in family law correspondence where many parents are planning weekends with their kids, who they miss, making them especially vulnerable to a re-negotiation at the last minute. By email at 5pm on the Friday before Saturdays 3pm kick off, Krasnopovich refused to allow Sam's weekend visit.

"*Sam is too young to go to a football game.*" And that was it. He was not dropped off at Celia after school on Friday. Sam never got to visit Selhurst park with me.

Clearly, had I said "OK, you can have £100,000," then Sam would have watched the Palace vs Sunderland home game with me. I still went to the game that Saturday. After the invitation I decided it would be rude to not show up at all, even if the intention, to bring Sam, had been a failure. Driving to Selhurst park was memorable. I could not understand why Krasnopovich was allowed to get away with it. I had reported it to my lawyer, David Clam. It was all so transparent. Celia knew. Everyone I knew, knew about this football last minute cancelation. I called Chris in South Africa and told him. He refused to allow Sam to be collected on the Friday afternoon to spend the weekend and attend this football game unless I gave him £100,000. Palace won that day. (3-0 V Sunderland). The manager, Ollie, was disappointed that the offer had failed to produce the outcome intended.

It was the saddest game I ever attended. I thought how much Sam would have enjoyed the Eagle they fly across the pitch before the game starts, Palace of course being called 'The Eagles.' Ollie signed a child size Palace football strip for Sam. I sent that by post along with the program for the day and the invitation by Ollie. I never found out if Sam received it though. I never had any doubt that Krasnopovich knew how much it would upset me to not be able to take Sam to his first premiership game in such a memorable way.

I sent a letter accompanying the football kit package, which I doubt he ever received:

Sept 2, 2013

Yiassou my beautiful Sam,

I have done a drawing for you from my friend who is the manager of a football team. His name is Ollie. I wanted to take you to see a real football game and I have sent you the program and the tickets of where you would sit to watch the game. A very nice seat in Ollie's own special box at the stadium. Ollie has written a message on it on it for you. Maybe before too long we can go to a game together and you can wear the same kit as the team.

I think you will enjoy meeting real football players in a team at a football match. Football is such a fun game.

Miss you,
Love you,
Mummy

And then after 13 weeks of this same 'no money no visit' nonsense, in which I was not even able to speak with Sam on Skype and had hopes raised and dashed every weekend in what was cruel and unusual punishment for a 4 year old child legitimized in the name of family-law, it was not difficult for Clam to convince me that bringing proceedings in Family Court, an Application for visitation, was the only realistic prospect of seeing Sam.

Copied here is the summary of that application, drafted by Clam. Who provided a cost estimate of some £5,000 for the hearing in family-court. I believed at least in this hearing I would have the opportunity to show that the parent, the member of family law, was blackmailing me for £100,000 before allowing any visitation. Eventually Mr. Clam's costs turned out to be £37,000 for what followed the application to visitation. This draft letter alone was billed at some £5,000. None the less, I paid up, believing that Family Court would now enforce the visitation my son had every right to expect. This was as clear cut as is imaginable. Sleazy family lawyers demanding payment before allowing any visitation, while asking all manner of irrelevant questions raising entirely inconsequential concerns. I had been to see a therapist for grief counselling? So what. There was no shred of concern that I was in any way a risk to my son or that staying with me would place him at risk. It was simply a tactic seized on by his family-lawyer father and his brazen accomplice, Tim Clock. That they would prevent the visitation they had delayed with 13 different excuses for 13 consecutive weeks, this time by saying that because so much time had passed, they would require 'phased in visitation'. I could meet Sam, supervised by his Mother? Of course Krasnopovich knew this condition would never be acceptable to me. Positioning me as unfit to be alone with my child. There was only one single reason why Sam was not being allowed to see me. I did not agree to their financial demands.

Here, for free, enjoy £5,000 of writing, for less than 1,000 words by David Clam. The notes for the application for visitation.

IN THE PRINCIPAL REGISTRY OF THE FAMILY DIVISION
CASE NO: FD 13P 0Z7089

IN THE MATTER OF THE CHILDREN ACT 1989
IN THE MATTER OF SAM LEANDROS
(DOB: X MAY 2009)

BETWEEN:

ANDREA LEANDROS
Applicant
And

NICO KRASNOPOVICH
Respondent

**APPLICANT'S CHRONOLOGY
FOR FIRST HEARING
DISPUTE RESOLUTIONS APPOINTMENT (FHDRA)
WEDNESDAY 30 OCTOBER 2013
AT 10.30AM**

---

16 June 2013   (Father's Day)   Nico Krasnopovich (**Father**) informs Andrea Lee (**Mother**) that he intended to leave her, saying that he no longer found her attractive and that he had "outgrown" her. He added that he would be taking their son, Sam, with him.

17 June 2013   Father and Sam leave the family home. Father and Sam move, temporarily, to the Father's own Mother's home in Surrey.

23 June 2013   Mother consults her general practitioner because she is so devastated by the separation from her son and is referred to a grief counselling psychotherapist at "The Priory".

[   ] June 2013   Mother begins a series of ten consultations, once per week, with psychotherapist at The Priory.

20 July 2013   Mother sees Sam for the first time since his Parents separated for just 1 hour; Sam has not seen his Mother since.

3 August 2013   Father and Sam move again and the Father refuses to let Mother know where he and more particularly where Sam are living.

17 August 2013   Father sends email to Mother in advance of contact on Saturday 24 August 2013 saying that he feels it is "*essential for Sam to have a better understanding of your health as this may affect him*", notwithstanding the fact that Sam is only 4 years old. Father adds that he needs to see a letter from the Mother's therapist in advance of contact taking place setting out the current state of her mental health and whether they consider unsupervised contact is appropriate or not.

21 August 2013   Mother's solicitors, Spoon LLP, write to Father who is at that stage unrepresented (Father is a family lawyer) seeking to confirm arrangements for contact including for the weekend of Saturday 24 August 2013 and for Saturday 6 and Sunday 7 September 2013.

23   August 2013   Psychologist confirms:

1.   She will not put her views in writing. For reasons of confidentiality.

2.   Ms. Lee had never shown any signs of any form of mental illness, in particular she was not disabled by depression when she first saw her and was not disabled by depression now.

3.   Ms. Lee had needed to see her as grief counsellor because of stress caused by the breakdown of the relationship, missing seeing her son and the circumstances surrounding that.

4.   There was no reason at all why Ms. Lee should not see her son.

5.   From Sam's point of view there was every reason why contact should take place.

28 August 2013   Four-page letter received from Father's solicitors. That letter states:-

1.   Father still requires a "short note" from The Priory that there are no concerns with regard to contact being unsupervised.

2.   Proposes contact on Saturday 31 August 2013 for 2 hours between 2pm and 6pm with 2 further contact visits of 4 hours each on 14 September and 28 September 2013 before overnight contact on Saturday 12 October and Sunday 13 October 2013 and thereafter overnight contact every 2 weeks to be reviewed in January 2014. This is notwithstanding the fact that there had previously been discussions with regard to overnight contact taking place on Saturday 6 and Sunday 7 September 2013.

10 September 2013 Father's solicitors write to say it would not be right to "*force*" staying contact upon Sam although Father might consider contact being extended from 10am until 6pm instead of 2pm until 6pm.

12 September 2013 Father's solicitors write again and propose that Sam should see his Mother:-

1.   On Saturday 14 September 2013 for the day.
2.   Overnight contact on Saturday 28 and Sunday 29 September 2013 which is described as a "*leap of faith*". The letter also seeks reassurance that Sam's bedroom was "all welcoming for him" notwithstanding that the Father and Sam had lived at the Mother's home from 2003 until 17 June 2013.

18 September 2013 Father's solicitors write again to say that he would consider overnight staying contact on Saturday 28 September (the Mothers birthday) until Sunday 29 September but only if 6 specific questions were answered by the Mother to his satisfaction.

19 September 2013   Mother's solicitors reply immediately dealing with those 6 points.

20 September 2013   Father's solicitors raise questions with regard to the Mother's Replies.

25 September 2013 Mother writes to Mrs. Celia Silver, a friend who is acting as an intermediary between the parents, asking the Father to confirm by the end of the day whether contact was or was not going to take place the following weekend which was her birthday. In the absence of confirmation from the Father, the Mother is forced to make alternative arrangements for that birthday weekend.

26 September 2013 Father's solicitors write. Firstly, the letter implies that the Father was no longer pursuing answers to his 6 points which were satisfactory to him. Secondly, the letter contains the unfortunate statement that the fact that the Father had by then commenced these Proceedings led to "*the only conceivable conclusion…... that he has issued his application for the purpose of causing distress to my Client rather than for any purpose involving Sam. This would be an abuse of process and I have instructions to apply to strike out the proceedings with an Order that your Client pay the costs.*"

26 September 2013 Mother's solicitors write to confirm that the Mother has had to make alternative arrangements for the forthcoming weekend but suggested that Sam should see his Mother on the weekend of 5 and 6 October 2013. The letter also gave the Father further reassurances with regard to his 6 points.

3 October 2013 Father's solicitors write to say that their Client is no longer prepared to agree to overnight contact starting immediately but instead proposes interim contact for 3 successive Saturdays with overnight contact on Saturday 26 and Sunday 27 October 2013 for a period of 3 months.

8 October 2013 Father sends email to the intermediary, Mrs. Celia Silver saying that the Mother's suggestion of one night staying contact did not provide any structure and that there needed to be a gradual build-up of contact, asserting that that was in Sam's best interests.

21 October 2013 Mother's solicitors write with further proposals suggesting that Sam sees his Mother on Saturday 25 October and then on both Saturday 2 November and Sunday 3 November 2013 and thereafter overnight on Saturday 9 and Sunday 10 November 2013.

23 October 2013 Father informs Sam's Godmother who was seeking to assist that he will "*see Andrea in Court*".

Dated this 28-day October 2013

12 CAFCASS and the application for visitation
David Clam and the £40,000 bill for alternate Saturday night visitation

In October 2013 acting on legal advice from David Clam at Spoon LLP, after months of Krasnopovich obstructing any visitation with Sam, I brought legal proceedings for visitation. A family court process. The initial application was for twice monthly overnight visits. Krasnopovich had over the course of the previous 13 weeks of obstruction to weekend visits seeing that, now introduced a new measure as the latest in his line of obstructive measure preventing visitation; phased in contact.

"You can have Sam overnight, but not until you have three supervised appointments of an hour each to make sure that he is comfortable with you."

"This will be waived if you pay the settlement figure" was the subtext, by separate letter. This from the 10% parent. Couching blackmail in convenient language that in no way concealed the fact that, had I agreed to their financial demands, then all these specious reservations offered as reasons why they opposed visitation would disappear. This phased in visitation clause was so transparently another of Krasnopovich's cynical legal manipulations that it became the last straw that led to the application in court much though I had resolved not to be drawn into family court where I knew his influence was real. Clam, my solicitor, made it plain that he saw very little prospect of Krasnopovich agreeing any form of visitation without a court order. He advised that we should proceed immediately. In this he was correct. 13 weeks of suggesting visitation would happen and then cancelling told its own story. There was no doubt that Krasnopovich would continue as he had set out to do. *"Pay me the money and then you can have Sam. Otherwise, bring it on. This is what I do."*

I had no doubt that they intended preventing any visitation by all means necessary unless they received payment of a specific written demand or if they received an order by the court. And even then, had I won a court order for visitation, I believed the corruption between these two was so advanced, there was a realistic chance they would find some new family-law efficient reason why visitation should not take place, even if they had to break the law to keep control of the visitation linked to the financial demand. I knew as clearly as words can make plain, their assurance that *'You will not see Sam until I have the payment'* was the sole determining factor in making visitation a reality. And as convincingly as my words here can make plain, I knew that to accede to this demand would be wrong. Giving into blackmail is the start of a pattern. I did not accept that it was in Sam's best interest that he be used as leverage for financial extortion. He has two parents. Each must behave as responsible parents. I believed words were powerful. They could not get away from the written word. Surely they knew that? The written word lasts forever. There is no statute of limitations on the written word. Surely these two knew that I would keep copies of their correspondence and record every aspect of what they were doing for a future publication. That I had all the emails showing the ineluctable truth. This lawyer and his family law member client were blackmailing a parent with visitation to a young child. Abusing a child for their own material gain. Crossing that line between what is allowed by family court within the law, and what is not. And believing that the law would prevent the child from ever finding out about their decisions. Or more specifically, how each parent behaved in 2013 in relation to a child's future. One voice stood out at that time. Chris, Sam's Godfather who spoke to me after my decision to pursue visitation in a Court Application. Chris as an older person with much experience of court, himself having been through a custody decision in which he raised a two-year-old child, had strong views on winning and losing in court. He did not share my view on the power of words. And the value of truth.

"You are making a mistake going to court. This is their home patch. They work there every day. They know the system. Doesn't matter what you say, they will lie as much as they need to. They are members of family law and they will use their legal position to their advantage. It has nothing to do with the truth. You are in their back yard. They can do whatever they want. Your words will disappear. Court is not where this should be decided. You lost when you let him take the child out of the house. Now he wants a hundred grand to give him back? That is your best way forward. Just give him the money. Don't think anyone will give one fuck about your words if you lose this hearing. These guys are the law. No judge is going to side with you against one of his own. Mark my words. Give him the hundred grand or they will fuck up Sam before they let you see him again. You think your smart Cambridge lawyer is on your side? He is not. He is there for a payday. He doesn't give a fuck about what happens to Sam. He wants you to go to court so he can get more money out of you. He is only on your side for as much as you pay him. Pay Nico his hundred grand demand and get your son back. Don't waste one more penny on lawyers. After that you can look at having them both disbarred or whatever you want to do about justice in family-law. Save your words for that. I know him. I have been talking to him. He is not going to stop until he wins what he wants and he wants £100,000 more than he wants Sam. That's why he has got a slick city lawyer to front it. If it was just a discussion about who raises Sam and visitation, why would he need an expensive aggressive lawyer? He knows you have some wealth and that is his goal. He told me that he wants ten grand for every year he was with you. That's how he works out the hundred thousand bucks. Meanwhile Sam is desperate to see you. Just pay him and get Sam back."

That was my binary decision then. Concede blackmail works and pay them their demand. Or try my hand in the lottery I already knew was family court. And yet, how could I possibly lose an application for just 2 nights a month? It was unimaginable. Once the court knew his blackmail role, I believed he would have to give up Sam immediately. I had even worked out the visitation I would agree for him. (As close to 50% as possible, although I expected he would not want more than the few hours a week he had with Sam to date.)

The court date was set with an impressive turn of speed, just two weeks away. Clam would represent me in this hearing, in which we would only apply for 1 night each alternate weekend, to be certain that no judge would object. It will be a no brainer. The cost indication he provided for this court hearing was £5,000. To a maximum of

£7,000 in a worst case. All of which I agreed with as eminently sensible and in the child's best interests. On paper it was clear. No way could a judge rule against me having my son for just one night on alternate weekends. Clam knew the material facts and would accompany me to the hearing, familiar as he was with the paperwork filed for this hearing. Once we had that judgment in place, Calm agreed with me, Krasnopovich would fold and allow Sam to return home with me.

In the week leading up to the hearing Clam told me to expect a call from CAFCASS. (The government agency advising family court on child issues.) And in that week I did in fact speak by phone with CAFCASS in what appeared to me as a satisfactory call by a most sympathetic, encouraging CAFCASS official who ended the call saying *"You can look forward to seeing your son next weekend."*

There was no indication from CAFCASS that there was any possibility that they would raise any objection to my son being with me. In fact, the person I spoke to made plain she was excited for me that I would be seeing my son the following weekend. The day before the Monday hearing, on Friday at around 3pm on 29 October, 2013, with all preparations made there was an ambush filing that turned the whole thing on its head. Clam phoned me, late afternoon just the day before the hearing in a state of high anxiety.

"We have a huge problem. Clock has filed a motion for costs. It is highly unusual at a preliminary hearing for visitation, in fact I have never seen this this before. In their costs they have included costs for a QC. (Queens Council. The most expensive level of barrister in British law.) *I know that I was going to represent you myself, but now I have to get you a QC. It will inflame things if I go in myself against a QC. I am afraid it will cost you a little bit more, but at least you won't have to pay to have me there all day."*

"But David, you know the whole story. It's very straightforward. So what if they have a QC. Just stick to the plan and you represent me. I don't want a QC at a preliminary hearing. Anyhow, what kind of QC are you going to find just a few hours before the hearing. They won't know the case. You do. Stay with the plan."

Clock was not to be persuaded. He was in a state of shock at this ambush. As a result, he simply refused to stay with the arrangement that he would accompany me to the hearing. Instead, in the last two hours of the business day he found an elderly QC available to represent me at a preliminary hearing for visitation. For just £5,000. Bear in mind, a preliminary hearing for visitation in a matter such as this where there are no allegations against either parent and no concerns over the child's wellbeing, is usually a straightforward affair based on the fact that the child has a right to see both parents. A judge in this situation has a simple decision to make. One parent wants to see their child. The other parent has raised objections. That in itself should be a clue to even a jaded slow-witted judge. A child, not yet five, has been taken away from his family home, and the parent has made an application for just two nights a month. (The child was not taken away for any reason other than the departing parent was pursuing a romantic interest.) Should you allow the child to see the parent, knowing there is not one reason in the application stating any concern over the child's well-being when with the applicant parent. This is, essentially, a model older parent of irreproachable character, making the application. A parent who was present in court, in an Armani suit, making it pretty obvious this is not a drunken hillbilly situation.

In this hearing two things stand out. If you were a family-court judge the first is;

It is highly unusual to see a QC (Queens Counsel, the most expensive level of barrister representation) contesting an Application for visitation of just 2 nights a month in a case where both parents seem pretty ordinary.

And second, it is unusual for a parent who is a member of family law, familiar to this very court in weekly visits, to appoint a top City firm with a reputation for acrimonious litigation, to prevent a 2-night monthly visitation for a child not yet 5 years old. The judge would also note that it is extremely unusual (if not unheard of) for one parent to defend an application for visitation by filing a motion for costs, after incurring significant costs (bringing a QC to a preliminary hearing) against the other side, who is simply trying to see their 4-year-old son for 2 nights a month. Why would any parent try so very hard to stop a child seeing his parent twice a month absent of any safety concern? I remain deeply concerned that this judge did not manage to see that Sam should have been allowed to see his Mother that weekend. Exactly as is usual when a child's best interests are being represented. That judge should, in my opinion writing six years later, review himself on that day and write a comprehensive letter of explanation to both my son and myself. It was a pathetic show of incompetence whose consequence is child abuse. Judge Berry.

That Friday before the hearing, I did not agree with Clams last-minute change of direction. I was deeply concerned by the sight of Clam, panicked and borderline hysterical. His voice had risen half an octave. He was flustered. He knew he was being played. We had prepared a strong case to present to the Judge that my son Sam, 4, should spend 2 nights a month with me and not be subject to the father's insistence on 'Phased-in Visitation'. To me it seemed a transparently clear case of simple blackmail by two members of family law using the child as leverage.

Simple Child abuse.

Why was Clam so shaken he was no longer willing to just stand up in court and tell the judge. That is what he was hired to do. Represent me in the application for visitation. Just go to the Court, standup when the time comes, and tell the judge the facts? Show the judge the 'blackmail' emails? So what if they were sent Without Prejudice. This was a child's life. These are members of family law playing the system. It's that obvious. I expected Clam to simply address the court with one question.

"Mr. Krasnopovich, is it true that you have written to Ms. Lee making plain that she cannot see her son unless she pays you the sum of £100,000? Is it true that if she agrees to give you £100,000 you will, as you have assured her you will, allow as much visitation as she likes?"

I showed up that day in the High Court convinced the court's duty was to support the child's best interests. It was unimaginable that preventing the child spending even one overnight stay with his mother was in his best interests. Unimaginable to consider that family-court would not award me two nights a month with my son. Learning that Clam was now not willing to attend my hearing, appointing an unknown quantity, a QC whose most notable quality was that he was free on the day and happy to pick up £5 grand filled me with the dread equivalent of no-confidence. Clam was already all too familiar with the particulars. All it required was to present the simple facts to a judge at the application for visitation. Two nights a month in the home where he grew up, with the mother who raised him, whom he was missing terribly. How was it appropriate to have to pay a QC (£5,000) to state the blindingly obvious? The hearing itself was quite predictably, a shambles. No proper order applied to the time for any hearings. People shuffling around this dank and depressing venue, looking homeless and gormless in equal measure. We assembled in one of the small rooms to the side which could not be booked, but served as the meeting rooms for those waiting to be summoned into Court. The place smelled; of body odor and unwashed damp clothes. And old woman perfume. Three of us waited. Myself, the elderly QC with the £5,000 payday for a few hours and the unpaid young assistant lawyer trainee sent by Clam to meet me at the court so I would know where to go. If children's rights are important, then this location and the people populating it suggested otherwise. This place was a smelly disorganized mess. To me it represented a low-value being attached to the structured order in which a child's best interests might reasonably expect to be represented. As will come as no surprise to anyone familiar with the process in family court.

In advance of the hearing, accompanied by my newly appointed, expensive QC who I had never met before and who had no clue about the child's background, or my background, or the dynamics of malicious intent motivating the other side, I was interviewed by an illiterate Ghanaian chap from CAFCASS, whose role in this story can best be described in two words; simply incompetent. By simply incompetent, I mean, functionally illiterate, unable to spell adequately and unable to speak English with even basic clarity. And significantly, quick to recognize my South African accent, giving me the clear impression that he, as a Ghanaian African has a preconception of what a White South African accent represented. This shabbily dressed gentleman asked me questions from a form, where after a five-minute stumble across writing my name with the correct spelling, we reached a key moment.
"Do you have any concerns over the child being with the father?"
I thought about that. Yes I did. Of course I did. The father was blackmailing me for visitation. He had tricked me into a situation where he removed my child from me. He had, for 13 straight weeks, refused visitation with last minute notice to make plain the fact that he controlled all visitation and would to allow it until his financial demands were met. The answer was very clearly. "Yes." But. Then I thought about Sam. His well-being at the mercy of this awful place and these shabby people. What if Krasnopovich answered the question in the same way? What if he was asked by this same shabby official, when it was his turn to be interviewed in advance of the hearing
"Do you have any concerns over the child being with the mother?"
I saw the picture unfolding. If both parents accused the other of being unfit, would the court place the child in foster care until the matter could be investigated? I had the image of Sam being taken, crying, by two CAFCASS workers, to be placed in a safe home until the investigation between these two unfit parents concludes. And so I answered no. *"No. The father is not unfit."*
That was my pre-hearing interview done. I recorded it, as I had my iPhone on record. Later I transcribed the recording. This CAFCASS guy from Ghana was exactly as I have outlined. Functionally illiterate. He would go on from that interview with me to interview Krasnopovich. And as I now know, when asked *"Do you have any concerns over the child being with the Mother?"* Krasnopovich answered yes.

Less than half an hour after my interview, we were all summonsed into Court. Before deputy district judge (DDJ) Beddy. He looked up. Looked at me, looked at Krasnopovich. Looked again at the two QC's. And sighed. Audibly. On the bench next to him was the CAFCASS official. The judge began his summary, at which point the CAFCASS guys phone went off.

"*I am sorry your honor*" he approximated in English with the strongest Ghanaian accent I have heard, before or since. So I am assuming that was his apology, although the thick accent means I cannot be certain. Perhaps he said "I cannot believe I am getting paid for this." I am certain though that his phone went off in the court as the judge was about to speak. The judge sighed again. I saw a very tired man, who really could not be bothered. There would be no hearing that day. He explained it this way.

"*I will not be entering any submissions. We will be here all day if I do. You are both way over represented. I will turn the decision over to CAFCASS and what he decides is this court's judgment.*"

Following which he invited the CAFCASS official to deliver his report. The Ghanaian CAFCASS official, having pointedly succeeded in turning his phone off then stood up and approximated in his best English emulation.

"*I find for the Father.*"

No further arguments were considered. A functionally illiterate virtually incoherent Ghanaian with limited English and lacking the nous to turn his phone off in court made the judgment. Given this authority by a family-court judge who simply could not be bothered. My application for visitation for two nights a month was denied by a CAFCASS official who could barely speak English and took a phone call in court? Even as I heard the judges voice ring away in the court, I was standing to leave, beyond outraged. What a con. A sham. A mockery of due legal process. The foul stench of gross injustice filled the room. My first instinct was to accuse the judge.

"*How in the name of holy fuck can you stop my child from being with his mother this weekend? It is your job to represent the child's best interests. Do your job properly. You can see with even half a functioning brain cell, there is nothing wrong with me that is so hideous it would place my child in danger being with me for two nights a month.*"

But I didn't. In that place and that time I knew I was being played. That to say anything would be unhelpful. And so I decided to walk out. I stood up, wearing what I am sure is the black face of furious anger and began shuffling along the bench isle towards the exit. Walking out, wanting nothing more to do with this circus act manipulation of a blackly comedic legal process by two professional liars, Krasnopovich and Clock, who were so transparently playing the system, with their slick underaged QC named Piers, with the lispy public school accent and the smooth baby skin cherub face. Piers, another member of family law quite willing and able to turn his expensive skills to play the system in what he knew all too clearly was against the best interests of the child. And there can be no doubt about this, because it was a contrived set up involving weeks of planning. Piers, the baby-faced QC of family law, knew exactly what he was doing. Being highly-paid to abuse a child.

For nothing more that the benefit of a friend, the family law member, and employer in the way that solicitors like Krasnopovich employ barristers like Piers in disputed family court hearing that we know, from the CEO of CAFCASS, Anthony Douglas, represent a 100% statistic of being parental alienation and child abuse. I could see what was going on as plain as day. I did not need the Anthony Douglas statistic to explain it. So could the family law QC I was forced to pay £5,000 to accompany me to that hearing by the no show solicitor, Clam.

Krasnopovich had obviously told the Ghanaian CAFCASS chap that he did not think the child was safe with me. The Ghanaian chap knew South Africa and made plain from the outset that he had an issue with race, remarking on my South African accent from the start of our interview. It did not take an international detective to work out how easy it was for Krasnopovich to get this unfortunately gormless fellow employed by CACFCASS to whistle to his tune. A bitter dash of racist discrimination to add to the cocktail of prejudices stirring and shaking my experience of family court. When I stood up to leave that court room, my first thought was that I was not going to see Sam that weekend as I had believed would be the case following my application. That disappointing realization was a blow to the pit of my stomach. I had so looked forward to that weekend. It had been some two months by this time. I missed Sam to my very core. I had to get him back. I knew Sam was experiencing similar feelings of deep, dark disappointment. He wanted to be with me. How was it possible that the very court there to prevent his kind of child abuse by a deviant parent was now complicit in the abuse. How would I ever explain to Sam what had just happened in Family court on the occasion of my application for Visitation in the months after fathers-day?

Before I got to the end if the exit isle, my £5,000 QC, whose name I can't even remember, such was the extent of his anonymous quality, stopped me leaving, placing his arm on mine and holding me back. Perhaps feeling ashamed at taking money for this debacle. He turned to the judge.

"Can I have a word in private with my client". He invited me back to the waiting room where he explained *"If you walk out now you will have played right into their hands. This has not just happened by accident. This is as clear a set up as I have seen. They want you to walk out and they will then apply for costs against you. You have been played."*

His advice was to say nothing and agree with the courts order, or face losing the costs application.

"I will negotiate the best deal possible for you. Just agree. Live to fight another day. You just have to accept that you have been played They know exactly what they are doing. Unfortunately for you, this is family-court."

I was astonished in that I never thought it was possible to award costs in family matters such as this. *"They do not generally award costs in family court because it increases animosity between the parents which is not good for the child"* Clam told me. But as events would go on to show at far greater expense, he was wrong.

Family Court as I was to learn later in Flaherty's court, the hearing that followed six months after my application for visitation, the revenge by Krasnopovich being his claim for 'beneficial entitlement', awards the maximum in costs when they benefit a member of family law against someone who is not. How this membership benefit affects the child abused by this process is open to your speculation.

After the Flaherty hearing that followed on as a second act to my application for visitation, I researched as professionally as is possible within the Freedom of information act to confirm; the costs award against me as a parent in family court are the highest ever awarded.

Six figures.

At 8% interest that continues 5 years later, at the time of writing. Because the winner was a member of family law. The loser though, was, at that time, a five-year-old child. After that court judgment, I never established regular visitation with my son. At the time of writing, we have not spoken for over 3 years. Quite a successful costs award if the intention all along was as the outcome shows it to be. I left court that after visitation hearing having failed to secure even 2 nights a month with my son. Soon after was presented with a bill of £23,660 just for that one single day from Clam LLP. After agreeing £5,000 costs estimate, at a maximum of £7,000. I was furious with Clam and demanded he progress an appeal at his cost, having made such a mess after the ambush on the Friday when he stood himself down from our agreed course. Of course Clam behaved exactly as you would expect from a member of family-law. This was the first big win for Krasnopovich in the tactic of forcing big legal costs onto me. There was never any need for a visitation hearing, if he had agreed to let my son see me. Throughout this entire period his constant approach was *"Pay me the money and you can see him whenever you want Not before."*

My overall legal costs in events surrounding this application to see Sam for 2 nights a month during that crucial early period following separation would reach £40,000. That is the reality of how determined Krasnopovich was to stop me using family court to see my son. I spoke to Chris after the hearing. He called Krasnopovich to speak directly about what he had done. Chris' reply to me was *"He said he told you that unless you gave him £100,000, you would not see Sam and now that offer is off the table. It's going to cost you more."*

Those costs visited on me by family law by Krasnopovich at the time of writing exceed £500,000. And rising, as he won interest on his costs at 8%. And of course, it has been years since I last saw or spoke with my son.

One curious aspect of the CAFCASS Court order in 2013 made in the application for visitation hearing is that it includes specific provision for removal of the child from the UK. It is a thing removing a child from the UK without the other parent's consent or approval. This specific provision by the court enabled either parent to remove the child from the UK within a pre-agreed set of conditions, written into that court order. (Which I had paid £23,000 for). This included the travelling parent giving the other parent a two-week notice period and details of accommodations and travel specifics. Despite this order of court Krasnopovich would go on to remove the child from the UK repeatedly without letting me know.

On several occasions following the court order of October 30th, 2013 I wrote to Clam to report that Krasnopovich had breached the Courts direction by removing the child from the UK without giving me two weeks-notice (or indeed any notice) along with the accompanying information required by the court order. Clam was entirely ineffective in raising my objection and it was never noted with the court that this breach (by a member of family law) had occurred as a result of his failure to follow my very clear instruction. In particular I had real concerns over Krasnopovich taking Sam to Dubai, during which time several emails were sent to Clam. At no time did I receive the information the Court Order provided for. Clearly, a breach of the Court order occurred. A breach by a member of family law. I was especially concerned at having Sam taken into Sharia Law countries. He has the same name as myself and I am the author of civil rights articles which have been banned in the Emirates. It is irresponsible to take a child with my name into this region where our laws do not protect him. Had Clam done as I requested at that time it may have given

Krasnopovich pause to consider not breaching the same Court direction 5 more times since Clam failed to put him on notice. Since I first reported this removal from the UK, in the first two years, Sam reported to me that he has travelled abroad with his Father on 5 separate occasions, including to the home in Geneva of a family law deputy district judge and Barrister Dia Mirza in December 2013.

I know Dia and her husband Fritz well, having been a guest in their home on many occasions, and Dia having been a guest in mine even more frequently. I was a guest at their wedding, which came about in no small measure after a very personal conversation in my home between myself and Dia. And so, months after the separation, when I was being blackmailed with visitation, I learned that Sam was to be removed from the UK to visit Dia in Geneva. It was Sam who disclosed this to me. Aware even then that the airport was a thing he should report back to me. As soon as I heard about this visit to Geneva, I texted Dia requesting an explanation. She did not reply. Dia is a DDJ and family law barrister and knew a child was a guest in her home in breach of an existing court order. One member of family law, Krasnopovich, breached a court order issued in family-court, removing a child from the UK without notice, taking that child to the home of another member of family law, who is a deputy district judge and a barrister member of family law.

Whilst David Clam, my solicitor and another member of British family law, had pocketed £40,000 for representing my son's interests to this level of incompetence evidently was not even capable of making a note of this breach for any future reference by family law.

It became clear the Court order could be breached with impunity by Krasnopovich, protected by other members of family law while my family law solicitor pocketed tens of thousands for total incompetence. Not for the first time and not for the last, Krasnopovich breached a court order. I reported it. Nothing happened. Family law did nothing about an offense by one of its own members. Which remains the case at time of writing. Eventually I wrote to the President of family law, who knew my case all too well, having sat as judge at the permission to Appeal hearing, where he found switch-judge Flaherty's judgment flawed. I detailed the clear breaches by members of family law, disclosing the specific dates, names and places. Although Sir Lord President acknowledged my concerns, even then nothing happened. This clear lack of accountability influenced my confidence in family law, reinforcing my impression that it was a money-making scam that simply took astonishing amounts for doing nothing more than benefitting members of what by any interpretation appears as little more than an organized crime syndicate. After the Ghanaian CAFCASS debacle, the very next day, I put my complaint in writing to Clam as well as raising it on three recorded occasions in telephone communications. I requested reimbursement of my costs from Spoon LLP in order that I could file an appeal in the hope of achieving visitation with my son on practical terms. Clam simply refused. There was no appeal. The events I have recorded here were allowed to stand unchallenged. Family law itself, did nothing about multiple breaches of their own ethical code by multiple members of family law. It is as if nothing ever happened. Such was the deafening silence meeting my complaints. And yet, it did happen and there are consequences. All actions have consequences. As a result of Krasnopovich and Clock's win in family court, the consequences included no regular weekend visitation for Sam. At this key time, in the first six months post separation. That opportunity for regular contact with his parent in the child's post-separation development passed and as events were to reveal, regular visitation never became a possibility again as events turned both our worlds around. In the first year apart, Sam got to spend 4 nights with me, at an average cost of £10,000 per night to Clam. Plus the costs of international travel and hotel accommodations, after my home flooded and entirely because of Krasnopovich's efforts, I was made homeless and unable to remain in the UK. This was all achieved by lies written into law by a switch judge in family-court. In a process that was un appealable.

As a footnote to this debacle, I began a complaint to the Legal Ombudsman. It was Clams advice that I follow this route, clearly intended to distract me from pursuing him for a refund of his fee for incompetence leading to losing two nights a month visitation. He led me to believe the Ombudsman might well act to have the court ruling reversed. (Because obviously stopping a child spending two-nights a month with his mother is a decision that reeks of something.) I come away from that experience, weeks of letter writing and phone calls, with the clear impression that the Legal Ombudsman's office is a waste of time. They could not have been more transparently disinterested. My local MP, Dominic Raab was spectacularly unhelpful.

The simple fact is I paid in the region of forty thousand pounds to secure regular visitation with Sam. There was no reason why this visitation would be denied. No history of violence, substance abuse or risk of kidnapping. It was a plain and simple case of a child's right to see his parent. The one who raised him for the first four years of his life in an atmosphere of harmony and joy. But that regular visitation never happened. Krasnopovich found it all too easy to not only prevent the visitation, but visit the maximum cost on me for even trying to use family law for access to Sam. After the hearing Jo asked Krasnopovich why he did that. His reply was;

"I had to nip it in the bud so Andrea doesn't get any ideas."

After that it was clear to me that to attempt visitation with Sam was to invite Krasnopovich's legal wrath. This could never be seen to be in Sam's best interests. Without further resources to fight a legal challenge, which I knew I could never win in a system I knew all too well after ten years of living on the 'inside' of British family law, I took the view that the most responsible thing was to take care of my own health. By this time I was feeling the strain of months of sleeplessness, chronic depression and anxiety, mostly arising from not being able to see my son and the terrible injustice of a system that can so easily be manipulated by its members to serve their own, child abusing agenda's. I decided to write to David Clam and after that letter, intended having no further business with British family law. £40,000 for what amounted to absolutely no contact with Sam and witnessing the debacle of a Court where the judge simply hands over the decision on a child's future to a semi-literate minimum wage Ghanaian while all sides pretend that they are doing a responsible job without even squirming with the embarrassment any ethically driven person would show when complicit in the abuse of a child's life in this way.

And best of all, these proceedings and this disgraceful conduct by all involved is protected by law as 'closed proceedings. With all kinds of threats made about leaking what actually goes on.

"She can't breathe a word of what I have done, or she will be guilty of contempt. I know what I am doing This is my job." Krasnopovich explained to Celia when asked if he was worried Sam might find out one day.

Small wonder they need that protection.

So that was intended to be that. I was going to visit the US and spend Christmas in the sunshine, focusing on my wellness. I left the court offer for visitation with; either Sam staying with me for term time and visiting his father on holidays, or him staying with his father and visiting me for holidays.

My letter to David Clam before leaving for my December trip.

Dear David,

Following my appearance in DJ Berry's Court, I write for the purpose of clarifying the outcome and summarising the prospects for my relationship with my son. You may include any part of this letter in any correspondence with DJ Beddy, in the event that it might be helpful to him.

As you know I believe leaving the judgment for contact up to the CAFCASS officer was a poor decision. My position on phased-in contact has been clear from the outset and you have first-hand experience of the obstacles and shifting positions that my son's father has placed in my path from the outset. In other words, I do not believe anything he says or agrees to. He is transparently dishonest. As you know all too well from your own dealings with him.

Unfortunately, I have found this disappointment in court depressing. I have not adequately recovered from the traumatic stress of fathers-day and in the interim have faced constant legal pressure and endless financial demands which have worn down my reserves of wellness to the point that I am, simply put, unwell. I am on prescription medication and have had to spend enormously on professional counseling. After all of this cost and effort and stress, I have not seen my son and the reasons for this are quite clear. Thirteen consecutive weekends of building up to having him visit and then having his father prevent that contact, usually at the very last minute, has been emotionally draining. I feel harassed by this endless letter writing persecution and the seeming inability to impact in any way on the family court system despite your best efforts which seem to be no more than draining whatever money I have for no visible progress in seeing my son.

In considering options for dealing with the health endangering stress and following medical advice, I have agreed to accept an offer of one month of sunshine therapy in the USA, far from the stressful nastiness of this persistent obstruction of visitation with my son

On my return I will not pursue the 'phased in conditional visitation' in this CAFCASS judgment for reasons that are self-evident. You know all too well the meaning of unfettered visitation. I may never recover my confidence in a system where I paid unspeakably ridiculous costs to have senior counsel represent my sons position, and watched him be discounted from saying one (1) single word, whilst the estimable Mr. Osei Agyemon of Cafcass, a semi- literate man barely able to spell my name inside 5 minutes of sweaty effort, became the sole arbiter of my son's future. You are already familiar with the grounds for my complaint and I hope that DJ Berry will become aware of Mr. Agyeman's interviewing techniques, although he evidently takes no offence at Mr. Agyemon receiving phone calls in his Court so I don't expect much by way of censure for Mr. Agyemon or this tired Judge.

It is unspeakable incompetence at its worst which prevents a child from seeing his parent in these circumstances while siphoning off what will be in the region of £40,000 in the process. Small wonder I am left feeling ill and distressed by British family-law. I remain as committed as ever to my son's welfare and believe this will eventually include a relationship with me. I will be available to take up whatever opportunities arise following my return from the US. If Krasnopovich continues to prevent this, I will not be pursuing any further legal expenses. I am fully aware of how pointless it would be to rely on this creaking, defective family court system, advantaged as he is by superior spending power and professional knowledge of the system. Most significantly, his willingness to use contact with the child as leverage makes me believe remaining in this adversarial position is never going to be the best thing for Sam. I will attach by separate mail the correspondence he sent to me this past Saturday, in which he makes clear;

'am not trying to issue you with any threats by saying this but if you continue to refuse payment the legal process is not going to stop.'

I do not believe it is in my son's best interest that he be passed between parents with such extreme differences during this period in which his animosity seems limitless. Consider a family law solicitor so determined to prevent overnight contact that he brought a QC to a preliminary hearing and then aggressively pursued an application for costs whilst being fully aware by the nature of his day job of the extent to which this would increase the animosity and its consequent effect on the child's best interest?

I now consider my son's best interests in light of the reality that his father is unlikely to ever change the way that he uses contact between my son and myself within his Tim Clock led adversarial 'war to the death approach'. Any judgment led visitation I might win now will always be subject to his controlling influence, with an inevitability that he will continue this pattern of controlling and obstructing indefinitely. Unless my son is returned to me on a basis that excludes Krasnopovichs controlling oversight, I cannot see any happy outcome from Krasnopovich being the residential parent.

I do however believe that the fullness of time will bring my son's father to the realisation the importance of not obstructing Sam's relationship with his mother. That he will choose to support this right rather than receiving the malign influence of Clock, whose serial abuses of SRA ethics code we have discussed at length, and continuing to use contact as the opportunity to commit theft, which remains at the heart of his objection to visitation. "Give me the money or the kid gets it" sums up their approach.

I have no doubt Sam will one day become aware of the lengths his parent went to prevent him seeing me.

My letter to him of 4th July, 2013, written for my son's benefit, leaves no doubt as to who drove the decision to end his relationship with me and describes with some prescience, the lengths he would go to toward this end. The exhaustive correspondence you have directed will serve this same purpose. The idea that he can conceal from Sam his decisions regarding his best interests and the animosity of his litigation forever, suggests he knows what he is doing is wrong but thinks he can depend on legal implements to protect his anonymity in this matter, in particular, from his own son.

He has repeatedly reminded me that Family Court is closed proceedings and can never be spoken of. To the extent that if I do so much as blog about it, he will "See you in jail." It is of course no less than plainly obvious that I was there to see my son on every one of the 13 weekends, and that the reason I did not see my son is because his father prevented that contact taking place. Our correspondence serves as a contemporaneous record of Krasnopovichs' actions. I remain convinced that actions have consequences.

During my absence I will provide contact details through Celia should any emergency arise with my son.

I will write to my son's parent through Celia upon my return in January with dates for visitation and examine the possibilities for having him returned to his Mother. In the meanwhile, I wish you well in your career and confirm you are paid up in full.

Regards,
Andrea

13 Street attack and the Clock claim

Harassed at home alone on a Friday night. Jumped in the street on a Saturday morning by a hired goon working for Krasnopovich and Clock. Attacked and physically injured

Following the expensive loss in family court my outrage that Krasnopovich was so easily able to stop Sam from even two nights a month with me grew. As did my disgust at the very fabric of British family law, an adversarial system in which all participants pursue their own version of self-interest without reliable ethical checks and balances to protect children who may become victim to those easily identifiable opportunities to abuse the child's rights in a process that relies on hearsay allegations without substance to enable flawed, prejudiced decision-making to prosper. Populated by members of British family law tasked as Judges, who in my experience of this role, include many transparently incapable of taking a common-sense child-centric view. I was seething with the injustice of it all and missing my son awfully. I saw in David Clam all that was worst about family lawyers. Judging is essentially no more than a decision-making process in which a basic level of competence can so easily be determined. Yet the Judges I met in family court were all too often simply not fit for purpose in a system where checks and balances for their competence were as absent as those for accountability after the fact.

It is clear to me that modelling family court on criminal court is a mistake.

The decision maker should not even be called a judge. The title confers undue status on those vulnerable by ego to the social uplift this title represents.

I had decided to walk away from the whole circus. Winter was fast approaching. My lawyer was clearly no more than a blithering dolt out to take every penny he could. My health was trending towards poor after months of applying my very best efforts to seeing my son and meeting a brick wall of obstruction, made worse by the outrageous demand for money that felt to me like a matter for the police. And criminal law. I was convinced family law was an ethical quagmire without regard for the child's best interests in which, much like a mafia protection racket, members of this mob would never find against each other. I would have to find a better way of seeing Sam than hoping everything I knew about family law and specifically, Krasnopovichs' practice in family law, was wrong. And to best approach the situation more holistically, I decided to focus prioritize my health, on getting myself back into a positive frame of mind before revisiting how to overcome the obstacles Krasnopovich had in place to obstruct Sam's visitation with me. It was around the time the clocks change in October and darkness comes before 5. Always a time when my energy needs some up-lift. Soon after arriving in the UK as a new immigrant in 1985 and seeing the effect of daylight-saving time change when, overnight it becomes dark at 5 in the afternoon, for the past 28+ years of living in the UK I made a point of travelling outside the UK on the weekend when the clocks change. Knowing the dark months lie ahead works subliminally on my good cheer and that added fuel to the depression flames. This year, more than ever, I did not want to be in the UK when the clocks changed. I decided to travel to sunshine. The consensus at that time from my network of friends and confidantes was to leave the UK and go get some sunshine and feel better. Or as they say in CA, pursue wellness. Philip agreed to host my visit and so, with my affairs in order (as they say in the UK), my flats rented out to good tenants and my music work obligations taken care of, I booked a ticket to California. 6 weeks of sunshine and wellness. Healthy food. A one-week Yoga retreat, visiting old friends in a drive up the costs to San Francisco. Therapeutic walks and tennis. And just hanging with old friends, some of whom I had known all of my life, in a place far away from the malign reach of family court and Krasnopovich. My goal was to arrive at the best way to pursue custody. Sam should be with me.

Shortly after Krasnopovich left on fathers-day with Sam, he rented a three-bed apartment house in Thameside close to his office, but refused to provide me with the address. The sequence of events was that my therapist emphasized the importance that I write to Sam. I emailed Krasnopovich asking for the address. He simply refused. My request resulted in a letter I was not expecting.

"Give me £100,000 first and you can see Sam as much as you want." and that is how the legal bills began. I knew better than to engage with family law. But this situation forced me. What do you do when you can't even get the address of where your child is for a letter?

I paid for Clam to tell me that I had the legal right to know where my son was at all times and that Krasnopovich was obligated by law to provide me with the address.

So far so good?

Clam wrote to Krasnopovich requesting this detail and only after £2,000 of legal bills charged to me by Clam for writing these demands for address letters did I finally received the address. I paid some £2,000 in legal charges just to find out where Sam was staying, while at the same time Krasnopovich had emailed me demanding money and including the assurance that the address and all other obstacles would disappear just as soon as he was paid. Krasnopovich drew out the costs to a maximum by waiting until Clam was on the train to the Court for an application before texting him the address. Literally e mailing him just the address one hour before his court visit. The outcome of that first precedent setting encounter in family law is that Krasnopovich faced no censure for a breach, withholding a child's address from a parent. I was left with a £2,000 bill payable to a member of family law. The pattern was established.

In the weeks after losing the visitation hearing, while I was making arrangements for my trip to California, I worked on fixing up my house. Reviewing the maintenance requirements at that time as a responsible landlord and preparing a works schedule. A new bathroom went into an upstairs flat. I replaced the balcony in the middle flat, which was a high maintenance wood finish mini conservatory, with a purpose-built one that was likely to be low maintenance and which meant low maintenance going forward. And happier tenants. I spent tens of thousands of pounds on upgrading my rental apartments, investing in reliable income over the next years where I foresaw, I would need reliable income to ensure I would be able to see my son. I was preoccupied by fixing the house, and winding down the days until I left for California. After my day's efforts, I would have dinner out every night with my circle of fine friends. Fine dining and fine tennis on the clay courts in nearby Thameside Club. Working my way towards wellness. Which began with having nothing to do with family law. That was Krasnopovich's world and he was welcome to it. The combination of vigorous exercise, weekly therapy sessions at the Priory and with the considered input from my wonderful friends meant I was making some progress in processing the trauma of having my son wrenched from my life.

Then just as I was stabilizing after the fathers-day event and being blackmailed to see my son, a tsunami rose out of nowhere and what little order I had established in my world was shattered. Unbeknownst to me, Krasnopovich and Clock had hired a process server and set up a scam claim. They would claim half of two of my flats, in so called TOLATA litigation based on his claim that '*She promised me 50/50 like we were married.*' They would claim 'Beneficial Entitlement.' That shortly after I met him, I promised him that half of everything I owned would be his. They then hired a process server to serve me with the court summons, personally, with maximum prejudice. In UK family law the correct procedure if you wish to serve a summons on someone is that you serve their lawyer. Makes sense if you think about it. No need to create animosity. Simply courier or DX the documents to the defendant's lawyer who will sign confirmation of receipt. That is the appropriate process for serving a summons in family-law. It is especially important in family-law where the focus must remain firmly fixed on avoiding causes of animosity between the parents because we know that increased animosity is always bad for the child. Krasnopovich and Clock chose instead to have me aggressively attacked with personal service in a matter that was unmistakably chosen to create maximum upset. Two members of the law society knowing no censure would follow the breach of ethical protocol, because, why would the law society censure its own members?

October 2013. It was 9 on a Friday night. Little more than one month before my California trip. I had arrived back from an early dinner and was alone in the living room, doing my meditation exercises on my guitar (scales at varying intervals at varying tempos) when I was rudely shaken from this reverie by loud banging on the external door to the property. The video buzzer inside 28A was ringing constantly as well. Someone had the entry button pushed down on hold while simultaneously banging the door so loudly it shook the house. I put my guitar down and went to the videophone point. On the six by four-inch color screen I saw the face of a thuggish looking individual, late fifties, like an East End Cray brother employee, eyeing the video camera, scowling, deliberately and provocatively, while hitting the door with his left fist. Hard and loud. With menace. The other hand pressed firmly holding down the videophone buzzer, both eyes fixed on the lens. The banging was loud enough to rouse the upstairs tenants, who appeared at the top of the staircase when I went into the hallway. Tenants who were good friends by now, and asked me "*Is everything alright. Shall we call the police?*" I shook my head. Remaining silent. I had no idea who this goon was, but no way was I answering the door to him. After some five minutes of this banging buzzing scowling, the house went quiet. The upstairs tenants went back upstairs. "*We are right here if you need us*", Alan, a 6.5 rower, reassured me, aware that this was an extremely threatening moment and that I was alone downstairs. I went back to the lounge and started my guitar playing again. My heart rate appreciably accelerated. What was that about?

By the time I had calmed down, fifteen minutes later, the buzzer rang and the banging started again. Banging for several minutes. Clearly I was not going to answer the door. This was not a social caller. It was aggressive, late at night and unmistakably hostile. I put my guitar down and huddled on the sofa. Blocking my ears with my hands. My heart was pounding. I hoped that the door would not break from the sustained banging. I had my phone in my hand ready to dial 911 when the fellow stopped hitting the door, released the video buzzer and silence returned. I sensed a touch of professionalism in his timing, stopping exactly at the moment I was about to call police as if previous experience had taught him this skill. Unpleasant enough. I wondered what that was about. I didn't sleep very much at all that night. The following morning I went for my cycle ride at 3am, returned for a shower and at 5 to 8, I set out for my usual 8 am coffee with Jo and Tom at the Steve's Café. Of course Krasnopovich would know all too well that every Saturday at 8 am I would meet Jo and Tom at Steve's Cafe. As I exited the doorway I noticed a thuggish looking individual standing on the other side of the road, at the bus-stop at the bridge entrance to Thameside, watching my house. He saw me, his head jerking in recognition and started to cross the road heading towards me. I realized immediately that this person was watching and waiting for me. It felt threatening. Like a hitman from a movie. I felt I was about to be attacked and chose flight over fight. I ran in terror. I thought I could make it to the coffee shop ahead of him, where many friends of mine were likely to be ready to defend me. Or at least, be witness to the assault I felt was imminent. He gave chase. I was sprinting from a cold start without warming up. I have long standing issues with my Achilles tendons arising from pronation. My Achilles pulled as I ran up the alley towards the Steve's Café. Painful, a tear of tendon just as I had experienced before in a tennis injury but the adrenaline of sheer terror kept me at sprint speed. A few steps later I was in the alley where two young local lads, big and confident, walking out of the alley appeared. As I saw them, I said *"Please help. This guy is threatening me."* They came to alert and I saw the thug pull up. I had a close look at his face. It comes back to me in nightmares to this day. Casting for the Cray brother's movie could have used his number. This was a determined assailant, but with two young men bristling with bravado between him and me, he pulled up, smirked at me, like a Cray brother's bodyguard before walking away. *"Catch you later"* he said with smirk.

Jo and Tom appeared from inside the café. They had heard the shouting. They witnessed the guy leaving the scene at a brisk and determined pace. I told them what had happened. Jo said 'Call the police." I started to dial, but thought, best call the lawyer first. Have a record of this in case it was linked to the family court business. To his credit, Clam answered the phone on a Saturday morning at 8.05. He advised me to not make a big deal out of it. *"If it is related to Krasnopovich, then don't give him the satisfaction of knowing he got you so upset. It sounds to me alike a process server. You will probably find some documents under your door when you get home. Sounds like a summons."* I didn't call the police.

We had breakfast, after which Jo and Tom helped me hobble home, and there on the floor of the entrance hall was a thick envelope with legal notices stamped on it. A summons. The date was exactly the same date as the transfer of title agreed for the freehold transfer at the Land Registry. The return of my freehold as agreed when I transferred his domain name titles and as he was required to do as a trustee bound by a trust agreement. My first thought was. *"Oh no. This means he is not going to sign the transfer of the freehold."* My second thought was, I should not have transferred his domain name titles when he asked me. That was a mistake, thinking he would honor any agreement.

I was unable to walk pain free for the next three weeks, requiring anti-inflammatory meds and sports injury massage to recover. It was an ugly experience. I felt injured emotionally as well as physically. It was an assault on my space. It made me feel like I was back in South Africa again, being emotionally raped by an untouchable system. Did Krasnopovich and Clock act inappropriately as members of family law hiring a with prejudice summons server clearly briefed to be as rough as possible? Does it matter?

Of course not. I reported it to my lawyer. Nothing happened.

I read through the documents the process server goon put through my door. It was an inch-thick batch of legalese that I found difficult to understand. It appeared to be a claim for half of my properties based on Krasnopovich's claim that '*She promised me 50/50 like we were married.*' Twenty thousand words of no relevance at all couching a legal demand for 50% of my home. Based on one entirely unsubstantiated claim.

'*She promised me 50/50 like we were married.*'

No date of claimed promise. No details. No motivation provided. No evidence of any kind in support of this 'promise.'
Seriously?

Aside from the simple fact that we were never married and that no one who knows me and the ownership of my house and Krasnopovich's status as possibly the seventh man to enjoy living with me there since 1986 for little or no cost, would reasonably accept that this was any evidence to award someone half of a house. An outlandishly ridiculous claim on the face of it. Especially given the magnitude of my generosity to him.

One that meant, if the claim prevailed and became a precedent in law, that anyone could simply say "*My boyfriend promised me half of his house*" produce no evidence at all, and just point to the case of Krasnopovich to show that, yes, all you have to do is say "*he promised me half of his house.*" Who needs evidence, or a factual matrix when you have a professional liar coming up with a 'promise' claim for the first time, weeks after writing a blackmail letter demanding money for visitation, weeks after appointing a city lawyer with a reputation for aggressive litigation? My thoughts turned to that common argument in family law when people start to speak badly of the other.

"*But you married him*".

Reminding us that hateful comments follow on from the obvious reality that at one time a degree of love and trust existed. But I did not marry him. For good reason. I took no comfort in realizing at that moment, in at least that much my instincts had served me reliably. Krasnopovichs' desperate need to marry had never presented as more than a meal ticket to a payday. More than one of my rock star buddies had asked me, after meeting Krasnopovich for the first time "do you know what a star fucker is?" More than one of my musical friends would go on to tell me "I saw it right away. Money grabbing lawyer." Faced with this legal challenge my wish to walk away from litigation, expensive lawyers and the foul stench of British family law was de railed. I had no option than to defend myself legally. And so another chain of costs began. Clever lawyering by Krasnopovich and Clock.

With hindsight, this level of litigation was out of David Clam's league. A provincial lawyer, with a conventional training in which he was outmatched from the beginning. I should have gone to a city firm, just as Krasnopovich had done in retaining Tim Clock of Souvla Raven Hogg LLP. But I was wrong in assuming that such a transparently baseless claim would require anything more than a cursory look by a judge. I thought the claim would be thrown out at the first look by even a half-witted judge.

"You want me to give you half of her multi-million-pound home and rental properties because you say she promised it to you and you have not so much as an email or a witness to back up that story. If I do that then anyone will be able to claim half of anyone's house on the same basis. It would be pandemonium."

Little did I know the underlying rot in British family-law and especially the dishonesty of Tim Clock, who originated not only the claim for beneficial entitlement on the flat that we lived in, 28A, but added in my mortgage free property, 28B Thameside to the claim, whilst participating in Krasnopovich's win in the visitation-hearing preventing my son from having even two nights a month with his mother. That vigorous defense, bringing a QC to a preliminary hearing for 2 nights a month visitation and claiming costs in a notice served at 3pm the day before the hearing. How could any judge not look at that hearing; the lengths they went to in manipulating family law to stop a 4-year-old seeing his own parent for 2 nights a month at a time when both the child and the parent were so very desperate to be with each other after weeks of separation where blackmail was attached to visitation. How could any judge look at the events of that visitation hearing and not draw the very obvious conclusion that one parent and his lawyer was going to extraordinary lengths to abuse the child, entirely motivated by commercial benefit by the transparent use of family law deceit to stop the child seeing the other parent.

What did Krasnopovich want and how did Clock advise him to get it?

I had 3 flats relating to my freehold title of 28 Thameside which I bought in 1986. When I first invited Krasnopovich to live with me, that occupation would include three flats. Starting with flat, 28C, my top floor apartment, where I was resident in 2003, when I met him and invited him to move in with me, rent free. The following year, some six months after he had moved in with me, when my tenant moved out of 28B, the flat below, I never re let, because I needed more space. I was earning well from music and not so dependent on the rental income and had a steady flow of visiting guests from abroad. I decided to use 28B as well as 28C while I worked on a house refurbishment plan. In part because I intended refurbishing works in the next 12 months and didn't want the nuisance of tenants during building works. That arrangement of me having no tenants and using all the space for my own guests lasted until I completed works to 28A in 2005, the bottom flat, where we would move once the refurbishment works completed. After which the upper two units were used for rental income. During those first two years Krasnopovich never paid a penny towards even his living expenses. Able to enjoy both 28B and 28C depending on who was visiting at the time. He enjoyed what may be described as "The life of Riley" because of my generosity. I set out to help a young person in all kinds of trouble, financially and emotionally. I did a fantastic job and enabling a whole new approach, including paying off his student debt and getting him passive income by enabling him to rent out his flat while living with me at no cost. Yet here he was, ten years later, claiming not only half of the flat he had actually lived in 28A, but also half of 28B, a flat valued in 2005 at £700,000 and most significantly, a flat with no mortgage. It was such a palpably ridiculous claim I couldn't imagine any judge misguided enough to believe such a 'promise' had any merit. At that time I could not have imagined that family law DDJ standards had fallen to the level of Cecelia Flaherty. Even though I had hosted many family law judges in my home for dinner and for parties over the years and had a good idea of the variance in their competence by personal interaction and in-depth conversation. One of my closest friends for a period was a barrister and deputy district judge in family-court.

Of course, to not mention here that it is never in the best interests of children to litigate and create animosity that is child abuse would be remiss. A family lawyer would know that. Is there any other way of interpreting Krasnopovich and Clock's decision to instruct such an aggressive service on the individual and not the lawyer than as intended to create maximum animosity by pursuing the maximum possible slice of my net worth. The Solicitors Regulation Authority publish a code of ethics for members. Within this prescription, service in a family matter should be to the other sides lawyer. There is no reason to effect personal service unless you intend causing distress. It is very clearly, a malicious act, in which Clock is as guilty as Krasnopovich of breaching the SRA ethical code.

This was just one more example in a long list subtitled; premeditated parental alienation, which in the context of what happened to the child, is child abuse.

Eventually, in defending this claim, my legal costs to David Clam would reach £189,000. And that was just the half way point in legal costs, as there would be a Permission to Appeal hearing. And new lawyers. And an entire new set of costs.

Before I wasted what I knew would be a huge sum on Family-law, in a situation I knew would be as corrupt as the well-earned reputation Family-Court enjoys, I wrote directly to Clock in the hope of settling without litigation. My intention was to represent myself. To present the facts of the matter and put an end to the nonsense before legal fee's spiraled. Of course, looking back, I can see how much he must have enjoyed receiving this letter, with all the ammunition it gave him to build his defense. The date of the 'personal-service' of their claim is significant. 21st November 2013. That was the date on the transfer of my freehold title document in which I had formally requested, in accordance with the trust agreement that had my title in Krasnopovich's name. Clam had prepared the land registry document and sent it to Clock for Krasnopovich's signature. The date for completing the transfer was 21 November. The buildings insurance on my home was related to that transfer. 21 November was a significant day for ending Krasnopovichs' hold on my property as well as his liability as Trustee, which would include Insurance cover. In law, Krasnopovich was obligated to return the title, which bound him to fiduciary responsibilities. His creative way of saying 'Fuck you' to the legal system was to serve his TOLATA Claim (beneficial entitlement to half of my home) on exactly the same date as the transfer of my freehold title back to me.

Smart lawyers Krasnopovich and Clock. A sense of timing that goes to credit.

14 Preliminary hearing. Clams contempt

How Krasnopovich got the claim to move forward and how David Clam made a calamitous error

In the letter to Clam that I hoped would end the nuisance claim, that I am copying below, you will see the reference to *'witnesses'* at this stage of the proceedings. Witnesses are hugely important, if not critical in understanding the flaw in Flaherty's judgment. Starting with the decision to allow witnesses in the first place. Bringing multiple witnesses was an integral part of Krasnopovich and Clock's presentation at the preliminary hearing. Given their cases was rice-paper thin – based on a word of mouth claim with no substantiation, they proposed to substantiate it with witnesses. This they could do in full confidence that there never would be a hearing because I would inevitably 'take a commercial view' and agree to their financial demands. They took the gamble to convince the judge of two things.

1.) To allocate sufficient credibility to the claim to allow it to go forward, because, they had witnesses to substantiate the claim that otherwise was nothing more than his word.
2.) To allocate sufficient time in the hearing to accommodate these multiple witnesses.

Obviously, because he was going to bring multiple witnesses, my barrister argued for the same allocation on my behalf. I knew I could easily find multiple witnesses and agreed that this would be the case. For this reason, initiated by his side, the judge ruled the case would need three days – in order to accommodate the multiple witnesses from both sides. Had he not claimed he had this evidence – these multiple witnesses – I say the case would have been ended there and then. That is how important these multiple witnesses were. He had zero evidence of this 'promise'. The proof was, he claimed, going to come from the multiple witnesses. With multiple witnesses promised, by both sides, the judge at the preliminary directions hearing determined the case could proceed and an appropriate time schedule was allocated.

Three days.

Obviously, this judge had to consider that in a case of 'he said she said', witnesses were crucially important. Which must be considered in light of Flaherty's very first ruling when she switched with the appointed judge to hijack the case set down for three days to accommodate multiple witnesses. In that 2015 hearing, after suddenly and surprisingly switching cases to take up Krasnopovich's matter on the morning of day one, Flaherty saw two things. First, that Krasnopovich did not have one single witness. Second, that I had six witnesses, including independent professional's privy to the financial details influencing the case she was to judge. Flaherty's first decision as switch judge was to exclude the only witnesses offering actual evidence in this claim. And overlook the fact that Krasnopovich had no witnesses. Having succeeded in bringing his case to this stage on the promise of bringing multiple witnesses to prove his claim. That is a summary of the first hour of day one in the 3-day hearing set down for Krasnopovich vs Leandros, to determine whether she did or did not Promise him 50% of her home. Under the rules representing British family law in 2013.

And this is the letter I sent to Clock hoping to end any litigation in the best interests of the child I was aching to see. I wrote this letter for Sam. Believing it would demonstrate that litigation is not good for the child's interests and that they should stop litigating and let my son see the parent who raised him with a full-time presence immediately. We can all reflect now that the advice from Chris that I not send it because it gave them fair warning of what was to come, was ignored at my own expense. But I meant well, thinking honest disclosure and words that could not be erased would bring them to understand their case was not going to succeed and was not worth risking Sam's life for.

By E Mail:
3 December, 2013
From: Andrea Lee
To: Tim Clock

Dear Mr. Clock,

I write in reply to your letter of 21 November.

As I understand it, your client is making a claim against me under the Trusts of Land and appointment of Trustees act 1996, in respect of his alleged interest in 28A and 28B Thameside. Apparently he is claiming direct financial contribution in that we shared common intention, throughout our (almost) ten-year relationship, that these properties would be owned in equal shares. That is something I refute entirely. Had that been true then surely we would have included the property your client owns in our agreement and in my opinion this omission is a fairly significant oversight in your clients claim.

You may be interested to learn that whilst living in my home at Thameside, your client made no direct financial contribution to my property costs. He made modest contributions towards a portion of his living expenses; including gas, electricity, council tax, television license, sky multi room, and so on, but the totality of that amount falls by far below the amounts I loaned him, for example, in respect of student loan repayment and equity partnership buy-in, that were never repaid. Your client has a diamond ring gifted from me, valued at £16,000, which alone by far exceeds the total of his contribution towards my costs in supporting his lifestyle.

There never was any common intention that the properties would be shared, neither in writing nor in conversation. Ever. There have never been any co-mingled finances.

There are no witnesses you will bring to any hearing because there is no story that anyone could have witnessed. Your case is 100% invention.

Consequently, I believe your clients application to the Court to be a malicious reaction to correspondence of Friday 21st, November and would advise you at this time that the content in your client's statement includes claims that are demonstrably untrue. In other words your client is seeking to mislead the court with deceit. This is essentially a mischievous claim, being lodged on exactly the same day of the deadline for the return of my Freehold title, failing which I indicated I would file a complaint with the SRA about your client's breach of trust in not returning my Freehold.

You are already aware that on 21st November, the date of your application, the house Insurance for my home became due and that I had Insured the property in my name having formally requested the return of my title from your client. Instead of returning the title, as obligated by the trust agreement, your client contacted insurers forcing them to place the policy in his name. As you are aware, this title was held in trust following your client's advice to me in 2003, when I barely knew him outside of the context of his profession. It is ridiculous to propose I gifted a person I hardly knew 50% of my home by giving them my Freehold title.

It was your client who approached me with a view to starting a relationship in February 2003, and your client who moved into my home just weeks after that and your client who less than three months after moving into my home and borrowing money from me to pay off his student loan gave me the legal advice to transfer the Freehold title to his name, as a thank you for my financial help to him, and for reasons of Insurance benefit. An agreement he knew very clearly was in Trust, made with the assurance that it would be returned in 5 years to my name when I could reinsure. I agreed to follow his advice after consultation with my Financial Advisor on the clear understanding that the title would be transferred back to me after 5 years. I had a lawyer draft this Trust agreement at my IFA's insistence. There is no doubt that your client knows the Freehold is my property. His obligation is to act as required in the trust agreement. It is his fiduciary responsibility to return my title as requested.

I am aware that a solicitor giving legal advice and then using that advice for personal benefit is a matter for the Solicitors Regulation Authority and you knew that following confirmation that this is precisely what your client has done by refusing to return my title deed, I intended lodging a complaint with the SRA on Friday the 21st November. I believe this is the reason why your client has made up this series of falsehoods for the purpose of bringing this application. And what has motivated this aggressive service, which is in breach of the SAR ethical code, as well as this ridiculous claim which is no more than leverage for blackmail in which I say you are complicit. If I had normal visitation with my son, then my claim in this regard would not be as transparently obvious as is the case. I have an e-mail from your client making plain 'Pay me £100,000 and you can see Sam as often as you like." I have not paid. And I have not seen Sam. I say, you are as guilty as your client in whatever the legal name is for this form of coercive conduct using a child's rights as collateral.

I turn in brief to the key points at this time:

1. As a result of the stress inducing aggressive conduct by your client towards me, including taking Sam away on fathers-day, and the extraordinary lengths he has achieved in denying me as much as a two night a month visitation, along with the tremendous stress arising from his refusal to return my Freehold title, I am medically unwell. Following medical advice, because it is clear from your clients conduct as well as yours, that I have no prospect of seeing my son unless I pay you a ransom amount, I am taking 6 weeks off to attend my wellness and will not be able to correspond during this time. I will notify the Court to this effect.

2. Your client earns £350,000 PA, owns his own home, which he could easily have moved into and has demonstrated the means to house his son. I am not earning as a consequence of, having invested heavily in establishing your client's career, housing him at no charge for the first few years when he moved from his hundred- thousand pound flat-over-a-chip shop into the million pound+ home I have owned since 1986, paying off his student loan, financing his equity partnership, managing his rental property and find that I am now unable to afford a lawyer to argue your client's disingenuous avaricious claims. I have borrowed against my home to finance the effort I made to have contact with Sam and take the view that your client's malicious application makes clear that he wants to ensure there is no prospect of Sam having a relationship with me before I pay him his ransom demand.

3. Outside of his imagination your client has no claim on my home, which I have owned since 1986. In fact numerous men have cohabited with me in the 29 years I have lived here, all of whom made some contributions towards living expenses, and yet your client is the first to try and claim ownership of my home. If he succeeds does this mean my previous partners have similar rights? If your claim succeeds does it mean anyone can claim 50% of anyone else's home based on a transparently deceitful unsubstantiated claim?

Your client paid a contribution in later years of our relationship toward costs of living. But never towards the mortgage and never as much as 30% of the lifestyle expenses we incurred whilst cohabiting. All of the building works to the property were paid for by myself. All of the decisions on the refurbishment in 2005 were made by the builder and myself, something that can be verified with ease by the builder. And the bank statements.

Your client was at work every day while the works were in progress, involved only to the extent of being asked if he liked the colour of the tiles. There is not one single item in the construction that your client paid towards. The full extent of his executive input into the refurbishment of my home, the fourth refurbishment of my home as it happens, after the expensive refurbishments I undertook in 1991, 1996 and 2001, is zero. That is, not one single Pound. Your claim that he contributed to the refurbishment in 2005 is a lie. For this reason I assure you, you will not find one single bank statement to substantiate his claim. Nor one email. Nor one witness. It is a bald-faced lie. And of course, in the court hearing, if you choose to continue suing me, you can produce this letter for the Judge, along with the bank statements, the emails and the witness statements to show that I have unfairly accused you of being a bald-faced liar. A bald-faced liar whose lies have knowingly harmed my child, so you can tell the judge; I called you a bald-faced child abusing liar. And you will have the evidence, the bank statements, the emails and the witnesses, to show I was wrong.

Your client's rental income from his own property in Hounslow was always far in excess of the amount he paid toward the living expenses in my home. In other words, he lived in my home enjoying a subsidized standard of living while I wound down my business to stay home, look after our child and support his career. Financially and executively. Living with me his income from his rental flat exceeded his outgoings for his expenses in my home.

Your client was never promised at any time that he would have any beneficial interest in my property. It was never even mentioned conversationally on one single occasion. Had it been my intention to give him part of my home I would have put his name on the mortgage. And invited him to contribute to that cost. Bear in mind at the outset of your client living in 28A my mortgage cost was £2,800 pm and my monthly living expenses averaged £2,000. On average each month it cost me £5,000 to live there, before you factor in my child support costs or the various causes I support. Your client contributed on average £500 pm. Less than 10% of my costs of living there. His contribution towards living costs equated to no more than 60% of only the gas and electric bills each month.

Your client is a lawyer and knows the importance of putting things in writing. Not once did he ask for any beneficial interest in my property, and if he had, it follows that I would have put it in writing to confirm this is the case. The information presented in your client's statement is factually incorrect and is no more than disingenuous invention.

For the first two + years of our relationship, while your client was on a modest salary, he never paid any rental to me despite the fact that he was renting out his own property and benefitting from that rental income. My goal was to uplift him financially, which I did through generous subsidy. In the first two years I would lend him thousands because he could not afford to make it from paycheck to paycheck. I never asked for any of that money back. Yet I have possibly six emails from him during that period reading "Honey, please can you lend me £3,000 until the end of the month". Tim, you have my assurance none of those helpful loans were ever repaid.

4. The arrangement we had for a joint property was that we were going to buy a home together in the future, based on his ability to qualify for a mortgage following two years accounts at our new firm. We had already looked at several properties with this in mind. My IFA Larry Chester had already secured a number of mortgage scenarios for us that substantiates this point. And it is true that I had agreed to marry him in December this year, in California. The purchase of the matrimonial home would follow that. Thameside was always my property, intended as a rental property in my sole name to provide me with independent income. Our family plan was to buy the matrimonial home as equal partners.

5. Your clients mention of 'witnesses' he can produce to confirm hearsay must be seen in its appropriate context. I have witnesses too, professional credible colleagues who have been aware of the arrangement between your client and myself from the outset.

My Financial Advisor has been a constant through the years and will confirm my position with regard to the ownership, the agreement with your client, as well as the transfer of the Freehold title in trust.

I will be most interested to see who the witnesses your client claims to have waiting are? I say to you here; this claim that you have multiple witnesses is a falsehood. There are no witnesses because the claim itself is a lie. I say you and your client have lied at the preliminary hearing with your claim of multiple witnesses to add some substance to a claim which otherwise has none. If it turns out that you have lied about this in court, and the multiple witnesses are revealed as no more than another lie told by yourself and your client in pursuit of a blackmailing claim predicated on a lie, told to a family court judge at the preliminary hearing to enable your baseless claim to continue without being thrown out for lack of any evidence, then the absence of multiple witnesses in the hearing will be your guilty plea.

It appears to me that your client's sole claim to this alleged agreement is not any written provable quantity, but limited entirely to her 'direct discussions' with me, which I can confirm, never happened. Further, I assure you I have multiple credible witnesses who will confirm, with documentary substantiation, that your clients claim is an invention, unconnected by fact to any truth.

Your client's entire declaration of reassurances that 'we viewed them together as our joint properties' is simply untrue. There was not one conversation referring to his ownership.

Another curious oversight in your client claim is the omission of the third flat, 28C Thameside. If the agreement as stated by your client was that 'we viewed them together as our joint properties' *why omit 28C, which is actually where your client lived for the majority of his time in my home.*

6. Because your case is being brought to court containing factual errors that your client knows to be disingenuous, and if lying in court is perjury, then is it not the case that your client is conspiring to commit perjury in bringing this application, and more importantly, that knowing this makes you complicit? Only the presence of your multiple witnesses will introduce the possibility that I am wrong. That you are not willfully encouraging your client to commit perjury.

7. It is true that I never progressed the transfer of the Freehold title back to my name at the five-year period we had agreed. This is because we had a flood in 2007, and again in 2008 and a large Insurance claim followed. It was not practical to change Insurers with a claim in progress. In 2008 we were living in Thames Road in a rental, where our relationship broke down and I moved out. This relationship breakdown was because your client was obsessive about having a child, which for me, in my forties, was not something I felt his lifestyle supported. He was frequently out late at night 'networking' and having dinners, often returning home demonstrating the effects of extreme alcohol use, and being unresponsive to the traditional accompaniments of a romantic relationship. He was obsessively declaring his life goal was 'Marriage and 2.4 children.' The distance between us led to a break up.

I moved out of the rental property in 2008 and considered that the relationship was over. Post separation, please note, there was no mention of any '50/50 like we were married.' A month passed and your client then approached me with a declaration of love, the assurance of reform, and the proposal to have a child which was centered on a detailed agreement. A parental agreement perfected over a period of several weeks, including specifics of a business plan addressing the costs of raising a child. My concerns were registered and addressed by your client. I would not undertake that level of cost of a child, privately educated when in my forties without a detailed business plan on how the costs would be met.

Together we agreed a career plan which would lead to the establishment of your client's firm in which I was the mentoring director of business. I set up the business effectively as an equal partner in terms of the business providing the expenses involved in raising the child. We spent many weeks drafting and perfecting a business plan to establish a business able to generate sufficient proceeds to meet the costs of raising a privileged child. For this reason I provided your client with (some) £40,000 to buy equity in his then firm MWT, and was instrumental in the formation of his own practice, Krasnopovich McDonald, paying the set up costs of some £18,000 out of my own pocket while your client worked his notice at MWT, on the very clear understanding that we were partners in this business, for the purpose of providing income to give the child a good life. In simple terms. We agreed to have a child and we agreed that the education costs for this child would be met by your client's business.

Additionally we had agreed that I would wind down my own music production business to stay at home for the child to have a parental presence in his life while your client invested the long working hours in establishing the new business. My support to him in this time was immense. We were a highly effective team. He would not have been able to start that Firm without my involvement and financing. And all the while I housed him in my home, accepting a small percentage of what our lifestyle cost by way of contribution and meeting all of the mortgage costs myself.

8. My primary income at this time is the rental I derive from my rental properties. If I were to lose that, I will literally be homeless and penniless. It goes to the character of your client that the thanks I get for entering into arrangements with him that have taken him to the position he is in now, with the child he wanted and the business he wanted, find me facing demands intended to bankrupt me and end any prospect of my seeing his son. All in the name of blackmailing deceit by dishonest lawyers trading visitation with my son.

I know that in year one of trading, the family law arm of Krasnopovich McDonald saw £350,000 in turnover, much of that arising from files taken from his former firm MWT, with my technical assistance, without which your client would not have had some £180,000 worth of files to transfer, and will look forward to the calculation on what I am owed from that. He would not have had those files without my input. They generated £180,000, much of which was processed on my Visa merchant account. I think, considering the costs your client has visited on me, that my 50% of that agreement, the £90,000 owing from that agreement alone, should be paid by return.

Yours sincerely,
Andrea Lee.

And in light of what happened in Flaherty's court, getting rid of the witnesses was crucial to the outcome. Think about it for two seconds. The claim is '*She promised me 50/50 like we were married.*" Consider, means motive and opportunity.

There is one of two possibilities. She said 'Yes' or she did not say 'Yes.' Witnesses say X. That she did not say 'yes'. There is no counter to X. How do you proceed knowing X will derail your case? You cannot prevail unless you get rid of the witnesses. There is a motive here to make sure that you do not sit in front of a judge who will allow the witnesses. What you need to do is switch judges. To a judge who will get rid of witnesses.is it a coincidence that on the morning of the hearing, the judge set down by the family-court system to hear a 3-day case with multiple witnesses from both sides, is switched. For a new judge who not only makes it her first decision to forbid witnesses, but also, a judge who my barrister declared 'Will guarantee that we lose.' Really? The insider in family-court, the professional barrister, knows this switch judge and discloses that she will judge against him.

That happened, but was it legal?

And if, as I accuse, family law members conspired to fix a hearing in favor of one of their own, how does accountability follow this transparently clear case of judgment fixing by DDJ Flaherty? It defies all coincidental probability that Flaherty's arrival and conduct in this case is innocent. This is a bent judge. Who made a bent decision. For which a child has not seen his parent for over three years at time of writing. With legal costs of £500,000 accruing interest at 8% in a costs award by that same judge in a family matter, awarded against the defendant? Whose child is clearly suffering as a consequence of this judgment. Financial consequences of this acrimony generating judgment, breaching the SRA ethics code, exceed £3 million and include 6 years of a boy's life with his parent.

How does accountability follow the child abuse that could have been avoided had Clock not pursued a claim he knew to be a lie, with all the evidence supporting this laid out in front of him in my letter copied above?

A letter which he did not even reply to.

Are lawyers who lie openly and are found out by events immune to accountability? So far it's worked out very well for Tim Clock.

15 Insurance renewal before flood

I paid for the usual policy cover for 2013/2014 with the AXA. 27ʰ year in a row. But all you need to know about the AXA Insurance is 'Jeff the Plumber dunnit."

In October of 2013 the House Insurance notice for renewal arrived. The date was 21 November 2013, and covered the year to 21 November 214. Because the Freehold was still in Krasnopovich's name land registry documents for transferring the title back to my name were sent by Clam to Clock, due to complete on 21 November, 2013, enabling me to insure in my name and bring an end to the freehold trust agreement. Clock had a duty to respect the law in advising his client to respect the law. There was then, and remains to this day, no question that my freehold title was transferred to Krasnopovich, not as a gift, or an indication of his ownership of my home, but simply for Insurance benefit, to be held in trust to be returned on demand. I had only known him for some 3 months at that time, making the idea I gave him 50% of my home just like that, patently ludicrous. I put the Freehold into his name for one simple reason and that followed a sequence of events in which there are multiple witnesses. The entire sequence of events relating to the freehold transfer and subsequent insurance policies was an agenda item at more than one meeting between myself and my IFA, Larry Chester, who was set to be a witness in the April hearing and made a statement confirming the facts. Larry was ready to attend the court hearing, having cleared his diary for the day, to discuss his statement and expose Krasnopovich's lying claim The title transfer was a trust agreement. The idea came from Krasnopovich. As a means to avoid paying high insurance premiums. In other words, for Insurance benefit, he would hold my title and take out the policy in his name, deceiving the AXA into providing cover for my home. Because, I had a fire claim on my Insurance history and for this reason, the AXA wanted to charge me a huge premium for Insurance cover. Putting it in his name meant a low Insurance premium.

Was it legal? He said it was. He was the lawyer.

Time passed. The 5-year blight on my name for Insurance expired and I asked for the title back. He did not argue when I asked for it back. Eventually it came down to the date for the reinsurance of my property in October 2013. My lawyer completed the paperwork to transfer the title back to my name. I would then take out the Insurance renewal cover in my name. That date arrived. The document transferring the title back to me at the Land Registry was on Clocks desk. Instead of signing the title transfer as he was required to do, Krasnopovich and Clock instead booked a summons server to 'attack' me on exactly the same date as the transfer of title. Serving notice of their TOLATA claim for 50% of my home because *'She promised me 50/50 like we were married."* Their way of telling me they were not going to honor the trust agreement and sign the transfer of title. And overlook the fact that I had transferred his domain name titles as agreed, on his word that he would transfer my title upon request. A quadruple double whammy of deceit. Consider all the lies Krasnopovich had to put forward to get himself into the position where he stood in Flaherty's court and claimed that he owned the Freehold to my home. Where he tried to sell it to me for £17,000, to show that he did in fact own it.

Here is my short form list of lies relating to Krasnopovich and the freehold:

1. 2003. He lied to me, advising me to put it in his name for insurance benefit. In a trust agreement to be returned 'upon demand'.

2. 2003. Lied to Larry Chester, the IFA about it not being Insurance fraud.

3. 2003. Lied to the AXA implying the property had never had a claim.

4. 2010. Lied to AXA in application form, omitting claim detail from 2008 flood. Caught out by Lars the Loss Adjuster.

5. 2013. Lied to me about transferring his domains attached to return of my freehold

6. 2013. Lied to Fairtimes brokers about being freeholder, to cancel my Insurance cover.

7. 2014. Lied to AXA about the flood claim of 2014.

8. 2014. Lied by way of fiduciary breach in refusing to return title upon request and spoiling insurance claim for flood.

9. 2016. Lied by way of fiduciary breach by claiming he owned Freehold to substantiate a claim for beneficial entitlement based on him being the owner of the freehold. Acting against my interests. Making him liable for all costs consequential to that cause.

10. 2015. Lied in Flaherty's court, saying he 'owned' the freehold.

11. 2016. Lied by way of fiduciary breach in failing to restore property to its pre incident condition and failing to make up shortfall in Insurance out of own resources as required in the Freehold agreement.

12. 2016. Lied by way of fiduciary breach and deceit by blaming 'Jeff the Plumber' as the cause for the flood, ending the Insurance liability for repair of the property.

13. 2016. Lied by way of fiduciary breach by failing to pursue Jeff the plumber for causing the flood when his Insurance would have paid upon request

14. 2016. Lied by way of malicious fiduciary breach in refusing to trigger claim for property damage from treefall at next door house. Where the responsible party agreed liability and was waiting to pay costs through Insurer, which Krasnopovich refused to authorize as the named policy holder. Leaving me to pay

£15,000 bill that was the liability of the neighbor, who had accepted liability. Which had to go through Insurance.

15.   2016. Lied by way of fiduciary breach in refusing to trigger claim for property damage

16.   2016. Lied by way of fiduciary breach in preventing me selling property as going concern – Freehold and three leases – for £2.5 Million.

17.   2017. Lied by way of fiduciary breach in forcing sale of property by court order based on lies dependent on the Freeholders authority

18.   2018. Lied by winning 'sole conduct of sale' preventing me from any interest in selling one of the flats he won, and then failing to sell it after 16 months of exclusive right of sale. Deliberately spoiling the sale opportunity I had with a different agent.

19.   2019. Historical lies in the matter of claiming to be freeholder resulted in my property having no flood Insurance, and being left empty for forced sale, which failed to materialize, while he accumulated 8% interest in a court costs win achieved by claiming ownership of the freehold. Leaving me to continue paying all costs on the empty properties, that because of the interest and costs element reached a threshold where the amount owing by me exceeds the possible sale price. Reducing the value to me of my £2.5 million asset to zero.

While the Freehold title in a property such as mine, a 19th century terrace converted into three leaseholds, is in itself essentially worthless, it is the instrument responsible for Insuring the building and for managing the joint tenant costs in the maintenance of the building. I have held buildings and contents insurance on 28 Thameside since 1986. Always paying the annual premium at the outset of each year. As a responsible property owner and mortgagee, I have had adequate building and contents cover in place for the 27 years to that date, always paid in full in advance of the commencement date. In 2013, after his fathers-day departure, the annual Buildings and Contents Policy was due for renewal through Fairtimes Brokers. The Insurer was the same as usual, The **AXA** Insurance. In due course, according to the usual timing in Insurance cover renewal, about one month before the due date the policy renewal notice arrived at my address. It contained the policy details for buildings and contents for the year 2013 to 2014. I contacted the brokers to advise that Krasnopovich was no longer resident in my home and that I would pay for the renewal, having the policy transferred from his name to mine. I explained that I was the Freeholder, that he was only ever the trustee, and that the transfer of the title back to my name was being dealt with by lawyers and would be effected by the due date of the policy cover.

One aspect of the policy cover relates to the policy holder being resident in the home. Obviously Krasnopovich could not take out that same policy cover as he was not resident in the property. But I was. And I was the legal freeholder as well. This type of cover for rental properties differs when the Landlord lives in the property.

By this time the 5-year claim history against my name for the fire claim was long expired and there was no premium charge or complication in issuing the cover in my name. The last flood claim was in 2008. This was 5 years later. With no claims in between. On the face of it then, this was making the best of a bad mess. The Freehold would come back to my name and I would take his name off the Insurance cover. The brokers were aware that Krasnopovich was a trustee. Every previous year's renewal bill had been paid by myself and I had on occasions called them to make modifications to cover. As was the case every year since 1986, I took out Buildings and Contents cover. I removed the £16,000 cover for his 'jewelry'. The policy was paid for and accepted, buildings and contents, and that was the end of that. The money left my account and life moved on. The litigation at that stage had advanced the date where my request to have the freehold returned to my name had been sent by Clam to Clock, awaiting signature by Krasnopovich. There was at that stage no indication that Krasnopovich intended not returning the title. It was a legal requirement which he was obligated to respect. In the meanwhile, the backdrop to the Insurance matter was Krasnopovich enmeshed in the 13-week long period where he would suggest a weekend visit for Sam was possible before cancelling at the end of each week. A cruel and malicious abuse of both Sam and my hopes of seeing each other. 13 weeks in a row. Building up Sam's and my hopes, before cancelling with the option of paying his 6-figure demand. It was a difficult and highly stressful time where finding my joy occupied the best of my efforts, so when I received a call from the Insurance Brokers to tell me they had cancelled my policy I felt sucker punched.

Fairtimes brokers reported to me that Krasnopovich had called them to say he was the freeholder, reminded them that he was a lawyer and demanded they cancel the policy in my name.

"How can that be legal" I asked.

"I have a policy accepted and paid for and in place. You cannot just cancel it on the word of someone who is not even resident in the property. I am the legal freeholder. Not him."

How can that be legal I am still asking five years later with not one penny paid by the AXA and my costs as a consequence now in the millions. I just wonder if that law, where you can just call Insurer's and cancel someone's policy, applies equally to individuals who are not members of family law? Do the AXA have specific wording in this regard? Krasnopovich cancelled the Buildings and contents cover and then took out a 'minimal' Buildings only policy in his name. Ostensibly to continue his masquerade as the freeholder, responsible for the Buildings Insurance. But knowingly and deliberately excluding the contents cover. Even if he claimed the freeholders title gave him the obligation to take out insurance, that same title gave him the fiduciary responsibility to act in my best interests. Quite clearly his actions were driven by bad faith and in support of his beneficial entitlement litigation. Because he cancelled the cover in my name I wrote to him advising that in so doing he was personally liable in the event that anything happened. That letter was dated October 2013. That document was ignored and still is to this day.

And as was somehow inevitable when considering the irresponsibility of Krasnopovichs' fly by night approach, on 8th February 2014 the Thames flooded and breached the tanking in my home, causing serious damage to the fabric of the building as well as ruining many contents. I had no cover in my name. Neither buildings nor contents. Krasnopovich, the responsible Landlord, had some buildings cover, but no contents. I was now homeless and reliant on the Insurance I had paid for to provide for remedy. To repair my home to the pre-incident condition and to house me until my home was once again habitable. Krasnopovich managed the Claim and in so doing deliberately ensured that I received not one penny. To make up the Insurance shortfall, just to get the flat habitable would cost me over £250,000. In the course of the post flood correspondence Krasnopovich was investigated by the Insurers, the AXA, after it turned out he had not disclosed a previous claim in one of the earlier applications in his name. The claim process, such as it was, was put on hold. And the net outcome was that I had to pay the costs to make the property habitable again. The Insurers appointed a specialist Insurance fraud City law firm to investigate Krasnopovich for making a false declaration on a previous year's application. Krasnopovich hired a weighty City firm to represent him, to fight fire with fire. Meanwhile, no work progress on restoring the property to its pre incident condition. I was left to pay both the rehousing costs and the works costs in mitigating the flood damage and later, to make the house habitable. My costs skyrocketed as I had nowhere to live and had to pay costs that would have been covered within the policy had Krasnopovich not ensured that this was not the case.

Eventually, with my home rotting away untended for over a year I raised a loan to have remedial works done to make the property habitable and enable me to mitigate further costs arising from leaving a building untreated post flood. By this time I was so far down in legal costs and repair bills and interest in loans that I couldn't even speculate at an accurate total estimate of costs. That sum in direct expenses relating to the Insurance shortfall, the absence of contents cover and the failure to repair the flood damage exceeds £250,000 by far. There would be three further damages claims raising the total owed in respect of the lessor's obligation to the lessee to £250,000. All of which Krasnopovich simply ignored. His standard reply to my requests being *'So sue me.'*

In raising the loan for the repair works I approached my IFA, Larry Chester, and went through the process of securing funds by way of a Mortgage on my property 28B, which had no mortgage. I was able to put in place a £500,000 loan, which would cover my legal expenses, enabling me to continue the fight to see my son, as well as pay for the remedial works post flood. And progress my legal claim with a City property lawyer for the Insurance shortfall Krasnopovich was liable for as the Lessor. I had every confidence that this loan would be repaid when the Insurance paid out, as they were obligated to do, and when Krasnopovich's nonsense legal claim was exposed. With that arrangement ready to go, I received a call from Larry saying *"We have a problem. Krasnopovich has placed a charge on your property at the Land Registry."*

Smart move. Cut off all funding. She can't sue without money to pay a lawyer. The question anyone reading the SRA guidelines might have for Clock is; did that litigious action increase animosity between Sam's parents? Is increased animosity between parents harmful to the child's best interests, being a layer of parental alienation? Is it worse still when that litigation is predicated on a lie. Can family law members ever be accountable for anything non-members might go to prison for?

Without doubt Krasnopovich and Clock placed a charge at the land registry on a property that was bought by myself in 1986, paid for entirely by myself, in which they had zero claim at all. Not one single shred of supporting evidence. Only the word of a professional liar that I had promised it to him, shortly after we met. Or possibly the year after that. Or, no hold on, it might have been the year after that. Who can tell. He couldn't even get that aspect straight under cross examination.

In 2008 after weeks of heavy rain the Thames washed over its banks at Thameside and the basement level of my home flooded. I came downstairs and felt a squish underfoot. Soon after water entered at the rate of about one inch an hour, covering the entire floor area, some carpeted, some tiled, with up to one foot of water. In 2008 Krasnopovich was still the named Insured party. He called the brokers within minutes of seeing the damage and his first task was to authorize the Insurers to talk to me from which point forward I handled the claim. The Loss Adjusters appointed were Gab Robins, the same as in 2014, and the Insurer then, as in 2014, was the AXA. In terms of a comparable circumstance for insurance purposes, this was as like for like as it is possible to imagine. The flood of 2008 and the flood of 2014.

In 2008 Krasnopovich was living with me and the policy was in his sole name. Two points are clear in a claim of this type.

1. A flooded property (with foul water, soaked carpets and no heating) is uninhabitable and

2. The property should be reinstated to its pre incident condition.

Obviously, one cannot live in a flooded property and the policy cover provides for alternative housing on a like for like basis. At that time equivalent housing in my locale was £3,500pm. I found a rental property within a day after the flood and Insurers agreed to pay rehousing within days of the claim progressing. We moved to a three-bed rental property, a short walk from my home. Convenient for monitoring the works progress and within a brief time to minimize the inconvenience to the affected residents. The Loss Adjusters arrived within two days following the flood. Following my instruction Krasnopovich had called the AXA and named me as the person authorized to handle the claim so I was able to run the claim directly.

The obvious cause of the flood was determined to be defective tanking. The remedy, to return the property to its pre-incident condition was to strip out the lining of the basement level and re tank it, before replacing the interior. An area of approximately 900 sq. feet including two top-spec bathrooms. The contents lost were all replaced as well. Approximately £50,000 of contents. The works took 9 months to complete. Insurers paid all the costs as laid out in the policy. Rehousing, replacing contents, and restoring the property to its pre-incident condition. The total amount of the claim with rehousing was some £300,000. Money paid by confirmation from the Loss Adjusters into the policy holders account. Nico Krasnopovich. The flood of 2014 was as close to identical in its nature to that of 2008 as can be imagined. It rained heavily for weeks. The Thames rose higher every passing day. And then on the 8th of February, the whole area flooded. An event so severe it made International news. TV news networks stationed cameras on the Bridge overlooking Thameside to record the moment when the water breached the road. In my home, exactly as in 2008, the basement level flooded, contents were soaked. Wall to wall carpeting under many inches of foul water. The tanking was breached. Water came in the drain side of the building, flooding the boiler area, and shorting out the boiler. (Irreparably.)

The emergency sump pump put in place to relieve pressure on the tanking, blew from the overload. This was an unprecedented amount of water rushing in, supplemented by the backflowing waste drains serving Thames Water. Once the sump pump was overwhelmed, the pressure relief on the fabric was ended, the water pressure rose to a critical level and the tanking was breached. The bottom level flooded, including foul water from the Thames water drains and with no heating to even dry the property out once the flood waters had been pumped out, the property became uninhabitable. Unlike the flood of 2008, in which I dealt with the Loss

Adjusters, this time it was Krasnopovich acting as the Insured party. And I was very much in his hands with regard to progressing the claim with an entirely predictable outcome.

Looking back five years later 'the facts' enjoy the benefit of hindsight. Krasnopovich ensured that the Insurance cover I had did not pay out one penny to me.

He achieved this by lying.

Repeatedly.

At the time of writing I have still not received not one penny for that flood claim. No rehousing costs were paid. Not even one night in one hotel. No contents were replaced. Not even the carpets soaked by the flood water. And it is a simple fact that the property was not restored to its pre-incident condition causing me consequential costs by now measured in millions. We can look back at several letters I wrote at that time to Krasnopovich in which I have detailed of his legal position as the Lessor and insured party because he had not transferred the freehold back to me, and had cancelled my Insurance cover.

In three separate letters he was given a cost-free opportunity to;

1.) return the freehold to me and let me take over the claim from there.

2.) be indemnified from any liability in the future relating to his fiduciary responsibilities as Freeholder.

3.) end his malicious and deceitful litigation and allow the child to see me.

He elected to reject that opportunity so that he could continue with his beneficial entitlement claim in which the only document supporting his claim was the freehold in his name. He chose therefore to accept full liability for all that followed, even knowing that being the named freeholder made him liable for the clause;

'*Make up any Insurance shortfall out of freeholders own resources.*'

My letters to him put him on notice of his fiduciary responsibilities as freeholder. To act in my best interest. By bringing an action against me as he did, he breached those fiduciary responsibilities. And did so on notice that the costs if it all went 'south' would exceed three million pounds. Which is exactly what happened. I say, he elected to accept liability for that bill by his decision to claim he owned the Freehold and proceed with an action so clearly at odds with the fiduciary responsibility of the Freeholder. At the time of writing, the bill breaks down as follows:

£250,000 in hard costs making the property habitable post flood

£3,000,000 in losses related to the failure to sell the property after winning 'sole conduct of sale' leaving me solely responsible for all costs
£1,000,000 for the loss of my rental income business. The income I would have had of Krasnopovich had not forced the eviction of my tenants and forced the sale of my property.

In addition, consider damages for the California breach of privacy offense (Krasnopovich by his own admission broke two penal statues in California law in 2014) and the Flaherty judgment in 2015 that indemnified Krasnopovich from prosecution in a foreign country, and labelling me as a compromised parent in her judgment, would have reached £1,000,000

The illegal use of copyright photos after legally accepting terms and conditions for use. £2,000,000

For damaging my son's life with his parent by lying and producing a court judgment that is child abuse, costing my son many years of life with his parent and causing him untold harm in this process, I say £10,000,000 is a minimum settlement figure.

Although, as I do not know at the time of writing whether I will even see my son again or what harm has been visited on him since I last saw him, that figure may well require upward revision to reflect the magnitude of the harm done as a consequence of actions in family-court by members of family law. All of this though is mere speculation because, the financial consequences of the events described mean I have no funds to pay a lawyer and without a lawyer to sue for damages, I am unable to accept Krasnopovich's offer to 'sue me'. All that I can do is record the numbers in case at some point in the future the law changes in the UK and the protection afforded the miscreants in my matter leads to formal accountability. While lawyers and deputy Judges remain above the law, no matter how egregious their conduct, I can do no more than record the what where why and how-much of the past six years. The total I have received to date is nothing. Larceny on a grand scale. Any number of frauds including perjury and breach of SRA ethical code. Breach of fiduciary responsibility in breach of a trust agreement by a member of family-law, and an officer of the court, expected to be held to a higher standard than a regular fraud. I imagine this achievement by Krasnopovich, Clock, Hazelwood and Flaherty goes down as the most irregular judgment in family-courts stained history.

The flood added a tremendous stressor to an already stressful time. I was suddenly homeless, living in hotels, looking at a minimum of 6 months of work to repair my home, and having to pay enormous legal costs to defend against Krasnopovichs' BE claim and now having to make up shortfall on Insurance out of my own pocket. In the first costs schedule, some £250,000 out of my pocket to make up Insurance shortfall. Plus interest, plus a great deal of bad feeling towards the AXA Insurance for being complicit in this conduct. As I was in year 28 of my ownership of the building and as I paid for Insurance cover that year just as I had every previous year, I called the AXA directly. In principle, here was a customer of 28 years standing with every right to expect the service paid for in full at the start of every one of those 28 years of policy cover. None the less, when I called the AXA they would not speak to me because they had an instruction not to.

"We can only speak to the named policy holder."

Although the Freehold agreement requires each lessee to be named on the policy, Krasnopovich had failed to do so. When he cancelled my paid-for policy in October 2013 he put the building cover in his sole name. And that was the end of the possibility of me talking directly to the AXA even though he was required as Landlord to name each Lessee (me) and the Lender (The bank) in the policy cover.

Depending on how you feel about paying insurance for 28 years, I suggest this decision may reflect poorly on the AXA's client care. I say it brings the AXA insurance into disrepute as I wrote to them detailing the circumstances of Krasnopovichs' fraud.

They were *'Unable to comment'* as I was *'not the named policy holder.'* But, I pointed out he had a duty to name me on the policy and was in breach of a legal fiduciary obligation by not doing so. But no.

The AXA chose not to pay anything.

Empowered in this way buy the AXA's decision to take instruction only from him, Krasnopovich deliberately spoiled the Insurance claim, in breach of the fiduciary responsibilities contained in the very title he used to cancel my policy cover, acting in bad faith to deliberately cause me maximum financial hardship to affect my position in respect of the litigation he was pursuing. His 'so sue me' reply was made knowing he could impose financial harm on me to the extent that I would not be able to afford legal redress. And that has proven to be effective, successful lawyering by a member of British family-law with a little help from his friends.

In the week directly before the flood I was in the USA, visiting restorative wellness activities in California that included daily vitamin D sunshine, positive reinforcement activity, like yoga and tennis and long beach walks, playing my guitar and enjoying a healthy diet. I had my return flight to the UK booked for February 20. My intention then was to return to family-court to win custody of my son. I had some savings left to enable this and I felt restored to my former confidence after my effective visit to California, far away from the constant stressors visited on me by Krasnopovich, Clock and their aggressive goon of a process server.

I learned about the flood on 8th February 2013 after a call from the house sitter, Richard, who was living in my home during my absence.

"I have some bad news for you" said Richard.

I returned immediately, literally, on the next flight. I was back in Thameside 20 hours after the flood and set about deciding what to do. Meanwhile Richard and my handyman, Gareth and the builder Cliff had all attended the flooded property and effected various remedies. Attempting to mitigate the flood damage. Krasnopovich had only three months previously cancelled my Insurance cover and refused to return my Freehold title. He had also already begun his house claim 'TOLATA' litigation, the *'she promised me half of her house'* claim, and his raging antagonism along with my awareness of his intrinsic dishonesty meant I understood all too well that he was not going to progress the Insurance claim in my interests.

No matter what fiduciary obligations required that he do so. He is after all, ruler of his universe. Untouchable in law. And by now I had learned that he would not stop at anything to win what he perceived was his right. To extract a six-figure sum from me before letting me see my son.

Back in England 24 hours after Richard's call, standing in the flooded ruin of my multi-million-pound home, I had to consider the wider picture; the most important aspect of which was ending litigation for the best interests of the child and then getting my home repaired. I spent an afternoon in my Hotel room on my laptop running numbers and after many hours of mindful considered thought, came up with the best-case solution. Based on; what is best for the child.

I wrote to Krasnopovich by registered letter and e mail on Feb 16th, proposing that;

1.) he not claim on Insurance. Instead,

2.) he should return the freehold to me, as he was required to do in any event, and

3.) I would repair the property without any claim against him.

4.) He would be indemnified for any future claim following from his fiduciary failures.

In return

5.) he was invited to end his bogus beneficial entitlement claim and I would not pursue any claim against his business or return of monies loaned to him.

A full and final end to any litigation. Enabling us to agree

6.) immediate visitation for Sam and me. Starting again with a clean slate, putting the child first. Entering into a discussion on who would be the best option for Sam's primary carer.

7.) Each side would accept their own legal costs to that point. And

8.) I would accept the costs in repairing my property. Keeping his name clear from Insurance claims. And keeping my property clear from raised Insurance premiums.

Even at that stage, on that date, February 16th, 2014, here was an opportunity for him to not litigate and put the child's interests to the fore. As well as to support his own best interests, being free of the responsibility that comes with being the Insured party on a claim that would likely exceed £500,000 and a fiduciary breach claim with a potential to exceed £3 million. He knew, from the flood of 2008, as well as my notice to him in my letter of February 16th, 2013, that The London Basement Company would charge in the region of £500,000 to re-tank the basement level. Quite how Clock saw fit to not seize this opportunity to end litigation makes plain that Krasnopovich and Clock were primarily concerned with causing me maximal financial disadvantage rather than settling any dispute with the child's interests as a factor. Having watched this process close up for the previous ten years, I knew my gamble would be on his paternal responsibility preventing Krasnopovich from playing the win-at-all costs game that is his model of family law practice. I feel foolish now, looking back and imagining I was still that naive at that time to think he would have considered the child's best interests. Of course he did not. He just ploughed on with the same demand. Pay me the six-figure sum and you can see Sam whenever you want.

I was living in a Hotel throughout this post flood period waiting for the rehousing money to come through from the Insurance policy. I chose a nice Hotel, close to my home, in keeping with my residential requirements. I had to have the facility to house Sam, should I win any visitation, as I expected would be the case. I knew that for some 27 years I had paid for Insurance that included like for like housing and was not prepared to move into a Holiday Inn. Finding suitable accommodations in the extreme short notice turned out to be a little bit more expensive than a bargain. I figured American Express air miles would be my compensation for fronting the costs that Insurance would pay. My bill on my credit card in the first month for Hotels was over £5,000. Of course all my usual bills on my home, like mortgage repayments, continued. The Insurance policy cover I had in place for the previous 27 years provided for alternate accommodation while the property was being restored to its pre incident condition and I saw no reason why this claim would be any different to the flood claim of 2008. After all, this is why we pay for Insurance. If you are made homeless you need a home to live in and Insurance cover pays that cost. This accommodations provision had been in every one of my Insurance cover policies for 28 years. I chose my accommodations responsibly within that understanding. After all, I had been with the AXA for well-over 20 years (at that time) and had a previous experience of being homeless and rehoused by Insurance, after my fire claim in 2001. When the AXA agreed to rehouse me within a day in a like-for-like rental accommodation. With an interim payment to cover my immediate costs. I knew what to expect from Insurance both because I had experienced a claim before and because I have a financial adviser guiding the extent of my policy cover.

Did I have rehousing on a like for like basis with the AXA Insurance for the flood of February 2014?

Yes. I believed that is what I paid for and what I expected and what the policy made provision for. I had no doubt that the AXA would pay out both my rehousing costs as well as the costs to return my property to its pre incident condition. Which I knew immediately would include re-tanking. Because; that is why the property flooded. The tanking failed. The only way to repair failed tanking is to replace it from scratch. I had already been through the Insurance company policy on this exact point before. With the AXA. Their surveyor had visited the property and confirmed 'The tanking was breached.'

Krasnopovich did not reply to my written offer. About two weeks later, he gave me his answer by triggering the Insurance claim, which I had made clear he should not do. (As he was the trustee freeholder and bound to follow my instruction.) Even if he disputed that, and claimed he was the actual freeholder and not a trustee, he was still bound by fiduciary responsibility between Lessor (The Freehold owner named at the Land registry, which was Krasnopovich) and Lessee (The Leasehold named owner named at the Land registry, which was in all three leaseholds, myself). Not only did he act against my request and my interests, he triggered the claim in a manner ideally suited to ensuring it would fail. Starting with the late notice of incident to Insurer. He delayed responding to appointment calls from the appointed Loss Adjuster. He used speculative language on the 'possibility' of an incident at the property in the notice to claim document. All clearly done deliberately to prejudice the claim, to cause me the maximum financial hardship this opportunity provided him with as the sole named Insured party, using his position to maximum effect. He was the sole named party because he breached the fiduciary obligation to name the Lessee and the Lendor on the policy cover. I found it hard to believe that Clock advised him to take that route. On the face of it, a malicious choice that so transparently abused a 5-year-old child, leaving me living in a hotel and requiring that I pay hundreds of thousands of pounds to family lawyers. A bankrupting position that at the same time exposed him to an enormous claim for the multiple breaches that placed both him and his lawyer in this position.

Why? Just for the money because he wanted a hundred grand?

Possibly yes, but more significantly, he did not want me paying a top-drawer family-lawyer, like a Fiona Shackleton, to pursue custody of Sam. Which would have been my next step if I had the funds. To win custody and be done with his disgusting child abusing deceits.

The more time passed without my seeing Sam because of Krasnopovich's obstruction, the more acrimony built towards him, from me and from my family and friends. My earlier hopes that he would at some stage realize the harm he was causing me in his use of visitation to win his financial goals would be upsetting to Sam, would override his adversarial stance and he would agree to encourage the relationship between Sam and the mother who raised him. More than once I realized that hope, whenever explored, only ever met disappointment. Not once since removing my son from my home in June 2013 has Krasnopovich encouraged as much as one skype call without attaching a financial demand. By not once, I mean; not on one single occasion. Krasnopovich and Clock have a 100% record in obstructing any and all visitation to the best of their ability, which, it turns out, as family law professionals, is considerable. All these years and countless letters later, the AXA insurance have not paid me one penny for the flood of my home in 2014. Not even reimbursing the invoice I paid for the emergency crew who went out on the day of the flood to put in emergency pumps and plug back-flowing drains, mitigating even worse damage. Eventually I went on to pay far in excess of £250,000 in making up the Insurance shortfall, to make the ground floor flat habitable. And that does not include the re tanking. By 2019, when the failure to properly repair was made clear in the failure to achieve any forced sale as ordered by the court, I calculated my losses arising from Krasnopovich, the named Insured party and the AXA failing to repair my property, to be in excess of £3 million.

As events unfolded, I was never able to return to my home. I stayed on in the rental agreement I had in California and then came the Flaherty hearing, ordering that it be sold with Krasnopovich given 50%, including no reference to the money I spent making up the Insurance shortfall. An acrimony generating judgment made by a competent, financially aware judge, considering the child's best interests?

Flaherty would later award her family law colleague '*Sole Conduct of sale*' on my property. (A property I bought in 1986, when Krasnopovich was 14.) With this 'sole conduct of sale' Krasnopovich appointed agents who succeeded in making the property the longest running listing on Rightmove without selling, even at a fire sale price. During this period, as months went by with me receiving no rental income, because Flaherty ruled the tenants had to be evicted for the forced sale, I had to keep paying the mortgage or default, which became inevitable after almost three years of following legal advice to support the sale and keep paying the mortgage. Another mistake that cost some £90,000 I could have avoided just by foreclosing the day after the judgment by switch judge Flaherty. During this process, from the end of the Flaherty judgment in 2015 up until 2019, I had to keep paying a property lawyer to argue every step of the way to ensure I received at least something from the forced sale of my property. Which he was now not selling. Evidently because he was earning 8% interest on the Flaherty award and benefitted more from not selling for the advantage it gave him in causing me financial hardship, knowing that without funds I could not hire a lawyer to win custody. To make the point clear, Flaherty wrote by court order that I was not even allowed to enter' my own home.

Did I mention that clever part of Flaherty's child centric order from April 2015? I was forbidden by court order from entering 28B. Her version of a just order included me having to pay to stay in Hotels if I wanted to see my son in the UK, while the flat I had owned since 1986 stood empty.

When I visited the UK, I found myself in the position of paying for accommodations, while paying the mortgage on a property that was no longer generating rental income for me, having been made vacant by court order, that I was not even allowed to enter. And at the same time, aware that every time I wrote a letter to Clock in trying to arrange visitation for Sam, he was making 8% interest on the huge costs award Flaherty gave him for abusing my son. Does that seem like the appropriate person to be negotiating visitation? Krasnopovich insisted on it.

What I saw throughout this litigation was one member of family law, a barrister who passed the Deputy District Judge exam, rewarding another member of family law, a solicitor, who hires barristers for family law work, both making handsome return out of abusing Sam. All done in flagrant disregard of the child's best interests and complete confidence in their mutual protection from accountability. Flaherty's confidence in the law protecting her anonymity being both complete and at the root of her deviant judgment. As the cherry on top of Flaherty's ill-considered judgment is this; consider that my primary income then was the rental income I received from the three flats I had rented out. Flaherty awarded 50% of the rental income from my properties to Krasnopovich. Obviously, when making this decision as a judge in family law, Flaherty knew that wouldn't in any way increase animosity between the parents. And as is obvious to even a casual onlooker, awarding 50% of my income to someone I had declared to be a liar and a thief for bringing this bogus claim against me, to the extent that I had multiple witnesses able to prove the dishonest foundation of his claim, was a decision made with the child's best interests to the fore? Meanwhile, his rental income from his flat was unaffected by Flaherty judgment? A decision by a sensible and well-informed deputy district judge happy to promote herself as *"Lawyer; Juvenile delinquent; lover of champagne and fun"* in her social media profile while ruling on cases in family court involving children's futures.

16 After the flood

27 years of paying the AXA for Buildings and contents cover. And now this

Months passed after the February flood in 2014 without any Insurance cover kicking in. Without even any interim payment towards rental of a temporary home, Hotel life was becoming beyond my credit card limit. Something had to be done. It was clear that Krasnopovich, the sole named insured party on the Policy was undermining the claim to maximize my discomfort. At the outset of the delayed claim, the Loss Adjuster originally agreed to the obvious rehousing request; that I needed rehousing because the flooded house was uninhabitable. After Krasnopovich triggered the claim, in March 2014 I had a meeting at my property with Lars the Loss Adjuster following which it seemed we were on course for the housing payment. I explained my rehousing needs, and the costs involved. It was obvious to Lars the Loss adjuster that rehousing was necessary because our meeting took place in a mold infested basement that stank of excrement and had no heating. Following that meeting in the property, Lars invited my costs for rehousing and having told Lars that I envisaged the costs of a like-for-like rental property to be more cost efficient than living in Hotels I contacted my letting agents to find a comparable let in the area. That letter from the letting agents arrived soon after and I forwarded it to Lars the Loss adjuster. The amount for a like-for-like similar property was £4,000 pm and I had a choice of one available for immediate occupation. We were at that time, on that day, ready to go. In the time between me locating the rental property and Lars inviting the rehousing cost, the named policy holder was consulted. Lars called Krasnopovich to confirm the rehousing position which I had only that morning gone through with him. The £4,000 pm rental available for immediate occupation two roads down from my property.

In that conversation I learned that Krasnopovich informed Lars the Loss Adjuster that I would not need rehousing on the basis that the property was habitable.

How do I know for a fact that Krasnopovich deliberately and maliciously stopped the payment of rehousing by Insurance, causing me a loss that would eventually reach £60,000 in rehousing costs? Because Lars wrote to me, to retract the proposal for the vacant rental nearby. In this letter he explained that he had learned from the named policy that the property was habitable. Krasnopovich told him that he did not agree that the property was uninhabitable and would not support a claim for rehousing. This deceit would get far worse when it came to my application to house Sam. I showed that the house had no heating, that black mold was creeping up the walls and that the stench of excrement permeated up to the first floor. I had an inspector from health and Safety visit and complete a report, in which the health risk was made clear. It is not safe to go into this property, let alone live in it. Black mold is toxic. No hot water. Etc etc...... yet when the time came where I finally had Sam for a four-day visit, I pointed out that I would have to pay for a Hotel, because it was not safe to house a child in this dangerously uninhabitable building, Krasnopovich stuck to his guns. Of course it will be fine for Sam to stay in that black mold infested house. Just as long as Insurance don't pay Andrea any money. That is a typically indicative example of his parenting consideration. On the face of it, gambling with his son's health just to win a point against me.

Denying me rehousing funds was an opportunist error by Lars, based on a lie by Krasnopovich. I pointed out that it brought the AXA Insurance into disrepute, making plain the exact factual matrix of why. Lars put forward that I could live in the upper level of the apartment. (Not withstanding that in a previous claim incident in 2008, the same Loss adjustor, Gab Robbins, and the same Insurer, The AXA, provided immediate rehousing for the duration of the remedial works. Because. Simply put, that is the Insurance cover I paid for and had every right to expect. Like for like accommodations until the property was restored to its pre incident condition.)

28A is a two-level home. The lower level was under water and smelling of foul water. The ground level was not underwater, but was not habitable. It was a damp mess that stank of rotting damp from the flood below. It had no bath (I like to bath), it had no heating and I like hot baths. The boiler was unrepairable from flood damage and it was deep in wintertime. It was abundantly clear that my flooded home was not a habitable dwelling but it is not difficult to see why a Loss Adjuster would take the opportunity to not pay out rehousing when the named policy holder says it is unnecessary. Especially when considering the cause of the flood was already known to be blown tanking and replacing the tanking would take a minimum six months. So Lars knew the rehousing was going to be a sizeable chunk of the claim. Saying 28A was habitable to Lars the Loss Adjuster was more malice by Krasnopovich and his way of adding more stress to my position when trying to defend against his court action for half of my home. It impaired my ability to see my son and the financial pressure it added to my situation was considerable. It is a simple observation here that if Lars the Loss adjuster believed the property was habitable and wished to dispute my assurance that it was not, all he had to do to remove any credibility from my claim was agree a meeting in the property. And show me that his confident assertions were in fact provable to the naked eye. He did not because? His claim of the house being habitable could not have survived a three-minute walk through.

This on top of all else is simply disgraceful fraud attaching to the reputation of the AXA Insurance. Taking advantage of the situation where the lying lawyer was the sole named policy holder and choosing to ignore my very real notice of the details affecting the claim.

It left me with a big housing cost on top of which I had no agreement to pay for repairs to the house which I knew would be a bill similar to the identical flood in 2008. The re-tanking alone would be a sum in the region of £500,000. The tanking was blown which meant the building had to be taken back to the soil, which required re installing new tanking, with everything put back afterwards. This included all the pipework for plumbing, the central heating boiler, the electrical wiring. Two top of range bathrooms with baths and showers. And everything you associate with a 900 sq. foot area of top of range furnishing. Knowing what I do about this type of claim in this exact property, there is no way that the Insurers could have seen off their liability for less than £500,000. Realistically with contents and fittings, a claim of £600,000.

In the identical flood conditions that occurred in 2008 (when Krasnopovich was living with me at no cost to himself), the same Insurers, the AXA, and same loss adjusters, Gab Robbins, paid to restore the property to its pre-incident condition. This included rehousing on a like for like basis as detailed in the policy cover. And that is when I moved to the Thames Road rental. In terms of precedent, this claim was identical in every way to the flood of 2008 excepting for one thing. Krasnopovich was dealing with the Insurance and not myself. As a result it was all too easy for Krasnopovich to sour the claim completely, meaning to date I have not received one penny from Insurers and to date the property has not sold because it was never repaired post flood. I say it will never achieve the target trigger price Flaherty listed for the forced sale because Flaherty has deliberately made a poor ruling based on her willingness to serve deceit. The liability for repairing my home formed a fiduciary responsibility for the Freehold Lessor. And that, as we know from his claim in Flaherty's court, was Krasnopovich. He claimed it was his in Flaherty's court. It is right there in the transcript. So – ether he is guilty of perjury – or he is liable for the shortfall in Insurance that forms a part of the Freeholders liability.

Clearly, in the Lessor agreement, the Lessor was obliged to make up any shortfall in Insurance cover out of 'His own resources.' On the one hand, he was claiming to be Freeholder to win a beneficial entitlement claim. On the other, he was now not liable for the obligations of the freeholder, because, it would cost him, potentially millions. What to do?

How about get his Judge friend to indemnify him in court from any claim I might bring against him after the hearing? Bear that one in mind for later in this story. Could it really be that transparent?

Remember, *Means Motive and Opportunity.*

He had the means with a family law membership.

He had the motive, because he was Freeholder, liable for a million-pound claim against him personally.

And he had the opportunity, when he saw Flaherty switch cases to enable him to get rid of the witnesses to his deceitful claim and accept he was Freeholder for the support it gave his beneficial entitlement claim, but ignore the fact that it was perjury in her court that also made him liable for a multimillion-pound damages claim. All he had to do was get Flaherty to make me promise to not bring any action against him. Making it a court order, so if I did, I would be in contempt. Except. I did not make the 'Promise' in her court. It's not in the transcript. They simply made up this most unlikely indemnity. That I would forgive this magnitude of debt for no reason, because that's how they roll. Who is going to challenge them, exposing this very clear lie, when its written as a court order? Ta dah. Contempt.

Meanwhile, after more than two months of living in Hotels, I was down over £10,000 in accommodation costs alone and I had not seen my son and I was facing an average of £10,000 a month in legal bills from my marvelous family law member, David Clam, who was looking increasingly like a flubbering idiot of a beached whale, incapable of winning me as much as one single night's visitation with my son while still able to generate monthly invoices in five figures. He was no help at all.

I had the help of my Priory therapist, and my neighbors and friends were amazing, but the truth is, I was homeless, and hemorrhaging money at an unsustainable rate and getting nowhere with seeing my son. I needed some help in a situation that could not go on and that is when the cavalry arrived. Philip stepped in, offering to rent me a level of his home on a six-month letting agreement, at the same rate as a UK rental, on a credit basis, to be paid when I received the Insurance payout, which was imminent. This credit agreement was truly a life saver. At least I had a roof over my head. And I had room for both sons to stay with me. I had a safe place to live where I could gather my thoughts and mount my defense against having my home, my primary source of income and my son stolen from me by British family-law members. This stressful unpleasantness of the Insurance claim dragged out over an 18-month period during which time I repeatedly asked from payments for my rehousing and for payments of the costs I outlaid in mitigating the flood damage. Invoices went in accord with the Lessor Lessee agreement from me to the Lessor, Krasnopovich, who simply ignored every request.

In the first six months after February 2014, I was down some £40,000 in legal invoices just trying to see my son and find out where he was; while at the same time I was down some £50,000 in rehousing and flood repair costs with not one penny paid. Letters and emails flew in one direction; from me to Krasnopovich and to the AXA Insurance. And then after about eight months of zero payments and zero proper cover by the AXA Insurance, the claim was suspended entirely.

What?

Insurers, the AXA, became suspicious of Krasnopovich after Lars the loss adjuster investigating Krasnopovichs historical dishonesty, located an Insurance cover application filled out by Krasnopovich in 2010 in which he had falsified information. In the application for cover he had not disclosed the flood of 2008, (A claim of some £300,000 that was paid by the AXA to Krasnopovich) which was required as a condition for the cover. It looked like Krasnopovich had been caught out at last.

This deceitful cover application was a repetition of the first Policy cover in his name, in 2003, in which he made the same erroneous claim however this 2010 incident was different in one key point. In 2003 he did not live in my home when the previous (fire) claim was made, so technically he was not lying in saying HE had made no previous claim then. This time though he was the one who made the claim in 2008, who lived in the property and who received well over £300,000 from the AXA for rehousing and repairs. Yet this same £300,000+ beneficiary had signed in 2010 that he had never claimed before.

Busted. In his own handwriting. I admit I felt a flush of relief. Finally this lying thief had been hoist on the petard of his own disingenuity. The AXA instructed solicitors to investigate Krasnopovich. And it looked like that was that. But no. Not so fast. This is a gifted liar, adept at playing the law game. Krasnopovich immediately instructed an equally weighty City firm specializing in this type of Insurance fraud litigation and the two city firms cancelled each other out. Four weeks of furious letter writing followed, in which I was excluded, because, I was not named on the policy and so they had no obligation to me (Apart from the fact I paid in full every year for 27 years and had disclosed the fact that I was in fact the owner and Krasnopovich a trustee freeholder obligated by fiduciary responsibility to follow my instructions, which he had breached.) The AXA chose to ignore me, although their lawyers did invite me to comment, assuming I guess that I would want to see Krasnopovich go down. I elected not to do this though. My property lawyer advised me to stay out of it. And that's what I did. Meanwhile the two City law firms ran up a nice bill reaching a commercial agreement. And once again Krasnopovich got away with it. A deal was made. But what deal I hear you ask?

Although this litigation put a hold on the claim for the flood repairs, whatever outcome was agreed between Krasnopovich and the AXA, through their City law firms excluded repair works to my home. I was not involved in that agreement and all I know is that the commercial agreement they reached with the Freeholder and his lawyers meant the AXA were off the hook in paying my cover for the insurance on the house.

Which I say speaks for itself and brings the AXA into disrepute.

For the avoidance of doubt, since the flood, at the time of writing, all these years later, I have still not received one penny from the AXA for the flood of my home. After some 27 years (at that time) of being a fully paid up Insured property owner.

The clear and obvious cause of the flood was identified by the Surveyor sent by the AXA at the outset, in writing, as a tanking failure following the huge pressure brought to bear on the shell of the building by the unprecedented rise in the Thames water table. Despite this written statement by the AXA paid surveyor, the decision by the interested parties, Krasnopovich, the Loss Adjuster and the AXA Insurance, with the two law firms on either side can be summarized in one line.

Do not pay Andrea, the owner, who has been insured on this property for 27 years with the same level of cover, one penny. Instead came up with one of the all-time greats in Insurance history. They called it '*Jeff the Plumber*' dunnit.

The legal matter between the AXA and Krasnopovich was settled when Krasnopovich reached an agreement with the AXA to not claim on the policy for 28A, restoring to pre incident condition and providing the full policy cover requirements, in exchange for them not pursuing him.

Win win for both parties. Far more cost effective than paying out on the policy. Accordingly, my lawyer received notice that the claim was now over. This was about 14 months post flood. I was still living in the rental in California, waiting for the Insurance payment to meet my rental debt and to repair my home so I could return to live in it. Shortly after this letter saying the claim was over, the AXA sent in a '*man in a white van*' to paint some walls and called it job done. For good measure, this chap, the man in van restoring the property to its pre incident condition to the Lessors satisfaction, left all the lights on, running up a £600-pound electric bill in an empty house. I only discovered this when I visited the UK four months later and saw the lights were on, which explained the £600 electric bill in an empty house. The cause of the flood had been modified to a new version of events in which Lars and the AXA explained that that the flood was not caused by the river Thames flood at all.

Their position, when I first heard about it made me literally laugh out loud. A whole new tack in ridiculous avoidance of liability that brings the AXA into comedic disrepute. What could they say about a property flooded after their own surveyor pointed out the cause that was quite obvious to everyone who knew the circumstances of the property and the flood of February 8, 2014, because of breached tanking?

My lawyer sent me their letter concluding any liability for the claim with their findings in full and final closure that ensured I received not one penny. And here is their finding. After almost two years and not one penny paid.

"Jeff the plumber done it."

They explained, very briefly, the flood was caused by Jeff the plumber who pierced the tanking and caused the flood. There would be no remedial works to the cause of the flood because Insurers expert had been with Peter Cox, the tanking company who did the work in 2008; and warrantied this work. These two interested parties agreed that the plumber had installed a pipe incorrectly, damaging the tanking, and that had let the water in. They referred to him as Jeff the plumber. (Not even spelling his name correctly.) Geoff (the owner of TED heating) the plumber who did the original fit, a £25,000 plumbing and heating job in 2005, was my first call when I heard this outlandish claim.

His reply, copied verbatim here;

"They're having a laugh Andrea. They are trying to con you. I do these fits with tanked properties a lot. I always go in before the tanking. Peter Cox, who did your tanking, went in after my piping. It is impossible that my work caused the flood because I was done before he began. And if I had in any way fucked up, I have insurance. I do this for a living and I have done it for a long time. I would have taken care of it if it was my fault. You know the people I work with. I'm not going to kill my reputation and my business I have built over fifteen years of hard work by dodging out on a claim if I made a mistake. I didn't fuck up. These guys are just trying it on. You know exactly why the property flooded. This is the first time I have heard of this. Don't you think they would have called me if they thought it was me, to discuss their story? They didn't. Ask yourself why. Because they are trying to con you."

I asked Geoff to put in writing his position and impression of the accusation against him, which he did. Geoff the plumber confirms that
1.) He did not cause the flood.
2.) He was never once contacted by Insurer or Landlord. And
3.) If he had caused any damage, he would have claimed repairs on his insurance.

For clarity. Krasnopovich signed off the Insurance claim because the cause of the flood was determined to be a bad fit by the plumber in 2005. They did not even bother to check the spelling of the plumber's name.
Beyond ridiculous.
This is the conduct of **THE AXA INSURANCE.**
The property had flooded three times since the original tanking job in 2005. The tanking was the cause of the flood. Here we have the tanking guy blaming the original pipe fitting when the tanking goes in after the plumbing. The tanking job in question in the 2014 flood was done by Peter Cox. Peter Cox stood with me in the property in 2008 looking at the flood damage after the flood that year and when I asked him why the property had flooded, his reply was *"There is only one reason a tanked property floods. That is an error in the tanking job."*
The AXA surveyor made the same observation when he came later the 2014 flood and put his find in his report.

'Our surveyor has now also confirmed that the tanking system previously installed was defective and/or inadequate which has resulted in the incident occurring.'

Hey, let's forget all that fact stuff. I know we have to provide policy cover that this customer has paid for for 27 years and thinks she has a right to expect, but we have this great opportunity here because she doesn't have her name on the policy cover and the named Insured party who we caught out making a fraudulent application, agrees to not claim So let's tell her *Jeff the Plumber done it*. What's she going to do about it? It's not as if the AXA Insurance will ever be called out to explain

The 'Jeff the plumber' dismissal of the claim raised concerns on several levels. If insurers identified the plumbing company as liable then it follows that they would contact the culpable party to complete the remedial works on their insurance. If they believed it was 'Jeff' (Whose name is spelled Geoff) they would have contacted the company owner, and at least learned how to spell his name.

Secondly, if the cause was deficient plumbing, then the repairs should show that this work to repair this deficient plumbing was done.

There was no plumbing repair. No documentation or evidence in support of this Jeff the plumber card. Just a blanket dismissal of the claim, signed off by Krasnopovich, with the AXA all too pleased to see the back of this headache claim. Secure in the reassurance that a lawyer was the sole named policy holder and able to provide the guarantee's they wished to hear to not pay out on the claim. Meanwhile though, despite washing their hands of the claim, the questions of the Insurance matter and freehold issues, in which the trustee of the freehold, and sole named policy holder, Krasnopovich had fiduciary responsibilities, would not go away. Not for me at least.

If the cause was 'Jeff the Plumber' then his company has liability Insurance and the fiduciary responsibility of landlord Krasnopovich would include having the plumbers Insurance pay for the works. None of this happened because Krasnopovich and the Insurers did a deal, exonerating him from the fraudulent application in exchange for not paying the claim for the 2014 flood.

Did Krasnopovich deliberately ruining my Insurance cover, costing me many hundreds of thousands and making me homeless in the UK increase animosity that is in Sam's best interests? Did handling of this policy by the AXA Insurance bring their company into disrepute? After 28 years of paying full cover for buildings and contents for my home with the AXA Insurance entitle me to cover for this costly flood damage? Especially as I had paid for contents and cover for the year including the flood. Building and contents. Accepted by the AXA and paid in full. Providing exactly the same cover as I had in every previous year. Like for like rehousing. And restoring the property to its pre-incident condition.

From the many letters written on this subject, here is one capturing the average flavor. From myself to Krasnopovich's lawyer, Tim Clock.

---

10 September, 2015
From: Andrea Lee
To: Tim Clock

Mr. Clock,

As your client has not proposed any intermediary for contact and as there are matters requiring his attention as the registered Lessor of my home I am sending this to you for forwarding to your client. Mr. Clam has already provided the opportunity for your client to provide an alternative intermediary which he has failed to do.

Nico.

1. Below you will see correspondence from Lars Richter. You will see that he proposes 'sanitizing' the downstairs. I confirm this was never done. Hence his reference in correspondence to this being no obstacle to living upstairs is exposed as a lie.

You will see that he claims '*our surveyor has now also confirmed that the tanking system previously installed was defective and/or inadequate which has resulted in the incident occurring*' and yet in his proposed schedule of works which you signed off on there was no re-tanking element.

Clearly this is irresponsible as you know the tanking failed and yet you signed off on works that simply patch over the failed tanking, ensuring that the property has not been restored to its pre-incident condition. This is in breach of your obligations as the Lessor.

You will see from his correspondence that Lars Eichman does not even know what the room arrangement is on the ground floor. ('*You still have two bedrooms, two bathrooms and a kitchen that have not been affected.*')

In fact as you know, there is one (small) bedroom and one (extremely small) shower room. There is no bath on the ground floor.) **Lars Eichman never once visited the ground floor of 28A Thameside.** How does he know what it is there? You have had the opportunity to correct him on this from the outset, yet you have failed to do so. You are aware that toxic black mold consumes the area and that the inspections to the property by Lars Richter's agents have caused damage to the interior walls.

They have torn away entire sections of wall. Who is responsible for fixing that? The property now remains as uninhabitable for my purposes as it has been since 8 Feb 2014. It has no heating. It has remained empty all this time, unheated, with mold thriving. Despite my frequent requests for rehousing as is provided for in the terms of the Policy I have had not one penny towards my costs. You already have an indication of where these costs are at this time. I have been renting at a market equivalent rate for 11 Months. This is exactly as per precedent in a claim of this type and in this property (in 2008) and with exactly the same Loss Adjusters and the same Insurers, all of which is subject to the provisions of the policy providing 'Like for like rehousing'. If I do not begin receiving rehousing and insurance payments soon my debt in servicing the loans I am living off jeopardizes my solvency. I require confirmation of your intention in this regard as a matter of urgency.

2. I have no indication of why 11 Months have passed without any payment for my losses from the flood or even the flood mitigation invoices. Please give me the reason why you have not made any payments as you, the Lessor, are required to do. It appears that you are willfully disregarding the law instead of upholding your legal obligation.

3. I have been requesting sight of the current buildings policy renewal since November 2014. You have refused to correspond with Murray Simpson as the (4th) intermediary and you have not replied to the last email he sent you leaving me with no other way of communicating with you than through your solicitor.

I have in the interim paid the same amount for building Insurance as 2013 (£920 paid in December 2014 by bank transfer) in the assumption that you have secured the cover you are obligated to do and that you have included my name in the policy as you are obligated to do under the terms of the lease agreement. Please reply to Murray's letter without further delay dealing as it does with Freehold matters that are your fiduciary responsibility.

This payment concludes my obligation as the lessee for Insurance cover going forward for the next 12 months. (October 2014/2015) I have arranged separate contents cover for 28A and trust that you will not call Insurers to have them cancel that cover as you did in 2013.

4. I accept that you have refused to allow Sam to attend Ski School in Switzerland in February. His flights are non-refundable so, well done. Another bill for me. Another disappointment for Sam. Two weeks with his Mother in beautiful Wengen with ten days in a world class children's ski school giving him a solid foundation in skiing at a key age in this development. I am sure Sam will grow to thank you for putting his needs above your own will to win.

You won. He doesn't get to go on the trip I booked and paid for as I promised him I would do. I will arrange to travel to the UK to see him for his one-week holiday from the 14th of February returning him the following weekend. I am flying to the UK solely for this purpose with a non-transferable booking. Please confirm that you will not obstruct this visitation.

5. I will be in London in April and hope to have Sam for the weekend of the 17th. I will write to his headmaster regarding one or two days off school to enable a trip to the Countryside for a long weekend. His godfather Chris is likely to be with us at this time and is looking forward to seeing him. Please confirm that you will not obstruct this visitation.

6. I have booked Sam's travel to be with me for one month in July following his term break up as you have agreed to only this length of time. As I can't afford the travel costs involved following your impact on my net worth and as you are a high earner, please will you contribute 50% towards Sam's travel costs. You will appreciate that there is considerable additional expense in fitting my visitation with Sam around your convenience.

7. I have advised Sam's grandfather that you have refused to allow him to travel to South Africa to attend his 80th birthday despite the school agreeing to a 5 day leave of absence for this purpose. Evan has asked me to relay his grave disappointment that you have denied what he believes is his last opportunity to see Sam. I am sharing with you now Maria's tremendous disappointment that she will not be seeing Sam again, as seems likely in view of her health complications. This is an awful thing you have done to your own son.

8. Sam has explained that he likes your partner Carol, is happy having her live with you and enjoyed your family Christmas together. However I am concerned that Sam may be left alone with someone I know nothing about. Please provide me with the background of Carol and the reassurance that she would pass a police check. Sam has explained that Carol is a smoker and I look to you for confirmation that you are not exposing Sam to the harmful effects of second hand smoke or modeling cigarette smoking to a 5-year-old.

9. It is a matter of regret that you prevent Sam from Skyping with me. I have asked repeatedly and do so again here.

Please allow Sam to Skype me at his will without your presence in the communication and without recording our conversations for your legal purposes.

Andrea

That letter was sent to Clock on 10 September 2015. Not one point raised was acknowledged. There was no reply to my request to know who this Carol Adrian, living with my son and modelling for him the lifestyle of a smoker, might be. I would write again on this subject and again receive no reply. Only when Sam arrived for a visit on one my trips to London to see him with a weekend bag in which I saw a pack of cigarettes and a lighter, that my letter to Clock finally produced details of his identity. It turned out in that reply that his girlfriend Carol Adrian is also a member of family law. Working for his former boss, the dinosaur of family law, Christa.

Clearly leaving cigarettes and a lighter in the overnight bag of a 6-year-old is no big deal if you are a member of family law. Perhaps that was Jeff the Plumbers cigarette box.

Nothing to see here.

17 Gifts, iPad, Skype and letters

I wonder where Sam is now? I wish it wasn't legal for a member of family law to conceal my sons address from me

Once I knew where Sam was living by the end of July 2013, after paying Clam's legal charges for finding out Sam's residential address and with a sense of the importance of post enhanced by my Priory visits, I sent letters and gifts by post. With absolute regularity. One valuable tip from my Priory therapist was emphasizing the importance to young children of postal deliveries.

"They love to get things in the post. So at this time where visitation is difficult, you should write regularly. On the same day each week. Possibly send drawings and invite him to send drawings back to you."

Off I went to an art supplies shop with Jo, my friend and fine-art lecturer, who advised me on how best to approach this art challenge. I bought supplies and opted to use colored pencils on thick 120 gsm art paper, which I would fold over to make a card with my drawing on the front and a handwritten message on the inside fold.

With my negligible skills in pencil art to the fore, I spent many hours developing the basics until I had drawings skills that enabled something like my intention and every week from then on, a minimum one letter would arrive in the post for Sam with words of love and encouragement and a drawing. Although, when I say, 'One letter would arrive' I mean, I sent one letter a week, but had no way of knowing of Sam was being given this correspondence.

Skype contact was my next goal. But how to get a Skype to him? Before I left for California in December 2013 I bought an iPad, with my Skype address preloaded, and left it with Jo to give to Sam when she next saw him in an existing arrangement to meet Krasnopovich where she would be giving Sam his Xmas presents. At this time Jo was still keeping on friendly terms with Nico as the best intermediary for Sam. In the course of that meeting when Jo gave Sam his Xmas gifts, Krasnopovich spotted the iPad and took it out of Sam's hand to return it to Jo. *"He is too young for an iPad."* (Despite the fact that at 4 Sam was a whizz on the iPad.) For the time being that meant no Skype was possible for Sam and me unless it was to be on Nico's own iPad. Which he could control. Never allowing Sam to speak to me without his presence in the background. From America post flood, I kept sending weekly letters to Sam at his Father's address. And almost every week would send gifts, some small, some less so, via Amazon. Books, Scalextric, Nerf Guns. Some gifts for him to experience the joy of the postman bringing something from Mum.

For Christmas of 2013 his Godfather Chris Andiotis and his wife, Maria, picked out a very thoughtful gift. A battery scooter. That cost many hundreds of pounds. Typically Chris and Maria would buy Sam expensive gifts as is quite normal with Greek Godparents and more so with wealthy Greek godparents.

Later that year on one of our visits I asked Sam how he enjoyed the gifts. It became evident that he was not receiving them. He never received the scooter and he never received a majority of the gifts I sent. I relayed this scooter story to Chris, who decided as one year had passed, he would phone Krasnopovich to ask why he had not given Sam his gift one year later. His answer was *"It is in the office and it's too heavy to carry on my own."*

To date I don't know if Sam ever received that, or any other number of gifts sent. The outcome with Chris after several further attempts to confirm that his gifts were getting through to Sam, was that he gave up trying.

"There is no point sending things that don't get to Sam" was his unarguably cogent conclusion. The same came of my own ability to send gifts. There is a special sorrow that comes from sending a thoughtful gift to your son only to learn months later that he never received it.

In my second visit of 2014 with Sam, we stayed at a hotel in the city. A five-star hotel chosen because it had a nice swimming pool. The trip was just to spend three days and nights with Sam, as agreed between the lawyer and the intermediary as Krasnopovich would not speak directly to me. (Unless I paid him a six-figure sum.) Philip came with to see Sam for that three-night visit. This was the time when Sam had his iPad and we were speaking regularly on Skype. Philip and Sam had been speaking on Skype even more than he had been speaking with me. There was great rapport between them. Sam kept reminding Philip that he was 18. (A humorous reference to his teenager enthusiasm.) They had a high energy between them. I loved listening to their banter. On this trip Philip was super excited to see Sam and he was super excited to see Philip. On one of the three days Clock had allowed Sam to be with us, Philip decided to treat Sam to the Hamley's experience. Sam had never been to Hamley's, the world's greatest Toy Store. Off we went by London cab. What joy for a 5-year-old. We got a shopping cart and he had the same experience I once gave his brother Evan When Evan was 5 I took him to the Toys R Us warehouse that had just opened in Woking, gave him a shopping cart and said 'choose whatever you want'. To have the experience of not regretting any poor choice of toy later. Because you can have every choice. On this occasion Philip gave Sam the same opportunity.

As kids do, he knew exactly what he wanted. Remote control car, Nerf guns, art supplies. Remote control helicopter. A shopping cart full of as much as we could carry. We left with three oversized bags filled with his new purchases. It was a happy experience and a great memory. Later, in a skype chat I asked him about his progress with the remote-control car. By the end of that chat it was clear that the majority of the toys from that Hamley's experience were gone. Why would I think Krasnopovich would allow Sam to keep any happy memory of his mother?

As a pattern, Krasnopovich would obstruct any reminder of his mother, or family. During Sam's single visit to California, he met Philip's mother, who became mesmerized by 'beautiful Sam' and his English accent. She seemed in awe of his radiant joy. As was everyone who met him on this trip. 'That child is so beautiful.' As a gift, she had a monogrammed Bathrobe made for him, with his name embossed in a cursive font. Sam, written in Greek blue. A nice gift for a 5-year-old. A month later in a skype chat I asked if he was enjoying his robe from 'Grammy'.

"What robe".

I expect that when Krasnopovich unpacked his bags on return from California and saw the robe, it went straight in the bin. That robe simply disappeared.

I kept sending gifts though right up until the last occasion when I saw Sam on 16 February, 2016, where it became painfully clear that I was wasting money sending gifts when the vast majority were not getting to him. I haven't sent anything through Amazon since. I haven't even sent a birthday present or called on his birthday. Neither has any one of my family or any-one who knows me. Another round won by Krasnopovich.

How did Sam get the iPad I bought for his Xmas present 2013? The iPad issue resolved in 2014. When I returned to the UK for the first time after the flood to my home. Philip accompanied me specifically to arrange a visit with Sam in the Hotel we became very familiar with, the Four Seasons in Hampshire. We enjoyed a wonderful three-night stay during which time I set up his own Skype account on his iPad and loaded up his favorite games for him. I explained that he was going to keep his iPad and we would be able to talk whenever he wanted with this iPad. He already knew that Krasnopovich had prevented him from getting the iPad for Christmas.

"But daddy will just take it away from me" he said mournfully as I was loading him up for his collection.

"Philip will talk to daddy" was my reply.

And Philip did the handover when Krasnopovich came to collect. Drawing his attention to the iPad in front of Sam.

"There is an iPad in Sam's bag so that he can Skype with his Mother." In that moment, in front of Sam, Krasnopovich seemingly had no alterative than to agree.

And that is how the Skype contact began, from March 2014, until the use of Skype conversations between Sam and me by Krasnopovich to benefit his beneficial entitlement claim in family Court led to the sight of Sam squirming uncomfortably in a Skype chat with me, parroting comments while looking up over the camera lens, where two voices could be heard clearly leading him the conversation. Krasnopovich and his fiancée Carol Adrian. It was pitiful and clear to me that I could not allow Sam to go through that level of discomfort again. That was the end of Skype chats for some time. Heartbreaking though it was for me to not even be able to Skype with Sam. Now no one on my side seemed able to get hold of Sam.

By April 2015 godmother Jo had not received any reply from Krasnopovich to 5 text messages requesting a visit with Sam. Chris Andiotis had not received any replies to his messages following on from the last gift he sent not being given to Sam to the extent that he no longer even tried calling. The message was all too clear. No one on my side had any contact with Sam. Krasnopovich was successfully preventing any contact between Sam and myself as well as anyone who knows me. Parental alienation and child abuse? Protected and, for this reason enabled, by the anonymity of family court? Although I stopped the Amazon gifts to Sam, I kept sending letters by post to the Thamesbury Gardens address. And then in June of 2016, A letter arrived back at my address in California.

"Return to Sender. Not known at this address. No forwarding address provided."

The next week another returned letter arrived and then another. I wrote directly by email to Krasnopovich requesting the address of where Sam was living. Krasnopovich did not disclose the address, saying instead;

"Don't write to me directly, write to my lawyer."

And so I did. The letter is copied below. For the record, on 16th December, 2016, after some nine months in which I did not know where Sam was and Sam did not know why the letters from Mom stopped, I received a letter in the post, addressed in Krasnopovich's handwriting containing a Christmas card written in Sam's handwriting. And that envelope had a return address (In Krasnopovich's handwriting.)

It bears repeating in its own paragraph.

The first occasion in which I was provided the address of where Sam was, was 16 December, 2016. Some 9 months after my letter requesting Sam's whereabouts. I relayed this information to my lawyer and we established from a Land Registry search that Krasnopovich bought this property in early April 2016, moving out of Thamesbury Park road in that same month. From April 2016 until 16 December 2016 I did not know where Sam was living and could not even send a letter to him.
About 9 Months.
My lawyer observed "A long time for him to say whatever he wants to by way of explanation of why mummy doesn't want to see him. I am afraid it's called poisoning the well.' You would think a family law member concealing the address of a child from that child's parent for nine months would be subject to some form of professional censure. But in that, you would be wrong.
Nothing to see here.

Here is the age-appropriate letter I sent to Sam via Clock in September, when trying to get Sam's address My intention was that there would be a record of why he was not receiving letters from me for his clarity, one day.

To: Sam c/o Tim Clock. Souvla Raven Hogg LLP
From: Andrea Lee

September 27th, 2016

My beautiful Sam,

I am writing you this e-mail letter today, 27th September 2016. I cannot write to you by post because I do not know where you are living so I'm sending this letter to your dad's lawyer Tim Clock, hoping he will pass it on to you.

I feel very sad that I haven't been able to see you or write to you and don't know where you are. I didn't know you'd moved from Thamesbury Park Road. I sent you three letters to that address and only found out you'd moved when the letters were sent back to me. They were marked *"Return to Sender. Address unknown,"* which is what the Post Office puts on letters when they are sent to the wrong address. (I think whoever lives in your old house in Thamesbury Park Road told the postman that you didn't live there anymore and to send them back to me.) That was on the third of August, almost one month after I wrote my letter of 6th June.

All came back marked; ***Return to Sender. Address unknown. Unable to forward***

Of course a lawyer who moved and left no forwarding address seems most unusual. But we have to believe that's true of Nico. I wrote to Nico the moment I found out you'd moved and asked for the address but no-one's told me what it is. I am writing now so you'll know that the reason you never received these letters from me is because I don't know where you are living. It's not because I've forgotten about you. Or because I haven't been writing to you. It's because I was not told that you were being moved and I do not know where you are because Nico will not tell me unless I pay a lawyer to force him. And I have no more money to do that with.

Do you remember, just after you left Thameside and moved to Thamesbury Road and I managed to get your address, I sent you letters? Every week you'd receive a letter in the post from me, with drawings and messages. I know this made you very happy because you told me the last time I saw you. That seems like a very long time ago now.

Every week for the past three years I have sent you a letter, with pictures and cards and even the certificate from your California Jedi School, reminding you about The Force! Every letter was reminding you that I love you and think about you all the time and that I can't wait to see you again - and, of course, reminding you that I am trying as hard as I can to make that happen. I know that one day you will be able to see just how hard I tried to see you and to have you with me.

You probably don't know this but I have been very worried about you. It's not usual for a father to move a child to a new house without telling the mum where the child is. This is what makes me worried.

It's very important that I know where you live and that you know why you're not getting the letters I'm sending you. I hope you get to see this letter, but if you don't I will copy it and show it to you next time I see you.

I'll keep the other three letters for you too - the ones that have 'Return to Sender' scribbled on the front, the ones that were sent back to me, the letters you never received.

I am very sorry that so much time has gone by without you getting any post from me. I hope you don't think I've forgotten about you. Because I haven't. I think about you every day and, even though you're not here, I say 'goodnight' to you every night before I go to sleep.

I hope more than anything that we will be together again soon and that at the very least we will be able to start writing to each other again.

I miss you more than words can say. Wherever you are, I am here for you. Whatever happens, I want you to know that I love you and always will.

Mummy

PS: *Everyone misses you and sends you their love. Especially Papou, Philip, Evan, Chris, Jo and Tom, and of course Mason, who has just made a movie and is doing very well at school.*

The first letter, sent on 6th June, 2016, returned to me on 3 August, 2016. I wrote to your dad the same day, Wednesday 3rd of August, asking *'Please will you provide me with Sam's address.'* Krasnopovich replied 5 days later, on the 8th of August. 2016

Verbatim

"I have passed your recent email to Tim Clock who will continue to liaise with you about Sam and with your lawyer about the house. I would prefer no direct contact with you so please continue to communicate through solicitors. Any direct emails you send to me will not be answered."

From: Andrea Lee
Date: Friday, September 30, 2016 at 9:02 AM
To: Roland Court

Subject: *Sam address*

Dear Roland,

I still do not have Sam's address even though Clock claims to have sent it on 10 August. He has no other means of contact with me. This is distressing.

We know Krasnopovich moved Sam sometime before June, which, assuming my letters were being given to him, means he has not heard from me since my letter of 11 April, 2016. I am certain this is as upsetting for Sam as it is for me.

Regards,
Andrea

After the failure to get any visitation with Sam for the summer holidays of 2015 I was in a new low of despair. How to explain to my beautiful son that I was not able to fulfil my promise to make sure that we would see each other soon. The complexities of devious legal manipulation made a challenging presentation for the comprehension of a six-year-old. I set out to write a letter to him and this took me days of sitting in various coffee shops, shaping a letter in age appropriate terms, detailing the events that conspired to prevent him being with me. Cecelia Flaherty featured prominently, for obvious reasons, as did Tim Clock. The lessons I learned from my Priory therapist and my Psychiatrist, Mark Zetin were especially helpful in presenting a picture that reassured him of both parents love without becoming the basis for a lifetime's resentment over what his father and his father's legal team had achieved by way of parental alienation and child abuse. After days of diligent work, I had a 5,000-word document ready to send to my beautiful Sam.

The connection between litigation and animosity is easy enough to understand. The connection between animosity and child abuse is its logical extension. It became clear that while Sam was under the unmonitored control of Krasnopovich, sending him my letter would only make him more of a target for his parental alienation agenda. And of course, the chances that Krasnopovich would let Sam read any letter without screening it first were zero. So the letter was never sent, but remains as a reminder of a tragic year in which Sam expected to spend his holidays with me, but never did. Krasnopovich was able to say to me "*pay the money and he can come*" without prejudice. In one of my last conversations with Sam on this subject he told me that he tried to get him to agree and kept asking him. Sam was reassuring me that he would convince Nico. "*I will keep on asking him until he says yes*" he announced with tremendous confidence. The final word on that approach was.

"*When can I see mummy*" to which Nico replied

"*That time has come and gone.*"

Throughout this acrimonious litigation brought by Krasnopovich, I have prioritized consideration for the consequences of acrimony between parents on the child's well-being. It has been clear to me and everyone who has followed this story of Krasnopovich's conduct towards me that Krasnopovich from the outset disregarded the litigation acrimony = child abuse balance on the basis that family law would enable him to act in anonymity. Repeatedly his correspondence reminded me directly, or attempted to get me to agree to confirm I would never discuss the '*breakdown of the relationship.*' Consistently Krasnopovich would act litigiously with creating maximum animosity being the intention, while concurrently relying on his belief that Sam would never find out about his actions. It seems to me that his belief that family law protects him from this accountability to the child has encouraged him to be more litigious still. This is one area of family law that cannot be allowed to continue without revision. To do so is to allow ongoing child abuse even after the child has reported the abuse. It is wrong to enable parents to deceive children knowing that deceit can never be disclosed to the child even if they are foolish enough to believe any law can overcome a growing child's interest in finding out the truth about their parents. The same charge is equally true of Flaherty and Clock. Who seemed convinced that the system indemnifies them from the child ever founding out either who they are or what they did. Secure in their belief that their conduct is protected by anonymity within the confidentiality family law provides for its members. Of course, when considering accountability, there is no simple measure by which we can calculate how damaging this period of time, over five years to date, has been for Sam or for myself. One possible up side arising from the tragedy for Sam and myself is if a lesson is learned and a legal system revised to protect children from similar abuses.

One reform of family law to eliminate this protection and the opportunity it represents for abuse is to make family law proceedings transparent. Read **Section 12 of the Administration of Justice Act 1960.** It provides family court judges with a broad-brush sledgehammer to conceal any manner of deceit in family court, being conveniently adaptable for any judge to keep judgments un appealable, safe from the checks and balances of a proper and just judiciary. It is the one-size-fits-all deterrent enabling the jailing of any whistleblower in corruption causing child abuse in family court.

In the meanwhile, Clock, Krasnopovich, Hazelwood and Flaherty freely carry on benefitting handsomely from membership of family law and the right it gives them to encourage parental alienation and child abuse for the enormous profit it represents. Family law provides an easy out, not only for offences against the child's best interests committed in family court, but for offences that are criminal outside of family court. Sam has been a victim of these abuses. As have I. Instead of reparations and apologies and lessons learned, we have the situation where no precedent can be set which shows up the deceit that underpins family court. And so instead, sledgehammer threats of legal punishment assure Krasnopovich and his allies that Sam will never know anything other than their version of what happened to his life after fathers-day 2013. In Sam's case, this underpins his lawyer parent's determination to prevent unfettered communication with his other parent, even though it is flagrantly a breach of the very legal process that pays him so much money.

By September 2016 I had not seen or spoken with Sam for seven months. My requests to Krasnopovich to provide me with his address had been unsuccessful.

'*Talk to my lawyer*'.

Whilst I wasn't prepared to do that, I opted instead to write a letter to Sam, knowing I would never send it. For the therapy. And here is that unsent letter. Much like a time capsule. I was exploring every possibility to keep Sam aware of why he wasn't seeing me or receiving any letters from me. That not seeing me was not in any way a choice of mine through lack of love or commitment to trying, as I promised I would, to have him with me, either for both long holidays or for school terms. I was not seeing him or writing to him because. I didn't have his address, and it seemed right to record that moment:

---

22 September, 2016

My beautiful Sam,

I am writing you this letter today, 22nd September 2016 and I will keep this letter for you to read in the future. I am sitting in a coffeeshop in California and I am missing you terribly. Writing helps me feel I am doing something when I have tried everything I can and still don't even know where you are.

A great deal has happened to us both since fathers-day 2013, when you were four. Now you are seven and aware that something has happened to stop you from seeing me. You know I would do everything I could to have you with me. But something has gone wrong. It is called family-law. Nico is a family lawyer. And he has chosen to use this system because he can.

Ours is a story you already know much about. Things like this – what has happened between you and me – do not just happen by accident. They are the result of a determined action. That is where people think about what they want to happen. And then make sure that thing happens. And in our case, you and me, they use family-law to make things happen in a certain way. Here are some examples.

Letters in the post.

Soon after fathers-day in 2013, when you were four, Nico took you away from our house in Thameside. He moved you to a rental property. I tried to get hold of you there. I wrote to Nico, but he would not provide the address. He said he would tell me where you were and let me see you as soon as I gave him some money. I had no way of finding out where you were unless I agreed to Nico's demand for a lot of money, which I was not able to do. I did not think it was right that he asked for money for letting you be with me. So I had to talk to a lawyer. A family lawyer, the same as Nico is. People who work in the business of family-law, making money out of children who are feeling sad because parents are fighting.

It turns out that family law has rules about one parent concealing the address of the child from the other parent. There are also rules about the residential parent asking for money using the other parents love for the child as leverage. I was very upset at not knowing where you were. I wanted to know that you were safe and I wanted you with me. I knew that you wanted to be with me and so I paid a lawyer a lot of money to use family law to make Nico and his lawyer Tim Clock tell me where you were. Although you know Nico is a family lawyer, for some reason he decided to hire another lawyer to represent him. That lawyer's name is Tim Clock. And he is known in family law as someone who likes to litigate. To go to court for winning money. I thought that was strange because all I wanted to do was to see you. Why would Nico need to a hire a money lawyer. I wasn't asking him for any money.

I just wanted to write to you so you would at least have some contact with me while Nico worked out his money demands. Nico decided that he wanted to be paid a lot of money from me even though I have given him a lot of money since I first invited him to come and live in my house for free and even though I did not leave the relationship with him and take his son away and charge money to let him come back.

My first lawyer, who Nico calls 'that idiot David Clam' is a member of British family law and a very expensive lawyer who charged a lot of money for every minute he spent trying to help you to see me, by writing letters to Nico asking for this information. The address where you were. But instead of replying with the address, as the law requires, Nico and Tim Clock did nothing and I had to spend even more money having David Clam take the case to family court. On the day of the court case where the judge would have ordered Nico to provide the address, because he had to, it is what the law says, which he knew very well as he is a family lawyer, he waited until David Clam was already on the way to Court before he emailed the address to me. He was clever in providing the address at the last minute because the judge would have known that he had been wrong in not giving the address. And family -court would know one of their own members was breaking the rules.

So why did he do that? Because David Clam charged me a lot of money to prepare the case. And I still had to pay his bill even though the judge never got to hear the story. You see, the lawyers charge by the hour, so Nico waited until David Clam was almost at the court before emailing me. I got a huge bill for David Clams time going to court for me and Nico made sure that the judge never learned that he was being malicious and obstructive. Deliberately causing problems for me in seeing you making sure that I had to pay family law lots of money as a punishment for not listening to him. He wanted his huge payment from me and that was that.

He was very clever, showing me how he could make me pay thousands of pounds paying David Clam to 'attend the address disclosure matter' with Clock just to get the address where you were so I could write to you. You can say that is very good law work by Nico and his expensive City lawyer Tim Clock, but it was not good for me not knowing where you were. I think you would have been upset to think that I was not even writing to you?

You may remember that once I had your address I was then able to send you letters. Every week after I had the address you would receive a letter in the post from me, with drawings and messages. I know this made you very happy because you told me when we met. There is something very comforting in sending and receiving letters. I enjoyed making cards for you with drawings and words. With all the ups and downs along the way, 'Letters to Sam' was always the one thing we could rely on.

Do you know, when Nico left with you, I was very sad and I went to see a doctor. A very clever doctor, a world-famous doctor, who knows the best way to deal with difficult situations, like when one parent makes it difficult for the child to see the other parent. That doctor, who is called a therapist, taught me that the one thing that children can rely on when things change so much during parents separating, is post. Getting letters in the mail. It became the most important thing so I had a way of getting through to you even when Nico made it difficult with Skype or phone calls. That therapist is also a child psychologist, who helped me to understand what you are going through.

Two years went by. I saw you very little. Our house in Thameside flooded and Nico made sure that the Insurance would not fix it. He was not very nice at all. So I had nowhere to live and no address for you to send me letters. That is why I ended up in America.

Philip rented me some of his house because I had nowhere to live and no money to pay rent because mummy made sure I had tremendous financial pressure. Paying every penny I had to family law. Philip was very kind to me. Especially so I would have a place for you to stay in when you came to be with me. I made sure that you would have a place to stay with me when Nico agreed to let you. And Philip agreed too. He missed you terribly. It wasn't only me who was sad in not being able to see you. Philip was very upset too. So was Papou. And Jo. All of your family and friends from my side of the family couldn't talk to you. Not even beautiful Maria.

This is because Nico and Tim Clock and family court did nothing to ensure that I was able to speak to you, or, for a long time, even have the address of where you were living. Boy, did that create animosity. I wanted to know where you were. I just missed you all the time.

In 2014 – when you were five – you spent three weeks with me and Philip in Laguna Beach. Other than that, we have spent just a very few nights together. Most of them in

Hampshire at the Four Seasons Hotel, with Oliver the black dog. There is a reason for this. You know that I love you very much and that it must have taken a great deal of effort and resources to stop me from having you with me.

Every visit we had, and I came to the UK 19 times to see you in three years, involved endless letters between lawyers in which without fail, Nico and Clock made it as difficult and expensive for me as possible, to the extent that I estimate it cost me about ten thousand pounds for every night you got to spend with me.

They knew that the more difficult and expensive they made it for me to have you with me, that eventually I would run out of money. Papou helped by sending money so I could stay in nice Hotels with you. Philip was amazing, making sure that there was always a place for you to live with us if we could get family court to agree. He even agreed to move to England once I got the Insurance money to fix my house.

I tried as best I could. But you should know that I met only resistance and obstruction from Clock that eventually finished all the money I could get to come and see you.

Do you know family law has charged me more money in legal fees than the cost of your entire education in private school and University. And still, after paying all that money to family law, I don't even know where you are?

It was more difficult for us than for most people because Nico is a family lawyer so it would cost him nothing to write letters. But I would have to pay a lawyer lots of money. Doesn't seem fair, does it? I can't even send you a book on Amazon because I don't have your address. And even if I did, I know that Nico would not give it to you, along with all the other gifts I sent you which we discovered you never received.

A great many words have been written along the way since Nico started this litigation (Going to family court) and it is only right that you should one day have access to the story of "Krasnopovich versus Leandros" and the opportunity to see how British family-law and especially a judge named Cecelia Flaherty can be manipulated. That is, tricked by people who do not have good intentions. Who are interested only in making money and will use any means necessary for this purpose. Who are dishonest.

In time, when you are able to see how events unfolded, you will see exactly how family law has failed us both. While Nico and his lawyer Tim Clock have made a lot of money along the way by stealing. I think of them as Rainbow thieves. You to me are like the treasure at the end of the rainbow of my life. It has been very difficult knowing that the best I could do to try and be with you was just squashed down by family court.

Here we are more than three years later and after all that has happened the only contact between you and me is through post. You probably already know why Skype is not possible after the recording of our conversations being used in Court to paint a picture that I am not a good parent. I think it was quite wrong of Clock to take private talks between you and me and cut out small pieces of what we said to show a judge to make them think I was a bad parent. And even more wrong that a Judge would be stupid enough to rule as you will one day read Flaherty ruled.

Just supporting Nico no matter what he did. Even when he broke the law. I think Cecelia Flaherty is not an honest person and should not be a judge making decisions for children. She is prejudiced and easily misled. I think, if the law is just, she should go to jail for the offences her conduct represents. The system cannot work when people break their own rules and get away with it. It is called accountability. It is when consequence follows cause. Without it, our whole social order sinks into a mire of ethical sleaze.

Every week I sent you a letter, with pictures and cards and even a certificate from your California Jedi School, reminding you about the Force. Every letter reminding you that I love you and think about you all the time, and that I can't wait to see you again, trying the best I can to make that happen. I have tried my best but I am not a member of family law and there comes a time when we have to accept my best has not been good enough in a Court system where lying is the most important thing. Who lies best wins.

I did not just give up easily. Only after 4 court hearings and legal costs to me approaching half a million pounds. Enough money to have paid for you to have the best schools and University in California. I even got to see the top Judge in family law, the President, and he looked at the judgment of Flaherty, which was where Nico lied and Flaherty made a judgment that let him have control over not only me seeing you, but also taking all of my money and my house. So I had nowhere to live and no money to keep paying lawyers to try and see you. Well, the family-law President looked at the judgment by Flaherty and said it was wrong. And there should be an appeal.

But that turned out to make no difference. It looked like because Nico is a member of family law, other members of family law all supported him. And that meant letting you down. And me too. Money was more important to them than your rights to be with me, and my rights to be with you. The system is endemically corrupt. Placing monetary gain above the best interests of a child in a process where the safeguards against this, called 'Appeal', in our case was absent. Judge Flaherty made an 'un appealable' judgment. And the long list of lies told by Nico and Clock just got swept under the table. You and me are no more than collateral damage in a system that abuses 10,000 children every year and still does nothing about reforming to the law to make liars accountable.

On Wednesday, 3rd of August 2016, I went to collect the post and in the post box was a letter I recognized. It was a letter I sent to you on 22nd June, and it had a big line across your name on the front saying
> **'Return to Sender. Not known at this address.'**
In the weeks that followed two more of the letters I had sent weeks before arrived back with the same message.
> **'Return to Sender. Not known at this address.'**
I realized that Nico must have moved home and had not left a forwarding address for post. I had no way of knowing where you are and so I wrote to him, Wednesday 3rd of August, asking;

'I have received returned post indicating that Sam is no longer at the Thames Court address. Please will you provide me with Sam's address.'

It is very unusual for anyone to move home and not leave a forwarding address for post. There is a very good reason Nico is not disclosing his new address. I think it is because he knows how much I want to be with you and that I will pay whatever I have to get your address. Here we are again with me having to pay lawyers to find out where you are.

This time I have a different lawyer, Roland Chambers, after I fired 'the idiot David Clam' for making some awful mistakes and not managing to win any time for you to be with me after I paid him so much money to do exactly that. Nico replied to my email asking where you were 5 days later, on the 8th of August. Telling me how to find you. Here's what his email said.

"I have passed your recent email to Tim Clock who will continue to liaise with you about Sam and with your lawyer about the house. I would prefer no direct contact with you so please continue to communicate through solicitors. Any direct emails you send to me will not be answered."

And so I have no way of finding out where you are unless I spend more money on lawyers. But where will I get that money? Nico and family law have stolen my house and my flats, which I used to rent for a lot of money. Exactly as happened in 2013 July, when Nico (and Clock, Nico's solicitor in charge of 'liaising with me about Sam') would not disclose your address.

It is not allowed in British family law to conceal the address of the child from the father, so what Nico and Clock are doing is wrong, both from your best interests, as well as from the legal point of view. But it is a clever decision by both of them to cause me the maximum distress. It has worked. I am very upset. I am curious on how they have explained this to you. That it was in your best interests to prevent you receiving any post from me or even letting me know where you are?

Or do they think it will always be a big secret that you will never hear about? That's what they have told me. I cannot ever tell anyone what they have done. Not even you. That what family-law says.

They must know that one day you will find out about what they did? Perhaps they care more about the money they have made stealing my house and rental business than what you will one day think about why they did it. Or maybe they believe you will never meet anyone who knows me, or even me, again. Then their dirty secret will be safe.

Lawyers are members of the 'Law Society' which allows them to charge a lot of money out of people's misery when families break up. You know lots of families break up. In England, 1 out of 3. This means a lot of people do not like family lawyers because they feed off people at their most vulnerable time. Often this is in family court, where they lie to win money for their clients. You would think that it was illegal to try and make money from people in this way. Especially when it ruins children's chances to see both parents without 'alienation'. Being given a bad picture of the other parent.

To regulate (control) this opportunity to benefit from what is called parental alienation and child abuse, The Law Society has a 'code of ethics. I think Nico and Clock should have provided me with your address as soon as they moved you. I think they breached the Solicitors code of ethics by withholding your address for 9 months.

By this time, we have lost so much time together that I feel something is very fishy with British family law. I wonder how many parents like me and children like you will be similarly affected by family law while the system is allowed to carry on as it is.

This is a question I have in progress with the family-law President, who is in charge of this organization, the President of British family law. I have written him a long letter. And I have a copy of that letter for you to read one day. To know that no one can say I didn't tell family court what was going on with you. I think what has happened to you is child abuse. What has happened to me is theft. A serious burglary. And to you as well. Your mother was been stolen from you by family court. It wasn't your choice and it wasn't mine. It was a judgment made in family court.

You, and my love for you, have been used as leverage against me to win money by a member of family law. Members of family law make money out of children's misery and if a judge says that is OK, they carry on doing it again and again. To other children and fathers just like you and me.

At the time I write this letter to you, 22nd September, 2016, I have had no communication on where you are. Yet clearly you were moved out of Thamesbury Road before June 2016. My solicitor did a search of the property register and it shows that Nico moved out in early April. That is nearly four months in which you have been moved and I was not notified. And after requesting the information from Nico, I was not given the address. Instead he told me to write to his solicitor. (Which would cost money. When all he had to do was e mail me the address.) So I wrote to Clock and guess what. I still don't know where you are.

What does the law say about this?

Nico and Clock have already cost me all the money I had including stealing the 'Old House' since this determined litigation started with them stopping you spending Saturday nights with me in Thameside.
    In October 2013, when you were four, just a few months after you were taken away from Thameside I tried to get Nico to agree to you spending Saturday nights with me in our Thameside house. Staying in your old room that you had stayed in just a month before. I asked the judge to have you spend weekends, just one night, Saturday night, with me. In that court case Nico and her lawyer Clock fought tooth and nail to stop you spending even one night a week with me. Even though you surely wanted to be with me and I wanted to be with you.
    But they won in family court. They won the decision by a Judge who decided that Nico and Clock were right. And that you should not spend Saturday nights with me.

So that is good for Nico. He won another case in family court. He is very concerned about winning. And this is what he thinks winning is.

But was that the right decision by the family court?

Was it best to stop a child from seeing his mother in this way? You will be able to decide for yourself when you read the story of how Nico and Clock won the child visitation hearing. Maybe one day you can sue for damages, such is the obvious reality of how corrupt the family law system was in your case. And they can decide what value to attach to the time they stole from you being with me. How much do you think that would be worth?

I don't think it was in your best interests to stop the weekend visitation. It was very upsetting for me. I became very sad that I couldn't see you unless Nico and Clock agreed. And they would only agree if I gave them a ton of money. Which wasn't fair. And wasn't right. One day you will see the movie "The Godfather" and see how mafia gangsters work.

As we know now, three years later, that judgment did not assist your right to be with me. It just made Nico and Clock more money, at your expense. And we were never able to establish a regular weekly contact to enable me to be a part of your life in England.

How the family law system worked for you and me is a whole story in itself and so I will be writing a book about it, with all the letters and the details of how Nico and Clock were able to use family law to win the position they have, where now I don't even know where you are after months of asking. And unless I pay a lawyer a lot of money, I have no other way of finding out. All Nico has to say when I asked him is 'Talk to my lawyer." Whenever I asked him to do the right thing with the house insurance when the house flooded, instead he cost me a huge amount of money which the law said he owed to me. His reply when I asked him was always the same. "So sue me."

He has not been honest at all. Perhaps he loves you so much he thinks he wants you all to himself and there may be reasons why Nico thinks he is a good father and doing the right thing for his son. I do not. I think he has made a serious mistake. And to start making amends, he will need to talk to you when you are old enough to have the conversation and explain what he was thinking when he stopped you seeing your mother and did the things you will read about in the judgment of Cecelia Flaherty.

You know Nico is a family lawyer so why did he hire another family lawyer to talk for him about you being with me? And one who has such a reputation for being 'aggressively adversarial' and 'litigious.' I don't think that was decision he made with your best interests at heart. We didn't get to spend weekends together after Nico and Clock won the 'Child visitation application in October 2013. That's was simply wrong. They asked me for a sum of money. Unless I paid it, they would 'fight' my visitation. That is called blackmail. There is nothing honorable about it. Or anything that can be confused with acting in the child's best interests. Greed is greed no matter how you cloak deceit in legalese.

After that Nico and Clock ended up winning a huge cost against me. More money than I had, so now, even if I wanted to pay a lawyer to get the address of where you are, I am not able to. I used to have enough money before fathers-day when you left. Now, after all the legal bills I have no money and have to borrow from Papou. That is not very nice for me and it means it is not possible for me to pay family law any more to try and see you. All I can do is write to your parent and ask him. He has won all control over my access to you.

The story of what happened to my house in England and why I had to leave for America makes another interesting chapter of the story you will one day be able to read in my book about this time.

I have to accept that family law has different rules for Nico and Clock and that there is no point in trying to take this any further. It is not in your best interests to continue hoping that family law will assist your opportunities to be with your mother without demanding another hundred-thousand-pound bill for lawyers.

But with this letter at least one day you will know why my letters stopped coming. Animosity is a word that means when people do not like each other.
    Litigation is when people take other people to court.
    They say in British Family Law that litigation only raises animosity between parents and is never in the child's best interests. But in this case, litigation has been very rewarding for Nico and Clock. And that reward for them is worth more to them than your right to be with your mother. Disregarding how you feel about this. Or how you might feel in the future when you learn about how you were used.

But I think you have the right to know why you are not receiving letters from me. Whether that happens now, reading this letter of 22nd September 2016, at this time, or whenever you read it in years to come, knowing you were not even told why I stopped writing, you will be able to take your own view on family law and how important it is to win lots of money if you can lie well.
    One day you will be able to read what Cecelia Flaherty wrote about me and decide for yourself about how family law works. And what Cecelia Flaherty means to family law. The deputy district switch-judge who describes herself on her Twitter profile as **"A lawyer, a juvenile delinquent, and a lover of champagne and fun"** *whilst at the same time making judgments like the one that ended your early life with me.*

While later on you will become aware of the words 'Parental alienation' and be able to see how both of your parents spoke about each other, I do not want you to be limited in your understanding by what you should and shouldn't be allowed to know about each parent. This is your life. Nico acted in one way. I acted in another. You can decide for yourself about who did what and why. It is a fact that Flaherty's judgment was reviewed by the President of family law, who found it flawed. And agreed to an appeal. Yet, no appeal happened because, I found family-law to be flawed. And people who lied the best won. Nico lied very convincingly. He lied and said "I promised him half of my house" and Flaherty agreed and gave him half of my house and my business and charged me the costs on court, which turned out to be more than 100% of everything I owned and ended my opportunity to stay in England, which was the home I loved very much. I think Flaherty knew this huge cost would mean I could not carry on fighting to see you. So she did it on purpose. Her judgment ended our hopes of being together until I can get back on my feet with money to pay another lawyer to get Nico to agree to let you be with me. Although, I think by then you will be old enough to decide for yourself where you want to live.

I hope that we will be together again soon and in the meanwhile, at the very least that we will be able to write to each other.

Until then, I think about you all the time.

I miss you more than words can say and I can't wait for the day that you are able to be with me. I won't stop hoping you will be with me soon.

You will always have a home with me, and with Philip, who talks about you every single day. And misses you terribly. Philip took what you asked him very seriously. "Will you be my daddy?" We are both always here for you. Whether it's for school or for holiday time. Whatever you choose.

Remember nothing is impossible.

One day you will be old enough to speak for yourself and you can decide where you want to live. I will always support your decision.

With all of my love,
Mummy

18 Visitation arrangements

You won't know where Sam is. And you won't see or speak to him until you agree to give me £100,000

The visitation timeline at the outset following on from fathers-day begins with no agreed visitation. I did not even know Sam's address. E mail requests for visitation were met with financial demands. That led to a court hearing, an 'Application for visitation' where I tried to have 2 nights a month agreed for Sam to be with me. Krasnopovich fought like a rabid dog to prevent any visitation. And 'won' the judgment to prevent Sam spending even 2 nights a month with me. Although this win was accompanied by an offer that I could still see Sam as much as I wanted. Irrespective of the Court judgment.

"Pay me the money and you can see Sam as much as you want."

After a few emails directly between Krasnopovich and myself, it became clear that no progress could be made when his position started and ended with "Pay me and then......". And so it was decided to use an intermediary, who could speak impartially between both parents, solely about visitation and who would always put Sam's interests to the fore. The first intermediary was Jo, Sam's 'godmother' and my neighbor on Thameside for the previous 28 years. We met most days over a 20-year period and including after Sam was born. Jo had a special relationship with Sam starting from visiting him on day one at home. They loved each other and met every single week of his life. Jo was very motivated to arrange visitation and took on the role with great enthusiasm and the highest intention to see regular visitation for Sam with me. As well as ensuring that she would stay in regular contact with him.

That lasted some three months during which time seeing the tone of Krasnopovich's letters made Jo feel ill.

Literally.

"I can't go on reading this toxic correspondence. It makes me ill."

Bearing in mind I have known Jo almost as long as I have lived on Thameside, where she lives 3 doors down from number 28, and where we have met almost every morning for coffee and breakfast for, like 20 years, for Jo to recuse herself from this role, being the only point of contact for Sam and me, means this was not simply 'Toxic' correspondence in the general sense of 'pretty nasty words'. It was far beyond toxic. Black moldy slime encrusted infectious excrement oozing from every syllable. Krasnopovich at the top of his game; being transparent use of visitation and Sam's wellbeing to achieve one specific purpose; to force me to pay him money. A blackmailing conman with membership to an enabling society where this conduct is validated. Anyone reading that sequence of emails between Krasnopovich and Jo would understand the extent to which the absence of any ethical paternal consideration in pursuit of specific goal, payment of a sum of money, would upset and deeply offend any parent familiar with the instincts that normally accompany parenthood. After Jo advised Krasnopovich she would not be able to continue as intermediary, a new intermediary was agreed. Krasnopovich ended the visits Jo had with Sam despite her best efforts to arrange visits.

The second intermediary was Celia Silver. Tony and Celia Silver knew us both socially. We would have dinners at each-others homes. Tony was my dentist and Celia has a South African background and similar interests in New Age kindness to me. She is also the mother of two.

A good neutral choice for intermediary. And for a few months Celia corresponded successfully on a frequent basis with Krasnopovich. Several times a week, towards setting up weekend visitation for Sam. Celia was warned that her predecessor in this role, Jo, was upset by the toxic correspondence. Despite being told in advance of the nature of Krasnopovich's obstruction, in which she would politely agree on a reasonable basis to proposed visitation before, at the last minute, sending some spurious reason why the visit could not go ahead, Celia found the same effect on herself. Identifying this conduct by Krasnopovich as 'Toxic' to her own understanding of putting the child's best interests to the fore. Placing a love of money above the more traditional maternal instinct to protect and nurture the child. Bearing in mind this child was with me all of his life so far, was now not seeing me at all, this was deeply upsetting to my friends who wanted to assist in arranging visitation but found the obstacles Krasnopovich presented to be insurmountable.

I have a folder of some one hundred emails between Krasnopovich and Celia from this period where, for 13 weeks, the week begins with the details for the coming weekend visit, and ends, on the Thursday or the Friday, with the e mail from Krasnopovich detailing why the visit will not go ahead.

On occasions backed up by a letter from Clock, validating Krasnopovich's position. None of which is copied here because, the toxicity contained in those emails is not worth exposing a reader too and, life is too short. This book would need another 100,000 words to include the nonsense Krasnopovich and Clock spent their time writing to send to me. All of which concludes with a very good reason why they have to cancel that weekends visit, on a Thursday or Friday, last minute. Every time the same outcome. Just moving a few words around to make it look like it was my fault that I did not want to have Sam visit. To a level that is so idiotic my take away is they believed those emails would never be read by anyone so they had no reason not to write idiotic ridiculous drivel. They were protected by family court 'closed proceedings.'

There is no upside to going on about how dark Krasnopovich's approach to trading Sam's visitation for money is. And never more so than at that time, early on after he removed Sam, when I was genuinely traumatized by not seeing my son, especially because I intuited how he must be feeling at missing me. It was so wrong on so many levels.

The simple fact is Sam was not allowed to see me for 13 straight weeks in which time Krasnopovich and Clock explained that I was obstructing the visits by not complying with Krasnopovich's very reasonable requests. Cynical legal speak as transparently disingenuous as the consistent thread of *"you can see him anytime as much as you want. Right after you pay."*

The premise of their toxic logic was that I was cancelling the visits because I didn't really want to see Sam. Not considering the consequences of stopping a four-year old seeing his parent. The net outcome of seeing this mind boggling toxic legal nonsense was; Celia recused herself from any further exposure to Clock and Krasnopovichs' words.

"When you told me about toxic correspondence and Jo, I was prepared for anything. But I just couldn't have imagined anyone would do this to their own child. It's upsetting."

Celia and Tony remain great friends and I remain very grateful for their efforts to help. Between us, with options by now somewhat limited, it was agreed that Philip would become the third intermediary. Krasnopovich knew Philip, had been a guest in his home and seemingly, respected his love for Sam as a motivator in seeing the best case for Sam. It was Philip who negotiated the first meet with Sam after Krasnopovich left. And so it fell to Philip as the last person who knew us both prepared to advocate for Sam in this matter. Krasnopovich initially wrote civilly to Philip, but very quickly it became apparent that he took against Philip through something Sam may have disclosed. Sam was very loving towards Philip. Krasnopovich very quickly demonstrated the full extent of his resentment.

By this time, Krasnopovich had won the visitation hearing, preventing Sam being with me for two nights a month and ensured that there was no visitation arrangement in place for the holidays. As by now I had lost my home in the UK, to foul malicious legal process and to a flood damage insurance claim Krasnopovich deliberately fouled. Now I lived on a different continent, I had requested Summer holidays and winter holidays with me and term time with him. Or vice versa. We were approaching summer holidays, 2014, his first holiday since the separation. He was now 5 and I was making every effort to arrive at the best outcome for Sam. Trying to encourage Krasnopovich to put the parental conflict to one side and the child's best interests to the fore.

Two scenarios existed to address the child's best interests as being to see both parents in as close to an equal amount of time as practicality allowed, as visitation unfettered by the prejudices of either parent. Sam spends terms with me and holidays with dad, or vice versa. With neither parent imposing their will on the other in the guise of the child's interests.

Philip has known Sam since shortly after his birth. He has a special relationship with him, as do many did when meeting Sam, who was the most charismatic and beautiful baby imaginable.

From the out, following fathers-day, Philip advocated for Sam's best interests with tremendous enthusiasm and concern. He assured me of his commitment to seeing Sam's best interests served. When considering the visitation, the time in California and the options to alternate holidays and term time, Philip agreed to support Sam's education in the US. I had calculated by selling my home in the UK and investing in an American rental property I would have sufficient funds to pay for Sam's education. At that time I had a buyer for my London property at £2.5 million. Enough for a good start in my new Country. Enough to support my son's education. And with Philip's obvious love for Sam, I had a willing partner in making this a real opportunity for

Sam. I researched schooling opportunities with the same diligence I had done in the UK for him two years previously.

In my conversations with Sam on Skype I remained convinced that the best thing for him would be to have me involved in his education. As I was from day one.

After I left the UK, driven out by the consequences of malicious litigation, having nowhere to live when the AXA Insurance declined covering my flood claim and being unable to afford anywhere in the UK, I accepted Philip's invitation to rent a level of his home, to be paid for when the Insurance payment arrived. That accommodation was arranged to enable housing Sam and providing him with an ongoing relationship with me, including my role in schooling him. Philip had committed to supporting Sam in this way. For a period of time while Skype was allowed, Sam would talk to me for an hour, and then to Philip for even longer. They never tired of talk. During this period, in the run up to the court case for their claim for beneficial entitlement to my home of a so-called promise I had made to him, Krasnopovich and Clock decided to aggressively pursue me for payment of Sam's private school fee's while at the same time applying maximum difficulty to my visitation every time I travelled to the UK to see Sam.

Ironic.

Their reaction to me offering to school Sam in California was met with a demand for school fee's in the UK. This would affect my interest in having anything to do with paying for Krasnopovich's choice of private schooling. Especially as payment of school fees was already the subject of a clearly defined parental agreement between Krasnopovich and myself.

At this time, 2015, Krasnopovich was living in a rental in Thameside, close to his office. Sam was attending his first year, reception, where he would be collected each day by nanny or granny. Nina had by now been 'let go' and Krasnopovich had temporary nannies who I would occasionally see on Skype chats with Sam. One of these nannies could barely speak broken English. This is who would sit with him until Krasnopovich arrived home from work to spend an hour or two putting him to bed. I was sorry that Sam was spending his afternoons with illiterate strangers when he could have been with me. Inspiring and motivating his education.

It seemed wrong that Krasnopovich was allowed to get away with denying his son the clear advantages and opportunities being with me presented, just to claim the win in having the child in a house with paid help changing TV channels for him.

Largely Sam was an afterthought to a career obsessed lawyer, aggressively pursuing marriage. His romantic aspirations had long since left the fitness instructor in his past and led to a new woman appearing in Krasnopovich's bed and in Sam's life. One whom Sam discussed with me at some length.

'*Daddy is going to get married. To Carol.*'

I became aware of this new presence in Sam's life when he disclosed Carol's name whilst effecting a smoker's inhaling motion. Suddenly Sam was intrigued by smoking? A smart way for a five-year-old to introduce a big new subject in his life. Pretending to smoke, inviting my reaction, knowing I had demonized smoking. I am a zero tolerance anti-smoker. Sam knew that. I had been grooming him into an anti-smoking position from the get go. 'Smokers are jokers'. I consider cigarettes the single most offensive drug (because of its passive smoking effect) and will avoid any environment where smoking is permitted. I have passed on this awareness to my son;

however, he had now learned something more about smoking and this would be our subject for that skype chat.

'Daddy smokes you know. So does his girlfriend. And she has a tattoo".

I do not admire tattoo culture. Tattoos are marks of submission, mostly suited to prison inmates. I don't feel tattoos are a subject appropriate for young children and I had indicated this to Sam previously. Certainly glamorizing and normalizing tattoos is not something I want for my son. So, as is my right and my responsibility as a parent, I requested details of this live-in partner. Concerned over the smoking and the tattoo references. I wrote to Clock formally requesting this information. The identity of the person living in the same house as my son. I waited for a reply. Weeks went by. I checked the email daily. No reply. I sent a reminder. Weeks went by.

No reply.

I sent a reminder. Clock did not reply.

Sam's life in the UK continued the 10% input from Krasnopovich, but could not in any way replace what I shared with my son. He was usually collected from school by nanny or granny, left with child-minders until 6.30 when his father returned, with a new smoking girlfriend. Who for good measure, was also a member of family law. A profession populated largely by individuals whose ethical standards I knew to be at odds with my own. Whereas there was the alternative opportunity to live and be schooled in California. It was clear to me that Sam would benefit far more being schooled in California, with me, and spending his holidays with his father, who could then take time off work to have quality time with him during holidays.

What would be best for Sam? Certainly living with me would not include encouragement in smoking, tattoos, or the money first ethics of family lawyers. Or being aggressively excluded from the other parent's life.

This matter came to a head after the first three letters to Clock requesting the identity of the tattooed smoker living with my son were ignored. I felt this was complaint worthy conduct by a member of family law bound by SRA ethical code, even though it was conduct typical of this particular member. Ignoring requests for details of the adult living in the home of a 5-year old child who reports being introduced to the appeal of becoming tattooed and exposed to second hand smoke.

I was deeply concerned.

This woman could be a registered sex offender for all I knew. Left alone in the house with my son. Yet Clock dismissed my requests.

Three letters.

Three delayed replies, which would not reveal the identity of this woman. Did it increase animosity between the parents by not providing me with this information? It did seem to me that Clock should have provided this information by return. Not provoke me with his bland provocative reassurance that *"You have nothing to worry about."*

During this period, two months after my first written request for the identity of the adult tattooed smoker living with my son and being left alone with him on occasions, I travelled again to the UK for a long weekend visit with Sam in London, where he arrived at the hotel with his little knapsack of clothes for the visit. His weekend knapsack, thrown together, obviously in haste, as packed by his father. When I opened the bag, in the central pocket, clearly visible, was a pack of cigarettes and a lighter. As if intended for me to see.

For fucks sake.

I was there for just three days with Sam. And this is how the visit begins. Of course no one will ever know.

"It will really mess with Andrea's head" seemed the clear intent by this engaged couple practicing family law. Sam saw the cigarettes. He was as shocked as I was. He understood something was going on. A message or a mistake? After I took a photo of the cigarette paraphernalia and sent it to Clock with my further strongly worded request for the details of the person living in the same house with my 5-year old son and putting cigarettes in his overnight bag, I finally received a reply from Clock identifying Carol Adrian, a solicitor employee of Christa Hast (Krasnopovich's mentor and former boss) at her London City firm. Carol was a divorcing mother of three children. It occurred to me then that here was another member of family law acting well within the ethical code of the SRA. Pretty upsetting for my hopes in raising my child in an ethical and mindful way.

Later I would observe the symmetry in my visit to family court where I saw a member of family law award half my home and my income generating business; along with the future of my child to another member of British family law to share with another member of family law. Not as if this would include any grounds for complaint to the President of British family law? It's not like there is any insider dealing reserved for members of British family law or anything of that nature.

It is of no interest to any regulatory body in family law that I had to write to Krasnopovich and Clock on three separate occasions over a two-month period urgently requesting details of the person sleeping in the same house as my (then) 5 year-old son during which time I was not only ignored, but taunted with the fact that I should 'not worry' because they assured me she was of good character. This approach, to respond provocatively, unmistakably intended to increase the animosity between the two parents, is child abuse. I can say though, to Clock's credit, at least this sleazy antagonism was entirely consistent through-out my dealings with his office. In no way at any stage can Clock's conduct be confused with anyone considering the best interests of the child. Not one single occasion he might be able to point to and say "There was this one time I tried to help Sam see you."

Wherever possible they (Clock/Krasnopovich) would deliberately ignore valid precedent in family law, of not supporting parental alienation, by treating Sam's rights to see his father with more than just total disregard. They consistently took an adversarial position towards each visitation negotiation. In the course of several different visitation arrangements, at a late stage, once they knew my flights were booked they would add an alternate night that fell outside of the fixed travel dates and then write extensively on how I was declining the opportunity to spend time with Sam. A constant drip-drip of nuisance obstruction, worded in legal letters that were, simply dishonest. Transparently building up a file of stand-alone references to made up dates offering visitation that was never a part of any visitation negotiation.

Here's a made-up illustration of how they presented the average letter which is a sketch of more or less exactly the version Flaherty accepted.

Your honor. I turn to Ms. Lee's email of 17 February 2015. In this letter we see the father has clearly offered the mother visitation for the night of 28 March. Once again we see a father trying his best to encourage the absent mother to see her son, but, I am afraid, that visit never happened. The mother never showed up. The child was heartbroken. And yet. Even despite all of those occasions where the father put forward opportunities for visitation, only to see the mother fail, repeatedly, to visit her son, the father still tries to the best of his abilities to encourage as much visitation as possible. Tirelessly. Consistently. From the outset his goal has been to encourage visitation. Your honor, I have in my hand a list of fifteen emails detailing fifteen separate occasions in which the Father offers visitation which the mother then dismisses outright. Fifteen instances your honor. Clearly, as the record shows, the mother is lying in pretending she wants to see her child, when we have this irrefutable written evidence that she repeatedly, consistently, fails to agree even one of the fifteen attempts shown in these emails by the father trying so very hard to encourage the mother to see her own son. After the father was forced to leave their family home by the mother, there was a period of thirteen weeks when the father tried so very hard, tirelessly, writing to an intermediary to arrange a weekend overnight with the mother. The poor child was dying to see his mother, but for thirteen weeks in a row, the Mother simply refused to have the child. I have the emails your honor. Although I can't show you, because its confidential and Without Prejudice, but honest, we are family lawyers, and we would never lie, so you can trust me. We have the emails to prove this. She wanted nothing to do with the child even though my client tried tirelessly to arrange weekend visitation. My client wanted nothing more than for the Mother to have the child with her. But she kept obstructing his efforts to arrange visitation. The Mother, your honor, is too busy galivanting around the world, living the life of riley with her boyfriend Philip, skiing and so on, in expensive ski resorts without giving a thought to the poor child. Left behind. While my client, the father, is left to do the best he can as a single parent in the absence of any support or interest by the mother who does not even write to her son. Your honor, this mother has not even written to her son for nine months. That is a fact. And she is unfit. She saw a psycho therapist at the Priory. Where mentally unstable people go. And all the while my client, who is struggling to pay the rent as a single parent provides constant written reminders to the wealthy mother, wherever in the world she might be travelling at the time, Verbier, Aspen, St Tropez, Geneva, Budapest, Yosemite, Tokyo, Paris, golfing on the Old Course at Saint Andrews. No matter where she might be at the time, my client tries, tirelessly to get her to allow her son to visit her. And yet. As these fifteen emails prove. Conclusively. The mother simply cannot be bothered. To take time out of her party schedule in order to give her son so much as a weekend of her time.

The last occasion I saw Sam in 2016 took considerable negotiation. As was inevitably the case. The dates for that visit were argued aggressively and extensively by Clock, down to the hour of collection from his School on the Friday and the return was determinedly set for no later than 5pm on the Tuesday. Friday night, Saturday night, Sunday night, Monday night. Return on Tuesday. Finally, after the dates had been exhaustively negotiated and agreed by Clock, I booked my flight. Arriving at LHR on the morning of the Friday, and departing hours after the agreed drop off time. Car hire and Hotel were booked according to the exhaustively negotiated 'down to the hour' time Sam was allowed. Possibly ten emails negotiating and agreeing the visit to the nearest hour. These e-mails to Clock would be included in the costs award by Flaherty on my bill. (At 8% interest charge until paid) meaning I was effectively made to pay the bill of the lawyer negotiating the visitation with my son. With the dates and times finally confirmed I was able to share with Sam in a Skype chat that we would be together soon. Yay. For four nights staying at The Four Seasons in Hampshire. A perfect choice of venue for our visit being just one hour's drive from his school, and with all the home comforts he was used to from our previous times together there. All my arrangements ran smoothly. Plane was on time. Hertz service was efficient. No traffic in the drive to collect him. I was there an hour early to wait. Timing it perfectly from leaving Laguna Beach to pick him up from school in Kingston. I was so excited at knowing I was about to see him. Philip travelled with me, equally excited about seeing Sam and the prospect of our four days together. We watched the classes being led out of their classrooms in single file, to await release to their parents. Sam spotted me on the side of the field, his face one solid smile as he jumped up and down with joy, waiting on tip toe for the teacher to call his name, after which he ran over with unbridled joy. A mirror of my own excitement at being together at last.

"*My mummy*".

He leaped into my arms. Hugs and kisses. I carried him all the way to the car. And in a breathless excited rush he shared the great news with me.

"*Daddy said I can spend a whole week with you.*" Imagine his excitement.

"*Sam, I wish we could spend a whole week, but we only have four nights.*"

"*But daddy said I can spend the whole week with you. It's OK.*" He nodded his head pleadingly. Reassuring me.

How do you answer that? My broken heart broke again. Krasnopovich had told him, as he dropped him at school that day, that he could send the whole week with me. And adult conning a kid in this way is brutal. Plane tickets are booked. Car hire is fixed. Hotel is booked. And the legal agreement in place is such that even if I had agreed to stay 9 nights it would be in the full expectation of that breach of visitation agreement appearing in some future litigation showing how I didn't return him within the agreed visitation period. My heart sank. Years later, it is still difficult to fully describe the effect of this very cunning cruel dig by Krasnopovich and Clock on my impression of their honesty and extent of their depravity in using the child to hurt me. The joy of our hugely anticipated meeting soured by having to explain what I saw as an awful and cynical manipulation of a child intended to cause maximum harm to our relationship. Intended to cast a shadow over our small amount of time together.

"*But mummy, why do I have to go back. Daddy said I can stay all week.*"

Sam could not easily understand why we could not just spend the whole week together. Daddy had said he could, just before he went to school that day. I could not tell him directly that his father and his father's lawyer had done what they had done. I knew I had to return Sam to his father as agreed and sending him back primed to reprimand his father for this deceit would not be in Sam's interests. I had to simply swallow my tongue and explain that I did not know about this and I had booked the airplane and the Hotel for four nights and that could not be changed. Did that raise the animosity towards Clock, the family lawyer, and Krasnopovich, the family lawyer parent?

That is just one of many examples of how Krasnopovich and Clock thoughtlessly abused my sons emotional state, deliberately and consistently in keeping with almost every previously negotiated visitation for no reason other than to cause me the maximum amount of harm. Without regard for the consequences for the child. It was consistent with a repeating pattern, intended to blight the time we spent together, that Krasnopovich had deliberately told him about this extended visit knowing that I would not be able to extend my stay. Krasnopovich had told Sam only as he dropped him off at school that morning that he could spend the rest of the week with me so that I would have the dual joy of having our time on this visit tainted by the disappointment of me telling him I couldn't spend the week with him, as well as having to explain why he could not spend the whole week with me in terms that did not disparage his Father. Deliberately abusing a child to score points in their typically adversarial way. Able to act in confident awareness that they are protected by legal privilege. No one will ever know. Beyond any doubt this tactic of agreeing strict visitation times and then telling Sam a different detail was intended to deliberately affect the visitation as well as challenge Sam's understanding of why I was choosing not to see him when Daddy said I could. Cynical parental alienation. The outcome is I could no longer negotiate any visitation with Clock. I was disincentivized on many levels by his conduct and it influenced my son's prospects for being with me.

Awful razor wire child abuse by two members of family law.

With the constant stream of angry, bitter, dishonest and nasty correspondence continuing with clear disregard for Sam's well-being, through Philip who was now the only point of contact between Sam and myself, having reluctantly allowed me to persuade him to liaise with toxic Krasnopovich and his lawyer Clock, only in the matter of Sam's visitation. I made a second written proposal to put Sam's best interests to the fore and agree either:

He spends the two long holidays with me and the school terms with his father, or the converse. School terms with me, and holidays with his father. Inviting a thoughtful conversation on this subject.

I include below the correspondence that followed. Not only did Krasnopovich not allow the whole holiday saying that 3 weeks is long enough to be out of the Country but when I proposed coming to the UK to spend time with him there, maximizing our time together, in this case travelling on a road trip to Scotland before flying back to the US, he prevented even that opportunity for Sam to spend time with me. This took place at a time when Sam was left every week day with child minders while Krasnopovich was out at work by day and dating his new girlfriend by night, a divorcee with three children. Another example of Krasnopovich simply obstructing visitation to flex his controlling muscles. Why would he not want some free time to follow his work and romance interests when the mother was ready and waiting to take the child and show him a great time. An educational great time. A week driving round Scotland including golf lessons for him at St Andrews. My plan to introduce him to golf as a life experience he would take forward. Not only did Krasnopovich not agree the term time vs school holidays split, he would go on to ensure no visitation at all. Cynically. With considered deliberation and by using legal deceits. An example is included here. An extract from the letter below, a Without Prejudice letter, a select line to show a judge towards establishing his claim that

"She has enough money to fund a private education in America so she should pay for school here."

The sequence of emails is self-explanatory. And includes, as was invariably the case, Krasnopovich spelling the recipient's name wrong. (Philip) In thirty + emails to Jo, Sam's godfather, whose email address is Jo@xxxxx, giving a clue as to the difference between Jo and Joe, Krasnopovich started every single one spelled Joe. This convention of spelling names incorrectly runs right through Flaherty's judgment as well. It is a constant in family law. Misspelling names with such consistency it defies all probability that it is not done intentionally. In Appeal Judge Le Clercs' Judgment he has misspelled both my name and Krasnopovich's on the cover page of his judgment. Two names. Both spelled incorrectly. Leandros and Krasnopovich. Spelled on his judgment title as: Leandros and Krasnopovich. A judge ruling on a child's future cannot even be bothered to spell either name correctly. Even on the cover page. Repeatedly they refer to the husband and the wife. We were never married. This slack jaw yokel attention to detail is a constant in my experience of every judgment in this process (Excepting the finding of the President of family-law, which was the sole exception.) That sums up the standard in family law where I have learned this misspelling of names is a constant that may hide a deeper flaw in competence.

Again, these are verbatim emails that were sent. This one from Philip to Krasnopovich.

From: Philip
Subject: FW: Sam
Date: June 17, 2014 10:45:07 PM PDT
To: Nico Krasnopovich

Dear Nico,

Without Prejudice.

Unfortunately I received your message too late to call so I will detail Andrea's position and then call you tomorrow (Wednesday) 8.30pm your time to discuss.

You have agreed Sam's visitation this July for only the three weeks in California. Andrea was quite clear about the connection between his travel dates and the trip to Scotland.

*For this year's visitation Andrea suggests **collecting** Sam on **Monday 14th July**. She suggests returning Sam the day after arriving in the UK. She arrives on Friday the 8th*

*and would like to spend the last evening with Sam, **returning** him on **Saturday 9th August**. Please confirm that this is agreed.*

Andrea has already told you the flight dates. She considers it unreasonable and intrusive that you demand to see the actual flight information, suggestive as this is that you do not believe her and wish to maintain a controlling interest over her affairs. She is traveling on BA on the dates she has told you. It is unhelpful demanding sight of her ticket. You have no basis to doubt her word and especially in regard to this travel plan which she is paying for in full and looks forward to as her very limited time with her son.

*Andrea has outlined the position in respect of the next visitation she can offer, being the three-week December holiday in California. She proposes flying to collect Sam on **13th December,** and returning him on Tuesday the **6th of January.***

I think it may be worth reiterating that Andrea can only offer the contact she is able to offer and not be guided by the only the contact that you choose to allow which appears, invariably, timed to cause her inconvenience and increased cost. The principle is that you are required as a responsible parent to support and encourage their visitation. Not obstruct by proposing alternatives which appear, quite clearly, to be timed for maximum inconvenience to Andrea.

If you wish to discuss this observation or any of these dates please feel free to call me. I am here to help. It is a simple matter involving a calendar and a principle. Encourage as much visitation as possible. That is in Sam's best interests. You have only to call me with a pencil and a calendar. I will take care of the rest.

In the matter of Sam's education; Andrea would like your agreement to allow Sam to attend school in California. We have identified a private school in Laguna Beach which provides an excellent standard of education which should be considered alongside the advantage he will enjoy being with his Mother each day. Andrea will drop him off and collect him and ensure he keeps his educational standards high. You are aware that Andrea is committed as a priority to his education, beginning from the parental plan you agreed for her to have this child.

Preferable I think to your having to pay costs for child minders to take care of Sam while you pursue your career goals. There will be health benefits in the sunny dry California climate for his bronchiolitis. This is a win-win situation for all three of you.

In this scenario, the Holiday access would reverse as would the payment of costs. Andrea will pay all costs for Sam and not look to you for any support in his schooling here.

For holiday visitation, Andrea would agree all of the long holiday and all of the second-long holiday; Summer Holiday and Winter holiday. Or as much of it as you want. Entirely at your convenience and aligned with Sam's best interests.

If you took up the entire holiday option, you would be spending some three months of the year with Sam in pure quality time and Andrea would take on all the costs of raising and educating. During term time you could Skype with Sam without constraint at his discretion. After the first year we could examine an ongoing situation if you saw that Sam was thriving in the American educational system. If not, you two could agree to alternate years. You share his upbringing 50 50 in every way. This could easily be achieved by Sam attending the American School in Cobham which follows the American Syllabus. I think this represents a tremendous opportunity for Sam with many advantages for both you and Andrea and I hope you will give it appropriate consideration. The term year here starts in late August so please respond in good time if enrollment is to be successful.

Your alternate proposal that Sam sees Andrea subject to your controlling whim which has achieved a total of 4 nights visitation in year one and is on course to achieve no more than 3 weeks in one holiday in year two can never be considered more in Sam's best interests than the proposal made to you here.

I look forward to talking with you.

Regards,
Philip

From: Nico Krasnopovich <NicorjKrasnopovich@yahoo.co.uk>
Date: June 17, 2014 at 11:19:16 AM PDT
To: Philip Parker Voula
Subject: Re: Sam

Dear Phillip
Happy to talk but no point going over old ground regarding the July week. I'm not changing the trip.
I just want to know if Andrea wishes to see Sam on 28th as she sought originally. Just sent you the emails regarding this. If she doesn't want to see him then for some reasons then I can obviously draw my own conclusions about how she is acting irresponsibly. In case she had forgotten she's been away for three months, very responsible of her.
I also want the flight information asked for, in writing.
If you feel the need to discuss those things then please feel free to call me at 9pm tonight on my mobile.
Cheers
Sent from my iPad
Please excuse any spelling mistakes

And then my reply following Phillips letter

Begin forwarded message:
From: Andrea Lee
Subject: Re: Sam. Please forward.
Date: June 17, 2014 10:25:36 AM PDT

To: Philip Parker Voula

Nico,

You may recall from previous correspondence the dates I offered to have Sam. In case you have forgotten I wanted to maximize the time we spent together during my visit, to include a week in Scotland. You declined. As a result I changed my dates for visiting. You already know this. At no time did I indicate I would have him on the 28th and 29th. If you have led him to be 'very excited' at the prospect then you have acted irresponsibly.

In the circumstances, I am prepared to change my travel plans once more to accommodate you if you will agree to let him travel with me to Scotland. It is a trip planned very much with Sam in mind and includes a golf day for him at the Old Course in St Andrews. A fine life experience opportunity at the right time in his development. A week of visiting the best of Scotland.

Consider this is a great opportunity for him to experience not only time with his mother but also a rewarding and educational cultural experience.

My position remains that I would like to see Sam as much as possible during this summer holiday. In view of the time sensitivity for travel plans, please talk to Philip and see if you can put Sam's interests first. He has over 7 weeks of summer holiday. You have agreed to allow him 3 with me. Even though I moved part of the holiday to the UK because of your limit on the time he spends in the USA. Why deny your son the opportunities on offer right here?

Andrea

My last meeting with Sam ended on 16 February 2016. The build up to that meeting involved lengthy negotiation and was soured by Krasnopovich and Clock programming Sam for disappointment on the morning of our visit. Sam was told, as he left the car to come and see me for an arranged four-night visit, that *"Daddy said it's OK for you to spend a whole week with mummy."* You decide if there is any possibility that a seven-night visit is proposed or offered in this letter finalizing the visitation detail.

From: Andrea <andrealee@#gmail.com>
Date: Wed, 06 Jan 2016 19:04:10 -0800
To: Tim Clock <timclock@XXXXXX.com
Subject: Re: Your client Nico Krasnopovich

Dear Tim,

It is unfortunate that you have chosen to indulge the adversarial and unnecessarily provocative reference in your letter.

The deadline you describe as 'arbitrary and unreasonable' is applied both appropriately and reasonably in light of the historical delays which form the character of your communication throughout our historical correspondence.

The absence of basic courtesy in your correspondence has been written about extensively by my lawyer and I can only confirm his observations on your aggressive obstructive adversarial approach which you already have in writing from his firm. You are a rude correspondent, operating at odds with the ethical code governing your profession. Your intention and its consequences is at its conclusion, child abuse. In my sons' case you have succeeded admirably.

It is for this reason entirely disingenuous that you would imply that there is no need for a time deadline in any correspondence with yourself or your client in light of my experience of what happens in correspondence with you, even when deadlines are applied.

I will not even begin to list live correspondence currently awaiting your reply, notwithstanding the history of extremely late replies in previous years. It is true to say in all fairness you are on record for consistently failing to reply in a timely manner even in matters relating to the child's well-being.

At the opposite end of the conduct scale, I have not on one single occasion been late with any reply. Usually, as is the case here, I reply by return and so for this reason, because you are habitually late in correspondence, it is entirely appropriate that I apply deadlines, given the organizational requirements necessary in planning this visit.

For reasons of historical irregularly as well as my wish to see this visitation succeed towards the best interests of the child, I have attempted to derail your clients ongoing systematic efforts in ending any visitation, by presenting a very simple invitation to agree one of two possibilities that invites no possible confusion.

The limit of choices to two in my letter is because Nico has previously serially obstructed my efforts towards arranging visitation for Sam, often by re-wording well intended correspondence in a provocatively misleading manner giving rise to a familiar outcome. I can refer you to visitation arising from Nico's negotiating Sam's right to see his mother limited to some three (3) nights in 2013 and eight (8) nights in the entirety of 2015.

This low amount if visitation is not Sam's choice, nor mine, and equally clearly, Nico's success in limiting our time to this extent cannot be confused with acting in his best interests. Sam wants to see me. I want to see Sam. The occasions in which our wishes have been met are directly in proportion to yours and Nico's success in obstructing our visitation.

Fueling this process is your basic adversarial and unhelpful rudeness in communication along with the untimely manner in which it is delivered. This is not my sole opinion or experience, but copied from another member of your family law community. Your reputation precedes you, which you will likely receive as a compliment.

It was entirely possible for Sam to see a great deal more of me than he has and it is tragically disappointing for both of us that your client has chosen the approach he has, the outcome of which is spelled out clearly in the number of nights we have had together.

Perhaps you will look towards your own contribution to this process, and if not now, at some future point in your life, especially if you have children of your own to consider, realise the harm that your approach visits on situations where basic courtesy would make all the difference. The consequence of your approach is child abuse. Essentially, that is how you earn your living.

But it is not for me to offer free advice on the connection between cause and consequence. The passage of time has its own way.

Your client's obstructive and controlling approach towards visitation has prevented Sam, on all but one 3-week summer holiday occasion in 2014, from being with me in California, where I am resident only because of the severe financial harm your client, with your guidance, has successfully imposed on my financial position.

This vindictive and baseless litigation in which you benefit handsomely at my expense with funds that might in the alternative provide advantages for my two sons also leaves me reliant on the kindness of my family, who now also feel the weight of Nico's ongoing vindictiveness to the extent that my 80 year-old father, in his failing health, refers to Sam in the past tense. All of which your client, previously a frequent beneficiary of my Fathers largesse and generosity, is well aware of.

I will not detail the many examples of that fundamentally dishonest representation here, but it is not inappropriate to refer to the last occasion which Sam was allowed to see me by your client, In September 2015 for 28 hours, which you may accept was an expensive 28 hours, involving my travel from the US for a 28 -hour period with my son. The visit was originally for 24 hours. You may recall the tremendous kindness Nico showed in extending the time by an additional four hours, against your written advice. Another example of your correspondence with me that speaks to the nature of child abuse.

That visit in September was followed by an offer in November to spend the same amount of time, a 2-night visit travelling from the US which your client would not extend on the grounds that Sam had to attend Greek classes on a Saturday morning, allowing me the opportunity to travel 12,000 miles for only one single night in full awareness that I simply could not consider flying 12,000 miles for no more than 24 hours with Sam. Because attending Greek lessons on a Saturday morning was more important than being allowed to see me? Bearing in mind I know it is extremely unlikely that he attends Greek lessons as in our last meeting it is clear he does not speak Greek.

It seemed to me Nico deliberately imposed this limit on the amount of visitation in full awareness of the likelihood that it would obstruct the visit and was abusive of Sam's rights, denying him this pre-Christmas visit on the spurious grounds of a Saturday Greek school appointment. Unfortunately, I interpreted this insistence on not allowing even two nights when I was prepared to go to those lengths (12,000 miles for two nights) as his way of affecting the visitation because that is exactly what happened. I could not justify the travel cost for one night. While this may appear as a triviality to you, the reality is that following that cancelation, I have not seen Sam for over four months. There is a clear pattern here and you are a part of it.

In the interim your client, acting on your advice, has disconnected every Skype contact on Sam's iPad with every member of my family, including both Sam's Godparents.

He has limited Sam's contact with me to one single phone call on Christmas day, which was extremely controlled, with his family in picture continuously and which gave rise to serious concerns over Sam's well-being.

I refer to what appears to be Nico grooming Sam to lie to me. I say that this is transparently parental alienation and child cruelty. And that you are both aware of it and as his legal counsel, you bear responsibility.

If you wish to explore specific detail of this decision by the father, evidently using a child to serve his commercial interest, then I welcome the opportunity to disclose that detail to you in full for your client to explore the opportunity for an explanation.

Turning to my offer to travel to the UK in February to see Sam and the expense this involves I would like to detail the consequences of your client's decision to deny Sam's travel with me in June of 2015 in the hope that this may advance his progress towards understanding cause and consequence. In so far as this affects future visitation with Sam.

I have already written to you on the subject of Maria Andiotis. (a letter that represents just one more absent reply from yourself or your client).

In June of 2015, Sam was aware of the South African trip and was even more excited about seeing 'Beautiful Maria' than attending his Grandfathers 80th birthday, which was funding that trip.

Sam was by then, as he expressed in our last conversation on 25 December, 2015, very concerned that Maria is 'very sick'.

Your client was aware that Maria's battle with cancer meant she had not long to live and that the June opportunity for Sam to see Maria, a woman he adored and had a close relationship with, would be the last time for both Sam to enjoy with Maria, as well as for Maria to enjoy with Sam. In fact the arrangement was for Sam (and myself) to stay in his Godfathers home, with Maria. I cannot overstate how disgusted I am with your client's decision to prevent this visit.

Shortly before she died last week, Maria expressed to me her sorrow at being denied the opportunity to say goodbye to 'my sweet Sam' by someone she viewed formerly as a friend. Maria admitted she was wrong about Nico and described him in less than favourable terms as *"The most dishonest person I have ever come across in my life."*

I chose in my letter of 4 January, 2016 to limit my correspondence to one of two possibilities, reflecting the fact that all correspondence with yourself and Nico appears to end the same way. In adversarial, rude confrontation that ends visitation.

I would like to point out to you that even in the letter I am replying to, you have chosen what appears as adversarial reference to 'arbitrary and unreasonable deadlines'. A choice of words that was unnecessary and cannot be seen as helpful towards supporting the visitation prospects.

My letter of 4 January 2016 was presented reasonably and without any invitation or provocation for this style of antagonistic reply.

May I respectfully request that if you are to continue as intermediary in Sam's visitation with me, that you adjust the tone of your correspondence to include the basic conventions attached to courtesy. Let's avoid this unpleasantly unnecessarily antagonistic approach if at all possible. I confirm that your intention to annoy me is a triumphant success. But is it in the child's best interests or a reasonable representation of your office, guided by the ethical code of the SRA.

Let's focus on placing the child's best interest uppermost and agree to move forward toward a common goal of encouraging the best prospects of success for this visit bearing in mind that *'Litigation leads to animosity between the parents which is never in the child's best interests.*

I understand that litigation is what you do and represents your best and most lucrative interest here, but perhaps on this one occasion you might consider almost three years of persistent damage to a child, now just 6, to be a sufficient measure of your success.

I remind you that the litigant in this separation and Sam's residential parent controlling his visitation options, is your client and our correspondence faces the challenges this acrimony represents.

Courtesy therefore should be uppermost in your consideration when writing to me for the benefits it represents to the child's best interest. Its absence would clearly be abusive.

If you reflect for a moment on my letter of 4 January 2016, you will see that I have described, in simple terms, two options.

Simply put Nico can either:

1. Arrange for Sam to have a half day at school Friday. Or.

2. Not arrange for Sam to half day at school

The return time is agreed for 6 pm on Tuesday. In other words, he will be with me from Friday afternoon, at one of two collection times, on Saturday night, Sunday night and Monday night.

In light of the uncertainty governing Nico's historical predisposition towards obstructing visitation, or imposing conditions that end visitation possibilities, I have not yet made the arrangements in respect of travel, car hire or hotel reservation prior to written confirmation of the specific details. This is the reason for a deadline. To enable me to make non-refundable reservations.

The confirmation I require before I make these expensive commitments is limited to one of two possibilities.

In my letter of 4 January 2016, the two possibilities relating to Sam's collection from School include either him having a half day off, or not.

I have agreed to meet the cost for:

1. Travel from LAX to LHR. And 2. Hotel for four nights.

What I am asking of your client is:

Allow Sam to have a half day (which his headmaster will surely agree. I have already emailed him). I will take Sam to a specified Hotel within 40 minutes' drive on Friday, and; return him for collection from Sam's Godmother Jo on the Tuesday evening at 6 pm. (Subject to Jo's agreement.)

I have explained that I have not yet consulted with Jo, Sam's godmother, because there is no point in securing her commitment towards this end in advance given Nico's historical reluctance to support the success of any proposed visitation. However, even if Jo is unable to assist, I am offering the reassurance that collection will be from a local address for Nico's convenience. Details to be determined following written agreement on the allowance for this visit.

Relative to the cost I am inviting to make this visit succeed, I hope you will agree adding the extra half day is in Sam's best interests.

For the purpose of clarity and avoidance of doubt let me repeat again:

In the alternative to no:

Will Nico agree a half day on Friday, for me to collect him, and return him at 6 on Tuesday at Jo, or a nearby family friend. For a four-night visit, to be collected locally from Jo not before 6pm on Tuesday.

Once I have this confirmation I can proceed with flight and Hotel arrangements.

Once I have a Hotel booking then I will be able to disclose this information. And the same applies to the return collection details.

Bearing in mind this is an extremely simple proposition, requiring very little thought, and entirely absent of arbitrary and unreasonable intent, I ask again for confirmation on the very clear terms proposed by no later than Thursday 7th January.

Post Thursday the simple fact is there will be no further opportunity for this 'Valentine's day' visitation because the opportunity to book late notice International flights and suitable Hotels will have passed. This is no more than an obvious practical reality.

I propose we put to one side the very clear reality that Sam's opportunities for visitation are serially obstructed, consistent with previous situations of an identical nature and on this occasion, and at this time place the best interests of a 6-year-old who is desperate to see his mother to the fore.

This letter is sent by return in all fairness to enable you to have the maximum amount of time to decide on whether to allow the visitation as outlined, or not, within the clearly specified deadline and considering that more than half the time proposed by this deadline has already passed without the seemingly simple yes or no answer required.

I hope I have addressed any concerns and offered every appropriate reassurance that there is no reason why this visitation should not proceed as outlined unless it is your support for your client's decision to once again obstruct visitation.

Yours sincerely,
Andrea

---

*From: Tim Clock **Date:** Wednesday, January 6, 2016 at 7:53 AM*
To: Andrea Lee
Subject: Re: Your client Nico Krasnopovich

Dear Andrea

Please confirm which hotel you have in mind. Provided it is local Nico will arrange for Sam to be dropped there for 4 pm otherwise you will have to arrange to collect him.

Whilst I have replied promptly I do not understand your deadline which seems to me arbitrary and unreasonable.

Yours sincerely

Tim Clock

And after that visit ended, 16 February 2016, I never spoke with Sam again. That was our last farewell. At Jo's house. Even my correspondence with him ended when Krasnopovich moved and refused to provide me with the new address. (For 9 months.)

It is clear that during that visit Krasnopovich would have been actively progressing the purchase of the property he moved into 6 weeks later, yet he never mentioned it, and had ensured Sam did not know he was moving imminently, to tell me while I was visiting with him in February. It would take a further nine months before he finally wrote, providing me with the address, enabling at least that amount of contact with my son. The start of twice weekly envelopes with three pictures in each, each with a handwritten story on the back.

Children love getting things in the post.

Three years would pass with nothing more than letters in the post. Twice every week. With four pictures in each envelope. With story's handwritten on the back. No one I know has any contact with Krasnopovich.

19 California visit for Sam. Breach of Privacy
Sam finally gets to visit with me

After the flood in 2014, being officially homeless, I arranged a six-month rental in California, intended at the time as a temporary let while my home was repaired. Philip had a level in his house that was available, providing me with a studio and a guest room for Sam and Evan to visit. There was no reason to stay in the UK while the works were undertaken by Insurance, as I assumed they would be and having lost my application for visitation meaning I had no prospect of seeing Sam unless I paid Krasnopovich a six-figure sum, which had now risen to £150,000.

I was particularly attracted to the sunshine in California, which I knew was having a positive effect on the depressive stimulus arising from the court case. Live vitamin D. Crucially, as I had not yet received any payment from the Insurance for rehousing, Phillip agreed to let me stay on the basis of paying him when the Insurance money came through. With my Hotel bill at £5,000 for the previous month, this housing decision became a no brainer.

Once in California, the initial plan was that Sam would spend his holidays with me in Philips home in Laguna Beach. During this time, leading up to the summer holiday we would speak regularly on Skype. Initially Sam would Skype me every day, after his return from school while his nanny was babysitting. A good routine emerged. His iPad was working and we had long chats each day. But then Krasnopovich found out. The iPad was taken away from Sam, and he was told he could only use it on weekends. With his father present, usually scowling in the background on camera.

Shameless.

Our Skype time was set by Krasnopovich at once a week, at 6pm UK time, for a maximum of 1 hour. At that time Sam would take the Skype to his room and I hoped that there was a degree of privacy in our talks. It was also clear that Sam did not want to talk when his father was in the room. On those occasions where we were chatting and he arrived, Sam's demeanor changed entirely. He would stop talking. We would stare at the screen in silence while Krasnopovich scowled in the background.

Meanwhile negotiations went on for the visitation. Between Clock and Clam. I wanted the summer holiday in full. I had not seen Sam for more than a handful of nights since the fathers-day incident and in our Skype chats it was very clear that he wanted to be with me.

My proposal was that I would collect him the day after his term end from school and return him three days before his return to school date. Flying from LAX for this purpose and returning him to London after his trip.

His reply was "*You can have him for two weeks.*" Extensive negotiation followed. Between my lawyer, Clam, and his lawyer Clock. Costing me literally thousands of pounds. Krasnopovich would not budge. As one part of his objection was that Sam would be outside of the UK for over a month, I offered to take him on holiday in the UK first. And to this end arranged a one-week trip to St Andrews. Driving up to

Scotland and visiting some of the landmarks in beautiful Scotland, in June. I thought this road trip would be good parent son time. The arrangements were made and the negotiations continued. It seemed for a while that Clock and Krasnopovich would allow Sam to be with me. A week in Scotland followed by a month in California. Not ideal, but at least some time for Sam to spend with me. Several expensive legal letters later and with tickets to include Scotland already booked, Krasnopovich refused all but three weeks in California. Sam was not allowed to join me in Scotland. My gamble on booking the trip in anticipation of Krasnopovich and Clock allowing Sam that time proved an expensive mistake. Once again my optimistic belief that no father would refuse his son a wonderful experience just to establish his authority and dominance over the mother while attaching a price tag to every visitation was proven wrong. The dates for his visit were eventually confirmed. Three weeks exactly, 21 days in CA. Sam was driven to my Hotel by Jo the night before departure to the US and the next day we flew together to LAX and from there to the rental in Laguna Beach. From the moment he saw me and we hugged he slotted perfectly into the character of our relationship. My beautiful son and his adoring mummy. This has been the case very time we met. Like a connection to the four years we were together all the time. That same emotional affectionate familiarity, unblunted by the enforced absences. We had a magnificent time together for those three weeks. With too many highlights to pick. He especially enjoyed Jedi School at Disneyworld, where he earned a Jedi certificate. He saw the schools in Laguna where he might attend if an agreement could be reached with his Father. He met Tommy the Turtle, Phillips brother with a farm in the countryside with animals and an overnight sleep in a tent in the American West where Sam heard Coyotes howling at night and discussed how he would deal with a Coyote attack. (With great humor.) He saw an owl and heard its night time cooing call.

He fired a real .22 rifle in a supervised and appropriate context, rode on a real BMW motorcycle down Coast highway, with his own fitted helmet, rode on a VESPA scooter, made good friends with Mason, the next-door neighbor, who showed him around the hood. Sam had weekly tennis coaching with the Laguna Beach kids' coach and became the host and lemon picker from 'his' lemon tree in Philips garden for the BBQ parties we threw for him to meet family and friends in Laguna. He visited musician and mouth organ maestro Hugo Fernandes at the Pelican Hill resort, where Hugo gave him a gift. A real professional Mouth Organ.

Sam especially loved being with Philip, spending one-on-one time every day practicing art and enjoying swimming with him. Philip proved to be the ideal swimming instructor for Sam's level of swimming. His progress under his tutelage was remarkable. And all too quickly it was over. I had to fly him back to London, delivering him to Jo's house on Thameside, for collection by his father from there.

I turned around and drove the 4-hour rental back to Heathrow, heading back to LAX the same day, feeling emptier than any selection of words can demonstrate.

Chronic depression hardly describes the net outcome.

I returned to California in a cloak of sorrow. The twin barb of not being able to see Sam while having whatever income I had deliberately drained away by family law acted very much at odds with the 'man up' approach to fighting. The injustice of being turned over by a beneficiary of my best kindness made the betrayal all the worse.

The realization that by fighting I was involving Sam in a fight that was not of his choosing and which could never have a positive outcome for him became conclusive.

If ever there was a claim to be 'using the child as a football in a game' then Krasnopovich and Clock held the Champions cup.

After Sam's departure from California, I tried Skyping him the day of my return. As I promised him I would. This was some 48 hours after I last saw him.

No reply.

I tried the next day.

No reply.

And the next.

No reply.

After ten consecutive days of no reply I grudgingly had to pay the lawyer, Clam, to take up the matter with Krasnopovich's lawyer, Clock. Writing to ask why Sam was not answering his skype. Shortly after that, some three weeks since I last saw Sam, came a letter from Krasnopovich containing a transcription of a recorded conversation between Sam and myself.

While Sam was with me in CA, Krasnopovich kept calling repeatedly to Skype. I had agreed that while he was with me I would allow him to skype Krasnopovich as soon as he asked, but not otherwise. Sam never asked, yet Krasnopovich kept trying to Skype. There would be five missed calls each day. After a week, he had Clock write an email to me saying "Nico is worried. Please get Sam to Skype him."

I replied to say. "Sam is having a great time. There is nothing to worry about. As soon as he asks to speak with his father I will ensure he skypes."

That wasn't good enough. He demanded to speak to him.

Although I did not accept this was reasonable in any way because Sam was obviously happy beyond words to be with me and had not so much as mentioned his father once, rather than allow things to escalate, I asked him to Skype his father.

He was initially reluctant to do so. Eventually he agreed. I left the room to allow him privacy.

After that call, which was extremely brief as it seems he was very clear about keeping time with me separate from time with his father, literally returning two minutes after he connected the Skype call, he came into the living room where I was sitting.

"*Mummy, why doesn't daddy like you*" he asked.

"*Because daddy has issues with me*" I replied in the same open and honest age-appropriate way that I discuss all things with my child.

The conversation ran for awhile, in which time I openly and in an age appropriate way gave some necessary and opportune perspective to a 5-year old who had seen his world so completely rocked by his father's decision to break up his family and then obstruct visitation so deliberately while litigating.

That five-minute conversation was between my son and myself. An important exchange on many levels. From my point of view, it was, as ever, extremely well phrased and communicated to Sam exactly what my intention was. Explaining his questions in the most positive and considered way. Sam absorbed my answers to his questions. Appeared satisfied and we moved on with our next fun activity.

Unbeknownst to Sam or to myself, Krasnopovich recorded that conversation, through the iPad. Without permission or consent. He transcribed the recording, word for word, and sent it in an email to Philip, who was at that time the intermediary between us as I had no direct contact with Krasnopovich.

What Krasnopovich did was a criminal offense in the State of California where it is a penal offense to Breach Privacy by recording someone without their knowledge or consent. And it is a second penal offense to share any information gained in this illegal manner with a third party. In this case, by emailing the illegal content to a third party, Philip. Because a criminal offense occurred I consulted a California State bar attorney, Dick Brando. Dick explained that two offenses had occurred. Reviewing the email from Krasnopovich to Philip as proof of guilt, effectively an admission of guilt in his own hand. Sending the email to Philip was proof of the second offense. Dick explained that the statutory award in each of the two offenses was $5,000 and that the claim for damages arising would be a calculation in a court hearing. The valuation would be relative to the harm this recording caused.

Did this recording damage my visitation with Sam and if so, what value can be attached to this? Because of the recording Krasnopovich was now preventing any skype contact and considering whether he 'would allow any visitation unless……..'

Clearly an offense was committed and clearly as a result of that offense, visitation with Sam was affected, meaning I now had to spend more money on legal fees to address Krasnopovichs' criminality. I paid Brando to prepare the case and file in California.

Was Krasnopovich guilty of two criminal offenses in the state of California? Clearly yes. Written by his own hand.

Unfortunately my lawyer, Dick Brando, made a technical error. He did not do his homework on jurisdiction sufficiently well. Krasnopovich was able to use a Newport Beach solicitor to first make an offer to settle at the mandatory amount for each offense, $5,000, and when that was not accepted, to argue jurisdiction saying the offense happened in England. Where the recording was made and not in California where the recording took place.

You decide. The offense was committed. That is not disputed.

Where did the offense happen? In London, where he pushed record. Or in California where the microphone was located and the conversation that breached our privacy was recorded.

Legal semantics which led to a judge deciding the offense did not occur in California and the Court did not have jurisdiction. This in part because Krasnopovich lied in saying that I lived in the UK, which influenced the judge in that this was a matter between two UK citizens. It was shrewd lawyering to make that claim, but it was untrue as I was already resident in the US. Which Krasnopovich knew. There you go Another example of a false declaration in court proceedings by a dishonest lawyer.

Brando should, I was told, have established jurisdiction before he filed for anything. Who knows. Law is what it is and everyone has an opinion.

Without doubt, the offense did occur. And without doubt, the legal semantics got him off on the technicality that the offense did not happen in CA, but in London. And without doubt, declaring that I was resident in the UK helped the judge find that the case should be heard in London, not Los Angeles.

The option then was to appeal the jurisdiction hearing on grounds that the offense happened in California, where the conversation took place. Not that the offense had not happened. It was accepted that it had. A practicing lawyer committed two offenses in the State of California, but got off through a technicality.

After consulting with a high-powered specialist in this type of law in Los Angeles, despite reassurance that clearly the offense did happen in California, and seeing precedent in similar cases that would be used to '*almost certainly, I would say 90/10'* win the jurisdiction issue, I was by this time out of funds to pay the retainer to progress. Krasnopovich broke the law in California, on two counts. Bang to rights. By his own written admission. And for good measure, in the April hearing he used his special relationship with Flaherty to present the case (In Flaherty's closed proceedings) that nasty Andrea tried to sue poor Krasnopovich in California for damages, when all he was doing is looking out for his son. Flaherty, in what appeared to me to be highly irregular conduct that spoke to an undeclared interest in supporting Krasnopovich, attempted to have me agree in her Court to '*not pursue any further litigation against Krasnopovich'*. Effectively interfering with Justice in the State of California by attempting to make me indemnify Krasnopovich from any prosecution for the two offenses which Krasnopovich was clearly guilty of.

The question I have relates to Flaherty's integrity and impartiality as a judge.
This legal offense in California had nothing to do with the matter before Flaherty. If it had, clearly Krasnopovich was guilty of a criminal offense. Why then did Flaherty attempt to use her position to make me undertake in court that I would not '*bring any proceedings against Krasnopovich.*' This happened, along with the reminder that these were 'closed proceedings' and so I could not tell anyone. The California proceedings were not in any way related to the matter in Flaherty's court. How did she even know about these proceedings, let alone decide to indemnify an offender in this way?

From the user side of this experience I can report it felt very much like a mafia visit. You do what we say or else. I wasn't asked to indemnify Krasnopovich from any claim in California. I was ordered to.

Who regulates Judges (Deputy District Judges) when they act outside of the law when they can prevent their actions being disclosed using the contempt law?

Here is Flaherty's wording on a criminal offense in the state of California committed by a member of British family law.

61. There is one unhappy postscript to this matter. It seems that post the hearing in April this year and at about the time when Ms LEE should have been complying with the orders of the court to subject herself to a psychiatric assessment on her mental capacity, instead she instigated appeal proceedings in America to revive the unfortunate and misconceived lawsuit in the USA about the so-called breach of the penal code when she was found to have been responsible for some very ill-judged and non child-focussed remarks to Sam about his father. I hope that this matter is no longer pursued but I would be very happy for this judgment to be released into those proceedings if it was of assistance.

It is not a '*so-called*' breach of the penal code. It is a breach of the penal code. On two accounts. That is not disputed by Krasnopovich. The 'confession' is by his own hand. The email admitting to the offense.

"when he was found to have been responsible for some very ill-judged and non-child-focussed remarks to Sam about his father."

Found by whom? Flaherty?

My conversation with Sam in my home was private and if there is any ill-judged aspect in this comment that credit is entirely for Flaherty. If Flaherty is commenting on the content of the illegal recording, then she is willfully breaking the law. Knowing that the recording was a penal offense in California. It is the subject of an illegal breach of privacy.

Worse. She is making a value judgment on my parenting that might be used against me in future proceedings if my son wishes to be with me. And she is making it based on a nonsense that was not even a part of the proceedings she was there to judge on. I dispute entirely that the conversation included '*non-child focused remarks*' *because* the conversation did not include any *non-child-focused remarks.*

Quite the contrary. I say Flaherty's words are a lie. Intended to cause harm to my child and myself. For the purpose of benefitting her fellow member of family-law. The conversation, illegally recorded in a breach of privacy offense in California, was completely child-focused. This comment in Flaherty's judgment is another transparent lie by a judge clearly relying solely on Krasnopovich's version of events and not offering even the pretense of establishing the facts behind this criminal act. Preferring instead to manifest her prejudice against me in blindly supporting a fellow member of British family law who has committed a criminal offense, by attempting to transfer the blame and use her position to interfere with due legal process in another country. Attempting to make it an order of court that Krasnopovich was indemnified from prosecution in California.

Putting on record that I was found to have made '*non-child focused remarks*' serves Krasnopovichs' interests in any future custody hearing. Bad mother Andrea. Good father Krasnopovich. Clever and responsible Judge Flaherty.

Even her observation that '**at about the time when Ms. LEE should have been complying with the orders of the court to subject herself to a psychiatric assessment on her mental capacity, instead she instigated appeal proceedings in America**' is off point.

I did not '*instigate appeal proceedings.*' Proceedings were already underway. An offense had been committed.
    Where does Flaherty get this stuff from?
With such incoherent incompetent interpretation of law intended to protect the best interests of a child, whilst relying on a spelling age of a ten-year-old and the logic of an adolescent. Psychiatrists identified for me to choose one from is glossed over to suit her convenience in making this point about '*what I should have been doing*'. That specific aspect, *the three psychiatrists*, is detailed later in the story. This point 61 of

the judgment, in every aspect it raises, is an abuse of Flaherty's position as a judge in family court.

It forms one further link in a series of lies that contribute to increasing the animosity between Sam's parents. Her claim seeks to establish 'on the record' that I am guilty of bad parenting and is another instance in which Flaherty is guilty of child abuse.

Or. I if am wrong then Flaherty is right to ensure that Sam should not have his mother in his life. And she has acted appropriately in this regard.

A judge presenting a demonstrably prejudiced pre-determination tailored to suit her judgment without regard for the truth of the matter. Willing to flaunt the same law that employs and empowers her.

Consider that I very much wanted to be present at the court hearing deciding my son's future in that add on day where I was hoping to travel to London, but was unable to for reasons of health. Unquestionably I was unwell. I had several doctors of unimpeachable character vouching for my health. Yet Flaherty devalued them by doing exactly that. Impugning their credibility. There was no pressing need preventing adjourning until I was well enough to attend. Instead Flaherty rushed through a poorly considered order that I see one of three psychiatrists to enable her to complete proceedings without me on an unrealistic timescale in which her own order to provide three psychiatrists was breached and even then she glossed over this breach to force through a revised version that contradicted her own ruling. I resent not being able to attend a proper and efficient court process determining my son's future. I believe it should have been my right as a citizen and as a parent to be present at the hearing. I feel offended that this was done in such an amateur way that it falls far below the level of laughable competence and yet, there is no provision to make this person accountable for actions that harmed a child. I believe it is more than just incompetence responsible for heinous child abuse and that Flaherty has a case to answer in law.

I reported Flaherty's comments to the law firm handling the Breach of Privacy offences in California. Here is their reply.

---

from: Dick Brando
Date: Mon, 6 Apr 2015 22:09:34 +0000
To: Andrea Lee
Subject: RE: Leandros v. Krasnopovich; Appeal.

Andrea,

Thank you for your email. Contrary to Mr. Krasnopovich's representation to the UK court as you described below, the CA case was not "thrown out" on the "merits" in California. The court did not reach the "merits" of the case.

To the contrary, the Orange County court has ruled only, as indicated in my email of March 27, that it lacked personal jurisdiction over Mr. Krasnopovich (a UK resident) to take up or consider the merits of the dispute here. As such, you are free to bring the case in the UK if you choose. That's what's called a procedural ruling only (and not a substantive ruling).

It's odd that Mr. Krasnopovich would take as a "victory" a mere jurisdictional or procedural ruling, while ignoring his underlying offense that reflects far worse on him—the unauthorized taping and recording of you and his son (apparently for litigation advantage or emotional harm or both)—than your good faith disagreement about whether CA has jurisdiction over him for causing these affects in California.

While the prospects for success are extremely high, predicting the result of any litigation, including appeals, is a very difficult, if not impossible, endeavor. I, and no attorney, can tell you in percentage terms precisely the chance success of an appeal. In this case, I think the court's analysis was legally flawed, and this is why I am confident, largely for the reasons stated in our opposition showing, in our view, that the CA court could exercise personal jurisdiction over Mr. Krasnopovich due to him causing the "effects" in California, among other things. For example, the trial court ignored analogous authority cited in the opposition where a New York woman, who made threatening and obscene phone calls to her ex-husband and his wife, both living in California, was found subject to California jurisdiction in an action for intentional infliction of emotional distress resulting from her phone calls. (Schlussel v. Schlussel (1983) 141 Cal.App.3d 194, 198-99 [190 Cal.Rptr. 95, 97].)

To answer your question about timing, the appeal would likely be decided within a year of filing. If the appeal were successful, then the case would be remanded to the trial court for further proceedings which would entail discovery, motions, trial preparations, court appearances, and unless otherwise resolved, a trial. I think all of this could very reasonably entail legal fees of approximately $50,000 to take a case through trial, but this depends largely on what the other side does in response to the case. The scale of the damages would reflect events since we first filed and I would expect to recoup your costs within this claim. It remains the case that two offenses were committed in the State of California by Mr. Krasnopovich. Reported in his own hand.

Thank you.

Sincerely,
Dick Brando, Of Counsel
Prescot Law Group, APC

20 David Clam. Solicitor

Member of family law. Invoiced me £189,000. Caused me losses measured in millions

In the first six months after fathers-day my legal bill from David Clam reached around £40,000. For which he failed to win me even 2 nights a month with my son. In year one I had my son with me for a total of 4 nights. That equates conveniently to £10,000 in legal costs for each night Sam spent with me.

During this time Krasnopovich wrote to one of the intermediaries saying *"Clam is an idiot"* and is the single occasion in which he spoke honestly throughout these proceedings.

In year two, the Financial directions hearing and the Flaherty hearing, Clam's bill to me was some £120,000. By the time I fired him after the appalling Flaherty hearing, his bill to me was £189,000.

Aside from his spectacular failure rate against Krasnopovich and Clock, there were many areas in which he was not only hopelessly remiss, but in which he failed to meet the ethical standards as laid out in the Solicitors Regulation Authority.

Here are a few examples.

Clam was late on a number of occasions with filing documents directed by court order. I was following proceedings with my full attention, as is not hard to understand. It was my life on the line and I was paying top dollar for a Cambridge educated family-law member to process my position in law. I usually replied to his emails by return on every occasion that he wrote. However, I noticed slippage on his correspondence requiring that I send prompts to him, reminding him of dates for specific disclosures. I wrote repeatedly on this subject during the course of our preparations. My legal position was reliant on his reply to emails, which all too often would take weeks. He was not in his office a great deal and often there would be unacceptably long gaps before his replies to me.

During the run up to the Financial Directions in October 2014, before DDJ Berry, Clam phoned me with notice that he would be missing a court deadline for submission of documents on my behalf because he was super busy elsewhere. He sounding convincing enough. He assured me that he would be responsible for any cost consequence arising from missing the court deadline and '*not to worry.*'

"It is highly unlikely that they will make any issue out of it anyhow. They have been late so many times and I haven't claimed against them so I don't foresee any problem, but even if there is, I will assume any responsibility. I will complete the submissions for you after my return in two weeks."

Months past with no further mention of this late filing and I thought no more of it. When I arrived in London to attend the Financial Directions hearing for the Krasnopovich claim, I sat down in the court waiting room with Clam and the barrister, who handed me a chronology to read before we went before the judge. In that chronology I noticed that I was listed as having breached a court order for late filing, been found guilty of contempt, and that costs had been awarded against me, some £2,600.

I realised at that moment that this referred to the late filing Clam had told me about with the assurance that he would take care of it. But here it was, on the record, with my name next to the offense and being listed as having been fined £2,600 for contempt in the late filing. It was a shock.

I had to re-read it carefully because I thought I must have misread it the first-time round. But no. There it was. Andrea Leandros. Guilty of late filing. Found in contempt of court. Fined costs of £2,642, payable to Tim Clock.

I immediately raised it with Clam, with barrister Richard Castello in the room. "David what is this finding against my name here?" I pointed at the notice.

"This is the call you made telling me you would take care of any consequences because you were going to be late filing. Why does it show as my name?"

Clam looked sheepish while Castello looked on with keen interest.

"Not to worry, I haven't invoiced you for that as I promised. I have paid the fine."

"David. That is unacceptable. You gave me notice that you would be filing late because you had business elsewhere. You assured me there would be no comeback on me. And now I see this?" I was furious and shoved the paper under his nose. *"You need to put this right immediately."*

Castello seemed bemused that Clam had allowed this to happen. I was referenced it with him directly. *"Richard, how do we put this right."*

"There's nothing we can do now. We are about to go in. But Mr. Clam can write to the court and have the record amended."

My barrister Richard Castello was aware of this error by Clam and weighed in with his recommendation for remedy.

Sure enough, the following week when I received my invoice for that cycle, I saw that a £2,600+ charge had been paid by Spoon LLP. Showing up on my invoice as NC. (No Charge). I assumed at that point that Clam had done as I demanded and as Barrister Castello advised, and contacted the court to set the record straight. However he did no such thing.

David Clam was solely responsible for that late filing and my name should not have appeared as the guilty party. That caused me actual harm. For which he is liable.

After the Preliminary hearing I wrote to Clam requesting confirmation that he remembered to contact the court and set the record straight. Clam then wrote a lengthy email (for which he charged me £120) in which he explained that it made no difference whose name was on the record and that as he had paid the fine I was not materially affected. I called him by return, explaining that this was not acceptable. And I wrote after that call placing in writing the same message. Demanding that he contact the court, admit he was guilty of the late filing offense, and have my name removed from the court document. He had already paid the court fine for the late filing. Effectively, to cut a long story of British family law conduct short, Clam ignored each one of my requests and never amended my name on the record.

When I arrived at Court for the April 2015 hearing before DDJ Flaherty, in a déjà vu moment, I was handed the barristers timeline chronology where the first thing I noticed was my name, highlighted, guilty of contempt for late filing. Having breached the order by DDJ Berry leading to the £2,600+ costs award against me.

To date my name remains on File as having breached the Courts order and as having been awarded costs against me. It is one of the first things anyone reading Krasnopovich's submission would see, highlighted as it was.

Would this lead any judge towards an adverse view of me?

Could this be used to my detriment in proceedings?

Is there any doubt that David Clam caused that evidential harm to my case?

As it happens, that late filing contempt was the first thing Appeal judge Le Clerc referred to in the Appeal hearing. '*But Ms. Leandros was late.*" The Appeal hearing began and ended with this point. The Appeal process I paid maybe £80,000 for lasted three minutes. Le Clerc reading that point and remarking "*Obviously Ms Leandros was late so what happened next really is her own doing.*"

I have no doubt that the Appeal was not allowed entirely because that point gave the Judge, Le Clerc, the opportunity to close a case he was all too keen to not open.

Here is the extract from Flaherty's judgment dealing with this exact point. *It was apparent that one of the issues in this case is the wife's allegedly frail mental health; her ability or inability to work and this has been given as a reason for delays in providing her solicitors with up-to-date instructions and her non-compliance with the directions for the filing of evidence laid down by DDJ Berry on 22.10.14 timeously.*

In her judgment Flaherty refers to me repeatedly as '*Wife*'. Which in the context of her awareness of the case is a telling oversight.

To be clear:

At no time was I late in filing. Clam was. Repeatedly. Clam paid the bill on the occasion listed in the Court record. Yet Flaherty and family court have penalised me and my son for an error by a member of British family law. Krasnopovich's Barrister Hazelwood would refer to that late filing at every opportunity and not once did Castello correct him. Including during the Appeal hearing before Andrea Le Clerc, where Hazelwood's submissions began with "*Ms Leandros was late.......*".

During the preparation for the April hearing, 6 witnesses were agreed as being significantly material to the facts. Including Larry Chester, the Independent Financial Advisor whose input would have been crucial when considering Flaherty's awareness shortfall in Financial matters and seeing how that ignorance has played out in relation to her Court order. The IFA's evidence contradicted the essence of Krasnopovich's claim and also provided independent verifiable documented evidence which would have disabled every avenue the prosecution would go on to present to Flaherty. Collating the 6 witness statements took some time and involved some expense. Eventually costing by my estimate some £12,000 of Clam's billable hours. And yet, no witnesses were allowed in the hearing by Flaherty.

The witnesses were set down by the previous court order allowing for multiple witnesses. They were all ready to go on the day of the hearing when the appointed judge was to start. And yet. Suddenly, the appointed judge was no more? A new judge had taken over the case right as the case began. Flaherty. Whose first decision was to prevent any witnesses? Her first ruling as the switch judge on the morning of day one was to declare that no witnesses would be allowed because Clam, with his usual turn of speed, filed the witness statements on the Friday before the Monday hearing. I knew nothing about this 'late' filing until the Monday hearing began. It was Clams job to file the witness statements appropriately. It was my job to pay for his work and provide the answers he required in connecting him with the witnesses. Which I had done. I realized later, during the visitation hearing, Clam had been ambushed by a late filing by Clock. When they announced they were bringing a QC to a preliminary hearing for visitation, and were claiming costs. Evidently, Clam thought he would play the same trick right back on the other side. Doing to them exactly what they did to him. Serving on the last day before the hearing.   The small details of what happened are all subsumed by this important fact. In this case of 'He said, she said' the only independent corroboration could come from witnesses. And those witnesses were there and ready to go. Beyond a shadow of doubt, this judgment could not have prospered as it did had the witness's information been considered. Worse still. I knew that the other side knew about the witnesses and how they would destroy his case. Because he knew who the witnesses were and what they would say. (For obvious reasons.) So it was clear that the only way their case could continue was by excluding the witnesses. I say therefore, that it is no coincidence that the witnesses were excluded. Hard evidence of collusion between a judge and a law firm to fix a judgment. In which my lawyer, David Clam, played right into their hands with his foolishly considered decision to file late. Just as they had done to him at the Visitation hearing.

At the Flaherty 'hearing' the opening submission by opposition council, Simon Hazelwood, was *"But here we are. There is, in my submission, absolutely no good reason as to why father's evidence was served as late as it was last week."* Flaherty nodded and dismissed the witnesses. It was that simple.

Flaherty's ruling to overrule the courts direction to allow multiple witnesses by both sides in a 3-day hearing was wrong. I acted exactly as the system required, paying the £12,000 I was charged by a member of family law for the statements and making sure that all the witnesses' statements were ready weeks in advance.

Ultimately, Sam was penalised for actions between two members of family law, Clam and Flaherty.

My complaints in highlighting this gross negligence have resulted in nothing whatsoever. Once again, British family law covers up its own mess and Flaherty got to note in her judgment;

"her non-compliance with the directions for the filing of evidence laid down by DDJ Berry on 22.10.14 timeously"

Had Clam filed the witness statements in good time it would not have presented Flaherty such an easy opportunity to dismiss 'them'. Witnesses who would entirely and comprehensively discredit her colleague Krasnopovich. Although, I have to say, I feel certain, even though Clam was foolishly incompetent in his approach, Flaherty was always going to prevent the witnesses. One way or another. Her case could not prevail otherwise.

How important were the witnesses?

Larry Chester has been my financial adviser since 1986. We are not social friends. He is a professional IPA who has also been responsible for my Building Insurance and every mortgage on my properties over a 28-year period at that time. He was appearing as a witness to present hard facts, with documentary substantiation.

Not only did he have the full background to my financial affairs at 28 Thameside, but he met with Krasnopovich on several occasions, advising on his investment requirements. He knew Krasnopovichs' financial picture and could demonstrate the financially planning showing 28 Thameside was my property and the financing never had any contribution from Krasnopovich. His picture of our mutual finances showed the precise details of who paid what and what the intention was in both my property as well as his property as well as his law firm.

Larry was present and a witness to the transfer of the Freehold to Krasnopovichs' name in 2003. Larry advised on the legality of transferring the Insurance into his sole name. He had a professional insight into my financial intentions as my financial adviser for 28 years and with the sole exception of the freehold transfer to Krasnopovich in 2003, I followed his advice to a tee. He guided every one of my decisions relating to 28 Thameside including the mortgages and including the freehold matters and buildings insurance. No one could be more useful to any judge looking to determine the honesty of Krasnopovich's claim.

Larry assisted with ensuring I had adequate Insurance cover since 1986. During the Insurance claims filed while he was responsible for the Insurance, he knew to the smallest detail the buildings and contents requirements for my situation as well as the exact details of previous claim history. He knew my intention to buy a 'matrimonial home' with Krasnopovich once his accounts from the new business became credible enough to qualify him for a mortgage. He knew my three flats were to become rentals and had already quoted on a joint mortgage for Krasnopovich and myself to buy a 'matrimonial property' following the proposed marriage intended for January 2014. He knew my pension plan was to pay off the mortgages within eight years and rely on the three flats as a retirement income. He knew the exact details of the policy cover I had with Fairtimes brokers which Krasnopovich cancelled, illegally, and had details relating to his fiduciary responsibilities in the Insurance cover. In any fiduciary claim against Krasnopovich, Larry had the precise detail of what amount was owed and why.

In simpler terms, had there ever been any '50/50 *like we were married*' agreement Larry would have been the first to know.

He was ready to swear in his capacity as an IFA who advised both of us together and separately, that this was never mentioned and more importantly, that there was a plan in place for a jointly owned property. In fact, in the months before Krasnopovich went for his fitness instructor led separation, we had visited two properties that were suitable for the 'family home' we had in mind. One a 3-acre property with a knock down-rebuild farmhouse and a large barn in Claygate, which would have provided me with studio space and a granny flat, which was a part of my house buying interest for my aging dad to have a place. Larry had prepared a mortgage offer for that property. Relevant because; it showed we were looking at buying a property together – one in which Krasnopovich would have 50% beneficial interest and be named on the title and the mortgage. Two obvious omissions from his claim on my property. His claim for 50% beneficial interest in my Thameside property was a clear fiction, which Larry was capable of articulating with some conviction, being in possession of all of the financial background.

Flaherty chose to not consider professional independent financial advice from the most informed professional person best equipped to provide this guidance.

When she made the order to enforce the sale of my property, had she considered Larry's advice, she would have had some idea of how best to go about that process without imposing a million pound loss on me through her uninformed ignorant judgment in which she would go on to award Krasnopovich 50% of my rental income as well and 'sole conduct of sale' of my home, at the same time as ordering that I was not allowed to enter my home. Foolish misjudgments leading to cost consequences that can be measured in the millions. By ordering 'sole conduct of sale' for Krasnopovich, whilst I was the mortgagee responsible, as ever, for 100% of the mortgage costs, all Krasnopovich had to do to profit best from this judgment, was nothing. Not sell the property which was made vacant by court order, meaning I had to pay all the costs with no income. After months that became years of meeting these costs or default on the mortgage, I realized how clever Flaherty's ruling was. And how effective. It made defaulting on the mortgage inevitable. Along with a hefty council tax ill for a property left empty and not generating rental income for three years while I am forbidden to enter it, if say, I wanted to see my son in the UK. Meanwhile, I keep paying 8% interest on the costs award and I have no say in the sale of my property, bought in 1986. The property meanwhile, has no flood insurance, because of the freeholder, Krasnopovich's fiduciary breach relating to the flood of 2014, and thanks to the indemnifier by Flaherty's court order, I am to believe that he is immune to any consequence for any of his actions as Freeholder. For good measure, I am required to keep paying a property lawyer to attend my affairs. To try and force the sale though, despite the huge loss I faced from selling I this way. Left to observe, at time of writing I am down well north of £ 3million, with no end in sight.

The judgment of Flaherty.

My Greek friend for 30 years, John Milos was another witness who knew me from before I bought Thameside and was present in my life throughout each of my property acquisitions with awareness of the specific details. He attended the party I gave when I completed the works to the last of the 3 flats I developed and John was aware of the various struggles involved in getting me to that point. He was a frequent visitor to my home through the years and one of my first friends to meet Krasnopovich when we started dating. He had a good insight into his character and the dynamic of our relationship. John as the auctioneer for the Onassis jewelry providing the £16,000 ring that I gifted Krasnopovich. John hosted Krasnopovich on his Greek Island home in one of many travels which I funded for Krasnopovich when he had only debt to his credit. John was a credible witness as to the arrangement in the relationship between Krasnopovich and myself, including being consulted on the parental agreement to have a child in 2008. John had input into the 'business plan' governing costs to raise a child and was frequently consulted and offered business advice on the set up of the law firm in Thameside. He knew and would attest to the agreement to fund the costs of the child by the law firm. He was one of several business savvy friends of mine who consulted in the set-up of Krasnopovich McDonald and who knew why I was so engaged in that business.

Chris Andiotis is Sam's godfather and has been a friend and occasional business manager to me for over thirty years. Chris was my close confidant following the break up with Krasnopovich and in the discussions and agreement to have a child. Along with his friend Jeff Jarred, a successful City lawyer for many decades, Chris provided detailed business advice on the set up of the legal business. As a multi-millionaire entrepreneur with many years of success in small business, his input was important and helpful in both my development and investment in Thameside as well as my investment and development of Krasnopovich McDonald. (The Law firm set up for Krasnopovich.) Chris had called Krasnopovich on several occasions, as an advocate for Sam, to represent Sam's interests as well as to broker a settlement when his litigation began. In this context Chris made valuable points to him that he knew the details of our life very well and knew that his claim was bogus and would be prepared to attend court to go through his statement to this effect along with the evidence he had from conversations between them in which Krasnopovich told him that

"It doesn't matter if she said she promised me anything or not. I will win in court. This is what I do. Either she pays me or I will bury her and she won't see Sam again."

Chris emailed me the content of one of their conversations, the last one which reads;

"Why do you think she owes you anything? She paid for everything. Every time you visited me here, she paid for everything. I know what she paid for his house since long before she met you and ever since then too. You live off her kindness. She bought that house twenty years before she met you. You're not on the mortgage. You're not on the title. And you only have the Freehold in your name because you frauded the Insurance company. You are a trustee in the Freehold and you had the duty to return it on request. You haven't even done that. When you asked for the website domain to be transferred from Andreas' name to yours, she could have said no and charged you for all that work, setting up your business, your website and all that she did for you. She didn't. She asked me for advice then and I told her to transfer the title back to you immediately. Because that's how these things work. You put the child first. You do not opportunistically look to take advantage of your child's parent. When you go adversarial it always ends in tears. Only lawyers win. You got what you want. You want out of the relationship. That's fine. I can't tell you what to do there. But you can't leave and then take the house with you. It's wrong. Do what's right for Sam now. Don't go to war over something that isn't even true. There is no upside. I will tell Andrea to agree to not claim anything from you and you agree to not claim anything from her. Put Sam first and get on with your life."

The first thing Krasnopovich did on reading Chris' witness statement was apply to have it excluded because his emails were sent 'Without Prejudice.' Which became a moot point when Flaherty just decided to exclude all witnesses.

Chris is a very compelling and credible character. Motivated very much by his love for Sam, he had arranged to fly on the Monday night (from his home in Johannesburg) to give evidence on the Tuesday, even though at the time his wife Maria was severely ill with cancer that would end her life just months later. He only learned he was not to be allowed to speak on the day he was due to fly.

My accountant was another witness who made a statement and was ready to appear. Able to show in numbers exactly how my finances worked and what my plans going forward were. There was no indication that I had given away 50% of my equity and income. To the contrary, he was aware of the forward planning for my property and knew that it did not include Krasnopovich. Our finances were never co-mingled.

My handyman/property manager wrote a witness statement and was set to give evidence on the Tuesday. John B was the handyman on 7 Thameside from 1986 when I first bought the building. He was from Durban and a real music fan who used to attend many of my gigs when I was a performing musician. We became friends. Aside of the handyman jobs, when I was busy as a music-producer I would hire John B for odd jobs in the music production business, which he enjoyed. Often involving driving stars to shows. I once booked John for a specific job. To meet fire regulations at the Shepherds Bush Empire, he was paid £150 to be responsible for dousing the fire hat used by Arthur Brown in his rendition of 'Fire'. A process where Arthur lights up his fire hat in a darkened theatre stage and starts up his hit song 'Fire'. *"I am the god of hellfire and I bring you… Fire"* after which the fire hat starts to burn his head meaning someone has to take it off him and make sure the flames do not burn down the venue. A responsible job which is one of many nice handy man jobs I put Johns way. All the while he continued as handyman at 28 Thameside until 2001 when he announced to me that he would not be able to continue looking after my property.

Why?
    "Because I have been silly. I noticed blood in my stool many months ago and I didn't go to the doctor. Now I have stage 4 Bowel cancer. I have 6 months left."
    I was shocked. This was totally unexpected.
    "What treatment options are there. Surely there's something?"
    "NHS say it's too far gone for chemo. They offer a surgery but that's an 80/20 I will not survive so not recommended. And if I do, no sex ever again. Not sure I want to live like that."
    "Have you gone for a second opinion?"
    "Yes. I sent the results to a top Oncologist in Durban who is famous for giving high dose chemo. It's so high its illegal here, but his prognosis is 50/50. Fifty percent likely the chemo will kill you."
    "Well, that has to be a better option?"
    "Yes but that's not on the NHS. They won't fund it. And he won't do anything without a £10,000 up-front payment and I don't have that kind of money."
    "If you did have £10,000, would you go?"
    "Like a shot."
    "Give me a minute."

I stepped around the corner and called my friend Leo Sayer. Leo liked John who had driven him on many occasions where I had worked with Leo professionally and wanted him safely transported.
    "Leo, just a quickie. John B, my mate who drives you, has cancer. Stage 4. Six months to live. But there's a chance with doctor offering a 50/50 using high dose

chemo. He needs £10 grand to get that treatment. I am prepared to front the money if you will agree a benefit show. I'll get the band to do it and take care of all the arrangements. I just need your buy in to the gig."

"Mate I am so sorry for John B. What a nice guy. Of course you can rely on me. Just let me know when."

John B left the next day for South Africa, where he came within a whisker of dying from the extreme chemo. He struggled for about 6 months which made him question whether he really wanted to live after all. He decided that he did and overcame tremendous odds to return to the UK free of cancer. To this day he is free of cancer and was still property manager of my property until the point where the court forced the sale.

The 4th July 2001 fund raiser at the local Hotel was a magical evening with a magical outcome, which reminds me of the mental fragility Flaherty identified in me.

After the John B fund raiser success, for many years I did annual collections for Marie Curie Cancer care in which I raised many tens of thousands for that worthy cause. Had I known then about my mentally fragility, as Flaherty ruled for my son's awareness,, I may never have had the confidence to do any of those sorts of things. It has rankled me persistently ever since, that Flaherty made the connection between my dishonesty and mental fragility, awarding my net worth to a family lawyer with a blighted reputation and fomented such animosity between separating parents that my son has not seen me since her 'mental fragility' judgment. For more than one reason John B was very keen to give testimony in the Flaherty hearing, not only because I helped him with the cancer fight, but because he was present for so much of the time that Krasnopovich was in Thameside doing building jobs and was for this reason privy to many of the most intimate conversations regarding the building, the costs of the building and the development in which Krasnopovich was not present.

I think John was a very compelling witness to the bricks and mortar element of my involvement and investment in Thameside and very aware of Krasnopovich lack of involvement and investment.

John also looked after Krasnopovich's rental property in Hounslow, at my behest and expense, which again, he did for me as a part of our relationship. Not because he worked for Krasnopovich.

I believed that the testimony of the witnesses would conclusively give the lie to Krasnopovich's claim and in the run up to the court case I tried to second guess what he would say, knowing who the witnesses were and what they knew.

My conclusion ahead of the hearing was the only chance he had in Court was stopping the witnesses speaking.

How exactly then did he achieve this so easily.

In a fair and honest hearing in a matter such as Krasnopovich's claim, witnesses were necessary and witnesses in this hearing were agreed at the Preliminary hearing where the time for the hearing was set at 3 days to allow for multiple witnesses. His case was only able to proceed at the Preliminary hearing on the assurance that he would bring 'Multiple witnesses'. And for this reason the family court judge set aside three days for the hearing, to allow for multiple witnesses. Yet it turned out at the hearing that he had no witnesses.

I knew he would have no witnesses all along. In all certainty. Because finding people to lie for you in court is not easy. Not even his mother would do it for him.

He had no witnesses because his claim was a lie.

Flaherty ruled *"Mr Castello also prays in aid that Ms Krasnopovich swore evidence about other witnesses who could attest to conversations about the beneficial ownership of 28A and 28B. I do not find this helpful. There can be many reasons why apparent witnesses do not give evidence and to speculate in this area is dangerous."*

When questioned about why he said he would bring multiple witnesses and brought none by Castello, he said he thought he would have a witness, but unfortunately that didn't work out.

Well. Why not. Why pray tell, 'let that one slide'.

Pressed further by Castello for details, he referred to our mutual friend Dia Mirza, a Family law Barrister and Deputy District Judge, saying he thought Dia would remember a conversation about this 50/50 claim.

But wait. That was a crock too.

When pressed still further by Castello he admitted Dia had no memory of any such conversation. Dia has no memory of any such conversation. So she cannot be a witness.

So, in summary;, the one witness Krasnopovich claimed he had at the preliminary hearing, had no memory at all of this claim? That is because Krasnopovich lied at the preliminary hearing. As the facts recalled here bear out.

Yet Flaherty's judgment skips over this point without pause.

"to speculate in this area is dangerous."

What?

Where is the speculation? There is no speculation outside of Flaherty's reference to this word.. Dia's absence confirms no such conversation ever happened. It does not invite 'dangerous speculation'. It confirms Krasnopovich claimed he had witnesses and it turned out that claim was a lie. He might just as well have said "I intended bringing the family-law President as a witness, but he doesn't remember anything." Bear in mind, Krasnopovich couldn't even get his mother or sister to even make a statement to this effect. Such was the magnitude of his lie.

I on the other hand had six credible witnesses with factual statements that entirely undermined Krasnopovich's 50/50 claim and, more significantly, would have made the claims he went on to make in her submission, perjury.

It was galling to watch Krasnopovich lie openly to Flaherty's encouragement when many of the individual points he made were contained in witness statements that she had excluded evidently for the sole purpose of enabling the lies Krasnopovich told leading to an award cost me millions, and costing my son his childhood with one parent, rather than leading to the arrest for perjury that would have been the honest outcome for the representations made by Krasnopovich for Flaherty's approval.

Knowing Krasnopovich's preparation style after ten years of assisting his legal practice, it is apparent to me that he had prepared his statement reliant on the witnesses not being a part of the case. This made me more convinced than ever that the judge was fixed for this hearing.

I would swear in a court of law that Krasnopovich knew the witnesses would be discounted. By hook or by crook. Winning his case depended on it. And I suspect this is because he knew he could rely on a friendly judge, who on this occasion turned out to be Cecelia Flaherty.

Flaherty was not involved in this hearing at 8 am on that Monday morning. Yet by 9 am she was and in her first act after becoming the self-appointed judge for Krasnopovich's claim, the witnesses were discounted.

My belief is that Flaherty replaced DDJ Burkes to fix the case according to direction from her colleagues in British family Law, Krasnopovich, Clock and Hazelwood.

It is a fact that Flaherty had taken against my barrister Richard Castello. He told me as much and it was clear from the moment he started speaking in her court. I will wager thruppence and a hapenny that Richard Castello could take the character perfect wife of a man convicted of seventy-two sex acts against minors for a visitation hearing in Flaherty's court and lose.

 She quite clearly had a personal agenda against this barrister. Castello's exact words to me were *"If we get Flaherty we will lose."* He knew her from a previous hearing where they fell out.

There is no doubt in my mind, or in the context of the blindingly obvious that Krasnopovich had to remove the witnesses or lose his claim. And I believe something untoward occurred whereby Krasnopovich/Clock/Hazelwood managed to bring in a friendly judge for exactly this purpose.

Did Flaherty's decision increase the animosity between the parents? Is increased animosity between parents in the best interests of a child, or is it child abuse.

I wrote to Spoon LLP extensively on this subject. It was raised on the first day of the hearing, in the presence of Richard Castello. Clam's reply was that *"The witnesses wouldn't have made any difference to the outcome."* If true, that contradicts his previous reply to my questioning his bill for the witness statements, that his £12,000 charge was *"money well spent"*. Only one of those contradictory statements can be true.

What is clear though is that the witness statements were important and should have been a part of the evidence considered for a fair judgment to occur. They contained information Flaherty bemoaned not having. She could not have made statements in her judgment that were firmly at odds with the witness testimony.

Then there is the matter of **Without Prejudice** and when it applies and when it does not. During the Financial Directions hearing I noticed that a paragraph in Krasnopovich's witness statement was a direct quote from a without prejudice letter submitted by Tim Clock of Souvla Raven Hogg. I believed it was not legal to quote from Without Prejudice documents and brought this matter to Clam's attention. Clam explained to me that it wouldn't matter because no evidence is submitted at this stage of proceedings and so it would not cause me any harm. At the very least I would expect the offending party to be censured for this ethical breach. But it seems Without Prejudice is not all that it appears in family law. In the course of these proceedings I have seen all of her 'Without prejudice' letters to me or my lawyers excluded.

Most gallingly, the letter he sent with his first demand for money in which he specifically refers to £100,000 to 'rehouse Sam', in which case I will be able to see

Sam whenever I chose. Clam would not allow that as evidence because it was sent Without Prejudice?

At that stage there was no mention of 'beneficial entitlement' or indeed anything other than simple blackmail. The idea to claim '50/50 like we were married only arose following his first meeting with Clock, some weeks after his without prejudice letters to me.

Quite clearly it was Clock's advice to Krasnopovich that he pursue this legal deceit, to increase animosity by lying in full awareness that this will harm the child's best interests. Succeeding in winning the endorsement of Flaherty who for reasons of loyalty to fellow members of British family law, or simple incompetence, and probably a combination of both, did not even pretend to have an impartial and fair hearing.

Her error strewn judgment arrived by email containing over thirty typos. And misspelled the name of Philip Parker Voula in seven different ways. Deliberate and transparent prejudice against Philip because by this time Krasnopovich saw Philip as being responsible for keeping me 'in the fight' after his successes with costing me my home and hundreds of thousands in legal costs. He was angry that Philip had loaned me funds to pay legal fees and carry on having representation in court.

The original cost projection for the April hearing that Clam sent at the outset of proceedings was between £40,000 to £50,000. Although he modified it upwards later it was never estimated higher than £80,000.

By the time of the April hearing (the Flaherty hearing) I had already paid him £130,000 and he was asking for a further £28,000. The reason for the overcharge, apart from the fact that Krasnopovich and Clock worked so diligently at causing unnecessary legal costs to impose financial hardship on me, has never been explained. It is my view that Clam simply invented items in the invoices that have no relevance to my matter. A typical example of how British family law operates and why their reputation is what it is. At a time when I was under enormous pressure, it was easy to add items to the lengthy emailed invoices that stretched pages with items like "E Mail of 12/09/2015. £55. E Mail of 12/09/2015. £75 E Mail of 12/09/2015. £25 E Mail of 12/09/2015. £40". Reams of invoice items. Eventually totaling £189,000.

By the end of the Flaherty hearing I had paid Spoon LLP some £160,000 in total. Including work for a visitation order with Sam in which he failed to win 2 nights a month with my son and as a direct result of which steady visitation was never established and now, years later, there is no contact between Sam and myself.

I believe I would still have a relationship with my son today if British family law was not corrupt. Clam presided over losing a claim made by the Father (wholly without merit or substance) for beneficial entitlement so completely that I saw an award made against me more than quadruple what the other side had asked for at the outset. And had costs awarded against me, which is highly unusual in family law. With 8% interest. Highly unusual. At odds with the guidance of the SRA.

Transcripts of the hearing, which I had sight of, for just another £5,000 to British family law, show that from the outset the lateness of submission of the statements by Clam were seized on by the Judge as an opportunity to dismiss my witnesses. As well as Clam's lateness in submitting the DDJ Berry documents, showing my name as the offending party, which was entirely Clam's error, both in being late in the first instance and paying the fine himself, and compounded by not rectifying this error on the court record in advance of the Flaherty hearing, leaving my name on record after I had made him (and Castello) aware that my name was still on the record for his late filing.

I wrote to Spoon LLP following the judgment outlining the specific complaints I raise here.

I subsequently appointed new solicitors to appeal the judgment by Flaherty which is quite clearly wrong. My new solicitors, who came highly recommended as a leading City firm, Friedman Oldfield Shutterworth, wrote to Spoon LLP requesting my files for the purpose of advancing the appeal, to which Clam replied that he intended placing a lien on my files unless I pay the £28,000 bill he claimed as still outstanding. For works done on my behalf after the April hearing?

Work I did not request and that I would not have requested following Clam's serial incompetence. A disputed amount that he raised deliberately for the purpose of using as leverage to dissuade me from reporting him to the Solicitors regulation authority, and/or the Legal Ombudsman.

Putting all specific points to one side, consider this fact.

How can it ever be appropriate for a family lawyer to bill £189,000 for nothing more than a parent wanting to see their child? Talk about kicking someone when they are down. And all done in the name of family law, without fear of censure, because: members of family law are free from any censure. It is an entitled clique with their own protection racket. All workable within current legislation.

21 Goodbye Clam LLP

How Clam blackmailed me to not report his malpractice to the Ombudsman's office

In May 2015, despairing at the poor service I was receiving by Spoon LLP, and the family law senior partner David Clam, I began beauty parading alternate representation. This was the period between the hearing and before the judgment. I was referred to another firm where I spoke with a recommended solicitor Simon Horowitz with a view to using their firm to replace Spoon LLP in receiving the judgment and in all likelihood, lodging an appeal, as I knew the judgment was going to be exactly as Barrister Castello had indicated to me before the hearing began.

Following a few phone conversations and email exchanges I liked the sound of their approach and agreed a way forward with them. To proceed taking me on as a client they needed ID. I was in the USA and to save time I requested Clam provide a copy of my passport for the purpose of identification to the new firm. I assumed Spoon LLP had a duty of care to release my Identity documents upon my request. *"Please will you send a copy of my passport to the following address."* A very straightforward request from a client to her lawyer?

I subsequently received a message from Simon Howrowitz saying Clam had called and raised *'serious matters'* which affected their ability to represent me. As a consequence of that call they could not take me on as a client.

Clam prejudicially disclosed confidential information to dissuade a rival firm from representing me and would not provide them with my ID document as was requested. After which he added upwards of £20,000 in billable hours which he sent me an invoice for.

Simply put.

I tried to appoint new lawyers. Clam spoke to them and convinced them not to take me on as a client. Disclosing information that breaches client privilege. An offense by Clam in law which he has got away with.

This gave rise to a delay in finding alternate legal representation and in that period Spoon LLP sent me a further £28,000+ of invoices. That I refused to pay.

Aside from all other considerations including the failure to consider the child's best interests, how is it fair that I was penalized in this way. British Family law charged me £12,000 for witness statements which formed the basis of my defense against a claim that had no substance. (And how do you disprove a negative.)

"She promised me 50/50 like we were married."

Well, here are a number of credible witnesses who know that is not true and willing to stand up in Court and share the facts of the financial planning that went into my property. Where the money came from. How the bills were paid. Who loaned me money. Who was responsible for repaying the loans? What were the terms of the repayment. What the agreement was for paying the costs of raising a child. What Krasnopovich had said in front of the Wills lawyer about his property ownership. The exact circumstances of the Freehold transfer into Krasnopovich's name. His refusal to return it and honour his legal fiduciary responsibility. His clear obstruction of visitation with Sam. His written offers, albeit made without prejudice, demanding £100,000 in a one-off payment before allowing unfettered visitation with Sam, with no mention at all of any Beneficial Entitlement. The fact that the beneficial entitlement claim only came to light after he retained Clock. The fact that he had suddenly invented an additional claim to 28B Thameside. He never paid a penny towards even living expenses for the months that he spent in that flat yet confusingly, he claimed 50/50 like we were married, including flat 28B in his claim, but not flat 28C? Why if it was 50/50 like we were married. And why was his flat – a 2 bed flat in Hounslow that he lived in when I met him – and immediately rented out for £800 pm after moving in with me for free – not included in '50/50 like we were married'.

For that matter, why did they exclude the business, Krasnopovich McDonald LLP which I financed and established as a working tech'ed up office while both partners were still working at MWT, (Caroline McDonald was working in the Property side of MWT, and Krasnopovich in Family) on the very clear agreement that this was a joint project in which I had a vested interest. That business would turn over more than a million PA, with possibly 25% of that being operating costs at most.

Why then does his promise of 50/50 against me not work as 50/50 the other way? Like we were married.

Because Flaherty says so? Who cares about logic. Or the blindingly obvious.

David Clam repeatedly failed follow my clear instruction. Knowing he was being fired he told Flaherty that I could not give clear instruction – inviting her to pursue a 'capacity' notice.

The hearing was adjourned at the submissions stage.

The Judge ordered three doctors were to be named for me by the other side. I was to choose one of the three proposed in the matter of determining 'capacity to instruct'.

Clam did not properly relay instructions from the court to me, making his own unilateral decisions. He disregarded the Judge's ruling that three psychiatrists would be identified for me to choose one from. Instead he identified one doctor and told me that this was the only psychiatrist in California suitable for this type of work. (In the area with the highest percentage of Psychiatrists anywhere in the World, Clam and Clock agreed there was only one available to sign a form for the Family Court.)

My own doctor, reputedly one of the leading Psychiatrists in California, wrote on the subject for the court's benefit clarifying the matter comprehensively. Fr. Zetin wrote to Clam and the court, detailing their practical requirements. Any commentary from Flaherty or the lawyers after that is simply ridiculous. A psychiatrist has determined 'capacity to instruct'. That is that. The end.

While Flaherty was making her desperately ill-considered three psychiatrist ruling, I had a psychiatrist who knew me and was more than qualified to complete the form required by the court. But Flaherty would not accept this practical and obvious facility to provide the form she needed. Instead she recanted her 'pick three psychiatrists and let Ms. Lee choose one' and agreed I should have no choice, but accept one doctor put forward by Krasnopovich and Clock' Flaherty wrote that was the only doctor who she would accept. A decision that is quite simply ridiculous and shows again the extent of her prejudice overriding the authority of a Deputy District Judge. A decision made with malice, that harmed a child. A child abusing decision by a child abuser representing British family-law.

Dr. Zetin did complete the form and also wrote for the courts benefit. An authority advising the court regarding *'the child's best interests'*. I had him send these two documents, the Capacity letter and his report, to Clam for the Judge.

Despite Clam assuring me in writing that he had admitted this letter from Dr. Zetin to the Court, it was subsequently revealed that he failed to do so.

A complete and utter mess is how this period can best be described. All the while, members of British family law were running up chargeable hours arguing over the simply ridiculous, incompetent direction of Flaherty.

This "Psychiatrist letter' is one example of many in which Mr. Clam has provided written assurances to me that have later been shown to be untrue.

His explanation in this case was that he felt showing the letter to the court would have been detrimental to my interests. This is demonstrably untrue. Precisely the contrary is true. It also fails to explain why he wrote to me that Dr. Zetin's letter had been sent to the Judge when it was not. On numerous occasions I requested sight of documents and never had my requests acknowledged.

One specific example of Clams failure to respond to my clear instruction follows my request for sight of the final submissions document by opposing Barrister Simon Hazelwood. For many months Clam simply did not provide me with sight of this document after four written reminders. Obviously a document I would need in an appeal. Clam simply declined forwarding it. After four reminders.

Another example is Clams email of 3 March 2015, in which he confirms he will send me a copy of the attendance note from the Fathers Will signing. An important document in this case as it says in his own words that he has no claim to the properties I own during his attendance at a will signing at MWT. I was never sent this document. I paid for it. I requested a copy. Where is it?

At that time my new solicitors were asking for sight of this document, being a featured point in the appeal. Clam instead indicated that he would not release my files and place a lien on them for the 'unpaid final bill'. Jeopardizing my appeal process significantly and in light of the time sensitivity and the importance of this document, appeared to me indistinguishable from blackmail.

I was left with a clear impression that this was a dishonest deceitful man, embodying many of the qualities of alternate truth that represents the bottom feeders of family law.

The clear and unmistakable message was *"If you don't drop your complaint with the Legal Ombudsman and the SRA and your claim against us for my incompetence, then I will not release your files for the appeal. Take it or leave it."*

This particular document, Krasnopovich's attendance note for his will signing, makes clear in his own words, that his claim that he was promised 50/50, or believed he was promised 50/50 like we were married, was a lie. Had he been promised 50/50, he would not have hidden this information from the lawyer drafting his will. He discloses all that he owns, and my properties do not feature there.

In fact he acknowledges in that legal document, "Andrea owns the 3 leases." How much more did Flaherty need than to see this admission in Krasnopovich's own words? The answer is, she moved swiftly over it in her judgment with a nonsensical alternate-truth assessment that would make a Trump Tweet writer proud.

One of my most pressing concerns is how Flaherty appointed herself to Krasnopovich's case. On the Monday morning of day one of the three-day April hearing the judge who was appointed for the Krasnopovich vs Krasnopovich hearing recused himself. (DDJ Burkes.) I was told this after the court hearing was due to begin, explained by Richard Castello as 'because he had previously been employed (as a barrister) by Krasnopovich'.

Subsequently I learned that this was not the case. And if he was compromised by a relationship with Krasnopovich, then he would have known this on Friday night when the Court hearings are farmed out to the DDJ's, and recused himself then, giving the court time to find an alternate judge. Why did Burkes not recuse himself on the Friday when he saw her name on the Case file if he was compromised?

My barrister Richard Castello was the first to announce to me on the Monday that, we may not have a hearing as the judge has recused himself. Then explaining that Flaherty might switch cases and we will have a hearing with her. And then saying "*If we get Flaherty we will lose.*" This he explained is because he had already sat before her in a similar case, where she had taken against him and he learned she lacked competence in financial matters. Something that became abundantly clear as time went on. He disclosed that he lost the previous case against her. And then minutes later explaining that Flaherty had switched to become the judge.

At that point, as I was jet lagged, having flown from California just two days before and suffering sleep deprivation along with side effects of the medications I was taking for a neck injury, anxiety and depression, I realized this was not going to be a normal court hearing. I could see clearly that there was no point in going ahead with the hearing. Castello had already pointed out that we were going to lose. Answering my questions on this subject left me in no doubt. He confirmed categorically.

"*If Flaherty is the Judge, we will lose.*"

He would later say to me "*I knew we had lost when she rolled her eyes at me*".

Recalling the eye rolling moment, I note here, that happened two minutes into his opening submission to Flaherty. He had barely got started with his opening submission and she rolled her eyes up at him. Clearly visible and for the benefit of everyone in the court.

Along with the absent witnesses, all the signs were that this was not a proper hearing in which a child's future could fairly be decided.

Beyond any reasonable doubt, this Judge, Flaherty had already ruled even before the proceedings began. Castello was not going to win. He knew it. She knew it. Everyone in that room knew it.

While we waited in the small room to one side of the Court foyer that morning, for Flaherty to read through the files, I asked Clam to have the case adjourned, at least until I was well enough to speak clearly and in a court where I was not given advance notice that the judge was going to find against me because of historical issues that had nothing to do with my case.

Quite clearly this hearing was not going to be fair. I knew it. I reported it to my lawyer and requested an adjournment.

Clam, with his usual turn of efficiency, did nothing. In his opening submission, Richard Castello said (as appears in the transcript. P5 16) Richard Castello: *Someone last week should have applied to adjourn this case*

This is absolutely correct. It was obvious that the outcome of the hearing was determined from the moment Flaherty took the case.

How did Flaherty's weakness in financial matters impact on the judgment and what cost consequences follow?

During the course of these proceedings my home flooded (In the Thames flood of February 8th 2014.) The Insurance policy was in the name of the Lessor, Krasnopovich, who as detailed in these proceedings, was the Trustee Landlord, holding my freehold title to the property since our agreement in 2003 to transfer it into her name for Insurance advantage. In breach of her fiduciary responsibilities as Trustee, Krasnopovich sought to blight the claim for the purpose of causing me financial hardship. My home was at this time uninhabitable and in need of expensive Insurance repairs.

Clam wrote extensively in his efforts to progress my Insurance claim following the flood. His efforts were poor although he charged top dollar for them. He is after all not a property lawyer, but was still happy to charge top dollar. I received not one penny by way of Insurance or rehousing whilst my home was uninhabitable. This increased the financial hardship I was under enormously. Clam's advice eventually migrated to '*Don't go after him for the Insurance because it will look bad to a judge.*' As a result 19 months after the flood I had not had one penny back from Insurance and had to outlay £125,000 (by that stage) for repairs just to mitigate the damage and protect my investment until the Insurance money was paid. None of this factored into Flaherty's thinking.

Beyond, that is, trying to force me to indemnify Krasnopovich from any action in pursuing him for his fiduciary failures.

Flaherty's judgment was delivered by email to the lawyers on 5 August, 2015. Mr. Clam sent it to me on 10 August. Five (5) days later. He failed to mention that the time period for registering an appeal was 21 days. Through this delay and omission over 25% of the time available to me for filing an appeal was unilaterally removed by Clam's decision.

Once again Clam was late.

During the adjournment delay for submissions I had written to Clam detailing my complaints and my dissatisfaction that he was not following my clear instruction and instead making his own unilateral decisions.

I explained my dissatisfaction with him invoicing me significant amounts for explaining to me why he acted the way he did rather than doing as he was clearly being instructed to do. I saw his role as acting on my instruction. Not billing me to explain why he would not.

His reply was wholly inadequate and ended with him sending me another bill for a further (approx.) £28,000, which he explained should be paid or else he would put a charge against my home.

When I appointed a reputable firm, Friedman Oldfield Shutterworth (FOS) to progress an Appeal against Flaherty's judgment, Clam refused to release my files to my new solicitors.

This is after invoicing and receiving payments in excess of £160,000 for his services in losing me 2 nights a month with my son and losing my home to a claim based on the word of a professional liar along with costs in a family court. A total monetary loss when considered with the flood damage far in excess of £1 million.

My threat then was to detail my complaint to the Ombudsman and to the SRA which I put into motion by drafting the list of complaints according to the guidelines on the Ombudsman website.

The total invoiced to me by Spoon LLP for this negligent and incompetent representation is £189,000. Of which he had been paid over £160,000. I say he made up this additional invoice knowing he had lost badly and knowing all too well that I was going to come after him for incompetence and malpractice. All he then had to do is use the law to place a lien on my files, stalling my appeal process past the 21-day limit, and he would be home clear. Knowing I had no means to go any further with litigation. Not untypical conduct by a member of family law.

Here is my letter to Clam following my decision to sack him.

Dear Mr. Clam,

Thank you for your letter of 26 October, 2015.

What is clear in your letter is that you favor a recollection that is very different to mine even despite the written evidence to the contrary as well as the very clear evidence of Philip Parker Voula, which in any event you do not dispute. Plainly, as you are want to say so repetitively, you are saying what you have to say to avoid facing the truth. I say you know all too well what the truth is. You have made a royal mess up, where you have been roundly beaten by Tim Clock and Nico Krasnopovich, failing spectacularly to win so much as two nights a month for me with my son and charging me £160,000 for a service so bad, I have lost my home and do not see my son. Which is down to you David.

You seem to be avoiding the very clear fact that I was charged some £40,000 for your representation in order that I might see the child I raised for the first four years of his life for 2 nights a month.

As a result of your failures, some two years since the judgment of DDJ Reed on 30 October 2013, and as a direct consequence of your handling of my affairs I have no contact at all with my son.

His Father is in a new relationship and has successfully prevented me from seeing my son by so easily legally manipulating the markedly inferior opposition he faced in the visitation for 2 nights a month. Marcus, the QC you hired for me, said
'This did not just happen. They have been planning this for weeks. You have been played'

Unfortunately you were not aware and when the surprise came, in their disclosure on the Friday afternoon, just hours before the Monday hearing day, you were unprepared and reacted poorly. At the hearing itself, you were absent and therefore unable to offer any advice at all. You had agreed to be there with me. You knew the particulars of my claim. You panicked, by an ambush tactic of late service, and you walked right into their trap.

You already know that same judgment provided for a 'removal from the UK' set of criteria which the Father has breached repeatedly. In fact the father is at this time in Abu Dhabi and the only way I know that is by third hand news from a friend because he removes the child from the UK freely without concern for the Court order following the lack of success you had in encouraging her to follow the court direction, despite charging me for this service.

In other words. You charged me for him to win a court order that he drafted entirely on his terms and when he breached that court order, you still saw no reason to do anything before first charging me £350 plus VAT, which you happily did, and even after that you still failed to prevent him from breaching the court order freely. You were hopelessly ineffective in the first instance and then saw fit to charge me more to be hopelessly ineffective again. My son is in Abu Dhabi right now. I have no idea where.

And you remain richly rewarded, fighting to defend your gross incompetence rather than acting as your professional regulatory body require you do. Or even with the basic common decency of a human being. How hard is it to just be honest? It not just about money. It's a child's life you have fucked up.

You are aware I did not go to court expecting to sign this agreement giving him exactly what he wanted in respect of control over the child. I went following your advice in the belief that I would win 2 nights a month with my son.

I hired you to represent me in the matter of 2 nights a month visitation. How complicated is that. How much can you possibly attach to the appropriate charge for a visitation hearing for a mother with ideal credentials to win 2 nights a month with the son she raised as a stay at home mum up till the age of four, just a few months after the separation.

It is completely realistic to believe 2 nights a month in my circumstances is a reasonable and achievable goal. How did you turn it into £40,000' of billable hours by not even attending court and losing the case so completely you had me forced (on pain of £20,000 cost penalty) to sign over exactly what he wanted or face paying his costs. This is incompetence that beggar's belief.

Instead of winning the 2 nights a month, as I was invoiced for by yourself and as I had paid in good faith with a reasonable expectation because, why wouldn't I have my son for 2 nights a month, I found myself presented with a 'sign this or else you pay £20,000 of his costs' court order written up by his lawyers exactly as he had prepared 2 weeks before the hearing and being told that I couldn't have my son for 2 nights a month unless I agreed to the very conditions he has put forward prior to the hearing.

This Court order remains in effect to this day even though he freely breaches the travel with child from UK clause. By allowing that Court Order to stand you have done me a tremendous disservice.

Why did you not prevent that from happening? That Court direction with removal from the UK clause is not why I hired you and not what I wanted. Yet even when he breaches that clause which exists wholly as a consequence of your sheer incompetence, you still do nothing.

On top of which you placed me in a blackmail position of having to sign the 'phased in visitation' they prepared or face paying his costs. You never told me this in advance? What you did assure me was 'They never award costs in a Preliminary hearing for visitation' and when on 30 October 2013 I was told otherwise and presented with this 'sign it or else you pay £20,000 of his costs' you were nowhere to be seen.

You never consulted me with legal advice on what my options where. You were not there. I hired you to be there. You charged me a great deal of money for representing me properly. And you failed on every layer of possibility.

Including your advice to me following my complaint right after 30 October 2013, where I told you this had to be appealed and that I was not in agreement with the Judges direction for reasons already detailed in previous correspondence, as well as my CAFCASS Blog, which has been read now by a UK audience of over 100,000, suggesting there is some interest in the failings of family law, tainted by rip-off lawyers who operate far below the guidelines of their regulatory body. I see on your invoice you have charged me over £500 for 'reading and considering blog. After I told you there was no need for concern. I did not name Krasnopovich or Sam. I did not ask you to charge me £500 to read my blog. Here, as so common in your invoicing practice, you simply write whatever you like and associate a ridiculous amount to the service. Whether I requested it or not. Whether I was notified of it, or not. Whether the outcome was a simple cock up, or not. You just fire away those specious invoice charges.

Your failures leading to me not seeing my son at all should, on the face of it should be a straightforward case of admitting you failed and proposing a compensatory element that can be mutually agreed.

You know that this was a failure, the facts of your performance are self-evident. You know that I am extremely unhappy about it yet your idea of client care and trying to remedy your own sequence of errors is first to deny any error on your own part and second to add further damaging delays to your bungling behavior in defense of SPOON LLP rip of fee's. Your master plan was to run up another £28,000 in costs I never asked you for, at a time I was looking to replace you in any event, and then position it so I appear as a bad payer I do not owe you that money. Your invoice is entirely made up and does not reflect on any agreement between us.

*In the stead of some consideration and remorse, you prefer an adversarial approach in defense of your failure and its consequences for my son who I no longer have any contact with by actually sending me the words **'he has not suffered in any way at all.'***

I believe you cannot defend your charges and your conduct in my matter as anything but ' rip off fee's, damaging delays and bungling behavior' and for this reason your conduct should progress to Publication by the Legal Ombudsman.

I have very little doubt that your late reply to the second part of my complaint, your rip off fee's, damaging delays and bungling behavior in the TOLATA hearing, will be as unhelpful as your attempt to address my first complaint without the need to seek compensation via complaint to the Ombudsman. I note here that your reply was promised to me by the 19th October 2015 causing further delay in my opportunity to further my complaint in advance of the impending Appeal hearing on November 9th. Spoon LLP are quite transparently guilty of 'Rip off Fee's, damaging delays and bungling behavior' as well as so much more in representing me at a cost of some £160,000.

Please reply to my complaint in detail as you said you would on October 19th in order that I can progress to the Ombudsman in advance of the November 9 Appeal date. Plainly Spoon LLP are in in breach of SRA guidelines on 7 specific points. In particular, you know I am waiting for your proposal on how you wish to advance review of the invoices. I have already written to the judge in the previous hearing and you indicated it needed to go in a different format. I have invited you to save time by telling me your preference for how we can best accommodate the review of Spoon LLP invoices. To be clear, these are the 'Rip off' invoices to which I intend referring and I hope you will not delay or continue to obfuscate this aspect further.

Yours sincerely,
Andrea Lee

I followed that with a formal complaint letter to Spoon LLP managing partner Valerie Spoon, following which my files were released to FOS for my appeal. Although by this time it was too late for them to be used in preparing the appeal file, which was all done at added cost to me by my new solicitor, relying on my own copies of proceedings. Clearly Clam withholding the files did impact on the Appeal.

To: Valerie Spoon
Spoon LLP Cedar House78 Molesey Road, Cobham, Surrey, KT11 1AB

Formal complaint about David Clam. 15 September, 2015

Mrs. Spoon,

................Conclusion paragraph

My son Sam has been adversely affected by Mr. Clam's failure to secure visitation for him and for losing the TOLATA claim that had absolutely no merit by leaving my name on his contempt of court late filing and failing to have the witnesses heard at the hearing (after charging me £12,000 for compiling the witness statements), and for now attempting to interfere with the appeal process by withholding my files.

In my view Spoon LLP must:

1. Refund the amount invoiced for the failed visitation hearing and all associated invoices, rounded down to £40,000
2. Refund 100% of the incorrectly and inappropriately invoiced charges for works in my April hearing. The minimum sum of £120,000.
3. Release my files immediately in full and final settlement subject to points 1 and 2 or invite my claim for costs going forward with my appeal against SPOON LLP and for damages arising from SPOON LLP' failures in the two pertinent matters. If my appeal fails, your failure to release my files to my new solicitors will be a factor.
In light of the pressing nature of the appeal I look forward to your decision by no later than close on the 22nd September, 2015 before proceeding with my complaint. I understand that you are required to respond within seven days. If you require any further information please email me.

Yours sincerely,
Andrea Lee

22 Settlement offers

So, there was actually a settlement agreed. Then what happened?

In the months leading up to the April 2015 hearing the tension rose significantly. Family law reality is that the costs spiral just before the court hearing and it is always better to settle. Clam and Richard Castello both used the words '*Take a commercial view*' on how much it would cost to go to Court and how much to just settle. By this time my contact with Sam was minimal. It was clear that Krasnopovich was present on every occasion he was allowed to speak on Skype. After a period of weeks passed without any reply on his Skype, he reached me on Krasnopovichs' iPad. He told me that

"My iPad is broken."

"What happened".

"I sat on it and the cable broke."

"OK, that's not a serious thing. Just get daddy to take you to the Apple Store and they will fix it for you. If it costs any money, I will pay for it. It can't be a big problem."
Months passed with no sign of his iPad Skype account active. I wrote to Krasnopovich via his lawyer Clock requesting him to ensure Sam's iPad be taken to the iStore with the assurance of meeting any costs. To no avail. What this meant in contact terms for Sam and me was that any Skype contact would be on Krasnopovich's iPad. His position was *"Sam's iPad is broken."* And that was the end of that. No longer could Sam and me speak without Krasnopovich controlling the skype chat.

During these talks on Krasnopovich's iPad Sam's discomfort was visible. Awkward and embarrassed replaced the huge and joyful smile from our previous 'private' Skype chats on his iPad. On occasion's he appeared much like a ventriloquist's dummy. Waiting for a voice above and behind the camera to instruct and then blandly repeating what he had been told. Krasnopovich did not even attempt to make it appear as anything other than prompts. Leaving me in no doubt that he had that control and wanted me to know he was prepared to use it. Knowing, I believe, how much it would upset me to see Sam abused in this way. My offers for him to visit California were flatly rejected.

I would propose possible dates for travel, at my expense, and Krasnopovich would interrupt. Appearing on screen out of nowhere.

"Sam will not travel to America."

No alternatives were proposed.

Not long after I travelled to the UK for a three day visit that Krasnopovich allowed Clam to agree. I asked Sam to bring his broken iPad with and so after all these months of talking about getting the broken iPad fixed I finally got to see it first hand when he pulled it out of his bag and handed it to me.

At first glance I could not see any damage to the iPad.

"Let me see the cable" I asked him.

The iPad to USB cable had bent on one end. Perhaps deliberately? In such a way that it would not enter the iPad power port. It took me all of three seconds to identify all it needed was a new iPad power cable.

It cost £9.99. All that time he never had an iPad because?

I concluded Krasnopovich did not want Sam to have his own iPad and be able to call me without him being present.

We lost four months of skype contact because of that. When he saw the solution to the iPad issue, Sam understood what had happened.

"*I asked him ten times to take me to the iStore*" he said in a thoughtful tone.

By early 2015, with over £150,000 spent in legal fees and with my home still unrepaired from the flood and while I was responsible for significant rent to house myself, still in California at Phillips property, I had to consider balancing how to do the best for Sam and how to get rid of Krasnopovich's vexatious litigation.

By this stage I the proceedings, my negative cash flow included ongoing financial commitments to home ownership, like mortgage, and meant I had entirely exhausted all my savings. The litigation and the constant worry for Sam meant my productivity in both writing and music was negligible affecting my traditional source of income. I was hardly playing music at all and not motivated to produce anything commercial. My mind was completely elsewhere. I was writing 5,000 words a day on average. The problem was that was all in legal letters and not towards paid work. As any composer will tell you, the Muse does not come calling when you are preoccupied with constant court related stressors. I had no enthusiasm for writing and recording any music knowing it would have sounded like an ode to bottomless sorrow. Not much of a market in that genre. My main source of income was the rentals from my two habitable properties. Both were rented to good tenants. At least that was enough to pay my bills in America.

My awful financial picture forced my hand in deciding to settle and to make a workable offer for Sam's sake. To end Krasnopovich's animosity by conceding to his financial demands. This was to take the form of a negotiation between the two barristers. Richard Castello for me, and Simon Hazelwood for him. Clam wrote with the various details and we worked towards a date for a telephone conference.

Before Sam was born we entered into a detailed agreement as parents. A proper, professional, considered parental agreement. Aside from the commitment to not bring another child from a broken family into the world, we agreed financial terms for his upbringing. Our business plan for raising a child focused on his income from law than my less reliable income from music. I had the house and would provide a home for us to live in. With enough income from royalties, my share portfolio and from my rental properties to enjoy a lifestyle where I would be the stay home parent. He would assume the costs for schooling and child care support. I agreed to support this arrangement financially (by assisting him purchasing equity at his previous firm MWT and then in setting up and paying for the new law firm) as well as in terms of executive input including setting up Krasnopovich's own legal practice to pay the child's education costs. Having seen the benefits of a British private education with Evan, I was determined that Sam would enjoy a good education in which I would play a hands-on role. I was by now convinced and excited by the prospect of having a child as an older parent with the time and resources to provide the best of everything.

Krasnopovich was equally keen to have a child and the financial arrangement offer came very much from his side in a parental agreement covering all costs up until 18.

The parental plan arose in the context of our separation in 2008. He persuaded me to get back together for the purpose of having a child on terms that were agreed only after considerable revision. At first I could see he had no clue about what costs were involved in having a child.

Krasnopovich and I differed in the matter of education. For me education begins with creating a passion for learning. A lifelong interest in acquiring information. I learned whatever I achieved along the way in my own life because I loved to learn. It is an attitude. A passion.

His was different. Hindsight shows this is a huge factor in parenting. How we choose to educate our kids. I believe in the formative years 90% of the interest and manner of learning is modeled for the child by the parent.

When Sam reached 3 we considered pre-schools. I was more than happy to keep enjoying the days with him and Nina, his nanny, where his learning curve was scorching, with wondrous opportunities arising daily, which he responded too with real signs of progress. But I understood the value in him spending mornings in a socializing environment with children of his age. From age three to four.

His first opportunity for pre-school was a Montessori, located in nearby Police College building. I agreed reluctantly because I did not approve of the aesthetic in the school's location. I let Krasnopovich take the lead, as he emphasized that he was paying for it. Krasnopovich paid the terms fee and along came day one. We both took him in together. I did the majority of the sales pitch to Sam, about how much fun it would be and meeting other kids and so on and the opportunity to learn some cool stuff. We arrived at the building and I held his hand taking him down the corridor for his first day. He took one look at the place. Surveilling from left to right. Getting the feel for the room and then literally jumped into my arms saying *"Get me out of here."* Of course I respected his decision completely. And after a short apology to the teacher, carried him out. He wouldn't let go until we were out of the building and he allowed me to put him down. Krasnopovich followed with a black face. Saying nothing.

Once Sam was out of earshot, he expressed his anger with me. He had paid hundreds of pounds for the term.

'All kids don't like their first day. He has to man up and face it'. And so on.

After his persistent insistence that we try again, the next day we tried again. This time he couldn't afford to take more time off work, and we agreed it would be better all-round If I went alone with Sam.

"Whatever happens leave him for the morning If he cries a bit, its normal. Don't' show weakness."

That day Krasnopovich left for work and we prepared for our drive to the nursery.

"I'm not going back to that place" was Sam's opening bid. As ever though, he listened and invested some trust in my words. The deal was *"Just try. Play some games. Have some fun. And if you still don't like it, tell the teacher to phone me. I will give her my number. And I will be right here to collect you. But please try your best to enjoy it. If you try for at least half an hour and you still don't feel good, I will be right there."*

"How long is half an hour".

Off we went. I had to carry him down the corridor into the classroom. With tears streaming down his face, I left him in the care of his fawning teacher, assuring me that *"he will be fine. We are going to have a great time. Aren't we Sam"*. I almost felt him thinking *"Don't patronize me you silly old cow."*

She seemed confident. He didn't. I told her our agreement.

"Sam is going to try his best. If he still doesn't like it in half an hour, please phone me and I will collect him. If he stays till the end of the day with a happy face there will be a very nice treat waiting for him."

I headed home with my phone on high volume. It rang half an hour later.

"Sam has asked if you will come and collect him" said the teacher.

And five minutes later he was jumping into my arms. His joy at seeing me was immense. No tears. Just sheer relief. I loved my son and he loved me. No misunderstandings.

"My mummy." He clung to my neck.

Fifteen minutes later he was at his piano, and especially receptive to instruction.

Do reh mi fah so la ti doh.

I called Krasnopovich with the news. He was angry. *"You can't just keep picking him up when he calls. He will never learn. What are we going to do now. I have paid for the full term and they won't refund."*

What I saw was that the Montessori nursery, which was located next to the Bar in a police college, had a dark energy. Walking into the classroom required walking past the open door of a smelly pub. I totally related to why Sam didn't find it comfortable there. And I would not be taking him back. If the child intuits a dissatisfaction, that is the end of it.

But still, the problem was, he would need a year in nursery if he was to get into one of the private schools we were interviewing for him.

What I was able to do is speak to Richard Nastase at the Lansbury Club where I had been a member for many years and played tennis in Leagues at least three times a week. At one time, in 2010, winning the league division one singles title.

The Club were launching a nursery. A professionally run, exclusive, expensive and oversubscribed one. We had tried before to get Sam in, but it was fully booked. But on this day I had a coffee meet with Richard and he pulled the necessary strings and a place appeared for Sam. Starting the next day. The next day I had no difficulty convincing Sam that he was going to a really cool place. A nursery at the club, where he already had a positive association as he played on the swings there regularly.

And off we went to Sam's first day of school. This time our experience of day one at school involved an excited walk hand in hand with a happy smiling boy. From day one he was happy to go to school. And every day when I collected him at 1, in the handover process that they do with 3-year old's, on seeing me in the line, he would jump up in joy. *"My mummy"*. So excited to let all his friends know I was his mother.

I don't remember one collection from that nursery school where he didn't jump into my arms and hug me. *"My mummy."* Well, I was the reigning women's champion in the tennis league so, perhaps that was it.

The Lansbury nursery year went very well. In which time we considered schools. Visiting the five best options in the local area. My friend and neighbor, Jo, knew the education system well having put her daughter through private schooling and she was a good reference for the possibilities.

A key for me was the religious aspect. I did not want him in a religious school. My own upbringing in South Africa, seeing the counter intuitive element of a religious education, existing at odds with my view that learning must be fun, meant I placed a secular aspect in the school manifesto as a priority. We visited three schools before we identified one as top of the options list. We went together to meet the headmaster who I liked enormously. He seemed a gifted teacher and I liked that he was in a civil partnership with a man. Indicative as this was of a liberal hierarchy in the school. I took Sam for his try out day. A morning session to see if the child and the school have a good fit.

This was a big day for me. His first day of 'real' school which would determine if he would even be considered for that school. Walking him down the corridors through the brick halls of that imposing old building to his classroom where his teacher waited along with a group of similarly placed children was a burn onto the memory banks. Krasnopovich stayed behind in the entrance hall and let me walk him to the classroom. He clung firmly to my hand and there were tears when I handed him over. From him as well.

But he came though that great and when both Krasnopovich and I collected him after that trial day, he was a picture of confident joy. I felt a landmark moment had arrived.

His first school and he liked it. That day was in April 2013, only a few months before fathers-day, 2013, which is when my parental involvement with Sam was hijacked.

When Sam started reception year in September of that year I was already excluded. I didn't even know where he was being kept. I have not played any part in his education at that school thanks to the conduct of Krasnopovich and Clock.

With the April 2015 Court date approaching came the need for two settlement proposals. One for Sam's future with me and the other for Krasnopovich's financial demands.

For Sam's future I proposed that he live with me and spend the two long holidays each year with his father. The law in this situation, where we were not married, is that both parents have 50/50 interest in the child. However Krasnopovich had very quickly effectively claimed 'ownership' by taking the child and attaching considerable financial cost to each visit. His legal brain seemed to apply a 'possession is 9/10ths of the law calculation'. He had latched onto the fact that I had seen a counsellor for depression to label me as unfit to see my own son.

Complicating matters considerably was my residential status. The fact was by this stage I had no residence in England as my home was flooded and Krasnopovich, who was the insured party on my home, continued doing an excellent job of ensuring that my home would not be repaired to cause me the maximum of financial harm at a time when the court case was approaching (And with it increased legal bills, meaning more pressure on me to 'take a commercial view' and give him some money.)

In the meanwhile I was living in California in Philips house, paying rent month by month on a credit basis, waiting for the Insurance to pay the rehousing cost and repair my home. Any visitation that they allowed me meant I would travel to the UK and book a suitable Hotel to spend time with Sam in. To keep up with the legal bills, and my lawyer would invoice regularly, sometimes running at £20,000 a month, I had to borrow from my family. Awkward and undermining to my confidence. Having been financially independent and earning my own money since my first 12 hour a day job in Johannesburg station aged 11.

For Sam's rights to see both parents by this stage there were two options.

That he attends school in the US, living with me, and spend summer and winter holidays with Krasnopovich in a small South London suburban house.

The second option was the converse. That he goes to school with Krasnopovich in the UK and have summer and winter holidays with me in California.

Considering that his commitment to his work in family law was such that he saw very little of Sam anyhow, it made sense that I schooled Sam, having the time, aptitude and enthusiasm for this process. I also felt that although little boys need their fathers, they need their mothers too. Gender discrimination in this area is inappropriate. With Krasnopovich's long working hours, having Sam in holidays would mean he could take time off work and enjoy some real quality time. Not just putting him to bed a few nights week. The 10% parent.

In the course of presenting these two options, Philip, by now the third intermediary advocating for Sam between his parents at that stage wrote a Without Prejudice offer. This letter outlined both scenarios. Living with one parent and holidaying with the other, and vice versa.

It was written with **WITHOUT PREJUDICE** very clearly highlighted and underlined across the top. It was, in all fairness, an objectively balanced presentation taking into account Sam's best interests at the fore. In no way a demand for anything inviting litigation.

None the less, as was common in the course of the proceedings with Krasnopovich and Clock, extracts from that letter were presented out of context with total disregard for the Without Prejudice position. Later I would learn that in family-court, nothing is without prejudice if it relates to the child. As long as it wasn't me doing it.

Krasnopovich and Clock presented the single point detailing my offer to pay for Sam's education in the US. *"She has the means to pay for a private education in America so we demand that she pay for his education the UK."* Krasnopovich and Clock's constant pressure to visit school fees on me had the unsurprising effect of putting me off having anything to do with their choice of private school.

Later they would apply to have a statement by a witness excluded because it was a conversation that took place 'Without Prejudice." The rules on how without prejudice works in their world are entirely subjective and unilaterally decided and reflect poorly on family law. Members can arbitrarily use WP extracts to suit their case with the same ease and opportunity as objecting to the other side doing the same thing.

The animosity this pressure point placed between myself and Krasnopovich/Clock cannot be over stated and is the core reason I am not involved in Sam's schooling. Payment of Sam's Private school fees in the UK was agreed between Krasnopovich and myself, forming a part of the child expenses budget we agreed regarding the costs of raising a child together, from the legal firm we set up with my investment and expertise, Krasnopovich McDonald LLP, in Thameside. Added to which I had voluntarily taken a back seat on my income generating work to support Krasnopovich increasing his. Done because we had a commitment to the child.

All that went out the window when his solicitor did the strategizing for him, and instead of honoring the parenting agreement he put forward, he targeted the hand that had fed him from the start. Blackmailing me with the one area where I was most vulnerable. My love for my son.

Although I flagged the Without Prejudice reference in Krasnopovich's statement as soon as I saw it, no further action was taken by either Clam or Castello. Later, when recalling this instance to Roland Chambers at FOS, I was told by Chambers that in family law, 'without prejudice' is admissible if it relates to the child.

So there you have it. When he, the member of family-law, makes without prejudice offers I am prevented from using it (in entirety or by select reference) whilst he was allowed to quote selectively and dishonestly from my without prejudice correspondence. And that's how the Law Society rolls. It fine to abuse the process without fear of censure as long as you are a member.

The second settlement aspect was his financial demands. To this end I was advised by my barrister Richard Castello that he would negotiate a deal with Simon Hazelwood and that I should authorize him to go up to a maximum figure. This he proposed at £160,000. Explaining to me what the legal costs would be in going to court, where he assured me it is very unusual that costs are awarded. I was shown the cost calculation for a worst-case outcome which reached £160,000. So rather than spend up to £160,000 on the Court case, with all the negativity this brings into the child's prospects, offer at least some of that amount to settle.

Much though that irked me, being in many ways evidence that Krasnopovich's bullying litigation based on an unsubstantiated lie had succeeded, I agreed to the proposed settlement with an end of the litigation and the animosity litigation brings uppermost in my thinking. I could approach the Insurance and freehold matter separately. The priority now was to end the litigation and to see Sam.

A series of calls followed; with me in California, Clam and Clock in London with Hazelwood and Castello, leading to an email confirming a settlement figure of £130,000. I felt this was highway robbery but none the less agreed it. Paying £130,000 to someone I knew to be a lying cheat who was simultaneously blackmailing me with access to my own child.

That settlement was confirmed in writing from Hazelwood to Castello in an email I have on file.

"Nico will accept a sum of £130,000."

Then followed the demand from Clock/Krasnopovich that I agree to indemnify Krasnopovich from all claims relating to his fiduciary failures whilst freeholder of my property.

I had still not been paid one penny for the flood damage and had in the meantime advanced my property lawyer business from the firm instructed in early 2015 to Roland Court, property law partner at FOS, to pursue my claim in respect of the Freehold and the House Insurance matter. I had taken the view that FOS would be best to handle both matters.

The settlement offer proposed that I would now take over the Insurance claim and pursue Insurers the AXA and not Krasnopovich, for the payments due.

Krasnopovich simply refused.

He demanded to be totally indemnified from any of his actions whilst freeholder of my property. I believe, because his actions in that freehold/insurance matter breached not only the Solicitors Regulation Authority ethical code but was also criminal fraud.

My reply was. "*I agree to the settlement amount. I agree that I will not claim against Krasnopovich for the fiduciary failures if, as he has assured the court is the case, he has not breached any fiduciary responsibilities in the course of the flood Insurance claim.*"

Seems fair? If he told the truth in court that he had properly repaired the property?

Of course it is true that Krasnopovich was in breach of fiduciary responsibilities and is the only reason he tried to advance a settlement. To be indemnified from accountability. I say this is evidence that he knew from the outset that he was committing an offense in claiming to be the freeholder as well as in spoiling the insurance claim to cause me harm and benefit his prospects in his fictitious beneficial entitlement claim.

And so shortly after the Agreement was made, it was 'unmade' by Krasnopovich. He was not willing to accept liability for the fiduciary failures that he knew all too well were a consequence of his actions, from not returning the freehold as per trust, from not returning the freehold when his Domain names were returned (in 2013) and from spoiling the insurance claim, ensuring the house was not re-tanked and blighting the Insurance cover as a result.

Instead he was determined to go to court and go for the jugular. How dare she try and take him on in his member's office.

Doubling down Trump style. And perhaps in his mind he had the idea that he would be able to find a judge to agree to let him write an indemnifier into the court judgment.

This might explain why Flaherty actually wrote exactly those words into her judgment where you will see a full indemnifier which claims, untruthfully, that I have undertaken to indemnified Krasnopovich from any claim.

Gosh. Is it that transparent?

Why yes. In Flaherty's own judgment where you have only to read on to see for yourself.

With the settlement offer withdrawn by Krasnopovich and his barrister the Court case went ahead in April, by which time I had paid out in excess of £160,000 in legal fees alone to the hapless Clam. On top of my legal bills, I faced losses through rental costs post flood, repair costs in mitigating the flood damage plus flights and accommodation to attend Court, totaling by far in excess of £250,000. This being my out of pocket losses. Not the actual cost of repair to the flood damaged property. Which would be an amount in excess of £500,000. The quote I had from the London Basement Company to redo the tanking and return the property to its pre-incident condition.

This is the email confirmation by Simon Hazelwood to Richard Castello of the settlement agreement. Verbatim copy.

From: "Simon M. Hazelwood" <Hazelwood@1xxxc.com>
To: Richard Castello <RCastello@1xxx.co.uk>
Subject: Krasnopovich - Without prejudice
Date: 22 April 2015 15:31:57 BST

Richard, Thank you for the e-mail.
Nico will accept a sum of £130,000.
If Nico is to settle on this sum with the attendant clauses we have talked about, the
payment must be made soon and not consequent on a sale of Thameside. Your client
could quite easily re-borrow money from his father or from Philip pending sale of
Thameside.
I have not taken instructions on secondary education but was keen to come back.
S
Simon Hazelwood
TempleLondon EC4Y 28BE

At the conclusion of the three-day hearing, as if in a passing comment, Flaherty, raised the matter of indemnifying Krasnopovich in respect of the Insurance claim. I was surprised at the time, thinking, this has nothing to do with the beneficial entitlement claim, why on earth is she raising this matter? I noted that she seemed cautious in her approach. As if she knew she was doing something wrong. Judge Flaherty. I felt it was clear to me she was going beyond her authority as a family judge to rule in an entirely separate matter, the fiduciary responsibilities Krasnopovich breached serially on the way to claiming his ownership of the freehold to my property. Which made him liable for a claim that might run to multiple millions. I was convinced at that time that she was aware that her attempt to introduce this indemnity was wrong. Her body language was that of a liar. Krasnopovich did the crime and here we have a judge trying to ensure he does 'not do the time.' In awarding costs against me Flaherty allowed Krasnopovich / Clock/ Hazelwood to write the wording and in the course of 'perfecting' Flaherty's costs order they added this:

IT IS RECORDED THAT:

2. In the course of his oral evidence to the court the respondent openly confirmed the following:
1. **a. That she would take no action against the applicant of any kind in any jurisdiction consequent upon his use by him of any photographs or other documents in these proceedings.**
2. **b.   That she would take no action against the applicant of any kind in any jurisdiction arising out of the Insurance of the properties and the property/properties at 28A, 28B or 28C Thameside including for the avoidance of doubt any action (existing or pending) relating to or caused by flood damage at those properties and the costs of renting alternative properties.**

Indemnifying Krasnopovich doesn't end there. The second attempt relates to the unauthorized use of copyright photos, in breach of terms and conditions for use. In these proceedings Krasnopovich/Clock and Hazelwood knowingly used copyright pictures which I own, represented for commercial gain by a professional agency by contractual agreement, which could only be accessed by agreeing a terms-of-use agreement which made quite clear that they were copyright pictures. Agencies who sell my photos include Getty Images and Alamy. None the less, they stole 20 photos and used them to create a case harmful to my defense, which again, had absolutely nothing to do with the matter before this court, and imposed on Flaherty to attempt to make me agree to not pursue any remedy for the illegal use of copyright photos. In the first instance, why would Flaherty involve herself in indemnifying Krasnopovich from a clear legal offense? This photo indemnification followed directly after the fiduciary failures with Insurance indemnification. Which followed right after the California penal offense breach. It appears clearly as if the Judge had a note saying; before you go just add these three indemnities, so if he tries to appeal or tell anyone about it, we can use *section 12 of The Administration of Justice Act 1960* to cover our backs.

Did they use copyright material in full awareness that this is what they were doing, relying on the knowledge that in family-court special secretive laws apply to protect members from perjury and breach of common law. That they deliberately broke the law knowing they could never be prosecuted for doing so because they have their own protection law? If they did nothing wrong in adducing these copyright pictures in presenting their case, why then would they try so hard to have the Judge intervene to try and release them from any legal consequence to an illegal act? If it was legal to use copyright pictures because in family law copyright law is not applicable then there would be no need to try and indemnify Krasnopovich from any consequences.

Krasnopovich did nothing wrong so why try and get it in writing that there will be '**no action in any jurisdiction, ever.**' What if Krasnopovich /Clock/ Hazelwood and Flaherty were acting in full awareness that they were breaking the law?

How were copyright photographs used?

What they did is adduce 20 pictures from a copyright source in which any reprinting without written permission by the copyright holder could not occur without first entering into a binding contract to respect the terms and condition by which the photos could be accessed. Using them is no less than an admission of guilt with a £100,000 per picture penalty for illegal use. International Copyright law is clear and these pictures were protected, with notification, as copyright owned pictures. Clear terms of use specified and were agreed by Krasnopovich and his team when they accessed the picture archive. They could not have accessed the pictures, protected behind an entry portal, without first clicking on that entry window thereby binding them to a specific agreement relating to specific terms of use. By clicking on that link and printing the pictures they agreed to the terms and conditions of use.

Why then would Krasnopovich knowingly steal 20 pictures and submit them after agreeing by virtue of accessing the pictures through the terms and conditions to pay a set amount per picture? In a terms and condition wording compliant with International copyright law. What were these pictures they were prepared to agree some £2 million to use in these proceedings? The pictures from my professional library of licensed photos formed a substantive part of Hazelwood's presentation to the judge. His 'Life of Reilly' feature, in which he discussed 20 pictures, showing pictures of me skiing, riding horses, riding a motorcycle, presenting the case that this was someone living '*The life of Reilly*' while at the same time claiming to have no money. While the poor father was struggling alone on an uncertain income to afford expensive private school that this mother simply found less important than living the 'life of Reilly.' My lawyer, Clam's, comment on all of this was *"Frankly I don't know why they are doing it. It proves nothing and does not serve their case."* To which my reply was *"why do you not invoice them for the £2 million they owe for the photo use?"*

In the hearing Flaherty took a keen interest in the photos but made no reference to the legality of their use. My side never mentioned to her about the Copyright breach and the £2 million owing. In fact, my lawyer Clam's advice when he saw the pictures in the disclosure was that it was irrelevant. "So what if there is a picture of you looking happy. This is irrelevant." And for this reason, the court was not told of the breach of copyright. No mention of it occurred in the course of the 'Life of Reilly' presentation. Something that came and went, like a damp squib, after which Hazelwood turned to his next item.

It is possible judge Flaherty had no way of knowing that these pictures were 'stolen' in breach of copyright because that matter never arose in her court.

Why then would Flaherty take such an interest in securing indemnity for Krasnopovich for this very offense? I suggest, it is in itself an admission of guilt. Firstly, it shows complicity between the judge and team Krasnopovich, because how else would the Judge know to add an indemnifier in the judgment for the breach? She knew and they knew that they were acting in breach of international copyright law. They agreed to a £2 million-pound payment for pictures they used only after legally undertaking this agreement. And they knew they could get away with it because they were going to get the judge to indemnify them in the judgment. Which is exactly what happened. Krasnopovich breached legal terms and conditions regarding the use of 20 photos in the April 2015 hearing. He agreed to pay £2 million for using the photos. I say it would be reasonable to apply the same 8% interest Flaherty awarded against me for the costs of trying to see my own son. 8% interest from the date of the hearing. £2 million.

One of those pictures involves skiing. It is a picture of a skier in Wengen, taken in To illustrate the devious nature of their approach, here is the **ski story**, being one single example from a list of dozens illustrating how Krasnopovich /Clock /Hazelwood and Flaherty's' lies become child abuse.

In February of that year, 2015, I had planned to take Sam for his first ski trip. I had not seen him over Christmas and the Breach of Privacy offense in California was still live. Now it was half term holidays and I had told Sam I would take him skiing. He was five years old and at an ideal age to learn. I envisaged a two-week experience. Ten days of instruction. I researched and found a children's course in Wengen ideal for young beginners. I was reassured and convinced that this ski school was ideal for a first time 5-year-old skier. I felt this experience would provide Sam with a foundation to develop a lifelong interest in skiing. One of my many wishes for him. Having exhaustively researched the details in this trip, I booked Sam in and made arrangements to travel to the UK to collect him. We would spend two weeks in Wengen during his half term. It was an expensive trip and I had to consider the cost carefully, but decided that for the importance of the occasion, Sam's introduction to a passion I hoped would last him a lifetime, as it has with me, I would do the best I could to make it work. I missed Sam and hadn't seen him for so long and this was an opportunity for some real quality time together, in a picture postcard Alpine village, that I believed Krasnopovich would not deny us on the grounds that, no parent in their right mind would stop their son enjoying this wonderful experience. The one issue was Sam would need to miss a three-days of school to make up the time for the ski school, which started on a set weekly cycle. I wrote to Sam's headmaster, detailing the 'life experience' opportunity skiing in the Alps represented with specific details of the ski school. I received his reply by return. This is verbatim from Sam's headmaster.

"No problem in giving him those days off subject to the father's approval. I am sure it will be a wonderful experience for Sam. He is a lucky boy."

Just as with the football invitation, I believed no father would deny his child this lovely age appropriate opportunity. Learning to ski in a top-quality ski school situation. I sent the details of the proposed trip through. And with all of that opportunity in place, with no indication that he would obstruct the visit to suggest caution, I booked the tickets and paid deposit for ski school, directly after which Krasnopovich refused to allow Sam to come with me.

With two weeks prior to departure, I took legal advice. I had the option of going to court to apply for this visitation but decided against it. I would win, but it would cost me thousands. By that time I had learned it was pointless taking anything to family court in Britain, where Krasnopovich could even choose the judge. Instead, I swallowed my tongue, metaphorically and as I had already paid for the trip, I went skiing for two weeks in Wengen. I reflect on some painfully sorrowful moments in Wengen when seeing the 5- and 6-year-old group every morning and watching their progress in the class. After my return to California, I posted a picture from that trip in my Flickr gallery. Protected by copyright terms and conditions. It was a nice action picture of me slaloming into a turn, in good focus, and with the stunning white powder framed by a line of fir trees. A great action shot. It has been used legally, earning me payment for licensed use by Adobe Images.

Krasnopovich /Clock /Hazelwood agreed the terms and conditions on that picture portal, before they printed out a picture and in front of Flaherty, Hazelwood drew my attention to a picture of me skiing and here is how they presented that photograph, copied in triplicate and included in File number seven of their court bundle. While I was being cross examined by his barrister Simon Hazelwood, in the course of the '*I Put it to you you are lying,*' professional-liar Simon Hazelwood produced my action skiing picture, lifted from a copyright source legally agreeing to a £100,000 payment. (For each picture used.) He flamboyantly flourished his exhibit.

"Now let us turn to File 7, page 62, Exhibit 17". And everyone in the courtroom, the judge, my Barrister, his lawyer, Clock, my lawyer, the idiot, turned dutifully, monkey-like, to File 7, page 62. Exhibit 17. A picture of Andrea Skiing. Turning into the slope with flawless technique in glorious Alpine winter light, framed by a shining snow-white backdrop lined by shimmering *Abies alba.*

A hush came over the courtroom. We are in a Court hearing for beneficial entitlement. Where a man has claimed he is owed half of someone else's multi-million-pound home and business because of a supposed promise made at an unspecified time, without any corroboration, yet here we are; looking at a picture of a woman showing some fine form in a downhill turn. And no one has made any mention that this same claimant claimed £100,000 for any visitation with the child?

Hazelwood puffed his chest out, Flaherty made a close study of the picture and then turned in expectation to Hazelwood. The court hushed to total anticipatory silence. All eyes turned toward me in the hot seat. The Judge spoke.

"Ms. Lee. Is this a picture of you?"

Hazelwood holds up the picture and pauses to ensure everyone has ample opportunity to take in every aspect of this rather excellent picture of a downhill skier turning hard on a steep slope where the splash of powder coming off the upturned ski edge has caught the light quite splendidly. No wonder that photo had a commercial value.

"Yes"

"Ms. Lee. Will you please tell the court what you are doing?"

"I am skiing."

"Ms Lee. I see this photograph is taken in February of this year. A year in which you have contributed absolutely nothing towards your son's school expenses. I ask you now Ms. Lee. Is it true that you were living it up in one of the most expensive resorts in the world, staying at one of the most expensive hotels. Whilst. And I say this with great regret. Being unwilling to contribute one penny to your own sons schooling?"

Hazelwood pauses and turns slowly to face the judge. Nodding twice, very slowly before turning back to look at me.

"It's expensive, isn't it. Skiing at top resorts. And for two weeks I understand. Where was Sam in your thoughts while you were away skiing. While his father was paying his school fees and left to take care of his son without any support from yourself?"

He paused again, turning his eyes back to the incriminating photograph. Flaherty eyes moved in the same way. Both looking long and hard at this photograph. Before he looked up abruptly, this time speaking at an accelerated pace and with increased volume.

"Ms. Lee. Have you ever heard the phrase 'The Life of Riley?" A hard stop. And a hard stare directly at me.

"Mr. Hazelwood, you do know that this trip was booked for...."

Before I had even said his name, Flaherty interjected.

"I can see who this trip was booked for. Just answer his question."

"Your honor, this trip was booked so I could ...."

"Ms. Lee. I will not ask you again. Answer the question put to you."

At which point Hazelwood took over.

"No need to answer the question Ms. Lee. We all know what the Life of Riley means. I would like you now to turn to File 7, page 63. Exhibit 18. A picture of yourself on horseback on a beach. Dated March 2014."

This was the *'Life of Riley card'*. They had stolen 20 copyright pictures from a site charging £100,000 per picture for unauthorized use. This use was not authorized.

Judge Flaherty would never know that trip was booked for Sam on her court record. Although I know she knew exactly what was going on. After all, it is recorded in her judgment. Krasnopovich prevented Sam going on that ski trip with me (and Philip) and I lost the price of his flight and ski course. (about £2,000.) And here I am watching a judge enabling the, frankly pathetic, 'I put it to you you are lying' child-abusing Hazelwood spin and ensuring I have no opportunity to place the photograph in context and no opportunity to place into context the illegal use of the pictures in the first place. They have broken the law in stealing copyright pictures. Used them for their purpose. And not even allowed me the pretense of explaining the context. And then written an indemnity into the judgment suggesting I can never pursue this offense by

Krasnopovich and Clock. At the same time they have not referenced the £100,000 blackmail using visitation as leverage. Nor have they mentioned one single instance in which Krasnopovich was in question.

In Flaherty's court this man was perfect in every way. The judge could not have shown more admiration for him if she had slipped her phone number into his hand with a condom and a knowing wink. Two members of family law. One a solicitor, who hires barristers for family court work, the other a barrister who gets hired by solicitors for family court work.

Flaherty nodded her head sagely. I imagined the cogs turning in her head.

"What a terrible mother. Off skiing rather than seeing her own son. Not even contributing to her son's private school fees. This poor man, the family lawyer who has had some bad luck in his business and is almost broke, is working day and night barely making ends meet while the mother is obviously too busy partying and going on expensive ski trips to even see her child. Obviously she must be richer than an Alaskan Coot farmer yet she gives nothing to her own child when all the poor father want's is for the mother to see her own son. This ends right here. I am going to get her good."

What I believe happened is that Krasnopovichs' lawyer Clock advised using the pictures, despite knowing the terms and condition of use in International copyright law, confident that there would be no censure. Because in family law, there is provision for anything that might relate to a child being harmed being allowed.

Obviously where a child's welfare is at stake, there is no need to respect copyright law. For example, a picture proving child abuse could not depend on privacy or copyright in family court. It is evidence. I understand that. However it is a fact the 20 pictures they used in no way related to any child offense.

They were stolen deliberately for malicious use, making them guilty of breaching a legal agreement they entered into by accessing the photo archive and using the pictures. They would have known a judge has discretion in her court and that they could rely on Flaherty to indemnify them, even knowing that the spirit of the law was breached. In no way did these pictures reveal anything that warranted over-riding International copyright law in the name of child protection. However, this assumption would rely on having a friendly judge. One who would go along with the set up. I say it is in fact ironic that they used these pictures illegally, to harm a child. This usage was unauthorized. In no way can the nature of these pictures be seen as protecting the welfare of a child at any risk and being admitted on that basis. The pictures were used to advance a financial claim for the benefit of the copyright thief. The offence compounded by the Judge attempting to indemnify the miscreants by firstly trying to bully me into a verbal commitment indemnifying Krasnopovich and secondly, by allowing Krasnopovich/Clock/Hazelwood to draft their own wording in a court record that reads **IT IS RECORDED THAT**. And then adding their own fabrication after that **BOLD INTRODUCTION.**

It is recorded that this is what KRASNOPOVICH /CLOCK/ HAZELWOOD wrote in this court document. I say it is further evidence that Flaherty has acted dishonestly. Manipulating arcane family court legal provision to breach international copyright law, knowing that the spirit of that law was being breached. It is clear. The pictures are copyright. To view them involved a tacit agreement to specific terms and conditions. In addition to trying to persuade me to indemnify Krasnopovich for the

Insurance matter, Flaherty worked hard to bully me into agreeing to indemnify Krasnopovich for copyright theft of 20 pictures, protected by international copyright law.

Here is the picture access terms and conditions Krasnopovich and Clock had to go through in order to extract the pictures they admitted as evidence and that Flaherty accepted as evidence that I was 'Living the life of Riley.'

Krasnopovich has used a total of 20 pictures from this source. Printed out and admitted (in colour) in court. Flaherty in turn imposed on me quite forcefully to indemnify Krasnopovich from any claim for knowingly entering into the agreement below. Why" If it is legal for them to override International Copyright law, would she need to make me 'Agree' to never sue for this breach?

Andrea Lee gallery pictures. Terms and Conditions.

These photographs are copyright. All rights are reserved. Entrance to the library confirms unreserved acceptance of Terms and Conditions. You may view them for personal enjoyment without the owners written consent by clicking the link below. If you wish to publish or refer to any of the pictures you can contact the owner HERE for written authority. If you choose to use any of the pictures without consent and this use is deemed harmful to the owner by the owner then you agree unreservedly to the terms of conditions by which you view these pictures.

Terms of use: The rights to all pictures that follow on the Andrea Lee account are reserved. These are copyright pictures subject to protection under copyright law and the terms outlined herein for their use. If you use any picture in a manner that might cause nuisance to the owner you agree to pay the sum of £100,000 for each picture used in any way whatsoever. You undertake to pay this sum without the need for any legal action and agree that the act of using the pictures in the commission of nuisance against the owner is a guilty plea enforceable in UK law, or, if necessary any jurisdiction in the world. £100,000 per picture. Do not use or refer to these pictures unless you agree that in so doing you are willing to pay £100,000 per use, be it in print, on a screen, or by reference.

Confirm agreement and click to enter here

I believed that international copyright law applied to members of family law. As much as to anyone. But no. In the judgment they simply write in BOLD HEADERS and then make up whatever they choose.

In point **b** that follows from Flaherty's judgment, consider why I would agree to the wording they spell out relating to my flood claim. Bear in mind, at this time, April 2015, it is over one year since my home flooded and I have not received one penny from Insurance, whilst being down, at that time, £150,000 in house flood repair costs. I had a lawyer pursuing the flood costs as a major priority. I had already spent £10,000 with his firm in the Insurance matter. Who can afford to overlook an Insurance claim that may well run to a million pounds, as is the case here?
Seriously.
Here is what Flaherty wrote; Verbatim.

TWO) b. That she would take no action against the applicant of any kind in any jurisdiction arising out of the Insurance of the properties and the property/properties at 28A, 28B or 28C Thameside including for the avoidance of doubt any action (existing or pending) relating to or caused by flood damage at those properties and the costs of renting alternative properties.

This is clearly the wording of a lawyer given free license to say what he feels best supports the opportunity to release Krasnopovich from the consequences of his actions whilst Trustee freeholder of my home. Actions in which he has breached fiduciary responsibilities on multiple occasions. Acted fraudulently in relation to Insurance matters, refused to return a title as prescribed by a legal agreement he entered into and, acting in bad faith with the insurance of my home to the extent that followed the flood of 2014 along with two further incidents in which Insurance should have provided cover.

My cost consequences arising from his conduct as freeholder, insurance policy named party, and litigant? I have paid over £250,000 in making up insurance shortfall costs (directly related to the February 2014 flood) that fall within the policy cover. And most significantly, in his conduct as the trustee lessor and insured party, causing a down valuation and a loss of income opportunity in the forced sale of my home that is in the region of £3 million and still rising. And worst of all, serially, from the outset, used visitation with the child to benefit his financial demands. Often, lying in this pursuit. As a result of which, since 16 February 2016, I have not spoken with, or seen my son.

I have two questions for any interested reader on the financial aspect of Flaherty's judgment.

If I am right and Krasnopovich was remiss to the extent that I detail above, why in the name of basic common sense would I *"Openly confirm the following"*. Declaring in Court that I will not claim anything against him. What possible motive would I have in forgiving a loss of this magnitude?

I put it to you, the rational reader as a test of this court's credibility; why would anyone *'Confirm the following'* being to overlook a multi-million-pound insurance fraud by a member of family-law for no possible benefit?

This is clearly dishonest use of a court process, to the best of my interpretation of what I saw with my own eyes, Flaherty allowing team Krasnopovich to perfect her judgment, (in the legal sense where the judge invites the winning side to 'perfect' the typo-strewn draft instruction with the fine detail) and in so doing put in any manner of words of their own choosing. It is a fraud.

Words that in this case are patently untrue and which, in the ridiculous nature of their premise, turn this Judge's ruling into a deceit whose function is no more than child abuse. A judge who is the worst triple threat; a fraud, a thief and a child abuser. As written in her judgment in the 2015 ruling of Krasnopovich vs Leandros.

Effectively on the monetary side, the award to Krasnopovich represented my entire proceeds from a lifetime of work towards achieving my real estate ownership and rental income business. Awarded by one member of family law to another without any evidence beyond 'his word' underpinning a judgment based solely on the opinion of the judge. A judge who has deliberately removed any evidence that would have challenged her judgment, by excluding the witnesses.

Talk about witness tampering to fix a court case. I believe the facts show Flaherty formed her judgment before the case even began. Flaherty's opinion was soon after reviewed by the president of family law, in the 'permission to appeal' hearing that followed some six weeks after Flaherty's judgment. The family-law President reviewed Flaherty's judgment and found it to be flawed. He awarded 'Permission to Appeal.'

This was a hearing Krasnopovich brought claiming '*50/50 like we were married.*' The Judge was there to answer that question.

True or false.

Did she promise to give him 50% of her property and business assets in an un-recorded conversation at an unspecified time, in which there is no written evidence, not even one email, and not one witness to any conversation, although, conversely, here are 7 credible witnesses to establish a factual matrix underpinning the claim to be a lie?

Why was this judge interested in involving herself in a separate Insurance matter that had nothing to do with '*he promised me 50/50 like we were married.*' That has crossed over into another area entirely.

I say because Krasnopovich knew there would be litigation which exposed him to a million-pound+ claim. Exactly as laid out in the freeholders' fiduciary responsibilities. He and Clock had already received notification that I would be pursuing an insurance claim for the flood of 8 February 2014. I had instructed a property lawyer and they knew, all too well, the extent of the claim they faced. They knew that Krasnopovich was the named party on the flood insurance policy and responsible, in their 'own words in Flaherty's court' for the fiduciary responsibilities that go with being the freeholder. Fiduciary responsibilities that cumulatively, when adding the same interest calculation that Flaherty used in her costs award against me, by far exceed £3 million.

It is ridiculous to believe that I would voluntarily or otherwise make the agreement recorded in Flaherty's judgment. It is a lie signed off by a family court DDJ who on the face of it is complicit in multiple offences relating to fraud, parental alienation and a child abuse. As a consequence, my son's life has been abused. We have not seen each other since 16 February 2016. During which time I continued to pay mortgage and maintenance costs on my empty home in the UK, (which I was not allowed to enter by Flaherty's court order) in a sales situation where Krasnopovich has 'sole conduct of sale' excluding me from the sales process, as a result of which he has, quite deliberately ensured no sale occurred in over two years of so called 'marketing', while interest on the costs award against me accrued at 8% giving him a tremendous incentive to not sell and face any litigation for his fiduciary failures that would follow on from the accounting for the sale.

Clearly this judgment could only end one way. With me defaulting on the mortgage. With no funds to pursue the fiduciary accounting by chancery court with FOS property law partner, Roland Court. Or pursue custody via family law. No money = no lawyer.

All he has do is continue with "*So sue me.*"

Secondly, does it not appear as transparent as day that the wording used in this Order made by Deputy District Judge Flaherty, sitting in Private is legalese. Does that word selection sound even remotely like something I would say in a hostile court of this nature?

Read the verbatim **BOLD RECORDING** from Flaherty's judgment further down this page and decide.

I say **IT IS RECORDED THAT** this is further evidence that Flaherty has acted dishonestly. Once again she has signed her name to whatever Krasnopovich wants (I recognize Krasnopovichs' hand in the writing of various points in the judgment) and in so doing demonstrates her unconditional support for Krasnopovich's position and her unrestrained prejudice against me.

IT IS RECORDED HERE that Flaherty's actions increased the animosity between Sam's parents immeasurably. In a matching balance of dishonesty, prejudice and incompetence. The conclusion of this causation is child abuse. And parental alienation by a judge who knew all too well that this punitive 'bankrupting' sentence would harm the child's rights to see one parent. I do not accept that Flaherty acts in good conscience. A good judge, simply worn down to incompetence by long hours in a hopelessly confusing heartbreaking job. Flaherty knows all too well exactly what she is doing. A vain woman, driven by ego, in a career notable for under achievement as a barrister, relying on the power vested in a judge's position providing protection from accountability. Secure that the secretive court that is British family-law with its selective code of confidential proceedings will prevent her conduct being reported. Even as a child abuser. She can depend on the sledgehammer silence of contempt proceedings.

By September 2015, the possibility of Sam spending summer holidays with me had gone. Countless skype chats and letters from me had promised Sam we would be together for summer holidays, just like the previous summer, only for '*The whole holiday*'. But as the visit date drew closer, the obstructive replies from Clock grew more adversarial. And it became clear the deadline for booking tickets was not going to be met. Sam had repeatedly assured me;

"*I will keep on telling him I am going to you for the holidays until he says yes.*"

When the deadline day had passed I asked Sam what he had been told.

"*I said when am I going to see mummy. Daddy said to me 'that time has come and gone'.*"

Sam reported this to me in a Skype chat. It was abundantly clear to me in our last few Skype chats that Sam was growing despondent. Missing the summer holiday visit was simply heartbreaking. A new quality was emerging in our chats that until then had been only 100% boundless enthusiasm at seeing each other.

Just as the obstacles to our being together had damaged my wellness to the degree that I had been diagnosed as depressingly unwell, I could see that the five-year-old boy was presenting as a shadow of his former super high energy positive self.

I had assured him repeatedly in our meetings that I would do everything I could to see him again. He asked and I replied.

"*I will make sure we are together again. Really soon. Whatever I have to do I will make sure we are together even if it's just for the two long holidays every year.*"

"*But daddy is hard*" he replied. His confidence was shaken.

I did not know what to do next. As the new year rolled around, I could not see any option I had not already tried. Family court had ruled. Nothing was happening with the Insurance. My lawyer was simply not acting as I had not been able to pay him the advance he requested to pursue the breaches attached to the Freehold fiduciary failures that would have at the very least provided the Insurance for the flood damage. My home was under a forced sale by the Court and I did not even have 'conduct of sale' which somehow the court saw fit to award to Krasnopovich. My rental income properties were all vacant, as ordered by the court, so my monthly income was ended while the mortgage and maintenance obligation continued. Even if I wanted to get a family lawyer to pursue visitation for Sam, I had no means left. Lawyers do not work without payment. Although they explained to me how very sorry they were about the 'horrible judgment' and the appalling failures of my previous solicitor, David Clam. I had by this time a £300,000 legal bill and felt it would be foolish to even try finding more money to pay family law in a court service that employs the likes of Flaherty, Clock and Krasnopovich.

Philip had provided Sam with the same reassurances.

"*We will see you in California real soon.*" Yet here we were, almost three years later, many hundreds of thousands poorer in legal fees and witness to the judgment of Flaherty ensuring animosity between Sam's parents continued its upward trend.

By this stage it was clear that in the UK there was no prospect of Sam seeing me while Clock and Flaherty represented British family-law's version of Sam's best interests. Countless attempts to arrange visitation for Sam to California failed. I wrote numerous letters directly to Clock. Coming away with the firm impression that if the family-law President, or even any reader of the Daily Mail was to see how Tim Clock conducts his business, he would be subject to the maximum censure for child abuse. I considered writing directly to the family-law President.

In many instances during email communications his job description would realistically read;

"*Ensure Mother loses every attempt at visitation. Ideally, none at all is the optimal outcome. At the same time ensure that she has to pay a maximum amount to send emails that refer, however improbably, to how she is to blame for not wanting to see the child. No one will ever know how I run my business. Winning money is everything. That kid will thank me one day for fucking over his Mother. This is so easy. Like taking candy from a baby. I can write whatever drivel comes to mind and no one will ever challenge me because I am a member of family law.*"

Summing up the options available to me by this time, as Sam was now in his 7th year and experiencing some difficulties at school, I went to great lengths, expensive lengths in which Clock argued every hour of our visitation down to the bone to leave me with the decision on whether to travel from LAX to London for a finely tuned 24 hours with Sam. This particular visit was specifically over a disclosure he had made to me about a personal issue at school. I wanted to be there to check on him. To interpret and offer guidance as a loving parent. The parenting circumstance was this: A school friend had come up behind him and shouted in his ear and he had wet his pants. Not a big deal. Just a conversation about motor functions and bad manners. I couldn't have this talk with him on Skype. I wanted to process the details in a proper talk with him without the pressure of being overheard on Skype. To be there for him in this important parental function of interpreting the confidence affecting event. That parental ambition required beginning another costly negotiation with Clock, which eventually led to their agreement I could see Sam for 24 hours. 48 hours of travel to spend 24 hours with someone. I still had to go through. It was a talk I could not miss. Arguing over visitation was Clock's special skill. Arguing visitation details by email is an effective way to run up your opponent's legal bill, making a lawyer write repeatedly over times and places and negotiate minutia of no relevance for no purpose other than to run up the legal bill. I would estimate over the course of my dealing with Clock (And Clam) that I was billed some £30,000 only in my efforts to arrange visitation with Sam. Did that raise the animosity?

Is that child abuse?

Is that within the code of conduct for members of family law published on the Solicitors regulation authority web page?

I travelled for my 24-hour allowance, LAX to LHR. Some 6, 000 miles. Generously, on this occasion, under pressure from Sam, Krasnopovich went on to extend the 24 hour visitation to 26 hours and so on 21 September 2015, I had an overnight visit with Sam, in which I flew to the UK, timing my arrival to enable me to collect a rental car, drive to collect Sam from the arranged pick up, and then return him 26 hours later, before driving back to the airport and returning to LAX.

We had a good talk. It was so worth doing. Sam loves me beyond my ability to describe it in words. Those neural pathways formed in our 4 perfect years together remained intact. But what was clearly showing, was the strain of these long separations and the constant hostility by Krasnopovich. Sam would tell me at length the nature of what he was being told by Krasnopovich and his new partner. And that raised the question of whether it would be in his best interests for me to speak to him at all. Would it be better parenting to wait until he was free to speak to me without fear of retribution by his controlling parent. During the three years this process went on I made 19 trips from LAX to LHR at an average of $1,200 for each flight. Almost without exception every one of those visits involved a negotiation with Clock/Krasnopovich who measured their success by the minimum amount of time they would allow for Sam to be with me. Whilst invariably building a paper trail by extending visitation time after the arrangements had been agreed and booking paid for, to show that I was turning down visitation opportunities. Deceit on a scale of deviance that encompasses child abuse as well as obstruction of justice.

I knew this type of visit couldn't go on, it was draining financially and emotionally, yet at least in this way I was able to keep some contact with Sam. But inevitably the time arrived where I could not see sending him back to his father as anything other than a failure to provide for Sam's best interests. I simply could not fool myself into believing Krasnopovich had Sam's best interests at heart. It is not easy to tell a child their parent is less than they might have hoped for. I could not risk putting either Sam nor myself through the pretense that there could now be normal dialogue as if nothing had happened. Even if I thought that was an option, which I did not. Sam's father is dishonest. Concealing this fact from Sam does not change the truth.

I did not know this 18th trip to LHR for a 24-hour visitation allowance would be my second last visit with Sam. My 18th visit, like every previous occasion, was so exciting for both of us. Although I had travelled this route many times before, I still felt excited at the thought of flying 12,000 miles in 48 hours to spend 24 hours with Sam. Initially, for my first visits to the UK I had no place to stay in the UK due to my flooded home never being repaired, and later, after paying the repair cost myself waiting for an Insurance payment that never came, I still couldn't stay in my home for my visits with Sam, because Flaherty's court-order forbad me from entering my own home (which was vacant while awaiting forced sale in which Krasnopovich had sole conduct of sale'. On every occasion I visited I would stay in hotels. Following the very good suggestion of my musician friend Alan, I chose the Four Seasons in Hampshire for my visits with Sam. It was less than an hour's drive from his school, and provided the variety of homely experiences that would be appropriate for our time together, bearing in mind by this stage each hour we spent together equated to roughly £1,000 in legal fees. Inevitably, it was raised by Clock that, obviously I had lots of money because I was staying at a 5-star Hotel. And that warrants some explanation. The fact is, my financial position made even a 1-star accommodation unaffordable. I should have stayed in my empty flat, 28B Thameside but I was prevented entering my own home by Court order. So, thanks to Flaherty's judgment on 'No right of entry' I had to stay in a Hotel. And as the time I had with Sam was so precious and so hard fought for, I could not take any chances on staying anywhere less than ideal for our purposes.

The Four Seasons was the best choice available to me as the closest thing to living in my home. It was the best choice of canvas for perfecting the memories of our time together at this point where I knew visitation in the UK would soon come to an end. The Four Seasons offered nice walks in nature, comfortable beds. Swimming in a heated pool. Mostly, a place where I could have quality time with Sam. He rode his first horse there. The Michelin star chef took him for a tour of the kitchen and prepared his meal for him himself, sparking his enthusiasm for food as art. We walked in the rain and the sun, through green watery countryside in wellington boots under grey skies and talked tirelessly. We kicked balls around. We fed chickens. We ate chicken. He got to know Oliver, the black lab who works as host there.

It became my favorite hotel in the 19 visits I made to the UK and would be Sam's favorite as well. On one visit asking me *'Can we come and live here together?'* After this particular visit drew to its close I felt confident of being able to articulate Sam's best interests and decided to write to Krasnopovich on the basis of both parents considering solely what would be in Sam's best interests at this time. Putting to one side the litigious animosity and putting Sam to the fore. Once again I proposed representing Sam's wish to attend school in California living with me. After all, Krasnopovich was obsessed with work and saw very little of Sam, who was effectively being raised by nanny and granny. Both equally uninspiring to a 7-year-old with a curious mind. The opportunity to be raised in California, taken to and from school by myself and tutored in the areas in which I have known strengths appeared to me as an ideal option for a young child. Far better than growing up in the cold of South West London with a working father whose role in breaking up his family was all too clear to Sam. It was also very much what Sam wanted. His declaration then was,

"I want to live in California with you and Philip."

The letter I sent follows. I never received any reply. Sam was not able to see me over Christmas for the third year running. Although, it has to be said of the ever-mindful family-lawyer Clock, that he very kindly began negotiations to enable me to have Sam for the afternoon on Christmas eve, (four hours on the 24th) and then for the morning on Christmas day, collect at 8am and returning him to his Fathers for 3 pm. Not at all unreasonable visitation times for a return journey from LAX. 24 hours of flying time over Christmas when flights are peak expensive, and a two-night hotel bill for a total of 6 hours with Sam.

Typical of his letter writing showing how reasonably they offered contact, which the mother then declined. What an awful parent she must be, turning down the chance to have her son for Christmas.

I did in fact come close to booking a two-night visit to the UK see Sam that year, but decided not to when considering the probability that once I had booked the non-refundable ticket Clock/ Krasnopovich would find a polite reason to change the visitation date. That was a realistic prospect in my experience of these two-family lawyers.

September 27, 2015
From: Andrea Lee
To Nico Krasnopovich

Nico,

I write further to my visit with Sam of 21 September. Thank you for allowing Sam to spend 26 hours with me.

During our visit Sam shared with me his thoughts at this time and I was able to evaluate his well-being from my perspective as the parent who raised him for the first four years of his life and who shaped most of the thought processes he now relies on. I am therefore able to comment with some insight on the extent of his development and make a record of Sam's wishes at this time.

Sam has not sparked at school. He says that he does not enjoy school and has no enthusiasm for lessons. His after-school routine is not assisting him and that is unlikely to change within the existing arrangement. Nanny and Granny.

Sam's says that his favorite part of school is Lunch-time. He makes this claim with a humorous intention which does not mask the reality that at his stage of his development he does not identify any lesson as a favourite.

This is not how I raised him and falls short by some distance of my hopes for his education and his prospects for developing into the best person he could be. I spent a few hours doing spelling and reading exercises with him and I see no improvement to the level he displayed when I taught him spelling and reading. Over two years later? I did numbers with him and report the same. I asked him about Greek and he showed me the extent of his improvement in Greek. He has regressed from where he was at 3 when he could comfortably count to ten. Now he cannot. It is clear that in our agreement that Sam would learn to speak Greek you have not succeeded.

Sam does not understand what has happened to him. Your explanation that these are 'adult matters' is as hopelessly inadequate now as it was when you first put forward this ridiculous under researched approach. This is his life and cannot be fobbed over with such a self-serving convenient expedient that is transparently inadequate.

The very first thing Sam said to me when he arrived on Monday at 4.30pm was "I am not allowed to talk to you about anything to do with Daddy." Placing this burden on a child of 6 is unsurprisingly poor parenting. What exactly are you thinking here. That Sam can never speak to his Mother about his Father's conduct? The clear implication is that you believe you can silence Sam's interest by your force of will or some legal edict. That you can act as you do believing your conduct, no matter how abusive it may be, is protected by some legal right to anonymity? Perhaps you can get him to sign an indemnifier to never ask you anything to do with mothering.

I have already introduced you to Frederick Douglas' observation 'It is easier to build strong children than to repair broken men'. You seem determined to prove the alternative. Sam has told me that the gifts I sent for his Birthday by delivery to your office, including a Wii game station along with games and other gifts, have not reached him. That was May. Over four months ago. He has never received the present his Godfather sent for his 5th birthday and understands why his Godfather didn't send him one for his 6th.

Do you?

You have alienated Chris and Maria to the extent that they see no point in trying to send gifts knowing that you will not give them to him.

I have concerns that much of my correspondence to Sam is being similarly diverted. I have long since learned how many of the gifts I sent to Sam by Amazon delivery were not received by him. At this time you have another opportunity to consider what will be best for Sam before more damage is done at such a critical stage of his development.

I repeat the offer I made from the outset. I will undertake responsibility for raising Sam without looking to you for anything. He loves me unconditionally and has never once told me to 'Go Away" as you will recall in his greeting for your return for so many months when he was 4, borne of disappointment at your parenting shortfalls. He has expressed to me his wish to live with me. As you would expect.

I am able to provide him with a good education in which I will participate extensively and most importantly, I am able to be there for him every day and help with his education. Something you have never been able to offer nor show any indication of offering. You have different priorities in life.

Sam is unequivocal in his expressed wish of attending school in California and living with me. The only obstacle to that is your unwillingness to place Sam's needs above your own. My responsibility for Sam's upbringing remains exactly as was agreed between us when we planned this child. At the very least for this holiday; Arrange for Sam to have 1 week off school. His headmaster will agree. I have already written to him. All you need do it authorize it.

E Mail Philip the dates and I will book a one month return ticket for him to LAX. I will collect him from the airport and return him to the airport. He will have a great time that will accelerate his learning and return to good cheer that can only be seen as a good thing.

It is vital at this crucial stage of his development that Sam spends time with me in my home. You have very successfully ensured that visitation cannot take place in the UK.

Sam demonstrated worrying health issues during our visit. He sniffles constantly. He says he always has a cold. He emulated smoking with a twig on a walk in the Park. I asked him what he was doing. He replied 'Smoking.' Obviously in light of the recent trip where he arrived with a travel bag containing cigarettes and smoker's paraphernalia smoking is being modeled for him at home. Second hand smoke is not good for developing lungs and Sam has bronchial issues. Why do you expose Sam to smoke and allow cigarettes to appear in his travel bag when he visits me?

Sam's health will only benefit from time in California where the weather will benefit his lung issue. I see the bronchiolitis has not fully cleared. You may also be assured that while in California he will not be exposed to any form of smoker and the ethical standards they represent.

This is a vital time for Sam's health. Exposure to cigarette smoke increases the likelihood that an infant will develop bronchiolitis and kids who have had bronchiolitis will most likely go on to become asthmatic. There is no doubt that Sam would benefit from a warm dry climate to aid his immune system in overcoming this health issue which, to be fair, is down to your poor decision making with a one year-old when you hired your aunts 17 year old recommendation who had no child-minding experience and took him out wet into the winter cold, causing the bronchiolitis, and to avoid being in a smoking environment, which you are not willing to undertake as a consideration for the harm you do to Sam's health.

I look forward to confirmation from Sam that he will be able to spend a Month with me in California this December along with the dates for Airport collection. I have explained to him that I will be writing to you to this effect. If you are willing to discuss Sam living with me in California then perhaps you will consider agreeing a one-year trial. I have no doubt whatsoever that this will provide Sam with a far better start to life than being collected by nanny from a school that he show no enthusiasm for in a rainy damp climate in a smoker's household.

I am willing to discuss feasibility for him to start school here in the 2016 year. Moving seamlessly from year-end there to start the next year here.

At this time a decision on December is paramount in importance and as ever, it is a simple yes or no that will suffice.

Andrea

Sam's skype message to me after that visit was so beautiful. It arrived on my Skype messages as I landed in LAX and the Internet service came on.

"The weld is betur for you."

The weld is betur for you

23 Tim Clock. Family law solicitor

"Clock is a nasty litigious idiot who gives family law a bad name" David Clam

In 2003 cheeky faced ambitious young lawyer Tim Clock worked his way up in low level libel law. But libel law is hard work and high risk. He soon learned he was no Peter Carter Ruck and soon after that found his way into the easy money that is family law. A court where he earned a great deal more than his average libel win by winning against me, first by preventing my son spending 2 nights a month with me, and then winning a completely untrue beneficial entitlement claim.

Along the way he paid a process server to serve me aggressively, rather than simply send the summons to my solicitor, in a process that caused me physical and emotional harm. His support in the Insurance fraud by his client that saw me lose my home and any Insurance payment, found me moving to America, where Ii had family able to offer me housing after Tim Clocks success in ensuring I became homeless in the UK. Tim Clock is a family law member who traded my son's life with his mother for a 6-figure payment and succeeding in having family law member, and deputy district judge Cecelia Flaherty award him costs against me, achieving, as I had predicted in email exchanges with him, making me pay his legal bill for abusing my son. A man who wrote on more than 20 occasions to me in the matter of visitation with my son, where without exception, he applied maximal hostility towards me, ensuring maximal animosity between my sons' parents. He was especially successful in blocking all overnight visitation in the first six-month period, post separation, as a result of which regular visitation never followed. His win at all costs approach including being complicit in the blackmail demand for £100,000 before I could see my son, which failed and then migrated, on his advice, into a litigious action for 50% of my properties based on an entirely unsubstantiated claim that "She promised me 50/50 like we were married." Not on one instance during my multiple exchanges with Tim Clock over a five-year period did he ever encourage an end to animosity and my sons right to see his parent.

My first awareness of Tim Clock came shortly after learning that Krasnopovich had instructed Clock to represent him. When David Clam told me about Clock, he described him as *"extremely adversarial, which is not a good thing because these people never think of the harm they do to children."*

In this one area Clam was quite right. Despite my overall disgust at Clam's deceitful incompetence for which he took £160,000 from me, I acknowledge Clam tried his best to deflate potentially adversarial situations in the hope of assisting the child's best interests. Sadly this approach was never reciprocated by Clock, seen instead as a sign of weakness that was exploited accordingly. Soon it reached a point where Clam's disgust at Clock's conduct caused a total breakdown in communications between the two. Having seen the correspondence I can confirm that in this aspect Clam was not wrong.

Clock is an abrasive young man, whose deliberately annoying negotiating style begins with the most adversarial position and works down from there. An old school Cambridge lawyer like Clam was a lamb to the slaughter in this approach, handicapped by his awareness and regard for the ethical code of the Solicitors regulation authority. Against an opponent who clearly not only knew his opponent's weakness, but exploited it fully. With extreme deliberation. Riding roughshod over all conventions of courtesy between lawyers as well as the guidance in the SRA ethical code, which he breached as a matter of course.

It was not long after proceedings began before Clam declared to me his utter despair at the ethics of his rival. "*That man is impossible to deal with*". Before long, Clam simply would not call or write to Clock, such was his assured expectation of an offensive reply. At the outset post separation, about 5 weeks after fathers-day 2013, I learned Krasnopovich had appointed Tim Clock. I was surprised that Krasnopovich instructed a solicitor.

Why?

He is a family law solicitor. I wasn't going after him in any way. (We weren't married and I had no designs on spousal support even though he was by now earning a big six figure amount with the new law firm). All we had to agree was visitation and the division of assets in which his investment was at best a few thousand pounds. Less in total than 50% of one single gift I had given him. A diamond ring.

With hindsight, his choice of solicitor was telling. Why he needed to retain a solicitor and who he chose for this purpose. Clock's first input into Sam's life was convincing Krasnopovich to claim 50% of two of my apartments. One of which I bought in 1986 and had paid of fully, meaning it was a 100% profit rental income property. Their claim was the guise of '*beneficial entitlement.*' Prior to retaining Clock, Krasnopovich had not made any reference to claiming beneficial entitlement. The financial arrangements in concluding our separation were initially done be email between him and myself. And it was not complicated.

We had no intermingled finances. Limited to a shared car that he insisted be sold to give him half the money, the repayment of money he had on my Amex card which was used for the Krasnopovich McDonald LLP bills, about £5,600 at the time (Which I paid off in any event as gift to try and be friendly and deflate hostility.) A £10,000 shortfall on a loan repayment I provided for his equity buy in at MWT in 2010. And the transfer of the title for his web domains, all in my name, and the transfer of my freehold title, in his name. Pretty straightforward. There was a sofa and a TV we bought together in equal shares. The value of which, second hand, was the price of 5% of the diamond ring I had gifted him. My priority was not to argue money, but to make the most appropriate arrangement for Sam's future. I did not initially instruct a solicitor, because I didn't think I would need one. The 'shared' assets between us were small change. The balance owing was almost entirely from him to me. At best he could claim the things he paid for totaling some £5,000, which he had in any event taken with him when he moved out.

He made no claim against my property until after taking Clock's advice. There was no mention of any '*50/50 like we were married*' until Krasnopovich retained Tim Clock. Initially, prior to instructing Clock, the claim from Krasnopovich was in a Without Prejudice email sent to me directly. He wrote claiming £100,000 for 'rehousing Sam' and that was basically that. "*Give me £100,000 and then you can have Sam.*" I understood that included me taking full custody. I believed his request meant if I paid him £100,000 he would encourage Sam living with me as his primary carer.

Any interest, imagined or otherwise in my other two properties was not mentioned. Only the one that he lived in with Sam, because it was the home where Sam lived and in family law the child had to have provision for a home. Of course, that made no reference to the fact he already owned a home and there was no case in which family law would make me pay to 'house' Sam in these circumstances

For clarity, dear reader, I had three properties. Valued at that time, after costs, at some £2 million net. Flats 28A, ground floor, 28B middle floor and 28C top floor.

When Krasnopovich moved in as my guest in 2003 I was living in 28C Thameside. He arrived in that apartment, because I had a long-term tenant in 28b. The flat below. This was to become an issue later when they chose to claim 50% of that flat, 28B, which had the highest equity value. A year later, when the tenancy finished, I kept both flats empty for my use. I had visitors from abroad and a steady stream of my close friends from California. I was planning renovation works so I opted to not have tenants in the house while I undertook renovations to the bottom two flats. A period I envisaged would take one year. And so for this second year with me, living rent free and having nice holidays paid for, Krasnopovich had the use of both flats, 28C and 28B. To support his claim against 28B, he agreed with Clock that he would say he lived there with me all along. And try to frame me as a liar for saying he lived with me in 28C.

Confused yet?

While Krasnopovich had lived rent free for a period in 28B and 28C, my two upper level flats, he had never paid any rent for the two years he lived there before we moved into 28A. The large ground floor apartment I spent 6 months refurbishing. If he was to claim something against 28A, the ground floor flat where he lived when he started paying £500 a month for living expenses, on the basis he paid a rental contribution, there was a thread of logic, even if that amount represented 10% of the living costs he enjoyed. But claiming on 28B was ridiculous. He lived there for free while accepting loans monthly. And the claim on that flat is made more ridiculous because as he did not claim on 28C as well. The flat he actually lived in when he arrived as my freeloading, money borrowing guest.

Why then did his meeting with Clock result in adding this flat to the claim?

This addition of 28B to his claim followed shortly after my first financial disclosure. Up until then Krasnopovich had no idea what my mortgage position was. Literally no idea. Why would he. We did not have that level of relationship. Position wise, I was the property owner, paying all the bills while he was the lucky chap able to live in a luxury accommodation for free. (For the first two years, and after that for a small fraction of the total overhead for that lifestyle.)

The mortgages were my business.

The property was my business.

He had his own mortgage on his little Hounslow flat, still rented at £800pm. That was his business. However that first court financial disclosure revealed to him for the first time that I had my principal mortgage on 28A and no mortgage on 28B. This mortgage structure was a decision made with the guidance of a financial planner, my long-standing IFA, and included tax advantages for my rental income. This was a property valued at £700,000 when I had the bank survey and valued the property in 2005. With no mortgage. And now, for the first time, Krasnopovich realized that is where the most equity in the property was. 28B It made good sense to claim against the property with the most equity. Great advice from his lawyer.

Even without any shred of credibility to the claim they added 28B to the 'promise' claim. A different property. Simply a cynical exploitation of a bluff principle that by adding the value of 28B to the claim, I would be more motivated to take a commercial view and settle based on the higher value of the claim. That the entire claim 'she promised me 50/50 like we were married' was invented is just another layer in the deceit. Why not add as many properties as you like if you're going to make up a story. If you're going to risk your reputation on a lie might as well make it worthwhile.

After deciding to proceed with the beneficial entitlement claim for two flats, 28A and 28B, Clock elected the summons serving procedure most likely to cause maximum animosity; having me door-stopped and served in a hostile street encounter causing me injury. An experience so unpleasant on so many levels it influenced my will to remain in the UK when the time came where I had to make a choice. A harassment that caused trauma. I certainly would not trust Krasnopovich and Clock to not repeat that behavior again. I see a value in being 12,000 miles and a different jurisdiction away from their opportunity to repeat that experience. Perhaps, if they had been brought to account for what was clearly in breach of the SRA ethics code, I would feel more secure. It is that they got away with-it scot free that makes me think there is no reason they would not repeat the same conduct. If they act is if they are above the law it is because evidently they are.

When lawyers serve notice of proceedings the correct procedure, in line with the SRA guidelines, even if creating maximum animosity is not the intention, is to have the papers delivered to the solicitor. It is obvious that serving an individual personally is unpleasant and increases animosity. Which is why family law makes plain, the correct procedure is to simply serve on the lawyer. It's not as if the outcome is any different. The lawyer accepts the documents and that is the legal notification of the summons. But Clock and Krasnopovich chose to send in a six-foot thug to approach me late at night in an aggressive and threatening manner. This was not an acceptable normal service of a summons. It spoke of deliberate malice. It was intended to increase animosity between a child's parents. It was in breach of the SRA ethics code.

It was a door stopping harassment and actual physical assault in the street after which I felt unsafe in my own home. Not long after which I left for health reasons to the United States. The ongoing harassment and actions by Clock clearly intended to maximize animosity by causing me financial harm, being direct causation as to why I am now unable to reside in the same Country as Sam. At no time have Clock or Krasnopovich faced any censure for having me served in the aggressive malicious way, very much at odds with the SRA directive. Certainly it is no exaggeration to say Clock's actions in representing Krasnopovich against me, specifically in negotiating visitation is the most significant factor explaining why I have not seen or spoken with Sam since 16 February 2016. From the outset of negotiations for visitation Krasnopovich and his proxy Clock were obstructive, controlling visitation whilst at the same time making ridiculous financial demands far beyond what the law provided for. There was no mistaking that the visitation possibilities were linked to his financial demands. And no mistaking that, if this is an offence on any level, ethically, morally or legally, then his lawyer was beyond equally complicit. Krasnopovich and Clock. Both members of the law Society. Both familiar with the SRA ethical code and equally familiar with their exemption from any liability for breach. I say it is blackmail. *"Pay me £100,000 and you can see Sam as much as you want. But not before."* The TOLATA claim was the lever to pressure me into agreeing the payment, because they could.

Soon after the separation, when I was denied any visitation, and even the address of where my son was unless I paid him £100,000, I retained a member of family law for an initial retainer of £20,000 (David Clam) and brought an application for visitation in family court. Clock succeeded in preventing my 2 nights a month application in family court to see my son. He brought a QC to a preliminary hearing for visitation, lied in the declarations to CAFCASS and recorded a win in stopping that 'soon after separation' visitation that was so important for the child. The first six months post separation is absolutely vital for the child's relationship with both parents. I recognize that Krasnopovich made it as difficult as possible in those first 6 months for this very reason. Imagine blocking 2 nights a month visitation application by such determined means it eventually added up to a £40,000 legal bill on me? Clearly stopping a child from spending two nights a month with his mother is a noble goal for any family lawyer that should be rewarded with top dollar invoices, that should be paid in a costs award against the losing parent, me, and with an 8% interest charge, as Flaherty would later determine was in the child's best interests. Seriously. How does that make sense. I applied for two nights a month visitation and they fought it and put in a costs application to boot.

The facts in Clock's conduct and approach to family law speak for themselves, embodying as he does the very worst qualities of the conscienceless exploiter of a poorly regulated system, determined to win at all costs by whatever means.
    That his approach harmed Sam's opportunity to have a relationship with me is undeniable. As is the logical extension that his conduct and its consequence for Sam is child abuse. Tim Clock has made a fortune out of abusing my son and DDJ Flaherty, a fellow member of family law, has rewarded him with costs against me at 8% interest. Had I been able to stay in the UK and had any realistic prospect of continuing 'fighting' to see Sam through family court, I would have completed a substantial complaint to the SRA on Clock's conduct. A man who generates many hundreds of thousands annually as a member of the Law Society by knowingly abusing children through litigation he constructs on the dishonest (certainly in my case and allegedly in others) bedrock of maximizing animosity. Aware as I have been from the outset that the most important thing in all of this is Sam, it is beyond disappointing to see members of family law get away with all that they have in Sam's case. It was never in Sam's best interests to have Clock negotiating his visitation with me. As countless adversarial provocative emails between us show, up until the last one that cancelled Sam's December 2018 visit. Invariably his emails set out to prevent visitation or to attach conditions to visitation for financial benefit. From a parenting perspective, it was a poor decision by Krasnopovich placing Sam's future with his mother in Clock's hands. In placement terms, it positioned financial interest above the child's best interest. Krasnopovich's choice at the outset to retain an individual of this character

demonstrates his intentions in reconciling his duty as parent and his priorities as a winner in family law. Since the outset of litigation by Krasnopovich I have corresponded directly with Clock in the matter of visitation with my son on at least 30 occasions in which his aggressively adversarial tone is so clearly intended to maximize animosity as to represent a constant transparent thread. In his correspondence with Clam, the same approach is all too evident. There is not even the pretense of elegant articulate discourtesy. It is a constant 100% nastiness.

Where a child is involved in litigation there is a responsibility associated with both sides in the dispute which should and must be subject to checks and balances within a working legal system in which the child's best interests are given the highest priority. Yet in this case before family-court and in the judgment, that is demonstrably absent. Worse still; despite my repeated alerts to the professional body running British family law, nothing has been done about any of the miscreants in my matter. Even after the President of family law ruled in a 'permission to Appeal' and after I sent him a detailed list of the conduct apparent in this case.

Tim Clock has to date continued to prosper handsomely by his interpretation of the Law Society's ethical code in 'winning' a victory for his client that began with ensuring Sam could not see his mother absent of a blackmail payment. That this victory was predicated on a lie – 50/50 like we were married - which I believe has its origins in legal advice from Clock to Krasnopovich makes the abuse of the child a co-venture. Being left with a costs award by Judge Flaherty in Clocks favor accumulating at 8% interest, cannot in any interpretation of the SRA ethics code be seen as acting in the child's best interest. More certainly, as I propose here, it is a clear line between child abuse and the profit won by members of family law.

I have chosen one example from my multiple exchanges with Clock to copy verbatim, in that it shows the average flavor of our correspondence. Wherein, he would never reply to my questions. But instead simply choose the most annoying word sequences to send in the stead of a measured and satisfactory address of the matter raised. Obfuscation is a euphemism for his disregard for an honest reply.

This letter is dated 25th January 2015, about three months before the Court hearing set for April 2015.

Of special interest in this letter is the reference to one of my witnesses, Larry Chester, who was set to appear as a witness in the April hearing, less than 3 months after this letter. Bearing in mind what happened 3 months later in Flaherty's court. How on earth would Krasnopovich and Clock get around this witness evidence in which several of his more serious frauds are listed with credible independent witnesses set and ready to appear in Court to testify?

From: Andrea Lee
To: Tim Clock
25 January, 2015.

Mr. Clock,

Thank you for your letter of 20 January written in reply to my letter of 8 January inviting you to be the 5th intermediary between your client and myself in representing arrangements for Sam's visitation with me, because no one else can perform this service without your charge.

Unfortunately your reply entirely disregards the urgent matters I have raised in my letter of 8 January. Once I have received your reply to my letter of 8 January, I will reply to the points raised in your letter of 20th January, 2015.

If you are to communicate directly with me as the intermediary in my son's visitation then my hope is that you will agree that the common convention by which correspondence between two parties prospers is by the civil and adequate reply to the matters raised in receipt being delivered in advance of the presentation of your own position. Aside from the conventions of professional courtesy, it is also an obligation of your office since the last time I read the code of ethics on the SRA website. To be clear, here is my understanding of the conventions you are required to respect in our correspondence.

From the SRA website code of ethics:
As a member of the law society I will:

Act in a respectful and courteous manner in all my professional dealings with others, taking particular care to avoid real or perceived acts that might be construed as prejudice, intimidation, harassment and/or unwarranted negative criticism of colleagues. Unwarranted negative criticism may include demeaning comments that refer to a colleague's level of competence or to an individual's attributes such as race, ethnicity, national origin, color, sex, sexual orientation, gender identity or expression, age, marital status, political belief, religion, immigration status, and mental or physical disability.

I do not see anywhere in this code of ethics *"I am free to be as aggressively adversarial and provocative to my opponent, without considering the consequential abuse this presents to her child, for as long as I can charge the absolute maximum of billable hours at £500 plus VAT and win costs against the mother. Who will have to pay my bill for abusing her own son. Raising the animosity between the parents by acting aggressively is the best way to achieve the maximum billable hours. And going to a disputed trial is, by far, in the best interests of the child/lawyer relationship."*

As you are now the 5th intermediary in correspondence between your client and myself you may notice that the letter you have written conforms entirely to your client's habitual disregard for these conventions in correspondence, preferring instead of replying to my considered and pertinent concerns over my sons wellbeing, with an unrelated series of questions, unmistakably governed by control issues over visitation rights for the child and total disregard for any matter he wishes to avoid. Plainly the intention is to ensure unfettered visitation does to proceed.

This approach, a well-established well documented pattern, which is indistinguishable from blackmail, using the child as leverage, while you obfuscate to confuse any paper trail, is, I hope you will agree from the child's point of view, a recipe for certain failure. Mr. Krasnopovich's habitual reliance on 'ignore and ask an aggressively different set of questions with a list of non-negotiable demands' has failed with each of the previous intermediaries, all of whom have identified your client's approach as 'toxic correspondence' for this reason. So here we are. You get to be paid top dollar just for agreeing times for collection and pick up. Because the father, a trained family lawyer is incapable of arranging this with a friend at no cost to me. Five times. He has alienated friendly no-cost intermediaries, a;; serious professional people with high standards of regard for Sam's best interests, by toxic behavior to the point of offense so serious they cannot continue.

You and your client write repeatedly in a fashion so at odds with basic honesty that the only surprise is that you believe any reader would be deceived by your approach.

I have on file upwards of 100 email examples in the course of your correspondence with Mr. Clams office demonstrating precisely this approach and for this reason I do not welcome or require more additions from yourself in the context of; disingenuous, unhelpful and pointless.

It is clear that your client

1.) Obstructs contact serially under the pretext that he is in fact, generously hoping to enable contact which I (unreasonably) decline.
And 2.) Would have allowed any contact I chose to accept if he received a lump sum payment in excess of £100,000. Trading visitation for payment. After retaining you that approach changed in number only. It is still blackmail, as the very fact I am writing to you in this way at this time demonstrates. If I accept your settlement offer, then I can see my son as often as I like. Not until.

What is equally clear is that your client and yourself are abusing my son by your conduct in correspondence deliberately intended for this purpose. You are participating in parental alienation and child abuse, motivated by significant monetary reward. If a criminal detective writer was to examine your child abuse in the traditional examination of Means, Motive and Opportunity, I say you would be found guilty beyond all reasonable doubt on all three measures.

In this awareness, if you are to correspond directly with me in respect of my son's visitation with his mother, as Mr. Krasnopovich's intermediary charging at your usual rate for a service traditionally associated with zero charge, then please respect the conventions of appropriateness in your position. I have sent a list of legitimate questions to which I expect an appropriate reply. I am requesting no more than you are obligated to provide by the terms of your law society membership.

Yet, in this letter I record, as has been the case on every previous letter I have sent you directly, you do not answer in a *"respectful and courteous manner in all professional dealings with others"* as required by your governing ethical code.

What I receive from you is indistinguishable from obfuscation and disingenuous nonsense. Admittedly, your grammar and spelling are fine. It is the content and intention of your words that is objectionable.

I am especially concerned that despite my request for information regarding the possibility that my son is left alone in his father's house with an unknown adult female, who smokes and for all I know may be a registered sex offender, you choose not to reply to my simple request for information, preferring instead to issue me with a set of instructions on when your client deems it convenient for my son to see me and titling it '*for my kind attention*' which I am trying to understand in context.

You are ignoring my concerns over my son being left alone with a stranger about whom I have no knowledge, who has been reported to me by my son as a smoker and may well be offering him second hand smoke, or more.

Then, despite being obliged by your ethical code as a member of family law to provide me with this important information relating to my child's well-being, instead you ignore my request entirely and send me a list of instructions, unconnected in any way with my request, under the heading 'for my **kind attention**'?

This appears from my end as both puerile and provocative. It is not in accordance with the spirit of avoiding antipathy and acrimony because it is never in the interests of the child. Yet it is your de facto position in all correspondence with myself and with Clam. I assume, by your reputation, that is your go-to position in family law.

'*For my kind attention*'. Is this some newly designated Clock invention, a style of attention giving tried and proven to annoy the reader to the maximum level? Kind, unlike common attention which is by your inference, not kind? The adversarial unpleasant sort of attention, bereft of kindness?

Really though, what do you mean by my 'kind attention'? It may be that I will adopt this approach for my own correspondence when I want to offend and antagonize recipients from the very first line.

I cannot in good conscience agree that I am giving you my 'kind' attention nor that I expect the same from you. I can confirm that you are extremely annoying and this approach is one of many reasons why I believe you set out to deliberately cause annoyance when it is your duty to avoid acrimony between the child's parents. Yet you clearly ignore this obligation by the SRA.

If this 'kind attention' to which you refer is indicative of your total disregard for both your responsibility in family-law as well as the important questions relating to the child's well being raised in my letter, then of course, it is neither kind, nor in keeping with the common understanding of attention. It is in fact, rude disregard that you offer, requiring in its stead, my 'kind attention.'

If my son is being subjected to second hand smoke, as he has reported to me is the case on the last occasion where Mr. Krasnopovich allowed him to speak to me on Skype, and despite my repeated requests to you in writing to establish who is smoking around my son then clearly this is a matter for concern. Not an invitation for you to list further demands before replying.

You are not putting the child's best interests to the fore. You are deliberately taking an adversarial position that is clearly abusive to the child, which you do with a license to practice family-law from the Law Society.

It is your duty to do an about turn on your historical position in respect of writing letters that do not represent maximum acrimony as your best-case intention. It is simple. Reply to my request for the identity of the adult living with my son. I asked. All you have to do is provide a name and a background. But after three requests you have not done as you are required. Instead you continue to do that thing you do, so much at odds with the SRA ethical code you serially ignore. That thing you do is child abuse, unacceptable even by the high standards set by your client in child abuse. I fail to understand why your client is unable to respond to such a serious concern without drawing the obvious conclusion. Is Carol able to pass a police check, ensuring that she is not a registered sex offender being left alone with my 5-year-old son? If there is nothing to hide, why not just answer the question. As you should have done the first time I asked. As you should have done the second time I asked. And as you should have done at my third request, leading up to this observation. You are not playing by the rules of your own office. You are abusing my son and you are abusing me by abusing the rules you are bound by in your profession.

I asked you a simple question about the person sleeping in the same home as my son; as is my right and as is my child's right. Who is Carol? Would she pass a Police check? Is her smoking exposing my son to harm?

What conclusions do you expect me to arrive at in the absence of any answer and seeing all Skype contact stopped by your client shortly after Sam revealed these details of the prospective Mrs. Krasnopovich, Carol?

As I have not had my legitimate concerns answered there are two possibilities. One is that Carol has something to hide. And may present a risk to my son. Or secondly, you are once again failing to reply, as the SRA ethical code requires from you, to deliberately cause maximum annoyance and increase the acrimony between my son's parents. Please will you ensure that I have sight of Carol's police check certification within seven days, (By no later than Monday 2nd February)

Would you agree that your comments are not likely to be best received as kind attention, whatever your understanding of the words kind and attention may be.

'I understand these proposals have been set out to you on several occasions and I am instructed they will not change' and *'I look forward to hearing from you with confirmation that these arrangements are agreed.'*

This appears to me as 'rude disregard'. Which would have been a more honest title for your email subject. Rude Disregard presented as Kind Attention does not in any way diminish your responsibility to provide an adequate reply to my letter.

I remain deeply concerned by your conduct in family law. I have raised serious matters relating to my son's welfare and as ever, you and your client prefer to ignore the issues and answer with a series of irrelevant cut and paste acrimony generating instructions, reliant on your client inventing a reality he can control in the hope that this will make the reality he wishes to ignore, disappear.

Turning to the issue of the **house Insurance,** please be advised it remains of the utmost importance. Your client's failures have directly contributed to me losing over £500,000 at this time. Particularly galling as it was your client's legal advice (in 2003) that I transfer my Freehold to his name to avoid high Insurance premiums with the deliberate intention of misleading Insurers (In this case the AXA Insurance) that is now being used to support your clients claim against my house. I have repeatedly requested the return of my Freehold from your client, as he is legally obligated to do. And I have repeatedly written to your client making clear the liability attached to the Freeholder. Your client has had every opportunity to walk away from liability for my house Insurance. He has elected, in response to a specific notice, to 'make up any Insurance shortfall out of his own resources'.

Unsurprisingly and predictably your client is now being investigated for dishonesty in an application for cover by the AXA in a procedure that may well lead to criminal charges. He is after all guilty of fraudulent representation to the AXA on more than one occasion. If the extent of his fraud is uncovered, the AXA will most likely seek to recover costs against your client, who has benefitted by over £300,000 paid by the AXA to him on a policy in which he knowingly misled them through non-disclosure in one instance and false disclosure in another. This occurred in 2007 and 2008.

I have always had the impression that members of the Law Society should be held to a higher standard. Obviously, Mr. Krasnopovich's dealings with me, breaching a trust agreement and offering legal advice to me which he then used to benefit himself, along with his dealings with Insurers; making misleading applications for Insurance cover and then claiming over £300,000 from these policies, indicate that he may not be maintaining the ethical standards one would expect from a Solicitor. Your client cancelled my Insurance cover with the AXA in November if 2013. This was in breach of his fiduciary responsibility as trustee freeholder. As well as being a simple fraud. You cannot call an Insurer and have an existing policy cancelled. Your client was on written notice after that event that if anything happened as a result of him cancelling my policy, that he would be liable. To 100% of the consequence of cancelling my policy. That is over and above his standing obligations as Freeholder, whether as trustee, or as he has amended his position following your advice, to claim the Freehold is actually his. You know the claim of ownership to the freehold is a lie, yet you encourage him to use it in the BE claim? This is a whole mess of criminality. And a whole mess of liability. He has signed his name to a commitment, he has been offered the opportunity to walk away from liability, and he has elected to maintain the fiduciary obligations that include restoring my home to its pre-incident condition. An amount, when added to the other 'Insurance shortfall' items, is already far north of a million pounds. I have it on record that your client was offered the opportunity to return my freehold, and be clear of the fiduciary responsibilities attached to her claim. Your client elected to continue with the nonsense BE claim and refused to return my title. Accepting 100% liability for all that accompanies being the Freeholder.
Continuing with your BE claim is not going to take away the fact that your clients misjudgment in cancelling my Insurance and then not fulfilling the fiduciary obligations in making up the shortfall in Insurance, is likely to be a figure by far in

excess of any win you might achieve, even if you did win a court judgment that his word is word, as a liar of note, is worth more than the independent professionals who will give evidence against his claim. Continuing with your claim when you have had the opportunity to withdraw and defuse the minefield of liability your client is exposed to is negligent. And it is the wring call for the best interests of the child. Settling is always best. You and your client had that opportunity with the Freehold return. You elected to continue.

Your client's reputation as a liar?

You know your client was summarily expelled from MWT, after an emergency partners meeting, which I attended, where they accused him of dishonesty, and had him escorted off the premises. Made to clear his desk under the watchful eye of a guard. And escorted out the front door. This is after he stole the MWT data-base, including the files of his clients, which generated £180,000 directly for the new business. And that is not even the reason he was expelled, as MWT did not know about the theft, or have sight of the documentary disclosure of this data theft (In my document disclosure) at that stage.

Your client's expulsion as a partner from MWT was for a different level of dishonesty, in breach of the articles of partnership of that law firm.

I do not know of many lawyers dishonest enough to warrant being expelled. It was an unusual sight, Mr. Krasnopovich, standing on the side of the road with a few boxes, having been escorted out of the building directly following his expulsion from his MWT office. This is a large law firm firing an equity partner on the spot, such was the extent of his dishonesty. Evidence of his dishonesty is by no means limited to that chapter in my court disclosure.

You may already be aware that my laptop containing emails from your client to his soon to be business partner Caroline McDonald was stolen from my home in a burglary in August 2014. The Police investigation identified your client and his then personal fitness trainer as the only two suspects. The emails on that laptop relating to poaching a 2yq solicitor, Belinda Rostock from MWT in breach of the articles of partnership may well have cost your client dearly with MWT.

Surprising then that this burglary happened in the coincidental way that it did. Interesting that the police investigated your client as they did. And reached the conclusion they did.

Surprising that the contents insurance which was in your client's name as per our Trust Agreement on the Freehold and the Insurance cover, did not pay the £1,800 for replacement of the stolen computer. As per the police report on the theft and presentation of the invoice for the replacement unit. Your client, as the named policy holder, is responsible for processing that claim. Yet I have still not seen the payment.

Indicative of a pattern? You client and dishonesty are well acquainted.

Dishonesty has accompanied your client's legal career since he first falsified his CV to improve his poor grades after receiving ten rejection letters since scraping through the bar exam. Happily the first letter he sent with the altered grades, a fraudulent job application, led to his first job, in Criminal law in Aldershot. I expect many members of the Law Society lie about their grades on job applications and get away with it so I am not intending following up on this point. It does however present a consistent thread to a career based on dishonesty. The skewed ethical compass arising, I believe, although because it is his word, who knows how true it is, from childhood abuse. The traumatic events of his childhood and the failures of subsequent therapy to find closure for this deep betrayal he claims, when he was 12. Whether his claims are true or not, and I suggest his behavior and anxiety issues may well be consistent with early life abuse, it is clear that from an early age your client's ability to reliably determine between right and wrong is inconsistent with what any psychotherapist would consider normal. A condition that makes him believe that his version of the truth is the truth, irrespective of the facts. Also generically referred to as cognitive dissonance. Plainly put, your client is a habitual liar, who makes a living out of lying professionally. Similar in this way to yourself.

Another example of unethical legal conduct by yourself and your client was hiring a goon process server to attack me in the street. As you know, personal service was unnecessary. You had only to send any documents to David Clam. Whose identity and address were well known to you. Instead you chose to have me personally served, with maximum prejudice.

You may be reassured to know the outcome was much as you intended. I was so traumatized by that attack I left my home shortly afterwards for sanctuary in the USA. It is really not nice being attacked in the street by a threatening goon. I had no way of knowing this thug approaching me was a legal process server. His intention was unmistakably hostile. Did you have to pay extra for that service?
Can you imagine any circumstance in which Debs would do this to you?

Is your conduct increasing animosity between Sam's parents?
Is increased animosity good for the child? In your estimation, would you say your conduct is serving the child's best interests?
Is deliberately increasing animosity that is harmful to the child, child abuse? You are the professional in family law so you would know better than me.

During the Preliminary Financial directions hearing your client admitted extensive quotes from a letter written '**without Prejudice**' by Philip Parker Voula, detailing opportunities for Sam's education. (Document email between and your client). It is my understanding that the ethical code for solicitors precludes using 'without prejudice' correspondence and I am surprised that you have so readily lent your name and reputation to such an obvious breach.

Why is your client able to disclose extracts from my 'Without Prejudice' letters, yet I am an unable to include content from her 'Without prejudice' letters to me, like, verbatim, "*You can see Sam as much as you want as soon as you pay. Until you do, this will not stop.*" Which I understood to mean, the rising legal bills, which you and your client deliberately increased as a tactic to place maximum discomfort on my position. It is your duty to assist children in seeing both parents. Not trade visitation for money to strengthen your negotiating hand. That would be an example of bad family law practice. It would present a case indistinguishable from that of a blackmailer.

You are aware your client holds the Insurance policy on my home and that the deadline for the Insurance works is 8th February 2015, despite which I have had no satisfactory reply to the matters relating to this deadline as presented by Mr. Clam in his correspondence with you. Why is that? This is my home. I am homeless until my home is repaired. Why the delay. You client is the Freeholder. There are fiduciary responsibilities that accompany his position.

Mr. Krasnopovich has breached a trust agreement by not returning the title on request, first in 2007, shortly before the flood then (detailed in my document disclosure), and again in 2013, when he had written notice that unless he returned the freehold he would be personally liable for any costs arising from her failure to do so. (Detailed in letters from myself to him and in correspondence with Mr. Clam.) He has had numerous entreaties in this regarding including from Chris Andiotis and from Philip Parker Voula. (Disclosed in Documents list.) He has serially refused and to this day continues to refuse to return the Freehold he holds in trust.

What kind of advice are you giving him? There is clearly very little prospect of Insurers honoring the claim now that they have established Mr. Krasnopovich's deceit in the policy application.

This is evident from the fact they have not paid one penny in 12 Months of asking. Once they (The AXA and their legal representatives) become aware of the deceit in 2003 as they will following the April proceedings where my witness Larry Chester has the independent verification as the IFA involved at that time, if they decide to pursue recovery of the amounts paid out arising from this deceit, the amounts they will seek to recover are in excess of £300,000. All paid to your client.

It appears to be no more than simple criminal Insurance fraud. Your client lied on the application for cover. In a clever move intended to 'steal' my freehold title. Which then backfired on him when the house flooded and he decided to claim. Any shortfall in cover as per the Freehold conditions. Fiduciary responsibility to make up shortfall in insurance out of his own resources. Surely you could have seen that was the best way forward for the child's best interests.

But that would have meant an end to litigation for you. And that's not where your interest lies. You may recall that while my Freehold title was in Krasnopovich's name, his business domain titles were in mine. When we separated he asked me for return of the domains, without which he was vulnerable. The titles were registered in my sole name. He received my reply that I would transfer the titles immediately and he should transfer my freehold back. I accepted his word that my freehold title would transfer back when Insurance renewal came up. That is why you saw the title renewal document sent by Clam arrive on your desk.

But for some reason, which may relate to his lifetime of serial dishonesty, although I transferred my part of the agreement, perhaps acting on your advice, no doubt you will let me know, your client did not follow through on his promise with the freehold transfer. Instead. On the very day that the title was set to transfer, you sent an aggressive summons server to doorstop me and cause me injury. Conveniently you overlooked the agreement that tied the transfer of the domain names to the freehold.

You will note that I have made every effort to protect your client by not discussing the offense in 2003 with the AXA solicitors. I am curious. If you as a lawyer are aware that criminal activity has occurred, are you not bound by your code of conduct to report that offense?

It remains surprising to me that Mr. Krasnopovich appears unconcerned that the FA who advised both myself and him at that time, (Larry Chester is a professional IFA with whom I have a long standing business relationship and who has extensive notes relating to my property ownership, Insurances along the way, and in particular, his comments in 2003 regarding Mr. Krasnopovich's advice), will come to court to confirm the exact circumstances in which my Freehold title was transferred to Mr. Krasnopovich as well as the exact detail of his advice regarding Mr. Krasnopovich's approach to misleading Insurers. He knows exactly how much Larry Chester knows. I can only attribute this to Mr. Krasnopovich's remarkable gift with masking deceit in denial. In cognitive dissonance.

Why would you knowingly invite prosecution for misleading Insurers unless you are now obligated by this information to do so?

I can report that I have had a surveyor in to value the property (January 2015) and establish its habitability and his survey reveals that damp has spread upwards from the flooded and untreated basement area up to the ground floor. The damage to the wooden flooring on the ground floor now requires treatment or possibly replacement due to the high damp content.

The fridge and dishwasher have both taken in so much moisture both have failed and need replacing. The walls show visible signs of damp requiring a course of damp treatment before repainting. Two of the bay windows have absorbed so much moisture they need repair, damp treatment and repainting. Most of the doors have absorbed so much moisture they need drying out and rehanging. To delay these works will increase the damage and the subsequent cost of repair, which is your client's liability.

All of these added costs arise from your client's failure to exercise his fiduciary responsibilities to me. Adding many thousands of pounds to the overall cost of repair. Obviously as you have been advising him, it is my impression that you have acted negligently, motivated by creating and maximizing animosity which has as its consequence, abused my son. As your client, the Lessor of my property, has failed to provide adequate insurance, not even having the damp removed from the basement some 12 months after the flood, the costs of repairing the damage arising from the spread of toxic black mold and damp throughout the property now affecting the ground level as well, will be added to the costs of repair. It falls to me to address these works as a matter of urgency to prevent the damp causing more damage to the ground floor level.

Your client is fortunate that I am mitigating the costs by taking this preventative action now at my own expense. (By borrowing even more.) I am undertaking those costs myself because is evidently pointless asking your client to fulfil any of his obligations as the Lessor in light of his resounding failure to pay even one penny toward his obligations as Lessor since 8th February, 2014, during which time my own housing costs/contents arising from his failure have reached some £100,000.

This is before we even consider the cost of remedial works to the tanking. (London Basement Company will do that part of the repair for some £500,000 plus VAT.) None the less, I ask once more. Please will your client provide an indication of when he will pay the money he owes for the works to my property and my rehousing and contents, covered by the adequate Insurance I have paid for.

I have made every effort to reach an agreement without the need to bring expensive proceedings against your client however it is consistent with his approach that he invites me to sue for the cost it imposes on me. (Disclosure email between me and Mr. Krasnopovich in which he replies to my demand for payment with the words '*Sue me*'.)

You are aware that I have not had one penny back on the costs I paid out. Not even the bill for the emergency crew who went out during the flood to block drains, put in emergency pumps and attempt to mitigate the damage.

I would hope that at this hearing any judge would award costs in my favour and that your ongoing failure to address my requests for information will support this decision. I cannot envisage how you will explain away your conduct to a judge in a court room when the paper trail you leave is what it is.

Your client's failures to pay are causing me extreme financial and emotional hardship. My house is rotting away, I am paying expensive rehousing costs, there is no schedule of works in place, no re-tanking quotes sought and no prospect of any date for completion for works that I can use to look forward to returning to my home. I cannot see my own son without costs of £10,000 per night whilst your client is more concerned with running me up a £200,000 legal bill on a story that he has invented, long after he moved out, about me making a 'secret promise' to give him half my house. One so secret I did not even know about it.

I believe you are the author of the lie this litigation is predicated on. You know there was no '50/50 like we were married' promise until you provided the words as a legal tactic. His first reference to this 50/50 promise follows after his first meeting with yourself.

Why did your client not accept my offer to return my freehold and not claim on the **Insurance** (Disclosure letter in March 2014 in which I detail the consequences for reinsurance and blighting the property as a flood risk) being far greater than the cost of restoring the property without claiming. Your client declined my offer and went ahead with the Insurance claim and failed to return my Freehold title.

In so doing your client accepted liability for all the costs arising from his decision to assume liability for the property insurance. This includes the lowered property value arising from the property now being zoned as a blighted property with a £25,000 Flood claim charge and with the annual premium doubled.

It has also meant that I now cannot get a mortgage on it as lenders are wary of a property that has no flood insurance and has a blighted status. All of which would have been avoided if your client had agreed to my offer in March 2014. This document is relevant in April for a number of reasons, not the least of which is to demonstrate your client's blind commitment to causing me as much financial harm as possible without considering the child's well-being at any stage.

Your offers usually link offers of visitation with the child in exchange for a settlement giving him a large lump sum of my home. (Document disclosure email from October 2013 with Celia Silver, showing your client agreeing to drop proceedings and let Sam stay with me if I pay him £200,000.)

Other documents disclosed refer to differing amounts. Mr. Krasnopovich has changed his expectations repeatedly along with the identity of which apartments he claims to have lived in and which she claims a part of. When he left he claimed nothing.

Later he claimed a lump sum of 28A. Later still he added reference to 28C and even later he added 28B. Is this because his memory suddenly became clear on what was 'promised' to him or is it just cynical manipulation of events to find the version most likely to succeed in a Court hearing?

Curious that these claims only appeared after he retained your services. After he had written a WP offer to me to 'walk away' for £100,000 to rehouse Sam and not claim any future child support. And of course, to then offer unfettered access, *as much as you want, right after receipt of the money*.

In the interim I can confirm that your client continues to obstruct the Skype contact I had agreed with my son with unfortunate consequences for both Sam and myself. I wonder if this is connected to his concerns over what Sam might tell me about Carol? Had you replied to any one of my three previous requests for information on the adult cohabiting with my young son is, there would be no need for this form of conjecture.

Obstructing Sam's opportunity to Skype me, as he requests and as was agreed, whenever he wants, is a stain on your office. As you are the intermediary between Sam's parents, as well as his legal advisor, this is work you can take credit for. Sam is five. Using him as the football for his game of blackmail does not bode well for his future or his prospects with your client as the primary carer. Perhaps you have heard the saying *'It is easier to build strong children than it is to fix broken men.'*

My document disclosure on letters between us that link his financial demands to my visitation prospects leave very little room for doubt as to your client's character. Witnesses, more than one, in the upcoming hearing will attest to this. 'Blackmailer' does not sound attractive as a parenting quality.

I will be arriving in the UK on the 14th February in the early evening so your client's collection instructions are not accepted. I will make arrangements in advance for Jo to have Sam with her for my collection from her home at around 8pm on the 14th and Jo will contact your client with the details.

I am disappointed to observe no change in your clients ongoing disregard for the child's best interests after some 18 months of serial and persistent avariciously motivated hostility; whilst his skilled ability to place his own material interests above all else, including regard for the truth continues to harm our child. That he chose you as his advisor is interesting. He is after all a family lawyer and the sole matter between us was the child's custody. I was not pursuing him for any financial gain despite my financial interest in his business.

I accept we have very different versions of the truth with mine being that the child's best interests come above anything else. At no time have I done anything other than place the child's best interests to the fore, and this is what I will continue to do. You on the other hand have one unmistakable truth. You are earning a great deal of money by abusing my child. Your truth is whatever generates the most billable hours.

I remain concerned that your client's version of 'what's best for the child' with your advice, cost me over £40,000 in legal fees (in 2013) in his legal efforts denying my application to have my son spend 2 (Two) nights a month with me. Bringing a QC to a preliminary hearing for visitation? Which he later justified as

"*I didn't want Andrea so get any ideas so I nipped it in the bud.*"

How would you describe one parent, a member of family-law going to such lengths in denying his child even 2 nights a month with his other parent? Do you believe you are acting in the child's best interests stopping twice monthly visitation?

It is quite obvious how that worked out as I now have no mutually agreed visitation schedule in place, do not even get to Skype with my son unless your client sets the conditions, including tape recording conversations and threatening me with the transcripts stating that he is '*considering whether it is in Sam's interest to have any relationship with his mother* unless I provide written undertakings to him.

I have to put up with ridiculous offers for visitation intended as nothing more than file entries in his case for showing how caring he is for his sons right to see his mother, like 'you can have him for half of Christmas, pick him up at 5 on Christmas day' when, quite obviously I am in a different Country and visitation arrangements need to reflect the realities of advance booking for long distance travel. My document disclosure on this is relevant because it shows that he presents facts in a disingenuous way intended to mislead. Using omission for the purpose of deceiving any reader, by deliberately presenting only one aspect of the overriding criteria. It is an ugly deceit, which harms a child A deceit in which you are complicit.

In this case, suggesting how reasonable he is letting me have half of Christmas, when I am 6 thousand miles away and unable to travel to collect him from his mother's house at 5 pm, to spend a few days with me in a hotel because a.) I am not able to pay £2,000 for the costs of travel at that notice and b.) I have no home in England (It is flooded and he will not pay the Insurance due to repair it) and refusing all the while to allow me to have him with me in my home in the US. C.) Hotels in England over Christmas are both booked up and super expensive.

Your client wrote a letter to this effect in December, offering me this very reasonable 50% contact over the three days of Christmas in full awareness that there was no possibility of me being able to secure travel to the UK for a few days and knowing that I was unable to meet the exorbitant costs of traveling to the UK at Christmas time for a few days in an expensive hotel.

The omission from your client's letter is that he persistently refused my request for alternate Christmas' on a 50% each basis. One year with me here and one year with him there. Pretty clever then to repackage the 50% principle in a way that could never work but makes him look like he is agreeing to 50%.

Does it not seem curious that, in December, a parent would send out a letter offering this appearance of a very reasonable 50/50 share of Christmas to the other parent? This letter (Document disclosure December 2014) I suggest is the work of a deceptive, dishonest and manipulative person, well versed in using legal process for these base intentions, acting deliberately to prepare a file to present a picture of how reasonable he is offering 50% contact for the purpose of preparing a case on how I am obstructing his every effort to encourage the relationship with his son's absent parent.

This is only one example of this type of manipulation of facts to prepare a legal file without any regard for what is best for the child. It is in fact, child abuse. In which you are the guiding advisor, both far more concerned with winning court cases than doing what's best for the child.

And all the while, can you imagine the effect on the child, who told, me repeatedly with great determination that *"I am coming to America for Christmas with you mummy."*

Good job Tim. That was worth getting into family law for. Imagine if you win costs against me, then I get to pay you for abusing my son.

Your client's deliberate actions in failing to provide adequate insurance for my home and not returning the freehold title to me to enable me to provide that insurance, and then cancelling the Insurance I did have which would have covered me. Instead I remain homeless (since Feb 8, 2014) and cannot even house my sons in the UK as a result of your clients malicious and vindictive use of his legal office to impose a legal bill on me that will likely reach £200,000 by the end of the April hearing, and has left me £500,000 in debt arising from his failure to meet his obligations as the Lessor of my property.

All done, as he explained to me, (And as forms a part of my document disclosure in correspondence) to show that if I don't agree to give him a lump sum, he would run up my costs to bankruptcy levels, encouraging me in this way to 'take a commercial view' and pay him.

An approach that is undeniably effective and that has succeeded in the first part, if not the second. You guys sure know what you're doing. Considerable premeditation.

What is the average legal cost in a separation in the UK between average people? I was not even married to this person, we had no joint bank account, no co-mingled finances, no joint mortgages, no joint property ownership and yet he has serially and deliberately used techniques that fit the description of blackmail, including using visitation with my son in this context, to ruin me financially.

How is it possible I have been presented with legal costs approaching £200,000 just to defend myself against his allegation that I *'promised'* him half of my house? A claim made entire without any substance.

That he is able to house himself and our child, either in the property he owns in his sole name or in the one he is comfortably able to rent for the convenience of being close to his office is beyond dispute. His record speaks for itself and I am hopeful his record will speak for itself at the April hearing.

I find it difficult to see this in any other way than a shake down. It's like a mafia hit, forcing me to pay extortion money or face bankruptcy by legal bill. Using visitation and contact with my son is especially cynical.

Hard to imagine that this is legal and even harder to imagine that any court will believe your clients version of events. Especially with the weight of witnesses able and available to discredit her. The story, and the court's decision is of wider interest than to just myself.

With the April hearing in mind, I am disclosing several documents detailing previous offers to settle which demonstrate quite clearly the malice in your client's intention behind these proceedings.

It is apparent from my tax returns and from my E1 statement that what your client already knows about my financial position is true. My cash-flow at this time is in freefall. My home is flooded. Insurance has not paid a penny. And I am having to deal with expensive legal letters from you on a weekly basis.

What commercial sense does it make for a lawyer earning £500,000 pa suing a musician who currently earns considerably less. Clearly the only sense that anyone can draw from this is your hope that by impairing my financial means to pay family law for custody of my son, you are serving your clients clear instruction.

This to me appears to be borderline psychotic as well as in clear breach of your professional office. It seems because you cannot get more than the CSA have ruled as my responsibility by way of maintenance you have chosen my home, being my most valuable asset to target and absent of a marriage certificate to make a claim, have invented the next best thing. The unlikely and transparently ridiculous claim of '*50/50 like we were married.*'

Surely you are aware of the witnesses who will give evidence to show just why you are unable to provide even one witness?

There is a deviant malice in your client taking the child I raised full time while he was there no more than 10% of the time, providing all his emotional and material needs while your client was out at work, pursuing his only real passion, high net worth clients at a vulnerable point in life. While demanding a 6-figure payment before he will allow me to see my son.

It is no coincidence that your client's application for the position of DDJ in 2010 was rejected. Those multiple-choice questions sure picked up something. The parental agreement between myself and Mr. Krasnopovich was Mr. Krasnopovich would set up a law firm with my assistance and input and this would pay the child related costs. That is the position now. I expect the child's school fee's to be met from the business I established and financed for this very reason.

It is not through any fault of mine that Ms. Krasnopovich became enamored by his tight, petite Fitness Instructor, finding his lustful interest in the 'incredible chemistry' they enjoyed more important than honouring his commitment to his family and it is certainly not my fault that he elected fathers-day as the appropriate occasion to remove my child from my life, deliberately causing me the maximum trauma, which I now see was the only way he could have removed Sam from my home, before launching a vicious campaign of litigation that may reach £200,000 in legal charges by the April hearing. While using you and your abrasive, offensive technique to argue every visitation down to the least possible amount of time, causing untold misery to both myself and the child who you continue to abuse in this way.

I do not believe Mr. Krasnopovich's recent actions negate the parental agreement we entered into for the having a child together and the costs of raising the child. I did not renege on the agreement to meet the child's expenses. Imagine after all of what I have done in the course of uplifting your client from where he was when we met (A £35K PA junior lawyer on the bottom rung of a career going nowhere in Reigate working for a woman he despised as 'the dinosaur of family law' whilst requiring therapy for major anxiety issues) to what he became when he left (A confident and high functioning owner of a law firm earning £500K PA in year one with a beautiful, balanced 4 year old athletic and intelligent son) having the gall to come up with demands for my house based, as is clear, on nothing more than the lie that I '*promised*' him half of my home.

On this same haphazard invention he has placed a charge on my house at the LR, preventing me borrowing money that I need to survive and pay legal fees, causing me serious financial consequences and grievous emotional stress as a result.

I am not sure how in all good conscience why, as his friend and lawyer, you have not pointed out to Mr. Krasnopovich that even if his deceit succeeds in court and costs are not awarded in my favour, there is no prospect of getting any money where there is no money.

Whatever money I had for Sam's future is gone in legal fees. Whatever equity I had in my home, one that I worked very hard to pay for myself, since first buying it in 1986, when your client was 12, is largely gone.

You and your client are hounding me for no purpose higher than malice and greed and along the way the net outcome is you are destroying a 5-year old's relationship with the parent who raised him for the first four years of his life, which inevitably, following these proceedings, will become the subject of further litigation. Clearly this is your intention. To use the child custody matter as leverage in a blackmail extortion racquet.

You cannot get away with what has been done to my son. It is abusive. He cries for me. On the occasions when his father allows him to Skype me, the first thing he says is '*I want to come live with you.*'

I raised this child for the first 4 years of his life while your client spent less time with him than socialising late on his 'networking dinners' leaving the most common question Sam would ask being 'Is daddy coming back tonight.'

My document disclosure being my letter to Mr. Krasnopovich of August 2013, detailing his awful deceit on how involved he was during those 4 years is entirely relevant in the April proceedings for obvious reasons.

Sam's father has serially prevented virtually all contact between him and myself from the outset. In the first year he allowed us no more than 4 (FOUR) nights together. Costing me a total in legal fees in those 12 months of around £40,000.

That's some £10,000 per night I had to pay for you and Krasnopovich to allow my son to spend a night with me. That's is quite an impressive achievement for you. I am sure you receive this information as complimentary recognition for your legal prowess rather than the deep contempt with which it is intended.

The blog I wrote (November 2013 in Document disclosure) details how he/you so vigorously opposed my application for just 2 nights a month with my son. Bringing a QC to a preliminary hearing for contact to prevent me having 2 (TWO) nights a month with my son and leading to my son not seeing me regularly at that important time, post separation.

Good job. An important win for your career in family law. That was a 4-year-old boy you beat down. Some top dollar billable hours.

The facts of the matter are that Mr. Krasnopovich has not behaved very well at all despite his transparently disingenuous claims to the contrary. Ironic for someone selling expensive advice to separating people, often with young children, often in the very court we will visit in April. I understand that you called Mr. Clam to propose a settlement, but that despite my willingness to agree a settlement, your intention is to pursue the threat of the April hearing with all vigour.

I remain as willing to settle as I have ever been. Of course, as the defendant in this matter, obviously it was never my desire to go to court in the first place. However at this time, with these extraordinary legal costs and my desperate financial position, it appears my only way forward is to proceed on the basis that I will win costs in April. I can't see how I will pay an £80 - £100,000 legal bill otherwise.

If your client wishes to settle then I am willing to agree on the following basis:

1. Your client end's all proceedings and establishes from Mr. Clam what he intends charging me for his work since the last hearing. That cost should be paid by your client in entirety.

2. Your client should agree to either let me have my son for the two long holidays each year that I have requested, while he has him for term time. Or vice versa. He should accept that it is a good thing for Sam to be with both parents for as close to an equal share as possible. He should enter into an open and appropriately intentioned dialogue on what will be best for Sam. Schooling in California and holidaying in the UK. Or vice versa.

Whatever it is you and your client understand in terms of what is in a child's best interests, I don't believe Sam would agree that his father acts in his best interests if he was asked at this time. Nor when he is asked in ten year's-time by his therapist.

You and your client are just plain wrong by any measure of acceptable conduct for a child's best interests. The only best interest you serve is your billable hours. I am certain that Sam will reflect on his father's conduct in years to come in light of the facts of his (and your) conduct. No amount of self-serving delusion will change that reality. Is it possible that everything really does come out in the wash? Parental alienation and child abuse is what you and your client are doing, lured in by that irresistible six-figure sum. That easy money that comes from knowing I would do anything to be with my son. I say it is clear that the many opportunities your client has had to mediate and to accept a settlement, ending hostility, were all passed up because he felt making money and winning fortune in family court was placed far above Sam's best interests.

The callous disregard that accompanies Mr. Krasnopovich's self-serving take on fatherhood ends with three real victims, which is unfortunate for Sam. And in the bigger picture of a successful life, especially for yourself. Sam has already lost a great deal. An idyllic childhood stolen for what? The thrill of sexual conquest and no more than blind monetary greed after seeing his first big payday with his new business in April. Just 6 weeks before he decided his newly empowered status warranted being with someone he 'had not outgrown' and was 'attracted to.' Never mind about Sam and his future.

Sam though has seen the prospect of a cheerful post separation relationship with his parent (4 nights in year one and £200,000 legal bill so far) lost to a litigious parents/member of family law, unwavering commitment to placing his material gain above all else and the unwavering commitment to winning at all costs, including causing me unconscionable financial harm.

Why not take this opportunity, in light of the disclosures above establishing you can never argue plausible deniability, say you never knew you were lying for material reward while causing harm to child, to reflect on the advantages to yourself in trying to make up to this victim of your avarice, a 5-year-old child, for what he has lost?

Of-course as events have shown, Sam's misfortune is yours and Mr. Clam's good fortune. Hundreds of thousands of pounds advancing a case based on the spectacular improbability that underpins Mr. Krasnopovich's claim, all done in full awareness that the child's place in all of this is secondary to Mr. Krasnopovich's unprincipled greed and willingness to deny him the opportunities having his parent in his life represents.

For now, it is 'nice work if you can get it' and you are a credit to British family-law that will in time, I am sure, make a good subject for a book. Perhaps even one titled 'Your Kind Attention' which I have to hand to you, is brilliant legal writing and much better than I could have come up with in the event of reversed circumstances. Although the idea of 'reversed circumstances' beggars any possibility, given the diametrically opposed ethical space we occupy.

With the assurance of my immediate attention I look forward to your reply to my mail of 8 January and the still unanswered mail of 21 December 2014, along with the time sensitive matters I have raised today.

Andrea

24 The three psychiatrists ruling

Let's see how easy it is to get another contempt charge against his name. We wil say there is only one Psychiatrist in California, and then ignore his very qualified Psychiatrist

In April 2015, approaching the hearing, I was not in the best health. I had been through a great deal of stress arising from not being allowed to see my own son or even skyping with him. And then there was the hemorrhaging flood of money in legal fees. To the extent that it affected my positivity. The medical diagnosis was chronic depression, anxiety and insomnia. I was unable to sleep for much more than a few hours each night. Although I had excellent medical care and prescriptions for the leading pharmaceuticals in this area of medicine, the extent of my despair at the loss of my child and feelings of injustice in a system that allowed the abuse of my child while charging me hundreds of thousands of pounds became moderately overwhelming. At the same time, my ability to work was affected. Creative work, writing music and writing books, relies on a flow that is diverted when you are submerged in all-encompassing sorrow.

From the outset of my traumatic stress evet I sought out the best of medical care.

Starting in the UK with my GP, Dr. Adam Simon. Then in California my GP Dr. Henry Ling who was sensitive to the cause of the stressors and pro-active with advice. For my chronic insomnia I had many consultations with leading California Sleep doctor, Ronald Roberts MD. And most significantly I had many highly productive sessions with leading California Psychiatrist Dr. Mark Zetin. An authority in Psycho Pharm, who was tremendously supportive and knowledgeable in child psychology. Dr. Zetin took a personal interest in my matter, particularly as an authority on similar law regarding child visitation in the US. Dr. Zetin, in the course of advocating for Sam, whom he believed was subject to abuse by the British family court process, would attempt to write to the court on behalf of my son. This professional source provided a good opportunity for Flaherty to learn from. But was missed, because she declined reading the opinion of a top California Psychiatrist. Compounding this foolishness is the irony that at the same time she was ignoring this on point guidance from a California Psychiatrist she was finding me guilty of not seeing a California Psychiatrist she appointed, in a nonsense court order intended only to abuse my son. This is the incredible story of the 'three psychiatrists ruling of DDJ Flaherty'. Which is another instance of a family court judge using family court to abuse a child.

Having had no medical attention in the misleadingly titled area of mental-illness in the past, since June 2013 I can reflect that since then I have had the best of advice by top medical professionals. I may have known very little before father's-day 2013. Now I have an experiential and scholarly awareness into mental health that is considerable.

This is not a coincidence. I have invested considerably in seeking the right advice, so when Flaherty's judgment found that I had no convincing medical letters, I believed her judgment was substantively short of credible.

Or something more sinister.

Her reading of mental illness and how she incorporated it in her handling of the hearing is a red flag on many levels.

It is for this reason worth detailing the factual aspects of my medical history.

Quite clearly, when I arrived in the UK for the April hearing, I was operating largely by strength of will. My determination was to end this awful litigation and focus on seeing Sam.

On the morning of the hearing there was a hugely unusual announcement to me. The appointed judge, DDJ Burkes, was being switched. The switch judge was named Cecelia Flaherty. The first thing I heard about her was by my barrister who said *'If we get Flaherty we will lose'*. Feeling pretty unwell to begin with, my first thought was that the case should at this point be postponed. I knew that I was not well enough to properly represent myself on anything but a fair playing field. What confidence I had in my reserves of energy went at that point. With news that we had a switch judge who was by reputation ignorant in the area this case involved, financial matters, and who was guaranteed to rule against me the moment she saw my barristers name, the matter of my health became critically important.

I requested that Clam move to postpone the case until I was well enough however nothing came of that request. It is a fact that one should have the right to speak in one's defense in court. I was made aware that I had no prospect of winning for reasons related to my case, declared that I was unwell and unable to continue for this reason, yet the case proceeded. From my position, it was clear at that point that this case was a fix. I knew as clear as day that Krasnopovich /Clock and their barrister Hazelwood had somehow shifted the playing field. The answer to my question of how they would address the evidence of the witnesses became clear with Flaherty's first pronouncement. No witnesses would be allowed.

Suspicious?

At 8 am I showed up for a hearing with DDJ Burkes with 6 witnesses set to appear by the courts ruling in a procedure that I knew was based on due process. By 9am I was at a hearing with a switch judge, Cecelia Flaherty, told I was going to lose because Flaherty had a historical gripe against my barrister, and seen this switch judge breach the multiple witness provision in the preliminary hearing by excluding my witnesses. On whom the entire case rested being a 'disprove a negative' basis.

From the outset of the hearing Flaherty's approach was to identify me in terms of my 'mental infirmity'. It became increasing obvious that she had determined this strategy in advance, acting on instruction, to repeat two lines consistently.

'Use the words 'mental infirmity' and repeat as often as possible 'I put it to you, you are lying Ms. Lee.' Flaherty did not even attempt to labour valiantly to discredit my medical records. She declared the doctors who all wrote in regard to my health were not credible and that's it. None of these doctors were worth her time. So she summarily dismissed all medical records, summarizing my condition in a convenient bubble she

determined would as 'mentally infirm' to suit her pre-determination that I was a liar and therefore should face a judgment ending my relationship with my son while awarding 100% of my multi-million-pound asset to her fellow member of family law. Who she found to be "*Wholly credible.*" Having discarded the evidence of his previous history in dishonesty that included being expelled as a senior partner by MWT, in 2012. Called into a meeting, summarily expelled as a partner for dishonesty and frog-marched out of the building never to return.

In one reference to a letter from my Californian Primary Physician, Dr. Henry Ling she referred to him as a her. A doctor with 22 years-experience. I formed the impression Flaherty did this often. She confused the sex of people as a common feature in her writing. She referred to me as the wife on several occasions, not because she was unaware we were not married, but seemingly, just to cause annoyance. I felt her approach was unprofessionally personal. An attack on my character way outside of what a family court judge should be allowed. Based not on anything I did or said, but rather on a predetermined conclusion. I would swear on a Richard Dawkins book of beliefs that this judge knew exactly what she was going to rule even before she switched to take the case on the day of the hearing. I would swear on that same device that she switched to take this case for that very reason. To affect the judgment that she did. From the first sentence, I felt belittled by Flaherty's deliberate and repeated use of '*Mental infirmity*' in the most offensive way. I found her adversarial antagonistic tone unmistakably 'in my face' from the moment she opened her mouth to address me. What I saw and understood from the off is this was someone who had made a decision, attached a prejudice firmly to the fore and was now working to make the storyboard fit the ending. And doing it without even making a half assed effort to conceal her intention. A course of conduct that can be summed up in one three letter word. A Fix.

My awareness of family law through friendships with many judges, barristers and lawyers is sufficiently familiar as to recognize that Flaherty had a brief and she was simply executing it. In no way was this a hearing in which two sides would present evidence and a thoughtful judge would determine the value of each in a decision-making procedure distilling factual evidence before delivering a judgment. I made no apology for being depressed and for seeking help. Yet this was used against me. Deliberately and with prejudice by Flaherty.

Everything that could go wrong, was going wrong. Plus awful jetlag having flown in two days earlier. My experience in family court felt like a rape. I was there because my child had been removed and I believed family court would assist my child in his return to his loving parent. Instead of being heard, my reality is, from the outset, I was positioned by the judge as 'the mentally infirm liar'.

I put it to you you are lying' started virtually every second line. I was worthy of only her scathing contempt with every glance and every word directed my way. At the same time, Flaherty embraced Krasnopovich with her supportive kindness, encouraging him through his cross examination. Interrupting Castello when he came close to calling him a liar. It was glaringly obvious and the complete converse to how rude and interruptive Flaherty was when it was my turn for cross examination.

If as a movie editor, in a metaphor of like and dislike, I could have made a ten-minute edit of Krasnopovich's appearance and mine, with five minutes of each, Flaherty would be seen hugging Krasnopovich with her one-sided affection and hissing and spitting with anger at me. It was that obvious to anyone in the room. I was watching excellent teamwork in an adversarial game. This is not a case of me being a sore loser. Or me moaning because a family court judge abused my son. It is an honest, recording of what I saw. An objective reporting based on memory of having been there as well as complete transcripts of the proceedings that I was able to use to compile this narrative. (After paying another £5,000 bill for the transcripts of the hearing.)

After the Flaherty hearing on the plane back to CA, I became more depressed than ever. Well. Wouldn't you? While we waited for the Judge to find time for the final submissions, I decided to replace my lawyer, the hapless Clam, by this time operating in the thin air of hysterical anxiety, all too aware that he had lost this case spectacularly. It was him who appointed the barrister (who the judge took against) and who made multiple costly errors. Filing late in the preliminary hearing and leaving my name on the contempt notice as well as filing the witness statements late (In a tit for tat mirror late filing by Clock in the application for visitation hearing five months prior. This late filing backfired though, giving Flaherty easy opportunity to breach the court order making provision for multiple witnesses. By forbidding any witnesses.

By this time Clam's tone with me was hysterical. Not funny hysterical, hysteria tinged hysterical. His voice on the phone was up half an octave. He kept interrupting himself with Uhmm's. There was to be a final day for the closing submissions as the three days had overrun. My instruction to Clam was that; I wanted to travel to attend the final day of the hearing. I was unwell and could not travel that week. He should postpone the final day of the hearing. To enable me to attend.

I provided the medical records to confirm my condition.

Yet the court letters continued and had to be addressed. At this point, because they would not allow any concession for health impediment. Flaherty seemingly did not believe that I was unwell. (Well she had me firmly labelled as a liar and mentally infirm, so hardly surprising). Her position was confusing and logically inconsistent. On the one hand I was not unwell enough to adjourn for. On the other, she couldn't get the words mentally infirm out often enough. Rather than agree to adjourn and allow me the opportunity to attend court and speak for myself, Flaherty issued a court order that is known as the 'Three Psychiatrist's'. She instructed that three psychiatrists be identified, for me to choose one from. The purpose of which was to determine my 'capacity to instruct'. Once the three doctors were named by Krasnopovich/Clock I would be able to choose one and that choice of doctor would complete a test on me to determine my 'capacity to instruct.' All within a tight timetable of 14 days.

This was unnecessary and unfair. Of course I had 'capacity to instruct'. I was depressed, but not catatonic. And I was a patient of seeing more than one doctor, including a leading psychiatrist, who could all attest to my condition. But Flaherty elected instead to proceed without having me present. The fact is I was unwell. Not simply depressed. I had a physical injury affecting my mobility. My GP had prescribed one month of rest, with no long-distance travel. An adjournment was no less than appropriate and reasonable. One month in the scheme of things was not a big ask. I wanted to be present. And I wanted a second opinion in law, as I knew Clam had made what is known in legal terms as 'an almighty cock up.' In this time I intended finding better legal representation.

None the less the law is; I had to comply with Flaherty's order and so I waited for the three doctor's names to choose one from. The clock Flaherty set ticked on and yet no names arrived until, three days from the end of her court timetable, when I received an email in which both Clock and Clam determined jointly that there was only one Psychiatrist in California suitable to carry out a simple 'evaluation of competency' for a Court. Just the one doctor capable of form filling a basic form. And no mention of the three for me to have some say in the choice? I was astonished at the transparency of this ill-considered and transparently malicious demand by a family court judge. Seemingly put in place for no reason other than to create a layer on paper of showing that I was not complying with court instruction from Flaherty by making conditions and then changing them without notifying me. Making it impossible for me to comply with her court order.

In a process of credulity stretching ridiculousness I received letters from Clam and Clock in which both, separately, confirmed that there was only one Psychiatrist in California, who I MUST see, or else, and that doctor (Suzy DuWee) was a three-hour drive away from my residence, and offered her services at four times the cost of my own doctor. Dr. Zetin was better qualified and better suited to this specific legal purpose. I had three days to comply with this court order, or I would be in 'big trouble with the judge.'

At no time was Flaherty's own court order, indicating three doctors for me to choose from, followed.

How is this not a breach of a court order?

Fine for family law to fine and censure people for breaching court orders, but when it's a judge breaching her own order, there is nothing to see here. One law for the members who are clearly, in this example, above their own law.

Aside of its legal impropriety, this idea that there was only one psychiatrist in all of California suitable for signing a standard evaluation document is patently ridiculous. It is no secret that California has one of the highest, if not the highest, number of psychiatrists per capita in the world. Yet here we are presented with the courts finding that there is only one Psychiatrist in California, and that one is three hours away from you and costs four times the going rate for a 'Capacity to Instruct' form filling exercise. And if you don't agree to see this unique individual, then the Judge will take an adverse view and find against you. Contempt of court.

Whilst this process unfolded I simply watched bemused. It was like being trapped in an alternate reality. While it went on my prospects of seeing my son were receding. If this family court was behaving in this way, with no regard for my son, and hell bent on processing a resounding win for Krasnopovich, what would that mean for my sons' future prospects? To make clear how ridiculous Flaherty's three psychiatrist' ruling was, consider, there was simply no need to 'establish capacity'. In the sense that she intended. In no way was I incapable of giving instruction. As a pile of emails to my lawyer Clam confirm. My mental ability was not the problem with travel. It was my physical mobility making it difficult to fly 6,000 miles to attend. Why not just accept the medical notice of this injury and extend for one month?

In the event, my doctor had written to Clam, agreeing that one month would be my realistic recovery time. I say that adjourning for one month was the correct legal procedure and that Flaherty acted in breach of her professional office by making this malicious ruling and then not allowing for medical advice in delaying the hearing day until I was able to attend. With a one-month time limit in place.

In the background to the 'Three Psychiatrists' rule by Flaherty, consider I had been seeing a leading California Psychiatrist. Dr. Mark Zetin, who was all too aware of my matter. When I heard about the 'Three Psychiatrist rule, I called to discuss the 'Capacity to Instruct' procedure. He confirmed it was no problem and he would do it for me in a 15-minute consultation. (Costing very little.)

I had a highly qualified Psychiatrist all too willing to complete the 'capacity to instruct' document, who knew me well and knew the particulars of the case. All of Flaherty's concerns could all to easily have been professionally addressed by; adjourning for 4 weeks to allow me to attend in person and, not bother with a 'capacity to instruct', which was so clearly a malicious nonsense. But even if we accept there was a valid need for a capacity document, Dr. Zetin could provide one. Any implication that this doctor was unsuitable for any reason at all is ridiculous. Dr. Zetin is a 'heavyweight' in the field, eminently qualified to complete this basic form filling role. Such was her determination to see through the judgment she made the moment she took on this case, against Richard Castello, a barrister she openly detested, Flaherty discounted the obvious practical remedy to her concern over 'Capacity' and in so doing deliberately and knowingly increased the animosity this litigation created between Sam's parents.

This is only one further instance in which Flaherty's prejudice and deliberately hostile conduct towards me flits with such fragrant convenience over the detail of her own previous order. Made worse by how a simple remedy for her concerns was so readily available. One that took into consideration the best interests of the child.

I say in that; in this single example, Flaherty acted with prejudice, outside of the logical minimum capacity necessary in a credible professional on the bench in a family-court, which served no greater purpose than abusing my son.

All done in full awareness that the factual matrix of her decisions would never be subject to further examination. Free in closed proceedings to act in full awareness that no accountability would follow her actions and as a result, free to act without consideration for any boundaries to her authority as a Deputy District judge in family court. Although there are many emails from this period, April and May 2015, I have chosen to include just one. Philip decided to write to Clam after being reading the instruction that I 'See Suzy DuWee and pay her 4 times the going rate bill, or else Flaherty will nail you.'

From: Philip Voulla Parker
To: David Clam   Spoon LLP

David,

I write in reply to your email of May 19, 2015, to Andrea.

In your email of April 28th, I see that Krasnopovich was required to provide a letter of instruction and three potential psychiatrists by Thursday April 30th.

I have had no sight of the three proposed doctors. Instead I see there is only one referral and it arrived on Monday 11th of May. Given the laxity with which court orders in these proceedings have gone by I am not in the least bit surprised that Krasnopovich once again appears to be getting way with breaching another court order.

Where are the three names and why the delay in communicating this court order?

*You will find attached Dr. Ling's letter of May 12th which is self-explanatory. I trust you will **deliver it in its entirety to the judge** along with the second attachment, which is Dr. Ling's referral to three Orange County Psychiatrists. Andrea's own Psychiatrist, Dr. Zetin is the obvious choice for this simple request.*

Manhattan Beach is some distance from here. Possibly three hours each way with traffic on the 405. Andrea cannot drive. You already know that the higher cost of this doctor places more burden on her. She has no means with which to pay unless the charge is lifted from her property so she can progress with a remortgage with Larry Chester. Without the charge being lifted she has no funds whatsoever for any purpose. Yet here you are asking her to pay an extortionate amount for an unnecessary service, that could in any event be provided by Andrea's psychiatrist Dr. Zetin.

To be clear, whatever happens in these proceedings, will not change the basic truth. Krasnopovich and his lawyer Clock are lying about any beneficial entitlement and in pursuing this lie, are harming Sam. That is the only truth that matters in these proceedings.

It is shameful that this court is damaging Sam's rights to see his mother by supporting a claim that everyone who knows the background to the story knows is fabricated. You yourself know all too well about Krasnopovich's historical dishonesty which you have raised in correspondence as well as in a formal complaint in family-law by your firm Spoon LLP against him for that business he has told the whole world about, the Trotter case, with the 60-year-old man and the 15-year-old girl from Panama whom he impregnated.

This court day should be adjourned until she is well enough to travel and represent her right to speak for herself. That she is physically unwell is clearly beyond any reasonable argument. You have seen the doctors report. That she has 'no capacity to instruct' is ridiculous. You know the strength of the intellect we are dealing with here. On top of which she has her own psychiatrist who is both qualified and able to complete this 'Competency' form from Flaherty. It is beyond ridiculous that this is being turned into a persecution of someone who is unwell precisely because of the actions of this court, who now seek to deny her even the basic right to speak in her own defense in a court hearing that will determine her child's future.

After our conversation on the subject of Andrea's health, I am disappointed that you interpreted that as an opportunity to send through your latest invoice.

I am deeply concerned by the consequences of allowing Andrea to give evidence on 14 and 15 April when she was so clearly unwell. I was present at the doctor's appointment today and I can tell you that we are all horrified by how Andrea was treated.

Early in that hearing, the judge Flaherty had a conversation dealing with her medication and was aware that this was someone sleeping for not much more than one hour a night while on a regimen of prescription medication for PTSD and depression. Medications that include with the prescription, "do not make important decisions whilst on this product."

What kind of responsible person does not at that point take a view of the health issue? You were asked to adjourn the case as soon as the barrister announced "We will lose if we get Flaherty" because of their historical antipathy. You did not demand an adjournment. And Instead Flaherty joined in on Krasnopovich's barrister calling him a liar by calling him a liar as well. This does not sit well with me. Here is someone not well at all, because she is not seeing her son, being bullied and called a liar by a family court judge, stopping her from seeing her son. It is a heinous abuse. Of both mother and child.

In one instance, when Andrea said she bought 28 Thameside in 1986, Flaherty attacked her saying she did not buy her home when she said she did. Does this not strike you as unusual? That a judge lacks the capacity to read a land registry document and comment accordingly? And accuses a vulnerable person who she repeatedly calls mentally infirm and a 'liar' of lying, while at the same time being demonstrably wrong in this accusation. Where is the apology and accountability for this conduct by Flaherty? Calling Andrea a liar, with a lie? You knew about her neck injury. Aside of all else she was in excruciating pain. At this time, she is completely immobile. This debacle has undone all the progress Andrea has made with her health since arriving in California. This family-court is like a persecution. Where the greatest loser is the child. And the winners are you and Clock. Getting paid these six figure sums for abusing a child.

At this stage all you are doing is harassing Andrea further, just as Krasnopovich has done from the outset, and just as this judge appears to be doing. I think your 'let's not inflame the situation' gently, gently approach was a disastrous tactic, given your awareness of the dishonesty of both Krasnopovich and Clock, an opponent who eats this wishy-washy tactic for breakfast, and in this case against you, has done precisely that. For many months now you have explained you 'Can't even talk to that odious man'. So how can you hope to prevail in litigation against him? Small wonder you have failed so spectacularly.

Krasnopovich has serially harassed Andrea from the moment he chose a father's day 'mafia hit' to obstruct her relationship with Sam. By hiring a goon sized process server to attack her outside her house and especially by running her up a £160,000 legal bill with a baseless claim deliberately intended to preventing her seeing Sam for even 2 nights a month by telling CAFCASS she was not fit to have her son overnight, winning a court order preventing Sam visiting his mother even on alternate weekends. Making sure that the crucial 6-month period after separation, Sam was unable to see his mother. Successfully breaking the continuity while you fluffed even a basic application for visitation?

How did you manage to mess that up so royally David? They served you on a Friday afternoon with notice of the QC and the costs application. You panicked and backed down from representing Andrea as you had agreed, sending in a late notice QC who simply confirmed 'This was a set up. They have been planning this for weeks'. You were roundly out thought there and your reaction was to try and get them back with

Friday service of the witness statements in the Flaherty hearing. That backfired on you too.

In baseball terms, you are batting at zero. They have won every single round. I have watched these proceedings from the outset. They play you like a buffoon. Every ball you have thrown has been knocked out of the park. Krasnopovich has cruelly manipulated the relationship in a way that is unmistakably parental alienation and child abuse. She used an illegal recording between Andrea and Sam to support her dishonest claim for money in Flaherty's court which Flaherty saw fit to blindly support despite the criminality of his representation. That recording transcript is a criminal offense in California. Its contents are private. Between a mother and her son. Yet a British judge has commented on its merits? Sharing an illegally obtained document of this type is a criminal offense. Why did you not make the judge aware that she was commenting on content that was illegally obtained?

Krasnopovich has harassed Andrea continuously in the US with threats and denials of visitation. He has ruined her Flood Insurance claim, costing astonishing amounts, and preventing her from having a home in the UK, actively denying her re housing money by telling the Loss adjuster that she could stay in the uninhabitable property and ensuring the tanking has not been repaired, compromising the value of his property significantly. This fellow has illegally claimed title of a freehold document in which he has fiduciary responsibilities which make him liable for enormous costs arising from his conduct. Yet despite charging for and being paid to pursue this matter, you have not.

On what level of reasonable expectation do you feel your representation is acceptable. Look at how much you have allowed him to get away with when their breaches in family law are so very clear. On top of all of this, now Andrea has to go through the whole ordeal again and this sorry business goes on and on. Krasnopovich has no claim. No witnesses. No written anything. He was never promised anything and all the evidence such as it is points solidly in this direction. Not even his own mother would come to court to lie for him.

He was caught out in the hearing after saying he was going to bring witnesses. This case progressed because of his assurance that he had 'multiple witnesses' in the absence of any evidence. As Andrea declared at the time, it is impossible he has any witnesses because this claim is a lie. Who would be witness to a lie in court? Not one person as it turns out. When challenged as to why, he explained he had identified only one, Dia Mirza, and was then forced to admit that Dia Mirza has no memory of this alleged promise. Why wasn't that alone the end of it? Dia is a family law barrister and deputy district judge. Who contradicts Krasnopovich's claim that she 'overheard' this 'promise'. Not only does he now have no witnesses. He has named one witness who openly denies his claim. You had this clear opportunity to end the whole nonsense.

I am especially disappointed with your performance because of the impact on Andreas' health. I am looking at someone who has been severely harmed by actions that should be illegal. It has had devastating consequences for Sam.

This is not family-law. It is amoral, unethical abuse of a legal system entitling a clique of entitled members to profit from abusing a child and destroying the lives of an entire family. Who love and support Andrea and her son's rights to see his mother. Krasnopovich and Clock have used Sam to cause upset to Andrea and her family. Unmistakably, using parental alienation and child abuse for the benefit of upsetting Andrea and forcing a financial penalty on her based on a lie. Deliberately and with forethought. All the while you have profited to an enormous extent in winning absolutely nothing for Sam's right to be with his father.

From where I am sitting this is someone who has been mugged by a system in which your six-figure bill is a factor. And a child who has been failed by the system that is tasked with representing children's best interests. And a father who has been rewarded for cheating on his family.

Although I accept Krasnopovich and his team have acted outside of the law and with tremendous precision in playing the weaknesses in family law, none more so that judge Flaherty, none of this would have happened if you had done your job properly.

Your errors are professionally embarrassing and costly. And have shaped the outcome. Why did you leave Andrea's name on the late filing notice at the financial directions hearing in the court of DDJ Berry, that you paid the cost for and know was a late filing of your making?. Not Andrea's. This was raised with you repeatedly. You filed late for your own benefit. You paid the contempt fine. Yet you allowed Andreas' name to show as the guilty party?

David, that is simply disgusting amoral behavior by a member of family law charging hundreds of thousands of pounds to abuse a child.

I see that last week, with the critical need for a lawyer to be instructed to progress Andrea's Insurance claim following the recent incident, you attempted to dissuade a rival firm from representing her by phoning them and putting them off when all you were asked was to confirm her identity. To enable them to take her on as a client.

You dissuaded a rival firm from representing Andrea when all you were asked to do is provide a proof of identity. You went out of your way to stop Andrea finding alternative, better, representation. I think in order that you could keep ripping her off with your exorbitant billing.

Andrea has written to you repeatedly on the subject of the Insurance claim and you have failed her time and again by not replying in time, allowing her to present correspondence in court as happened with the Shoosmiths letter, which was entirely at odds with the reality of the Insurance situation.

Andrea had replied comprehensively to that letter for you to pass on however you failed to pass the instruction on, choosing instead to moderate her reply, playing straight into Krasnopovich's hands when he presented the Shoosmiths letter showing that he had been diligent and responsible all along and it was Andrea who failed to play ball.

In general you have delayed and moderated her replies on the basis of not wanting to 'rock the boat' with disastrous consequences as she has not had one penny from Insurers, she is out by tens of thousands in damage mitigation costs and her home is not repaired.

What is your excuse on this occasion? You were happy enough to invoice and be paid for your service in this regard. The net outcome of which is?

I have had no reply to my letter of May 4th, 2015, with the time sensitive issues presented there still unaddressed. Has Andrea's notice of the neighbors fallen tree damage to Thameside been passed on, and if so why was I not copied in for awareness?

Andrea has not seen or spoken with Sam for too long. It seems inevitable there will have to be more proceedings for visitation which would not be necessary if you hadn't botched the visitation hearing so spectacularly.

Please reply without further delay to the very important points raised in my letter of May 4th.

There is a tremendous mess been made here and I cannot see how you will find the means to clean it up. You have been roundly bettered by Clock superior tactics. To the extent that you have disclosed 'I cannot talk to that man.' That's really helpful David. You have brought a feather to a knife fight. And then charged hundreds of thousands for failing. Even when you had clear sight of his offenses for an SRA complaint. You still bottled that.

David, I could not be less impressed with English family law than the picture you have shown me of its members. In my view you have no place working in any legal system representing children.

Philip Parker Voulla

And David Clams reply. Sent by his trainee assistant.

From: Darcie Trellis
Date: Mon, 11 May 2015
To: Andrea Lee
Cc: Philip Parker Voula , David Clam
Subject: TOLATA (Spoon LLP Ref:815/23)

Dear Andrea

As I understand David has previously explained to you, at the return hearing on 28 April the Judge ordered that an evaluation take place to deal with concerns over your capacity to give informed instructions to your legal representatives.

It was agreed at Court that as you are currently residing in California that this evaluation of your capacity to give instructions should be undertaken by a psychiatrist based in California.

It has taken some time to find a suitably qualified psychiatrists who is available to do the evaluation within the tight time scale the Court has ordered. We have though now had confirmation that a very experienced psychiatrist, Dr Suzee DuWee is able to conduct the meeting and evaluation. I attach a copy of Dr DuWee's CV.

Dr DuWee is based in Manhattan Beach.

The Court ordered that the evaluation of your capacity be provided no later than 22 May 2015 and therefore it is necessary for you to meet with Dr DuWee as soon as possible, ideally this week.

Dr DuWee has availability this Thursday 14 May at 4.30pm, which will hopefully work for you. Please let me know as soon as possible so that I can confirm this with Dr DuWee.

We will be providing a joint letter of instruction to Dr DuWee which will be agreed by the Court. This is yet to be finalised but will be provided in time for the above appointment.

Finally, the Court ordered that you are to be responsible for the costs of the meeting/consultation with Dr DuWee and any associated costs for the certification of whether or not you have capacity to give informed instructions.

I look forward to hearing from you soon

Kind regards

Darcie

For David Clam

25 Cecelia Flaherty. The switch judge

If we get switch judge Flaherty, we will lose. And she will make her judgment un appealable. Because you can in family-court

For the Krasnopovich v Lee hearing in April 2015 Family court deputy district judge (DDJ) Burkes was set by the court process that allocates judges to cases. However on the morning of day one DDJ Burkes quietly disappeared and Cecelia Flaherty was announced as the switch judge for my case. No explanation was offered. Just the assurance from my barrister during the two hour-long waste of allocated court time while they switched judges that

"*If we get Flaherty we will lose.*"

"*Why is that.*"

"*Because she does not understand financial issues.*"

That from a reputable family court barrister on the inside of family law. Later my barrister confirmed he had previously fallen out with this DDJ, Cecelia Flaherty, and for this reason knew she would ever find in his favor. Clearly, in that two-hour period of waiting outside the court room, with the barrister and the solicitor and Philip, it became increasingly obvious that something unusual was happening.

Why was the hearing set for three days?

At the financial directions hearing, the Judge set the case down for three days. (DDJ Berry) This time allocation as agreed by both sides following Krasnopovich's claim that he would 'bring witnesses'. A conversation followed and it was agreed that 3 days was ample time for multiple witnesses to be heard. Consequently, a court order followed, providing for multiple witnesses. From both sides.

The hearing in April was to start on a Monday. I flew from LAX to LHR the Friday before and went directly to Clam's office where I learned the judge had been named for the hearing.

DDJ Burkes, according to both my barrister and my solicitor, was a good choice for me as he was a well-respected Barrister and familiar with Financial issues. Clam was in good spirits and appeared optimistic, repeating his earlier view that "*He has been foolish to bring this case.*"

Clam required a further invoice payment of some £20,000 directly before the hearing, which I had agreed to drop off by cheque at that meeting. Reassured by his confidence, Philip and I went to our Hotel in the City. Philip had chosen a leading five-star hotel, close to the Court, so that I would be in good spirits for the hearing set for Monday morning at 8am.

Philip located a Michelin star restaurant walking distance from the hotel and I ended that Friday feeling as positive as was possible. Very loved and supported in what lay ahead. I could not have been better prepared for the hearing. I had googled the Judge, DDJ Burkes, and I knew in all probability, this man would be the one to stop Krasnopovich in his dirty tracks. And censure the odious Tim Clock, for his abusive unacceptable conduct in my case. I had notes prepared for him, disclosing specific examples of Clocks conduct. The court should know about these two child abusers and their lying ways. I was looking forward to referring to those notes at the right moment in DDJ Burke's court.

On Monday morning, the first day of the three-day hearing, I arrived at 7.40am with Philip accompanying me, by taxi at the Ghee Street Court, to be met as I exited the taxi by my appropriately dressed mortician barrister, Richard Castello. Alarmed that *'we may not have a hearing. There is an issue with the judge. It seems Burkes may have recused himself.'*

What?

That morning, for whatever reason was not apparent to that judge on the Friday when he knew he was appointed for the Krasnopovich vs Lee hearing, I was told by Castello the appointed judge, Burkes, had recused himself from the hearing.

No specific reason was given. "Perhaps he had previously worked as a barrister for Krasnopovich's firm and was therefore conflicted" I suggested. But no. Barrister Castello had written to Clam directly after the appointment of Burkes to request he check if there was any possible conflict. There was not. The email confirming this passed between Castello and David Clam. One year later, at the Right to Appeal hearing before the family-law President I learned from my FOS lawyer, who knew DDJ Burkes that this judge *"never worked for Krasnopovich. That's not the reason he was changed."*

So why did DDJ Burkes recuse and get replaced by Flaherty on the morning of the hearing?

As events unfolded in the hours of Monday morning, I formed the very clear impression that Flaherty drove the process of appointing herself to replace Burkes. To adjudicate Krasnopovich's matter. Two members of the same Law Society, one, Krasnopovich, a family law solicitor who hires family-law barristers. The other, Flaherty a family law barrister who gets hired by family-law solicitors. Commonalities abound. Common interests make it unfeasibly distant from impartiality. Crucially. Flaherty would have seen Richard Castello's name on the listing. Flaherty has a history with Castello. Should a judge not recuse if there is a history with a barrister in which she is known in advance to be prejudiced? In this case it appears the judge chose the case, switched with the appointed judge even knowing who the barrister was. Why?

In what I witnessed over the following three days it is clear that Flaherty made her judgment before the courts door even opened. I saw it in her eyes the first time she looked at me. The eyes don't lie. Hers were lying eyes. (As all Californians know, you can't hide those). Aside from my own experience being there and seeing what I saw, there are a few specifics I raise here in support of my belief that Flaherty was, in that hearing, abusing my child in family-court, causing me to form the very clear view that she is unfit to serve as a Judge, lacking both the intellectual capacity to take wise decisions in matters affecting people's lives as well as possessing and displaying personal vanity at odds with an impartial decision maker in a matter as serious as a child's future. A significant portion of the qualities associated with a caring judge, and specifically, the responsibility to represent the best interests of the minor child, were absent, while all the worst qualities of a lower vibration human, prejudice, antipathy, dishonesty, ego, self-interest, irresponsibility and abuse of the responsibilities of office, were represented in abundance.

In assessing her capacity as a decision maker, I found her to be frivolous and unable to follow a thread to its conclusion. She clearly had the opportunity to familiarize herself with the details of the case, having 7 large lever arch files in front of her. But she elected not to bother. Instead she referred to a single hand-written page which she had evidently compiled in the two hours we were kept waiting for the switch judge to 'get up to speed.' I formed the very clear impression that Krasnopovich had an input into that hand-written page of instructions. Each time she referred to that page and looked up at me, she began with one of two positions. 'Mental infirmity' or, 'I put it to you you are lying'

Flaherty's approach in one sentence. The page kept her on track. Repeating one line of reasoning over and over. Not reacting to answers being presented in evidence.

At number one in the *list of irregularities* accompanying this judge's appointment to this case: Barrister Richard Castello's observations in advance of the hearing.

Richard Castello said to me on the Monday morning when Flaherty was being considered as a last-minute change *"If we get Flaherty we will lose"*. He left me in no doubt this was because Flaherty lacks experience in financial matters and makes decisions outside of the facts of the case. I asked him

"Is she incompetent".

"I can't answer that directly." Rolling his eyes upward.

"Have you sat before her in the past?"

"Yes." He confirmed he had sat before her in Court and that he had lost in that hearing. That there was a history between them. I formed the view, from his own mouth, that Castello would never win a case in Flaherty's court in a Month of Sundays. At that point I asked him to have the hearing adjourned. It was clear to me that this judge could not objectively work with this barrister in light of their historical animosity. A year later, in the Appeal hearing before Judge Andre le Clerc, while chatting with my second family law fee earning partner, Roland Chambers, Richard Castello said *"I knew we had lost the case when Flaherty rolled her eyes at me."*

Flaherty rolled her eyes at Richard Castello approximately three minutes into his opening submission. I remember at the time thinking; this is highly unusual. Like a petty school mistress rolling her eyes at a naughty boy. Flaherty did not like Richard Castello. It was obvious from the get go. She interrupted him repeatedly through his submissions, with what was clearly irrelevant distraction intended simply to interrupt his flow. Quite clearly a busy barrister (and Richard Castello was an in demand junior barrister at that time) on the inside of family-law is informed during the first sentence of his submission, before he has even raised any facts in the case, that the Judge has already ruled. This is a judge who has evidently appointed herself to a case at the last possible minute before the hearing should have begun. And who has determined the outcome before one word is spoken.

My reaction, in the waiting room at around 10, in light of the Flaherty story was. *"This case must be adjourned. I am not up for going into a court room where I am told I am going to lose. I don't feel well to begin with and I now have no confidence in this court. Let's adjourn and get an impartial judge. Come back again when we have the prospect of an actual impartial hearing."*

Second most interesting Flaherty decision.

The 7 witness statements. Over the months leading up to the hearing we discussed witnesses to disprove the negative. From a pool of maybe 20 potentially significant witnesses, Clam selected 7 based on their specific relevance to the claim *'50/50 like we were married.'* Each one was interviewed and Clam set about preparing 7 witness statements which reflected on my invoice at some £12,000 of work.

In a case based on no more than hearsay, his word that *'She promised me 50/50 like we were married'* it seems likely that credible independent witnesses, such as Larry Chester, an Independent Financial Advisor who acted for both myself and for Krasnopovich, would shine considerable light on the truth in what otherwise is no more than *'she said, he said'*. This was the same IFA who had arranged my mortgages since 1986. He knew the financial picture the court was being asked to decide on in substantive detail. With a host of memos from meetings and quotes for mortgages that related to the matter.

Why would any judge looking for the facts in a dispute dismiss the witnesses and discount the only independent source of information that related directly to the matter she was asked to judge? Flaherty's first action after appointing herself to hear Krasnopovich's case was to refuse the witnesses. The reasons given for refusing the witnesses are, simply laughable. Clam evidently filed only on the Friday before the hearing, unbeknownst to me or Richard Castello. Which doesn't in any way change the fact that the witnesses had important evidence entirely germane to the matter Flaherty was asked to adjudicate on. Clam was simply mirroring the late notice by Krasnopovich/Clock in the application for visitation, where they filed at the identical 'late' stage. This is not a murder trial. So what if you file late. The other side knew we had these witnesses. They knew what he witnesses would say. Because Krasnopovich knew what the truth of the matter was. In the case of every witness. There was no 'ambush.' After all, in the application for visitation, Tim Clock had filed at exactly the same time. The last day before the hearing. This was the identical timing as used by the other side in the previous round of litigation.

Unless there is a fix in play, why then is the submission allowed by their side and not by mine? The answer is. Because it is an integral part of the fix. This case could not have gone forward with any prospect of success had the witness's evidence been considered. The point of the hearing was to establish whether Krasnopovich claim was feasible. Here was a series of credible witnesses including the Financial Advisor who directed every mortgage and buildings insurance policy on the property since 1986. The entire defense in 'disproving a negative' was based on the witnesses. The court order at the preliminary directions hearing provided for multiple witnesses. This was at Krasnopovichs' insistence because he promised he would bring multiple witnesses. The reason the hearing was set for 3 days was because there would be multiple witnesses. The only reason his case was able to proceed in the shape it had was because he promised to offer substantiation to his clearly implausible hearsay claim by way of 'multiple witnesses'. On this promise, the case was allowed to move forward.

From Flaherty's judgment in her own words.

The time estimate for the hearing was three days. This did not make any allowance at all for pre-reading or judgment writing. It was obvious that, whatever these additional witnesses had to say, it was bound to involve cross-examination, save for the evidence of the mother's father who is aged 79 and lives abroad. A civil notice had been served in respect of his evidence and he was not going to be called. To have allowed in these statements would have meant adding five additional live witnesses to the father and the father including Mr. Parker Voula, but excluding the seventy-nine-year-old Mr Leandros. This would, on any view, have had an impossible effect on an already very tight timetable.

11.   I made it plain that I had read none of the disputed statements, before hearing the application about admissibility. I also asked about the most recent evidence on the respondent's father's mental health. It was apparent that one of the issues in this case is the husband's allegedly frail mental health; his ability or inability to work and this has been given as a reason for delays in providing his solicitors with up-to-date instructions and his non-compliance with the directions for the filing of evidence laid down by DDJ Berry on 22.10.14 timeously. I was directed to read a letter from a medically qualified individual Ronald A. Samuel whose qualifications are given by initials only "M.D., FAASM, FCCP". He is described as Diplomat American Board of Sleep Medicine. This letter is dated (in American styling) 17th March this year. The other medical evidence within the case relevant to the father is contained in two earlier letters. One is from Dr Surnam who appears to be a General Practitioner at whose surgery the father is or was registered and it is dated 28.11.13. The other is from someone named as Hayden Ling "DO" and dated 15.01.14 from Aliso Viejo Family Medicine. This appears to be a medical practice in the USA. There is no evidence from any psychiatrist. The mother has been prescribed differing quantities (from time to time) of antidepressant medication. She also stated that she has significant problems with sleep. The medical evidence in this case is deficient. There are three different individuals voicing brief opinions in letters. There is no medical report as such and there are no CVs from any of these individuals explaining the nature of their expertise and / or their respective experiences to voice opinions. I am asked to accept these letters as sufficient justification to explain why the mother did not comply with the order of DDJ Berry and as a reasonable explanation for the delay. Most notably there is no psychiatric nor psychological evidence about the respondent father, as I would have expected to see.

Starting with her first line. '*The time estimate for the hearing was three days*'. That is correct. It was 3 days to allow for multiple witnesses. There was an entire debate about the time estimate in which Krasnopovich required 3 days in order that he could bring multiple witnesses. That is why it was set down for 3 days. Ample time to hear multiple witnesses from both sides. His proof in the claim was to come in the form of the 'multiple witnesses'. The claim may well have been struck off at the preliminary hearing stage for lack of credibility. But no. He had witnesses. Multiple witnesses. So the claim progressed to a full hearing.

The reference to non-compliance in the Berry hearing is down to Clam. It has nothing to do with me. Yet Flaherty has not bothered to get to the heart of this complaint that has been well documented from the moment I found out that Clam had filed late on a court timetable, by his own previous admission to me that he would have to do so as he was busy on another case. Clam assured me would pay any fine in the event that a fine was ordered for late filing. It was paid by Clam but, Clam allowed my name to show on the court order for filing late. He was notified and on several different occasions in the proceedings this error by Clam was introduced in evidence along with my written request that he rectify the record.

Now, in her own hand, here is Flaherty punishing Sam for her own mistake. David Clam filed late in that contempt notice by DDJ Berry, not me. Flaherty had the duty to listen to the evidence and get to the truth of this court record which could easily have been done. Clam was in the room. Flaherty had only to ask him.

"Is it true that the contempt order against Ms. Leandros is in fact down to you Mr. Clam?. Did you file late and pay the fine because the late filing was 100% down to you?"

Instead Flaherty used that error by a member of family-law to punish me and my son. Opportunist that she is in the judge's chair, here in her own hand is clear evidence that she is opportunistically choosing to use a provable lie in order to reach a judgment. By electing to not consider the facts that were available to her with less effort than it took to prevent the facts being heard. The reference to 'allegedly frail mental health given as a reason for delays' is wrong. I did not delay anything. Whether I have mental health issues or not. Flaherty is using this as a justification when it has no basis in fact.

It is a lie, set out in family court, affecting a child's future. Ultimately benefitting members of family law with a multi-million-pound payday. Money which would otherwise have been available for my son's future.

It was apparent that one of the issues in this case is the wife's allegedly frail mental health; her ability or inability to work and this has been given as a reason for delays in providing her solicitors with up-to-date instructions and her non-compliance with the directions for the filing of evidence laid down by DDJ Berry on 22.10.14 timeously

I am asked to accept these letters as sufficient justification to explain why the mother did not comply with the order of DDJ Berry and as a reasonable explanation for the delay.

This is, in legal terminology, a 'load of bollocks'. Starting with '*The wife*'. How can this judge not know that we were never married. Is this not central to the issue at hand? If we were married then the husband could expect '50/50 like we were married.' In community of property. We were not. This level of attention to detail falls far below the minimum one has every right to expect in a matter as serious as passing judgment that will determine the future of a child. Failing in this basic competence fails the child and the consequence of this failure is child abuse.

Flaherty dismissing the medical records as inadequate warrants some background.

The three doctors to whom Flaherty refers are Dr. Adam Simon, (she has not even spelled his name correctly) my NHS doctor for the past 15 years and as credible as it gets with a local GP.

One is from Dr Surnam who appears to be a General Practitioner at whose surgery the mother is or was registered and it is dated 28.11.13

He appears to be? There is doubt?

Rubbish. Complete and utter drivel presented as words in a judgment by a family court judge. The doctor she refers to is a 25-year veteran general practitioner who had been my NHS doctor for 12 years prior to writing the detailed note he sent for the courts benefit. There is no misunderstanding either his credibility or the content of his letter. Information that could so easily have been verified even if Flaherty really did doubt his credibility. For example, simply phoning his surgery and asking to speak to him. Or. Googling his name and seeing his professional profile as a general practitioner of medicine with 25 year's-experience. Instead, this judge has chosen to dismiss a doctor's report because it doesn't tie in with the fix she is there to put together, to ensure that the child whose future she is judging on received the maximum harm her dishonest dismissal of the facts visits on him.

The second doctor she dismisses, not even getting the gender right, is Dr. Henry Ling. Easy to see how a 'Henry' could be mistaken for a woman. Dr. Ling wrote as my GP in California. He replaced my UK doctor when I moved to the US in 2014. He is a reputable, in demand medical professional with his own practice and decades of experience in medical practice. His letter to the court regarding my health is accurate and reliable. This is how medical records to court work. A doctor, in this case my primary care physician, delivers a legal notice for the court relating to the private and confidential matters of the persons health. It is simply breaching the outer limit of ridiculous when Flaherty questions his professional stature and the clear medical diagnosis he provided the court. His details as a professional are freely available on the internet. Again, Flaherty has dismissed a professional report simply because it does not tie in with the fix she wishes to write into her judgment.

Flaherty has discounted his credibility without offering any explanation. She also refers to Dr. Ling as a 'she'. Even the briefest of glances at his picture in checking this doctor's credentials would make plain his sex. Calling him a her, Flaherty shows she did not make any effort to check the credentials of this doctor before dismissing him as being lacking in credibility. Another glaring nonsense. The Judge has a duty to consider the medical advice even if it contradicts the pre-determination she is depending on to make her judgment.

The third doctor she dismisses speculatively and without any credible reason, Dr. Samuel, has worked as a doctor in California for over thirty years after graduating in Medicine at USD. After 25 years as a pulmonary doctor in Los Angeles, Dr. Samuel became a specialist in sleep apnea, working as a consultant in sleep related matters. I have experienced extreme anxiety related insomnia (because I was traumatized by Krasnopovich blackmailing me for visitation with my son, who I missed terribly) and I consulted with a leading doctor in this field.

Flaherty scoffed at the idea of a 'Sleep Doctor'. As if she has caught me out in a lie. Pretending to be insomniac and making up mumbo jumbo. *"I put it to you Ms. Lee that you are lying. There is no such thing as a sleep doctor."*

And as for the Psychiatrist. Flaherty's words go beyond 'just plain wrong' into the realm of the mentally unwell. I had at that time weekly appointments with a highly-reputable Psychiatrist, one who I began seeing early in my visit to the US in the matter of my PTSD, depression and anxiety. A doctor who came very highly recommended by a previous therapist as 'the best in California'. Which, in my experience of therapists, I confirm may well be true. Dr. Mark Zetin is a top-level professional with a long CV one google click away from revealing that Flaherty's dismissal of this man makes no sense unless; her intention was to paint a picture in which this medical input contradicted her predetermined view.

Although since my trauma inducing life event commencing on fathers-day, 2013, event I have met with several therapists and doctors of the mind, including the best the UK has to offer, at the Priory in Barnes, undoubtedly in California Mark Zetin is a leader in Psycho pharm and a tremendous authority on both PTSD and children matters and especially, the link between the two. He was a good fit for me. His insights into parent child dynamics helped me tremendously in my approach to coping with not seeing my son and working towards winning his right to be with me.

Aside from his work as a consultant Psychiatrist Dr. Zetin was also an in-demand University lecturer and a published author who took a personal interest in my case. For this reason, Dr. Zetin wrote at some length to Flaherty for the benefit of the court and specifically in the hope of preventing the ongoing abuse of a child.

Beginning soon after our first session, this medical professional with a powerful academic familiarity with child matters was visibly moved by my story and took a personal interest in my matter. He offered insight into Sam's prospects for recovering from the harm visited on him in this dispute and how I could approach the various strands this abuse visits on a child at that age and stage in development. And especially the consequences for a developing child in relation to child abuse of the kind Sam was experiencing by both his parent and the family court process. In most, if not all of our sessions, I shared details of the family courts process and had the opportunity to receive advice exploring the consequences of this court process on the child's development. This gifted, erudite doctor provided me with a balanced analysis of the parent's motivation and a professional medical view of the degree of his accountability in relation to the child's developing awareness. How I would go on to make decisions in Sam's best interests was in no small measure, the product of insights gleaned from this professional advice.

Near the end of the Flaherty trial, around the time Flaherty was railing to have me choose one of three psychiatrists to sign a 'competence' assessment, in addition to providing this basic function which his office qualified him for in terms of the British Court requirement, Dr. Zetin offered to advocate for my son himself, by writing to Flaherty. About my son, who was missing his mother and the likely consequences arising from the decisions in family court. A letter written for the judge detailing to a high level of academic and experiential insight, the harm that this process would be causing the child along with his personal professional insight into the harm it was causing the mother.

He was moved to this degree of involvement because the conduct of Flaherty's court was so transparently deviant that even an independent doctor and professional in psychiatry relating to family law matters was moved to go on record in challenging Flaherty's competence. Child abuse is what it came down to. But of course, Flaherty had no interest in learning from a superior intellect. Instead she simply dismissed this doctor along with the previous three who wrote in the course of this litigation brought by a family law member to trade visitation for financial benefit.

Flaherty's various comments in her judgment on the medical aspects are simply wrong. As a result of which a child has suffered. For whatever reason, too much fun, too much champagne, too much juvenile delinquency, Flaherty saw fit to dismiss the medical advice in the same way as she had the witnesses. For no other reason than that it would interfere with her judgment. All four of these doctors are real, credible professionals who write for the courts benefit on the subject of my medical health. Not only are they real, each one is an accredited respected professional at the top end in their field.

Either all four are lying or Flaherty is.

Most notably there is no psychiatric nor psychological evidence about the respondent mother, as I would have expected to see.

Flaherty routinely dismissing this doctor in her judgment is wrong. Wrong and lazy and deliberately negligent. It is in its effect, child abuse, by a member of family law. Motivated in effect by benefitting another member of family law.

It would have been a simple matter of establishing the credentials of these 4 medical professionals. Including, phoning them? Or how about googling their names to establish that they are exactly what they are. It was her choice to ignore the facts, because they interfered with her predetermined finding. That my ex-partner, her colleague in family-law, should be rewarded financially without regard for the child's right to see his own parent. Instead she inserted her deliberate tactic, the label 'mentally fragile' in the alternative to accepting that four doctors of high standing had not arrived at this same conclusion.

Flaherty's judgment awarded every penny I ever earned along with a costs award with interest at 8% against me that would make me homeless and indebted to the extent that I could not even remain in the UK. And crucially, the financial consequences of this acrimony generating judgment meant I no longer had the means to fight for custody of my son.

That is her motive in this deceit.

Her means?

She was the switch judge in the court, empowered to make unregulated decisions without accountability to a review process. Able to make an 'un appealable' ruling.

Her opportunity?

Family law in the UK allows for this conduct. Closed proceedings. Un appealable judgments removing the checks and boundaries of an appeals process.

How Flaherty considered my child's rights in her judgment is a matter of opinion. You decide.

Here is the first page of her 12-page judgment. "*The Mothers case is she has always had a susceptibility to mental fragility.*" These are her words. Of all the words she could have used, including the correct medical terminology for PTSD and depression, she has repeatedly chosen the pejorative and prejudicial term 'mental fragility.' Profiling.

KRASNOPOVICH v LEANDROS

FD13P04082 &
FD13F00913

JUDGMENT

1.   This is the final hearing of two applications made by NICO KRASNOPOVICH against his former partner   ANDREA LEANDROS. The parties are the parents of their son who is SAM LEANDROS and who was born on XX.XX.09 and is therefore going to be six years old in May.

2.   The two applications are a claim under the Trusts of Land and Appointment of Trustees Act 1996 in relation to a property at 28 Thameside - the precise details of which will be set out later in this judgment - and a claim brought under the Schedule 1 of the Children Act 1989 for support relating to the upbringing of Sam. The Children Act application is dated 21.11.13 and the Trustees of Land Act, which I shall shorten to the title "the property matter" is dated 22.11.13.

3.   The applicant father has been represented by counsel Mr Simon Hazelwood and the respondent mother has been represented by Mr Richard Castello of counsel. The two applications were listed together by DJ Reed on 14.07.14 and further directions were given about evidence on 22.10.14 by DDJ Berry on 22.10.14. There has been considerable delay in complying with those directions resulting in the respondent mother producing evidence, including seven additional witness statements and her own very late statement, late on 08.04.15. At the outset of the trial I ruled on the admission of late evidence. I refused to admit all but one statement. Before I explain my short judgment about that preliminary issue I need to give a brief history of this matter so that there is some context.

4.   <u>The history in brief</u>
The father and applicant is a 41-year-old solicitor practising in family law. The mother is 47 years old and is not in work. She currently lives in the USA. She is a musician and, when receiving remuneration, she worked as a musician having a record label and specialising in producing music to be used while meditating. She also dealt in a modest way in shares and she produced and wrote music. The parties had a child, Sam who, as I have said, will have his sixth birthday at the end of May.

5.   The parties met in 2003 and some time later that year they started to cohabit in the property at 28 Thameside, the subject of the property matter. This property is divided into three flats comprising the basement and ground floor flat, which is 28A; the first floor flat, which is 28B and the top floor flat which is 28C. The father claims a beneficial entitlement to one half of the properties at 28A and 28B under the TOLATA property matter. The father also seeks a housing fund from the mother under Schedule 1 of the Children Act 1989 if he is unsuccessful in relation to the property matter. The combined equity in Flats 28A and 28B is £706,000 (gross of CGT) therefore the father's claim in the property matter has a value of approximately £350,000. He sensibly concedes that, if he is successful in that claim, he will not seek a housing fund pursuant to Schedule 1. Ms LEANDROS (the mother) had acquired these flats at different stages of her life. Flat B was acquired in1991 after her divorce from her first

husband in 1991 and flat A was bought from its owner in 2004 / 05 from someone called Derek Bowfield.

6.   The parties separated in July 2013 and the father and Sam moved out of 28 Thameside. The mother's case is that she has always had a susceptibility to mental fragility and that the separation caused her to receive treatment, including out-patient treatment at The Priory and medication. By around December 2013 she had moved to stay in California with a Mr Philip Parker Voula.

So many errors in Flaherty's words, along with the typos. I will try to get straight to the point.

Point 6. Parties separated in July 2013. Parties separated on fathers-day, 16 June 2013. Is it important that judges get date's right?

Ms LEANDROS (the mother) had acquired these flats at different stages of her life. Flat B was acquired in1991 after her divorce from her first husband in 1991 and flat A was bought from its owner in 2004 / 05 from someone called Derek Bowfiield.

Starting with the basic factual errors. I bought the freehold and the leasehold to Flat B in 1986. Is it important that judges get dates right? Or even basic facts?

Flat A was not bought from 'someone called Derek Bowfield'. Again, that is simply wrong. A sloppy error that could so easily have been verified. Once more here is a judge stating a fact in her judgment that is wrong. And can so easily be shown to be wrong. Just read the land registry title.
   Because it can so easily be shown who I bought 7A from, clearly Flaherty is arrogantly lazy. A judge who has not bothered to do even basic diligence on the history of the title to the flat she is ruling on. She does not need to bother to put any work in because she knows there will never be an examination of her judgment because family law will enable her to make an unappealable judgment. She has no real incentive to even try and cover her tracks. She can lie with impunity on a matter as simple as this, without fear of being caught out. I suggest, having been told by several members of family law, because this is her modus.

Consider point 4. "**The mother is not in work**". That creates an impression. But is it deliberately misleading?
   At the time of this court case and as disclosed in my witness statement which Flaherty could and probably should have read, I was a director and owner of a record Label and the sole owner of a property business generating an average of £6,000 pm. With a self-managed Stock portfolio valued consistently over £200,000 generating dividends of some £20K PA.

I have never been '*in work*'. That much is true. But this is semantic. It is misrepresentative to imply that is the whole of my position regarding work. I have worked very hard my entire life without ever being 'In work'. I have never had a 'job'.

At the time Flaherty is writing this summary of my 'Not in Work', I am working exactly as I have done for the past thirty years. Because it is technically true that I have never had a 9 to 5 job, Flaherty has taken the opportunity to describe a lowered-character description of someone seemingly a 'layabout unemployed'.

Why?

Because that is more likely to fit the profile of someone who would lie to prevent a member of family law from getting the 50% of the property promised to him by this jobless person who somehow owned 100% of a £2.5 million+ property? Hold on. Where is the logic in this finding? **The mother is not in work**. How did I get to own my own home and business then? The observation in her judgment is misleading and indicative of a prejudiced determination to create a specific impression. To be able to fill in the blanks of a worthless unemployed loser? Living off the largesse of the self-made family-law member, Krasnopovich, who has a proper job and obviously pays for everything because the mother has no job.

It may be that my previous income, often in the region of £10,000 a month from rental income, book and music royalties, was small change in the bigger picture of a divorce lawyer's earnings, but for a musician and writer, I certainly did not feel like an 'unemployed loser.' I believed I had done reasonably well in my choices of career and remuneration because I had put in a great deal of work. But no. Flaherty has explained to the world that I am an unemployed loser who is mentally infirm.

While I have never had a job, I have worked hard, since my first money earning opportunity at age 11. Through working for myself, with a solid work ethic, I owned, outright, after mortgage, £2 million+ in property assets, a music label with many hundreds of copyrights, and in the course of my working life employed and helped a great many people along the way, albeit I was technically, as Flaherty says, unemployed. Flaherty's ruling conveniently avoids that one aspect of my work was my rental income properties, choosing in her judgment to award those to the ex-boyfriend as well. Her colleague in family law. The one on the other side to Richard Castello. It is pretty shitty to read this scandalously profiling judgment of this person and know that it has been written in a way that family law deems to be 'un appealable.'

She gets dates and facts completely wrong again. Provably wrong. One has only to look at the US immigration records to see that this is simply a lie. She wrote;

By around December 2013 she had moved to stay in California with a Mr Philip Parker Voula.

I went on Holiday to CA for Christmas in 2013. On a tourist visa. I did not 'move to stay in California'. I returned to my home in the UK however, in February my home flooded. I became homeless. I was living in Hotels for the rest of February and March into April of 2014. This judge knows all too well that I was made homeless by her clients failure to act with fiduciary responsibility as the self-declared freeholder and sole named Insured party. Both accomplishments reflecting a deceitful origin. As, thanks entirely to his deceit, I received no Insurance for rehousing, and was spending some £5,000 a month on Hotel accommodation while at the same time spending on average £10,000 on legal bills forced on me by Krasnopovich and Clock, I ran out of money to pay for accommodation and accepted the offer to rent a part of Phillips home in California on a credit basis. The factually accurate wording, if Flaherty was not seeking to mislead in her judgment, would read;

by the end of April 2013, after two months of living in Hotels while waiting for Insurance to pay rehousing on her flooded home, in a claim that was obstructed by Mr. Krasnopovich, the sole named insured party who prevented payment of rehousing money by claiming the flooded property was habitable and declining to pay rehousing costs to Ms Lee as provided for in her policy cover for 27 years standing, he was investigated by the AXA Insurance for attempted fraud and the claim was put on hold. Ms. Lee then accepted the sole residential opportunity available to her that did not require up-front payment, renting from Mr. Parker Voulla in California. As I now realise, because I was the judge in April of 2015, writing this judgment in late 2015, when the facts of this Insurance fraud by my client were all openly available simply by inquiring from the AXA Insurance, or by asking Ms. Lee directly, Ms. Lee never did receive one penny from Insurance. Mr. Krasnopovich perjured himself in my court, claiming that he was the freeholder while at the same time I ruled in my judgement that quite clearly he was the trustee freeholder, breaching his fiduciary responsibilities in several instances including bringing these proceedings in the first place. But I cannot disclose these facts which fly in the face of my predetemined opinion led judgment and so I will just sweep it all under the contempt laws table and say:

By around December 2013 she had moved to stay in California with a Mr Philip Parker Voula.

Third in the most interesting list of Flaherty's judgment is the matter of the **Will attendance notes**.

In 2010, a year after Sam was born, Krasnopovich asked me to make a will. He explained that he felt insecure because he was living in my home, had no title and had no rights to stay in the event that I died. He expressed concern that if I died, my Evan would inherit my properties (true) and that his father, my ex-husband, would then motivate Evan to evict Krasnopovich, leaving him and Sam homeless. *"We would be out on the streets"* he assured me. I knew this was a nonsense, I had made provision for Sam in my will and there was no possibility that he would be left disinherited, but I accepted that Krasnopovich felt insecure with no rights to the property and decided to make a legal allowance for him to stay on in one of the flats in the event of my death, which would be left to Sam, to do with as he saw fit.

He offered to pay if I went to his firm to have a will made. I agreed.

At that time I had a will. My clear intention was to leave my estate equally to my son, Sam, and Evan and made provision for Krasnopovich to live in 28A until Sam turned 18. The executor of my estate would be my father, and should he pre-decease the requirement, Chris Andiotis. My sons Godfather. To address Krasnopovichs' repeated nagging concerns over Evan's father forcing him out I agreed to have a will done at MWT. (Reassured that he would pay for it. At no expense to me.) Off we both went for wills at MWT where the lawyer made an attendance note, in which he spells out the advice being given. In my attendance note the ownership of my property is made quite clear. There is no mention of giving 50% to Krasnopovich. Obviously. Why would there be?

Consider, the year at this time is 2010.

Krasnopovich has claimed the '50% promise' was in either 2004, 2005 or 2006. If that promise was true; then why did he require me to make a will when he already owned 50%. Why would he not just say *"Andrea, would you mind writing down the promise you made to me about half of your properties, just in case you die?"* And even if you move past that obvious flaw in his construct, why is there no mention in either of our Will attendance notes of this 'promise'. In 2010.

Surely, if he owned 50% in a trust agreement (or whatever random promise he later claimed) he would disclose this in his attendance note to feature in his will? It defies the outer limits of impossibility in probability law that he would not mention this asset in making his Will. During that lawyer meeting, I was persuaded to leave part of my estate jointly to Krasnopovich and Sam because of his youthfulness. (Rather than just leaving the title to Sam with Krasnopovich having right of dominion in 28A until Sam's 18th.)

Whereas before, all of my estate was left in equal measure to both boys, with Krasnopovich given the right to live in 28A, meeting the costs for so long as he stayed there, after which it would transfer to the boys along with the other two properties. Following the advice from the MWT solicitor I amended my will.

The two mortgaged properties, 28A and 28C were left jointly to Krasnopovich and Sam. And the most valuable one, 28B, was left to Evan as it was uncomplicated by any mortgage. I had no plans of dying in any event.

It is of course obvious that **if** Krasnopovich owned 50% of 28B as he claimed happened prior to this will attendance note, that I could not have left Evan this flat as 50% would have belonged to Krasnopovich. The lawyer would have pointed out the obvious. *"You can't leave 100% of an asset to someone when you have already promised 50% to someone else."*

Did Flaherty overlook these Wills documents deliberately as a part of her corrupt judgment, or accidentally for reasons of a mentally sub normal day making her unable to see the obvious Elephant in that particular room. Either way, this Will note episode is a red flag as to her competence and suitability for this particular line of employment. I say it is clearly evidence that she knew her judgment could never be appealed and so could make up any nonsense she saw fit. Which is exactly what this is. A corrupt family court judge.

Similarly, Krasnopovich made his Will, in which there is also an attendance note, in which he too confirms that he has no interest in the 3 property's I own. In his will attendance note, which went before Flaherty it reads *"Andrea owns the three leases."* These two will notes that were admitted in proceedings provide clear evidence from two separate lawyers in two separate attendance notes that there was no mention of any 50/50 agreement when declaring assets in a legal office. And in fact there is specific reference to the ownership of the properties confirming who the owner is.

We have in Krasnopovich's own hand notice that '*The three properties belong to Andrea.*' And that post-dates his claim of a promise by some 4, 5 or 6 years, depending on which date for the promise you prefer.

Flaherty's explanation for this being '***neither here nor there***' is a jewel of logical incontinence. Reaching a conclusion that would be impossible absent of deep prejudice or monumental stupidity of which I think the former is more likely, for reasons of respect to monuments. If Krasnopovich owned half of a 3 million-pound asset "50/50 like we were married" when making this will which post-dates his 'claim of entitlement', then why would he need to make a will at all? He owned, 50%, and along the same logical thread, why would he not disclose this ownership in his will. Would a lawyer in this position not simply record that 'Andrea promised me '*we jointly owned 50% of the properties, like we were married*' and make his will directions accordingly. It is simply unacceptable conduct by a family court judge to gloss over this obviously flawed judgment made worse because this judge is concurrently posting her character on social media as;

'*Lawyer; juvenile delinquent; lover of champagne and fun*'.

Flaherty has made serious errors in judgment that have caused tremendous damage to many people's lives, most significantly, abusing a child terribly. And she has got away with-it scot free. Still working the bench causing who knows how much more harm this approach to family-court judgment visits on other children because in the law she was able to make an unappealable judgment. Ensuring that her transparent factual errors and her corrupt opinion based prejudicial judgment, would not be examined on appeal.

I say there is no statute of limitation on crimes against children.

Fourth most interesting was how the judge encouraged Krasnopovich when he was being questioned by Richard Castello. And how clearly she encouraged his barrister, Hazelwood during my cross examination, even interrupting my replies to make corrections of her own which were factually incorrect. One glaring example from early on in my cross examination. This relates to dates. Are they important in a court of law?

I bought 28 Thameside in 1986.
28 Thameside is a Freehold title.
I also bought 28B Thameside in 1986.
28B Thameside is a leasehold title to a two-bed flat. This is a fact. To avoid any doubt dear reader, in case there is a child reading this who is not fully at home with 1 + 1 = 2. I bought two (2) things. One (1) thing was a freehold title. The second (2) thing was a leasehold title. Two separate things bought at the same time.

During cross examination by Hazelwood he asked me about my ownership of 28 Thameside. I started with "*I bought 28 Thameside in 1986*" intending to continue with the details of my acquisition of the three leases which explained how I came to own all the leases as well as the freehold. However no sooner had I said those words than I was rudely interrupted by Flaherty. With a correction. Spoken loudly, with a tone of irritation, as you would address a stupid kid in class telling a big fat fib. Stopping me in my tracks.

"*You did not buy 28 Thameside in 1986. You bought 28B Thameside in 1986.*"

I was left in no doubt that Flaherty was looking through her veil of '*I put it to you Ms. Lee that you are lying*' prejudice to find something to catch me out with to support the judgment she had already made. Whether that pre-determination was factually accurate was of no concern to Flaherty. The motions she was going through required no attention to detail. Either that is the case, or she is practicing as a Judge in financial matters, including multi-million-pound property matters, without a basic understanding of the distinction between a Freehold and a Leasehold, or even understanding the possibility that one person could own both.

Either way, this is a red flag to the competence and impartiality of a judge.

Although in this example Flaherty fell below the awareness standard one should expect from a member of the judiciary this was not an isolated instance of Flaherty interrupting me with a distracting lie. She would go on the rule not only that Krasnopovich was owed 50/50 like we were married, based on no evidence. (In a judgment which repeatedly refers to me as the wife). But also that she should be awarded her costs, ostensibly because I had received help from my family in defending the case. Despite the guidance from the law society that awarding costs in family-court only ever increases animosity between the parents and is never in the best interests of the child Flaherty, motivated by what I saw as personal vindictiveness, made a costs award against me. A sum far in excess of £100,000 which, for good measure, she then added an 8% interest to. To date I have not paid (because I have no money, so the 8% interest is a sum accruing over a 5-year period and beyond as it is an amount I will never be able to pay having had my source of income forcibly stolen by the same judgment.)

Add to that the fact Flaherty added 50% of the rental income from my properties, also at 8% interest, and you arrive at a sum of money that is quite remarkable. And then consider Flaherty forbad me to enter my own property, 28B Thameside, which I had bought in 1986. When I wanted to visit my son Sam in the UK, I had to pay to stay in hotels because I was not allowed, by court judgment, to stay in my vacant home, which was vacant awaiting forced court sale. But which never was sold. Just sitting their empty, rotting. After the judgment of Flaherty.

Either Flaherty is unaware of this costs = acrimony = bad for child, calculation, which goes to competence, or she is aware of it and deliberately abused my child in this way, which goes to competence. Of course she knows what she is doing.

I say there is no statute of limitation on crimes against children. The total cost consequence of Flaherty's deviant judgment on myself is measured in multiple millions. The cost on my son's life cannot be properly measured or compensated for. That would require a lengthy term in prison to even begin addressing cause to consequence for Flaherty's actions. Having made this 'judgement', Flaherty would then go on to allow Krasnopovich to draft the final judgment on his own terms. This is known as perfecting the order. Having drafted and edited Krasnopovichs' legal letters virtually 5 days a week for ten years, being one of the elements of support I offered him during our ten-year relationship, I am all too familiar with his writing style. The inner and outer limits of his literacy. I recognize his hand as an author from some distance. His word selection. The logic behind each structural argument in every sentence. The less is more. Or in this instance, the more is best.

There is no doubt many sections of the Flaherty judgment were authored by Krasnopovich.

The same person who made up this lie "*She promised me 50/50 like we were married*', said he would bring multiple witnesses to prove his word was good in the absence of any evidence, blackmailed me with monetary demands for visitation with my son; won a visitation hearing preventing me having my son for two nights a month and won costs in court approaching £500,000 against me, was empowered by family court to write the judgment against me in his own hand. Where he seized the opportunity to indemnify himself from three serious criminal charges not even related to his beneficial entitlement claim. (The fiduciary failures and perjury relating to ownership of the freehold, the copyright photograph theft, the breach of privacy offense in California).

The financial consequences of the Flaherty judgment meant a forced sale of my properties in circumstances that ensured a fire sale price. That is a significant loss arising from the sale by court. Say £1.5 million below market just on that alone, although because the property was never repaired by the Landlord post flood, that is not the full extent of the loss. The valuation Flaherty accepted and set as the trigger for sale amount is incorrect. As I pointed out at the time. As a result, the forced sale cannot hope to succeed. As I said at the time. However, Flaherty's response was to award sole of conduct of sale to Krasnopovich in a way that ensured I could only, eventually, foreclose. Flaherty awarded Krasnopovich 50% interest on the rental income I made from my property along with the 8% interest due on the cost award to Krasnopovich. She ordered the eviction of the tenants, leaving me without income, having to pay the costs of the property, and I still had a huge mortgage on 28A, which I had to pay month in month out or lose my credit rating. In 2018 alone, paying mortgage and maintenance on the two properties, 28A and 28B cost me over £22,000. While the properties rotted. Empty awaiting sale by the 'Sole conduct of sale' appointee by court order.

Flaherty's award of 'sole conduct of sale' to Krasnopovich meant all he had to do to win maximum harm against me was not sell the property. Once he appointed his own sales agent for the sale, two years passed in which not one offer was made. The listing became the longest running stale listing on Rightmove. For all I know it is still on Rightmove. The agents clearly cannot sell the property at the trigger sale price set by the court. The reasons afflicting Flaherty's sales order were made plain at the Flaherty hearing. However she chose to ignore my views on the valuation of the property, because as Flaherty has ruled; I am a mentally infirm liar. Why believe me and these pesky facts when you can just make it up to help out your fellow member. Even to the extent of endorsing perjury, "I own the Freehold" to indemnifying the perjurer from any liability as the freeholder.

At this time of writing I have been paying the mortgage in an empty property that he does not sell, for 27 months. I could just stop paying the mortgage and ruin my credit rating. Or I can keep paying the mortgage, because really, Flaherty's ruling is wrong. It has caused financial consequences, including the interest I have had to pay on loaning the money to keep paying the mortgage.

It is a fact that I travelled to the UK to see my son and I could not stay in my own vacant property because Flaherty made it an order of court, one written in the hand of Krasnopovich, that I am forbidden to enter my home. This is a family court decision made according to family law - with a child's best interests above monetary gain for members of family law? Bear in mind that after my home flooded in 2014, Krasnopovich went to some length to ensure the Insurance did not pay, leaving me literally homeless, paying hotel bills. 28A was uninhabitable after the flood and would require hundreds of thousands of pounds to make habitable. Money that I borrowed at considerable expense to make the property habitable. Flaherty's judgment ended any possibility I had of remaining in the UK. With no home to live in and no money with which to buy a home. And left paying off a high 6 figure loan attracting interest at a rate that is best summarized in Bruce Springsteen's line '*debts no honest man can pay.*' But still, I kept on paying the mortgage. Adding debt to debt even though this was a family-court judgment I say did not properly consider my sons best interests. A maliciously prejudiced opinion expressed as a legal judgment by a decision maker who chose to dismiss credible third-party evidence and gloss over the evidence allowed in a manner that is transparently dishonest.

My most enduring memory of Flaherty is her first comment to me when 'I took the stand'. Looking directly at me with twinkling gloat in her eyes and a contemptuous sneer in her tone of voice.

"*We are dealing with your mental infirmity here.*"

That was no way to start an objective hearing on the future of my child. I resented being profiled as mentally fragile and identified it immediately for what it was. A judge who had already made a decision. My medical history is what it is. I have no apology to make for experiencing PSTD and found it inappropriate and offensive that a Judge should start her hearing by making this prejudiced observation.

Why, if you believed someone to be mentally fragile, would you start virtually every question by referring to their mental fragility? If for example, I had lung cancer, would Flaherty have started every other sentence with "We are dealing with your weak approach to breathing here". Profiling the individual by way of a medical condition is unacceptable and offenders must be brought to account if we are to see any repair to a broken system. From my side, in the context of dialogue between a family law judge and the defendant, I was inflexibly courteous and softly spoken. Deferential even. I spoke in a monotone at a measured pace, as you would expect from someone qualified in voice training at the highest level. But clearly that is not what she saw or heard.

Later I would read in her judgment:

59. I have dealt with the issue of Ms LEANDROS' mental health. The evidence she produced was very limited. I find, because it seems agreed, thats she is a woman of mental fragility.

Consider the wording in points 15-17 of Flaherty's judgment.

15. When counsel came before me shortly after 10.00 on the morning of 28.04.15 I was told by Mr Castello on behalf of Ms LEANDROS that both Mr Castello and his professional client were concerned that Ms LEANDROS no longer had capacity to give instructions. Such an assertion from sources of integrity could not simply be dismissed, especially where mental fragility appeared to be an agreed element, but I asked what further instructions were necessary, given that the evidence was closed. I was cautious in my approach so as not to trespass into potentially privileged territory. However Ms LEANDROS mental fragility was, as stated above, a known matter and issue in this case. An investigation of this issue was inevitable, given that the case was not concluded. I made directions for the preparation of a certificate of capacity to see whether there was evidence to rebut the presumption that because Ms LEANDROS had capacity.

16. I directed a tight timetable for the instruction of a suitably qualified expert to provide the certificate. This was done because Ms LEANDROS had returned to the

USA with Mr Parker Voula. In brief because Ms LEANDROS refused or failed to meet the jointly appointed expert. The court was faced with the only evidence available from the father's side that he had capacity and the presumption remained in place and not rebutted.

17. Accordingly I finally received closing submissions from both counsel dated 12.06.15. I should explain that Mr Hazelwood for Mr Krasnopovich had already provided me with closing submissions for the earlier date of 28.04.15, but I gave him the opportunity to revisit / renew those submissions if he wished. It is now 04.08.15 - 05.08.15, for which I am sorry, but this case has not been easy and I have had to await a vacation period in order to have sufficient time to prepare this judgment.

Why would Flaherty say *Ms Leandros had returned to the USA with Mr Parker Voula.* I had been in the USA since December 2013. I had not had a home in the UK since February 2014. I had been paying rent for a residence in the US since April 2014. I travelled to the UK 19 times during the course of this litigation, often staying as little as three nights before returning to the US. Why specify that my return to the USA is 'with Mr. Parker Voula'. I was in the UK for 5-day period, three days of which were spent at the Court hearing. It is a curious choice of words to say 'I returned with Mr. Parker. Voula.' Impartial factual reporting if any was necessary on the matter, would read, Mr. Krasnopovich returned to his home after the hearing. But of course, canny judge Flaherty does not like handsome Mr Parker Voulla. She has formed an opinion based on what she has been told outside of the courtroom by Krasnopovich. This much is clear from the questions asked and the inferences of a romantic link. And yet; is it appropriate for one side to discuss gossip details for a judge to then use in child proceedings that have nothing to do with either parents romantic interests.

In the course of correspondence between Krasnopovich and with Flaherty, Philip Parker Voula has come up many times. Because he has supported me from the outset and because it was Philip who succeeded in persuading Krasnopovich to allow the first visit with Sam in July of 2013, and who subsequently acted as advocate for Sam, calling Krasnopovich on his irresponsible tactics of gambling with the child's wellbeing for petty financial benefit, Krasnopovich took a fierce dislike to his former friend. Enraged especially by the thought that there might be a romantic interest developing, despite the obvious fact that he left me for a (much) younger woman. When Philip acted as intermediary for visitation, by my estimate, 45 emails went between Philip and Krasnopovich. In every single one of those emails Krasnopovich spells Philip's name wrong. This was the same with the first intermediary, where Krasnopovich spells a four-letter name wrong every time in some 65 emails. It is a thing with family law. They spell names wrong a lot. But not when it is people they like.

And now the simply fabulous Flaherty 'three psychiatrists' judgment.

In brief Ms LEANDROS refused or failed to meet the jointly appointed expert.

Flaherty requested a doctor's certification that I had capacity to give instructions. This is a standard form in which a qualified doctor, in this case a Psychiatrist, meets the individual and determines whether they have capacity to give instructions. To be clear.

No one on any side of the planet could have any doubts that I 'had capacity to instruct.' The very notion is ridiculous. And was used by Flaherty deliberately as a device to create a situation in which she could find me in contempt. And bulldoze through her deviant judgment. At this time, the three psychiatrists and the capacity to instruct order, I had a very good professional relationship with a leading Psychiatrist in California. Dr. Mark Zetin. One face value, according to the Court, Flaherty had concerns over my 'Capacity to instruct'. So what to do? Why not ask a question such as "I require a Psychiatrist note to confirm capacity. Will Ms. *LEANDROS* provide one within x time period.*"*

No. That would be far too simple. Because then, clearly, Andrea would give her psychiatrist the form to complete and, as everybody and especially Flaherty knew, the document would confirm what we all knew. The mental infirmity Flaherty was repeating ad nauseum was no more than a standard and unsurprisingly common degree of PTSD and depression arising from being force separated from my child. My capacity to instruct in a legal sense was never in question by anyone other than Flaherty. Whose grounds were baseless. For this reason, because she had a higher purpose for her 'Three Psychiatrists idea' Flaherty ruled that Clock and Krasnopovich should provide the name of three Psychiatrists in California and that I should then choose from one of those names. Within a tight set time-period. A flurry of emails from Clam and Clock followed, in which British family law discovered that only one Psychiatrist in all of California was capable of completing a 'Capacity to Instruct' document.

This episode with the Doctor to appoint capacity was unfortunate by Flaherty. Her point was to have a *"suitably qualified expert to provide the certificate"*. Instead she allowed the ever-adversarial Clock to turn this simple direction into a breach of something leading her to observe that

Ms LEANDROS refused or failed to meet the jointly appointed expert.

The issue here is. Did I provide a certificate from a suitably qualified expert? To provide a specific court ordered document 'To capacity'. The answer is yes. That document was provided in good time.

Flaherty's court order directing the naming of three experts for me to choose one from never happened. Her court order set down 'Three psychiatrists will be named and Ms. Leandros will choose one." If we are to respect the importance of court directions, then the direction to send three names was a breach by Clock. We cannot, with any regard for good sense, leap from the order of three doctors, to an order saying, only Suzy DuWee can sign this document and if you do not see and pay her bill, then, you will be in contempt of court. And then to write the 'jointly appointed expert' adds idiocy to a lie. Jointly appointed? By who?

But that is what Flaherty did. Another line of lies in Flaherty's judgment.

Did her process increase the likelihood for animosity? Consider all she required was notice from a doctor that I was able to give legal instruction. This really is a simple 'Doctor's note. With very little opportunity to introduce any legal obfuscation. Was it necessary to escalate this simple process in the way that she encouraged?

Was there a simple practical remedy available that would cause no time slippage and no animosity? After all, she knew I was seeing a psychiatrist for therapy in grief counselling. And had received similar therapy in the UK at the Priory. Who better to provide this certification than my own, imminently qualified, doctor?

Did the decision to pursue a capacity-document in the first place, and then compound it with this foolish 'three psychiatrist's proviso increase animosity between the child's parents?

Is increased animosity a good thing for children?

Is knowingly increasing animosity harmful to a child to the extent that it is child abuse. Premeditated child abuse?

I say, if any one of the experts on parental alienation and child abuse who I have read and referenced in this book were asked, the answer would be straightforward. Throughout Flaherty's judgment there is bitter consistent prejudice. Opinions incorrectly expressed as fact. Flaherty cannot have been unaware that in ruling so aggressively against me, notwithstanding all the factual flaws in her judgment, she was ruling to end Sam's relationship with me. The animosity she fomented between Sam's parents is premeditated child abuse that brings British family court into disrepute.

During those court proceedings, I was accompanied by Philip. For emotional support as well as for medical reasons. I would not have been able to travel and attend without any support. I cannot properly describe the hateful conditions being forced to visit family court imposed. It is not dissimilar to physical and emotional rape happening concurrently. I did not want to go to court. I knew enough about family law after ten years supporting a family lawyer, to know what to expect. I went for one reason only. It was my sole hope of winning visitation with my son. But at no time was I blind to the reality that is British family court. My doctor advised that I do not travel alone into such a stress generating situation. Especially as I would be traveling to the UK and not able to see Sam during this visit. Which has a particularly depressing effect on me. Being in the UK and not able to see Sam is not workable for my wellbeing.

Philip had another reason for coming, besides my emotional support. He wanted to see Sam. He had communicated with Sam directly and assured him that he was going to visit him in England 'soon'. Philip and Sam had their own loving relationship independent of me. Philip had provided Sam with his own assurances as to 'everything's going to be alright' much as a father would to a son.

A date was set up for their visitation and Phillip allowed an extra day after the hearing to facilitate our meeting with Sam. On the Thursday after the hearings end on Wednesday, we would spend lunchtime and the afternoon with Sam before going to Heathrow. This visitation arrangement was agreed with Clock and Krasnopovich. I agreed it on the basis I believed I would win the hearing and be able to share the good news with Sam, and discuss with him directly how visitation was going to work going forward. It is a fact that on that day Krasnopovich refused the visitation for Sam. Offering instead, an hour in the Park with his Mother supervising the visit. He missed not one opportunity to obstruct any visitation to the maximum he could. Knowing from experience what supervised visitation implied.

From Flaherty's judgment, complete with typos. This relates to the point that Krasnopovich had no evidence. And would, as a lawyer, be more likely to have evidence of being given a million pound + gift.

49.   One of the major criticisms of Mr Krasnopovich's credibility was that, as an experienced family solicitor, how could he have allowed himself to think that his interest was secure without anDeed of Trust setting out exactly what his beneficial interest was. On the contrary, I found this part of his evidence something that assisted with his credibility. He was so convinced that the mother of her child meant what she said that he felt there was no need to have any documentary evidence. I recall in his evidence that he said it was a case of "physician, heal thyself" and it only reinforced the opinion that I formed that he was telling the truth.

During the hearing (barrister) Castello raised the obvious matter of why a solicitor, who has just been given the largest fortune of his life has never recorded this in any way. Not even telling his mother. Or his sister. Bear in mind, in one account, Krasnopovich claimed this happened in 2004. Less than one year after I met him. When I was housing him and paying his lifestyle expenses entirely, paid off his student loan, and helped let out his flat to start a second income stream for him. Is it even vaguely possible that I would have promised someone 50% of my multi-million-pound property? My fifth live in boyfriend in the past eight years.

Krasnopovich was struggling in reply in one of the better moments Castello enjoyed while cross examining him. At which point Flaherty interjected once again, to assist Krasnopovich.

"*Was this a case of Physician heal thyself*" she offered, deflecting Castello's cross examination. Krasnopovich noddingly agreed and Flaherty carried him though that aspect of the cross examination.

"I recall in her evidence that he said it was a case of "physician, heal thyself" and it only reinforced the opinion that I formed that he was telling the truth."

Those words originated from Flaherty who for the convenience of her judgment fitting her predetermined decision, reinvents the source. It was a lot like watching a double act at work. One feeding the lines to another at a tricky juncture in the performance. If her case is she believes Krasnopovich was telling the truth because he did not bother to get anything in writing and this '*assisted with his credibility*' then I suggest this is insufficient grounds to award a decision of such animosity generating hostility that ends a child's relationship with his mother. It may be that the gap between 'beyond all reasonable doubt' and 'balance of probabilities' is stretched in this conclusion beyond the ridiculous to the criminally negligent.

It is absurd. **On the contrary, I found this part of his evidence something that assisted with his credibility.**

That is verbatim from Flaherty's judgment.

The other factor in the evidence that I found very significant was Ms LEANDROS vehement attempts to suggest that Mr KRASNOPOVICH' had never lived at 28B. This was not believable for a number of reasons. The refurbishment and significant extension of 28A would mean the necessity of living elsewhere within the building; the flooding in 2007 would necessarily have involved staying out of the mess. Mr KRASNOPOVICH' remembered living at and in 28B Thameside as early as 2004 when he received the news of her father's death, and that evidence I found credible. I am persuaded that Mr KRASNOPOVICH on more than one occasion said to Ms LEANDROS that he owned both 28A and 28B "fifty / fifty like any married couple".

When Krasnopovich moved in with me I lived in 28C Thameside. He paid no rent, and made no contribution to expenses. He was the beneficiary of extraordinary largesse from me, including not just food and board, but international holidays and experiences commonly associated by beneficiaries with tremendous gratitude.

A few months after Krasnopovich moved into my bedroom at 28C, the tenant in 28B moved out, for a period of about 1 year, I kept both flats for my use. Four bedrooms instead of two. My father visited annually. Evan visited regularly and he needed his own room so when I was between tenants in 28B, I enjoyed using it myself for the extra living room. There were times when I had four bedrooms occupied by my family. During the two years before I completed the downstairs flat, we lived between 28C and 28B. My official address in this time was 28C Thameside. 28B was the higher earning rental.

In this matter of *'Where did you live'*; I hosted Krasnopovich, who made no contribution to anything for 2 years during which time he stayed in 28C and 28B Thameside. Before the refurb of 28A completed and we moved there.

Why is this of any relevance whatsoever? Where does the confusion arise? Simply put, he was living there for free and receiving high value gifts. Why target one flat above another as the place of residence? I paid for everything. It was my home where he was a guest not only paying no contribution, but also accepting significant amounts by way of gift and unpaid loans. During this period he spent time in both 28C and 28B. But they targeted me saying we lived in 28C to show how big a liar I was?

Well. We did. Live in 28C. Simple. We also lived, for a lesser time, in 28B. I owned both and decided when I needed the space for personal use above rental income. Further, it is factual flaw in Flaherty's finding that **'we lived in Flat B'** in any kind of exclusive way because for 6 months Flat B was uninhabitable. During the period when I had extension works underway. It was a back to brick building site.

Once again here is material hard evidence that Flaherty is not adhering to the commonly accepted version of truthfulness. Flaherty is writing a judgment in which her findings are untrue. Another lie by a family court judge causing further abuse to a child.

When Krasnopovich first left with Sam on 16th June, 2013, there was no mention of any interest in beneficial entitlement. His first requests for money made no mention of beneficial entitlement. Only after I retained a lawyer and tried to establish the address where my son was kept did he retain a city lawyer, Tim Clock, and only brought proceedings for this newly invented 50/50 claim, his beneficial entitlement, after I brought proceedings for visitation. Apparently a punishment for daring to challenge him in family court. The actual date when I was served with the beneficial entitlement claim is identical to the date that Krasnopovich was to transfer my freehold title back to me. Sending a clear message. Why then, if he stayed with me for the longest time in 28A, did he also claim for 28B, but not for 28C? He spent more time in 28C than he did in 28B.

The reason for the inclusion of 28B in the claim at this later time (November 2013) and the reason why Flaherty has labored such a seemingly irrelevant point, which of two flats did we live in, despite the fact that I paid all costs, is because up until then Krasnopovich did not know what my mortgage position was. 28B had no mortgage and is for this reason the most valuable of my properties. It is clear that Krasnopovich initially decided to try and claim 28A, based on the fact he had made a contribution to living expenses in the past few years while living there with me, and that is where Sam was housed, so he could use family law relating to the housing of the child. The family act where the parent has to pay to house the child if the child has no safe housing possibility. Only later, in financial disclosures, Krasnopovich found out the extent of the mortgage on 28A (which has a big mortgage) and the equity in 28B (Which has no mortgage). Only after consulting with Clock, did I hear about their claim to include 28B. To support this claim they latched onto the fact that I referred to us living in 28C Thameside and labored that Krasnopovich always stayed in 28B and never in 28C.

At no time did I say Krasnopovich never lived in 28B. To show me up as a liar. *"..... Ms Lee's vehement attempts to suggest that Mr Krasnopovich had never lived at 28B".*

What?

That is untrue. Whey hey. Another lie in a judgment by a family court judge. A lying judge whose lie count was in double figures before the first days lunch break. Krasnopovich lived in 28B, rent free with me. And, in what for Flaherty appears to be an unfeasibly complex arrangement involving one flight of stairs, he also lived in 28C rent free with me.

Flaherty suggests that I am lying about Krasnopovich never living in 28B and therefore he should get 50%? These are words written in a judgment that ends a child's life with his parent. Yet they are clearly predicated on convenient delusion. Misleading and plain-wrong. All that's left to conjecture is whether this was a premeditated decision by a corrupt judge, persuaded to switch cases on the day to benefit colleagues and fellow members of her profession or an instance of gross incompetence by an underqualified one. Consider – when she saw the barristers name on the other side, she should have declared herself prejudiced. She knew she had a history with barrister Castello. Yet, apparently, she volunteered to take the case and displace the judge set down on the day. The judge I knew by reputation to be strong on financial matters, replaced by one who we knew had a historical prejudice against my barrister.

Flaherty recalls *"Mr Krasnopovich remembered living at and in 28B Thameside as early as 2004 when he received the news of his father's death, and that evidence I found credible"*

During his cross examination in the 28B vs 28C matter, again Castello was making good headway into Krasnopovich's credibility. After all, it was never in dispute by me that he spent some time in 28B. And it was clearly evident that the works to 28B took 6 months, during which time, there was only one habitable flat in my house. 28C. Where he cohabited with me in 2003 and again for much of 2004.

At this stage, Krasnopovich rolled out his prepared memory of how he remembers being in 28B when the phone rang and he learned his father had just died. At which point, he sobbed, bravely fighting back the tears of this painful memory. Flaherty was visibly moved.

"Take a moment my dear." Spoken in a soft tone. At a slow pace. This extract from courtroom theatrics, intermediate level 2, could not have been more transparent. We go from this anguished painful memory moment to asserting the

'vehement denial that Mr Krasnopovich ever lived in 28B.'

The use of the word '**ever**' here is wrong. Deliberately misleading. Most relevantly. Did Krasnopovich ever pay one penny towards his living costs with me during this time. Whilst enjoying the £800 pm he was renting his own flat out for while living with me for free. Seems like a thin straw to grab at. Claiming 50% of a flat that you stayed in for a few months, for free. So how does Flaherty make the connection between where Krasnopovich may or may not have lived at a time when he was in any event being supported entirely by myself to conclude that

"I am persuaded that Ms LEE on more than one occasion said to Mr Krasnopovich that he owned both 28A and 28B "fifty / fifty like any married couple".

And here we have a mess of words.

The refurbishment and significant extension of 28A would mean the necessity of living elsewhere within the building; the flooding in 2007 would necessarily have involved staying out of the mess.

What is Flaherty's thinking here?

We never lived in 28A before the refurb. At the very essence of this point by Flaherty, there is a factual error. I only moved to 28A when the property was ready for occupation in 2005. After the refurb While that work was underway we lived in 28C. (The top flat.) 28B was a part of the refurb at the same time as 28A. It was a building site until late 2005, when the works completed. For that 6-month period, the only unit that was habitable was 28C Thameside. Once works completed, I moved from 28C to 28A after which time the newly refurbed 28B was rented as was 28C. So what is the connection to *"the flooding in 2007 would necessarily have involved staying out of the mess."*

Flaherty has confused dates and events again. In a confusing way indicative of something less than accurate awareness of the facts. Deliberately choosing to present a conclusion even when the factual matrix exists to show the conclusion is fallacious. The facts were clearly available to Flaherty, who chose to ignore them in her judgment. The facts are:

One.) The flood in 2007 did not result in a move. I had an empty flat at that time, inside the house. We only needed it for less than two weeks.

Two) The builder, a friend of mine, (Biff) started the refit right away. No re-tanking was done. Just a dry out. And new carpets. I just moved us upstairs for a few weeks, and straight back down when the repairs were done. By memory, a maximum of ten days.

Then in 2008, one year <u>after</u> Flaherty's reference date, the property flooded which *'necessarily involved staying out of the mess.'* This refers to a different flood entirely. That flood, in 2008, led to 9 months of work, re-tanking the property, during which time Insurance cover paid like for like rehousing accommodations in Thames Side. (£3,500pm X 9 Months.)

What exactly does her conclusion that "*the flooding in 2007 would necessarily have involved staying out of the mess*" mean? Consider that after the flood of 2014, a way more damaging flood altogether, it was determined by Krasnopovich that it was **"entirely unnecessary to stay out of the mess."** These guys just make up shit as if no one will ever compare their invention to substantive fact.

Once again, Flaherty's wording is confusing, based on a skewed factual matrix. Deliberate corruption or simply gross incompetence. Or both.

25.   Then Mr Krasnopovich was cross-examined. He was asked questions about the nature of his practice and accepted that he has been advising cohabitants since 2002 and that this has increased since *Stack v Dowden*.   There had been extensive work done to 28A Thameside and he was asked questions about the work.   His evidence was that he had asked if they could put the property in joint names, but Ms LEANDROS said "No".   28A was purchased on 17.12.04 and there had been a discussion about joint names at that time.   The works on the property started shortly after

Here Krasnopovich says, and Flaherty believes, that "**he had asked if they could put the property in joint names, but Ms LEANDROS said "No".**

But later we find Flaherty says I 'promised her 50/50 like we were married.' So if he asked to put the property in joint names, why then would I have not put Krasnopovich's name on the title when he asked? These two events cannot logically co-exist. If I had promised 50% - then when he asked to have his name on the title – I would have put his name on the title. If I had promised him 50%.

In 2004 I paid under £200,000 for the lease of 28A and then spent well over £300,000 on the refurb. Which also took some 6 months of my actual time, working many hours a day while Krasnopovich worked 8 hours a day in an unrelated field. His family law work with MWT. Krasnopovich spent £0 on either the purchase of the lease or the building expenses. Which begs the question. Why would he ask to have 50% of my property?

By this time, as a high earning lawyer, would you not think the conversation might have gone, '*can I contribute to costs in any way, perhaps a lump sum for the improvements, or a contribution to the mortgage, in return for a percentage interest'*. No mention was made of any interest for Krasnopovich in my properties. Quite the contrary. We were actively looking at property option for a joint property that we would move into on a 50/50 mortgage. 28 Thameside was mine and at no time was there any indication that it was intended as anything more than mine and an inheritance for my son.

If Krasnopovich had asked to have his name on the title believing that he had been promised this '50/50' deal and the answer had been no. Then surely a lawyer of such reputation for litigation and financial ambition would have been, at the very least, more insistent. Would you not think he might say '*But, you promised me 50/50 like we were married'* so why not put it in my name?' Even to the point of sending one (single) email or telling one (single) person who might corroborate this remarkable claim.

Certainly, you would reasonably assume that the opportunity provided by the Will signing in 2010 would have tempted him into disclosing this wonderful gift?

There is no thread of evidence this request was ever made because it never was.

No promise of this sort ever existed prior to the meeting between Krasnopovich and Clock sometime in October 2013, when they devised this tactic, intended to exploit my want factor for my child to extract the maximum amount they felt they could in exchange. The money or the kid ploy. A classic of family law.

And the second lie in this thread of Flaherty's judgment is that he asked to have his name on the title. Knowing not even one email that one would expect to follow such a disappointing exclusion from a promise to half ownership, existed. This alleged request by Krasnopovich is a bald-faced lie by a professional liar, advised by Clock to make this claim in the hope that it would erect another layer on the foundation lie, the '50/50 like we were married' claim.

Because this lie led to the judgment by Flaherty ending my son's relationship with me, I feel let down by family-law. I feel that a professional judge should have done better with a child's future at stake. I feel that this level of conduct by family-court is child abuse. And that is what it is. A judgment that abused my child.

If I was to describe my personal feeling about this hearing, I would use the comparison of rape. When I left Flaherty's court I felt that I had been raped. A rape of all logic and common sense. A rape of my belief that Britain's courts are bastions of fair play. A shocking realization that there is such a thing as an unappealable judgment in a hearsay judgment. And a rape of my child's life with me.

It was a deeply traumatic experience.

It is for my son, a deeply traumatic experience.

I am including my briefing letter to Roland Chambers, who was at that time my newly appointed family lawyer at FOS following Flaherty's judgment. Clam was by this time fired and I had retained a top London firm to represent me in the appeal against Flaherty's foolish judgment. This was my letter to my lawyer ahead of the 'Permission to Appeal' part of the process as we prepared for an appeal to an unappealable judgment. Roland Chambers did not tell me it was unappealable. He was most encouraging that we would overturn this 'Horrible' judgment and I would expect to see Sam again right away.

From: Andrea Lee
To: Roland Chambers

Krasnopovich has got way with lying and manipulating family law to the extent that is matched in its extreme only by the ease with which he was able to do it. It seems clear to me that Cecelia Flaherty is complicit in assisting her colleague Krasnopovich beyond the remit of her authority as a deputy district judge in family law. This judge has failed in her duty. Her actions in the April hearing were simply wrong and have had grievous consequences which includes the abuse of a child.

She quite obviously decided before a word was spoken that she would support her colleague in family law and had ruled accordingly even before a word was spoken.

This was obvious to Richard Castello, who confirmed on two occasions to the effect that **"If we get Flaherty we will lose, because she is incompetent."**

And **"I knew we had lost when I saw her roll her eyes at me"**. *Which happened just 3 minutes into his opening submission.*

Clearly something happened in that hearing. Why did DDJ Burkes recuse? He knew on the Friday night that he was listed for the hearing. The reason given to me for him recusing is that he had worked with Krasnopovich previously. I have since found out that he never worked with Krasnopovich. If he had worked for him, he should have recused on the Friday when he learned he was listed.

Here is the Email from Castello to Clam relating to that very point, asking him to check Burkes' history with Krasnopovich.

From: Richard Castello <RCastello@xxxxx.co.uk>
Sent: 10 April. 14.38

To David Clam
Subject: Monday

Dear David,
I understand we are listed at Gee Street on Monday.
Also we are before Donald Burkes (of garden Court). It strikes me that he is a good call for us
However I think you need to ask Tim Clock as a matter of urgency whether Nico Krasnopovich or him have instructed him in the past,
Regards,
Mikhael

Richard Castello
Barrister

Why then did Flaherty replace Burkes on the morning of the hearing?

I suggest there has been collusion between Hazelwood's side and the switching of the judges. That Flaherty is not an honest character is evident to me by her conduct in the court and her subsequent judgment is unmistakable in its profiling by mental health and dishonest inferences. She has misled the process with her own prejudice. Presenting opinion as fact.

There was no hearing in April. Simply Flaherty stealing my assets to award to her colleague, while betraying my sons right to a life with one parent in the process. I believe Anthony Douglas is entirely correct in his description of exactly this type of outcome as no more than legal child abuse endorsed by the family-law court service who allow Flaherty to continue with her inappropriate professional conduct, paying her to work with vulnerable children. During cross examination Flaherty led Krasnopovich in his replies with regularity. Friendly low voice pitch, measured comforting reassurance. She interrupted me repeatedly in mine, pitch rising, tempo accelerating, volume increasing; on more than one occasion correcting me on a point in which she was 100% wrong. Labeling me as a liar with her own lie.

Example: In the historical context of the building I answered a question by the 'I put-it-to-you-you-are lying' Hazelwood to the effect that "I bought 28 Thameside in 1986."

Flaherty interrupted, very firmly, to correct me. "You did not buy 28 Thameside. You bought 28B Thameside."

*Obviously it is a fact, contained in the documents in front of Flaherty, that I bought the Freehold to 28 Thameside as well as 28B Thameside lease at that time. Either Flaherty awareness of property title precludes understanding the difference between freehold and leasehold, or she did that deliberately in one of many interruptions based on the Hazelwood's approach of "I put it to you Mr. Krasnopovich that you are lying." The approach she endorsed and joined in on without regard for either appropriate impartiality by a judge or the actual truth in the matter. She wrote of me in her judgment "**I find, because it seems agreed, that he is a man of mental fragility.**"*

Agreed by whom?

From the SRA website code of ethics:
As a member of the law society I will:

Ensure that I maintain fairness and due process in research administration and Society activities in which I am engaged. I will not practice, condone, facilitate, or collaborate with any form of discrimination on the basis of race, ethnicity, national origin, color, sex, sexual orientation, gender identity or expression, age, marital status, political belief, religion, immigration status, or mental or physical disability.

There is proper medical terminology regarding PTSD and depression. 'Mental fragility' is not an accurate or acceptable label for me or any mental health issues I may have. It speaks to prejudice and profiling by this judge.

*Her judgment contains 13 instances of the word mental. She repeatedly refers to me as **mentally fragile** and that is discrimination.*

Fragility is *1. Easily broken, damaged, or destroyed.*
   2. Lacking physical or emotional strength; delicate: a fragile personality.
   3. Lacking substance; tenuous or flimsy:

"The father's case is that he has always had a susceptibility to mental fragility."
Cecelia Flaherty

"However Mr KRASNOPOVICH' mental fragility was, as stated above, a known matter and issue in this case." Cecelia Flaherty

This is an unacceptably prejudiced wording of a medical condition chosen deliberately with clear intent to serve a personal agenda, being pejorative in a way that makes Flaherty's lack of impartiality clear.

At no time have I been diagnosed as mentally fragile, nor has that been the truth at any time in my life. The first time in my life where I heard that description of myself was by Flaherty that day.

It is, by Flaherty, unacceptable and offensive profiling, which without redress will leave family court open to the commonly held view that there is inherent corruption in secret courts abusing children for the profit of members. And gives the lie to the claim from the department of justice that family-court can be trusted to be gender neutral.

I look forward to hearing from you,

Regards,
Andrea

As is the case with many of my South African peers, our generation grew up with 100% conscription of white males in a time of bitter war. It was especially challenging for anyone not right-wing conservative-Christian racist. I overcome challenges in my life which would not have been the case with anything less than adequate mental strength.

Not yet 21 I emigrated to the UK with for a new start in a City where I knew no one, with virtually no money and with no employment opportunity other than playing music. I was able to buy my own home within 12 months of arriving, as a musician with no credit history in the UK. And I was able to work successfully in a highly competitive area, music, for thirty years, often with some of the world's leading musicians. I have a reputation for many things.

Mental fragility is not one. Quite the contrary. This was the first time in my life someone labelled me as mentally fragile and the first time in my life I have seen anyone start virtually every other sentence to me with "*I put it to you you are lying*".

Like showbiz but without the show. Junior Counsel they are called, and junior is appropriate. Like junior court room drama by B graders. Today I think I will start every question with "*I put it to you you are lying. That ought to get her pissed off.*"

Flaherty has labelled me as mentally fragile at every opportunity. And even where there was no opportunity she still reverted to that pejorative insult. She has used the description 13 times in one judgment that is 12 pages long. Coming from a judge tasked with prioritizing a child's best interests it is especially offensive when that prejudice underpins a malicious judgment that in the same breath makes me homeless, penniless, indebted and unable to see Sam until those measures are repaired. All of which Flaherty has done in full awareness that the consequences will end Sam's relationship with his parent. The animosity Flaherty has fomented is child abuse. The cost she has imposed on me is theft. The manner in which she has achieved both outcomes is deceit. It diminishes an institution, family-law. The location of her offenses is family court. Cecelia Flaherty has lied repeatedly. And to this day there has been no accountability even despite the President of family-law, reading the judgment and awarding 'Permission to Appeal.'

I put it to you, the reader, that the facts are self-evident.
   Consider means motive and opportunity.

Judge Flaherty, self-proclaimed on social media as a *'juvenile delinquent lover of champagne and fun'* is also, foremost, a liar. An abuser of children under the protection of family court law. When considering her effect on my son's life, Flaherty is also a thief. Someone stole his future with me.

A rainbow thief.

26 Evan and Maria

My elderly parent and Sam's favorite beauty, his first crush

21 June 2015 was my Father, Evan Leandros' 80th birthday.

Evan lives in Johannesburg after moving there from Greece in the sixties. He grew up in post-war ravaged Greece. Having survived many ups and downs in a life rich with tragedy and joy in unequal measure, reaching 80 was a big occasion and I planned to be there and to take Sam with. Sam's arrival was a big thing for his grandparent. He was crazy about Sam. Evan has two grandsons. My boys born twenty years apart. At the arrangement stage for our visit, three months before the big day, considering the distances involved there would need to be some considerable attention given to flights. I would fly from LAX to LHR to collect Sam, and then onwards, later that same day, to Johannesburg for the big day as part of a two week visit to Johannesburg. A trip that was equally important in representing Sam's last opportunity to see 'beautiful Maria' about whom more follows.

My travel proposal for the summer holidays was sent for consideration by Clock and Krasnopovich. I explained the two reasons for visiting South Africa and that following the trip to South Africa, I would then take Sam to California, before returning him at the end of the summer holiday. I would collect Sam from the UK, spend two weeks in Johannesburg seeing his grandad, (Papou), his family in South Africa and especially, Maria Andiotis, Sam's first great love, beautiful Maria, 31, who knew then after years of Chemotherapy that the remainder of her life was a matter of months. That this would be her last opportunity to see Sam. A final farewell that she was prepared for. From Johannesburg we would travel via Atlanta to California for a month of Sam's summer holidays, after which I would return him to the UK for the start of the school term. A six-week period for Sam to be with me and see the family and friends who had missed him enormously. It had been an entire year since he last visited with me and I knew this was of vital importance for him. To have a good period of time with me. He would have just turned six. There was much for us to discuss. Evan, my father, was looking forward to Sam's visit for this milestone occasion where all of his family and friends would be present. His guest of honour, as he had announced for his guest planning, his two grandsons would be seated next to him. On his left would be Evan and on his right would be Sam.

Evan grew up in Piraeus during the war years where, in common with the vast majority of Greeks during the German occupation, he experienced tremendous hardship and deprivation. The Germans who occupied Athens in 1941 were brutal fascists, most of them Catholic, acting without thought for the children and civilian population. They would, for example, take whatever food supplies existed, quite literally leaving the population to starve. My father as a young man of 7 recalls walking to school, stepping over the bodies of his school friends who simply dropped dead from starvation.

The road they lived on would later be renamed Distomou Street, commemorating the awful Nazi massacre of 218 Greeks on the 10th June, 1944 in the village of Distomou, near Delphi. Awful, unspeakable barbarism by men doing their jobs, including bayonetting pregnant women in the stomach and bayonetting 2-month-old babies in their cribs. This was a punishment for guerilla attacks by the Andartes – the Greek Communist led resistance who harried the occupying Nazi forces continuously. My father's developmental years were spent entirely consumed by the horrors of war.

Here is one story he tells on occasion.

In a population dying of starvation, once a week the local Church would stage a meal specifically for young orthodox children, for whom this would usually be the only proper nutritious meal of the week. My father lived in their small house on Distomou Street, with his mother, Panayiota, his father Christos and his brother Elias, 5 years his junior. These were unspeakably desperate times to be a young person growing up in Greece. Evan would attend these life sustaining feeding sessions on Sundays where the condition for all the children being fed was that they would have to finish their plates before leaving the dining room. He learned on each successive Sunday, how to finish his plate before saying 'Thank You'. At which point he would place the last mouthful of meat into his mouth as he left.

But he would not chew it.

As soon as he exited the church he would regurgitate that last piece of meat to carry home to his mother, being the only protein she would have to survive on for another week.

The family survived on very little. Mostly lentil soup on most days. Near neighbors were not so lucky. As the war wore on the ever more desperate German occupiers behaved as we know from our history books. Commonly they starved the occupied countries. I learned many war stories first-hand from my father and my uncles who participated in WW2.

In 1944 Piraeus was a frequent target for allied air attacks. The harbour was a vital center for supplies serving the German occupiers. As Elias would one day show me visually when I visited Distomou street with him, an allied attack on a nearby strategic installation in Piraeus harbour missed and the massive bomb overshot the target landing fifty meters, away, plumb in the middle of the residential area, flattening five entire blocks filled with civilians. Distomou was the sixth street in that impact line, where the family lived in a 51-meter sq. house, was the outer boundary of the impact zone. The end of the blast wave flattening houses to dust, was the other side of the road to their home. Where I stood with Elias showing me the line, I could see it was a distance of less than 5 meters. How close I came to not ever being born because of a British bomb. The family escaped by a whisker. They spent that day with everyone else who survived helping to move rubble to extract the body parts of their neighbors for delivery to the church, for burial. A ten-year-old boy and his five-year-old brother, malnourished, starving, working tirelessly lifting rubble with bare hands to recover pieces of their friends and neighbors in order that they could have a proper burial. Necessary in the orthodox tradition.

And when you might imagine it couldn't get any worse for young Evan, it did.

In 1944, after three years of occupation by the Nazi's, when he was ten and younger brother Elias five, he recalls with tremendous clarity how they were standing in the kitchen watching their father Christos prepare lentils for their nightly meal of Lentil soup. They were alone with their father as mother Panayiota was out at the local church looking for the next food ration. There was a knock on the door. Two men in uniform, one with a rifle.

"Would you come with us to the Police station".

"Why".

"Nothing important, just a few questions for you."

"Now is not a good time. I am alone with the children. My wife has gone to the church to get some food."

"We must insist, please come with us now."

The two young children watched their father led away. They would not see him again for 18 months.

A neighbor, the father of Nikos, an older boy in the street, was trying to get Nikos a place in the Police force. To improve his credibility with the British backed right-wing leadership, and bearing in mind the majority of Greek resistance was led by Communists, he had denounced Christos as a communist. There as a value in turning in communists. That won him a promotion. Churchills strong anti-Communist position post war that saw him betray the Resistance who defended Greece so bravely also created a climate in which hearsay was enough to have anyone arrested as a communist and sent for 're education.' (Ironic that I would face a corrupt hearsay trial myself in later years.)

My Grandfather was arrested and detained. Later I learned he was taken along with Giorgios, the father of Yiannis Varoufakis, the former Greek finance minister, similarly denounced. Christos was taken to a holding pen in Piraeus harbor where he joined thousands of others denounced as communists and incarcerated without any contact with their families. Mother Panayiota arrived home from her daily food scavenging mission at the local church to learn about this arrest. With the two kids in tow she rushed to the church with enquiries; learned about the holding pen where the 'Communist's' were held, to be boarded on a ship for a concentration camp in Crete, and rushed over there. But despite rushing along the boundary wire calling out his name, they could not find their father in the enormous numbers. What they did find was Nikos, a newly appointed young policeman, standing guard over the prisoners.

"Nikos, you must help us they have arrested our father. Find him and explain he is not a Communist."

Nikos hung his head and said sorrowfully "*I cannot help you. I am sorry*." They had no knowledge of Nikos' betrayal at that time. He was just a friendly kid from the same road. Eventually defeated by impossible odds, the Mother and her two hungry young children trudged back to their ruin of a home, one road down from the flattened bomb site, where they struggled from day to day for the next 16 months to survive on the mouthfuls of meat my father could regurgitate after leaving the church-feeding and the small amounts of basics the church provided Panayiota to feed her family.

Mostly lentils.

They were all extremely thin. They all prayed a great deal. The Church played a significant role coordinating both hope for survival as well as basic charitable sustenance, enabling survival ration foods for the poorest.

Years later, I was standing on Distomou road in Piraeus, overlooking the Church where these events unfolded, Elias told me that the local priest in was in fact an English spy. A Greek agent had been put in place in the Piraeus church 1939 by British intelligence in the event of a German occupation, where he performed the role of a fully qualified Greek priest for the duration of the war, successfully sending intelligence back to Britain throughout without being discovered. After the war, his role was exposed and he returned to the UK. But for the locals, this news had consequences. This man had for 6 years performed all the religious rituals in his parish. Greek Orthodox rules often exceed national law in their importance. This man had conducted dozens of marriages in the church. Now it turned out he was not an official empowered in this important role.

What to do?

So many marriages invalid in the eyes of God. Kids born, technically, out of wedlock. Should they be cast out as bastards because of this technical error. What a mess. One countries hero became another's villain.

Apparently it all worked out though. The memory of prevailing over the common enemy was placed above the sin of heresy. He was grated honorary status in his church decisions because of the war. And his religious warranties were honored.

Twenty years passed and now it is 1964. By this time my father and Elias, his younger brother, had moved. One to University in Crete, the other to the Air Force. Their parents, Christos and Panayiota lived on in the same house in Distomou street, by now in their sixties. What happened that day twenty years before would became clear when the father of Nikos requested a meet with Panayiota (my grandmother) in his Piraeus home, one street down from Distomou street. He explained he was dying and wished to clear his conscience. Curious as to why this man wanted her to visit at the time of his imminent death, she agreed to visit him in his what was evidently his death bed.

"I was trying to help my son Nikos to get a job. I was the one who denounced Christos as a communist and they gave Nikos the job. But I was wrong and before I go to meet Jesus, I want your forgiveness"

My grandmothers reply was apparently *"No one can give you forgiveness but God himself"*.

After the war years, Greece was in ruins and eventually Evan emigrated to South Africa. Evan is my dad and provided for me all of my youth as best he could, but we were never close in that 'love you, love you too' way. He was not capable of emotional displays, mostly because of his awful experiences growing up with the horrors of Nazi atrocity. I understood that. And got on with my own life.

And so here we were in 2015. Evan approaching his eighth decade in a good place, comforted by a powerful ethical concern for sharing in which helping the less fortunate has rewarded him enormously. Charitable help and a comforting reliance on cigarettes proved to be winning combination for him.

I had long since given up trying to persuade him to give up. *"There is no science supporting ill effects from moderate smoking. My father lived to 88 and he smoked 60 a day."* He said in Greek. We always speak in Greek. To this day.

He was very aware that at the age of 80 this gathering of friends and family might well be his last meeting with his daughter and his two grandsons. He raised his energy accordingly. My father was ecstatic at the prospect of seeing his daughter and his grandsons for his 80th. So much so that he paid for all the flights involved. My travel itinerary was from LAX to LHR to JNB to Atlanta to LAX to LHR and finally back to LAX. Sam's from LHR to JNB to Atlanta to LAX to LHR. These were non-refundable pre-booked flights. Sam's journey alone totaled some $6,000 of airfare. Worth it in light of the circumstances. I couldn't wait to see my baby. My father couldn't wait to see his. So much anticipation for reunions from so many sides.

For this trip Evan was not alone in a great anticipation for seeing Sam.

Another was Sam's godfather and my very dear friend Chris Andiotis. My old friend, who I introduced to Krasnopovich the same week that we started dating, for his approval, as is the way with us Greeks. Chris knew Krasnopovich extremely well. And Sam even more so. Chris was an ever present in Sam's life, who knew Krasnopovich for one week less time than myself.

At this same time Chris' lovely wife Maria Andiotis was entering the final months of her life.

Maria was a beautiful, smart, tall, slim, young woman who married Chris when she was 29 and discovered just months later that she had stage 4 cancer. But before that sad news was the happy occasion of their wedding. I was still with Krasnopovich at the time, and Sam was 6 months old. I flew to Johannesburg with Sam to attend the Andiotis wedding in Johannesburg in 2010. It was a grand occasion. Philip joined us there, flying from California to meet Sam for the first time and celebrate with Chris and Maria. After the wedding, every few months Maria and Chris would visit Sam in the UK and my son very quickly concluded that '*Maria is very pretty.*' Soon after which Maria evidently became Sam's first crush. When Chris called on Skype, which was usually once a week, he would rush over and ask him "*Can I speak to beautiful Maria.*" And when she came on Skype he would become coy and bashful. I have some photos of them together that are just stunning. One of those photos would go on to be used at Maria's funeral. Beautiful Maria hugging beautiful Sam. A beautiful relationship for both of them. One of those special relationships for a developing boy. With each subsequent meeting Sam became more enamored with Maria. Seeing them together was a beautiful thing. Not least because they were both so attractive. Wonderful to see for everyone except Krasnopovich. There was a tension between Krasnopovich and Maria. Chris noticed it too. He remarked that Krasnopovich was jealous. All this affection for someone else was made especially noticeable by Sam's absent attention for his parent. I didn't understand what Chris meant.

Again, at age three Sam travelled to South Africa, spending two weeks visiting in Bryanston, (where I was raised) visiting his Grandpa (Papou) Evan and seeing Maria every day. On his second visit to South Africa we stayed at the Andiotis home in Dainfern. And that was where he enjoyed spending time every day beautiful Maria.

After the first cancer diagnosis the extensive chemotherapy appeared to have been completely successful. And Maria became pregnant. Very exciting for both Chris and Maria. All looked well until 7 Months into the pregnancy when the remission ended. A C-section followed to enable more chemo. We were in touch on an almost daily basis, Chris calling me, or me calling Chris. But although she looked great, Maria's treatment was unsuccessful.

In May of 2015 Chris called me with the bad news. With the best medical care Maria had less than six months. Possibly three. Baby Anna was going to lose her mother aged around two. And my friend Chris was going to lose the love of his life. With all the loss going on in his life already, Sam was soon going to lose 'beautiful Maria'. All very sad, yet here was one silver lining. I would be able to take Sam to say goodbye to Maria. And Maria would have the opportunity to talk to Sam herself. I had this conversation with Maria who was very much in reality about what was happening next and was preparing; looking forward to talking to Sam about it. It seemed important to me in Sam's development that he would have this opportunity to say goodbye appropriately. I booked the travel to South Africa arranging for Sam and myself to stay with Chris and Maria, in their lovely home in Johannesburg's Northern suburbs, so she could have some quality time with Sam. We would all attend Evan's birthday party together. With the tickets booked, both Evan and Maria were excited about seeing Sam for very similar reasons, both believing it would be a final farewell.

I cannot fully describe the scale of disappointment Krasnopovich's decision to refuse allowing Sam to travel represented.

Of the many poor decisions Clock and Krasnopovich made as representatives of family law, preventing Sam travelling in the summer of 2015 is right up there.

After cancelling that visit, summer of 2015, not only did he miss out on my father's 80th and saying goodbye to Maria; Sam never again had the opportunity to stay with me. (For more than a few scattered nights when I had to travel to the UK to see him. On one occasion allowing me only 24 hours.) To all intents, that late notice cancelation ended any prospect of holiday visits between Sam and myself. Sam has never spoken with his grandfather since and obviously, never with Maria who died in December of 2015. A magnificent, comprehensive win for Clock, Krasnopovich and Flaherty. One for the annals of the family-law winners circle in which all members can rightfully take enormous pride. Despite the disappointment of Sam being cancelled, I still travelled to South Africa for Evan's 80th and was able to spend what I would call precious time with Maria. Evan's party was memorable. An 80-year-old with such a story surrounded by friends and family all of whom knew the story of Sam's father and enjoyed the day despite the ghostly presence of the absent child. Maria attended the party, looking marvelous, hiding any signs of discomfort from the chemo she had undergone that very morning like the champion she was. She died not that many months later having made wonderful provision for the upbringing of baby Anna. Sam has never met Anna.

I never had the opportunity to explain death to Sam at this sensitive time of profound loss for a 5-year-old. It was the same with William the dog. I regret that I never had the opportunity to articulate what death meant through the passing of the dog to the developing mind of a young child. I used to wonder how Krasnopovich explained these two losses in his life to him, but haven't done so for some years now. I find the summit of all wastefulness to be conjecture into how the mind of Krasnopovichs' rationalizes the harm that he does. After the episode of Sam's June visit being cancelled, Evan found a truly awful resentment towards Krasnopovich.

"What he has done is unforgiveable."
Evan hasn't been able to speak with his grandson Sam since. The same is true of all my family who Krasnopovich prevents Sam speaking to and the overwhelming likelihood is that Sam will never see his grandfather. He is well into his 80's now and does not travel. He refers to Sam in the past tense. He does not refer to Krasnopovich at all. He 'ceased to exist' for the old Greek thinking.

Maria shared a tear with me when I told her of Sam's plight. *"I really don't understand what's wrong with him. All this just for money?"* she said of her former friend.

"Does he think one day Sam will thank him?"

Did Sam want to travel with me to see Papou and Maria and Chris and spend a month in California with me and Philip? Should Clock and Krasnopovich have prevented Sam from travelling? Clearly, the absence of any censure means their conduct adequately represents the ethical code of family-law members.

Two years had passed by now since Krasnopovich left Thameside. And by this time, the sorrow of separation between Sam and myself was immeasurable. Far beyond my descriptive skills as a writer. I had also by this time seen over £200,000 of legal bills. Although the Flaherty judgment had yet to be delivered.

27 Post judgment. Insurance claim

Typos and child abuse by the holidaying champagne drinker having fun being a juvenile delinquent

Flaherty's judgment took 3 months to arrive. When it did, it was by email, containing 74 typos. I counted them. Twice. Within its pages she spelled the name of one person, Philip Parker Voula incorrectly in nine different ways. There is a flippant tone throughout, evident to any reader. This is a missive written in full awareness that it will never be read in scrutiny relating to accountability. The author knows she is writing an 'un appealable ' judgment.

56. *I have been asked to look again at the wills and attendance notes that accompanied them and I did so [(what else are summer holidays for!)].*

The poor dear. Having to put her champagne flute to one side because 'what else are holidays for' than judging the lives of young children to be an incumbrance on your fun time. The completed order included many errors.

19. *Ms LEANDROS is the sole legal owner of three leasehold properties, 28A, 28B and 28C Thameside which is a large Victorian property on the banks of the River Thames near Thameside. The freehold to this property was transferred into the name of Mr Krasnopovich in 2003 as a result of difficulties in obtaining insurance as a result of an earlier flood damage claim.*

This is not true. It is a factual error. Another convenient lie. There was no earlier *'flood damage claim.'* It was a Fire claim.

The Insurance went into Krasnopovich's name on his 'Legal' advice (less than three months after I met him and moved him into my home where he lived rent free for the first two years) because Larry Chester, who owned the brokerage providing my Buildings insurance, could not get me coverage in my name after my home burned down in 2001 giving rise to a large claim.

Because I faced large Insurance premiums when disclosing the Fire claim of 2001, Krasnopovich proposed putting the title in his name and applying for insurance in his sole name by claiming no previous claim history. Larry Chester told me this was basically Insurance fraud, strongly advised me against it and would have attested to this in the hearing had he not been prevented by Flaherty from giving evidence.

Simply put. Krasnopovich convinced me that it was legal to apply for Insurance if he answered *'No previous claims'* in his name as that was technically true.

"*Just put the Freehold in my name. The I take out the Insurance, and when the five years are up on the Insurance in your name, I just transfer the title back to you. Simple. It won't cost you one penny in legal fees. I will do the Land Registry transfer.*"

On that basis he secured Insurance cover. The policy was in his name, although I paid all the costs. He was a 'trustee landlord'. Obviously no money changed hands in this arrangement and at no time was he led to believe he was anything more than the Trustee Freeholder. Doing me a favor for Insurance benefit in exchange for the years of free housing and expensive travel I had gifted him. He was obligated by the agreement in which he became Trustee landlord and for almost 5 years all was well. There was no claim on Insurance to test the validity of his application. Then the house flooded in 2007, and again, more seriously, in 2008. Krasnopovich had to claim on the policy in his name. He received some £300,000 from the AXA Insurance. But was his original application for cover in 2003 honest?

He certainly did not want Larry Chester (My financial adviser and mortgage arranger) disclosing the information relating to his name appearing as Freeholder and lessor responsible for the Insurance cover in the Flaherty hearing. On top of this historic offence, Krasnopovich was investigated following the 2014 flood claim for a similarly dishonest application. The AXA had some idea that something was amiss with Krasnopovich. They hired a top City firm to investigate him. All of which was substantiated in the evidence of Larry Chester.

Here we see a clear motive in preventing Larry Chester from giving evidence. Which I say relates to the appointment of Flaherty as switch judge for this very purpose.

Then there is a question relating to the "I will bring multiple witness to the hearing" claim made in DDJ Berry's court, when he evidently had no evidence and the case should, in the normal course of law, have been thrown out as a hearsay anecdotal claim made with malice by a bitter ex.

Who are these multiple witnesses?

Well. There were none. As I said, because obviously;

1.) There could not be any witnesses because the claim is a lie. It never happened, so that explains why there are no witnesses. And

2.) Krasnopovich could not convince anyone to even lie in court for him. Not even get his mother to say "I think I heard something about that in 2005?"

Nobody. Nada.

And when this point about multiple witnesses came up in front of Flaherty, I say, it should have been a red flag. Krasnopovich squirmed away under cross examination, and came up with this explanation.

The Dia Mirza story.

Dia Mirza was a mutual friend for many years. Krasnopovich met her in court, where she worked as a family law barrister and we were invited to Día's fortieth birthday party. After which we became friendly. I liked Dia a lot and we enjoyed many deep conversations. We would have dinner together usually once a month, at her home, or at my home. She was single and wanting more from life than her current lifestyle as a hard-working member of family law, hearing occasional cases as a Deputy District Judge. I was a good listener for her deepest hopes and we had many heart to heart talks in which I was performed something of a 'life coach' role. I helped her with advice I know had an impact on her life. (There is more to life than just work.) But none of that is the reason Krasnopovich chose to name Dia Mirza as the witnesses he meant when he said he would bring Multiple Witnesses to a court hearing to prove his claim.

The reason he chose Dia has nothing to do with her witnessing any such 'claim of 50/50' and everything to do with her credibility as a witness because of her position.

Dia is a family law barrister and Deputy District Judge. If you were going to bring a witness to a hearing on hearsay evidence, then bringing a family court judge and barrister is about as good as it gets. I expect Krasnopovich thought just mentioning her name as a witness would be enough. Not expecting that the case would actually get as far as the hearing. After all, the claim was made to put pressure on me to pay. Not to actually go through with a baseless claim. He needed to name a witness to get the preliminary hearing in play, and in that moment I guess he thought of the most likely person he could persuade to support him as a fellow member of family law.

"Can you tell me why Dia Mirza is not here, giving evidence, as you said she would?" Asked my barrister Richard Castello in Flaherty's court. The answer, delivered in a liar's monotone, which incredibly Flaherty acknowledged with a nodding head.

"Because Dia says she has no memory of any such conversation."

Let's recap.

The single shred of corroborating evidence promised in Krasnopovich's entire case is the word of a DDJ and barrister in family law. Dia Mirza, 48. Krasnopovich says Dia is the only witness to a conversation in which Andrea promised Krasnopovich 50% of his home. He has brought his case in a preliminary hearing to allocate the court for his claim where he has declared *"I will bring multiple witnesses."* Yet Dia Mirza says this conversation never happened. This is true. Dia never heard any such mention because it never happened. On the face of it, a damning, terminal indictment of a dishonest claim.

Yet Flaherty sums it up in her judgment as follows:

Mr Castello also prays in aid that Ms Krasnopovich swore evidence about other witnesses who could attest to conversations about the beneficial ownership of 28A and 28B. I do not find this helpful. There can be many reasons why apparent witnesses do not give evidence and to speculate in this area is dangerous.

The judge has dealt with the Dia Mirza evidence by saying '**to speculate in this area is dangerous**'. The plural promise of multiple witnesses is simply avoided altogether.

By the time the Flaherty judgment arrived I had already taken the overdue expedient of seeking more reliable legal advice. I knew from my experience of the participants, Flaherty with her open prejudice and my lawyer David Clam, with the late submissions and the serial errors leading to costly consequences to myself and my son, that the judgment was likely to be the worst case. So I started the process known as 'beauty parading' legal representation.

The best option came after to the introduction from my cousin and Knightsbridge resident, John Milos, to leading London Firm, Friedman Oldfield Shutterworth. (FOS) A top five City firm with famous lawyers as partners. John set up an introductory consultation call. So here I was, talking to one of the most senior members of family law, before the judgment arrived. I detailed the sequence of events. The first issue that became apparent is why a civil claim, that is, a claim against my property for beneficial entitlement, was even being heard in family court in the first place. That is a civil claim.

By the end of my consultation talk it was immediately clear that David Clam had made significant errors by way of incompetence and negligence. And also in the process of switch Judge Flaherty's ruling, excluding witnesses and so on.

My top-level advice from a top-level member of family law in a top London firm was to appeal Flaherty's 'horrible' decision, if the judgment was as I expected. And it was. In this period, the month while I was emailing Clam to ask after the judgment, which we were awaiting from Flaherty, Clam appeared a desperate man. He knew what was coming. When he received the email judgment from the holidaying Flaherty, it took him several days to even send the email on to me. Late again Clam. When I received the judgment, it arrived along with an additional £28,000 invoice from Clam. For his services post hearing. I had not instructed him 'post hearing'. I was going to change lawyers. That much was clear to him. And I intended claiming against him for his gross negligence. Certainly paying him another £28,000 was not a realistic proposition. It was a deliberate legal ploy by a scheister to leverage my ability to file a formal complaint by holding my files with the Appeal clock ticking. The three-psychiatrist nonsense and his failures in that episode were the formal end of our relationship. By that time he had received around £161,000 from me. My goal was to progress the appeal with my new solicitors. And to do that I needed the files sent to the new firm. Clams delay in forwarding had already wasted 5 days of the 21 days allowed for 'notice of appeal.' Meanwhile, I notified Clam that I held him responsible for the errors he made. I itemized the errors he made. And I made him an offer. To repay me 50% of the money I had paid him, and I would not pursue damages for negligence. From the date of the judgment, there was a 21-day period in which to file an appeal. That clock was ticking. If I was to file the appeal, my new lawyer, Roland Chambers, needed the files in good time. By Clam refused to release the files. Using the £28,000 fake invoice as leverage. *"Pay me the money and I will release the files."* Family law and blackmail. It's a commonality in members approach. This is a typical, unsurprising example of a family law member in UK family law acting within the SRA ethical code.

By this time I was receiving advice from my new lawyers who suggested I contact the Legal Ombudsman. And report the conduct of Clam and his firm. Beyond a shadow of doubt David Clam made multiple critical errors that had direct consequences on the Flaherty judgment. My claim with the ombudsman would be for the £161,000 I had paid in legal fees as well as damages arising from his negligence. That sum would have been far in excess of £1 million. Including his botched handling of the flood insurance claim.

Unfortunately for me and for Sam, I very quickly learned the Ombudsman process takes many months and as I had already learned from previous experience with CAFCASS and the ombudsman, it is a grand waste of time thinking the ombudsman's employees will act swiftly and efficiently against the very business they owe their salaries to. Although I could have progressed my claim via the appropriate channels, the Legal Ombudsman, their reply would not have come within the time available to me for the Appeal deadline.

Clam knew this.

So, pressured by time to get the files to FOD, my lawyers, for the Permission to Appeal hearing, with the days counting down to the limit for filing, I had to make a deal with Clam.

I agreed to drop the Ombudsman complaint and my damages claim in exchange for Clam releasing my files to FOS immediately. It was a 24-hour offer. He agreed. Withdrew his bogus £28,000 invoice claim and later that same day I heard the files arrived at Roland Chambers office. Our final correspondence was his Hail Mary letter requesting that I sign a non-disclosure agreement. I made clear that was not a part of the agreement and that I intended speaking openly about his conduct in a book. Much as is the case here. I copied his managing partner in on the correspondence. Valerie Spoon. I guess she must have been impressed with his conduct in the firm's name? I noticed not long after my letter to his managing partner that Clam no longer works at Spoon LLP.

David Clam received some £161,000 in payment from me for services which included a late filing down to his schedule in which he paid the contempt of court fine, £2,600, but left my name of the court record as being responsible. With disastrous consequences.

Clam charged some £12,000 to prepare 7 witness statements and then filed them late, mimicking what Clock had done to him at the Visitation hearing, only to find that gave the switch judge, Flaherty, grounds to exclude the witnesses.

The list of errors goes on. If there is any justice in British family law, David Clam and his firm at that time should pay damages for their errors in handling my case commensurate with the harm they brought to my case.

How do you attach a value to losing your son?

Or losing £3 million in hard earned money.

Or the trauma of going through this mugging by a corrupt gang of family law members. I say, for his part in this chapter of British family law, there should be accountability in the form of being judged by his governing body with appropriate damages being paid.

Dealing with my new law firm FOS was a very different experience to Clam LLP. As Roland Chambers was quick to point out *"It is a real pity you didn't come to us at the outset. You wouldn't be in this mess now."* He was all too aware of Clams blunders against the big city lawyer, Clock. My error in choosing a 'Provincial' law firm. Sadly for me and Sam, at the outset of this litigation while I was still stunned by the events of fathers-day, I did not imagine I would need the services of a top family law firm. I had no idea that I would even need a lawyer. It was quite clear that Krasnopovich wanted to leave. He had a net income (after tax) that year far in excess of £250,000 and he owned his own home. We had an agreement to raise a child together and the payments for that agreement were clearly defined.

Why would I need a lawyer?

My home, the freehold title, was bought in 1986 and the three leases were in my name. I only met Krasnopovich in 2003. He did not even know the details of my mortgage arrangements, let alone have any name on any title or any loan.

He may have elected to end the relationship with me, but the commitment to the child, our parenting agreement remained very much in place from my side.

What we had agreed when deciding to have a child was not affected by separation.

For the practical aspects of separation, we had no co-mingled finances. I made clear that I was not going to pursue him for maintenance or any share of his business, even though I had set it up with him, paying the costs, and worked for the business on a daily basis. In my traumatized state, I did not consider the possibility that I would need a lawyer because Krasnopovich might use visitation with the child to extort a six-figure sum from me. All of my focus went into planning a new life for me and Sam and making the practical arrangements for this. I had sufficient means by way of income from my two rentals and my music business to continue unaffected by Krasnopovichs' departure. All I expected from him was to honour the pre child parental agreement which made provision for the school fees. To be paid from the law firm I invested in setting up for this purpose.

Sadly, within weeks after fathers-day it became clear from Krasnopovich's 'Without Prejudice' letter that he wanted a six-figure sum or else I *'would not see Sam again'* and would have to face him in Court. At this time he simply refused to provide me with the address of where Sam was. During this period he disclosed to Chris in a phone call, if I did not pay him, we would find out how *'Shit hot I am at what I do'*.

That was the moment I realized I would need a lawyer. When Chris told me *"You will have to get a lawyer. He is going after your house. He is going to use visitation with Sam to blackmail you. Mark my words."*

Chris is, as everyone who knows him will agree, a smart and prescient reader of human nature. I did not believe him at first. *"No way will he try and stop Sam being with me."*

But when Krasnopovich continued refusing to provide Sam's address, and started with the demand letters, I had no choice but to find a family lawyer. That turned out to be harder than you would expect for someone with multiple family lawyers, barristers and judges as personal friends. The first four I spoke to would not take my matter because they knew Krasnopovich and the general reply was *"I wouldn't want him representing my ex against me so we show each other that professional courtesy."*

I have a good friend who is a top flight City lawyer, Geoff Gambino, and very much in the know about the current who-is-who in UK law. We spoke and he recommended a city firm I knew had no dealing with Krasnopovich. I contacted them and was turned me down because they would not go against a family law member. After my call, they made a few calls, and came back to me declining to take my case. Krasnopovich has a reputation in family law circles.

After that Geoff called to tell me *"You are going to have a problem finding a top firm because family law is quite small. They all know each other."*

That is largely why I ended up with a provincial lawyer and not a top city firm, as Geoff had advised. Although I knew my cousin John Milos was friendly with a leading family law partner at FOS, who are a top London firm, I also knew that would involve a 6-figure bill. John's advice was that this top lawyer would require a retainer of £100,000 to take on my matter. At that stage I thought there would be a very small legal bill because mine was a very small matter. Of course, if I could go back to that moment, I would have retained that name solicitor and this story would have been very different. But at that time I had no intention of going to court. I knew that the average cost of a divorce in the UK is £20,000. And I was not even married so I was not overly concerned about any need for family law. Just extremely alarmed that he was preventing me from even knowing where my son was and then demanding money for visitation. I was slow to see the writing on the wall. Because I could not believe a parent would abuse his own child in this way.

The first family lawyer I went to see for my initial one-hour £400 consultation warned me that although Krasnopovich had no claim, we were not married and he paid nothing towards my properties and was not named on any title, he might well tie me up in court nonsense that would cost him nothing while running me up a bill as high as £20,000. I thought it ridiculous that I would have to pay as much as £20,000 for Krasnopovich's decision to breach the agreement we made to have a child and pay for his upbringing, just to have sex with his fitness Instructor.

While I was ruminating over finding a lawyer to get some help with finding Sam's location, because at that time Krasnopovich would not disclose the address where Sam was, I was cleaning up the annex in my home where Krasnopovich had stored his overflow files from Krasnopovich McDonald and I came across a file he had discarded with the name TROTTER on the cover.

I remembered the Trotter case, in which Krasnopovich had represented the wife of Mr. Trotter. I am working by memory of what was for a period, Krasnopovich's favorite dinner party story. He told it as follows:

This guy, Mr. Trotter who had sold his successful business for many millions (Garage doors I think by memory, from somewhere up north). He was married to the same wife for decades. Newly rich, the moved south, South West London. They bought a nice home in a prosperous suburb where she, Mrs. Trotter could complete the upbringing of the children while he, Mr. Trotter, bought his dream yacht which he registered in Panama, where, he would spend increasing amounts of time without his wife, who did not share his enthusiasm for sailing. Whilst in Panama, he started an affair with an underage girl, having several children with her. The punchline of Krasnopovich's story is that Mr. Trotter named the Panamanian children the same as his children in the UK. By Krasnopovich's description, this was an unsavory individual and Krasnopovich was at his aggressive best representing the poor discarded Mrs. Trotter.

His entertaining recollection of his fine multi-million-pound win for Mrs. Trotter, honed to a delicious fluency by its frequent feature on Saturday night dinners with friends including family law members, included his memorable catch phrase from the Trotter case *"I like to remind him that he shouldn't be fucking 15-year old's."*

Looking at the Trotter file that day, I remembered from that story that Mr. Trotter's lawyer, one David Clam, had filed a formal complaint against Krasnopovich, for freezing a bank account of his client which he relied on to pay his bills in Panama. Something that he was not empowered to do in family law practice and which placed Krasnopovich in breach of some family law ethical code. After this formal complaint against him was lodged by David Clam, Krasnopovich became concerned. I spent many hours in working through possibilities with him. Possible consequences if the complaint was to succeed. I also knew this was a multi-million-pound case and so assumed that, Mr. Trotter must have known something to choose David Clam, who must be at least reasonably good. I googled his Cambridge Degree, and considered that he would be motivated to take my case as he already knew the character of Krasnopovich. After having been turned down by five lawyers by this time, David Clam seemed my best option.

I saw his phone number in the Trotter file and on impulse, there and then, called Clam. By the end of that five-minute call he appeared all too eager to represent me, starting with a £20,000 retainer. We met at his Cobham office. I explained my position. He seemed to be drooling at the prospect of getting even with Krasnopovich which I thought related to the Trotter case.

"He has to provide you with the child's address. It is the law" he told me with such confidence I decided to retain his services. At that time my financial picture meant I had £20,000 available and so I paid it even though I remember thinking, that's the same price a divorce would cost and we are not even married. I could not have imagined then seeing legal costs as I do now of over £500,000 going to family law because of what happened next. And seeing first-hand how threatening family-law members become when they want payment for their services.

After my failed visitation hearing, hoping to win two nights a month with my son in family court and running up a £40,000 bill watching Clam trying and failing to win more than a few nights visitation, Krasnopovich and Clock prepared a summons, demanding 50% of two of my properties in a legal device, a civil claim called 'beneficial entitlement' based on his word and no other evidence. Unless I paid Krasnopovich a six-figure sum, he would pursue this litigation and obstruct visitation with my son. It seemed ridiculous to me. Beneficial entitlement? Much as if anyone could claim anything just by saying it was promised to them. Surely you need evidence in some form? An email. A witness to a conversation. A letter. A recording. Something? But no. Not in family-law. As the Flaherty ruling makes clear. Jumping forward to after the Flaherty judgment, I spoke with Chris Andiotis, who was involved in advising me from day one. He was incredulous and his comment seems to mirror what I have heard repeatedly from people hearing this case.
"Come on. He can't just say that. You need evidence to make a claim on property. How can you just say 'She promised it to me so it's mine'. It makes no sense in law. You need evidence. You need witnesses."
And so as 2015 came to a close, I was in for another set of legal costs, only this time with an impressive firm with a reputation. FOS. At the same time I migrated the Insurance claim from the lawyer I had retained to pursue the Insurance matter that was by now causing me tremendous financial harm, to FOS as well. (The AXA Flood insurance claim for the flood of 2014).
This is when I met FOS property law partner, Roland Court, who would address the various threads arising from Krasnopovich's fiduciary responsibilities as Trustee Freeholder and his liability arising from failures to claim following the flood and two further insurance claim matters. The first stage was the Permission to Appeal hearing and a date was set for that with a one-hour schedule. At the Royal Courts of Justice. Roland Chambers prepared the notes for the hearing. He decided to use the same barrister, Richard Castello, who had handled the first case, despite my reservations after seeing Richard unable to have the hearing adjourned when he learned Flaherty had taken the case, knowing he would lose. I flew to London for two nights, arriving the night before the hearing and leaving the day after. Roland Chambers and Richard Castello were there and in a late change of Judge, two hours before the hearing, we were told that the family-law President himself would hear the case.
I was dressed in a new Armani Black and white outfit with an Armani cashmere overcoat to ward of the British winter cold. Philip treated me to it for the occasion. I felt good. I was looking forward to my moment in Court. Surely Flaherty's awful judgment could not be allowed to stand. Soon I would get my costs back. And I would get my son back. I had no doubt at all.

28 What are holidays for. Amateur Psychology

Cecelia Flaherty settles back with her champagne glass filled with holiday cheer to dispense with law

When Flaherty's judgment arrived over three months after the hearing, she disclosed her findings are made while on Holiday. Because *"What else are summer holidays for"*. Refreshingly honest professionalism reassuringly weighted in consideration of a child's best interests.

56. I have been asked to look again at the wills and attendance notes that accompanied them and I did so [(what else are summer holidays for!)].

42. There was a lot of detailed evidence explored about the uses of the three flats at different times over the course of the ten year relationship; the mortgages raised; estate agents used as letting agents; the input Mr KRASNOPOVICH had given to MS LEANDROS over the letting out of a property in her own name; the builders used in the major works carried out to 28A and 28B Thameside and to the assistance she had provided to MR KRASNOPOVICH when he set up his own firm of solicitors - Krasnopovich McDonald LLP. Ms LEANDROS, in the course of her evidence was not always sure what had happened. for example there was considerable confusion over mortgages that had existed. The net effect of this confusion was that there were additional bundles (five Lever Arch files and a smaller file known as the "Small Bundle") that were referred to frequently in the course of cross examination. This is not meant to be a critical observation, but it is the reality of a case where it is necessary to look at the way a couple, during their relationship, have used monies. This was a ten-year relationship where fortunes, as between the parties, varied. The star of Ms LEE was in decline while the star of Mr Krasnopovich was rising.

"Not always sure what had happened". What does this mean? I knew exactly what happened. I still know exactly what happened.

It is Flaherty who very clearly does not. The typo that follows is consistent with the standard of consideration in this point. What happened is. I bought a property in 1986. I had a professional IFA, Larry Chester. Larry knew how to shop around for the best loans. Through the years I took out several mortgages, benefitting from interest rate changes and increasing value of my properties. I am an above average intelligence professional person, using the services of a professional IFA. I know exactly what happened on every one of my business decisions on how I paid for my home. If there is any doubt about that, Flaherty had no need to take my word for it. She could easily ask the IFA who made all of the loan agreements for me, had a full statement made and was ready and waiting to give evidence in Flaherty's court. In detective terms, the means Flaherty had enabling her to lie in this way, her *'Not always sure what happened'* point, is only because Flaherty prevented this key witness from giving evidence. Larry Chester would have provided the certain surety of exactly what happened. Removing any possible doubt Flaherty associates with my version.

Flaherty was able to play this two-step move;
1) Claim the defendant doesn't know what she is saying and
2.) Exclude the witness who proves what she is saying is true, because arcane family court contempt law protects her deceit from the light of day, preventing anyone in her court from disclosing specific details of her conduct. Effectively, this contempt law entitles thieving liars to lie and steal without any fear of censure. When these lies cause abuse to a child, then it is safe to say, family-law contempt protects child abusers who know this and can abuse children with impunity. Flaherty as much as told me this directly in the course of her judgment. In so many words;

"I can make an un appealable judgment and if you say anything about what I did in this court I can have you jailed for contempt."

"The star of Ms Lee was in decline while the star of Mr Krasnopovich was rising."

This is the judgement in a child case in family court. Flaherty, a third-rate barrister with almost no demand for her services, has taken the deputy district judge exam, enabling her to earn £500 a day, less than I paid my carpenter to lay my Appalachian walnut floor, and now has the opportunity to share her advanced insights into my sons parent. She has determined that I am a *"star in decline?"* Is that an appropriate observation to make in a family court judgment? Where is Flaherty going with this bubblegum analysis. What does stardom have to do with a claim for '*50/50 like we were married.*' Does this tack lead to a decrease in animosity between the parents to assist the child's best interests? Is it pointlessly and unnecessarily intended for no higher purpose than to establish the supreme authority of this elderly woman for who stardom was never an option or a reality. Certainly in terms of achievement, comparing mine to hers, let's face it, Flaherty's connection with any suggestion of stardom is at best, invisible.

In the matter of stardom, success and failure, the rise and the fall. In how it relates to Flaherty's judgment, my star was Sam. My success in raising Sam as the stay at home parent was quite the opposite of a '*star in decline.*' By any measure, if my material star was in decline, as appears to be the basis for Flaherty's 'declining star' conclusion, I was still successful to the point of a net worth of some £3 million, generating a top 10% in the UK income, without needing to work because it was intentionally developed as passive income, with which I was able to choose my lifestyle being financially independent to the degree that I had never felt further from poverty consciousness in my entire life.

Even if Flaherty's observation is not a misleading convenient lie, and it is true that my '*star was in decline*' none-the-less, I was free to choose from a position of some opportunity that is not available to the vast majority of people whose '*star is on the rise*'. I was financially independent to enable lifestyle choices arising from a passive income making very little out of my reach.

I chose to invest my time and resources in raising Sam as a full-time parent. This was not an expression of failure, of a 'waning star' defaulting into unemployment as a stay at home loser. I was in fact by any measure a successful Landlord, managing a profitable dividend paying stock portfolio, writing books and producing music. Socialising with 'stars' and enjoying the wonderful experience of raising a planned child to be the best he could be. I was happier than ever before. What greater measure of success is there. Especially when that joyfulness is free from financial pressure. And allows for creative expression as my writing and music composition did. Why in the name of fuck would a second rate lawyer claiming £500 a day from that ethical trough of unregulated opportunity called family-court, whose social media claim to coolness is being a 'juvenile delinquent' choose to label me as a 'star in decline' for the decision I made to give 100% of my attention and means to raising a child with every opportunity? Which I believe anyone would agree represented a great success.

Krasnopovich's star was rising. That can be seen as true. From when we met and his low position as a trainee solicitor, until he left as a millionaire owner of his own law firm, it is clearly not inappropriate to refer to his growth as a 'star rising'. What Flaherty has omitted throughout her judicial commentary is the extent of my input and my financial assistance. It is a simple fact, one that Flaherty could have determined for herself by reading the statements in this case, that his 'star rising' is in no small measure, a consequence of my input. Making the Flaherty point of 'stars rising and falling inappropriately foolish in both references.

Just months before Krasnopovich left on father's-day, in April of 2013, he saw the first years accounting with the new firm. He had gone from £35,000 PA trainee working for Christa in Reigate when we met, to £350,000 in ten years as the owner of the firm I paid for and set up for him. This was his first experience of having 'real money'. It took him just a few months from experiencing that thrill, seeing six figure deposits in your bank account, to lose weight, become sexually fixated on a younger, more petite, fitter, fitness instructor, and break up his family for greener pastures, blackmailing the mother by withholding visitation to her son. That is the reality of this particular 'rising star'. He got to rise his star in a younger fitter model. A story he recounted as 'the Pole.'

If we are to relate success to the analogy of 'Stars rising', then Flaherty's use of this cliché is both inappropriate and incorrect. But unsurprising coming from someone whose Twitter ID reads "**Lawyer; juvenile delinquent; lover of champagne and fun.**" Her idea of fun evidently includes abusing children in the legally protected shadows of family court in typo laden judgments based on prejudiced opinion and profiling without researching the facts.

50 Her evidence about the decision to have a child was wholly unconvincing and the criticism - not even veiled criticism - of MR KRASNOPOVICH and his general immaturity, of which I neither saw, heard nor read, exemplifies the overall finding I make that MS LEANDROS has looked back on the relationship with MR KRASNOPOVICH in the light of her unhappiness at its breakdown and has reinvented the past. Quite simply it is my judgment that she has lied on many occasions in her evidence before this court.

Flaherty makes the judgment that I am a liar. This is the evidence in support of her judgment. All of my references in the parental planning matter, one which is documented and a simple fact not even contested by Krasnopovich, are 'lies.' The facts in this case are clear. He says '*she promised me 50/50 like we were married.*' Which flies in the face of the evidence in this case, the word and documentary substantiation by the witnesses, the simple common sense in the fact that if I intended giving him 50% I would have:

1.) Married him
2.) Put his name on a mortgage
3.) Included this information in my will
4.) Seen him include this information in his will that post dates the 'promise'
5.) Accepted money from him for the purchase of the flats he is claiming, bearing in mind 28B, in which he is claiming 50% was bought in 1986, fully paid off and irrespective of how much time he spent staying in that apartment, he never paid one penny towards anything.

"Ms LEANDROS has looked back on the relationship with Mr Krasnopovich in the light of her unhappiness at its breakdown   and has reinvented the past." (The spacing typo is in the original document)

Returning to the theme of Flaherty's penchant for bubble gum amateur psychology. If I 're-invented the past' why is Krasnopovich's name still not on any titles to my properties? A legacy from that reinvented past.

Why is his name not on any mortgage (I had 2 mortgages during the time he was living with me.) Why did he not even know the details of my mortgages.

Why is his promised ownership not evident in my will. Or his will.

Why would 7 credible professionals my witnesses, with insight into Krasnopovich's finances, perjure themselves by giving evidence in court.

And why, if Flaherty believes the past was reinvented by a liar, did she pro-actively obstruct witnesses from showing the evidence she knew they had? Offering impartial documentary evidence in the facts underpinning the very claim she was asked to judge on.

I say again. Because Flaherty made her judgment before a word was spoken and adjusted her words in the written judgment to fit her deliberate deceit, in which the glaring contradictions and opinions expressed as fact can never be confused with someone considering the best interests of a child. Flaherty has formed an opinion guided by a predetermined arrangement to make an award to a fellow member of family-law. Where the facts have interfered with her opinion, she has sought to get rid of the facts entirely, and where that has failed, has set out to blur factual clarity with nonsense, confident her errors would never be examined in an 'un appealable' judgment.

Flaherty is guilty of child abuse. There is an enormous irony in a professional liar of this caliber calling me a liar. Quite simply it is my evidence that Flaherty has lied on many occasions in her conduct in the court hearing which she switched with the appointed judge, DDJ Burkes, on the first morning and that her judgment is a series of lies, written to a low standard of literacy by a professional liar whose lies can be transparently revealed by material evidence, that remains as available today as it was when Flaherty ruled it should be excluded. Flaherty is a lying child abuser, by the definition spelled out by CAFCASS CEO Anthony Douglas, hiding behind family law statutes to protect herself from accountability for the consequences of lying. While concurrently promoting a persona on social media of a party loving champagne guzzling juvenile delinquent.

43. The final point of MS LEANDROS' evidence that I should note is the evidence that her plan for earning money is that she is writing a book about her experiences.

My 'plan for earning money' was to continue exactly as before in my income generating business. How curious that Flaherty should choose to include 'my plan for making money' in her judgment. Obviously done for a reason other than judging on the matter before the court. Why would she need to comment on any other plans for making money when she knew I had a sizeable rental income business.

There is no reason she would comment on my *'plan for making money'* unless it was her intention in advance to take away my money generating source of income. I had no modification or alternative to my previous financial plan, developed over a 30-year period. Generating rental income as a landlord of the property I owned since 1986, making musical recordings and writing books.

Flaherty had already decided that my source of income in Land lording was going to be given away to her colleague. Hence her one-line observation that ignores any reference to the source of the bulk of my income.

Writing the book about my experiences is not something I do for money. Rather it is a service I offer in the name of civic duty. To expose corruption. To not remain silent in the face of child abuse. To leave a record for Sam to know who did what and why. To assist every parent who experiences the shortcomings of a court service that allows people like Flaherty to validate their failures by punishing happy children. Curious that Flaherty would seek to note this comment in her judgment? Clearly building a precautionary reference to a contempt charge. *"You write a book about what I have done here and I will put you in prison. What I do in my court stays in my court."*

27. In relation to the will MR KRASNOPOVICH accepted that he was never asked any question about his beneficial interest. He didn't consider he had any interest in the property because he had the freehold. As he had the freehold he was the legal and beneficial owner. It had been transferred to him in order that it would mitigate the insurance premiums. MR KRASNOPOVICH said, in a most adamant fashion in his evidence *"She did not ask for it back. Absolutely not true"*.

In the matter of the Freehold title. The facts. Why this is perjury by a member of family law.

In 2003, months after Krasnopovich moved in rent free with me the issue of my house reinsurance arose. He convinced me to transfer the Freehold title into his name, in the context of legal advice. A declaration of trust was drafted, on the advice of my IFA, although I discovered much later, he did not sign it. At all material times it is a fact that Krasnopovich was a trustee. Bound by the Freehold contract between lessor and Lessee. With fiduciary responsibilities.

The agreement between us was clear. It would come back to me in about 5 years. It takes some 5 years before the Insurance policy application becomes clear of a claims history. That is, when the question, "Have you had a claim in the past five years" can be answered positively. The fire claim was paid to me in 2002. 2007 would be the five-year mark. The agreement to transfer the title back to me was made in anticipation of it coming back to my name, at no charge, in 2007. In 2007 my IFA checked in with me that this was the case and progressed a new Insurance application in my sole name in anticipation of the transfer. All dated at the time of the Insurance renewal.

Here is written confirmation by an independent third party that the freehold transfer was requested and in the process of being transferred in 2007. Then, one month before the Insurance renewal date, 28A Flooded. It was not workable to transfer the title with an Insurance claim in progress. The transfer date for 2007 was suspended. A new date was agreed between myself and Krasnopovich with the awareness of Larry Chester, for five years later, 2012. And then after the house flooded again in 2008. Another agreement followed, diarizing the return date for 2013. These dates are in Larry Chester's statement. Krasnopovich was aware of this statement as was Clock. What could they do about this? They were relying on saying the Freehold was given to Krasnopovich as proof of his beneficial entitlement. *"Look, she put his name on the title of her home. We have proof in writing. That shows she meant to give him 50% like they were married."*

Yet, clearly, this claim of being the actual Freeholder carried with it a host of consequences. Fiduciary responsibilities. Plus, the IFA was ready and waiting to give evidence on the factual background of how the title came to be in Krasnopovichs' name. How could they work their way around this in DDJ Burkes' court?

In 2013, within a few days of Krasnopovich's departure, aware that I held his domain names and his business website in my name while he still had my Freehold in his name, I wrote requesting the transfer of the title. Soon after, I returned his web domain titles in my name, in a linked agreement, which extended to my lawyer, Clam, writing to his lawyer, Clock. There are many e mails crossing confirming that the (Freehold) title return was requested. The subject arose repeatedly in correspondence, including Chris Andiotis observing (in his statement to the Court) that Krasnopovich had a duty to return the title and should not use it deceitfully to support his beneficial entitlement claim. There were multiple correspondences in legal demands made to Krasnopovich's lawyer by mine, David Clam, which included the paperwork for the transfer at the Land Registry being sent in full anticipation of the titles return in advance of the Insurance renewal in October 2013.

Hence *"He did not ask for it back. Absolutely not true"* is perjury. By Krasnopovich, verified by Flaherty.

Clearly a member of British family law has committed perjury while another member of British family law, one who in her own words claims to be a 'juvenile delinquent who loves champagne and fun' who has prevented the court-agreed witnesses who would show the paper trial proving this lie by Krasnopovich from testifying, has ruled that;

"I found the evidence of Ms LEANDROS on every point wholly unpersuasive. I found the evidence of Mr KRASNOPOVICH credible and persuasive."

But would the judge set down for this case have found *every point wholly unpersuasive?* Would DDJ Burkes have allowed the witnesses? I say Flaherty has ruled that Sam's best interests should be served be generating the maximum animosity possible by allowing a member of family law to profit from perjury. I say this is child abuse by a family court judge in her own words. More importantly, I say one day Sam will read the judgment of Flaherty and be able to decide for himself.

58.   I find that there is ample evidence to support the case that Ms Krasnopovich had a beneficial interest in 28A and 28B Thameside. Now comes the question of the quantification of such an interest and I have no hesitation in concluding that the interest was 50% in both properties.   This was what I find Mr KRASNOPOVICH said on more than one occasion; this was what Ms Krasnopovich had been acting towards; this is what her more than generous payments were buying into. She should have one half of the equity in both flats.

Yet, where is even one example of '**evidence**' however ample?

There is not one piece of tangible evidence beyond repeatedly calling me a mentally infirm liar. The sole evidence Flaherty has presented is her own opinion, formed by clearly disregarding the evidence, the factual matrix that was available, yet disregarded by Flaherty in her first ruling after switching with the appointed Judge to take this hearing.

There is no evidence from Flaherty. Only the opinion of one prejudiced member of family law, disregarding her primary function, to support the best interests of a child, by endorsing a perjuring fellow member of family-law in a financial claim that is based on exploiting the maximum harm to the child's best interests.

My evidence is that both of these members of family-law used, and quite probably continue, to use their position to abuse children. For their own personal enrichment.

29 I want to come with you

Sam has a plan. And he is ready. And so am I but

By the end of February 2016, in total I made 19 visits to the UK since leaving months after the flood of my home in 2014. I was effectively a US resident from shortly after the flood of my home as I had nowhere else to live and could not afford to continue paying Hotel charges to remain in the UK while, thanks to Krasnopovich, the Insurance did not pay. Usually the reason for travel was to see Sam for brief negotiated visits. Visits negotiated between intermediaries as Krasnopovich would not talk to me directly. On the occasion in late 2014, the first in which I was to collect Sam from his School on a Friday and return him to the intermediary for collection on the Sunday, the effects of our long separation were weighing heavily on us both. We still had some Skype contact at that time and had talked about what we would do on this weekend together. All planned meticulously to maximize our time together. I arrived in the UK on the Friday morning of the visitation. I would collect him from his school on Friday, spend two nights in our nearby Hotel, the Four Seasons in Hampshire, just forty minutes away, and then I would fly out hours after returning Sam to Jo's home on the Sunday evening.

With an arrangement hammered out in lengthy emails limiting time, place, and distance from school to accommodate the legal bill for Clock to feel properly rewarded for his significant input (several hours at his hourly rate) which can be measured exclusively in targeting the minimum amount of time his negotiating skills would enable towards facilitating this visit with Sam, I arrived at Sam's school in good time and waited in the courtyard with the mingling mothers, an attractive group of well-dressed affluent looking women aged between thirty and forty five. The kids were led out in a long line, classroom after classroom, to await their release notice, one line at a time. I was tingling with accelerated heart rate excitement.

Eventually I saw Sam's class crossing the sports yard. And he saw me. His beaming face radiating incandescent joy. He was bouncing on his feet with excitement. It was all I could do to stand on the sideline waiting for the teacher to excuse each child in turn. When released by his teacher he bounded over to me and leaped into my arms.

"My mummy".

Unrestrained joy. Hugging me close. How much we had missed each other.

As we walked towards the car with me still carrying him, he was trying to tell me his news. Gathering his pace, to make his intention clear.

"Listen to me". I stopped walking to listen with my full attention.

"I told Dexter that I am not coming back" he said quite seriously.
Determined that I listen properly to what he was saying. His hand went to stroke my cheek. His eyes staring intently into mine.

"Why did you tell him that?" I asked.

"Because I am not coming back here. I am going to stay with you."

I did not know how to reply. I kissed him and hugged him. He tried again.

"I am not coming back. I am going to stay with you. In America."

Earnest eye contact. Pleading. Resolute. Determined.

By this stage in the litigation and the animosity with Krasnopovich I felt for the first time defeated. How could I answer his request. I looked away so he would not see my tears.

Sam and I spent every day of his life before fathers-day 2013 together. It is erring on the side of caution when I say I spent all of his parental time with him whilst Krasnopovich barely spent 10% and post separation, still spent the same amount of time. Some 10% at most. Sam at this time was being raised by a new nanny and an old granny, collecting him from school until Krasnopovich returned from work at 6.30, spending an hour with him on the nights when he was not out networking. And pursuing his romantic interests. Our bond was strong. Sam is my mini-me in so many ways, emotionally and in appearance. And yet despite giving everything I had to the legal fight to see him, the simple truth is, Sam's best interests were not represented in the adversarial process that is British family law.

It was indescribably difficult to have the conversation with him, just 6 at that time, on why he could not stay with me.

I couldn't explain it to myself.

Perhaps eventually, with the writing of this book and the passage of time in Sam's development, his understanding of why we could not leave together as he wanted that day and as I wanted just as much, will be easier to understand.

That was a landmark moment.

That was also the last time I collected him from his school.

The disappointment of knowing Krasnopovich's malicious presence hung over every arrangement was damaging and not in Sam's best interests. That was my call as a parent and I have had no reason to reconsider. Krasnopovich saw Sam's time with me as a defeat. He would get his vengeance. I did not want Sam to be a part of Krasnopovichs' dysfunction. Our relationship was under the cloud cast by Krasnopovichs' legal position. He had the power to direct every moment we spent together. And every subject we were or were not allowed to discuss by his judgment.

Perhaps parents with experience of placing a child's best interests above their own at times of immense animosity with the 'winning' parent will find it easier to relate to what may appear as gross exaggeration, but the pain at being separated from a loved child is indescribable and equally true for the child. In backing away from any engagement with Krasnopovich and British family law, I concluded the chances of their ongoing abuse of Sam would be lessened.

It was beyond heartbreaking to have arrived at that point. The date was February 2016. After almost three years of total child abusing bullshit by Krasnopovich, Clock and Flaherty. My hopes that Krasnopovich would eventually reconcile his understanding of winning with Sam's best-interests had disappeared under the weight of Flaherty's judgment, Clock's ability to charge me thousands for every drop kick to the side of Sam's head and Krasnopovich's paternal negligence. Because Flaherty awarded Krasnopovich's legal costs against me, in actuality, Clock was paid by the court-order making me liable for his costs to obstruct visitation with my son. The injustice was overwhelming.

I can compare it to a court order forcing a child rape victim's parents to pay the rapist damages. It is true to say this decision by Flaherty did cause animosity. It harmed my son's best interests in equal measure to the financial benefit it gave Clock and Krasnopovich. Whatever prospects existed for placing Sam's best interests to the fore had to be considered given he had been apart from me for longer than he was with me. This crucial period in his development; along with the development of our relationship, can never be paid back. I am a tremendously compassionate, accomplished and committed parent. I love my son and placed raising him at the center of my world. How, I wondered, could a judge be made accountable for a loss of this magnitude?

A truly dreadful series of abuses to a child's rights have occurred at the heart of which members of family law have transferred every penny of my estate, including my home and source of income, into obstructing Sam's rights to be with his mother. That this was achieved by a lying member of family law endorsing another member of family laws' lies is just one of the areas in family law I consider in need of reform if we are not to look back in 25 years and wonder how we allowed this barbaric amoral victimizing profiteering into our culture. Lying judges should be made accountable by an appropriate measure commensurate with the extent of their deficiency and not protected by anonymity in unrealistic, counter-productive contempt law.

I understand that there will come a time when Sam will be able to emancipate himself and believe that Krasnopovich's opportunities for alienating him from his mother will not overcome the bond that is there. I was reassured in the course of therapy, particularly by my psychiatrist Mark Zetin, that the neural pathways of children are well developed by age four. I believe Sam will never forget the loving bond between us. Even if it takes him until his teens to find me. My parental responsibility following my decision in February 2016 became to be well in myself. To move on from the raped experience Flaherty, Clock and Krasnopovich left me with. To walk away from the material loss in the UK and work on starting again to provide a beautiful loving home with schooling opportunities for Sam when he is able to find a way to get there. And in the meantime, to keep sending him the twice weekly letters and photographs. Even despite the 9 months in 2016 where I did not have his address and he had no way of knowing why I was not contacting him.

The 9-month period when I was unable to find out where Sam was, thanks to British family law, ended in December 2016 when Krasnopovich finally provided me with Sam's address. Since then I began writing twice weekly. Whether Sam receives my letters is open to speculation. I sent them none the less. Three or four photos in each one. With stories written on the back. I dated them, and photograph them, and created an archive in case he never saw them. A laborious process that was fun at first, but, absent of any reply as the months wore on, became less so. It's became a huge pile of pictures and words. One day he will be able to tell me how many of them reached him. Perhaps he will enjoy reading the ones he might not have received.

And then we reached the events of December 2018. It seemed I would have Sam for the December holiday. 2 or 3 weeks. Depending. Once again my hopes were raised. I thought it was going to happen right up until the email from Tim Clock making plain that it was not. At the same time I realized my letters were not getting to Sam. That became the decision to stop allocating 2 hours every Monday and every Thursday to the process of getting photo prints and writing messages and sending them via post from Los Angeles to London. Instead I decided to write online. Letters to Sam. I set up a blog and allocated two hours every Monday and Thursday to writing to him. At age 9 I thought this might provide a good opportunity for reading and writing. His interest in reading would be piqued. I would write mindful of assisting him with new words and ideas. Influencing his literary education in this modest way, where I had hoped to be far more of an influence as a parent. At this time of writing 'letters to Sam' attracts 2,000 readers daily. Speculation on whether he is reading these weekly posts is abundant. I believe, eventually, he will have found the resources to access the internet and follow the blogs. Certainly, every week I set aside two hours to write these letters to him with a feeling that it provides a contact between us. Our virtual visitation.

As a consequence of Krasnopovich/Clock and Flaherty's comprehensive victory in family court and the misfortune of a flood to my home, I have found myself starting again in a new country, at fifty, with my fourth nationality. I thought I would be able to remain in the UK for the rest of my life. I was happy as British citizen and resident. I am unhappy that Flaherty's judgment ended my opportunity to remain in my home in my home country. However, from this new beginning I am comforted by the lesson I take from my experience in family court and my opportunity to share it for the benefit of others.

Children of separated parents are vulnerable in ways that are widely recorded.

Litigation causes animosity and animosity is never good for children. But litigation in family court is good for members of family-law.

Very good.

The family-law members, lawyers, barristers and DDJ Flaherty have won collectively many hundreds of thousands of pounds directly in charges from money I will now never have to spend on my son's future. Sam's childhood with me has at no time been considered above the value of litigious persecution for enriching members of British family law. Whether karma is real or imaginary, Sam knows where he fitted within the context of the decisions I made. And equally, Sam will know how he featured in the decisions made by Krasnopovich, Clock and Flaherty. And the greedy incompetence of the hapless David Clam.

After that weekend visit where I was unable to provide Sam with his clearly expressed wish, in which he was aware of what it was he was asking and ready with whatever responsibility a 5-year-old could muster to commit unconditionally, drew to its melancholy close, I explained our situation as best I could. I had to return with Sam to Jo's house in Thameside, from where Krasnopovich would collect him (an hour after I would leave to ensure not seeing me). It was a sad journey to our last farewell, in the entrance hall at Jo's house on Thameside. He said very little until we faced each other. "I have to go now." And we hugged. A hug where we both burst in to tears. He clung on so tightly.

"*I miss you so much*" he said.

"*I miss you so much too*".

He cried onto my shoulder. Heaving heartbreaking sobs of sorrow. Eventually I had to prize him off. I handed him over to Jo, and walked out to the car to drive to the airport. I was still unable to stop the tears by the time I reached Heathrow. The words heart-broken could never be more accurately placed. I felt bereft of all hope. Focusing on one breath at a time. Jo texted me half an hour later to assure me that Sam had stopped crying and was playing a computer game. She was a great friend at that time to Sam and to me.

I flew back to LAX in a haze of tearful numbness. Philip collected me from LAX and for days afterwards I felt incapacitated by grief. Deep, absolute, heartbroken sorrow. I felt very strongly that Sam was experiencing a similar emotional wrench. Rationalizing his pain in the context of culpability brought me to a specific conclusion. It was clear Krasnopovich and Clock would continue with their litigation come what may. My unrealistic hopes that Krasnopovich might see Sam's sorrow at missing me, or even the benefit to him so clearly associated to his time with me, were dissolved in the acid reality of this acrimonious litigation.

I was finally convinced his assurance that it '*Will not stop.*' (Unless you give me a six-figure sum) was never going to be mitigated by any concern for Sam's well-being. I determined that my hopes he was capable of acting as a responsible parent were past. I saw him in the reality of what he was. And that was difficult. How do you best explain to a young child that their parent has behaved as is the case with Sam's parent.

30 Doctors. What do they know

In breaking alt-truth news, deputy judge determines doctors can be discounted on the grounds of 'does not suit my narrative'

Common comments from well-intentioned friends that I would hear throughout this five-year trial by British family law included '*I don't know how you cope.*'

I cannot start addressing this point without referencing family-court deputy, switch judge Flaherty's judgement that I am 'mentally infirm'. The repeated premise by switch judge Flaherty that underpins her judgment, whether observed as an ironic reference, or as an actually real thing. If she is right, I am mentally infirm. And how I have coped with the trauma of this family court judgment validating the blackmail payment for visitation with my son and ensuring that I am not able to even speak freely with him on Skype, must be seen in the context of how the mentally infirm cope. Irony prompts me to observe that my challenge would have been all the more difficult if Flaherty's judgment was in fact correct. And I am mentally infirm.

How I have coped, whether hampered by mental infirmity, or not, depending on the extent of Flaherty's lie in her judgment, is a subject worth sharing.

I will start with one of the first lessons I arrived at during my work as a young child coping with my first profound loss. I loved my dog Heidi. I was 10 when I lost one parent. But I had a German Shepherd, named Heidi. She was my constant companion. And then, just weeks after my 11th birthday, Heidi died. She cut her paw, and started bleeding. She was on the edge of life and death overnight. And the next morning she died. I was 11 and I was bereft.

At this difficult time, instead of receiving parental help with advice and guidance, I found the blank canvas of my own imagination to provide my own therapy. Looking back, I realize I unwittingly became my own psychotherapist. My resource pool was music and books. Clearly, god and prayer did not cut it in my predicament, where the power of magical thinking and imaginary friends was already discounted. I needed sensible rules to live by to make sense of profound loss. And understand the finality of separation. In this maudlin time and place I worked diligently towards my own set of rules to live by. Discrimination came early in that process. There was no shortage of people looking to offer free advice. And yet I learned, everybody has an opinion but that of itself, meant very little.

I would discriminate on who I took advice from. That started me on a path that I have seldom strayed from. Choosing friends wisely. Choosing teachers wisely. And choosing pupils wisely. I have throughout my life been tremendously fortunate to have attracted many friends who have revealed themselves to be kind and wise. We attract the information we need if we discriminate wisely in receiving advice.

Without undervaluing my gratitude towards the many without whom I would not be here today, (literally, this attack by a family-law member hell bent on winning at all costs was a life-threatening experience) there are several medical professionals who were significantly instrumental in informing my position and in particular, my position regarding 'parental alienation'. Enabling me to measure appropriately the disclosure of personal details in the context of what is best for the child, and particularly avoiding any reference which might contribute towards alienating Sam from his Father.

Sadly this consideration was never reciprocated. Not by the father, his lawyer or his friendly lying family court deputy district judge, the champagne and fun-loving juvenile delinquent. It became clear to me that Krasnopovich acted as he did reliant on the belief that he was protected from his son ever finding out. He could freely abuse the child and engage in the accepted version of parental alienation, but if I disclosed details of his conduct, I would be committing an offense?

This deceitful double standard in family law was raised from the outset by Krasnopovich, in his first email blocking the original weekend visits proposed in July 2013 that '*You can never talk to Sam about anything to do with me.*' Because it is obvious (from Sam's disclosure as well as in Skype examples) that Krasnopovich has presented prejudiced views in the context of parental alienation, I have not varied in my consideration of how best to present age appropriate detail in Sam's best interests.

Simply put, I have been aware of parental alienation from the outset. And at no time have I compromised my relationship with Sam by opportunistically using parental alienation in any of our exchanges. On the one hand, clearly I have to provide answers to Sam for the questions he has, including those already raised. On the other, his age and the dynamics of acrimonious litigation making the likelihood of agreeing a mutually workable age appropriate explanation on why Flaherty ruled as she did against his best interests, requires consideration on many levels. Starting with basic contact with Sam.

My first specialist professional advisor after my GP, was my therapist at the Priory in Barnes. This structured my thinking along how to remain in contact with Sam when the weight of Krasnopovich and Clock's aggressive litigation made every opportunity to visit a trial by fire.

Even defeating my application in Court for two nights a month, and explaining that decision to Sam's Godmother, Jo, as "*I didn't want Andrea to get any ideas so I nipped it in the bud.*"

In simple terms: Directly after leaving, Krasnopovich refused to provide me with Sam's address and when I brought a court application for visitation, he went to extraordinary, unprecedented lengths to prevent Sam spending even one night with me. As a member of family law he was able to play that game – using a QC and applying for costs with a last minute 'ambush disclosure' and the willingness to lie to the CAFCASS official. All of which family law allowed him, even though I spent top dollar, £40,000 in pursuit of even basic visitation that the law provides for free for even dead-beat parents who barely know their own children. This is a child not raised 50/50 by both parents, but easily 90% only by myself. The fact that I was defeated in such a basic application for such a small amount of time with my son stands in isolation as an example of how easily Krasnopovich was able to abuse both the spirit and the executive function of family law in an abuse so transparent words fail me.

This guy stopped his son seeing his mother by lying in court. By spending astonishing amounts, bringing a QC to a preliminary hearing for visitation, and costing me astonishing amounts just to win one night on weekends for my son to return to his bedroom, all the while putting in writing and in reference to family tying to help as intermediaries, that unless he got £100,000 he would 'not stop' doing that thing he is 'Shit hot at.'

Those Priory sessions at that time established that regular letters in the mail to a child caught in 'acrimonious litigation by one parent' is one constant that cannot be overvalued. I realized during that same course of therapy with a professional of the highest order, that the only way to openly and honestly address what happened is to openly and honestly address what happened.

It is Sam's right to know. He has been the victim of abuse by family court and by members of family law. He should have the details available to him to enable him to reach his own conclusions on who did what. My duty is to report the facts honestly and openly. Whether it contravenes family court secrecy law or not. The highest purpose here is providing the information for the child own assessment. Be it now or later in life. If the conduct of Clock and Krasnopovich and Flaherty's ruling is not parental alienation and child abuse, or irregular abuse of a child's rights in any way, then it will be clear to Sam as it will to anyone else looking at this judgment and the circumstances around it.

If they acted in Sam's best interests, then the facts will be self-evident. And the need for them to be protected from Sam finding out, irrelevant. If they all told the truth then there's no reason to hide behind anonymity in the guise of protecting the child.

Bearing in mind the first six months post separation are crucial for the child relationship with both parents. It was this first six months where Krasnopovich went far beyond what is acceptable to ensure Sam could not have unfettered time with me. And once he succeeded with that, the damage was done. No one made him accountable. He knew he could get away with anything.

Soon after arriving in California I consulted a Psychiatrist, who was referenced in relation to my PTSD and grief counselling therapy. Mark Zetin, who became a valuable sounding board in the many considerations affecting my life.

Mark was referred as a leading California doctor. Bearing in mind I am particular about who I take advice from and have a low threshold of tolerance for less than brilliant therapists. I liked Mark from the get go. A sensitive, articulate, sharp, informed mind. And very relaxed with it. There appeared to be a mutual admiration. He showed real interest in the workings of British family law. He took a real interest in my story and I recognized he was offering a high level of well-informed professional medical advice. He became a great sounding board in formulating an informed position with respect to the balance between looking after my own health and making the right decisions in respect of Sam's best interests. He was even generous in his charges to me, reflecting his personal interest in my sons circumstances.

I can summarize Dr. Zetin's overview following his insight into Sam's treatment by British family law as being staggered. *"I am staggered by the ignorance of this court. You should not consider this normal or acceptable conduct."*

As time went by, the 'Three Psychiatrists' moment arrived. The astonishingly abusive debacle by Flaherty, with her court order for three psychiatrists to provide a reference on my ability to instruct a solicitor. (Capacity for conduct.) Dr. Zetin's opinion based on the detail he was shown of Flaherty's conduct was that Flaherty was clearly unfit to represent children in court. Had this been in the US, he explained to me, based on his own experience, she would have been removed from the case. And quite probably prosecuted for negligence and child abuse based on an expert witness (such as himself) reporting her misconduct.

While I was receiving these frankly ridiculous contradictory emails about '*capacity to instruct*' and '*three psychiatrists and you choose one*' and then '*there is only one psychiatrist in California and you must see her*' I was having weekly sessions with a leading Psychiatrist who could not only attest to my 'capacity' but who was up to speed with the proceedings and had a valuable insight to offer in respect of the child's welfare.

There is a connection between acrimonious litigation and a child's best interests. That connection resolves to the understanding of child abuse. Any family-court judge tasked with decision making on a child's best interests has a duty to be as informed as possible. Turning away information that relates to and assists the child's best interests in negligence. It is willful child abuse.

Dr. Zetin wrote at length to Flaherty. Flaherty's comments on Dr. Zetin appear in her judgment. Dismissive. Unconvinced. Disregarded. And this judgment is from a lying judge happily promoting her social media profile as "*Lawyer; juvenile delinquent; lover of champagne and fun.*"

My observation is that – Flaherty was caught out by a medical professional who outranks her significantly in the business of child psychology. Her defense against this negligence in considering the child's best interests is evident in her own hand in her judgment comments on Dr. Zetin. She is not convinced he is a real doctor because she is not seeing what she would expect to see.

One other medical profession discounted as unworthy in her judgment is Dr. Samuel. A leading sleep doctor in California, who has helped with my sleep disorder. I have insomnia issues. The traumatic events of fathers-day and the persecution by family court, being attacked in the street by a goon hired by Krasnopovich and Clock, and the constant barrage of aggressive letters costing me hundreds of thousands of pounds, affected my sleep patterns.

What cannot be overstated in my experience and that of anyone going through similarly traumatic child related stressful litigation, is insomnia. Without proper sleep the cumulative harm to mental wellness is considerable.

This condition affected the Flaherty hearing in that for the duration of that hearing with all the shenanigans going on around me, I was operating on virtually no sleep. By the time I was on the witness stand, I had not slept for many days and was on prescription medication that meant I was not able to draw on my usual resources in calling a group of child abusing liars exactly what they were.

This is not a case of mental infirmity. It is a case of having the right to be represented in court. In the circumstances of Flaherty hijacking that hearing and dismissing my witnesses and then attaching me as she did with every cynical, snide comment, I would have considered it no less than fair to adjourn, as I requested until I was well enough to speak without the disabling effects of being sleep deprived and affected by the obvious shenanigans of being told she had a gripe against my barrister which guaranteed we would lose, and then seeing her forbid any witnesses.

In such an adversarial arena, disadvantaging one side so completely obliterates all notions of fairness and equality. Quiet clearly, as anyone interested in appropriate conduct by a family-court judge, reading the sequence of events leading up to that switch judge hearing will conclude without reservation; that hearing should have been adjourned. Until I was well enough to speak articulately. Surely it is a right in law to have the opportunity to defend yourself without undue impediment?

Although I had a medical-records from three specialist doctors in California, along with the letters from my UK GP, Flaherty dismissed all as not being credible. Rather than respect the authority of the office behind these letters and the process where it is unreasonable to place a disadvantaged person into a dogfight, which is what family court appears as. All Flaherty had to do was express an opinion, her opinion, no matter how unscientific and absent of fact that opinion might be, and she was able to direct events to suit her purpose. And for that there was no accountability. In fact, this hearing has promoted her career and she continues to sit as a deputy district judge.

It is a fact that, despite google being freely available to source background checks to establish whether the doctors she dismissed as not credible were in fact exactly what they purport to be, Flaherty did not take this obvious remedy to doubting the credentials of the doctors.

Instead she dismissed medical accounts, which you can read in her own words in her judgment, as a result of which we have yet another instance of Flaherty presenting unsubstantiated opinion as fact. Even though the full weight of evidence suggests the four doctors she finds 'unconvincing' are;

1.) An NHS GP of many years standing and my GP for 15 years.

2.) A California GP (Primary physician) of many years good standing. Still my PCP to this day, winning user review awards as best Physician in the area for a number of years.

3.) A leading California Psychiatrist, author and lecturer.

4.) One of the leading Sleep Apnea specialists in California.

Flaherty's case is that all four of these doctors conspired with awful Andrea, the mentally infirm liar who promised poor Krasnopovich half of his house and then withdrew that promise to make up stories, which clever Cecelia saw right through. She was far too smart for their grand conspiracy. In the court of Flaherty a medical report is only as good as Cecelia's opinion of that medical report. If she decides to exclude it, it doesn't exist.

Either these four doctors are real and what they reported on in my case is true. Or Cecelia Flaherty is a liar who deliberately discounted all four doctor's reports in order to bulldoze through her dishonest predetermined child abusing judgment that rewarded he colleague in family law with multiple millions.

It is either one or the other. Both possibilities cannot co-exist.

My very clear opinion is that clever Cecelia is fundamentally dishonest. A "Lawyer; *Juvenile delinquent; lover of champagne and fun*". A trivial person using her position having passed the Deputy District judge exam to support parental alienation and child abuse by being grossly incompetent, and not even doing that with any competence. Without the key tool in her skill set, the lie, her role in my case would have been very different. I expect when she saw the word JUDGE before her name, her vanity went through the roof. Her years of low achievement in the lower reaches of occasional work as a family law barrister put behind her with this new cloak of invincibility. A Judge. All powerful in her court room. Able to live out her fantasies of being the person she had never been able to before. Time for champagne and fun.

I continue doing the best I can for Sam at this time currently making a record of events primarily for his benefit. I have however come up against a powerful obstacle and an immovable force. Unscrupulously committed to taking any opportunity during communication between me and Sam, be it in a Skype chat or a Without Prejudice email, to aggressively litigate. Sam is been aware from the outset that he is the subject of litigation and has on more than one occasion repeated '*I don't want to be used like a football.*'

The best I can do to protect him from further abuse is to disengage from any contact between Krasnopovich and Clock. Neither has Sam's best interests at heart.

After the 9 month wait until his father sent me the address, the sole contact between my boy and me was twice-weekly letters that I sent by post, containing photographs and reminders that I think of him all the time and miss and love him. However, in December of 2018, when it looked very much as if he was to be allowed to visit me for the December holidays before that hope too was dashed, I realized the letters I sent were not getting to him. I decided to keep writing and sending pictures, but to do it online, in a blog. I have no idea if these letters get to him and assume that they do not while I hope they do. Hope for the best and plan for the worst. I suppose one day I will find out if he received some or any of them.

In paper, envelope and stamp terms before I went digital, I estimate to date with over 5 years past since he was removed from my home, and allowing for the total period of some 12 Months in which Krasnopovich refused to provide the address to prevent the postal correspondence, let's say I have for 48 months sent two letters a week. That is eight letters a month – with three photo stories in each. Per month – 24 photo stories. In total that is I don't know. 48 months X 24 photo stories. About 1,152 photos with stories. Wherever I go I find pictures that represent this moment in my life and my love for him, and write a story on the back. The switch to digital has made it easier.

31 New lawyers for appeal

John introduces me to a top City firm who agree to overturn Flaherty's 'horrible' judgment and take on the property matter for the Insurance, freehold and fiduciary failures

On 13th May, 2015, after the Flaherty hearing but before her judgment, which took more than three months to reach me, John Milos, my Knightsbridge based Greek close friend for 35 years recommended I prepare for the worse, that Flaherty was going to judge as we all expected, and get ready for an appeal. John introduced me to a top City firm, Friedman Oldfield Shutterworth, and arranged a preliminary consultation by phone. With a senior partner. During that call he identified the distinction between the Civil law aspect of claiming Beneficial Entitlement and how it was introduced into family Court for the advantages it would give for the more personality-oriented judgments in family Court, which is exactly what Krasnopovich/Clock/ Hazelwood intended when filing a TOLATA in family Court. His beneficial entitlement claim had no business in family court.

That consultation chat with FOS gave me some confidence and I resolved to fire Clam and wait for the judgment before deciding on my next move. Concurrent with the family law matter, I had the freehold and house insurance litigation causing many problems in my life. I had still not received one penny from Insurance and was by this time down over £200,000 in making up Insurance shortfall. Whilst awaiting the Flaherty judgment, which I expected would reflect the very clear impression I arrived at three minutes after the hearing started, I prepared a background document for FOS. As a result of which I was to be represented in the family side by Roland Chambers and in the Property side by Roland Court. Both younger partners in FOS. A 'top' London firm. Here is the briefing email I sent.

From: Andrea Lee
To: Roland Chambers, Roland Court
Ref: Krasnopovich vs Lee

Nico Krasnopovich TOLATA claim.

Some background regarding current proceedings with DDJ Flaherty.

The three-day hearing set for April 13th over ran. My solicitor, David Clam was dreadfully incompetent. To the point that I believe I have a very strong case for negligence and a complaint to the Law Society over his billing.) *Example*: He charged me over £12,000 for 6 witness statements, all-ready weeks before hearing date. For reasons known best to himself, he filed on the Friday before the Monday hearing. (Possibly because this mirrors the ambush timing of what Tim Clock did to him in their last encounter, a preliminary hearing for visitation.)

As a result the judge Cecelia Flaherty, (A stand in late notice appointment, replacing the appointed judge, DDJ Burkes, on the morning of the trial), in what appeared to me as alarmingly suspicious, made her first ruling in dismissing the witnesses. Responding to Hazelwood's claim they were an 'ambush' because of Clam's late service.

Being undoubtedly crucial in a he-said-she-said case with no evidence presented by Plaintiff, this was quite wrong of Clam to not ensure the witnesses were allowed. The barrister, Richard Castello agreed that it was an 'ambush' but also said the judge was wrong to not admit them and this would be grounds for an appeal. If this judge, who was clearly prejudiced from the outset, rules against me then I believe the witness statement failure will be an important consideration in what follows. There was no excuse for serving late. Clam just didn't get around to it until the last day. He was late on several occasions, in breach of the court direction. Whoever is most at fault here, Clam for filing late or Flaherty for refusing witnesses, the most important matter in this case should be, what is best for Sam. And by slanting the outcome so deliberately one direction, Flaherty has harmed Sam's prospects immeasurably. The hearing was set out for 3 days to allow for multiple witnesses at the preliminary hearing. He brought no witnesses. I had 6.

Meanwhile Krasnopovich's TOLATA case is built on nothing. Only that he says I 'promised him half my house. But only half of two out of three flats I own which adds some mystery to the confusion. (Flats I have owned since 1986 when he was 14.) He brought no witnesses and has nothing in writing. It is a bogus legal tactic devised by his solicitor Tim Clock, inviting me to take a commercial view and settle. Krasnopovich has made me WP written offers before he retained Clock which demand money but make no mention of any ownership promise. That post-dates his appointment of Clock. He said in the Preliminary Directions hearing that he was going to 'bring witnesses. The witnesses she referred to turned out to not exist. They were witnesses in his imagination alone, impulsively referenced at the preliminary directions hearing as a threat now exposed as a lie. When asked why there were no witnesses he revealed he intended calling a witness, and that witness was a dinner guest who Krasnopovich claims overheard me promise to give her half my house. That sole witness turned out to be a barrister and DDJ Dia Mirza, a friend who I was extremely kind towards in the past. It then turned out that Dia did not show up as a witness because she had no memory of this conversation ever taking place. The reason for this is because no such conversation ever did take place. Flaherty simply glossed over this in typical style. Where the facts don't match her pre determination, she simply offers some amateur psychology interpretation, placed somewhere at third grade level. Bland opinions expressed as facts only because they are her opinions and she is a judge. So it must be true.

Even on Krasnopovich's own position not only are there no witnesses as he said there would be, but the sole witness he refers to says this conversation never happened. Even if it beggars all sensibility that I would have only ever made this multi-million-pound gift promise on one occasion to one 'witness' who happens to be a Barrister and a DDJ. Dia was not prepared to lie on Krasnopovich's behalf.

On the face of it, this aspect alone completely discredits Krasnopovichs' lying claim.

Not one shred of evidence at all. He doesn't even provide a reliable date this alleged promise took place (Answering at different times in different statements as 2004, 2005 and then 2006.) But not able to say exactly when, although this would have been the biggest windfall of his entire life by some margin and you would expect a lawyer putting themselves forward as expert in co habitation law to have something in writing even if just a diarized form. Krasnopovich has not one note of any kind. Because no such conversation ever took place. How is this not as obvious as the light of day?

This is just a desperately wrong situation. In which a young boy is prevented from seeing his mother by a judge who has erred repeatedly. Who quite clearly made a decision before the doors of the court opened.

My lawyer David Clam is at fault on many levels. He has been paid over £160,000 in fees and still wants more as we now have a day of submissions to come. Submissions are delayed for reasons of health. I have a doctor's note confirming that I am unwell. The stressors caused by this persistent ridiculous litigation preventing me seeing my son unless I pay a ransom amount has affected my positive outlook and left me depressed. Medical records confirm I should not have given evidence in court (April 14 and 15th) as I was medicated and traumatized by the events unfolding before my eyes. Suffering from debilitating depression, extreme insomnia and extremely anxious, triggered by the news from my barrister that there might be a switch judge, followed by If we get Judge Flaherty we will lose' Followed by the sight of Flaherty fluttering her eyes at Castelo two minutes into his opening submission in a way that suggested, we might as well all go home now; the judgment is made. As such my ability to speak was affected. I was not able to answer questions on un related matters with access to my usual recall of memory. My right to a defense was impaired. Confirmed by medical evidence. I found the experience surreal. As if I was being mugged. I was asked by Philip how I felt later that night when the hearing adjourned, and my honest answer was '*as if I have been raped.*'

It was simply an awful abuse of a system. Unrelated to the ethical standards we associate with a fair and transparent judiciary.

The stand in judge, DDJ Flaherty, suggested she was going to make it an order of court that I am not allowed to sue Krasnopovich for the house insurance or the breach of copyright. It seemed to me she was trying to interfere with justice in California by trying to make me indemnify Krasnopovich from any wrongdoing there. Krasnopovich broke the law in California by recording me without consent or permission. Called Breach of Privacy, in which he has pleaded guilty by writing about this recording to a third party. A second offense in California in which he is bang to rights guilty. I don't think that is in the Judge's power to rule on a case in the USA, although as the case is adjourned, no judgment has yet been made. Surely the whim of a family court DDJ cannot overrule the rule of law. If she does rule that I can't sue for my home to be fixed, then it would be a breach on many levels. I pay Insurance premiums to have my home repaired in an incident. An incident occurred. I have the right to pursue liability against the responsible party, in this case the Lessor, Krasnopovich. Who is in any event a trustee of my Freehold title and bound by that agreement to fiduciary responsibilities which he is clearly in breach of on a number of different levels, including bringing proceedings against me based on a lie. Clearly Krasnopovich has used the breach of his fiduciary responsibilities to cause me maximal financial harm. I am not sure how a DDJ has the authority to make a ruling on a property law matter. A property matter that has no bearing on the claim being heard in her court. Is this not clear evidence of prejudicial collusion between two members of British Family law?

Unfortunately DDJ Flaherty became taken with Hazelwood's B actor approach of starting many questions with "*I put it to you Ms. Lee, that you are lying when you say…..*" joining in the spirit of this aggressive approach which, even if it was the truth, would still be aggression towards one parent by the other which can only ever increase the acrimony that is never in the child's interests. None the less, even the judge found this appropriate, happy to lie whilst by calling me a liar. Example: when I answered Hazelwood's question saying 'I bought 28 Thameside in 1986.'
'I put it to you that you are lying he said' I said. 'That is not correct I am not lying'. At which point Flaherty interjected with
"*I can read Ms. Lee. Plainly you bought 28B Thameside in 1986. 28 Thameside is the whole house. You only bought one flat.*" Simply put. This judge is calling me a liar on a fact in which she is completely wrong. A liar is lying to call me a liar? Absent of working checks and balances and any prospect of accountability?
Realising that this judge didn't have a basic grasp of Freehold/leasehold I became all too aware that explaining that I was telling the truth because **I did buy 28 Thameside in 1986** and that a simple look at the Land Registry records confirms this would alienate the judge irreparably. How foolish do you have to be to not understand that someone can buy a leasehold title, in this case 28B Thameside, whilst at the same time buying a freehold title, in this case 28 Thameside?

If this was a legal hearing then there is much wrong with British family law.

I pointed out the dishonesty in the cross examination along with the risible credibility of the judge's interruptions to both Castello and Clam, who told me that these are closed proceedings and I cannot repeat anything that goes on in court. So, they can do as they choose, lie without any concern over censure? Present opinions as facts. And there is nothing to be done about it? I formed the clear impression that the proceedings were no more than the barrister and judge taking turns to call me a liar and had nothing whatsoever to do with the reason for the hearing. The plaintiffs lying claim for beneficial entitlement. I essentially gave up any hope of being heard at that point and became something of a bemused spectator. Voiceless.

Essentially, exposing someone like myself who is traumatized to begin with to a traumatic adversarial attack in the name of the Law designed to represent the best interests of children being used in this case specifically for the monetary gain of a member of British law, lying in a British family court, has proven in this case to be spectacularly harmful to the interests of my son, and is in my view child abuse. Conversely, Krasnopovich lied repeatedly without any word from my barrister. During my oral testimony, during the repeated lying accusations, I told the judge I was unwell and we discussed the medication I was on. The judge had already read the three doctors notes relating to my medical condition and should have known from this disclosure that I was not medically well enough to be in court and at the very least needed some protection from this over-measured adversarial approach, being called a liar over and over again. She said '*everyone who comes to court is depressed'* trivializing and minimizing my medical condition. Repeatedly starting lines with reference to my 'mental infirmity'. Profiling me. Clearly this judge seized on my traumatized state as something to use against me rather than respect the opportunity any defendant has to be properly represented in court.

Wherever she was able to insert the words, 'mentally infirm' in a sentence about me, she did. There was no way of misinterpreting her aggressively hostile manner towards me. From the first words spoken. Conversely, when Krasnopovich gave evidence, she repeatedly interrupted to assist him. And when Krasnopovich broke down in tears recalling the trauma of his father's death, Flaherty was visibly moved, offering words of consolation and caring. My barrister Richard Castello didn't call Krasnopovich a liar even once, even, as was so often the case, when he was lying. I was extremely disappointed to note that Castello appeared to give up about two minutes into his opening submission when Flaherty rolled his eyes at him. His body language spoke of accepting defeat. His subsequent efforts did little to dispel this clear impression from the outset of the hearing. I formed the impression this was his idea of *"You win some, you lose some. Either way, I'll still get paid."*

There was a clear and transparent disparity between how the judge treated the member of family law, the plaintiff, and how she treated me. I think that if you keep badgering a witness with unfounded accusations and especially one who is unwell, sleep deprived and medicated then it is a matter of concern for the court that no one said anything. After the hearing I have felt traumatized, on top of the ongoing trauma of not being able to see my son. It feels a lot like being raped. Physically and emotionally. How did it get to this where he has a realistic chance of winning half of one or even two of my properties? And how is it that I cannot see my son without having to spend a fortune on lawyers every time. How is it he can breach the visitation order, removing the child from the UK at will, without any censure. Ever.

Especially after I spent over £160,000 on a lawyer who assured me he had no case; that I had the right to know the address of where my son was living and that I could expect to have regular visitation immediately. I am now in the position where I may have to sell my home. All three flats just to pay my legal debts. On top of which the flood costs are ridiculous. Possibly £500,000 to restore the property to pre flood condition. I will have lost my primary source of income, my rental properties, and I will have no place to live and no means with which to rent a place to live. And no prospect of seeing Sam again without litigating, which I now don't have the means to do, and having seen how the family court system works, I have very little confidence that even if I could raise the money to pursue visitation through court, there is very little prospect of success.

All because a dishonest divorce lawyer worked the system so well, and a polite but ineffectual older generation lawyer, David Clam, failed so spectacularly to match Krasnopovich's legal performance despite charging me over £160,000.

My summary:

Along the way I have made several attempts to settle to end the awful acrimony so detrimental to Sam's prospects. The last attempt on the day before the proposed submissions hearing which was accepted by Krasnopovich and confirmed by

Hazelwood before being 'un agreed' in favor of more animosity generating litigation. The obstacle to settling is that Krasnopovich knows the Insurance claim he is currently liable for has issues and will not settle unless I waive all rights to pursue him for anything. Indemnifying him for his fiduciary failures as Lessor. Bringing this BE claim against me whilst the Lessor is itself a breach of his fiduciary responsibilities. He has clearly acted in bad faith with the flood claim and is responsible for seeing that I have received nothing from the AXA, causing me tremendous financial hardship and meaning the house has an Insurance issue. It is clear that he has lied in the course of the Insurance matters.

He also knows now that 28A Thameside, which was his only claim originally for beneficial entitlement, may well be worth less than the mortgage owing if the re tanking bill is not paid by Insurance following his fiduciary negligence. So he could be left with having to pay a bill rather than receiving any money if I am forced to sell 28A Thameside without the re tanking work. He has placed charges at the Land registry for 28A and 28B to prevent me remortgaging and he is trying in these proceedings to have a controlling interest in me letting 28A and 28B. That prevented me funding a legal defense and caused me considerable financial harm. Right now I need to raise money by re-mortgaging 28B Thameside, which has considerable equity available to me and which my IFA was ready to release. (I had a £500,000 loan ready to go.) However he has placed this charge at the LR and I cannot progress that remortgage. I say he has no claim on 28B and that he has made this claim illegally and should be prosecuted by the LR for making a fraudulent application.

28 Thameside Freehold and Insurance matter for Andrea Lee.

All letters and documents referred to in this letter were available to be introduced as evidence. At all material times Nico Krasnopovich (NK) is the Freeholder, the Lessor in the lease agreement and the sole named Insured party on the current policy. I (Andrea Lee) am the Lessee and the occupant of 28A Thameside, who has not received one penny by way of Insurance since the flood of 8 February 2014 made my home uninhabitable, whilst concurrently being forced into a completely unnecessary legal bill by NK's unsubstantiated litigation for 'Beneficial entitlement' to my home, which at the time of writing exceeds £200,000.

My objectives with this litigation are to pursue fair accounting by the letter of the law in the fiduciary failures by the dishonest Freeholder. And win costs for the dishonest litigation that has obstructed my visitation with my son. Restoring my rights to be with him as close to 50% of the time as possible. And restoring my financial position to its pre incident condition.

Time line.

December 2003. Nico Krasnopovich agrees to take on the responsibilities of the Freehold for 28 Thameside in a Trust agreement with myself, Andrea Lee, the owner, since 1986. A Declaration of trust is drafted and agreed, but, deceptively, never signed by him. Only by myself. The Trust agreement provides for a return of the Freehold on demand, which is understood to be after I am able to resume building Insurance in my name following the large claim in 2001 (a fire claim) that motivated the transfer of the title into NK's name which enabled lower Insurance premiums. No money changed hands for the title transfer. My IFA Larry Chester advised throughout this procedure, as he was involved with the existing policy that was to be replaced by the one in NK's name, and he is aware of the trust agreement and the Declaration of Trust document and a witness to this effect.

NK then insured Thameside in his name while I paid all the Insurance bills. This continued annually going forward.

In 2007 the 'claim history' for me Insuring in my own name expired and I approached IFA Larry Chester to reinsure the property in my name. I advised Larry Chester that I had agreed with NK that he would transfer the Freehold back to my name for this purpose. Larry Chester set about preparing Insurance quotes for the cover and confirmed by memo that the freehold was to be returned into my name. However this policy was not taken up because 28 Thameside flooded before the transfer could occur. In that two-week period, before the Insurance renewal and transfer of the title, the property flooded. An Insurance claim followed and the title stayed in NK's name for this reason. In 2013 I requested the return of the title again and in anticipation of its return took out buildings and contents cover with Fairtimes Insurance Brokers at a cost of some £1,400. This was timed to replace the expiring policy in NK's name, in November 2013. NK was not resident in 28A Thameside at is time.

The policy was paid for and accepted. Two weeks after the acceptance date and the renewal of the new policy date, Fairtimes brokers contacted me to say they had been contacted by NK to say that they had to cancel my policy as it had to be issued in his name because he did not intend returning the Freehold title. He claimed then he was the Freeholder. Without consultation or agreement with me the brokers cancelled the policy on NK's instruction. NK took out a buildings policy on 7 Thameside, but cancelled my contents policy without notification and did not renew the contents policy. I wrote to NK shortly after this, in November 2013, with written confirmation that he had cancelled the policy without my authority and he would therefore be accountable for any costs should he refuse to continue withholding the return of the Freehold.

Just three months later, on February 8th 2014, 28 Thameside flooded. 28A became uninhabitable. I was not in the UK at the time, but returned to examine the property. It was immediately apparent that the property had flooded because the tanking had failed, confirmed by Insurers surveyor who cited 'Breached tanking' as the cause of the flood. It was clearly apparent the property was uninhabitable. There was foul water included in the flood and the boiler appeared to be terminally damaged. No heating and no hot water, and initially, no electricity either.

I undertook **emergency remedial works**, restoring the electricity, and having the property pumped out and attempting to mitigate damage arising from allowing foul water to stand. Two invoices were generated from these works. One by the property handyman (Garret Bowden) who arrived on the scene within hours of the flood to attend and was a daily presence in the clean-up and the other from the house builder, Murray Clifford, who arrived within hours and brought in man-power and assistance including a pump to relieve the water pressure after the existing sump pump was overwhelmed. He took care of cleaning out the soaked carpeting. Both these invoices were paid by myself in expectation that I would be paid by Insurers however neither has been paid to date. Nor has the Lessor paid them himself as requested. In other words. Not even the cost of pumping out the water has been paid back to me by Insurers, the AXA. Despite the fact I had at that time been insured with the AXA for 26 years, covered for all eventualities.

As at late February 2014 NK had not yet filed any claim with Insurers. In late February 2014 I wrote to NK to propose that he return the Freehold title to me and **to not register any claim with Insurance**. This is because I was aware that there had been a significant flood claim in 2008 and that following a claim for this flood, the property would suffer problems with **reinsurance** that would exceed the costs of repairing the property myself. I offered to undertake the costs of remedial works on this basis. This letter of February 2014 made clear that if NK did not return the freehold and pressed on with making a claim, that he would be liable for any increase in premiums arising from his decision.

He had the ideal opportunity then to return the freehold and not claim on Insurance, in which case I would not be writing this letter today, nor would I have lost many hundreds of thousands of pounds along the way. His motivation in not agreeing to return the freehold was malicious, intended to cause me financial harm, and demonstrates if nothing else, a very active interest in increasing animosity through litigation that is at odds with a child's best interests. A father whose material gain is significantly more pressing than the benefits of a child's best interests. In early March 2014 NK started a claim with the AXA for the flood damage. At this time I presented him with the costs for my rehousing and the two invoices for remedial works, expecting them to be passed on to her Insurers. I was staying in hotels which cost a great deal. The priority became to take out a lease on a suitable property to mitigate the cost of Insurance and to address my immediate rehousing concerns until the repairs to the property could be complete.

Initially the Loss adjuster, Gab Robins, requested the rehousing bills from Hotels giving no indication that they were not prepared to pay rehousing. I met with LA Lars Eichman at the flooded property and went through the extent of the damage. He appeared quite willing to pay re housing as is normal in these circumstances. Lars Eichman did not examine the ground level at all and no-one entered the ground level to examine the conditions there. The ground level has separate deadlocking and no one connected with Insurance has at any time entered there. Relevant because later they were to say that the ground floor was habitable. This conclusion was reached on one sole assurance. NK, in another blatant lie now exposed, told them it was. Deliberately to undermine the claim in order that I would experience financial hardship, with his expense generating litigation uppermost in her thinking. I contacted letting agents and set about looking for a rental property. A letting agent visited 28A Thameside and provided a written confirmation that to locate a similar property in the area for rental, the costs would be some £4,000 pm. That letter was sent to Insurers. (And was in the evidence bundle.) Soon after the letting agents located a property for me, available for immediate occupation at £4,200pm. I wrote to the LA explaining that I needed to take a lease immediately and would need the agreement on the rehousing as a matter of urgency. To encourage this process and show willingness to mitigate the claim, I offered to pay 25% of the rehousing cost myself, in the hope that the agreement for rehousing would happen that same day. Bearing in mind I was living in a hotel at that time paying over £300 a night. I needed a place to live to provide for my housing needs, including housing my elderly father, my son and nephew. I knew from the same type of flood in 2008 that the remedial works would take a minimum of 6 months. During which time I would need a place to live.

However, after telling me he would contact the freeholder and progress the rehousing payment, I heard nothing from Lars the LA for several days. After which the LA wrote to me to say that they would not pay rehousing because they believed that the ground floor of 28A Thameside was habitable and that I should live there. This was of course, untrue. Based on the instruction from the policy holder. No one had visited 28A ground floor in the interim, or indeed, at any time. This information on its habitability can only have come from NK. I believe NK was negligent in his position by telling the LA that the ground floor was habitable, even when it was not. It was a lie told by someone with a legal fiduciary responsibility towards me, to cause me financial harm at a time when he was prosecuting a claim against me which piled enormous legal costs on top of every other stressor not seeing my young son entailed.

I replied, confirming that 28A ground floor was not habitable and outlined the very clear reasons why. I also pointed out that even if it was habitable, even if it had heating and did not smell of standing waste, one bedroom and one shower with no bath is in no way adequate for my housing needs, nor is it 'like for like' rehousing as covered in the policy and as I expected as a part of the 'adequate Insurance' which I had paid for and which I believed I was entitled to. I also pointed out that in identical flood circumstances in 2008, Insurers had paid rehousing immediately and got on with the job of repairing the property, including re tanking, without any delay. The precedent in the Insurance I paid for and expected was established in fact. The difference though to 2008 is this time I was not named on the policy covering this flood claim. Unbeknown to me, after cancelling my insurance cover, a minimal buildings only cover was taken out solely in NK's name (In breach of the leasehold requirement that the Freeholder name each tenant in the Insurance policy. As well as the lender, who was not named.) The policy was being run by NK and the LA was taking instruction from him. It mattered not what I said I was not named on the Policy and instruction in this claim came from the named policy holder. Krasnopovich. Breaching his fiduciary responsibility as the trustee freeholder.

The LA did not pay for the two remedial works invoices, some £4,000 for the team who went in on the day with manpower to pump out and attempt to mitigate damage, and remove all soaked carpeting. And they did not pay any rehousing. By this time months had passed and I was experiencing severe financial hardship as a result of having to pay my own housing costs and not being reimbursed for the funds I outlaid post flood to assist the repairs. I received no notification of any works pending and as I was experiencing a high level of stress and anxiety arising from the deliberate obstruction of visitation, masterminded by Tim Clock to great effect, clearly intended to cause me maximal distress, (cancelling proposed weekend visits on the Friday afternoons) I decided to rent accommodations where I was able to secure credit on the rental agreement until such time as the Insurance paid my rehousing. I had paid my hotel bills until 30 March myself and started the lease agreement from 1 April 2014.

I tried as best I could to pursue repayment for my housing and costs outlay from Insurers with no success. They took instruction only from the named policy holder. Krasnopovich. And his instructions to them were clear. As the amount paid shows clearly. Meanwhile, the house was rotting away, without any treatment to the foul water flood elements, and without any heating to help dry it out in the cold damp winter months, which made matters significantly worse encouraging the damp to spread to the ground floor which is now damaged as a result. I wrote repeatedly to the Freeholder and pointed out his responsibility to make up any shortfall in insurance out of his own resources. However after 6 months I had still not received one penny. Shortly after this the Freeholder took out a legal action against me for a beneficial interest in my home based on his claim that I had promised him half of my home during the course of our relationship. To substantiate the total absence of any evidence to his claim, including not even one single witness or email or indeed anything at all supporting what is a clear deceit, he referred to the Freehold being in his name as an indication that he had a beneficial interest in my property. I believe this is what motivated him to breach the trust agreement requiring him to return the freehold, with the knock-on effect that he wished to cause me maximum financial harm by ensuring I received no money from Insurers. He has succeeded in this as I have not received 1 penny since the flood. It is however the case that in the terms of the Freehold agreement, there are fiduciary responsibilities. That he has not acted in my best interests is clearly obvious as well as quantifiable by way of damages.

Why then has a family court judge attempted to force me to indemnify Krasnopovich from any consequences arising from his illegal actions? Is that representative of the impartial and fair reputation for a family court judge?

At his point, mid 2014, I faced significant legal fees defending a TOLATA case based on nothing as well as meeting the costs arising from the flood damage. Along the way, Insurers, The AXA, hired specialist Insurance fraud lawyers to investigate Krasnopovich in the belief that he was not telling the truth in the matter of the claim. I was then advised **they had suspended the claim** whilst they conducted investigations. Evidently he misled them on an application form by not declaring a previous claim. Meanwhile although the cause of the flood was clearly a failure of the tanking, NK agreed with Insurers that they could commence works that did not involve re tanking. 'Patch over crack' repairs that do not address the cause of the flood and cannot be confused with the 'adequate Insurance' to which I am entitled. He agreed works that contradict the AXA surveyor's own assessment of the cause of the flood.

In April of 2014, the LA wrote a letter to NK in which they confirm the 'cause of the flood is tanking failure' however following the legal intervention by the AXXA's lawyers and NK's subsequent use of his own aggressive city firm specialising in Insurance fraud to defend himself against their claim that he was being dishonest, suddenly without me being aware at any stage in these Insurance fraud proceedings against Krasnopovich, an agreement was reached whereby Insurers would simply 'paint over the cracks' in the basement and not re tank the property. (A cost differential representing a saving to Insurers of some £500,000). No mention was made of my re housing either. Without consulting me on any aspect of works NK evidently agreed that Insurers could simply 'paint over the cracks' in full settlement of their liability in this claim. I believe this too is negligence by the Lessor. It is my belief that I am entitled to adequate Insurance and that the only way of ensuring that the property does not flood again is to re tank it. I did not sign off on Insurance 'painting over cracks.'

I have precedent to support my view as an identical claim occurred in 2008, where Insurers accepted the only remedy was to re-tank, and agreed to rehouse me in this period (£3,500pm for 9 months 'like for like' rehousing at that time.) I have paid my Insurance premiums exactly as required in the Lease agreement. I believe I am entitled to adequate Insurance as a result. Adequate Insurance must restore the property to its pre-incident condition and meet my costs along the way.

The specific areas of my claim are as follows:

1. Re-tanking.

> The flood happened because the tanking failed, exactly as it did in 2008. To restore the property to its pre-incident condition, it must be re-tanked.

I wish to have my home restored to its pre-flood condition as per policy cover I had in place for some 26 years. This includes replacing all contents lost in the flood.

2. Re housing costs.

Following the flood, 28A became uninhabitable. This includes the ground level. The property has no heating. It has toxic black mold creeping up the walls. It has a high damp count which has caused damage on both levels, especially having been left untreated for fifteen months in an uninhabited property with no heating.

> a.) I have provided (at my own expense) professional Environmental Health certification that the property has failed 27 counts with regard to health and safety. (Toxic black mold is not good and high damp is not good either, nor is untreated sewage flood damage. They confirm that '28A is uninhabitable' and it would be a breach of Health and Safety law to occupy this property. Elmbridge Council rated 28A Zero for tax because it is uninhabitable.

> b.) I have written confirmation that the boiler was irreparably damaged in the flood and by standing idle for so long has no prospect of repair. There is no central heating and no hot water. To this day.

> c.) Elmbridge Council have examined the property details and confirmed that 28A Thameside in uninhabitable and is charged zero for council tax until such time as it is once more habitable.

I continue to pay rehousing costs to this day and wish to be reimbursed my housing outlay, along with interest for the delay it has taken paying me up until the date my home is considered habitable once more and I am able to terminate my lease agreement. I have been paying £4,000 pm rental accommodation since April 2014 and I paid hotel bills between 9 February 2014 and March 2014, which I can provide when necessary, totaling at almost £5,000pm. Amounts based on the cover I am insured for. Like for like housing.

3. Increased premiums following this claim.

> Because I wrote in February 2014 requesting that NK not claim on Insurance, in full awareness that the claim would cause premiums to rise

dramatically and that flood cover would be difficult to obtain following a claim, thereby affecting the valuation of my property, I gave clear indication that he would be liable for any increase in premium arising from his decision to;

1.) Not return the freehold enabling me to take care of the problem myself and
2.) Proceed with claiming in 2014.

I wish to attach any consequence in respect of increased Insurance costs or its impact on the value of my home in the event of a sale, to NK's decision to accept liability following that notice in February 2014. Any shortfall on the sale price will reflect the Insurance blight and be the liability of the Freeholder exactly as outlined in the Freeholders fiduciary obligations.

4. Contents claim.

I believe NK was negligent in contacting Fairtimes brokers in November 2013 and making them cancel my policy (without my knowledge or consent). As a result, I had no contents cover. I have clearly lost between £40,000 and £50,000 as a result of having no contents cover. I had contents cover in place and had paid for it and my payment had been accepted. I did not agree to cancel it. Someone has to be liable, whether it is NK for instructing the brokers, or the brokers for cancelling it without my consent. Either way, I believe NK as the Lessor, was negligent in cancelling my contents cover. I would like to claim contents to the sum of a minimum £40,000 for my losses in this flood.

5. Contents claim for burglary in August 2013.

Following the burglary in my home in August 2013, I requested that NK, who was the named policy holder for the contents policy in place at that time, claim for the Laptop that was stolen. The police report was provided along with the details of the burglary, in which NK was himself interviewed by Police. (Attended by Surrey Police DI Kevin Bridge. Reference. ELD11 5412.) Police advised me that the only realistic suspects in the burglary were the two they interviewed. Krasnopovich and his fitness instructor. The replacement cost of the top of range MacBook is £1,800. If NK has failed to provide adequate Insurance then he must make up any shortfall out of his own resources in accordance with the terms of the lease. I paid my premium in full and I have not received any payment in respect of this claim.

6. Works required before 28A is once more habitable.

Firstly, the property needs to be re-tanked. That is the basement level. The London Basement Company quote is in the region of £500,000. The delay in addressing the damp and mold aspects on the basement level have impacted on the ground level as well.
Damage to ground as a result of rising damp and mold includes:

1. Wooden floor needs treatment. It is 90 m2 of valuable Appalachian Walnut sourced and laid at considerable expense. (Over £20,000)
2. Walls needs redecorating and damp course
3. Bay window has visible rot and damp needing attention by carpenter.
4. One radiator (In lounge area) has rusted up badly. Plumbing job.
5. Kitchen areas have visible mold and bacterial rot. Two electric appliances have rusted and need replacing. Fridge and dishwasher. (Both almost new items.)
6. Kitchen has a dry wall section broken through damp and rot and needs replacing. (Plastering job.) Needs damp course and decorating throughout. (Decorator job.)
7. Boiler does not work. (Plumber job. Plumber has told me it is beyond repair. Requires new boiler.)
8. External sump pump needs replacing. It blew during the flood and it is the safeguard against a pressure build up without which the house is not secure. (Expert pump company job.) This is obviously urgent.
9. Non-Return valve needs to go into the drain that back-flowed the foul water waste to avoid foul water waste back-flowing next time water table goes high. (Plumber job)
10. Basement level needs the concrete floor recovered with similar wall to wall carpeting and underlay that was there pre flood.

Once these works are completed, 28A will be habitable and I can make arrangements to move back home. Re housing costs should continue until my home is once more habitable. The re-tanking alone is likely to take 5 months. With decisive action the repairs could be complete in 6 months.

7. Freehold.

I would like to request the freehold return without further delay. The timing of the transfer must accommodate the Insurance cover. He must agree to transfer the freehold as soon as the Insurance claim is settled in full and I am able to reinsure in my own name.

NK is a member of the Law Society. He undertook the agreement to hold the freehold in a declaration of trust. (The original declaration of trust exists and even though he never signed it, he does not deny that the transfer in 2003 was done in Trust for Insurance benefit.) His position at this time is that he accepts it was held in trust but that I did not ask for it back and for this reason he believes he does not have to return it. Firstly, I did ask for it back, in 2007 and in 2013, and in 2014, and in 2015. Secondly, he entered into a declaration of trust that did not say after any period of time the trust falls away and ownership becomes his. His claim is a thinly veiled deceit.

I say that not only is he causing me real harm by not returning the title as he undertook to do, but that it was his legal advice in 2003 to transfer the title into his name with a declaration of trust to protect me that brought about the transfer. The Solicitors Regulation Authority should know that a member is acting in a way that is, in my view, criminal.

In June of 2013, when we separated, the title to his business domains was in my name. And the web hosting was in an account in my sole name. He asked for them back. I agreed to transfer them immediately at the same time as he transferred the Freehold title back to me. There is a witness to this particular agreement. (One of the witnesses, ready to attend court in the April hearing.) I transferred the title back to him, at my expense. He had the freehold title ready to sign over on the agreed date, prepared at my expense by Clam and sent to Clock in readiness for transfer. Instead on that exact same date, he had me personally served with his TOLATA claim. He would go on to claim in Flaherty's court that he owned the Freehold because 'She never asked for it back ever'. Which is clear perjury. The freehold needs to be returned with consideration for the existing Insurance position subject to my agreement on the timing of when to take it back. Bearing in mind the unresolved claim from the 2014 flood.

8.   Following the **tree accident** on 3rd May, 2015, at approximately 7.30pm, I have incurred cost in remedial works to mitigate the damage. NK as the Lessor and sole named insured party needs to arrange for Insurers to progress this claim without delay. To date he has not contacted Insurers and my attempts to do so directly with Insurers have met with rejection as '*We cannot talk to you because you are not named on the policy.*'

Conclusion.

At this time because of the legal costs imposed on me by NK's litigation for 'Beneficial entitlement' and costs in rehousing myself on borrowed money, I am faced with no alternative than to sell my property once it is complete. My property 28A Thameside is presently valued by the court appointed surveyor at £794,000. This valuation assumes that it has flood Insurance and is safe for any new occupant. This judgment is likely to force the trigger price for a sale of this flat alone at this sum. £794,000. I have repeated ad infinitum that the re tanking is not done and will affect the sale price. Hence, the very premise of this forced sale stands of feet of clay written into law by the unfortunately challenged Flaherty. I believe that without re tanking the property is likely to flood next time the water table rises. Only the addition of powerful pumps to the side of building have prevented it flooding already. (Forming part of the £200,000 I have had to spend making repairs to 28 Thameside post flood.) If Insurers do not complete the re tanking, then, despite the view of Judge Flaherty, I am unlikely to sell at anything close to full price (Which absent of any Insurance blight is closer to £1 Million) until the re-tanking is complete and I believe the costs of re-tanking, as well as my subsequent rehousing costs while the re-tanking takes place must be met by the legal entity responsible for providing the adequate insurance to which I am entitled.

If Flaherty proceeds with forced sale based on this low amount, £794,000, without accepting the need to first complete the Insurance works, the property will not sell. Not even at the amount it owes the mortgage. I will be left paying the mortgage. And when the time comes to default, Flaherty will likely be indemnified from any action making her accountable as she should be for ignoring the facts to make an order of court based on her willful ignorance, made despite having my full disclosure available for her consideration.

I would like this recorded in the event that the passage of time exposes the credibility of our differing views in this point where a judge is ignoring facts seemingly for no higher purpose than to punish a non-member of family-law, (myself) for the very clear benefit of her fellow member of family-law. (Krasnopovich.)

I am experiencing grievous financial difficulties arising from the total lack of any payment for rehousing or my costs and some form of interim payment must be made as a matter of urgency until this matter is concluded.

Andrea Lee

32 Presidents Permission. Appeal judge Le Clerc
The President of family-law rules on Flaherty's judgment. But

The Permission to appeal hearing was set for 9 November, 2015. I travelled from LAX to LHR for a two-night stay, arriving on the 8th in London. The venue was the Royal Courts of Justice on the Strand. The Judge was the President of family law himself. I was excited to meet the family-law President. A man who appears often in Publications where he is referenced as the reformer of British family law. At last I could have the shocking conduct by members of British family-law exposed to the boss. My lovely new City solicitor Roland Chambers had prepared a file for the permission to appeal and Richard Castello presented it while Roland and myself sat on the bench behind him. The grounds for appeal were limited to 15 points. The witnesses and the Will attendance notes at the top of the list. The Royal Courts of Justice is quite a spectacle and I felt reassured on this occasion that I would be seeing the head of British family law, President, Lord, Judge, Sir President sitting on high, surrounded by paneled walls rising several stories from the ground, the ache of generations oozing their pain through the tired leather seats. I was immediately impressed by the judge, the President himself. First he questioned Flaherty's validity. *'Who is this DDJ Flaherty'* he asked. Establishing that she is in fact sufficiently qualified with what seemed to be some surprise.

There is a technical factor here where Krasnopovich and Clock played the Family law system. Krasnopovich's claim for '50/50 like we were married', the Beneficial entitlement claim is called a TOLATA. It is essentially a civil claim and it is not a matter normally determined by family-court, where the staff are not specialized in financial matters as you would expect in Chancery Court. I was not married to Krasnopovich so even on that level, why was this being heard in family-court? By joining the TOLATA claim to a family act claim (Housing for Sam – the act that (essentially) protects children thrown out of their home with unemployed dependent mothers by the primary earner.) This law means the child must be housed at the primary-earner parents' expense. This law arises from a traditional model in past years where the father goes out to work and the wife stays home and raises the child. When the relationship breaks down, the wife has no means to feed the child without the primary breadwinner's support. Excepting this was not the 20's. This hearing was in 2015, where in Krasnopovich's case, he was earning over £250,000 pa net, and owned his own home. So this was not a law designed or intended for his circumstance. But by joining it to the TOLATA, he was able to have a civil matter heard in family court. Which is his home domain. It is also an abuse of the system.

The President took about fifteen minutes in conversation with Castello before declaring the case should be appealed. And taking a moment to offer Castello some advice.

"If I may Mr. Castello. Keep it brief. You don't need these fifteen points you have raised. Just the first three will be enough. Don't confuse the judge."

Words I would recall later when Richard Castello explained his decision to use the *scattergun* approach that so clearly confused Appeal Judge Le Clerc as much as myself. After the President ruled, we went back to FOS offices where I met with the property law partner, the well dressed and well-educated Roland Court, to advance the Insurance claim and Freehold matter, still on hold until a final ruling in the TOLATA hearing.

This was my first meet with Roland Court, the partner in property law who would represent my claim against Krasnopovich. I found Roland's direct approach, absent from the hypocritical reserve so common in family-law members, confidence inspiring. I liked his reassurance that *"They will know we are coming after them"*. We concluded our talk in about an hour in the FOS boardroom. Next up would be the appeal and then the accounting for the money owed on the house for the flood claim. I left Heathrow the following morning in good spirits. Although I had not seen Sam on that trip, I had seen the wheels of law grind. It seemed to me that at last the law was catching up with Krasnopovich. The head of family law had looked at Flaherty's judgment and declared that it stank. Awarding the permission to appeal as well as offering my barrister good advice on how to win the appeal.

And then, one month later I was back on the LAX LHR 11-hour, 8-hour time difference overnight journey. (In economy.) For the Le Clerc Appeal hearing. I flew back to the UK for two nights to attend to one day set aside for the Appeal. From the off something smelled fishy. Roland Chambers looked nervous. Richard Castello spoke about his trip to France to following morning with considerably more enthusiasm than his strategy for the presentation, which I was obviously interested in. I had received an email from my former lawyer, David Clam, relating to our dispute. In that he disclosed to me that Richard Castello had told him *"Flaherty's judgement is unappealable."* I wondered if he was telling the truth. Just to be nasty at this stage because I had fired him.

And then we were up and running. Andrew Le Clerc, Appeal court judge, took about five minutes of listening to Castello to look bamboozled. Instead of following the President's advice from the 'Permission to Appeal' hearing to keep it simple and go with three or four key points, like the witnesses, and the will documents, a hyper manic Castello rose with a stream of consciousness ramble he later described to me as 'The scattergun approach.

But Richard. That was precisely what the President advised against. Had I not known better; I would have given more attention to my impression that Richard did not want to risk another day in the Appeal hearing interfering with his early departure for France the next day. With his scattergun bamboozle leaving everyone including myself confused, the other side rose to speak.
Simon Hazelwood, Krasnopovich's barrister, started with the late filing at the preliminary FD hearing.

"As you can see, Ms. Lee was fined £2,600 for contempt after a late filing".

Delivered slowly with confidence.

"And then you can see this business of the witnesses? Well, again she was late in filing."

Another thespian B grade pause.

"But Ms LEANDROS was late repeatedly and so DDJ Flaherty was right to dismiss the witnesses. This situation is all of Ms. Leandros' own making."

That impressed Le Clerc. In that moment it was clear he decided there would be no appeal. This was too easy. There in black and white was notice the Appellant has been found in contempt of court for being late. There was no mention that the solicitor David Clam was the one who was late. It said clearly *"Andrea Leandros found to be in contempt for late filing."* Although I was never once late. Why would I be? No one wanted this nonsense to be over with more than me. I had nothing else ahead on my to-do list than – attend the litigation process. I was aware that I had legal costs over quarter of a million pounds, with no income other than my properties, and my only hope was to win this litigation and win costs. Of all parties involved I had the most to gain by seeing this through to a just decision by the courts, to get my money back in costs and to see my son again.

I firmly believed that Krasnopovich's lying claim was going to be exposed and that I would be awarded costs. I wanted that day to come as soon as possible. In other words. I had absolutely no reason to be late. Quite the contrary. The opportunity to label me as 'Late' was opportunistically seized on by Hazelwood /Clock /Krasnopovich after Clams late filing in the run up to the preliminary Financial Directions hearing. Clam filed late on that occasion, after telling me he would be and that if there was a fine attached, he would pay the fine. Clam allowed my name to appear on the court record as being late, and having to pay a fine. This 'Late filing by Clam after promising to 'indemnify me' for his decision to file late has been repeatedly raised, with Clam, his firm, Spoon LLP, and Richard Castello, the barrister who on that day simply sat with his head in his hands, transmitting to the judge that he was done with this case.

To date my name appears on the record for Clam's late filing, which the invoice shows, he paid, as he told me he would when telling me he was going to file late as he was busy elsewhere.

Once again in Le Clerc's Court this error by Clam was churned out without being corrected. *"Mr. Krasnopovich filed the witness statements late."* Said Hazelwood. No rebuttal at all from Castello, who by this stage was transparently already on the French beach he was booked to travel to the next day. Apart from anything else, I did not serve the witness statements late. My solicitor David Clam did. Conflating the late service by my solicitor with any contemptuous action by myself was just wrong. But no one commented. My barrister, who I believe should have, did not.

And this to me is the real vulnerability of the legal process in family-court where a judge need only spend 5 minutes on a subject and make an impulsive finding that is no more than an opinion. I was present but not allowed to speak. That was a double agony.

Barrister Hazelwood lied. It is a lie to say I filed witness statements late.' I did not. In so far as I was involved in the witness statements, that is to say paying the £12,000 bill to Clam's firm for preparing them, I was on time. Clam, for reasons of his own, filed on the last Friday before the hearing. Exactly as Hazelwood knew his team solicitor, Tim Clock, had done during the Visitation hearing. David Clam was, almost certainly, simply getting the other side back for catching him out with a late filing in the visitation hearing, which had proven so successful then. Now it was his turn to use the same tactic. Yet, through no fault of mine, both these acts of incompetence, by Clam and Castello, the first late filing that Clam paid a fine for but left in my name on record, and the late filing of the witness statements offered Hazelwood, in his own words 'Manna from heaven.' Able to not only convince switch judge Flaherty to remove witnesses from the hearing, but also able to paint a picture at appeal of me being responsible for my own misfortune because I was late. Sitting in Le Clerc's court listening to this happening while Castello sat ineffectively enjoying the £60,000 or so that he charged me for sitting so ineffectively left me with a clear impression of what is worst about British family-law.

It seemed that right after Hazelwood's reference to my serial lateness in the hearing, the 'mood music' from Le Clerc changed to; This is ridiculous. Over £400,000 of legal fees to get here and now they want to start again with another court case? There simply isn't the money for that. So I will go with what the judge who heard the case said.

This is an un appealable judgment.   Case dismissed.

I was not able to speak at this hearing. Only the barristers were. Hazelwood spoke in his usual way, about the liar who was late and tried to ambush his poor client by serving witness statements late which the Judge, quite rightly, dismissed. Castello was startlingly incompetent. The man with the scattergun. And a French beach to get to. I gave ore thought to David Clam's email, confirming that Castello had written to him with his belief there was no prospect of winning the appeal against the unappealable judgement. (Clam copied me the actual email from Castello.) Just as Castello knew there was no prospect of winning the Flaherty hearing from the moment the proceedings began. Why take a case if you believe you cannot win? Especially as in the Flaherty hearing, it was her historical grudge against him that assisted her predetermined judgment. He knew then that "If we get Flaherty we will lose". So why did he not recuse himself?

I had flown in for two days for this hearing and was leaving that very night. After exiting the court, I left I went for a debrief coffee with Roland Chambers. I had on my iPhone the last drawing Sam had sent me. A beautiful declaration of love written on paper with colored pencils, a drawing he had made with me and him with William. I had scanned this powerful image into my phone. I had used that to look at in moments when my spirts sank, to remind me of why I was going through this actual nightmare. Sam knew that I was going to be 'trying my best to see him real soon.' In that coffee shop, instead of starting with words, I put Sam's drawing on full screen and showed it to Roland, who was all too aware that losing the case meant losing the means to continue pursuing visitation with Sam. I had mentioned more than once that unless we won with costs, I could not realistically see a future for Sam to be with me. A fact he confirmed as the motivation for his best efforts. He really did seem to care that I won, and was then able to see Sam again. Roland had the good grace to appear misty eyed looking at Sam's picture. In my reminder to him before the appeal that the real loss would not be the house, but Sam, because I would not have the means or even the residence in the UK to continue using family law to secure visitation, Roland's reply was "*As I am all too painfully aware.*" That was my best impression of family-law. A lawyer able to shed a tear for the child victim of this brutal system.

Richard Castello said goodbye to me outside the Court with a stiff handshake and the words '*I don't expect we'll meet again.*' In his defensiveness he came over as quite aggressive. Nice work if you can get it Richard. £60,000 for which I remember seeing him laughing with Simon Hazelwood outside Flaherty's court; telling me that he knew we would lose the case the moment Flaherty was announced as switch judge. And again that he knew we had lost when she rolled her eyes at him less than 3 minutes into his opening submission. Clearly expressing the belief that the judgment in the Flaherty hearing was made before a word was spoken. During the run up to the Appeal, Clam forwarded me a letter he received from Castello regarding prospects for an Appeal. In this letter, Castello says '*No prospect of Appealing Flaherty's judgment. She made it un appealable.*' Yet when Roland Chambers approached him to take on the appeal, he was quite happy to pick up another £20,000 for showing up. His French holiday money.

Later that night, in what can be fairly described as a state of shock, I flew out of Heathrow with the same feeling I had when I flew out of Johannesburg in 1985. Off to start a new life in a new country, never to return. It was hard to not see the similarities between the legal system that drove me from South Africa then, the ethically deviant Afrikaner Nationalists who made up their rules in Court and acted quite legally in what happened next, and the same ethical paucity underpinning British family law that enabled Krasnopovich, Clock, Flaherty and Hazelwood to get away with what they did. Stealing my child's future with me. Stealing my home and my income source. By lying. In an old system, a judiciary operating on legal statutes hopelessly inadequate in this current age, even if it had been well reasoned legislation when first laid out a hundred years ago.

By the time I landed in LAX I made the decision to make the best of starting again in the reality that British family-court had taught me a lesson. For a price measured in millions and the cost of my beautiful son, the center of my world, I realized in its current form, family-law is never any more than *Who lies wins*.

After the ruling by Le Clerc and facing another round of hefty billing from FOS, I sent the following email to Roland Chambers, which references the traditional definition of insanity. I did not want to pay one more penny to British family-law.

From: Andrea Lee
Sent: 13 June 2016 02:10
To: Appeal lawyer
Subject: Re: Draft Judgment of Mr Justice Le Clerc

Dear Roland,

Thank you for forwarding me the draft judgment on Friday and your letter. I am copying my reply to Roland Court.

Richard Castello

Reading the judgment my first thought returns to the 'Richard Castello' emails sent shortly after the hearing. March 29th, March 30th and April 3rd, which deal with my concerns over Richard Castello's competence in my matter.

Justice Le Clerc's draft judgment validates those concerns quite clearly. From the 'scattergun' decision to the wrong dates, to each of the specific points I have previously detailed.

In my experience Richard Castello has repeatedly failed to provide the duty of care his office requires from the outset of his appointment by David Clam to represent me against Simon Hazelwood. Their friendship appears to me far above the value he attached to my matter. His various failures, especially in not ensuring that Clams 'late filing indemnification' would have removed my name from the courts record for Clams later filing, did me a disservice. He was present when we both saw that notice on the court record and agreed that Clam was obligated to correct the court record to remove my name from the contempt finding.

I accept that I allowed you to convince me to use his services again after I had already seen the extent of his mishandling in the Flaherty hearing, in which he announced from the outset that we would lose "if we get Flaherty" who had a historical issue with him, and after he had already written to David Clam confirming that he 'knew there was no prospect of success at Appeal' yet was happy to take payment to put in the shoddy job that followed.

But for the avoidance of doubt; I do not want Richard Castello having any further input in my matter. His negligent incompetence has cost me dearly and I will not underwrite any further payment to him.

Procedure for the 18th July

In the process leading up to the Final judgment on 18th July I think we should consider the advantages of me representing myself.

One definition of insanity is the willingness to repeat the same thing in the hope of a different outcome. When I look at this Judgment and start considering a reply, I see that once again, I will be paying someone to make corrections of such a basic nature it would be insane to continue on this same path.

In Justice Le Clerc's draft I am referred to as 'the wife'.

Why should I pay someone to explain to Justice Le Clerc that I never married KRASNIPOVITCH or KRASNOPOVITCH.

On the cover page of his Judgment Le Clerc has spelled both Appellant and Respondent's names incorrectly. **LEANDRIS and KRASNIPOVITCH.** *It reads much like cut and paste judgment. Sloppy. Laced with typos.*

How is it a Judge, responsible for the future of a 6-year-old child, cannot even spell the name of either parent correctly and is unaware that the parents were not married? Le Clerc is ruling on the future of a child whilst incapable of even spelling his name correctly. And to add a cheerful cherry to the top, I am expected to pay your premium rate charge to correct these typo's.

This reminds me of DDJ Flaherty's misspelling of one name, 'Philip Parker Voula', in seven different ways during her judgment. One three-word name spelled incorrectly seven (7) times which I had to pay my lawyer and barrister to correct, whilst being reassured that it means nothing when a judge lacks the literary competence of a 12-year-old English student.

While it may not seem important to you that a judge would be unable to spell the names he is judging on correctly, or even accidentally consider that we were married, to me it is an all too familiar reminder of a standard I do not wish to pay one more penny towards.

Shoddy unprofessional and worthy only of contempt. The outcome of this judgment abuses a 6-year-old. I sat in Le Clerc's court and saw what I saw. This is a con. A racket. Everyone involved makes a ton of money and my son loses his life with me. British family-law has abused my son and all involved have been handsomely paid for this purpose. I am not sure there is any point in continuing to the end of Le Clerc's judgment with you. Procedurally, if I am to represent myself, I would like to consider the implications aside of the legal-cost saving.

Firstly, despite facing costs of some £300,000 for legal representation in attempting to see my son Sam and in defending my property from the very clear lie by Krasnopovich that he was promised half of the home I bought in 1986, when he was 14, and although I value your input enormously in full awareness that the professional damage was done by Clam and Castello before your involvement, the simple fact is that I could not have achieved a worse result if I had represented myself from the outset.

This judgment and the enforcement of the Flaherty judgment has two significant consequences.

1. I face losses following a forced sale that will leave me effectively bankrupt. I will have no home to return to and no source of income and no means to repay the debt I owe arising from Krasnopovich's dishonest and criminal conduct. You already know some details of this.

2. My son will not see me again until he is of age to emancipate himself. He is now 7. That means, effectively, after 4 years of being raised with me as his stay at home parent, he will now be raised by Krasnopovich's partner, Carol Adrian, a family lawyer, as his maternal role model.

There is no reason to believe these two-family lawyers will not continue to project onto Sam the same toxic version of his absent mother that means he will need to be an adult before he can muster the means to understand what has happened, process it in an appropriate context, and come to find me. At my age, and with the developmental aspect of nurture versus nature to consider, let's be realistic about the fact that this judgment and the parental alienation it represents in all likelihood ends my relationship with my son as a child.

I know this outcome is not in Sam's best interests and is not what he has chosen and yet in British family Court, DDJ Flaherty has visited this future parenting decision upon him and Justice Le Clerc agrees by ignoring the President's advice entirely, while both have done so without correctly spelling the name of the child they are affecting in this way. And I have to pay you £400 an hour (plus VAT) to correct their typo's.

British Family Court has failed Sam and the process into which I have been dragged by a dishonest member of British family-law has ignored Sam's rights completely, handing over his male parenting role to another member of British family Law while bankrupting his mother in the process and ensuring with unmistakable determination that no future visitation is possible. In the course of these proceedings, lasting over two years, which began with my attempt to see Sam for alternate weekends, I have seen a member of the law society lie under oath repeatedly. I have seen and listed numerous specific instances of negligent, if not criminal, behavior within British family-law that I have reported repeatedly, without any reaction beyond the generating of another legal bill.

Even after the visitation hearing order imposed specific limitations on either parent taking the child out of the Country, Krasnopovich repeatedly did exactly that. On one occasion, knowingly taking him out of the country without informing me, to the home of a DDJ (Dia Mirza) who lives in Geneva. Dia Mirza is a DDJ and barrister who works in British Family Law who knew that the child she was hosting was being taken out of the UK without consent. She knew because Sam managed to call me from Geneva and tell me where he was, after which I wrote to Dia Mirza and confirm that she knew Sam was the subject of a Court hearing, yet did not see anything remiss about enabling him to travel outside of the UK to visit her without (even asking for) my consent? It will come as no surprise to you that nothing came of my complaint about this either.

A British family law DDJ and barrister knowingly invited a child who was being removed out of the country without legal consent by a family law member, Krasnopovich, who knew an order was being breached in this process. The net outcome? Another £1,000 of legal cost for me for another member of British family-law, Clam, to explain to me that there is 'nothing to see here.' Krasnopovich removes

Sam from the UK at will and has not on one occasion sought my consent to do so. I do not even know where he lives now.

Perhaps you will advise me that I have the right to find out, for just a little more than £400ph?

As an aside, after Krasnopovich moved out with Sam in June, 2013, he refused to provide me with the address of where Sam was. I was presented with a demand for payment of £100,000 (rising twice) before I could see or speak with him. I had no way of contacting him and this is how the litigation began. I had to spend around £2,000 on a family law member, Clam, to make an application to Court requiring the Father to disclose the whereabouts of the child. Which he did only when the solicitor charging me had written numerous letters on the subject over a period of several weeks in which he did not provide the address, waiting until the lawyer was literally on his way to Court before sending it through. Maximizing my expense, using my want factor to see Sam as the lever.

This entire litigation has been underpinned by a member of British family law negotiating his financial advantage based on my want factor to be with my son, succeeding, as you have seen for yourself, in ending the relationship entirely, with the predictable financial consequences.

The Flaherty judgment

I believe that DDJ Flaherty has gone beyond the authority of her office, flaunting International copyright law by using copyright pictures that were subject to a usage agreement which clearly prevented their unauthorized use and seeking to impose restrictions on my rights in matters unrelated to her office. I am concerned that under the protection of closed proceedings shielding her from accountability, she has brought British family law into (further) disrepute. And I have seen both Hazelwood and Castello lie repeatedly, knowingly, including in your presence.

I have reported that Krasnopovich and Clock adduced extracts from a Without Prejudice document which was considered by the Court in a process where Richard Castello and David Clam were both aware, but did nothing. While I accept your assurance that nothing can be withheld when a child's welfare is at stake, quite clearly the use of this confidential information has absolutely nothing to do with the child's welfare. It is adduced exclusively for the financial benefit of a member of British family law, done in full awareness that she is protected by this same Institution. Why, if you can allow Without Prejudice in Family law proceedings, was I not allowed to disclose his original offer for "Give me £100,000 and you can see Sam as much as you want." Or any of the other WP documents in which he contradicts what was said in Court.

I have numerous similarly illegal instances that show the extent to which British family law has been abused by a liar, supported by professional liars and throughout the process Krasnopovich has prevailed without censure at any point.

Clearly if you are a member of British family law you can copy selectively from a Without Prejudice Document and admit that in a hearing as evidence, and not only is it allowed to stand, but when it is reported, nothing happens. It goes without saying that I on the other hand was prevented from using Without Prejudice documents by Krasnopovich in which she clearly contradicts evidence she would later go on to give to Flaherty's court.

The list goes on. A member of British family-law protected by his own in his own home patch with no regard as to the child's best interests. Personal gain has been placed over the deleterious effects of litigation on a child's best interests. All involved, Krasnopovich /Clock /Hazelwood /Flaherty have knowingly acted towards increasing animosity, in full awareness that the central claim '50/50 like we were married' is ridiculous in its merit and probability, and in full awareness that the outcome of winning Krasnopovich's financial gain is at the expense of Sam's future. They are for this reason child abusers, for profit.

The option of an SRA complaint or Ombudsman report seems pointless to me at this stage. How many times do I need to report this deviant conduct by members of the legal profession to other members of the legal profession before referring to my previous observation of 'Insanity.'

That Justice Le Clerc has simply upheld a judgment which has involved perjury by a member of Family Law and a clear factual matrix following the incompetence of the solicitor and barrister representing me, is a story that may assist reform in British Family Law. That is the only positive I can see arising from this situation. A court that abuses children for the members benefit must be exposed and changed.

You may recall from previous reference, Richard Castello told me that 'If we get Flaherty we will lose' on the morning of the three-day hearing. That hearing lost half of day-one because the judge recused. That delay was cited as a reason why my witnesses could not be called. (Witnesses whose statements were ready many weeks before the lastminute filing by David Clam, with Richard Castello's awareness that this may be considered and 'ambush' and dismissed, meaning the witnesses in a hearsay case were dismissed. I say because Clam and Castello failed in their duty of care to present my case efficiently. Le Clerc's judgment bears out my point about Castello in relation to this specific negligence.)

Richard Castello would go on to tell me that he 'knew the case was lost when she rolled her eyes' at him. This 'eye rolling' event happened just minutes into his opening submission. Here is a barrister failing to get crucial witness statements admitted, in the hour after admitting to me that the case was lost by the choice of Judge and then confirming he knew the case was lost just moments after he began his submissions. This is a corrupt system. Flaherty's judgment is the product of a corrupt system.

The fact is Flaherty's judgment was made before I even entered the Courtroom. This cannot in any way be considered a fair hearing in which evidence was examined and a sound decision reached. Flaherty made fundamental factual errors during the hearing (You did not buy 28 Thameside in 1986?) and has awarded 50% of a home I bought in 1986 to someone who was 14 at the time, who was a freeloading guest in my home for two years, during which time she never paid one penny towards anything to do with that flat. How is that beneficial entitlement and detriment?

This judgment, validating Flaherty's judgment, is simply plain wrong. British family-law has robbed me of my livelihood and ended the relationship with my son. While members of family-law have broken their own rules so transparently, I would be staggered if I didn't already know what I do about British family-law. An institution rotten to its core in which members profit handsomely from abusing children.

My representation for the 18th July and my means to pay a legal bill

I have already disclosed to you the extent of my financial position and my ability to pay any further legal bills. I do not expect you to work for free and in view of this judgment and the clear fact that British family law will not find against one if its own members, it would appear to make sense that I represent myself for the 18th July. Aside from saving costs, I will have the opportunity to write to Justice Le Clerc. The very least I deserve as a consumer of a very expensive product that has proven unfit for purpose.

This correspondence with Justice Le Clerc, supplemented by my detailed, substantiated recollection of my experience in Family Court, from the outset when 1.) my son was removed from my home with my request for his whereabouts met with a demand for £100,000, leading to 2.) a (£40,000) visitation hearing where my son was prevented from having the alternate weekend visits I applied for (because a member of British Family law told the CAFCASS officer that Sam would not be safe with me and the CAFCASS officer was the judge that day) leading to 3.) the current situation ending the prospect of any further relationship between my son and myself, I believe, can only assist the President's awareness of the Court system over which he presides. And consequently, make changes to prevent similar abuses continuing to ruin children lives, even if that means fewer high earning opportunities for family law members.

This may take the form of an open letter in so far as my intention is to assist any other children abused by the system to the extent that my son has been. British family law has failed my son, who is now being raised by two members of British family law, who have achieved this control over his future by 'bankrupting' me, using a court process in which it has proven all too easy for them to prosper with deceit.

In this process I have been assured by Members of family law that they can act with impunity and without regard for accountability because these are closed proceedings (His claim for beneficial entitlement and detriment is somehow a matter for family law and not a civil claim?) and if I write or talk about it in any way, I will be committing a criminal offense? However the offenses committed against my son by members of British Family Law cannot go unreported. I would be an accomplice if I do not, at the very least, detail the extent of my experience to the President. As you have already explained to me, there is no confidentiality where a child's welfare is concerned.

Details of how to advance the Flaherty judgment

Turning to your letter and the options available to me having accepted that Krasnopovich has prevailed completely with exactly what he set out to do on fathers-

day 2013. Remove Sam from my life and ruin me financially unless I accepted his financial demands.

I am not interested in pursuing any further appeal by funding any more special advice by members of family law. I have no resources and, more significantly, no confidence that this will make any difference to the reality that family law will not find against one if its own members.

In the event that you agree to the advantages of me representing myself at this stage, in the course of my letter to Justice Le Clerc I would draw attention to the shortfalls in the draft, including his explanation on why 28A and 28B but not 28C. By missing out 28C out completely in his summary of my property and his beneficial entitlement his awareness of the position is fundamentally incomplete. Why was he not curious about 28C? The omission of 28C from his claim is significant.

Le Clerc listened to Hazelwood and Castello for a few hours three months ago. As the judgment records, Le Clerc did not find Castello convincing at all. He found for Hazelwood on the day, which was quite clear to me as it was to you in that Court room.

    Richard Castello was hopelessly inarticulate and Le Clerc found Hazelwood convincing. It seems that this conclusion forms the totality of the notes Justice Le Clerc referred to 3 months later when writing his draft. He has not considered the facts in the matter leading to the Judgment being appealed. He simply records the failure of Richard Castello's scattergun approach.

British Family Law has ruled on my son's future, decided by a Judge who has not even spelled his name correctly on the title page of the judgment that puts an end to his relationship with his parent. Of course, why would I expect for one moment that any Judge in family law would consider my son's future. It would have been a first in the course of my experience if he had. It is after all British Family law. Who lies best wins. No one makes money without acrimonious litigation. As Krasnopovich has shown, the more acrimonious the litigation, the more money is won.

    That a parent would do this to make money out of their own child is one thing, that Clock would do this for money and get away with calling his child abuse, a career, is quite another.

How exactly will a forced sale work. The flats are rented out. What about the amount I invested in making 28A and 28B habitable post flood? What about the fact that I paid 100% of all costs for 28B from 1986 onwards and he paid not one penny. 28B has had significant expenditure even since the separation, without which it would not be worth even what it is now. Event he valuations she has applied are wrong. They will not fetch the amount she has indicated in a forced sale because Krasnopovich failed to repair the property and the Insurance blight will affect the sale price. Why is she allowed to ignore this very obvious reality from the owner of the property? Who knows better than I?

My claim against Krasnopovich with Roland Court

With this judgment made the only way forward for me is through the civil matter; the Freehold/Insurance claim with Roland Court, to which I would like to add the natural flow arising from the '50/50 like we were married' judgment. And possibly include the Breach of Privacy claim which is detailed below.

As Lessor in the Freehold of my property Krasnopovich has a fiduciary responsibility towards me. He could and should have returned the freehold when he decided to bring an action against me.

The causation of my financial losses through these proceedings is predicated on his abuse of the Freehold title. His litigation has cost me £300,000+ in legal fees, whatever other costs are awarded against me, and the down value of my home of £800,000+. And that presumes it will sell at all, which I doubt. In which case I stand to lose 100% of two flats that would have been worth £1.5 million but for Krasnopovichs' fiduciary failures.

The failure to provide adequate Insurance since he cancelled my policy in 2013 has caused me out of pocket expenses on my home of £250,000+ as the immediate shortfall in Insurance cover and making my home habitable.

In addition to the costs he has forced on me in the alternative to honoring his fiduciary responsibilities, we have the matter of the down value in a forced sale, which will now have a fixed figure to attach to my claim. Once the house sells, I say the shortfall is down to his causing the down value. The base price for my property absent of the flood damage, as a going concern with tenants is £2.5 million.

Had he returned my freehold as requested, or had he properly completed the insurance claims, the property would be worth what it was valued at. Instead of the £2.5 million it would be worth now, I expect it will realise not even 50% of that amount. This down value is caused by his action, by not returning the freehold when requested and deliberately ensuring I have not received one penny in Insurance to this day.

In addition, I have had serious financial implications in having to borrow the money to make the property habitable. Since he cancelled my Insurance policy, in 2013, I have had to borrow what is now, with interest, far in excess of £500,000 to survive and maintain the property. And keep paying the mortgages on 28A and 28C.

Obviously he has not paid one penny towards anything.

I would like to examine how best to pursue my losses arising from the Freehold/Insurance fraud by Krasnopovich. It seems to me that she had a duty to return the freehold in 2013 when it was requested. She did not, and instead caused the financial harm you see unfolding.

In 2013 October, he called an Insurance broker where I had contents cover and instructed them to cancel my policy. Without notifying me or seeking my consent. Almost five years later no action has begun against him?

Financial settlement now that we are 50/50 like we were married

Now that we have a judgment in which I am referred to as 'the wife' (Really?) which confirms we are 50/50 like we were married which is the finding of Flaherty and which is to be made an order of the Court, then what is the reciprocal.

If it's true then 'Like we were married' is community of property. Including, but not limited to the following:

50% of Krasnopovich McDonald LLP, in which I invested significantly. Both in financing and in executive business skills.
50% of the investments and pension funds
50% of the Equity payment return from MWT (Which I paid £40,000+ when he bought in as equity partner.)
and 50% of his flat. (Which was I looked after with maintenance and rental.) He frequently referred to 'Our property portfolio' in his claim although never mentioning any of his assets in that context.

You know that when he moved in with me in 2003, I supported him entirely for more than 2 years, helping him let his flat out for some £800pm. Over ten years that adds up to over £90,0000. Money he had only because he was staying with me for free. And yet he claimed he suffered detriment?

I gave up most of my commercial musical work to raise a child and placed reliance on my 50% share of the law firm's income. At least in so far as meeting Sam's school and travel costs. I have consciously put to one side out of home work commitments since the agreement to have a child together in which I would invest my time and resources towards establishing a business which would pay for the child's upbringing. I have not been able to return to work. Not because I am mentally infirm, as the judge determined, but because I am traumatized by this awful blackmailing theft of my child and my home by thieves walking in broad daylight. Clearly I have suffered detriment as a result of relying on his assurances.

Flaherty has awarded Krasnopovich 'Detriment'. Really. Why does detriment work only in his favor?

And it is worth noting that the correspondence I had showing the work for Krasnopovich McDonald, which would have been used in support of my claim, was on the Laptop I used for this purpose. This information on that laptop drive included the entire business plan for the formation of the business. From the first draft with cashflow showing no loans from any banks because my business plan involved me fronting the money to start up the new firm.
That laptop was stolen in a burglary of my home in August 2013, within days of my email (From me to Krasnopovich) requesting payment of money owing to me from Krasnopovich McDonald LLP

Police investigated the burglary. In August of 2013 a DI from Surrey Police, interviewed the two suspects identified in the course of their investigation. Krasnopovich and his then girlfriend. (The young fitness instructor.)
The circumstances of the burglary left the investigating officers in no doubt that there were no other suspects. I have no doubt that Krasnopovich was behind the

burglary. He had the motive. And the personality. The documents of the police investigation and the SOCO report exist and enable professionals in this type of crime to draw the obvious conclusion.

Krasnopovich was all too aware from then that he was going to bring an action and that I might well have countered with a claim for half the business in relation to my contribution to Sam's maintenance. The only reason no action followed is because Police could not find the evidence. So we can credit Krasnopovich with enough intelligence to not have left the stolen laptop on his work desk when the Police arrived to interview him.

Surely if the court has already ruled beneficial entitlement and detriment, on the basis that '50/50 like we were married' is the precedent then my claim has already been decided in the same ruling.

I would like to be clear that these proceedings have ruined me financially. My actual losses are in multiple millions. My sole prospect of any financial survival is through seeing a claim against him succeed. If there is no prospect of any success in any of the matters I am raising in this letter exceeding the legal costs, then that will affect my decision going forward.

I currently have two of the three flats empty, and have just had to pay out over £8,000 to repair flood related damage to 28A, which has caused 28A to be uninhabitable, costing me lost rent. I am continuing to pay the mortgages only because I hope that there is a prospect of winning the Insurance matter.

Conclusion

I am available to chat at your convenience, any time after 4pm your time, however I would prefer a written reply to the central issues I have raised, with any questions, however brief, in advance of that chat to determine how we are to progress most effectively. Particularly, the specifics of how a forced sale works. I have no other assets in the UK and no income other than the rentals.

Especially I am interested in Roland Courts intentions at this time. I see that since the initial letter regarding the May 2016 claim, there has been no further correspondence. I face a further £8,000+ cost in repairs and loss of around £5,000 in rental (so far) while the house is uninhabitable, which seems to have gone unrecorded, leaving me concerned that my claim may be compromised by delay.

Regards,
Andrea

And then, some months after to three-minute Appeal hearing, came the judgment. Here's Roland's letter to me. The reference to Roland Court, the property law partner, would be to pursue the fiduciary failures in the Insurance claim, an amount potentially higher than the loss of the properties.

From: ROLAND CHAMBERS
Date: Fri, 10 Jun 2016 18:57:34 +0000
To: Andrea Cc: ROLAND COURT
Subject: Draft Judgment of Mr Justice Le Clerc

Dear Andrea

Draft Judgment of Mr Justice Le Clerc

I hope you are well.

Please see attached letter and enclosure (which is a copy of the draft Judgment now circulated to Counsel by Mr Justice Le Clerc).

It is, I regret to say, as anticipated but do, please, have regard to what appears in my accompanying letter which has been considered and endorsed by Roland Court, who is copied-in.

Very best

Roland
Roland Chambers
Partner
Friedman Oldfield Shutterworth Solicitors

33 Post Le Clerc Accounting
How do you account for the money spent making the property saleable when there is no court agreed formula allowing the winner to have 50% which in reality becomes more than 100% when including the payments?

Le Clerc's rubber stamp for Flaherty's judgment gave Krasnopovich 50% of my home as well as 50% of my rental income from the time of Flaherty's judgment. This 50% was not limited by the common sense understanding of what costs go into rental income. In property letting the gross amount received is by some distance not the same as the actual profit. Commonly this would include; Agents commission, repayment of mortgage costs, maintenance costs and replacing broken items. Yet here we have a judge awarding 50% of gross rental income. Did I mention that Richard Castello said on the morning of the trial when Flaherty appointed herself as judge, that '*She does not understand financial issues.*' The same person charged with making a financial settlement on my home and income and future contact with my son describes herself as "*Lawyer; Juvenile delinquent; lover of champagne and fun.*"

The mess of Flaherty's making extends far beyond just the calculation of the rental income percentages.

Flaherty awarded costs against me and Le Clerc responded to Hazelwood's request that he 'punish' me for renting out 28A when the judgment called for immediate sale, with a £10,000 fine, which would attract 8% interest charge if not paid immediately. I did not attend that hearing. I learned about the £10,000 fine from Roland Court. Well good luck with that, was my first thought. These members of family-law are definitely enjoying the SRA ethics code about not awarding costs because to do so creates animosity and that is never good for the child. Here's a guy who has never even met me, fining me £10,000 at 8% interest because I am doing the same thing I have been doing since 1991 as my business. Land Lording. What, I wonder, was he imaging the upside was of making this ruling? Clearly he knew I had a £500,000 legal bill, and had lost my home and income business in a court order. How would fining me more when I clearly could not pay, help the situation?

Background: After the Flaherty ruling I had 28A rented out. Krasnopovich attempted to stop the lease going ahead by threatening my letting agents with litigation if they progressed with the lease of 28A on my behalf. He actually showed up in their office, a lettings agency with whom I go back some 20 years in the Landlord/Agent business, and fronted my letting agent with threats. This meant I had to pay Roland Court at FOS to indemnify the letting agents before they would complete the tenancy. More legal charges for me. In fact, Roland's legal charges in the time it took exceeded three months rental income. But the tenancy went ahead. I had a big mortgage to pay. That was my sole means to do so.

How this action places freeholder Krasnopovich in his fiduciary responsibility to me is open to your speculation. Was it in my best interests?

After the appeal that never was, there was a costs hearing. I did not bother flying in for that. Mathew Chambers made plain that because I could not pay the next round of fees he was going be on holiday at that time.

By now I had lost all confidence in anything to do with British family court. It is beyond a simply unbelievable scam. It is basic daylight robbery by a gang of lying thieves. Thieves walking in broad daylight. Playing a legal process built for their winning convenience at the expense of any notion of justice and fair play. I refused to agree a barrister to attend this costs hearing and in the end my property lawyer, Roland Court agreed to attend on my behalf. Motivated I expect by the possibility of being paid from the accounting process following the forced sale. I thought his intentions were good in representing me at that costs hearing and that there was some hope of winning at the very least, accounting for my costs in the property in advance of the distribution of the '50%' award to the liar. The £300,000+ I had spent fixing 28A post flood in the absence of Insurance. At least I might get that back. By paying Roland the bulk of it. Something would be better than nothing, even if he wouldn't take on the damages claim for his fiduciary failures, which was a far more realistic amount for Roland's hourly rate, being in the multiple seven figures.

I had some confidence that his self-certified skills as a litigator would lead to a hearing making Krasnopovich accountable for the various breaches since he cancelled my Insurance in 2013 and refused to return the freehold. In legal terms, his fiduciary responsibility as Freeholder meant that anything he did that was against my interests, including bringing this beneficial entitlement nonsense claim, was his liability. That as well as the loss of my property and rental income business.

At Le Clerc's costs hearing Krasnopovich/Clock/ Hazelwood made a case that because the judgment awarded him 50%, I should not have rented it out in advance of the forced sale. (Even though Flaherty had awarded him 450% of my rental income as well). Le Clerc agreed with their request to fine me £10,000. At 8% interest until paid. Obviously I didn't pay it. How could I with no income. Somewhere on some family-court clock that £10,000 fine is racking up 8% interest to this day. Once more I observe family-court being sensitive to Sam's prospects of seeing animosity between his parents assist his best interests. Because I had nowhere near £10,000 available to me, the only outcome would be that I would be in breach of his order because I couldn't pay. So the Flaherty costs award of over £100,000 for Clocks fee's plus the Le Clerc £10,000 fine both attract an ongoing interest charge because obviously in family law, awarding costs at 8% interest is always in a child's best interests, generating animosity between the parents.

And in an unsurprising twist, after that costs hearing and fine, Krasnopovich/Clock made an application regarding the forced sale. He wanted *'Sole conduct of sale'*. Again, I was not going to travel for this hearing, which I did not recognize as valid. I had Roland Court representing me at that hearing. He relayed to me that the application was made and he would let me know the outcome. Much to my surprise, Krasnopovich and Clock were able to choose the judge for that hearing.

Guess who the judge was?

The same Flaherty who was the switch judge at the April hearing. Roland Court got to meet her in person having heard so much about her. Of course she ruled in Krasnopovich's favor once more. More money for champagne and fun.

So at this point, he had won not only 50% of my properties, but with the costs and the interest and the 50% of the rental income, selling at the price set by Flaherty in court meant I had no prospect of receiving one penny after the payment of the mortgage and the £500,000+ legal fees. But I still had to keep paying the mortgage and maintenance. Which I only did because Mathew Court was going to pursue the accounting. (In invoices I paid relating to the flood claim alone a sum of some £299,000. Excluding any interest calculation.)

Or so I thought.

Did the award of costs plus interest against me assist Sam's best interests? Any more than ruling to force the sale of my home, using criteria that ignore the facts I disclosed, ensuring the property will not sell, leaving me not only homeless, but without the means to buy a home with all remaining equity gone in legal fees. The result being, my prospects of returning to the UK were not just affected. They were determined by this ruling.

By now we are up to early 2016. After the Le Clerc hearing which (property lawyer) Roland Court attended for me without a barrister in a cost saving measure, I received a demand for payment from FOS. By this time, having paid out close to £300,000 in legal fees I had literally no funds to call on. My rentals from my 3 properties not only didn't meet the costs of litigation debt repayment, but thanks to Flaherty and Le Clerc, I owed 50% of the rentals to Krasnopovich. As any landlord will tell you, there are always costs in owning a rental property. In my case, with the flood damage at 28A never having been properly addressed by insurers, the outcome was that 18 months of leaving a property rotting away in standing water meant things failed. And bills to fix those flood related problems often exceeded 50% of the rental income. The Flaherty judgment made no provision for the accounting reflecting the difference between gross and net. I was forced to retain a lawyer to argue that. And that lawyer was some £500 an hour. Adding up with every letter from Clock.

And the costs added up. In 2016 the staircase footing to the basement level collapsed when a plumber went through it while headed to repair a leaking toilet pipe. The stair frame had rotted through having been left so long in standing water post flood. eroded the wood bracing. Shortly after that the tiled floor in the master bathroom showed cracks. That floor construction involved 2X4 wood frame on which the tiles and bathroom fittings stood. This rotted after having stood in water for some 18 months. Weight on the tiles caused cracking. Examination showed that the entire floor had to come out, the wood frame replaced, and the tiles re-laid. All caused by leaving the property in standing water for so long without Insurance repair.

Electrical problems abounded. In one month alone my bill to the managing agents for electrical call outs was £1,200. Plumbing problems arose most months. The flood had shorted out the boiler and until I had a new unit installed 18 months after the flood, the pipes stood as they were. With standing water in freezing conditions. As a result there were multiple problems with the pipes. Including the radiators where standing water in the heating circuits required numerous call outs.

Firstly, all of these costs should have been paid by Insurance when the house flooded. There was an Insurance policy in place. And a named policy holder. And a lease agreement that bound the Lessor in a fiduciary responsibility to make up any shortfall in Insurance out of her own resources.

Secondly, the house was only habitable because I spent some £250,000 after the flood on making it so. Le Clerc's costs ruling awarded Krasnopovich 50% of the rental income. What about the costs I faced in respect of;

1.) Making up the insurance shortfall before tenants moved in and;

2.) The costs I faced repairing problems arising from the flood insurance failures while the tenants were in. This alone accounts for more than 50% of the rental income. But the ruling by Flaherty and Le Clerc does not consider this.

The two options I had at that stage were:
1.) Just walk away, let the house go into foreclosure and let Krasnopovich and the lawyer's squabble amongst themselves for another ruling by Flaherty to decide who gets what. Or;
2.) continue to honor my mortgage commitments and have a lawyer argue the accounting, including the historical Insurance and Freehold issues, towards a best-case sale scenario.

A conversation followed with Roland Court and Roland Chambers in which a demand for payment was made, with the mention that they were under pressure from FOS 'Management' to collect on the outstanding legal fees, an unspecified amount which was not sent by invoice, possibly because I have no fixed address for postal delivery. Unfortunately in this conversation they did refer to placing a charge on my home, which did little to change my impression of lawyers. None the less, having conclusively established that I really did have no money at all, instead of sacking me as a client they had a 'we are human' conversation in which Roland Court agreed to continue representing me towards the sale of the house and completing the accounting on the understanding that his bill (still unspecified) would be paid from the proceeds of sale of 28A and 28B. On one hand I hope his intentions were as he claimed, that he felt terrible for the way I had been treated by family-court, and wanted to see justice done. On the other, his only hope of getting any payment lay in the sale of the property where there was equity. 28B. He already knew that 28A, the one Flaherty had valued at £794,000, was not going to achieve what Flaherty and Krasnopovich claimed, because, they were lying all along, just as I said they were while they were calling me a mentally infirm liar for pointing out what the passage of time has made abundantly clear. They lied in that April 2015 hearing. And the trigger prices set by Flaherty, despite being at a vastly lowered level from the formal valuation, would never be achieved. Just as I said at the time I was discounted as a mentally infirm liar.

On this basis Roland Court continued with the final stages of negotiating the remainder of legal issues surrounding this forced sale. This led to a frustrating period of many months in which very little activity followed while I kept paying the mortgage and maintenance costs that arose from an empty property. Eventually the extent of his promised involvement changed to no more than ensuring the sale went ahead as quickly as possible without any commitment to following the original agreement to see through the accounting. Meanwhile, the costs in maintaining the property and meeting the mortgage payments added up to considerably more than I was earning. By this stage I had been forced to offer 'vacant possession' for the forced sale which meant, no rental income. I had to pay the costs despite knowing that absent of the intervention of a lawyer forcing 'accounting' on the moneys owed to me, I would get nothing from the sale. As time passed and every month saw the costs rise further, it became inevitable that a threshold would be crossed where, unless Roland committed to an aggressive demand for costs against Krasnopovich, the only source of revenue would be from the sale of the properties, and at the low amounts being proposed, that would not even pay the mortgage on 28A. Meaning I would lose my creditworthiness on top of everything else. All because a judge made a judgment in family court based on a lie.

When Roland Court attended the Le Clerc hearing on my behalf he made the point of approaching Hazelwood, as he assured me he would do, to confirm that

"This firm will pursue the accounting whatever happens, in full awareness that Ms. Lee is without funds."

When he told me that I felt reassured. At least there was someone in British law representing me. I was feeling very grateful to Roland Court for convincing me he was really going to see the claim though even though I could not pay him in advance for the legal work. And so I decided to keep on paying the costs to keep the sale possibility alive and continue to a hearing for accounting on the fiduciary failures. The costs in that claim against Krasnopovich would by far exceed the costs I had faced and I would then be able to retain the leading family law name in London to pursue custody of Sam. The extent of Krasnopovich's exposure in the matter of the fiduciary failures surrounding the freehold and the Insurance fraud, in which his conduct in cancelling my policy cover and blighting the claim, has seen possibly £500,000 in re-tanking plus £300,000+ in the costs I made up to make the property habitable, makes him liable. Along with the loss of the value of the property arising from the forced sale that his litigation has caused, being clearly a breach of his fiduciary responsibilities as Lessor (Freeholder) to act in my best interests. In a legal contest, the claim against him would easily be far north of £2 million. If it turns out perjury is also punishable with damages, then that sum would increase dramatically.

However, lawyers, like prostitutes, seldom if ever act without money up front. So Roland Court's enthusiasm to litigate diminished noticeably when we went onto the 'we are human' arrangement. Months would pass without any return calls while the tenancies expired and the property became vacant. At which point, there was no income at all to pay the mortgage costs. None the less, I can reflect that at that point the only member of the law society willing to represent me knowing the extent of my impecuniousness was Roland Court. Of course, when considering the mortgage of the property Flaherty awarded Krasnopovich 50% of, it is a fact that Krasnopovich has never contributed one penny towards, and even after he won 50%, still did not contribute one penny towards the mortgage I kept on paying in the years following the judgment to 'force-sell' my property.

I remained then, as ever, the only person paying the mortgages, in my sole name. Flaherty had ruled that she believed Krasnopovich's claim that he 'thought' he was paying towards the mortgage to be true. Although this was not supported in any basic evidence like bank statements, but anyhow. When Krasnopovich left he did not start any payments towards the mortgage. Why? If as Flaherty determined in her judgment, he contributed towards the mortgage, and owned 50% as a result, then why didn't he ever pay anything towards the mortgage. Especially at this time when he had won the court order giving him half the home. As ever, no reply to this query followed. I just had to keep on paying all mortgage and maintenance costs while he had 'sole conduct of sale.' And would have received 100% of any proceeds if they sold at the price Flaherty set as a sale trigger price.

If one could be bothered, say someone from the SRA or from a government office investigating fraud and child abuse, the list of obvious inconsistencies in Flaherty's judgment, flying in the face of concrete forensic detail as it does, would be long and the commonalities would glare. Prejudice. Reliance on opinion over fact. Serial breach of the SRA ethical guidelines. Reliance on anonymity to protect transparently disingenuous comments from the form of examination towards accountability for failures in even basic competence. Excluding material evidence.

It did not sit comfortably with me a that at a time like that, where the lawyers were in full awareness of the failures on family-law surrounding my matter, including their own part, they seemed more intent on getting paid than winning anything on my behalf. Perhaps I have been unlucky with lawyers and not all lawyers are the same. None the less, it is a fact that without Roland Courts ongoing involvement, I would have no representation at all and no prospect of seeing any payment from the accounting following the sale.

Here is the email I sent to FOS following that 'We are human' call.

From: Andrea Leandros
To: Roland Court

Dear Roland,

Thank you for our talk yesterday, 25th June. I write to summarize in brief.

We discussed moving forward with you representing me for the 18th July Judgment by Le Clerc and assist me in the resolution of what has become the ruinous litigation by Nico Krasnopovich.

We discussed the outstanding bill with FOS and the costs for the options going forward towards winning accounting for the various strands relating to fiduciary failures and Insurance matters being secured by means of a differential fee agreement, secured against an interest in one of my properties. I proposed the one with the highest equity, 28B Thameside. The best value in a sale would be the whole property with freehold at a figure around £2.5 million to an investment buyer. Three rental properties, each with tenants. Selling each individually, as per the court order – especially with disputes ongoing –attracts only fire sale buyers. But that is how it appears we will have to progress the sale. You indicated the motivation to assist me was largely on a human level borne of concern by yourself and Roland Chambers for the misfortune of my experience with family-law, in relation to the financial claim against me, my claim against Krasnopovich and the harm this visits on my 7-year-old son Sam. Thank you for making this point so well. I expected a better outcome from the Appeal process. Especially following the family-law President's ruling.

We did not specifically detail how the legal costs going forward will be allocated beyond my understanding that you will take on the matters as they arise on a success-based ratio to your usual fee, some of which, including the call on Friday, may be not charged, at your discretion. I am proceeding on the basis of trust that it is your intention is to prevail in my best interests rather than simply charge me what remains of my home equity until bankruptcy. And in the hope that whatever advantage is gained is not less than the legal cost involved. We mentioned the appeal process, the advantages of attacking Le Clerc's judgment, sending the file for a Chancery barrister opinion, and that you would secure a quote for this service which must be pre-paid. I indicated that despite having no access to funds at any level, in the coming week I anticipate the lease for 28A commencing and shortly after that I should receive the rental which will be some £2,000 which I could allocate for this purpose.

My understanding is that if this Chancery advice shows deficiencies in Le Clerc's judgment, then following the order on 17th July, I have 21 days to file an appeal, and that it may be that I can do this as applicant in person for reasons of cost and for time advantage. In this event, a hearing for this purpose might be subject to a delay.

We discussed in part the matters raised in my letter of 13th June, will be dealt with as appropriate by yourself. Specifically, the accounting process for the hearing on the 18th July. We did not raise the other points from my letter of 13th June, outside of specifics in Le Clerc's judgment, but which I believe must have a value. I would like to collaborate with you on somehow including these elements in this stage for Le Clerc if you require any detail on any of the points.

For example: His refusal to allow me alternate weekend visits with Sam unless I gave him £100,000, and succeeding in Court in preventing my application for overnight visitation by fighting tooth and nail to prevent my son seeing his own parent.

The exclusion of my witnesses in the April Tolata – through no fault of my own – and especially the IFA Larry Chester, who would have provided compelling hard evidence that Krasnopovich lied about the Freehold, about his interest in my properties and about the insurance history. Larry would clearly detail his separate finances and investment property of his own (his flat in Hounslow) and application to buy more investment properties of his own. There has never been a less '50/50 like we were married' couple than me and Krasnopovich. Everything was separate. There were no co-mingled finances. Loans only ever went in one direction. I was the financially established older person in the relationship who helped a low earning beginner up the ladder.

I had my witnesses' statements ready weeks before due date. Consider that I had nothing more important in my life than to conclude this matter. I had no motivation to be late with any filing. Clam and Castello filed on the Friday before the Monday hearing. Possibly because in the previous hearing, the application I made for visitation in 2013, the other side, Krasnopovich and Clock filed late on the Friday before the Monday hearing. It may be that Clam was simply trading tactics with them.

Whatever the reason, late filing, a judge who was switched to perform this precise function, the fact is the court is penalising my son for something neither myself nor my son is responsible for. And the judgment is wrong because of that omission. IFA Larry Chester was booked and ready to visit Court and testify, directly contradicting with substantiation claims Krasnopovich went on to make and which Flaherty accepted. Clearly perjury by Krasnopovich. If the judgment stands and we accept that an agreement was for '50/50 like we were married' then what of his property and assets.

This conclusion by the judge is not even mathematically or logically accurate because she didn't even include 28C Thameside, my third property, let alone his rental property. (So even in 50/50 like we were married, it's not representing 50/50 like we were married.) How does that make sense? 50/50 like we were married but only parts of my 50% of the marriage applies in this promise? If you are deemed to be 'married' it is 50/50 of everything.

I am proceeding in light of the choice I face between giving up now and allowing events to unravel without incurring any further legal costs, or placing my trust in your expertise in the hope that you will succeed in improving my position.

I identify this aspiration as getting rid of Krasnopovich's claim altogether, prevailing in my claims against him and by remedying the consequence his negligence has caused to my home. By restoring my financial position to what it was before his litigation, enabling me to return to the UK and raise my son. And at the minimum, getting the best-case outcome from the sale of my properties and the repayment of the Insurance and freehold consequences in the shortest possible time.

I look forward in the hope that at some point Krasnopovich will not continue getting away with lying and manipulating the legal system as he has done from the outset, removing my son in the way that he did, and that the Court system will not ultimately endorse the failures I have experienced leading to this position for my son and myself.

With best wishes,
Andrea

34 Final bill to family-law for visitation

Extracting the syringe of family law from the artery of my bank account.

By the end of 2015 I realized Roland Chambers (Family law at FOS) was not going to make any headway against Clock. Not without a £100,000 deposit to fund the case. The sheer brick wall Krasnopovich/Clock and Flaherty's obstruction placed in the face of any conventional approach left me in no doubt that '*working from inside the* system' continuing to pay family-law was not going to serve any purpose higher than more money to family-law. And more parental alienation and more child abuse. And more mortgage payments. Any complaint I have with Roland Chambers is placed in context by his comment "The damage was done before you came to us." David Clam was that damage. And now there really was no point spending $1 more on British family law to try and see my son.

Here is the last letter sent relating to visitation from my family lawyer, Roland Chambers, after seeing his appeal file fail so completely, followed by my reply.

From: Roland Chambers
Date: Wednesday, October 28, 2015 at 12:06 PM

To: Andrea Lee
Subject: Sam

Dear Andrea

Sam

Thank you for your email dated 26 October and the accompanying copy correspondence (of the same date) addressed to you from Tim Clock.

First, let me emphasise that from both a professional and personal perspective you have my every sympathy with your current predicament whereby Sam has enjoyed precious little time with you over the course of this year.

At the risk of stating the obvious, the current practical difficulties flow in large part from the fact that you are currently living temporarily in California and Sam is, of course, at home here in London. Inevitably, it will be said on behalf of Nico that the principal reason that Sam is not seeing more of you is because you have chosen to base yourself in the USA rather than finding alternative accommodation more locally to his home with Nico in Thameside-upon-Thames.

I am very conscious from our previous discussions and having regard to some of the lengthy (and acrimonious) history of your disputes with Nico that you have a very low regard for the family justice system in England. And, as I say, in many respects, I understand and sympathise with your frustrations and dissatisfaction with the process.

That said, however, and as a practitioner with some considerable experience of dealing with children matters in the family courts, my overriding advice to you (and anyone in your position) is that you must (albeit reluctantly) accept the constraints of the environment that you find yourself in, and you must operate within that environment in order to obtain the best outcome that may be achieved for you (and for Sam). In other words, there is little to be gained from seeking to resist the conventions and the procedural and legislative process that govern Children Act proceedings. Or, to put more colloquially, to make any progress you must 'play by the rules'.

As I say, I am already well aware of your dissatisfaction with the events of 30 October 2013 and the Consent Order made on that date by District Judge Beddy

I have, of course, considered DJ Beddy's Order very carefully. And, I am bound to say, that on the face of it the schedule of contact annexed to the Order is (objectively speaking) eminently reasonable.

I understand that you took exception at the time to (and remain exercised by) the fact that as part of the schedule of contact Nico demanded that two visiting contacts take place prior to overnight contact commencing. Obviously, as matters stand, I do not have sufficient information or insight into the proceedings or the events of 30 October 2013 to understand why Nico (and his advisors) were requiring this precondition to staying contact. Especially in circumstances where, as I understand the case, you had (on your own account) *"played an active and full part in Sam's upbringing and was intimately involved in the vast majority of his care up until [your] relationship with [Nico] end[ing] on 16 June 2013"*.

However, on the basis that these arrangements are all made in the context of a Consent Order (and I do appreciate and understand that you feel you had no option in this regard due, I think, to the possibility of a costs order being made against you), it appears to me that the advice that you would have received on that occasion would have been driven by pragmatism, and informed by the knowledge and understanding that after the two visiting contacts had taken place, the regime for Sam to spend time with you soon thereafter was what might fairly be described as entirely conventional (if not generous) insofar as it provides for Sam to spend alternate weekends with you as well as half of all his school holidays.

I should also say that the usual regime in Children Act proceedings is that each party bears their own costs, and I am unclear why you felt that if you did not agree to sign up to the provisions now enshrined in DJ Roberts Order that a costs order would be made against you.

As matters stand (and this is something which you and I may need to discuss over the telephone), I do not understand why the contact arrangements recorded in the schedule to DJ Beddy's Order were not taken up (other than your objection to the two 'conditional' visiting contacts).

Difficult though this may be for you accept, I must advise you straight away that regardless of the rights or wrongs of this analysis, mothers who find themselves in your position must take up any contact which is offered to them either voluntarily by the father or by way of an order. It is (and I re-emphasise, rightly or wrongly) regarded by the Court as entirely contrary to a mother's position for her to fail to take up any such contact.

As I say, in your situation, your initial difficulty in any further Children Act proceedings would be explaining to the Court why it is that you have determined to spend such a long period of time residing in California instead of basing yourself more locally to Sam. Inevitably (and regrettably given the complexity of the situation) this would doubtless take us back to the financial proceedings between Nico and you, as well as issues relating to your health and financial circumstances.

Of course, the Court can make orders which accommodate the fact that one parent may live overseas and sensible, practical arrangements can be fashioned in such circumstances. Your immediate difficulty is that DJ Roberts Order was made in circumstances where you and Nico were living locally to one another, and in light of subsequent events the contact arrangements have not been adhered to. The current relevance of DJ Roberts Order is therefore questionable (save only to record the fact that he was in October 2013 clearly content to agree that Sam spend extended periods of time in your care - and this is important).

Turning to your email and the specific queries that you raise; my comments are as follows.

First, in relation to overseas travel, please be conscious that at paragraph 2(A) DJ Beddy's Order provides both of you with permission "*to take Sam out of the jurisdiction temporarily during the time that he is respectively with each [of you]*". It goes on (I need hardly remind you) at 2(B) to say that "*for the purposes of any such travel out of the jurisdiction, the travelling parent shall provide to the other parent at least 14 days before the date of travel details of the proposed trip, including travel, destination and accommodation abroad*".

If, as you say, it is the case that Nico is taking Sam out of the jurisdiction (and has recently travelled with him to Abu Dhabi) without providing you with this information then clearly that does him no credit (particularly bearing in mind his professional occupation), and is a breach of that provision.

However, bearing in mind the fact that both of you have leave to remove Sam from the jurisdiction (i.e. there is no requirement to seek each other's consent each time Sam is removed from the jurisdiction of England and Wales for the purposes of a holiday) she is not, as would be the case absent the provision at 2(A), guilty of abducting him.

Similarly, if it is indeed the case that she is not providing to Sam the photo book and other gifts which you have sent to him, this is both unattractive and divisive.

By the same token, I note that Nico's agreement to facilitate telephone contact once a week at 6pm on a Wednesday evening is recorded on the face of the Order (I understand that the circumstances have changed entirely since October 2013 but nevertheless this provision remains).

Has there been any explanation as to why telephone contact and/or direct contact via Skype has deteriorated and broken down?

So far as what you refer to as the "*Sam File*" is concerned, you must approach this with great caution. Inevitably, it will be said in the context of any further correspondence or proceedings that you are seeking (albeit at some stage in the future) to embroil Sam in the dispute between his parents. I understand, of course, that at some juncture – most likely when Sam is himself a young adult – he may wish to know some of the narrative behind the circumstances of his own upbringing. However, if I were acting on your behalf in relation to children matters at the present time I would advise you very firmly to refrain from any further overt reference to the Sam File. Any Judge who learnt of the existence of this document would, I am afraid, regard it in a very dim light.

Similarly, on a related note, Tim Clock's request for written confirmation from you that you will not discuss "*with Sam such matters as legal process, arrangements over Christmas, moving to America or future visits to America*", is (I am afraid) entirely conventional. Indeed, it is frequently the case in Children Act proceedings that both parties agree and/or undertake not to make disparaging remarks about the other parent in the presence of the children or to discuss with the children the proceedings or the issues between the parents etc. etc.

Here again, if you were formally instructing me in relation to children matters, my very firm advice to you would be to agree to this provision albeit this would be in the context of a wide ranging letter to AFP addressing Sam's arrangements more generally (both in relation to Sam's direct and indirect contact with you going forward) and including our seeking Nico's agreement not to make disparaging remarks about you to Sam etc. etc. There is, of course, no reason why the kind of assurances sought by Clock should not be made on a mutual basis.

Based on what appears above, you will appreciate that my advice to you would be to see Sam at every opportunity that is offered regardless of how unreasonable you may think it to be. This is because you must, if you are to succeed in moving matters forward, demonstrate that you are taking up such contact which is offered and, conversely, not turning down opportunities for Sam to spend time with you.

In other words, to move forward in this environment you must behave in such a way that your conduct is seen to be unimpeachable and beyond criticism.

So far as your proposals for November are concerned, I would therefore not seek to remove Sam from school even for three days (as this request inevitably will generate controversy) but make proposals which accommodate the fact that he will be at school on the relevant days. Certainly, my advice to you would be to make realistic proposals for Sam to spend time with you whilst you are in the UK, however briefly.

I do take your point that if you 'bit the bullet' and made arrangements for the one night on offer, Nico may then retreat from this and cancel the contact at the eleventh hour. But, that is a risk you must take. You may then 'bank' the occasion of him having frustrated contact, as opposed to allowing him to 'bank' a further example of you declining to take up contact which is offered.

I anticipate that you will not like some (or all) of the contents of this note, but I hope you will appreciate that it is incumbent on me to provide you with objective advice as to what is realistic within the framework of Children Act litigation.

Once you have had the opportunity to consider the contents of this email, one way forward may be for me to let you have a draft letter to consider so that you may see what I would propose to say to Tim Clock if you instructed me to do so. The difficulty (and Nico is obviously all too well aware of this) is that adopting what would be a long-term strategy to instruct FOS to assist you in moving Sam's arrangements forward will be time consuming, may involve further litigation and will, inevitably, be expensive.

An alternative way forward is to consider the possibility of mediation in relation to Sam's arrangements (as encouraged by the Court on 30 October 2013), but it may (unfortunately) be the case that your relationship with each other is currently too polarised and toxic for mediation to be a realistic possibility.

I am, of course, more than happy to discuss this issue with you over the telephone but, as I say, I am additionally very conscious of the cost consequences.

Kind regards.

Roland
Roland Chambers
Partner

And the final letter from myself in relation to family law. Following advice I should write to Clock to arrange visitation options. And just pay family law more money to 'bite the bullet'.

From: Andrea Lee
Date: Wednesday, October 28, 2015 at 6:08 PM
To: Roland Chambers
Subject: Re: Sam

Dear Roland,

Thank you for the time and thoughtfulness you have put into your reply and especially the second line.

I do not propose to go through the points individually. I understand 'Bite the bullet or else' and will attempt to clarify my position in as brief a way as possible towards accepting the conclusion is best reserved for another time. Of course, as you say, I am aware of the cost consequences with your time.

I have learned through experience that family law operates within rules and guidelines. Nico is a lawyer and for over ten years I had first-hand experience of both the inner workings of family law as well as his interpretation of how to transfer this knowledge into billable hours.

For this reason, while I am tremendously grateful for your common sense approach towards explaining to me that 'the best outcome is achieved by operating within the environment' I would like to be clear that I understand and agree with you entirely. At the same time, for the best interests of my son and his relationship with me, you are quite wrong.

I am not interested in operating within the environment because I have a very different priority to that which the environment represents. Aside from the reality that working within the environment costs me on average £500 an hour and is very much what you would say if financially motivated, my priority is Sam's best interests. Yours is billable hours.

I believe that litigation generates acrimony and acrimony between parents is never in the child's best interests. (This is why I tried to settle/mediate etc.) Because of the nature of Nico's litigation in which he exploited the environment by perjuring himself while so easily manipulating the family justice system which puts forward a judge of Flaherty's ability, able to be so easily deceived and who so clearly disregarded Sam's interests on any level, you quite rightly point out that I have 'frustrations and dissatisfaction' with the process. Much of this arises from seeing how Nico keeps getting away with it. It is true to assume that I believe the family justice system does not place the child's best interests in the proportionate role.

None of which exists above my overriding priority; which is Sam's best interests.

I do not feel it is in Sam's best interests to be a victim of compromise in his rights regarding his relationship with his father following the very clear insight I have with my experience of family law, and in particular Nico Krasnopovich's position in determining what is best for Sam. This is someone I know to be an ethically toxic human being, who lies for a living and who has lied consistently through these proceedings, including on the record. (Which I thought was perjury, but evidently not when a family-lawyer does it in closed proceedings.)

I note in many instances you are working off written record. This does not tell the full story. For example, you observe in the matter of costs;

"I should also say that the usual regime in Children Act proceedings is that each party bears their own costs, and I am unclear why you felt that if you did not agree to sign up to the provisions now enshrined in DJ Beddy's Order that a costs order would be made against you."

To be clear, I faced a situation of **'sign this or you will face a costs order.'** It is that simple. My QC, hired by Clam to represent me at the visitation hearing after a late on Friday ambush notice, which is another example of a cost forced on me as I did not agree to hiring a QC in the first place, made clear that *"This did not just happen by coincidence. They have been planning this for weeks. I am afraid you have been set up."* So, while I appreciate enormously your moderate interpretation of events based on reading documents arising from Nico and Clock's way of working family-court, the fact is a great deal more straightforward than your analysis on how fair and generous the judgment by DDJ Roberts was.

The fact is, for 13 straight weeks I was denied visitation with my son, usually at the last minute, on the Thursday night before. As a result my lawyer, David Clam advised an application for visitation. Very straightforward. Pre-hearing interview with CAFCASS confirming no reason for any concerns. In fact assuring me I should look forward to seeing my son the weekend following the hearing. As the parent who was with the child 100% of the time, as opposed to Krasnopovich who was at best there 10% of the time.

Briefly: Krasnopovich and Clock played the system. Served ambush notice on Clam just hours before the hearing, on the Friday afternoon announcing they were bringing a QC to a preliminary hearing for visitation and taking an extremely offensive position in a cost's application against me, that led to Clam crumbling, and appointing a last-minute QC for me. Against my instruction. In that so-called hearing, the judge did not allow either barrister to speak. He simply deferred to the CAFCASS official. So that ruling which you describe as generous was made by a Ghanaian CAFCASS official of limited ability, who took a phone call during his 'judgment invitation' by Beddy, in which he reflected the father's disclosure that I was 'unfit' for overnight visitation.

Had I answered the same question to the CAFCASS official that day, Sam may well have been taken into care. I was aware that this was the case. When that fellow asked me 'Do you have any concerns over the child being with the father' all I had to do is say yes. As he did about me. He gambled with the child being taken into care as both parents reported the other as being unfit. I found myself being told by my QC. Either agree this document and sign it, or you will be hit with the costs. It is in this context that I find your reference to a voluntary agreement inadequately informed. I was coerced by extreme prejudice. It was, and remains, a disgraceful abuse of family-court by Krasnopovich and Clock. As a result of that court order ending what should have been regular visitation, events have moved on, and Sam has never had regular visitation with his own mother. Because Krasnopovich and Clock fought so very hard at his preliminary hearing to ensure that there would be no visitation. Bear in mind this was the first six-month period post separation and a crucial time for the relationship with my son. Making the deliberate obstruction of that relationship heinously offensive. Giving context to your opinion that the ruling was 'generous'.

Now, I have to decide what I am able to offer Sam and I have to determine where his best interests lie based on my authority as his parent and as a thoughtful person of good conscience and considerable insight into precisely this kind of situation.

I do not accept that either the various judges and lawyers in this process have superior insight into what is best for my son and nor do I accept their judgments as representative of Sam's best interests. Quite the contrary. I feel that I have been no more than a silent witness to parental alienation and serial child abuse by a gang of thieves protecting their own little job-for-life entitlement and a perceived status as members of an empowered elite.

I write now, as ever, with my child's best interests at heart.

In view of the acrimony that litigation visits upon embittered parents and with my experience of how diligently Nico uses his legal experience to exploit the residential parent position to trade visitation to suit financial expedience, I have no confidence in the family law system supporting Sam's best interests. The suck it and see approach you propose will not work because I have sucked it and seen. It is a toxic , diseased pill. Laced with deceit and monetary benefit for members at the expense of children's rights to see both parents.

It is far easier for you to offer me advice to keep paying £500 an hour to repeat the cut and paste training advice that enables you to charge me this rate in these circumstances than it is for me to see any value in doing so.

Sam has himself expressed his sorrow (on our recent visit when speaking to Jo, his godmother) of being used as a football by his father.

I am clear that no matter what I agree to or whatever compromises I might make, while litigation goes on and Nico controls 100% of the 'game' he will not agree the unconditional and unfettered rights for Sam to be with me and enjoy the benefits arising from our mother-son relationship. An area in which I have a great deal to offer. Children need their mothers.

Family-court has gone to great lengths to interfere with my sons' opportunities in this regard. Perhaps refresh your memory by looking at the costs plus interest award against me?

Looking to the past as to why the order by DDJ Berry was not followed is time wasting. My house flooded. I had no home in the UK. Nico along with Clock's firm paid a thug process server to confront me in the street. Around the time of that Court order Nico was getting away with terrible behavior while I was injured and homeless, quite literally, as a direct result of his intention. There was no possibility of DDJ Berry's order, the one I recognize as written by the hand of Nico, being adhered to. It is the product of a deceitful con by members of family court, used to prevent my son from spending weekends with me at a time when it was especially important in his development that he be allowed to see his Mother. There is no defense you can offer that changes that fact. They obstructed visitation at that crucially early time post separation (unless I paid them £100,000, in which case there would be unlimited unfettered visitation). And now, there is no regular visitation, which I suggest will show, in the fullness of time, their deliberate intention.

It is ridiculous to speculate that I voluntarily agreed phased-in contact. Clearly the very reason I went to court is because I did not agree to phased-in contact. The words 'unfettered contact' appear from the outset of my demands on my sons behalf. I wanted my son to be with me without delay after a period of 13 weeks where Nico blatantly offered me visitation if I paid him £100,000. It is that clear cut.

"I can stop you having Sam overnight easily. Unless you give me the money I will ensure you don't have overnight visitation."

You have only to read the timeline leading up to that hearing and the correspondence exchanged over those 13 weeks to see how clear cut this is. Nico and his lawyer played the system like a slot machine. The emergency QC I had to pay £5,000 to attend the hearing told me as much. Not a bad return on a £5,000 payment to British family-law.

My intention is to be clear about what Sam's best interests are. My belief is that Nico will not stop using visitation with Sam as leverage to affect me until the litigation is over. That is what I want to do for Sam's best interests. Win this fiduciary/Insurance matter and get back on track financially to where I was before being mugged by Nico the lying family-solicitor.

I have been clear from the outset that I will provide what is best for Sam. What that turns out to be in terms of visitation, emotional and financial contribution is my decision. (The financial part is not my decision, as the CSA have already ruled.)

It remains the case that I will do what is best for Sam and at this time, what is best for Sam is being removed as moving target in family-law litigation. When Nico is ready to allow Sam to enjoy the opportunities I represent for him as his mother, then it will take the form of unfettered visitation within the terms I am able to offer. Not in a legal gagging order written and controlled by someone I know to be a psychotic liar, with his use of parental alienation and willingness to abuse the child. What I am able to offer is a quantifiable set of opportunities all of which are subject to one concern. My health and wellness, without which I can offer nothing at all.

You mention the adverse effects of me moving to California as if it is a choice I made that '*reflects poorly on my visitation prospects*'. Again this appears to me as cut and paste training advice that ignores entirely the facts of why I became unable to remain in the UK. I did not elect to move to the USA. It was a circumstantial consequence forced on me by the actions of Krasnopovich., the flood of my home, the fiduciary failures of the trustee freeholder and the forced sale of my home and income generating business in the UK by a family court judge. It was not my choice to leave the UK. I loved living in the UK. I was forced to leave as a consequence of a determined and deliberate approach by Krasnopovich and his family-law associates. I am unable to return because 1.) I have not received any payment for the appropriation of my £2.5 million money generating asset. And.

    2.)   I cannot risk being in the jurisdiction of Krasnopovich who has already paid to have me attacked and gotten away with it without so much as a warning letter from the SRA. I have valid reasons to believe he represents a clear and present threat to my well-being that is best served by locating myself outside of the jurisdiction he is able to manipulate to serve his deviant purposes at will.

The fact is that his actions required my spending hundreds of thousands of pounds on litigation to see my son, and ensure, by insurance fraud and breach of fiduciary responsibility, that I have no home in the UK, no place to live, and feel unsafe following the historical conduct of members of family-law. Hiring a 6-foot goon to doorstop me, alone in my home late at night. Roland, that has left a mark on my confidence. He has faced no accountability for any of this malicious, criminal conduct. I am labelled by the English court as a mentally infirm liar. Why would I want to remain in a jurisdiction that stole my home, business and beautiful son, on this chalice of bitter deceit.

There can be no conversation on what I can provide for Sam if I am not well and clearly this must remain my first priority. My decision to withdraw from fighting over visitation is with my health in mind as much as with Sam's best interests. This family court business has made me ill. It feels very much like abuse of the worst kind. For myself as well as for my son. I have already used the analogy of rape and there is no reason I can see to review this appraisal of my experience in British family court. I conclude that there is very little point in challenging Nico for any visitation in 'his own back yard', that is British family-law, because not only are all the cards stacked in his favor, but because I know that he will put his fight for money above Sam's best interests every time. In this regard he has a 100% consistency level. I can observe here that in the Appeal hearing, you were fidgeting and sending the Judge a visibly distressed message. For all of your good intentions and reassurances, the fact is, aside from presenting some sizeable bills and being a first-rate lunch companion, your net effect on my matter has been inconsequential.

With the benefit of my considerable forethought and paid advice from professionals in child psychology I feel confident that I am acting for the highest good in Sam's best interests in a well-informed, responsible way.

I accept there will be a period of time in which Sam will not see me and I understand that Nico will present this in the most opportunistic manner, both to him with the clear and ongoing intention of, as you say, 'poisoning the well', which I call parental alienation, as well as in any litigation where he is able to refer to his reasonable and measured approach.

I believe the 'Sam File' will be a tremendously valuable resource to Sam as a young man when working with his therapist because let us not be in any doubt about where this process leads. The statistics in regard to this matter do not lie. It is very much in Sam's best interests that he will one day be able to see how events unfolded and why all those moments happened. Why mummy forgot to send him the Wii Games console and the games she promised she would for his 6th birthday. Why mummy never sent those gifts she said she did. Why mummy didn't take him skiing when she said she would. Why mummy didn't take him to see Maria when she said she would.

This pervasive system of selective, convenient filtering of information to protect the aberrant parent as well as the child abusing judge from having their actions reviewed by the child in the course of his understanding what happened cannot fairly be left hidden under arcane contempt laws. Sam has been lied to. By his father. And by the judgment. While it may be that contempt and defamation laws protect the offenders at this time, the damage their actions do will in the fullness of time become subject to the child's own judgment.

At this time my next opportunity to review visitation possibilities for Sam will follow November 9. If the judgment is as we fully expect, it will end any prospects of visitation for Sam with me until the Fiduciary /Insurance matter is concluded. As I have already made clear to you, I will be unable to pay to see Sam anyhow, so it will be a mute-point.

Or, perhaps, there exists in family-law some self-policing element which will intervene to examine exactly how these members of family-law have got away with the multiple breaches of not just the SRA ethical code, but using parental alienation and child abuse in exchange for profit.

Nico will have prevailed in what was his intention from the outset. I have no doubt at all that every decision he has made since choosing to leave on fathers-day is to set up a new life with a new partner in a new family in which Sam seeing me would only ever form an obstacle. He chose the optimal time to leave to cause me the most upset, to remove the child from my home. He demanded a sum of money when he left. He worked out how much he thought I was good for. And when he didn't get it he used every means at his disposal to litigate, without on one single occasion pausing to consider Sam's best interests. A deviant child abuser enabled by a broken system. Switch judge DDJ Flaherty didn't even pretend to conduct a fair and balanced hearing. It was so blatantly fixed. Castello told me '*If we get Flaherty we will lose.*' Because he knew it was one member of family law giving license to another. He has been 100% correct in his predictions of Flaherty's conduct.

The beneficial entitlement claim arose from a demand for money in exchange for me seeing Sam. It is at the heart of his litigation. Fist a blackmail demand for money in exchange for visitation. And then a BE claim based on a spuriously improbable promise. Did this promise ever occur? Not on a range of possibility of infinity to the power infinity was he ever even led to believe there was a chance of him being promised '*50/50 like we were married.*' It is a cold lie devised by two manipulative members of family law to play the system after the saw the blackmail for visitation effort had not produced the payment they sought. And the outcome is what it is. Parental alienation and child abuse.

Now we all live with the consequences of our actions. For me that means a new life in a new county, starting from zero, with a huge debt arising from these proceedings. For Sam it means waiting until he is old enough to find me. Not a day passes without my thoughts turning to Sam and his welfare. I believe it is the same for him. For four years, from birth, we were together all the time. The neural pathways in the parent child symmetry were perfectly formed to connect us. I believe he will one day find me.

Since fathers-day 2013 I have seen Sam for a few nights here and there, possibly a total of 9 nights, but only once have I had him for one prolonged visit, a 3-week period, and after that visit (August 2014) he stopped all Skype Contact and started another round of litigation. (This followed on from Krasnopovich tape recording my conversation with Sam in California in breach of the California Penal Code that makes Breach of privacy by recording without knowledge or consent a criminal offense.) Krasnopovich has successfully stopped all contact at this point and so that is that.

Once he succeeded in preventing my 2 night a month Application for visitation in the Months after he left in 2013, spending tens of thousands in family-court bringing a QC and applying for costs just for this purpose, the continuity in regular visitation was broken, in that first crucial 6-month period, and as we now see, that opportunity has never come again. Imagine how many letters I have written, how much I have spent in lawyer's fees and how many disappointments I have experienced in canceled visitation and interrupted Skype contact. And then I hope you will see why I believe my decision is best for Sam as well as the only choice I have for my own health. This is not a fair fight. I have seen close up, an inherently corrupt system. You are aware of how many clear breaches of court order have occurred. Yet you cannot point me to one example of Krasnopovich being censured. Offenses, like removing the child from the Country, that would have ordinary parents in serious trouble. I could list 15 specific dated instances of breach of court direction by a member of family law, supposedly held to a higher standard, right now. And still not one of my complaints has seen any censure at all. He lies and gets away with it. Every time. Your reply is 'The judge will take a dim view.'

Thank you for reading the detail on my matter and replying to me. Let's not run up any further costs because as you say it *'may involve further litigation and will, inevitably, be expensive.'* Similarly, your observation that's relations are *'too toxic for mediation'* is accepted. I have proposed mediation many times. Why would he mediate when he can do whatever he chooses in family-court.

Please let me know how best I can assist with any preparations for November 9th. Perhaps Richard would like my input into his submission in advance?

Regards,
Andrea

35 The freehold, fiduciary responsibility and the AXA
The lying judge and the Insurer who does not pay a legitimate claim

I have already detailed how Krasnopovich's advice came to place the Freehold title to the home I bought in 1986, into his name shortly after meeting him in 2003. This gave him the opportunity to deceive Insurers in securing policy cover in 2003. The agreement between Krasnopovich and myself, bearing in mind I had known him for a matter of weeks when this situation arose, was in a declaration of trust in which he would return the title to me in 5 years. He would go on to convince DDJ Flaherty that he 'owned the freehold' to my home because I gave it to him, and the follow on "*50/50 like we were married*" to a young man I had met a few months previously, who I was clearly helping financially to an enormous extent. Of course anyone with a £2 million+ property would give half to a virtual stranger two months after meeting in an agreement made with such complete secrecy that not even one single person knew about it. And not one single email referenced it?

Seems completely plausible?

Flaherty believed him when he said in court of his spurious claim to be the freeholder of my home; "*I own it.*' Having first taken the precaution of excluding the witness testimony of our financial advisor able to show documentary evidence that this claim was a lie.

The freehold trust agreement was based on the 5 years it takes for Insurance to 'forgive' previous claims. When applying for building Insurance the application form reads *"Have you claimed in the past 5 years and if so, give details."* In 2007 five years had passed and I was reminded by a call from my IFA Larry Chester to take care of the transfer of the freehold back to my name and to go in and see him about re-insurance for the building. The Annual Insurance date for 2007 was approaching. I met with Larry and agreed his Buildings Insurance advice (Which was his firms' brokerage though the AXA Insurance.) All that remained was to Krasnopovich to transfer the title back as per my email request.

I told him about Larry's proposal and the timing for the re insurance. *"We will transfer the title back to my name and I will do the Insurance directly from next month."* At exactly which point the house flooded, in 2007. I arrived home from tennis and went downstairs, barefoot, and felt the wetness creep up between my toes. Within minutes the water was rising above the level of the carpet. It had rained heavily for the past few weeks and the water table was high. The Thames was right up against the road. My first thought was *"Fuck. The tanking has failed"* which of course it had. That put paid to the return of title at that time. While Krasnopovich was the named party on the policy cover it would have been imprudent to change Insurance cover with a potentially huge claim in prospect. Larry's advice was to leave it as it is for now. Flaherty explains it as follows.

19.   Ms Lee is the sole legal owner of three leasehold properties, 28A, 28B and 28C Thameside which is a large Victorian property on the banks of the River Thames. The freehold to this property was transferred into the name of Mr Krasnopovich in 2003 as a result of difficulties in obtaining insurance as a result of an earlier flood damage claim.

Firstly, once again, Flaherty is factually wrong. In saying "**earlier flood damage claim**". There was no flood damage claim in 2003. This is typical Flaherty inability to get even get the basic facts right when the future of a child is at stake. Attention to detail is not a strength for this DDJ. Or even, evident at any stage of her summary. This is just one more in a long list of factual errors a judge known for her 'weakness in financial matters' can expect to get away with.

Fire, flood, what's the difference. Who cares. It's family court.

By assuming that Flaherty is guessing and considering the facts from that period of time, it is plausible to assume she has confused the fire of 2001 with the flood of 2007. Easily done by when you work on holiday. What else are holidays for, sipping champagne, having fun and knocking out a quick judgment on the side. Details? Pah. Who needs all that extra work reading statements. Not when there's fun to be had and champagne to be enjoyed in a juvenile delinquent lifestyle by a holidaying judge. It might have taken as much as three minutes to locate the information in the Mothers statement. But considering Flaherty has determined the Mother is an inveterate liar and mentally infirm, she could safely assume no point in wasting valuable fun time verifying any details by reading her statement. And of course, what difference would it make. No one would ever be allowed to read this judgment for the purpose of identifying this error.

It is though for me upsetting to record another example of Flaherty's cavalier approach to completing a judgment without bothering to check even basic facts. Available to her just by turning a few pages in one of the seven folders her job required her to read.

Although this may appear as one small thing, it is one more thing in a long list of small things in a long list of things small and not so small which demonstrate the extent of Flaherty's incompetence. A basic laziness. Her error strewn judgment had ruinous consequences. It abused a child. It made me homeless and meant I could no longer live in the UK after 29 years. And yet this error strewn judgment is made un appealable. She has licensed herself to be this lazy because the checks and balances that we associate with a working judiciary are absent. She knows no one can ever read the detail of her deceit.

I have hearsay confirmation from members of family law familiar with her work in family-court, as well as her work record as a barrister, that Flaherty has presented similarly incompetent uninformed opinions, turning evidence to suit her convenience, ruining the lives of other children. If appearances matter, then I suggest, just looking at her tells a story.

Here's what happened leading up to the Insurance claim preceding the transfer of the title into Krasnopovich's name. All of this evidence was available to Flaherty. But I guess reading through details while you're on holiday drinking champagne and having fun and posting on Twitter doesn't leave much time for getting to the bottom of what is really a significant part of the claim. The only evidence Krasnopovich can show of anything in his name is the freehold. He had nothing to back up his claim of a promise worth x million pounds. No emails. No witnesses. Not one family member prepared to say they *'remember Nico telling them about this promise.'* Just zero. As is the way with fabrication. This is why he clung to the Freehold with such determination, even after the flood when it became apparent the fiduciary responsibilities exposed him to 'make up insurance shortfall' that would far exceed his claim. He doubled down in the hope that he could ignore any Insurance requests, with a *'so sue me'* approach, knowing he could exhaust my means to pay legal fees for this purpose long before that day came. In her court, Flaherty was aware that Krasnopovich claimed he owned the freehold. It has his name on it. She also knows there is some dispute because I say the freehold is mine (I bought it in 1986, as disclosed in the Land Registry documents Flaherty had sight of) and was only ever held in trust by Krasnopovich, to be returned on demand. Which Krasnopovich has not done. Even after agreeing to do so to ensure I transferred his business Web domain names titles in June 2013.

He has not returned the title as required and as he had agreed to because it is the sole document supporting his beneficial entitlement claim that he was 'promised 50/50 like we were married.' He has viewed the risk of going to court without one single shred of anything supporting his unsubstantiated claim, as greater than the risk of being made accountable for the responsibilities of the freeholder as the Insured party. So the circumstances of why the freehold is in his name are important. Especially because since the litigation began, Krasnopovich refused to return the title as required by law, illegally cancelling the policy in my name, months before the house flooded, giving rise to a half million-pound claim that continues to rise with every day while the property sits unrepaired from the breached tanking. By claiming to own the freehold, the fiduciary responsibilities inherent in that contractual agreement make him liable for all that followed in respect of the harm it caused me.

One witness who Flaherty refused to allow, my IFA for 29 years, Larry Chester, was ready to provide an independent professional review backed up with memos from the time and quotes for House Insurance including details relating to the freehold transfer. Documents that implicate Krasnopovich in insurance fraud, essentially exposing the substance of Krasnopovich's claim. Why then would Flaherty not only refuse to allow this witness, but when preparing her judgment, not even read up on the background of this integral piece of Krasnopovich's claim. The statement by Larry Chester was admitted to the court and Flaherty could all to easily have simply; opened the document. Read the contents. And used the information set down by a respected professional for no purpose higher than to inform the court on exactly the issue being adjudicated. Flaherty did not look into this matter, as is made clear by her inability to identify the nature of the claim leading to the freehold transfer. I think, speaking from personal experience, there is a significant difference in fire and flood. Both experientially by the person being burned or flooded as well as by the demands on the Insurance cover. Flaherty chose to bother-not on even finding out why it was important she be aware of the fact it was a fire claim. A significant detail as that fire claim is the very reason the Freehold went into Krasnopovich's name.

Here is the sequence of events leading to the transfer of my freehold title, bought in 1986 when I bought 28 Thameside, into Krasnopovich's name.

In 2001, my home burned. I became one of the 25% of Brits who experience a home fire. My home was built in 1896. It was wired for electricity in 1920. At a time when homes ran very few electrical devices. Electricians then could not have foreseen the growth of electrical equipment and the demands they would place on electrical circuits. On that Friday, as I was laying back watching the movie on the VHS with a friend. Out of Africa, with Meryl Streep. At 9.02 we were interrupted by a loud CLACK. William the Schnauzer jumped up and started barking. It was about the same volume as Ringo Starr using a 5a Vic Firth drumstick to smack a piccolo snare. I got up to investigate. I thought it came from the kitchen. After a few minutes of looking around without finding any clue, we decided to take William for his evening walk to the Kings Head. I pushed pause on the VHS and off we went, down Thameside to the Kings Head, where we were for some 35 minutes, before setting off back home to carry on with our movie. As we turned left into Thameside I noticed a small crowd outside of my home. Getting closer I saw my upstairs tenants standing looking up at the building. They saw me.

"The house is on Fire".

I looked up and saw no flames. But I did see that the lights were out, and the windows looked too dark. Possibly black? I elected to inspect the condition inside. The fire department had not yet arrived. My friend held William while I opened the house door and went upstairs to the first level. I unlocked the door to 28B. There was no flame. I smelled smoke. I knew that my studio equipment, all my master tapes and client files, stood just inside the next door, and on a stand just thirty feet away, stood my new hand-made Taylor guitar, bought only a month previously in Los Angeles. The most expensive and best guitar I had ever owned. An object of great value.

I decided to make a run for it. Into the darkened room – grab the guitar – and run out. It was only some thirty feet away. Although in darkness, I knew exactly where it stood. I tiptoed in readiness for my flying start into the darkness. And then it became very clear to me that something was very wrong with the color of the darkness. It had a red glow. A swift change of plan followed. I withdrew, closed the door and made my way downstairs thinking, darn, I only had that guitar for a month. I could have made that run into the darkness.

The fire brigade arrived about five minutes later. Two big red engines. The leader looked at the front of the house. The crew put on tanks and masks. Still no flames. And no action by the Fire fighters. I asked why they weren't going in. Too dangerous was their reply. Another twenty minutes passed. I was by now quite unimpressed by the Fire Department. Thinking they could have save a lot of damage by going in and finding the fires epi-center and extinguishing it. Eventually, the chief explained what they were going to do. "We will break the window to the middle flat. That will let air in. Once the fire gets oxygen it will ignite in a fireball. Then we know what we are dealing with and we will go in with foam. Not water because that will ruin everything below. He took a long pole with a metal extension on its tip and in one swift smack, broke the large bay window of 28B. A roaring sound followed accompanied by a red flash of flame. Three firemen in full body suits with tanks and masks went up the stairs, carrying super-sized foam spray extinguishers. Ten minutes later it was all over. They had smothered all hot areas. I walked over the bridge to a nearby Hotel and spent the night there. They didn't charge me for the room. The following morning, early, I went back to the house, by appointment with the Fire chief, who had to accompany me. One reason being the importance of a forensic report for any Insurance claim. He warned me that going into my home to see nothing but wet black mush would be traumatic. It was. It stank. I looked around and basically, 28B was incinerated. Just black floor, walls and ceiling. The Taylor guitar I almost grabbed was no more. I found the strings in the black mess on the floor. The only part of the guitar that survived the immense heat.

Later the Fire Department forensics guy arrived and got to work determining cause. Meanwhile, with William in the passenger seat I drove to Weybridge to the office of my Insurance broker, Ken Quigley.

My IFA, Larry Chester had introduced me to Ken Quinton in 1986. His company, Firndowne Insurance had handled my Insurance ever since. Ken was simply great. He sat me down in his office, brought me a cup of tea and William a bowl of water and said;

"Don't worry about a thing. You are covered. We will get everything sorted for you".

The Insurer was the AXA. Lucky me. A reputable Insurer. Two hours later all the calls were made and I was cleared to find a rental property which Insurers would pay for. Like-for-like accommodations. I called a lettings agent I knew, George, and he talked me through a few comparable properties. That same day I had found a place, in West End, Esher. Moving was easy. I owned nothing so just me and William showed up. Insurers also rehoused my upstairs tenants and paid me the rental income I was losing so I could pay for them to be rehoused. Exactly as per the Insurance cover I had been advised to take by Larry Chester. This was my first experience of buildings and contents cover. It showed that I was well advised and had appropriate cover for my needs, including covering my loss of rental. And my like for like rehousing.

Inside of 6 months all the remedial works were completed. All of my contents were replaced as the cover provided. Forensics showed the fire was caused by an overload on a Bakelite switch, the original Bakelite circuit breaker installed in 1920 located under the floorboards near the kitchen. The circuit breaker snapped and interrupted the circuit to the fuse protection. That was the snare drum smack we heard. While we were out in the pub, the wires underneath the wooden floor overheated. The dust of generations around those red-hot wires started to smolder. Soon a critical heat mass was reached and the floorboards began to combust, sucking up all the oxygen in the room. The heat rose and went up through the floor of the upstairs flat 28C. The tenants in there smelt it and raised the alarm by running outside. And that's when I arrived back from the pub. As the temperature inside the house was rising to furnace level. Once the house was fully reinstated to its previous condition I moved back in. By now it was 2002 and the Insurance came due for renewal. Ken Quinton explained to me that Insurers were bound by law to reinsure after a big claim for one year, but that we should expect problems the year after that because they don't like to insure high claim properties and were not bound by law to continue cover as was the case in year one post big claim. So it proved, in 2003 when Insurance renewal arrived Ken told me that the AXA would not reinsure. We would have to go with a high-risk insurer the bill would go from £400 a year to £2,500+. Oh well. The issue that flagged the problem was the claim application wording;

"Have you claimed more than £50,000 in the past 5 years". Obviously I could not answer No to that one.

And around this time in my life I met Nico Krasnopovich. The ambitious young lawyer whose every second word was Uhm. When this Insurance aspect arose in conversation he had some legal advice for me. Put the Freehold in my name and I will get cover because I can answer No to that question. *"I have never claimed over £50,000 from Insurance. If I have the freehold in my name, I can answer no. And in 5 years-time, I'll just transfer the title back to you. No harm done."*

I checked with Larry Chester. He laughed out loud. *"You can't do that. Its fraud."* I relayed this to Krasnopovich.

"Who's the lawyer? Larry is not. I am not lying. It's the truth I have not claimed £50,000 in the past 5 years. I have checked with a property law partner at MWT. This will work."

I agreed to go with Krasnopovich's advice over Larry's. My mistake. Krasnopovich makes a very convincing liar, after all he does it for a living and this approach would save me £2,000 a year, for four years. Krasnopovich agreed to complete the transfer of title at the Land Registry and take out Insurance in his name. Aside from the verbal agreement to transfer back in 5 years, following Larry's advice, I had a declaration of trust done by my local law firm, Infields. A simple one page 'Declaration of Trust'. As advised by Larry this document noted that the date for transfer would be at the time of Insurance renewal in 2007. (Or upon demand.) A date he would put in his calendar and remind me of in 2007. No money changed hands for this Freehold title transfer. Just a favour for a friend, who was housing him for nothing and treating him to expensive holidays abroad. Once the 5-year blight on my name and the Insurance history passed, he would transfer it back to my name. He had the paperwork done, and I signed over the title to his name. All of which was memo recorded by Larry Chester in the context of his advice to me and the change of Insurance. Krasnopovich applied for Insurance with a different broker, not disclosing any claims history and hey presto. Low cost Insurance. Larry Chester never spoke to me for a year after I placed Krasnopovich's advice over his. The only occasion in which I never took his advice on a financial matter.

Life moved on. 4 years passed. Here we are in 2007. Larry Chester called me with a reminder. It's been 5 years since your claim, put that title back in your name. Come see me about the reinsurance for the house.

So the process began.

I told Krasnopovich this is what we were going to do. I don't recall his reaction but nothing stands out. Larry quoted for reinsurance. And in that period of time, after Larry quoted for reinsurance but before the transfer of the title back to my name had completed, the house flooded. No point transferring title now. The claim for that flood went through in his name.

Then in 2008 my home flooded again, this time a serious flood. The building was still Insured in his name. The AXA was the insurer. Gab Robbins the loss adjuster. A surveyor arrived. Established blown tanking as cause And in no time at all they undertook the repairs to return the property to its pre incident condition. In total they paid out some £300,000 to re-tank and replace contents. All paid to the Insured party, Krasnopovich. The agreement terms of the freehold imposes a fiduciary responsibility towards the leaseholders as is common in freehold leasehold assignations of this type. When in 2013 Krasnopovich cancelled my contents policy with the AXA, he claimed to be the freeholder. If this is true, irrespective of any trust agreement, the Lessor (The freeholder) is bound by the specific terms of the agreement. This spells out clearly what is required. And that is, to make up any shortfall in Insurance out of own resources. Or to paraphrase. If the Insurance does not pay out in full to restore to 'pre incident' condition, then the freeholder is personally responsible for making up the shortfall.

While I had Insurance cover for Buildings and contents with the AXA, Krasnopovich successfully had my cover cancelled. But even so, as the freeholder he was liable for providing the insurance. However when the house flooded in 2014, I received nothing. I became homeless having to pay hotel bills, while negotiating with the Lessor, Krasnopovich, to either return the freehold and let me handle it from there, or to take on responsibility as freeholder and make up any shortfall out of own resources. He did neither. He simply made sure the claim did not succeed. As a result had to pay out some £250,000 to make 28A habitable. Making up the shortfall in Insurance knowing that the Lessor had the fiduciary obligation to pay.

Then in May 2015, the next-door neighbors tree surgeon miscalculated and a large tree fell onto my home, causing £15,000 damage. I notified the lessor and Insured party. He refused to claim. He also told the AXA they were not authorized to talk to me. I was not named on the policy cover. (Itself a breach of fiduciary.) I ended up paying the repair bill myself. To be claimed later at the accounting process.

The same when the stairs and bathroom collapsed in 2016 from damp rot from the standing water post flood, causing £8,000 of damage. No Insurance claim went in. I had to pay the costs myself and hope my lawyer would follow through in the accounting process, which he would only do when he was paid following the sale. Aside from receiving nothing from the AXA, I had to make up all the costs in these three claims. A sum now north of £275,000 excluding any interest calculation. And excluding the £90,000 I would go on to pay in mortgage and maintenance while the property was empty awaiting 'sole conduct of sale' by Krasnopovich. Costs wise, on the house matter I was down almost £400,000, and in legal costs down £500,000 increasing at 8% interest. And I had nowhere to live in the UK. And was prevented by court order from entering my own flat. (Flaherty's order.) This all only happened as a consequence of Krasnopovich claiming in Flaherty's court that he was the freeholder. And her accepting this was the truth. Which is it then? If Krasnopovich is the freeholder, then he is obligated to make up the shortfall in Insurance. Flaherty accepts Krasnopovich is the freeholder, for as long as it suits the TOLATA claim, but rules in the end that the freehold is mine? Making matters more interesting for Flaherty is that she attempted in court to make me agree to indemnify Krasnopovich from any Insurance liability.

Why? If he has done nothing wrong, then why try and get me to indemnify her colleague.

I wrote a blog about the AXA, in the attempt to get the AXA to talk to me directly. I linked it to a Twitter # to ensure their swift reply. On the basis that I had then been a paying customer for 28 years. The AXA did not respond, choosing instead to block me on Twitter. The Insured party was Krasnopovich. And they would only talk to the insured party. I was not named on the policy even though that was a condition in the Freehold/Leasehold obligations. Pretty shabby conduct by a big insurer. With whom I had paid full premiums in full annually for 28 years by that point. I believed they had a duty of care to me to see past the fact I was not named on the policy because of an aberrant Lessor guided by malice.

Here is the Blog: Read by over 100,000 as at September 2017. From the Point of view of a long-standing customer who has paid Buildings and Contents cover for 28 years (at that time.)

AXA Insurance. Original blog posted September 29, 2014 · By Andrea Lee

Update: December 2016.

The AXA Insurance and my flood claim from 8 February 2014.

I confirm I have not had one penny in Insurance almost three years since my home flooded. No contents has been paid, although I had a paid for contents policy. No Buildings cover has been provided and no rehousing has been paid. I have had to raise over £250,000 to date to effect repairs myself to make the house habitable. However because of the delay in repairs – some two years – the effects of leaving the property standing unheated in damp conditions has led to costly breakdowns since. Most recently, June, 2016, the collapse of the staircase as the footing was standing in water and rotted, and the collapse of the bathroom flooring because the wooden frame on which the floor tiling was supported rotted through. I requested a claim for that cost. Still waiting for a reply. And yet I have paid for full Insurance cover for some 28 years on this property.

The AXA and the buildings and contents cover for my home

My Thames side home flooded in February 2014 in an event that made the news and was for me a traumatic experience. (BBC: 10 Feb 2014: *Thousands of homes along the River Thames are threatened with flooding as waters continue to rise. Aerial footage of the river between show the extent of the flooding.*) Lots of sewage and Thames water washing through my beautiful home. I wasn't even there at the time, being away on holiday.

Lucky for me my Lessor, a professional lawyer, Nico Krasnopovich, had buildings cover with AXA Insurance. I have had cover for my home since 1986. Fully paid up annually in advance, buildings and contents.

First off I needed immediate **rehousing**. Obviously living in an excrement flooded dwelling with black mold appearing on the walls was not going to be an option for me, with family members including a 5-year-old son and my 79-year-old father. The building not only stank. The boiler was damaged beyond repair by flood water and the electrics did not work for some time. Also, it is cold in February. After initially inviting my hotel bills and quotes for a 6-month lease while works were undertaken, following a meet with the Landlord, Insurers reversed their position. Saying the house was habitable and as such they would not pay the rehousing stipulated in the policy. I was assured that I should put my fears that it might be a breach of health and safety law to one side and consider living in the flooded property as 'adequate rehousing'. That there was no heating, as well as no electricity initially, did not seem to the AXA to be at odds with providing 'like for like' housing. It seemed clear there was some collusion between the Loss Adjuster and the Landlord in undermining the policy cover.

The market rehousing equivalent of my home is £4,000 per month. Given the urgency with which I needed rehousing, I was staying in Hotels, paying on my credit card, while I waited for a suitable lease, I took the first feasible option, a 3-month lease at £4,000 pm. I was prepared to pay 25% of the cost difference myself and made this offer to the AXA to encourage a swift agreement. I thought at worst the repairs would be effected within 6 months. I had an identical flood situation in 2008 and so knew all too well what the works would require. Not for one moment was it an option to live in the flooded and unheated property. It stank of poo for starters. For another, the AXA buildings policy provides for like for like rehousing when the property becomes uninhabitable.

When the flood happened I was out of the Country and sent in my building handyman to try and mitigate the damage. He successfully blocked the back-flowing waste pipe that was spewing excrement into the incoming water by sticking his hand under water into the drain to block it with a towel, effectively plugging it to stop further waste egress. He spent several days at the property working to mitigate damage, place dehumidifiers in, assist with drainage and so on. Vital work in mitigating the damage. 8 months later his bill was still not been paid by the AXA. To date, December 2016, none of the bills which I paid, relating to the immediate remedial and mitigating works, like the truck to pump out the flood water, have been paid by the AXA.

Throughout this first 8-month period the <u>AXA</u> did not pay me one single penny. Because I am not named on the Insurance and the decisions reside with the named party, the Landlord, Nico Krasnopovich. Yet the fact is, the AXA know I have been paying Insurance with this reputable Insurer for well over twenty years. In full. At the start of each annual cycle. This information is all too readily available. Instead they chose the convenience of listening to the deceitful landlord and named party on the policy who has his own reasons for using the Insurance to cause mischief.

I have had to pay all my rehousing myself with unsurprising financial consequences. My home meanwhile rotted away with black mold enjoying a good 8 months to take hold of the entire property. Without heating and through the cold winter months damage to the plumbing and electrics was to be expected. At the time I began writing this blog, (8 months after the flood) I still had no indication of when the restoration works might begin, let alone a completion date for me to aim at moving back home on.

I suggested to the AXA that their proposal that I house my family in an uncleaned foul water flooded property where they know black mold is present might represent a breach of Health and Safety Laws which would bring the AXA into disrepute. That is of course the truth. Their reaction as a large Insurance company who know I have been a loyal customer paying premiums every year, including the year in which the claim fell, was to give me a written assurance that I '*be advised that Black mold does not represent a health and safety risk*'. This is the AXA Insurance writing to a flood victim who has a 5-year-old child and a 79-year-old father expected to live in a flood damaged property with sprouting black mold, where Insurers have not even paid to have the foul water cleaned up.

With my family's health being dismissed in so cavalier a fashion, I thought it reasonable to request sight of their qualified experts report confirming that black mold is not dangerous to health. A professional report from a Health and safety professional accredited body, who had visited the foul water flooded black mold infested dwelling, just to reassure myself that I would not be placing my 5-year old's son's health at risk by living in a contaminated property (Even though it was transparently obvious to anyone visiting that living in this space was clearly not possible).

I expected that the AXA would not provide me with written reassurance that no Health and Safety laws were being breached by their rehousing arrangements without first taking the precaution of a professional report and so imagine my surprise when it turned out that they had no report to send me. This is because they had not commissioned a report. The AXA was the Insurance company. Gab Robbins was the Loss adjuster. Instead of a report by an Environmental Specialist in Health And Safety I got Lars the **Gab Robbins** Loss Adjuster assuring me that his mate told him that it was OK to house a family (with young and elderly) in a poo infested untreated black mold-rich property without hot water or heating. This is not an exaggeration. The words relayed to me instead of a reliable and credible specialist written report were;

"Lars Eichman has clarified there is no written report but an assessment by their surveyor who attended the property as to risk which was in turn reported back to him then to me. There has been deemed no risk by a professional surveyor."
Verbatim from the AXA to myself.

My further inquiry revealed the 'professional Surveyor' to whom they refer turned out to be another employee of Gab Robins who rebranded toxic black mold as Mild Mildew. Lars from Gab Robins is making it up as he goes along. I am recording here that the AXA are guilty of dishonesty with potentially serious health consequences for a young child, in the hope of exploiting a dispute between the Lessor and Lessee to avoid paying a claim likely to exceed £500,000.

If this is not the case, then obviously, I would have seen the report I requested confirming that Lar's assurance is based on reliable and credible professional evidence. To date, December 2016, I have never had sight of any confirmation that the property was professionally evaluated. And so I paid for the leading environmental health company in the area to send an inspector to review the property. He commented as follows:

"In terms of the Housing Act 2004 'Housing Health and Safety Rating System (HHSRS)', I have identified a Category 1 Hazard, this is because the extent of the hazard in this case cold & dampness and its potential to cause harm being high, warrants immediate action in regards to remediation. As a result of this defect your property fails to meet 'the Decent Home Standard' and is uninhabitable in its current state. I recommend that you engage a damp-proof specialist who can undertake the necessary work to remedy the situation. You will need to provide heating and electricity to the property, therefore I would recommend that approved contractors are used to test and repair both systems."

With a Health and Safety concern as significant as the one described and as you see pictured on this page, do you not think any responsible party would consider as a minimum precaution the commission a professional report, including a laboratory analysis of the black mold, which has the potential to be toxic, before insisting that a family should be forced to live in these conditions? And if so, what kind of professional loss adjuster decides to go ahead and say 'there is no risk' just to defend not paying for rehousing? The answer in law is, they knew I was not named on the policy. They were answerable to the named policy holder. Krasnopovich. Who, clearly, encouraged them to not pay out on the policy wherever it was in his power to do so, for the advantage it gave him in causing me financial distress at a time when he was litigating furiously. Burning through what resources I had in legal fees to see my son. I had however notified Lars the Loss adjuster as well as the AXA in writing that Krasnopovich was acting with malice. That the housing matter was extremely urgent. That I wanted to house my 5-year-old son and to do so in the flooded property exposed him to life threatening risk. The house was flood damaged and no money spent on repair. They even had a professional Health and safety officers report confirming the bio hazard element in a flooded property with no heating. Yet, the AXA simply refused to pay a penny. Months dragged by. Not one penny paid. Not even my first two invoices for the initial clear up and water pump out.

Krasnopovich was either unaware, or unconcerned by any fiduciary responsibility relating to his name on the title, because he knew I could only force accountability by legal action and he knew the extent to which I was being exhausted of any funds. His 'So Sue me' approach depended on me having no money to ever do that. "So sue me" coming from a lawyer with the resource of his own law firm with a property law department, meant he knew with some confidence that I would not have the resources to effectively sue for damages. In the case of the Insurance claim, by blocking the claim and ensuring I never received a penny, he was quite clearly breaching his fiduciary responsibility as Landlord to act in my best interests. This breach alone would potentially give rise to over a million in costs. His motivation in causing me maximal financial harm was clear. The AXA's motivation in agreeing to not pay out on a valid claim was equally clear. My name not being on the policy gave them a perfect excuse. They only had to take instruction from the named policy holder. It is a breach of his fiduciary responsibility as well as a breach of the Freehold contract. But, Krasnopovich has never been held to account for this, or any single one of the other multiple instances of breach during his smart stewardship of the opportunities being a member of the Law society provides.

I found the AXA's position to be unreasonable even though I understood why they were able to act as they did. What insurer wouldn't grab any opportunity to not pay out on an expensive claim in similar circumstances. But at least they could have made the effort to get a certified environmental health expert to go in and take a look at any health issues before dismissing my concerns out of hand. The AXA's conduct effectively placed a young child's health at serious risk. The property had toxic black mold growing abundantly. And they assured me it was safe to house a 5-year-old child there? It is a fact that it was not safe to house a child there. Which they would have known all too well when they wrote legal mumbo jumbo inferring that their surveyor, Lars friend who worked for the same company, said the house was safe to house a 5-year-old. In this instance the AXA have lied. It may be that I was not named on the policy but the AXA would know from their records that I had paid buildings and contents in good faith since I bought the building in 1986. It's not that hard or that expensive, as I found out when I commissioned a site visit and professional report with analysis of the black mold by an accredited professional Environmental health company sending a surveyor with a PhD to write a report. Which cost about £700. Surely the AXA could have taken this basic precaution? Even at that stage, (8 months post flood) given the total failure to provide any reasonable insurance cover, either by way of my rehousing costs until the works are complete, or by paying the mitigation works invoice, or by actually completing the remedial works to enable me to return to my property, I had very little confidence that the AXA actually would make any payment. It was clear that Krasnopovich's wider agenda was to cause me maximum financial harm and with the Insurance policy in his name, the opportunity was there on a plate. Then after 8 months of fobbing me off with offensively dismissive nonsense, the AXA suspended all dialogue in relation to the flood claim while they investigated the named policy holder, the Landlord (Krasnopovich) for fraud. He had filled in an application form dishonestly and the AXA retained a top London property firm to investigate Krasnopovich. None the less, while that investigation went on, I continued having to rehouse myself at my own expense and to house my 5-year-old on the occasions I had visitation, with a custody battle raging in the background. My home continued to decay as mold rose up untreated walls. And wooden frames remained untreated after foul water intrusion. And the AXA Insurance simply refused to speak to me beyond defending their position that I could safely house a 5-year-old and a 79-year-old in this toxic flood zone, without any heating, in the cold of winter. Month followed month with not one penny paid.

Whilst we are accustomed to Insurers trying to pay out as little as possible, especially given that many people were affected by the flood, I think that in my case the AXA have taken avoiding liability to a new high and I do not feel that I have been treated fairly.

8 months. Not one penny. No rehousing. No works underway. No completion date.

Andrea https://twitter.com/AndreaLee #theaxainsurance

PS: Now its 9 months later. Still no payment. Just nothing at all.

PPS: Now it over 2 years later. And not one penny has been paid. The financial consequences have been dire. I believe fraud has occurred in which The AXA, Gab Robbins and the named Freeholder of my home have conspired to fraudulently avoid payment.

PPPS: Three years later. I have had to pay over £250,000 to make the property habitable myself. Additionally two further claims for damage have arisen. One a tree fall from next door property causing £15,000 damage to fabric of building and another £8,000 damage when staircase left in standing water and bathroom floor wooden bracing collapsed having never been treated post flood. Neither claim was even triggered despite repeated requests through solicitors. The AXA declined speaking with me. The Policyholder, my ex-boyfriend, deliberately did not trigger a claim for either, acting in bad faith, in this case Nico Krasnopovich has deliberately fouled three Insurance claims leaving me with costs currently in excess of £270,000, whilst refusing to return the Freehold title that gives him the control over the Insurance despite being in a trust agreement requiring him to do so and in breach of fiduciary responsibilities that accompany his name on the Title. The AXA have at no time spoken with me directly about the fact that I am the property owner relating to the cover they provide, and have paid the costs of Insuring with them for the past 28 years, never once late in payment, always the full year ahead of time. To date, 2017, I have not received even the repayment of the bill for pumping out the property after the flood.

PPPPS: After the investigation for fraud, Krasnopovich met with his lawyers, the lawyers from the AXA and the tanking company owner, liable for the breached tanking. The case against Krasnopovich was dropped and the claim was ended. The property was not restored to its pre incident condition. Following this meeting it was determined that 'Jeff the Plumber' dunnit. And so that was that. Everyone walked away happy. Except me. I received nothing but the disappointment of seeing the AXA Insurance avoid a claim by now in the region of £1 million, by inventing a patently ridiculous claim that 'Jeff the plumber ' dunnit. Geoff the plumbing company confirmed that 1.) he was never contacted by anybody to claim on his cover, had he been responsible. And 2) He finished his plumbing work prior to the tanking going in. It was impossible that he was the cause. 3.) he confirmed that 'They are trying to con you Andrea.'

It seems poorly thought through by the AXA to not even spell the name of the Plumber they were pinning the blame on correctly. And one must wonder why, if they believed this to be the true cause of the flood, they did not contact the plumber; Geoff Howes of GHP heating, who had full insurance cover for this type of job which he does professionally on many jobs exactly like my one . One might consider not restoring the property to its pre-incident condition on such spurious grounds, to reflect poorly on the AXA Insurance.

Ten months after the flood and ten months after Lars the Loss Adjuster invited my costs for rehousing, the AXA wrote to Krasnopovich. The letter shows that ten months after the flood the claim was still not in progress and that Krasnopovich was under suspicion for dishonesty. Being investigated by a top London law firm specializing in Insurance fraud, retained by The AXA in the matter of Krasnopovich's dishonesty. The letter also spells out the reason for the flood. After this letter, correspondence followed between Krasnopovich and Insurers via lawyers. As a result of their negotiations the claim was simply whitewashed. Krasnopovich hired his own top London firm specializing in Insurance fraud. The two firms met and a deal was done. I found out that there would be no claim when I was notified that a new cause was found for the flood. Their creative think-tank came up with a doozy to contradict the AXA surveyor's observation following the initial visit to the property that *"the building flooded when the tanking failed"*. Now they had come up with a classic in Insurance avoidance creative thinking where there is flooding involved.

"Hold up chaps. Why don't we blame the plumber. After all it's a leak were talking about. Plumber cause leaks, right?"

The old 'blame the plumber card'. And that was what I received instead of the 'restore the property to its pre incident condition' provision. A letter saying. Sorry. Nothing to see here. We have decided it was the plumber's fault. So, sorry, no Insurance payout for you.' Insurer, The AXA and Landlord, Krasnopovich, the insured party, agreed that 'Jeff the plumber dunnit." And signed off the claim. With not one penny paid to me for the costs I incurred in repairs. And even though it was a transparently ridiculous change of tack from their surveyor's written report identifying breached tanking as the cause. When I learned of this outlandish claim I called "Geoff the plumber" (yes they didn't even bother to check the spelling of his name) who said;

"They're having you on. It's impossible. For one thing, if it was me, I have Insurance and that would cover any fault of mine. But it can't be a fault of mine. My plumbing goes in before the tanking. And anyhow, this is the first I have heard of it. Don't you think Insurers would have contacted me if they thought I caused the flood? They are trying to stich you up."

Jeff (Geoff) the Plumber showed, in writing, that it was impossible his work, which went in before the tanking, could explain the breached tanking. I say, very clearly, that a fraud has occurred involving a member of the law society, Nico Krasnopovich, a Loss Adjuster named Lars and The AXA Insurance. I sent Geoff the Plumbers report off to Krasnopovich, but none the less, I still did not receive one penny. Not even reimbursement of the money I paid on the day of the flood. Krasnopovich lied and lied again. The AXA continued refusing to speak to me. Their deal is done with Krasnopovich.

So to recap. My cover was cancelled by Krasnopovich, illegally. When he phoned the brokers to cancel my policy, in my name, paid for and accepted. My home flooded. I spent over £250,000+ in repairing it to make it habitable again. Although I was Insured with the AXA and had paid the policy in full, as I had done the previous 26 years, I received not one penny in Insurance. And then a family court judge awarded him half of my home, but none of the costs in the Insurance claim, which the same family court judge tried very hard to have me indemnify Krasnopovich from in any future proceedings. Throughout these events, Krasnopovich was the trustee of my Freehold title, bound by specific fiduciary responsibilities. The DDJ Flaherty must have known what fiduciary responsibilities are. Why did she go to such lengths to attempt to have me indemnify Krasnopovich from liability to a claim against him which will in probability exceed a million pounds. It does appear to be prejudicial conduct by a judge. Lacking both relevance and impartiality in a claim of this type in family court. I say the attempt by the judge to bully me into an indemnifier is clear evidence of corruption. Why else would Flaherty assist a fraud by Krasnopovich in the Freehold Insurance matter.

And as has been the case in a career based on dishonesty since lying on his CV to upgrade his Law exam result and get his first job in this way, Krasnopovich continues to prove that family law remains a fertile and rewarding place for professional liars. My complaints only ever received a three-word reply.

"So sue me".

Bearing in mind at the time of writing my legal bill approaches £500,000. It would appear that Krasnopovich is a pretty effective lawyer, unrestrained by conscience or contrary interpretation of law.

Below follows the letter to Krasnopovich from the AXA that led to the investigation for dishonesty. They lawyered up. So did Krasnopovich. And in that process a deal was done where I got zero (In Pounds) but the repair bills, by this time over £250,000. I also got to keep paying the mortgage and the repairs to the property. Krasnopovich walked away from any fiduciary responsibility. And I was informed that 'Jeff the Plumber done it' although no one thought to call Geoff the Plumber to tell him. This letter confirms the 'tanking breach caused the flood' (No mention of Jeff the Plumber) and shows that the AXA found Krasnopovich to be dishonest enough to set lawyers on him. It shows Krasnopovich accepting that he is *"the freehold owner of 28A Thameside, Thames Side (the "Property")"*. The fact is, the Freeholder has fiduciary responsibilities.

Our Ref: 1130591J
18 December 2014

Mr Nico Krasnopovich
666 Strand Street
Thameside Upon Thames

Dear Mr Krasnopovich

Policy Number	:	**MDFF06115**
Subject	:	**Water ingress at 28A Thameside**
Date of Incident	:	**8 February 2014**

I write regarding the above incident.

As you know, you have made a claim under your Midal Crown policy number M08724295 underwritten by AXA (the **"Policy"**) in respect of loss and damage arising from the above incident.

The purpose of this letter is to explain in detail the concerns that AXA currently has with the Policy and your claim, and to invite your views on those concerns.

We wish to emphasise that no final decision has been made and detailed consideration will be given to any representations which you or your representatives wish to make.

1. **Circumstances**

    1.1   You are of course familiar with the circumstances of the claim.

    1.2   Very briefly, you are the freehold owner of 28A Thameside, Thames Side (the **"Property"**). On or about 8 February 2014 the tanking system at the Property failed resulting in an ingress of water into the basement.

    1.3   Following a claim being made under the Policy, AXA appointed loss adjusters (GAB Robins) to handle the claim on its behalf.

1.4   During the course of GAB Robins' handling of the claim, certain facts and matters have come to light which raise questions about the information you provided to underwriters prior to inception of the Policy in December 2012 and renewal in December 2013 (discussed in more detail below).

2.   **The Policy**

2.1   Under cover of a letter dated 29 October 2012, your broker (Fairtimes Insurance) sent to you a quotation for insurance with Midas Underwriting (underwritten by AXA). Enclosed with the letter was a Statement of Fact, which included the following information:

Date of last flooding (if applicable)   01/01/2005

> *Have you or any other proposer to the insurance made any claim in the last five years for the type of risk now proposed or suffered from an incident that insurance would have covered should it have been in force?   No*

2.2   Your broker's letter asked you to check that the information contained in the Statement of Fact was correct. The Statement of Fact itself contained the following disclaimer (in Bold type):

THIS STATEMENT OF INSURANCE DETAILS THE INFORMATION YOU HAVE SUPPLIED WHICH INSURERS HAVE RELIED UPON WHEN ACCEPTING THIS INSURANCE. IF THERE ARE ANY INACCURACIES OR OMISSIONS PLEASE CONTACT YOUR INSURANCE BROKER IMMEDIATELY, FAILURE TO DO SO COULD RESULT IN INACCURACIES AND/OR OMISSIONS BEING TREATED AS NON-DISCLOSURE OR MIS-REPRESENTATION AND MAY ENTITLE INSURERS TO VOID.

2.3   On the basis of the above information, the Policy was incepted on 2 December 2012.

2.4   The Policy was renewed on 2 December 2013 and the water ingress occurred during the currency of that policy year.

3.   **Misrepresentation / non-disclosure**

3.1   Contracts of insurance are contracts of utmost good faith. Those insured under a contract of insurance are in the best position to know the risk and so must disclose to the insurer all material information affecting the risk which the insurer is agreeing to insure. Further, every material representation must be true. This duty arises at various times including at inception and upon each subsequent renewal of the contract of insurance.

3.2   During the course of GAB Robins' handling of your claim under the Policy, it has come to AXA's attention that the information supplied by you (or by your broker acting on your behalf) to underwriters prior to inception of the Policy in December 2012 was untrue. Specifically:

  3.2.1   The date that the Property had last flooded was not in January 2005 as represented but, rather, in January 2008; and

  3.2.2   It was incorrect to say that no claims had been made within the last 5 years, as an insurance claim for flood damage had been made in or about January 2008 (i.e. just under 5 years previously).

36 The forced sale of my home
Larceny by any other name

After the Flaherty ruling and the Le Clerc rubber-stamp confirmed that my home was to be sold by a court order, I wrote to Krasnopovich. A very simple email intended to save another £30,000+ legal bill. My goal was to get the house sold asap and move on. I was by then a US resident and there was no prospect of my return to the UK after the Flaherty judgment. I wanted the properties sold to end my ongoing financial commitment in paying the mortgage and the maintenance costs on empty properties. My best-case scenario was to sell as quickly as possible, at the best price achievable. I knew the local agents well and could have had the sale listed on Rightmove within days. I had buyer interest for the entire building including freehold. As a going concern based on ROI. Not sold as separate units as per the court order.

"To avoid unnecessary legal costs in the sale of the property you have been awarded in court, let's agree a sales agent between us without going through solicitors."

He declined. Why? The properties could have been sold quickly. This was before the Brexit market collapse. Demand was high. I had to keep on with the prospect of paying Roland Court. This would add, significantly to my legal cost. Enough to generate even more animosity between my son's parents. Even at that late stage I identified what appeared to me as a psychotic need to entirely destroy the opposition. Winning everything was not enough. He had to destroy any possibility that I would receive even one penny from the sale of my home and rental income business as a result of his litigation. Mostly so Sam would never know.

Various legal arguments followed regarding the sale, Krasnopovich spoiled the most lucrative possibility, selling all three leases along with freehold, tenanted as an investment property. Especially after Brexit meant the weak pound made UK real estate attractive to foreign investors. I had my own buyer in this regard, ready to pay a total sum of £2.5 million. All included. (Freehold with 3 leaseholds.) E mails went back and forth with my property lawyer Roland Court. At that price I could still have survived the enormous loss at that stage, if my expenditure was accounted for in advance of a 50% payment of 'beneficial entitlement.' That amount meant I could get out of this legal mess by paying my mortgage, my legal fees, and having a six-figure sum left over, which was earmarked to pay my lawyer Roland Court to pursue the Freehold fiduciary failures by Krasnopovich. A claim I valued at £2 million+. And enough to pay a decent City lawyer to ensure I could see my son 50% of the time.

Roland approached Krasnopovich and Clock with the request to agree selling the property as one unit – freehold and three leases. They refused. Their win award from Flaherty gave them 50% of two of the three leaseholds. More importantly, the freehold was still in Krasnopovich's name and so I could not sell without his consent. Of course, why would they agree to a sale where they would receive the maximum amount their 50% win allowed for. It would benefit me. So instead, they went back to court to insist on selling the leases to 28A and 28B separately and for good measure, applied for and won '*sole conduct of sale*' for 28B. Think about that for half a second. The court ordered the sale of the home I bought in 1986, that Krasnopovich contributed not one penny to, but lived in that particular flat for a few months as my guest back I 2004, and now he had won the sole right to sell without me having any say in the sale. Thieves walking in broad daylight. Of course he was not going to sell it as he assured the judge he would do. His plan was to prevent any sale, allow the interest to accumulate on the costs award, and wait until I ran out of money to keep paying the mortgage. I informed my solicitor that this was his intention. Above all else to prevent me getting any money out of my property because I would then be able to afford to pay a lawyer to prosecute the fiduciary failures that exposed him to a multimillion-pound loss. As well as, quite likely, being disbarred as a lawyer.

They won the right to choose the sales agent as well. And, without any input from me allowed by order of the court, they made sure that neither of the two flats, both highly desirable riverside properties on the Thames in a highly desirable area, remained unsold. While I continued paying the mortgage and the maintenance costs. Supporting my view that the goal was a psychotic need to destroy the opposition rather than just win money in court.

Months passed. I kept paying all costs for my property, just as I had done since 1986.

Months turned into years. The house sat empty. I kept paying the mortgage or faced losing my credit rating. In 2017 my costs were around £25,000. In 2018 my costs were more. £50,000+ just in keeping the court order alive for Krasnopovich to sell, while he benefits from 8% interest on his cost award. And I had zero prospect of getting anything from the sale.

In her wisdom, Flaherty ordered not only sole conduct of sale to Krasnopovich, but also that I was not allowed to enter 28B Thameside. This meant, when I travelled to the UK to see Sam, I had to pay to stay in Hotels. I was not allowed, by court order, to enter my home. While I continued to pay the mortgage and all other costs.

Motive in spoiling the sale?

To be sure I would have no means with which to come back at him for custody of my son. And no means to pay a property lawyer to sue him for the fiduciary breaches in the freehold fraud.

Overall, the amounts being offered by this stage for the sale of the three units as separate flats were a long way off the £2.5 million selling it as a going concern (With freehold.). It was as I knew it would be, a fire sale. Simply a theft of my home and source of income for the benefit of family-law at the expense of a child's best interest. Once the option of selling as a going concern was ended, and he won the 'sole conduct of sale' I sold the one flat I still had free from his claim, the top one, 28C Thameside. It took one month to sell at the fire sale price by my agents.100% of that amount went to pay legal charges. My hopes of getting money from my property lay in the more valuable two that he won in the court hearing. 28B and 28A. Flaherty had made an order. Set a trigger price for sale. And excluded me from the process. Now, as I had said all along, her foolish ignorance, so easily confused with malicious intent, became manifest in the failure to sell.

By February 2019 I realized there was no prospect of them ever selling at a breakeven price and could not continue paying the mortgage. It was time to fold the tent on any hopes of seeing one penny from the forced sale of my home and rental properties. But before I did that I took advice from three people. My UK bank manager, my financial advisor and my business friend Chris Andiotis. I also reached out to my lawyer Roland Court for advice, however he declined to reply.

In 2017 I had no contact at all with Roland Chambers on the family law side. No point running up more money on having a member of family law rack up more billable hours to arrive at the same conclusion. Especially when his last advice was to engage with the family-lawyer behind the litigation on the other side, to carry on paying into that system. As if I would ever waste one more moment talking to Tim Clock inviting him to further opportunity to abuse my son. Tim Clock is the author of some 50 emails to me relating to visitation with my son. The best that can be said of them is they are unwaveringly consistent. As he was appointed to do by Krasnopovich, in every single contact I have had with Tim Clock he has been determinedly, maliciously obstructive. The fact that Flaherty awarded his costs against me, at 8% interest, means I have to pay my child's abuser. I found paying a family law solicitor Roland Chambers to offer me advice to 'work within the system by dealing with (and paying) Tim Clock very much at odds with sound legal advice. And was the last straw in my interest in respecting the acuity of Roland Chambers. Who made plain he could not help me unless I paid in advance, and if I did not pay, would place a lien on my home. A far cry from the '*Lets sort out this horrible judgment by Flaherty for you.*' The same man who shed tears after the appeal hearing because he knew that meant the end of Sam's prospects for being with me. Funny how money works on family-law solicitors.

Krasnopovich and Clock set out to trade visitation with Sam for money and succeeded beyond their wildest dreams. Thanks to that switch judge. All that remained after the properties went on the market was to have a costs hearing, to determine the costs I would have to pay and the interest calculation. And to tie down the sale accounting.

What is 'The Accounting'.

The award Krasnopovich won from Flaherty was 50% beneficial entitlement. That entitlement is to profit on the (forced) sale. Simply put, the net proceeds after the costs in the sale. What then are the 'costs' in the sale. For example, the £250,000 I raised to make 28A habitable post flood? The £15,000 for the tree fall damage. And so on. Realistically approaching £300,000 in total. The amount that would have been paid by Insurance if he had not cancelled my Insurance. Also the 'shortfall in Insurance' that he as liable for as Freeholder. Surely, common sense suggests, you don't award 50% of the gross amount of the sale.

Then there's the mortgage. The total I paid since the ruling is just under £100,000.
    You calculate the costs relating to the award. That is 50% '*like we were married.*' And that is the net amount. Factoring in the costs of owning and maintaining the property.

It was clear from the outset that Krasnopovich and Clock never intended agreeing as much as one penny by way of accounting. My property lawyer Roland Court was monitoring that aspect. All he met with was constant obstruction. With all units empty after the court order that I end my rental income tenancies, it remained the case that all the bills, mortgages and maintenance were down to me, without any income from rental. Proper Accounting would only follow if I paid a highly specialized property lawyer for this purpose. These costs were rising each month. As was the debt for legal fees at an interest rate of 8% as awarded by Flaherty against me.

At this point in the process, to cause me maximum financial harm all Krasnopovich/Clock had to do is nothing and invite litigation. Having never paid one penny towards the mortgage ever, Krasnopovich continued not paying one penny towards the mortgage of a property that according to Flaherty, he owned half of. Flaherty's ruling incentivized and enabled them to simply sit back and watch the interest accumulate while I had to either keep paying the mortgage costs, or lose my creditworthiness as well. I say, obviously, Flaherty's judgment was made with the child interests uppermost. The outcome is proof of her wise judgment. None of the above-mentioned consequences of Flaherty's judgment could in any way be confused with an incompetent dishonest ethically flatulent fraud causing immeasurable harm to a child. Causing me losses measured in millions and standing as a monument to the rotten core underpinning British family-court.

I didn't see Sam at all throughout 2017. All I had to look forward to was selling my home and clearing enough to pay off the mortgages and the lawyer. It was then, as it was from the moment Krasnopovich decided to go knob his fitness instructor, an awful mess. A triumph for Krasnopovich, Clock and Flaherty, knowing Sam had no prospect of seeing his parent, who was left with no means with which to bring any action in family-court for visitation. And who wasn't even able to remain in the UK following this forced sale.

Krasnopovich was by now married to another member of family law. A smoker. My son was being raised by this dual pillar of ethical excellence, who had managed to let 9 months pass without disclosing to me where my son was. After they moved in April of 2016, one Month later, I learned in May that I did not know where my son was when my weekly letters arrived back with 'Return to sender address unknown." I wrote to Krasnopovich requesting the address. 9 months after he moved, I received the address in a letter sent on 16 December 2016. But that's not a thing if you are a member of family law. The laws about disclosing the whereabouts of a child do not apply to parents who are members of family law. Nothing to see here for any complaint to the SRA. Even though it is a second offense in terms of disclosing the address of the child from the parent.

Throughout 2017 I continued sending weekly letters to my son. I can confirm that as the months turned to years with this steady drip of family-court malice costing me more than I was earning, in mortgage payments and maintenance charges, while knowing the costs award accruing at 8% meant that any equity I did receive from the sale would all go in this way, my feeling towards my sons parent and his colleagues in British family-law declined to a level of disrespect that I would equate with Larry, Mo and Curly's contribution to world culture. It was clear that Krasnopovich, Clock and Flaherty had misrepresented the ethical guidance of the Solicitors regulation authority to a degree that could only be remedied by a significant damages award, in multiple seven figures. And by a legal accountability involving an appropriate period of incarceration. Aligned with the scale of the offenses they knowingly committed. Larceny, fraud, abuse of office, incompetence, breach of fiduciary responsibility, deceit, child-abuse and parental alienation just for starters. Accompanied by front page coverage of their trial. To encourage support for the change in litigation to ensure this kind of abuse of children for the profit of the family-court gang, ends.

During this period, throughout 2017 and 2018, while I was paying for a house I no longer owned by deviant court order, I also had to deal with adapting to a new life in a new country. No longer able to remain in the Country I loved living in for 29 years. Having to start again in my fifties in a new market, in a business, music, where my success happened mostly in my twenties, when I looked like an attractive 20-year-old. Starting again in a competitive, presentation specific market like the USA has not been easy. Especially when the music world I trained for and prospered in no longer exists in the fake-music era of Kanye West and Donald Trump.

Having a lifetime of responsible financial planning attached to long work hours stolen by a deviant judge has not been without its problems. Underpinning my motivation to start again with a positive outlook, was my belief that love will conquer all. And my desire to have a home for Sam to live with me if he could ever find his way. I had to accept my efforts to win visitation were unlikely to succeed given the historic efforts of family court. As he was soon to be ten, I set my hopes on the fact that the child I raised had qualities that would endure the tests placed in his path by that abusive family-court judgment and would find his way to me. My hope and goal was to be able to provide a stable happy home for him to join in a new family, much like his family up until daddy chose to knob his fitness instructor. With a mummy and daddy who both loved him and showed it.

The annual attempts at visitation, every summer and every winter holiday since his sole visit in July 2014, almost resulted in a visit for December 2018. Clocks achievement in spoiling that proposed visit led to the end of even the written letters I was sending Sam twice weekly through the post. No point writing if you know the letters are not getting there. Instead I decided to start writing online. At least that ensured my letters would not end up in Krasnopovich's bin. I started "Letters to Sam", online. Aged ten, he could likely find them somehow. If not now, soon.

The consequences of Flaherty's family-court judgment continue to affect my life and that of my son to this day. It is only right that Sam should be aware of the facts of why he is not able to be with the parents he chose to raise him.

37 Three years of no contact

He tries. I try. But more than three years go by. And we both still cry. While the miscreants lie

"If you want out of a marriage, earn your way out. Turn over every stone. Investigate every avenue of rehabilitation, so when the day comes that your child looks at you and says, `Mom, Dad, why did I have to grow up with just one parent?' You don't have to say, `Well, we just quit having fun. You need to be able to say, `Look, we did everything we could do. We went to counselors, we read books, we prayed, we did this, we did that, and we decided it was best for everybody if we lived separately but loved you kids together.'" If you can't say that with peace in your heart, you're not ready to get divorced."

Dr. Phil, the popular American TV show host wrote that.

Some six years have passed since fathers-day 2013. I wouldn't immediately recognize Sam in the street now. He has been apart from me longer than he was with me. 16 February 2016 is the last time I held him in my arms. I no longer live in the UK. My home and my income generating business was awarded to a liar in a judgment that saw me receive not one penny even within the provisions of that court judgment. I have a new life in California where not a day goes by without my thinking about Sam. Or a night where I don't wake up thinking about Sam and how it was possible that he has been so successfully removed from my life. I still wake up thinking it was all a dream. That didn't really happen.

The aspect of Britishness that I most admired and which drew me to emigrate to Britain in 1985, with which I felt at home and happy for almost 30 years, the sense of justice and fair play, the cricket analogy of meeting the ball with a straight bat, of valuing intellect and critical thought above all frivolous considerations, has gone.

In its place I reflect on a slime encrusted judiciary owned by greedy amoral charlatans who routinely trade the best version of a child's life for a handful of dollars. An old school branch of a class system in which an empowered sub-elite urinate over the simple ethical basis of 'fair and equitable' in a transparent judiciary. As a citizen, ethicist and student of British history I feel obligated to disclose this corruption in the heart of a society I consider myself a part of and indebted to for my education. I deserved better than this. My son deserved better than this. Britain's reputation deserves better than this. Allowed to stand unreported, this same abuse in British family-court is reflected worldwide. It affects millions around the world. Imagine if we can fix family-law. Put children above all considerations. Stop treating parents as criminals. Stop treating criminals as judges.

Imagine any parent who would trade their own child's parental future for money whilst relying on the same system that enabled this deceitful theft to protect their anonymity and accountability to the son they betrayed. Imagine people, members of a society protected by secretive laws, who make a very profitable living out of lying to encourage parental alienation and child abuse. Safe in knowing there is no accountability. When is the last time you read about an SRA inquiry into dishonesty by members leading to disbarment of solicitors, barristers or DDJ's, who profit from winning by lying, parental alienation and child abuse?

Placing financial reward over a child's best interests, even when not predicated on deceit, should be illegal. It is not.

There should be accountability. There is not.

There should be reform of the legal system that enables stories like my sons and mine to unfold. At the time of writing there is not.

There is only the deep irony of a Solicitors regulation Authority ethical code in which it is suggested that '*Litigation breeds animosity between parents. Every effort should follow to avoid litigation. The animosity it creates is harmful to the child.*' Awarding costs is pretty likely to increase animosity between parents. Willfully doing so makes one thing certain. The child is harmed. Flaherty awarding costs might just as well have tattooed '*child molester and loving it*' across her forehead. I find it hard to believe she is still employed in family law, but a recent google search confirms she is. I wonder how many more children's lives she has abused since she got away with the judgment in Krasnopovichs's case.

Is there any chance of imminent reform towards to a child-centric model? I say, if not now. When. Are you going to look back in 25 years and wonder '*That was us. Those 10,000 children every year getting fucked over by family law judgments. We knew what was going on and we let that happen We made that happen by our inertia. The roaring silence of those ministers charged with responsibility to ensure the ongoing efficiency of family-law.*'

It is past 6 years since that 'fathers-day' and I with the distance I have to reflect on what happened, I know I tried my best for Sam knowing that I did try my best; taking advice from leading professionals in every relevant area. I did the very best I could with no reservations. Educating myself in child psychology and development. Considering what would be best for him, from age four at 'ambush' separation and with every passing year where he was obstructed from being with me. In so far as I have taken expensive professional advice, I have learned a great deal to supplement what was already a twenty-year experience of the subject. It has been my good fortune, by design, to meet and interact with great minds on the subject of parenting, child-psychology and family-law. I am not alone in seeing the consequences of the ethical paucity so commonly associated with lawyers and especially family lawyers, working a unique legal footprint intended to protect the anonymity of children, but that has now become so easily abused by feeble minded judges and corrupt lawyers, that the list of stories validating this claim is endless.

Right now, on this day of writing, there is a man in jail in Virginia. A divorcing father of four. He cannot be bailed, as is the law in Virginia for those held in contempt by family-court judges. He is in his third month of working in the kitchen of a Federal penitentiary for $20 a month. He will remain there as long as his wife decides he should be. This could be years. Why?

Her lawyers Facebook friend, the Virginia family-court judge, found him in contempt of her ruling. A ruling that they share their 3 assets; House, business and car. He tried to sell the car at the trigger price. But could not find a buyer. Meanwhile he was paying the storage costs for this fine vehicle month after month, trying to achieve the price the judge set as the trigger sale price. It was too high. No market interest followed.

He says he phoned his wife to request that the costs be taken into account at the point of sale, before the 50/50 split. And that they sell at best-market price. He says she agreed on the phone.

He sold the car at below the trigger price, to the only buyer in the market for this specialized vehicle. (A muscle car conversion of a 68 Camaro.) The sale price was below the trigger value set by the judge. The malicious wife told her lawyer. He called his friend the judge. The judge ruled, contempt, for selling below value, he was arrested and taken straight to jail. In Virginia, this is an offence that does not qualify for bail. The facts of malicious mother syndrome, that are clear from the historical animosity in this case, are ignored. The judge gets away with putting a good man in jail indefinitely. And that is just one story of family law in Virginia. Every state has its own similar examples. When parents split there is a special animosity. Malicious Mother syndrome. Judges and the family court network in each jurisdiction use the opportunities this legislature provides to exploit Malicious Mothers, to win large fees in prosecuting wins in family court, in which, invariably, the children suffer the loss of one parent.

This happens all over the world. Wherever family law enables and empowers amateur 'deputy' judges to act knowing contempt laws, intended to protect children's identity, can be used to conceal their own corrupt, profit motivated abuse of children.

Whatever happens in the future, it remains my firm view that Sam would have enjoyed a far better upbringing with me in California, with a parent there for him all the time, than what Krasnopovich has provided for him in a small suburb in Greater London. Close to his office. It remains the case that when Sam was asked who he wanted to live with at that time he was unequivocal in his desire to be with me. It is a fact that in his life with me all of his parental time was with me and for months, he greeted the return from work of his 10% parent with "Go away."

It is clear, beyond any reasonable doubt, Krasnopovich has not acted in Sam's best interests at any one of the many points in the past 6 years where he could have put selfish greed behind his best interests and replaced vindictive malicious deceitful and dishonest litigation with reasonable respect for a child's rights to see both parents equally. Instead he has, without one single exception, chosen to use Sam's relationship with me, and my love for him, as a negotiating lever. Secure in the belief that a crushing victory in a court judgment with a junkpile of legalese words showing how very hard he tried to settle and act in Sam's best interests will shield him and his co-conspirators from the facts of action and consequence. And that brings this story round to where it began.

Will Sam take a kind view on the conduct of his parent and the collusion of a system designed for this exploitation to the extent that the CEO of CAFCASS is on record saying "100% of disputed cases feature parental alienation and child abuse." We know the system is broken. And yet they continue defending the indefensible.

DDJ Flaherty, that "fun loving, champagne guzzling juvenile delinquent" is still a judge in family court. Will those areas of family law that need reform react to Sam's story by continuing their blind defense of the indefensible or by embracing the reality that change is vital. And reparations essential.

Starting with making family-court child-centric and removing financial adversarial opportunities from family law. End the easy money system that attracts the avariciously unscrupulous to profit from the misery of people at their lowest ebb just by membership to an enabled society. By applying firm accountability to parents avoiding the best-case principle of the child's right to access each parent. And, crucially, removing those liars hiding under protection of anonymity in family-law from this profession blighted by the numbers that measure the extent of their deceit. Over 10,000 children every year. 100% of children in disputed cases in family law are subject to parental alienation and child abuse. Don't do the crime if you can't do the time. The law must be equal for all. Including those charged with representing the law.

That figure could, and should be zero. 100% of the time where disputed cases reach family court, the outcome is child abuse. There is your clue. The entire structure of family court in relation to children's rights must be changed. It is arcane. It is a broken system being exploited with predictable regularity by corrupt members, like Flaherty, like Clock, like Krasnopovich. Like David Clam. All of which is unnecessary. The answer is not blowing in the wind.

The three-word answer is. Stop the rot.

Make the child abusers accountable and once that is done, begin a new decision-making process staffed by qualified individuals, capable of making child centric decisions with one priority. If children are indeed our future, then the cost cutting measures that led us to CAFCASS reflects that we need to spend more. To make a better system that works for children.

The issue of Child maintenance in this decision-making process I see replacing family-court is entirely separate to visitation and the child rights to see both parents. I accept this is a weighty consideration and one that is best reserved for another book, but solely in the context of my own experience in Flaherty's court I observe that Judges should be prevented from imposing their own prejudices in any judgment affecting children. Allowed to make un appealable judgments evading the checks and boundaries of the appeals process. As was obviously the case in Flaherty's court. That reform process begins with making historical offenders accountable. Allowing greedy parents to raise financial claims guided by avaricious money above all solicitors in family court is a recipe for disaster. Krasnopovich clearly targeted the use of the child as leverage to make financial demands. Instead of seeing the obvious – that this was always a demand for money attached to visitation, by any other description, blackmail using a child, Flaherty has ignored the guidelines in place for the office she occupies. Litigation does cause animosity between parents. That animosity is never good for children. Ruling as she has is child abuse. It defies possibility that this grown woman, working as a family court judge did not know that her punitive judgment was abusive to the child. That is neither a lie nor a prejudiced opinion. It is a fact of life. It is the reality. The consequence of Flaherty's judgment. Made in clear breach of any number of the published guidelines for members of family law published on the SRA website.

Has family-court Judge Flaherty really gotten away with-it scot free?

Are there any prospects of family law policing its own and reforming the law to prevent reoccurrence? Populated in part, as CAFCASS published statistics make clear, by braggadocios dishonest incompetents colluding with avaricious child abusing liars.

Sam already knows much of what has happened to him, starting on fathers-day when he was 4. Whatever version of events Krasnopovich has presented to him in the years we have not spoken to each other will one day be evaluated by an informed adult consciousness able to interpret parental alienation and child abuse. Sam will not be the first child to grow up and consider the efforts each of his parents made on his behalf. Eventually, in the course of a lifetime we must all own our conduct. Cause and consequence. It is true that every action has an equal and opposite reaction. Denial and cognitive dissonance are short term solutions and not really solutions at all. Lying in a legal system is one thing. The judgment of a flawed individual can bring matters to the illusion of an end. A 'final' judgment.

Lying to yourself is another. That truth emerges at the top of any convenient interpretation of what truth means. Lying to yourself has consequences. Eventually, be it some understanding of karma, or just the passage of time, self-deceit which harms others, especially children, has a way of balancing the value of one's life.

This epilogue is also the epilogue on a time of life. While Krasnopovich and his family-law member wife control Sam's upbringing to exclude any opportunity to be with his parent, and continue to withhold the unfettered contact that is his legal right and my expectation, I have had to draw a line under how much more I can do in Sam's best interests to provide for him the opportunities he deserves. Bearing in mind the consequences of the litigation. Life is a show that must go on, for Sam and for me. With every month that passes by another month less exists for us to be together.

If I may, through the passage of time and the timeless permanence of the written word, address my beautiful Sam in conclusion, having spent the years on assembling this book to be the honest truthful record of events for his benefit.

"I did my best. The facts speak for themselves. Krasnopovich, Clock and Flaherty beat the best I could do. David Clam chose to not own his incompetence and skulked away with more money than your entire education would have cost in private school. A sniveling lying thief. All these members of family-law can reflect on what happened to you as their victory. And in that they are right. They won. The best I had wasn't enough. I told the ministry of justice. They said 'They trust family court judges to make good decisions.' So the law confirms, they are trustworthy and make good decisions. And their decision is that we should not be together. This conclusion comes from Judge Flaherty. One day you might write to her and thank her for doing such a great job representing children in family court.

I wanted to be with you more than anything. I know you wanted to be with me more than anything. Despite losing everything I had in this unhappy experience of family law, I have no regrets in fighting to have you in my life. But I have one regret that haunts me. And for which I owe you the biggest apology.

I am sorry I let your family-law parent take you away that day. Fathers-day, 16 June, 2013. It is the biggest regret of my life. I let myself be ambushed and caught wrong footed. And I wasn't able to stop him taking you away. I was outsmarted. I could and should have done better even though I was so devastated by what happened. 16 June 2013 seems a long time ago. Not one person who knows me has heard from you in a long time. I have no idea how you are or even where you are.

During this time, on two occasions you were moved to a new address without me being told. Quite possibly, even now, my letters do not get to you. None the less, every week I choose photos and write a story for you. In this way I spend some time with you and there is a record of that time when I get to tell you that I love you and I miss you and I think of you all the time. I know you think of me every day.

I will keep writing my weekly "letters to Sam." If you don't see them now, they will always be there for you later. I know it is crucial for your responsible parent to keep from you the details of what happened in family court. The conduct of Clock and Flaherty. And for me, it is important that you know why I disappeared from your life. It is not easy to describe in one line what it took to stop me from having you with me. That is why I have written this book for you.

I hope you read my letters and know I will always be here for you. I don't know what tomorrow might bring but I never give up hope that it will be the day I see you again. You can always demand the same shared custody I have been trying for. Holidays in California, Summer and winter, and school in New Malden. Or School in California and Holidays in New Malden. Soon you will have the confidence to make that decision for yourself knowing I will support you in whatever you choose.

Do you know how many people go through what we have? They have a name for it. Parental alienation and child abuse. So many children just like you and parents just like me have so much of their lives blighted because family law fails. Human nature has frailties. Few areas welcome and benefit human frailties more than family law. Where members are allowed to place monetary gain above the child's best interests. It is a broken system. And it will change. If not now, because of what they did to you and me, in the fullness of time. Change is inevitable.

Until I see you again I know that I will think of you every day. And every night. For any good to come out of what has happened to you and me let's hope that change comes to the legislation protecting children. It is easy to see what needs to be done."

Considering the prospects of seeing Sam again, after this book and the fact that people who know and work with the people involved will have to take a view on whether accountability is necessary.

My closing observation is this:

From the outset, visitation was traded for money by members of family-law knowing they could act with a degree of impunity because reporting with a minor child involved assures their anonymity. The formula was *"Pay the money and you can see him as often as you like."* And so, now, six years later after the layers of animosity have piled so high, I cannot imagine meeting a lower vibration human than

Krasnopovich; and I have met some of the world's lowest human beings. On opposite sides in this ring of huge animosity are both of Sam's parents. Both guilty of something that brought us to this place. Even now, six years later, how does Krasnopovich approach visitation?

"Does he think Sam will thank him one day?"

Having used a lie to underpin his claim for money in exchange for Sam seeing me, is there any accountability for this choice? His friendly family court judge Flaherty has said that I am the liar. Krasnopovich told the truth in everything. I believe this is quite obviously another lie by another lying member of family law.

Let's not forget the one moment of honesty in family court, the Permission to Appeal hearing in the Royal Courts of justice, when the President of family law ruled that Flaherty's judgment is flawed. That should have led to the successful appeal of her flawed judgment. That it did not does not mean that Flaherty's judgment stands; that I am a liar and Krasnopovich is not. And that awarding costs pus interest against one parent is not harmful to the child's prospects of a relationship with both parents.

It means, as I have laid out in this book, that there are layers of weakness in the legislation called family-law that allows liars to prosper.

Family-law operates on a simple formula. Who lies Wins. A skilled liar will always beat a defendant unfamiliar with this courtroom ability. The truth does not always out in that arena called a courtroom, governed by laws made hundreds of years ago. When the skills of liars were not as developed as they are now. The truth is what the family-court judge decides is the truth. And that position often rests with a deputy district judge who may be less ethically qualified than a London cabbie, assured that in making un-appealable judgments their failures cannot bring them to accountability.

Starting from contesting and preventing twice monthly weekends together in my application for visitation in 2013. And lying consistently to win money in exchange for visitation. Unsurprisingly, once the judgment went his way he presented a paper trail of offers for '*as much visitation as you like.*' Confirmation that he is true to his word, when he said at the outset "*You can see him as much as you like once the money is paid.*"

One problem following the damage done by this litigation is that there is no coming back to any degree of trust for Krasnopovich. How will he arrange for Sam to see his mother. The answer is, it will be difficult absent of a gagging order forbidding me and anyone who knows me from disclosing to Sam what his parent did. Actions which have crossed from family-court to criminal court.

Krasnopovich no doubt has given Sam a version of events. As Roland Chambers referred to this common aspect of parental alienation 'poisoning the well.'

Explaining why I stopped sending him presents.

Why I stopped sending him letters by post for so long.

Why I don't live in the same Country any more.

Why we never speak on Skype.

Why I have no fixed address.

How then would I answer Sam's questions without incriminating Krasnopovich in parental alienation and child abuse? The truth is Krasnopovich did what Krasnopovich did. I am not going to lie to my son by pretending otherwise.

And where does that leave the best interests of the child.

If the parent has lied, trading money for the child's relationship with the other parent, lying, stealing, breaking international law, is it all good and well now to resume a co-parenting relationship and call it a 6-year hiccup free from any explanation to the child, now ten?

Is it in the child's best interests to learn the objective truth about the litigious parents conduct? Is it in the best interests of family-court to not adapt its process to accommodate accountability for the multiple deceits falling under the heading parental alienation and child abuse. What is the appropriate consequence now?

Did I *'promise him 50/50 like we were married.'*? Is there any element of doubt? Is this claim true. Or is it a bald-faced lie presented by a professional liar with an impressively consistent pedigree in lying.

Flaherty said I made this '50/50' promise, repeatedly. And everything that followed is down to that.

Krasnopovich presented the lie in court.

Flaherty transformed it into a legal judgment.

Is Krasnopovich liable for the consequences of claiming ownership of my freehold title and the subsequent conscious effort to spoil any Insurance payout following the flood and other damage, which made me homeless and cost me so many hundreds of thousands of pounds. Depleting all my means with which to remain in the UK and fight for custody within the family-law system. Flaherty's judgment forced the sale of my assets, ended my income stream, awarded sole conduct of sale to Krasnopovich and made me liable for all costs in mortgage and maintenance despite my pointing out the facts of her valuations being wrong. Three years later, the properties still had not sold and, as was inevitable, I had to default on my mortgage. Ending up with nothing as a result of a judgment that ended any prospect of visitation with my son. Here's the thing though. That claim was, demonstrably, a lie. On every level, any objective person with a double figure IQ looking at the 'evidence' cannot reach any other conclusion. The entire litigation was predicated on a lie; a complete fabrication contrived by Clock and Krasnopovich to manipulate family-law in pursuit of a financial windfall in which Sam, a child, was used to introduce a chancery court financial matter into family court, as well as to pressure me into agreeing to pay in exchange for visitation in a blackmail situation. *"First pay me £100,000, then you will see the child as much as you want."*

Curiously, if not downright suspiciously, the judge appointed for the hearing, who had a good reputation in financial matters, DDJ Burkes, was replaced at the last minute for no good reason, by DDJ Flaherty. Whose reputation in financial matters is the opposite. A switch that was announced to me by my family-law barrister with the assurance that *"If we get Flaherty, we will lose"* because the barrister had a history with this judge. A judge whose first decision having taken on the case was to overturn the courts own ruling that allowed for multiple witnesses. Clearing the way for her to invent a sequence of improbabilities to underpin a predetermined judgment.

In the course of appealing what I was told by my barrister was an unappealable judgment, the President agreed Flaherty's judgment was flawed, and awarded 'Permission to Appeal' along with specific guidelines to my barrister on how this should work. To bypass the 'Unappealable' element.

I am certain that Flaherty knew the 50/50 claim was a lie.

I was there and I saw what I saw. And heard what I heard. And felt what I felt. It is there in the judgment, in black and white. From the outset, the evidence of her conduct shows this beyond any reasonable doubt. Flaherty removed the witnesses ready and waiting to show the extent of the lie in a case based on hearsay evidence, which required disproving a negative, she discounted the actual Financial advisor with the records relating to the matter she elected herself to judge. A witness who had signed off his statement and cleared his diary for the day in readiness to give evidence and produce the documents referred to in his statement, made available to the court weeks before the hearing. She massaged the judgment to exclude any relevance to the clear facts showing the lie. Including glossing over the Will attendance notes in which Krasnopovich reveals in his own words that he has no interest in the properties which were all in my name. She offers a nonsense bypass around the revelation that the 'multiple witnesses' Krasnopovich intended bringing was not 'many witnesses' as he claimed in the preliminary hearing, to prevent the unsubstantiated claim being thrown out at that point, but in fact, refers to just one witness, Dia Mirza, who never appears as a witness because Dia confirms she has no memory of the claim Krasnopovich said she would be witness to. A double bust, not only did he have no 'multiple witnesses', but the single witness he named to get out of admitting he lied about any witnesses at all, says that conversation never happened.

There is not one single credible element in which Flaherty could justify her finding that '*Ms. Lee promised 50/50, repeatedly.*'

This is a lie that is so obviously a lie that allowing it to stand as a record of how my son lost his relationship with his parent and how I lost my life in the UK after 29 years of happy, mostly musical, helpful, kindness-based achievement, is to fail in my duty to 'tell the truth.' Remaining silent in the face of gross child abusing injustice.

So here we are. From the mess of family-court, the lying plaintiff parent. His lying solicitor. His lying barrister and his lying colleague in family law, the Deputy district judge, with the maximum acrimony costs award with 8% interest and sole conduct of sale awarded to the liar whilst forbidding me entry into my own home. What now for Sam's best interests? Either his litigant family-law parent is, as Flaherty ruled, telling the truth. As the freeholder to my property who was promised 50% of two flats and was bound by the fiduciary responsibilities of being freeholder, in which case he is liable for the costs arising from every decision made whilst freeholder that was not in my best interests, which includes bringing this claim in the first instance, and this trustworthy honorable member, the family law professional, can now be trusted to do what is best for Sam with visitation.

Or I am making all this up. Flaherty was right. I am a liar and every charge I make in this book about family law and my experience, is a fabrication by a mentally infirm liar, in which case she is quite right to end Sam's relationship with such an awful parent. Her judgment then is not abusing the child, it is saving the child from any exposure to a mentally infirm liar. And Cecelia Flaherty, who loves champagne and fun, has made extraordinarily good use of her opportunity as a deputy district judge to save a young boy from seeing this unsavory parent.

It does make sense of you look at it from Flaherty's point of view as the judge making a decision on what's best for Sam's life. What kind of parent would make up such a story. Accusing the other parent and his family-law associates of serial breaches of the SRA ethical code and what amounts to criminal extortion. As well as criminal offenses in another country. (The California Breach of Privacy offence that Flaherty wrote an indemnifier for in a British Court.) Accusing an elderly deputy district judge of incompetence indistinguishable from deliberately and willfully lying to abuse a legal system charged with representing a child's best interests? Relating a judge's actions to consequences including child abuse? Suggesting there is corruption inherent in the very fabric of family-court? Flaherty clearly believes it was worth switching cases for Krasnopovich's hearing to award costs against the defendant parent having established mental infirmity was such a risk to the child's well-being, being prevented a relationship with the child was the right judgment for a family court judge. She didn't need evidence, or witnesses, or any corroboration, because her extraordinary wisdom meant she knew just by looking at the words 'Mental infirmity' that the child's best interests would be served by the judgment she made as surely as the best interests of family-law would be represented by her magnificently informed opinion, albeit it at odds with the SRA ethical code.

Then there is the possibility that Flaherty was wrong. That she is in fact the incompetent liar that I detail in this book, often in her own words. Consider the possibility that the verbatim extracts from her judgment are in fact, real. That Flaherty is exactly as I have outlined, the author of a judgment that is as flawed as the President of family-law concluded when reviewing Flaherty's judgment in the Permission to Appeal hearing. What if the facts are as they stand and we have a corrupt judge sitting in family court making corrupt unappealable judgments that ruin children's lives? What if, after you read this, that same judge goes on to make similar decisions, ruining other children's lives? Does your failure to act now make you complicit in ignoring child abuse? Even if that action is simply calling your MP and demanding an explanation for why family-court judges can make un-appealable judgments and pre determine the outcome to cases they switch to at the last moment, where the barristers know and declare before a word is spoken, the judge has already ruled.

What if it is true that Nico Krasnopovich is a member of family law, who did prevail in opposing a preliminary application for visitation, preventing a five year old child from having even 2 nights a month visitation with his parent by engaging a QC and applying for costs in a last-minute ambush disclosure, imposing what became a £40,000 legal bill just for trying to see my son on alternate weekends. In a court process where he knowingly, willfully, told the CAFCASS official that the child was not safe with the mother, in what was a blatant lie that, had it been reciprocated by me making the same allegation to the CAFCASS official at that time, could have seen the child taken into care whilst the parents contrary claims were examined? A tremendous gamble for a parent to take with a child's wellbeing at stake placing into context that parents' value in ethical decision-making for a child's best interests. And for what good reason? Just to win control over Sam spending two overnight visits a month with me at the outset of the separation. So that he could continue demanding his £100,000 payable before any visitation.

The advice of Tim Clock has been exactly as I have disclosed. The extracts from Flaherty's judgment are unaltered in any way. Flaherty ruled as she did and discriminated as I have described, without embellishment. What if every disclosure in this book is unflinchingly connected to a central truth. What if members of family law operate on the ethical spine, exactly as this book records?

Attaching a fair and appropriate value to the consequence this litigation has visited on my son, my health and wellness, as well as those close to me, Sam's family and friends on my side, is a challenge. The financial consequences of this claim can be measured in millions of pounds. I no longer even live in the UK. I own less now than I did when I was 18, although I admit that may not necessarily be a bad thing. But all material considerations pale as to nothing when compared to the unforgivable and immeasurable consequence of this story .

The damage to my son's life with his parent.

How much he could have learned from me in these formative years. How much I could have learned from him as his loving parent. How many opportunities for life lessons were denied to him and to myself for no higher purpose than a family-court payday. This has been a life challenging experience for both of us. And it does not end there. The consequences of this legal deceit. The damage done by family-law members has impacted on many lives. And will continue to do so.

Awfully.

For some, who have passed during the time Sam has been prevented from being in my life, like Maria and Mark, it is too late for any reparations in this lifetime.

The residual animosity that exists between myself and the Krasnopovich, Clock, Flaherty family-law gang places a real obstacle on any future visitation. Absent of a formal accountability hearing leading to appropriate damages and censure for the miscreants, I cannot see why these family law members, whose actions are indistinguishable from child abusing lying thieves, will have any reason to not continue as they have done with my son and me. Lying their way to profit from the misery of children, placing monetary gain above all other considerations in this arcane legal system that makes it all too easy for them to carry on making big money with business as usual.

I remain certain that *unfettered visitation* is the minimum requirement for Sam to be able to rebuild his relationship with me. We have six years of hard evidence of what happens when the control over visitation is left up to members of family law.

Going forward, given what has gone before, would I now believe one word they say about visitation? Dialogue can only follow accountability. And agreement on what is in the child's best interests that I can have confidence in.

Who Lies wins. Sadly for Sam and for me that is the reality of family-law.

I can only imagine the consequences of being raised by two members of family law, as is Sam's reality now. But, it was the same for me, when I needed to find courage in adversity, at the age of ten, when my parent died and I found myself effectively parentless. I found my Greek DNA brought me the confidence I needed to determine right from wrong. There is such a thing as the highest good. In any decision making. And there is consequence for every action that relates to the highest good. Anything that goes up must eventually come down. You can always trust mathematics and the laws of physics. Actions have reactions. When he is able to speak for himself, his parent is waiting. Perhaps he will yet enjoy the opportunities arising from being raised by his missing parent, in California.

It remains the case that Sam is always welcome to be with me for school terms and his other parent for the two long holidays. Or vice versa. There is no reason he should not spend the two long holidays with me, if He considers it best for his education to stay in the UK for school. That could easily measure up to 8 weeks in summer and 3 weeks in winter. At least 11 weeks each year. That he could have been enjoying from the outset. But has not because one parent has gone to extraordinary lengths, serially breaching the very legal system intended to provide for children's best interests, without censure on one single occasion.

As a result of which it now falls to Sam to make the ruling for himself.

School term in California and Holiday in New Malden. Or School term in New Malden and Holidays in California. I will agree to whatever choice Sam makes.

38 Mr. President. About family-law
My letter to the President of family law

From: Andrea Leandros
To: President of the Family Courts

Royal Courts of Justice
Strand   WC2 A2LL
By Post and E Mail

9 May, 2018

Subject: <u>Managed expectation.</u>

Dear Sir,

I am writing to you directly three years after you ruled in my permission to appeal hearing, presented by Junior Counsel Richard Castello and my solicitor Roland Chambers from FOS LLP. It was Leandros vs Krasnopovich. Appealing the judgment of DDJ Cecelia Flaherty. A family court claim for beneficial entitlement brought by my ex-boyfriend and solicitor member of family-law, Nico Krasnopovich.

My purpose in writing is to follow up on your judgment, when you heard my Permission to appeal in in my presence in the Royal Courts of Justice and found it to be flawed. I write to record details of multiple breaches of the SRA ethics code by three solicitor members of family law, along with a desperately unjust child-abusing judgment by DDJ Cecelia Flaherty.

I am aware of the statistics and the scale of child abuse and parental alienation in family-court.100% in disputed cases. My purpose in writing today is, above all else, to offer whatever assistance I am able towards seeing child-centric reform in family-law to prevent more children suffering the abuse that befell my four-year-old son when the evidence shows this occurs for no reason more than financial benefit for members of family-law. In my case, the process of family court has abused my child. I have not seen or spoken with Sam for two years now. I have faced almost £500,000 in legal charges from family-court, including a six figure costs award against me in family-court. (Accruing at an 8% interest charge.) My home of 29 years was awarded to my litigious ex-boyfriend, Nico Krasnopovich, a notoriously dishonest member of family law, once expelled from equity partnership in Surreys largest law firm for 'dishonesty' following a dishonest claim leading to a flawed judgment causing a court-ordered forced sale which gave him 'sole conduct of sale' which will never see any actual sale at the prescribed figures because, again, his dishonesty has convinced the Judge to make a flawed decision even on the sale price. I am not even able to remain in the UK following this court order after being made homeless by an order that prevents me even entering my own vacant property. Meaning, if I could visit my son, I would have to pay to stay in a Hotel while my home sits empty and I continue paying the mortgage.

Nico Krasnopovich has deceitfully manipulated family-law to cause financial losses for me far in excess of £1 million, likely to increase when my property that is subject to forced sale by the Flaherty court order does not achieve the trigger price she set down despite my contrary assurances, as well as ensuring with considerable deliberation that I would be not be able to see our son. In the course of which along with his solicitor Tim Clock, he has lied repeatedly and serially breached the SRA ethical code.

My background before family court prevented all visitation with my son. The judgment resulted in the loss of my home and income business, ensuring I am not able to even remain in the UK to continue the fight to see my son following a legal bill of £500,000+ (Accruing interest at 8% by judgment of DDJ Flaherty.)

I am Andrea Leandros, 52, Greek, born. Raised and educated in South Africa. I emigrated to UK in 1985, aged 19. Twelve months later, 1986, I was able to buy my home, 28 Thameside. A freehold terrace overlooking the Thames. I owned the building; freehold and the three leases to a property that some 30 years later, in 2016, was valued at £2.5 Million. This reflects a consistent work ethic for the 25 years following my arrival in the UK working as a musician, a music producer, a studio owner, a record label owner and as an author. I have raised funds for Marie Curie cancer charity for ten years. And have been first responder for vulnerable elderly in home care for Elmbridge Council for a total period of 9 years.

Unfortunately in 2003 I met Nico Krasnopovich, a struggling young divorce lawyer, 10 years my junior. I saw in him the opportunity to share my experience and provide life changing assistance, driven by the Greek quality called Philotimia. He was at that time 29, earning £35K PA, working at an entry level position as a trainee in family law at MWT Solicitors in Epsom and struggling to pay off his student loan. I moved his into my home at no cost, and provided financial and emotional support that saw him very quickly pay off his student loan and progress well in family law. In 5 years becoming head of the family law department for Surrey firm MWT. And becoming an equity partner of MWT in 2010.

In 2008 our relationship broke down. He wanted marriage and children. I did not. I already have a child, privately educated, to a high level. I knew the costs of a private education, the challenges of raising a child in a broken family and determined never to repeat that possibility. We separated in a clean break which notably made no mention of any demands as would be the case later. Post separation in 2008, in a tremendously skillful presentation accompanied by a written agreement, Mr. Krasnopovich convinced me to have a child with him within a carefully predetermined parental plan. A proposal where I would stay home and raise the child, enjoying the opportunity to raise a child. He allayed my concerns over having to start again paying for a child's education in my forties, having just finished paying towards the high costs of my son Evan's education with the reassurance that his work in family-law, and my assistance in setting up his new firm with financing and experience, would pay costs for the child's education and upbringing. Leaving me free to be the constant presence parent. With this clear understanding, he moved back into my home and in May 2009,

Sam was born. To be frank. I had independent means and he was broke, although with prospects of career improvement

For four years I had an idyllic opportunity raising this beautiful child, Sam Leandros, to be kind, mindful, enthusiastic, thoughtful, inquisitive and athletic. And musical. By four was reading Greek reasonably well. Alphabet and numbers. A fifty-word vocabulary and enthusiastic interest in his Greek lessons with me. His confidence reflected his nourishing attention, in which I was an ever present whilst his Father was around at best, 10% of his waking time. My son was growing up beautifully until fathers-day 2013.

A day tactically chosen for maximal upset by an experienced member of family law with a skill in creating profitable separation leading to disputed hearings. Also a date arriving shortly after his new Law firms first year accounts showed a £250,000 net profit for Mr. Krasnopovich. Empowered by a new financial independence and enamored by a new romantic possibility, (his much younger fitness instructor) he left and took the child with him. The ambush separation left me distraught. And in that anxious time he successfully removed the child from my home. With hindsight, he very skillfully caused maximum trauma in the breakup to create the window of opportunity, without which I would never have allowed him to take my son from my home.

Post departure, he rolocated close to his law firm, and would not disclose the address he moved to, demanding a payment of £100,000 before he would do so and allow visitation. This is when the legal charge to family law began. Along with his solicitor, Tim Clock, they contrived a fallacious claim that shortly after we met and I housed him at no charge, *'She promised me 50/50 like we were married'*. That claim lead to an offer to withdraw the TOLATA claim if I paid a six-figure sum in settlement following which I would enjoy 'unfettered access' to my son. The second phase of blackmail after the first 'without prejudice demand for £100,000 had not succeeded.

Devastated by the 'fathers-day mafia hit' removing my son from my home, and then blackmailing me for visitation I turned to family-law. Hiring a provincial lawyer, David Clam, paying him some £40,000 to 1.) locate the address of where my child was and then 2.) to progress a visitation hearing. An application for alternate weekend overnight visitation through family court.

Mr. Krasnopovich resisted attempts to agree visitation furiously, hiring a famously adversarial and litigious city lawyer, Tim Clock of AFB LLP. They brought a QC to a preliminary hearing for visitation, where my solicitor, David Clam failed to win me as much as two unsupervised overnight visits nights per month, explaining that Krasnopovich and Clock had serially breached SRA ethics code in achieving this win. Although his sympathy did not extend to refunding the £40,000 he charged for what, on the surface, is no more than the duty of any parent, let alone a family law member. To provide the address of the child and to allow the child visitation with his parent. As a result of this expensive, unnecessary litigation and its outcome, achieved by deceit by two members of family law all too familiar with family law procedure, my son lost that early opportunity, during the first six months post separation, to have regular visitation with me. Hindsight now reveals that regular visitation never came.

Their tactics were as successful in achieving a win with a large legal bill against me as they were abusive to the child's future.

Further litigation and acrimony followed. I kept trying to see my son through family law. In the first year my solicitor David Clam won me 4 nights with my son, charging £40,000 for this work. £10,000 for each night my son was able to spend with me. Charges made necessary by the obstructive approach of Tim Clock. Knowingly and deliberately using the weaknesses in the arcane structure of family law to play the system like a mafia hit man. His mark in this case being a 4-year-old child. Child abuse by any interpretation. That is my reality of the family-court service you preside over.

What followed was systematic running up of legal costs by arguing every visit down to the hour. Krasnopovich and his lawyer took an adversarial position at every opportunity, calculated against my desire to see my son. They attached a monetary value to my parental feelings, first £100,000. Then after I applied for visitation, they raised it to £150,000, made in WP correspondence from Mr. Krasnopovich to myself. I became depressed. I missed my son to the extent that it had a deleterious effect on my health. I learned through extensive research that my reaction is not an isolated consequence of corruption in family court.

During the negotiations for visitation and my efforts to provide the best-case outcome for Sam's upbringing, I presented a proposal in Sam's best interests: I would raise him and he would have him for holidays. Earning six-figure sums by now with his own law firm, Mr. Krasnopovich's habit was work long hours. I felt that his conscienceless appetite for placing monetary awards above any other consideration, and especially the child's welfare, represented a very poor model for a growing child. As I had been the ever-present parent for the first four years, and very much in tune with the child, I felt it would be best for him to remain with me, allowing him the quality time to make arrangements for spending more time with him during school holidays. I included the converse in my custody proposal. Holidays with me, term time with him.

The negotiations ended when Mr. Krasnopovich had me served with a claim for beneficial entitlement, (having me aggressively served at home in what turned into an injurious attack in the street outside my home rather than sending the papers to my solicitor) claiming that I had *"promised him 50/50 like we were married."* Of a home I had bought in 1986. When he was 12.

His was an unsubstantiated claim. On the face of it, laughable in its improbability. Simply another instance in a lengthy list of lies by an accomplished liar with a reputation going back for decades. Since he falsified his low exam results to land his first job in law. This claim was evidently made more to encourage a 'commercial view' settlement than to actually stand up in court. And why family court? Surely this type of material claim against property is a civil matter.

This was a clear cut a case of nuisance opportunistic litigation brought to family court, made worse by the blackmail for visitation, in breach of the SRA code of ethics. For my troubled son, this was child abuse. For me, it was criminal extortion and deeply traumatic obstruction of my relationship with the son I raised for the first four years of his life while his father was working making hundreds of thousands PA exploiting parents at their most vulnerable with huge legal bills to see their children. Highlighting all that is worst in that business of charging vulnerable people £500 an hour to debate the time for collecting a child and encouraging disputed cases arriving in court because financially they are incentivized for this purpose.

Certainly, my attempts at a mediated settlement were dismissed out of hand. They set out an absolute. Pay the money. Or we go to court. Even after a settlement was agreed in the weeks prior to the hearing – in writing by his barrister with mine – he reneged and forced the matter onwards to a court hearing, Lying again in the costs hearing that followed claiming that it was me who refused to agree. Despite the evidence of emails between the barristers that show this lie clearly. The commonality in their position has been to lie and then accuse me of the thing they lied about. As if knowing their lie would never be tested in any appeal context.

Mr. Krasnopovich and Tim Clock's beneficial entitlement claim was to be tested in family-court in April 2015. The Judge set down for the hearing was DDJ Burkes. In the advance financial directions hearing two relevant instances occurred.

1. The preliminary hearing court judgment provided for multiple witnesses, from both sides at Mr. Krasnopovich's insistence. He intended bringing multiple witnesses to prove this promise was made. Without that assurance to substantiate his word of mouth claim, I suggest it is unlikely the case would have continued, given the high degree of improbability in a claim with not one scrap of evidence behind it. However, when tested his claim to have 'multiple witnesses' turned out to be a lie.

2. The second item of procedural malpractice relates to my family law member with the £189,000 bill. My first solicitor David Clam.

In the FD hearing I noticed that my name appeared in the chronology for a contempt, filing late, with a fine attached. The late filing occurred after David Clam called me some months before, telling me that he was extremely busy on another case, that a court deadline for submission was due, but he would not be able to file in time. If, and he doubted there would be, any consequences followed, then he would be liable. This was in acknowledgment to my request for confirmation that he had received my replies for this particular court deadline for disclosure in good time.

I first learned of this late filing consequence was when I saw it listed in the chronology at the financial directions hearing. The Judge, DDJ Berry has found me guilty of contempt in late filing, and fined my costs of £2,600. However. This late filing was the work of David Clam. I was never on one occasion late. I wanted this hearing as urgently as possible. I was motivated to see my son. My invoice from David Clam during this cycle of payments shows the fine for contempt in late filing as "No Charge." (£2,600). True to his word, David Clam paid the fine. However he left my name on the record for his offense in late filing. This late filing remains on the record against my name to this day. When I sought to make David Clam correct this error, he was evasive and claimed it made no difference as he had paid the court fine. This contempt finding against me was listed first in both the April hearing and in the Appeal hearing. It formed the basis for the Appeal being discounted.

I say this misconduct by a member of the law society is in breach of SRA guidelines. Being extremely damaging to my case as in the two hearings that followed both judges would see my name highlighted in a red circle on the submissions from the other side. It remains an offense that requires redress. Especially as David Clam has been paid more than £160,000 for representing me in a matter that was never more than an unsubstantiated claim reliant on one person's word, flying in the face of all common sense. In other words, it would require a remarkable degree of incompetence to lose a case based on someone's word that;

'She promised me half of her house, but I don't remember when and there's nothing in writing and I have no witnesses to any conversation, although the case moved forward when I promised these witnesses and she has 6 witnesses to show my claim could not have happened. I have historically borrowed £60,000 off her, forgetting to repay some, and have been censured for dishonesty in my profession many times. In 2012, I was expelled from equity partnership at MWT for dishonesty, and escorted directly to clear my desk and leave the building.'

The fact is that I was never late at any time in these proceedings. More than anyone, I wanted to get this court hearing over with and see my son. The two significant references to lateness, by DDJ Flaherty and Appeal Judge Andre Le Clerc both refer specifically to this single incident, the contempt fine for late filing, caused by David Clam.

At no time in these proceedings (which I attempted to settle on several occasions, offering mediation which was serially rejected), did I believe it was possible that the court would not see the truth. The record of Nico Krasnopovich's career shows both formal and informal complaints over his dishonesty and aggressive tactics. His practice in family law is based on deceitful misrepresentation. Yet in DDJ Flaherty's judgment you will find this curiously all-encompassing observation. "**I found the evidence of Ms. Leandros on every point wholly unpersuasive. I found the evidence of Mr. Krasnopovich credible and persuasive.**"

This is the reference in Flaherty's judgment to that late filing by David Clam.

It was apparent that one of the issues in this case is the wife's allegedly frail mental health; her ability or inability to work and this has been given as a reason for delays in providing his solicitors with up-to-date instructions and his non-compliance with the directions for the filing of evidence laid down by DDJ Berry on 22.10.14 timeously

When I switched solicitors for the appeal and fired David Clam I prepared to report his conduct to the Legal ombudsman. In that process I wrote to his managing partner and as a result he wrote to me claiming a new invoice meant. Unless I paid him, he would not release my files to my new firm, with a clock running on time for appeal. He only released my files when I agreed to not pursue the complaint with the ombudsman. What is it with your members and blackmail?

Turning to DDJ Cecelia Flaherty.

The switch judge.

Cecelia Flaherty

@Flatulent666fla

Lawyer; juvenile delinquent; lover of champagne and fun

Joined September 2016

Tweet to Cecelia Flaherty

The hearing was set for 3 days. The appointed judge, DDJ Burkes was, according to my barrister, a good choice. Strong in financial matters. After all, this claim was a civil matter. A financial claim which had nothing to do with family-law. At this stage it seemed highly likely that justice would prevail. My 6 witnesses were ready. My case was strong and the judge was known to my barrister for his competence.

Then on the morning of the case something irregular happened. My barrister told me that the judges were switching. He appeared panicked. He told me that Cecelia Flaherty might be taking the case. That "*If we get Cecelia Flaherty we will lose*'. Then we did get Cecelia Flaherty. No credible reason given. Before a word was spoken in the hearing that would determine my son's future with me my barrister assured me that we would lose the case.

He gave me two reasons.

1.) Flaherty was 'unfamiliar with financial matters' and

2.) He admitted that he had a falling out with her in a previous hearing where she ruled against him unreasonably, at odds with the law.

At that time, before we entered the court, I was assured that the switch judge Flaherty, meant that the case was lost. There was no point even going through the motions. I asked that the case be adjourned. Why continue with a hearing where you are put on notice that you are going to lose because the barrister has an issue with the judge who has evidently switched to take this case solely to ensure the outcome will be as my barrister indicated. My barrister was completely right. (So why did he not recuse himself). The outcome was exactly as he indicated in advance. By this stage I had paid David Clam £160,000.

1. *The witnesses.*

The first thing Cecelia Flaherty did after taking Mr. Krasnopovich's case was exclude my 6 witnesses ready and waiting to give evidence. 6 witnesses whom David Clam had charged me £12,000 to prepare statements from and prepare to give evidence. Including an Independent Financial Advisor, Larry Chester, who previously represented both myself and Mr. Krasnopovich separately and knew our forward planning details did not include this fictitious promise of giving someone 50% of my home and income generating business. Mr. Chester knew precise details relating to this claim and had documentation, including contemporaneous memos of meetings to show the circumstances of the freehold/Insurance transfer that took place in 2003. He had arranged every one of my mortgages and had all the details of those loans. His evidence would have proven Mr. Krasnopovich's claim to be false. And exposed him to the real possibility of being found out for Insurance fraud. An independent financial advisor of high standing, professionally engaged by both parties with a file of documents incriminating Mr. Krasnopovich was ready and waiting to give evidence which Mr. Krasnopovich and Tim Clock knew about, yet the switch judge appeared out of the blue and made her first order simply cancelling the witnesses. It is that simple.

2. The ruling in advance of a word being spoken

I watched this 3-day hearing in horror. Cecelia Flaherty was clearly decided from the outset in favor of Mr. Krasnopovich. It appeared to me that she had taken this case deliberately to fix the enormous credibility gaps in the claim. It seemed clear as day that the switch was a fix for this purpose. All the contradictory evidence to Mr. Krasnopovich's claims were simply excised by Flaherty, or glossed over with platitudes. Throughout the hearing DDJ Flaherty's conduct towards me was unpleasantly unacceptably amateurish. Transparently partisan and hostile. I was sitting in a room with a woman who evidently despised me, was rude to my face and displayed arrogant superiority, shutting me up when I tried to make my case. She profiled me as 'mentally infirm' and repeatedly called me a liar, even when her point in this regard was itself a lie. Simply put, she called me a liar, on more than one occasion based on her lie. She did not bother to make any effort to conceal her deceitful intent in this process, finding 100% in favor of her colleague in family-law, was pre-determined.

After the hearing barrister Richard Castello told me "I knew we had lost when she rolled her eyes at me." This moment occurred in the third minute of his opening submission. Confirming his assurance to me before the start of the hearing. Clearly, this judge had received direction before the case, upon which she had reached a determination. The process of a so-called hearing was a mockery of due legal process. Nothing was heard that impacted in any way on her predetermined opinion. Any evidence contradicting that predetermination was simply excised.

3. The will attendance notes.

DDJ Flaherty was presented with the will attendance notes from both of us in 2010. In his attendance note Mr. Krasnopovich makes plain that 'Andrea owns the three leases.' In my will attendance notes I make plain my intentions for my three leaseholds. On the face of it, overwhelming evidence that no promise was made in advance of 2010. (Mr. Krasnopovich initially claimed the promise was made in 2004, then corrected it to 2005. And later still, accidentally referred to it as 2006.)

Clearly if he felt he owned 50% of a £2 million plus asset, he would have noted it in his will, or at least somewhere in some email or conversation. Even if, as was revealed in cross examination, he made three separate references to when this promise was made, that would have been the biggest windfall in his life by a 7-figure margin – so it is unrealistic to the point of impossibility to imagine that he couldn't remember the occasion when it happened. Yet he is on record caught out in Cross examination, as giving three separate dates.

In her judgment Cecelia Flaherty fluffs over the point. Comically so. **"I remember the evidence of the wills at the time and wondering in reality where it got the case"** Here is the extract from her judgment on this very clear point. She read them but '**does not find this to be the true position'?**

In his own hand in a solicitor's office, where Mr. Krasnopovich is declaring his net worth for his will, he fails to mention that he has been 'promised over 1 million in real estate' as well as saying in writing "*Andrea owns the three leases*." This event happened 5 years after his claim this promise was made. Why would a lawyer in this position fail to record his ownership of a million-pound+ asset?

Further, why would a judge reading this very clear information declare as you will read below, (complete with typos) from her (typo strewn) judgment; unless, as I suggest is clear, this case was fixed and Flaherty is guilty of deliberately misrepresenting facts to enable her predetermined decision to award her fellow member of family law a lottery win.

56. I have been asked to look again at the wills and attendance notes that accompanied them and I did so [(what else are summer holidays for!)]. I re-read them and feel that they do not support what I find to be the true position. They talk about the future not present interests. Both wills were made in contemplation of marriage I remember the evidence of the wills at the time it was given and wondering, in reality, where it got the case. The way they chose to deal with this property or the absence of identifying the legal and beneficial interests that existed at that time I find unhelpful and not persuasive. In my judgment it neither goes to support Ms Leandros' case nor to discredit r. Krasnopovichs' case.

4. The multiple witnesses referred to in the FD hearing

When Mr. Krasnopovich was asked by my barrister about the multiple witnesses he intended bringing, he admitted he had only one in mind After further prompting he admitted that witness (Dia Mirza, also a member of family law, a barrister and a DDJ) had no memory of any conversation. It transpired that, despite claiming at the FD that he intended bringing multiple witnesses, as a result of which the Judge set down three days for the hearing to accommodate multiple witnesses from both sides, when it came down to it in court, Mr. Krasnopovich was unable to produce one witness. And not one piece of evidence. Not one email. Not even his mother willing to lie on his behalf and say she heard something. Although he had promised in his threats that he had "*Multiple witness ready to show up in court*." Here we have one witness referred to, Dia Mirza, a family law barrister and judge herself, who says she has no memory of any such claim. It is ridiculous to propose that I made some secret promise which I went on to hide from everyone I knew, including my financial advisor, my accountant, my business manager and my son. Or my mortgage lender. Or even, myself in my will.

It is a fact that this claim by Mr. Krasnopovich appears for the first-time months after separation in 2013, and only after I had declined his demand for £100,000 before he would agree to allow visitation for my son. And only after he had retained Tim Clock, who I know by the chronology of events to be the author of this claim.

5. Financial settlement. The freehold/Insurance claim. SRA breaches.

Post separation we approached agreeing a financial settlement before any lawyers became involved. As we had no financial co-mingling this was a simple matter. He owed me some £15,000, in loans and charges on my Amex card which he used for his law firm Krasnopovich Macdonald LLP. I took a generous approach in offering him the opportunity to pay what he felt appropriate. I made clear my interest was in making the best agreement for the child. The two co-mingled elements were:

a) His business domain names, paid for and registered in my name. Hosted on my web server.

b) My freehold title, put in his name following his advice in 2003, for Insurance advantage, with a declaration of trust and with an IFA, Larry Chester in possession of documentation and memos confirming the transfer 'In trust' to be returned upon demand.

Post separation I requested, in writing, my freehold return, and he requested the return of his business domain names. We both agreed this was the next step in avoiding any acrimony post separation. All of which was documented in the witness statement and would have been personally verified by my witness. (Chris Andiotis, Sam's godfather, who was flying from South Africa to attend the hearing.)

Whilst I transferred his titles as agreed, Mr. Krasnopovich failed to transfer mine. I wrote repeatedly to Mr. Krasnopovich about returning my freehold, establishing that by doing so he was in breach of a number of legal offenses. Including SRA ethics, where as a lawyer he should not be breaking a trust agreement for personal gain. And that by keeping the freehold in his name, he would be liable for the provisions in that leasehold agreement, fiduciary responsibilities, which included making up any shortfall in Insurance out of his own resources.

As fortune would have it, three months later my home flooded. And an Insurance claim became necessary. Mr. Krasnopovich doubled down on his freehold claim, by not progressing the Insurance which was in his sole name, leaving me with what has become a damage and costs liability in respect of that Insurance claim exceeding 1 million pounds. His motive in doing this was to cause me maximal financial harm, impacting on my ability to pay lawyers to contest his beneficial entitlement claim in family court. And ensure I could not pay family lawyers to force the visitation he simply refused on the terms I was able to provide.

After the hearing, Flaherty made several reckless procedural decisions. By this time, largely in part because of the animosity between Mr. Krasnopovich and myself following the significant insurance claim for the flood to my home, which had left me homeless and living in Hotels, the financial pressure on me was immense. Mr. Krasnopovich used the opportunity of being the sole name on the Insurance policy (another fiduciary breech, he was required to include interested parties on the policy, the lender as well as the lessee) to foul the claim to the extent that I not only never received one penny from Insurers. Instead, after long delays requiring expensive lawyers, I had to pay out some £250,000 myself to make the ground floor apartment, 28A Thameside, habitable.

Having been made homeless by DDJ Flaherty's ruling, who ordered the forced sale of my home and which specifically forbids me entering 28B Thameside, another of my flats, unaffected by the flood. DDJ Flaherty would go on to give Mr. Krasnopovich '*sole conduct of sale*' of 28B Thameside.

Towards the end of 2015 I had seen my son for just a handful of nights, costing an average £10,000 for each night he spent with me in legal fees to family law. Because Flaherty's judgment made me homeless in the UK and awarded my income generating business to Mr. Krasnopovich, I had nowhere to live in the UK, lost my primary income stream affecting my ability to pay Hotel bills, and that is the driving reason I now live in the USA. Where I have family housing me on a credit basis until I have the means to pay, based on my expectation that the Insurance will pay, as is required by the policy cover I paid for. (Annually over the previous 27 years.)

In Flaherty's court Mr. Krasnopovich claimed of the freehold that he 'absolutely owns it'. A perjury. He is aware of the fiduciary responsibilities implicit in this title towards the lessee (myself). Bringing this action against me and using the freehold as evidence is itself a breach of his fiduciary responsibility within the provisions of the leasehold agreement. I believe it follows all costs in these proceedings are Mr. Krasnopovichs' liability. I have pointed this out to him, repeatedly, in writing. His consistent reply is '*So sue me.*' Unsurprising as he is a lawyer with his own law firm, knowing he has successfully run me up hundreds of thousands in legal charges whilst preventing my Insurance payment for the flood to my home.

During the April hearing, switch judge Flaherty went to unusual and suspicious lengths to bully me into agreeing to indemnify Mr. Krasnopovich from any consequences arising from the freehold fiduciary.
Why? She was there to judge the merits of a beneficial entitlement claim. Which shouldn't even have been heard in family court as it is a civil matter. I say this is not dissimilar to mafia style conduct. Which I suggest demonstrates switch judge Flaherty was there to get rid of any evidence against a fellow family law member.

Judgment point 27.
In relation to the will Mr. Krasnopovich accepted that he was never asked any question about his beneficial interest. He didn't consider he had any interest in the property because he had the freehold. As he had the freehold he was the legal and beneficial owner. It had been transferred to him in order that it would mitigate the insurance premiums. Mr. Krasnopovich said, in a most adamant fashion in his evidence *"She did not ask for it back. Absolutely not true"*.

Mr. Krasnopovich claiming that "*She did not ask for it back. Absolutely not.*" Is perjury. The IFA Larry Chester, whom Flaherty forbad giving evidence had noted in his statement, and had intended confirming in his witness examination, the notice in 2007 when I requested the return of the freehold as the Insurance blight on my name had reached the 5-year mark. And I could at that point Insure my building in my own name. Larry Chester had prepared the buildings insurance policy for this purpose and the paperwork was underway to transfer the freehold back to my name, in accordance with the trust agreement. Mr. Krasnopovich and Tim Clock knew this evidence was in Larry Chester's statement. I suggest this gave them a tremendous motivation to have this witness excluded. I believe this is the blindingly obvious reason why the judge set down for the hearing was switched to a judge whose first decision was to forbid the witnesses.

Simply put, If Larry Chester had been allowed to speak, Mr. Krasnopovich would not have been able to make this claim of ownership. And would not have been safe to perjure himself, knowing that his deceit would not face legal examination. As his advisor Tim Clock was all too aware. Yet his solicitor, a member of family law, still recommended he perjure himself with this claim. I say both have clearly breached the SRA code. I was a witness to perjury. By a member of family law in a family law court. Now reported to the president of family law.

6.   **Amateur psychology by a frivolous DDJ reliant on profiling and dishonest prejudicial summation to support a judgment made before a word was spoken.**

DDJ Flaherty took many months to rule, during which time she was active on social media and enjoying the celebrity of her status as a judge.
Her social Media Profile reads;

Cecelia Flaherty: *Lawyer; juvenile delinquent; lover of champagne and fun*

Flaherty's judgment point 42 is an unfortunate jumble of incoherence, even spelling my name incorrectly.. Which I would like you to read again.

Judgment point 42.
The evidence about the identities of the three flats was very confusing. Ms Leandros was adamant that Mr. Krasnopovich had never lived with him at 7B. This was the flat where Mr. Krasnopovich had recalled the distressing moment when she had heard the news of her father's death and had taken a bath to comfort herself. There were also items of correspondence and bills addressed to Mr. Krasnopovich at 28B Thameside. Ms Leandros was asked to explain how he had estate agents confusing the identities of the flats when the estate agents were, from time to time, letting them out to tenants. He could give no particularly convincing explanation of this, beyond saying that he never particularly set any store by the address and often had post addressed to him at 28 Thameside. There was a lot of detailed evidence explored about the uses of the three flats at different times over the course of the ten year relationship; the mortgages raised; estate agents used as letting agents; the input Ms Leandros had given to Nico Krasnopovich over the letting out of a property in his own name; the builders used in the major works carried out to 28A and 28B Thameside and to the assistance he had provided to Mr. Krasnopovich when he set up his own firm of solicitors – Krasnopovich Macdonald LLP. Ms. Leandroes , in the course of her evidence was not always sure what had happened. for example there was considerable confusion over mortgages that had existed. The net effect of this confusion was that there were additional bundles (five Lever Arch files and a smaller file known as the "Small Bundle") that were referred to frequently in the course of cross examination. This is not meant to be a critical observation, but it is the reality of a case where it is necessary to look at the way a couple, during

their relationship, have used monies. This was a ten-year relationship where fortunes, as between the parties, varied. The star of Ms Leandros was in decline while the star of Mr. Krasnopovich was rising.

There is no confusion over the three flats. I bought them. I lived in all three. I paid all the bills in all three whenever I lived there. Everything was in my name. There is no factual basis for indicating any degree of confusion exists. Nor is there any doubt in the various accounts confirming my address. For example, Bank accounts, Thames water accounts, Council tax accounts. As I owned the freehold I used 28 Thameside as my generic address. As I owned all three leaseholds I was liable for Council tax unless the flats were rented at which time the tenants would have to pay the council tax, and they would refer specifically to the flat number. 28A would refer to 28A and so on. There is no confusion unless the intention is to make up a confusing nonsense point. The reference to confusion over mortgages is seriously misleading. And misrepresentative of the truth. I say, in light of how un-confusing my property ownership decisions really are, that by presenting this confusion point, Flaherty is deliberately weaving a web of deceit. Conversely, there is not one document of this type, services, council, telephone, that places Mr. Krasnopovich at my address. He lived as my guest, accepting my generosity in providing him with a cost-free lifestyle.

The truth is extremely clear in its simplicity; I am the only mortgagee. All my mortgages though the years since 1986 have been professionally advised by my IFA, Larry Chester. I have paid my mortgage without fail since 1986. I have paid the Council tax on every property throughout as appropriate when they were not let out. There is only ever one name on those payments. And even now, long after I have been forced to vacate my tenants by Flaherty's judgment, I am still paying the mortgages on an empty property. And solely liable for the mortgage.

I say this mortgage waffle is deliberate obfuscation intended to cloud the judgment in confusion where there is none. As I have already pointed out, the IFA who assisted with of all my various mortgages, Larry Chester, was ready and willing to appear as a witness. Had DDJ Flaherty been occupied by any valid basis for 'confusion', she could easily have spoken directly to the mortgage broker, or even read his statement, which was available to her. It would have occupied the work of mere minutes to locate the statement of Larry Chester in one of the files before this judge and read his timeline of the mortgages he secured for me through the years, since the first in 1986. Her judgment engages amateur b-grade bubble gum psychology in describing my '*star as on the wane*' and speculating on the dynamics of my relationships when in fact she is describing the happiest most successful time in my life, raising my son and working on creative projects of my own choice, with financial independence arising from my previous work decisions. Another instance in which her judgment is no more than deceitful folly. It has grievously abused the relationship between me and my son. It is child abuse.

7. *Mental fragility, profiling a medical condition, and ignoring professional medical reports by accredited medical professionals*

Almost the first thing DDJ Flaherty said to me at the start of my cross examination was "*So you are depressed. Everyone who sits in that chair is depressed. But there we have it, you are mentally infirm"* She would go on the include the words *'mentally infirm'* at every opportunity and even when there was no opportunity. In her 13-page judgment she profiles me with these words some 24 times.

Why? Because my GP diagnosed me as depressed after my child was removed on fathers-day and recommended I see a therapist for grief counselling. Yes, I was upset that my partner presented this separation announcement out of the blue and before I surfaced from the shock of his presentation, my son was removed from my home. That was depressing. As is appropriate in times of trauma, I took professional advice. Yet this was used against me. And is, I suggest, the very reason by Mr. Krasnopovich effected this manner of traumatic separation, giving no clue that anything was wrong before timing his departure with the child for fathers-day.

Here is one example of how Flaherty writes in her judgment, strewn with typos. (In her judgment she spells one person's name incorrectly seven (7) different ways. Literary incompetence I have never witnessed before outside of primary school English class.)

Judgment point 59. I have dealt with the issue of Ms. LEANDROS'mental health. The evidence she produced was very limited. I find, because it seems agreed, that she is a woman of mental fragility.

The evidence she produced is very limited? This is the judgment of a judge who dismissed the evidence of the 6 witnesses waiting to give evidence in the specific matter the judge was tasked to adjudicate. On the one hand dismissing evidence and on the other bemoaning its absence as if I am responsible for her folly? The issue of mental fragility is offensive to me as much as to every medical professional I have shared this conduct with. It is profiling of a medical condition that is unacceptable. I became depressed following the deceitful ambush separation removing my child from my home and the complete failure of family law to provide me with the address of where my son was without spending a fortune in legal fees. It is not an offense to be depressed and to see a therapist, yet that was used directly against me. In person during the hearing and in the judgment.

I was profiled as 'Mentally infirm' and discriminated against by a judge for this reason. This is a grave offense on many levels, not least of which is impacting on my suitability as a parent. Cecelia Flaherty's dismissal of the medical professionals who wrote on my behalf is harmfully wrong. I had notes from fur medical professionals of unimpeachable credibility, all of whom were dismissed as unconvincing by Judge Flaherty. Based on?

Her opinion.

No actual effort was made to confirm the identity of these four doctors.

Dr. Adam Simon, (she spells his name wrong – typo 27 of 44) was my GP in Thameside who has known me for 15 years as my GP and is as good as it gets for an NHS GP. He wrote a detailed medical note for the Court.

The second doctor giving evidence was my primary care physician in America, Henry Ling MD is, again, an experienced and established medical doctor. As good as it gets as a GP. He wrote a detailed medical note to the court. Judge Flaherty referred to him as a her in rejecting his report on my health.

As I experienced insomnia I consulted with a leading sleep specialist in California. (Over a sleep disorder arising from being mugged by family law.) And because I had anxiety and depression affecting my sleep pattern. I attended grief therapy sessions; first at the Priory in Barnes, which was tremendously helpful, and then in the USA with a leading doctor, Dr. Mark Zetin, a well-respected Psychiatrist and lecturer who took a special interest in my case and wrote at length to assist the court.

All four of the medical professionals who wrote on my matter are reputable, excellent professionals, with untarnished reputations, all of whom have seen DDJ Flaherty's comments and reacted with grave concern over her competence.

With these facts in mind, consider Cecelia Flaherty's judgment. (Where she refers to me as wife throughout. Piling up the idiot-level errors at a rate that defies probability without deliberation.)

It was apparent that one of the issues in this case is the wife's allegedly frail mental health; her ability or inability to work and this has been given as a reason for delays in providing his solicitors with up-to-date instructions and his non-compliance with the directions for the filing of evidence laid down by DDJ Berry on 22.10.14 timeously. I was directed to read a letter from a medically qualified individual Ronald Roberts MD whose qualifications are given by initials only "M.D., FAASM, FCCP". He is described as Diplomat American Board of Sleep Medicine. This letter is dated (in American styling) 17th March this year. The other medical evidence within the case relevant to the father is contained in two earlier letters. One is from Dr Shimon who appears to be a General Practitioner at whose surgery the father is or was registered and it is dated 28.11.13. The other is from someone named as Henry Ling "DO" and dated 15.01.14 from Mission Viejo Family Medicine. This appears to be a medical practice in the USA. There is no evidence from any psychiatrist. The mother has been prescribed differing quantities (from time to time) of antidepressant medication. She also stated that he has significant problems with sleep. The medical evidence in this case is deficient. There are three different individuals voicing brief opinions in letters. There is no medical report as such and there are no CVs from any of these individuals explaining the nature of their expertise and / or their respective experiences to voice opinions. I am asked to accept these letters as sufficient justification to explain why the father did not comply with the order of DDJ Berry and as a reasonable explanation for the delay. Most notably there is no psychiatric nor psychological evidence about the respondent father, as I would have expected to see.

Firstly: The order of DDJ Berry is the David Clam late filing at the FD hearing (also where he provided for multiple witnesses) that remains outstanding. I have repeatedly raised this point and it remains ignored and features as a defining aspect of a deficient judgment. This judgment abuse of a child through incompetence, or deliberately as I maintain, has been reported. Yet nothing gets done. I was never late once in any submission. Not one single instance. David Clam was late after announcing his reasons for a late filing on a relatively minor issue that was in any event comparable to late filings from the other side. He assured me that if there were consequences he would be responsible and sure enough; he paid the contempt fine. It appears on my invoice as "No Charge". Some £2,600.

I have written to the legal Ombudsman about this. Barrister Richard Castello was a witness when this contempt item was first disclosed to me, at the preliminary hearing. There are four emails to Clam demanding that he contact the court and clarify the contempt judgment he paid was his error, not mine. This member of family-law simply ignored my instruction, with grievous consequences for the outcome.

Four highly qualified doctors, each one an experienced reputable medical professional, wrote to the court. Judge Flaherty had a full report sent by my psychiatrist Mark Zetin. She evidently elected not to consider his report. I suggest, because her tactic of excluding anything that contradicted her pre determination in finding I was a 'mentally infirm liar' and therefore should have the maximum weight of censure against me, irrespective of the harm it visited upon a 5-year-old child. And irrespective of how it breaches guidance for judges in making animosity awarding judgments that harm children's best interests. She wrote in her judgment; **Most notably there is no psychiatric nor psychological evidence about the respondent father, as I would have expected to see.** That is because Judge Flaherty simply declined reading the extensive report by the highly qualified Psychiatrist who wrote at length on my behalf, for the courts benefit. In which he details the problems arising from precisely the kind of child abuse Judge Flaherty invites with her approach. This from a specialized medical professional whose seniority and expertise in the field of child psychology and the law far exceeds Judge Flaherty's.

While DDJ Flaherty prepared to deliver her judgment, there was to be a day in court for the closing submissions. I wished to attend that hearing day and planned to travel to the UK for this purpose. However I was unwell and immobile at that time. (After suffering a neck injury that left me immobile). I requested a delay until I was well enough to attend. I had my primary care physician, Dr. Henry Ling, my GP in California write to confirm that I should not travel for at least one month. I believed I had a right to be present in the court deciding my son's future. Instead of simply agreeing a delay on health grounds DDJ Flaherty accused me, once again, of '*mental infirmity*' and demanded that I see one of 3 Psychiatrists in California, on an unfeasibly short timescale to identify whether I had *capacity to instruct* solicitors. In order that she could proceed without me present.
Her direction was that Mr. Krasnopovich's side should identify three Psychiatrists and I could choose from one. Mr. Krasnopovich's solicitors failed to identify 3 Psychiatrists in the state of California, where there are more Psychiatrist's per capita than anywhere. Whilst I awaited the identity of the three names the judge had ordered I choose one from, no names arrived. Not three as ordered. Not two as would have been one less than ordered. Just nothing. The law had taken the week off.

Clearly there is an enormous credibility gap between the written direction from Flaherty and the nomination of 3 doctors for this purpose. Making this debacle more farcical still is the fact that I already had a Psychiatrist who was by reputation a leading doctor in California. Dr. Mark Zetin. A professor, lecturer, author of the book 'Overcoming Depression' used as a text book in medical circles and a doctor who I had been seeing since arriving in America suffering from the stressors of not seeing my son as a result of family court. Advising me on my son's likely mental state arising from this child abusing litigation. Information enabling me to make informed decisions placing my sons' bets interests uppermost.

A doctor way overqualified to fulfill the requirement for DDJ Flaherty's 'capacity' certification. It is for this reason ridiculous that this judge writes; **Most notably there is no psychiatric nor psychological evidence about the respondent father, as I would have expected to see.**

As DDJ Flaherty requested a capacity to instruct, and as I had not received the three names she had directed be given to me, I raised the matter with Dr. Zetin who agreed to complete the 'capacity to instruct' form for DDJ Flaherty. This is a standard one-page document, that he completed exactly as required by this court procedure. That, by any definition of compliance with a legal order, was more than adequate. Judge asked for a professional 'notice of competency' and Judge received one.

At the same time, given his insight into this case, a senior American doctor and expert with court experience in child matters, familiar with the specifics of my sons experience in family-court process, wrote and attached a tremendously thoughtful insight into the importance of allowing children to see their parents, representing American legal experience in this matter which provided Flaherty with an enormous opportunity to improve her professional knowledge on a subject she is employed to judge on in family-court. But no. She preferred her familiar approach of not allowing any evidence that might contradict her intention. And her intention here was to create a 'Three psychiatrist' deadline in order to find me guilty of a contempt, and push her judgment through.

For your awareness, in the course of my sessions with Dr. Zetin, the subject most often visited was family-court and my sons development challenges arising from the animosity in family-court. Privy in this way to the case on an intimate level, Dr. Zetin assured me he was astonished by the conduct of the British family-court. He found it highly unusual to the point of negligence that DDJ Flaherty labelled me as '*Mentally infirm*' 24 times in a 13-page judgment. He described it as 'astonishing profiling'. His assessment to me on Flaherty's credibility was "*This woman should not be representing children in family court.*" I could not agree more and hope you will take this review under advisement.

Considering that I had a 'name' psychiatrist who wrote to the court, please reconcile point **15** in Cecelia Flaherty's judgment. I had made it plain that I wanted to be present in court. I had provided medical evidence of my incapacitating physical injury making it impossible for me to travel. I requested my right to be present in Court. It would have taken no more than a one-month extension, which might be considered in the context that it took Flaherty 3 months to deliver her (typo strewn) judgment. (And only then by pointing out she was on holiday – and what else are holidays for.)

15.   When counsel came before me shortly after 10.00 on the morning of 28.04.15 I was told by Mr Castello on behalf of Ms Leandros that both Mr Castello and his professional client were concerned that Ms Leandros no longer had capacity to give instructions. Such an assertion from sources of integrity could not simply be dismissed, especially where mental fragility appeared to be an agreed element, but I asked what further instructions were necessary, given that the evidence was closed. I was cautious in my approach so as not to trespass into potentially privileged territory. However Ms. LEANDROS'mental fragility was, as stated above, a known matter and issue in this case. An investigation of this issue was inevitable, given that the case was not concluded. I made directions

for the preparation of a certificate of capacity to see whether there was evidence to rebut the presumption that Ms Leandros had capacity.

16.   I directed a tight timetable for the instruction of a suitably qualified expert to provide the certificate.   This was done because Ms Leandros had returned to the USA with Mr Parka Voulla.   In brief Ms Leandros refused or failed to meet the jointly appointed expert.   The court was faced with the only evidence available from the mother's side that she had capacity and the presumption remained in place and not rebutted.

Dr. Zetin's letter made no difference. DDJ Flaherty has simply bulldozered over reason to set out her own position, where even by her own account, 3 doctors were not identified, so her court order was not complied with from her side. **An investigation of this issue was inevitable, given that the case was not concluded.** The issue she was investigating was the subject of a letter – along with the 'Capacity' document, sent by Dr. Zetin. The simple fact is, this judge has not told the truth in her summary of this 3-psychiatrist chapter of her sorry judgment. DDJ Flaherty ignored this psychiatrist letter, just as she ignored all the witness evidence and doctors' letters in the hearing.   And used her own 'tight timescale' to force through the predetermined judgment she made agreed to when switching with DDJ Burkes to take on the case of Krasnopovich, the member of family law.

Ignoring medical evidence to the contrary, Flaherty proceeded with the submissions day without my presence and found me guilty of a contempt for not seeing the one psychiatrist I was ordered to see, in breach of her own three psychiatrist rule. Recording her conduct as I do here finds me scarcely able to believe our judiciary allows individuals of this caliber to continue abusing children and even our commonly held understanding of due legal process, to this day. Judge Flaherty's punishing judgment certainly raised the animosity between Sam's parents.   It was, as Flaherty knew all too well, a judgment that gave control over my son to the father and for this reason ended all visitation between my son and myself. That this abuse arises from a judgment based on lie upon lie, disregarding material evidence available to clarify points she would describe as confusing for lack of evidence, makes it a matter for wider consideration than just my sons' disappointment at losing one parent.

As I know Mr. Krasnopovichs' writing style all too well, I confirm here that I recognize Mr. Krasnopovichs' hand in the writing the judgment.   It is clear DDJ Flaherty has given Mr. Krasnopovich open license to write up the judgment as he chooses in the guise of 'perfecting' the judgment. Items appear in the judgment which formed no part of the hearing and whose origin can only be the opportunity Krasnopovich enjoyed to write whatever indemnifier he chose into the judgment.

In this process Krasnopovich and his solicitor member of family law, Tim Clock have seized on the opportunity to write indemnities for three legal offenses they have committed in the course of these proceedings.

Another offense I believe affects DDJ Flaherty, Nico Krasnopovich and Tim Clock. These are three members of family law protecting each other's interests. Serially breaking the law. And no one will ever know. Because I can't talk about it. Thanks to *Section 12 of the Administration of Justice Act 1960*. Ironic that they can use this law intended to protect children from abuse, for precisely the opposite purpose.

8. *Dishonest claims on income and Insurance liability. Fiduciary responsibility*

DDJ Flaherty fluffed over the Insurance element forming an integral part of Krasnopovich's claim. He was after all using the Freehold title to substantiate his claim that I promised him '50/50 like we were married.' The fact is Mr. Krasnopovich, in his role as Freeholder and sole named policy holder after calling the brokers to cancel my comprehensive Insurance cover just three months before my home flooded, dealt with the Insurance element by ensuring I received not one penny. And had to pay out £250,000 to repair my property myself, an amount which Mr. Krasnopovich then included in his award to himself in the judgment. I declared in that hearing that the property was not repaired to its pre incident condition and that the valuation of the property would be affected as a result. Flaherty did not consider my evidence and arrived at valuations for a forced sale which I knew could not be achieved, premised as they were on the deceit that Krasnopovich had discharged his fiduciary responsibilities by restoring the property to its pre flood condition. As events have shown beyond all possible argument, Flaherty was wrong. The properties did not sell. I say they will never sell as per the court order because the court order is simply wrong. All that happened was

1) She awarded Krasnopovich sole conduct of sale

2.) She made me liable to keep paying all costs.

3) years later the properties had not sold and I had lost £75,000 more in paying the mortgage on an empty property. In the same time I lost £200,000 in rental income by being forced to evict my tenants. All the while knowing that their forced sale was not going to work, requiring me to retain an expensive property lawyer

I believe, because Judge Flaherty had the information available to her to not make this deviant judgment whose outcome could only have led to me defaulting on my mortgage, that she should be liable for the costs arising from her deviant judgment. She caused those costs. Making judgments at odds with the guidance for her office, depending on her opinions being protected by anonymity.

21. Mr. Krasnopovich claimed to be the Freeholder despite overwhelming evidence contradicting his claim. To maintain his claim as being Freeholder, in October 2013, he called my Insurance broker and successfully cancelled the insurance cover for my property. Three months later it flooded. He was then liable for repairing the property. He did not. I received not one penny for the flood claim.

Mr. Krasnopovich did not 'deal responsibly with Insurers The AXA.' He deliberately fouled the claim. He was then investigated by the AXA, who hired solicitors and wrote to Mr. Krasnopovich accusing him of dishonesty. (2014) This letter from the AXA Solicitors DIC Beachcruft, was included in my disclosure and Flaherty knew then that;
1.) Mr. Krasnopovich was investigated for dishonesty and
2.) That I never received a penny from Insurance, despite paying all premiums in reasonable expectation, because Mr. Krasnopovich first – cancelled the policy in my

name, illegally, and then did not 'responsibly deal with the claim' as is evidenced by the fact that I have still not received one penny. And that the properties will not sell at the amounts Flaherty has ordered. Because she has disregarded the evidence in the flood damage not repaired by the 'Lessor'. Mr. Krasnopovich. Who perjured himself in the hearing saying he owned the Freehold.

9.   I had buildings and contents cover paid for and accepted at renewal time in 2013. Mr. Krasnopovich cancelled both, illegally.

In October of 2013 the buildings Insurance for 28 Thameside came up for renewal. In anticipation of the agreed transfer of my freehold from his name to mine, in a trust agreement and in an agreement made post separation in which I returned a title of his held in trust in my name, I had renewed the policy in my own name. Paid the annual fee and had the Policy accepted. With the AXA Insurance. Two weeks passed. I received a call from the Brokers (Fairtimes Insurance brokers) telling me Nico Krasnopovich phoned them and forcefully, dishonestly convinced them to cancel my Insurance. Mr. Krasnopovich did not take out the like for like replacement cover. Although he did take a reduced minimum policy for the buildings cover. (Which proved to be inadequate.)

I wrote to him then to confirm that what he had done was illegal and that he was now responsible for anything that might arise in relation to the house Insurance. I was furious that he appeared able to get away with this seemingly illegal conduct. He was bound by the Freehold clause to 'make up any shortfall in Insurance out of his own resources."

A few months later my house flooded. (February 8th, 2014.) And I had no Insurance. In every possible interpretation of leasehold law Nico Krasnopovich is liable by fiduciary responsibility. This is a member of family-law acting like a vindictive common criminal. The consequences to me are immense. I reported this offense. I paid a top flight city lawyer a significant sum, Roland Court at FOS. To date I have not had one penny back from Insurance. Or from the fiduciary failures of the trustee landlord, Nico Krasnopovich, who claimed to be the freeholder in Flaherty's court. The reason is, it appears, because I have run out of money to pay legal fees, Roland Court does not appear to be willing to pursue the accounting on my home matter without a significant advance payment.   As with every other offense by Nico Krasnopovich, he has got away with-it scot free. Being a member of family law appears to be the ultimate get out of jail free card. And in Flaherty's judgment, she writes that I have agreed to waive any claim against him for this? That is another lie, presented in a judgment. It also begs the question – why would I voluntarily agree to indemnify the miscreant in a matter as serious as this? Legal liability for a million-pound Insurance claim against a Freeholder bound by clear fiduciary responsibilities. The answer is. I did not. A judge has simply allowed the solicitors to write whatever they want into the judgment she signed

10. Nico Krasnopovich and Tim Clock. SRA breaches including parental alienation and child abuse.

Throughout this litigation Tim Clock corresponded in a manner that was aggressively combative and increased acrimony between the child's parents with every word written. His attempts to argue down visitation time include one instance where I was given 24 hours with Sam. Flying from California to London to be allowed just 24 hours. All visitation was obstructed, without exception, and related to financial demands argued like a rabid dog with a bone. I can list multiple separate clear breaches of the SRA code by Tim Clock upon request. It would be more challenging to locate correspondence between myself and Mr. Clock that does not place him at odds with the SRA guidelines.

Repeatedly Mr. Krasnopovich would tell Sam one thing about visitation just before he came to see me, to deliberately project a downward mood on our visitation. On one occasion that included leaving a pack of cigarettes in his overnight bag, to be the first thing I would see. (I am a fervent anti smoker and Sam was then 5.) Another specific example: Agreeing 3 nights with me in painful detailed specific expensive wording following which I would book return flight, (LAX to LHR return) hotel and car hire (linked to flight details), spending way beyond my means to ensure this quality time visit could progress for these three days in the best way possible. Knowing how important it was to keep up regular visitation with my son. Then, while dropping this excited 6-year-old off to see me for the agreed 3 days, Mr. Krasnopovich told Sam he could stay with me for a whole week. He ran to jump into my arms, radiant with joy, announcing *"Mummy I can spend the whole week with you."* How would I explain to him that I could not change all the arrangements for a week visit. I confirm this felt like mental cruelty as well as parental alienation and child abuse.

After this hugely rewarding 3-day visit, I was in the plane back to California when Tim Clock lost no time in putting on record *"It is unfortunate that you did not see fit to have your son for the week that was offered to you."* I have no doubt, had I found the means to pay the costs of staying for a week, his letter would have read *"It is unfortunate that you have breached the agreed visitation dates"*. Without exception these two members of family law argued visitation to the child's detriment with absolute disregard for the direction on the SRA website.

Speaking on behalf of my son, I can say that their compulsive obsession to interpret every aspect of visitation as an opportunity to 'win one over' on me to prove some excellence in family-lawyering is an awful abuse of a child. And consistent with their conduct in terms of visitation from the outset. Borne out by the fact that I do not see my son. Although I wrote on a weekly basis I have no idea if he receives my letters. I have seen in both of these members of family-law the worst kind of child abuser, acting at odds with what I have read on the SRA ethics code, allowed to carry on practicing family law, where I feel certain I am not alone in observing both members as demonstrably unsuited to represent any child's best interests. Both measure success in billable hours from high net-worth clients in which children's interests are simple negotiating levers. Cynical conscienceless manipulative liars, free to trade children's lives for their idea of big money. Enabled by their membership of this self-protecting clique, family-law. I wonder if, as President, you are already aware that there are bad apples in your number presenting this impression of family-law, or whether I have been unfortunate in meeting what represents just a handful of corrupt exploiters of the system?

In the weeks after Krasnopovich's fathers-day departure, with Sam with him, he refused to provide me with his address unless I paid him £100,000. I had a documented series of exchanges with two intermediaries who agreed to facilitate the visits to avoid legal costs. For 13 straight weeks Krasnopovich cancelled weekend visitation at late notice, invariably linked to his financial demand. As a contextual aside, on one weekend I had discussed my family-law issue with Ian Holloway, then manager of Crystal Palace FC. Ian very kindly invited me to bring Sam to attend his first football game as his guest. In the managers box. *"He won't be able to say not to that"* was suggested. I wrote via the intermediary to Mr. Krasnopovich requesting that he allow Sam to come with me to his first premier league football game as a guest of the manager. His reply was *'Pay me the money and he can go with you.'* I did not pay him the £100,000 and he did not allow Sam to see me that weekend. I can say this was the talk of the Crystal Palace dressing room that day. What kind of a father would do that to his own son. Refusing to allow him to attend a premiership match as a guest of the manager? Thirteen weeks in a row he made the pretense of agreeing to a weekend visit, and then cancelled it at late notice. That is why I brought an application for visitation in family court, which ended up costing me £40,000, as a result of which I had my son for a total of four night that year. £10,000 a night is how effective these two members of family law were in associating cost to visitation.

11. Non accountability in secret courts with no appeal process. Permission to Appeal.

After DDJ Flaherty's judgment, my barrister Richard Castello, an established member of the family law circle, confirmed that it was un appealable. In writing. *'Flaherty will make her judgment un appealable.'* I did not believe this possible. Surely the appeal process exists as a safeguard against precisely this level of fixed court judgment. Evidently not in the hostility that exists between Cecelia Flaherty and Richard Castello.

After the Flaherty hearing and during the wait for the judgment, I changed lawyers. David Clam was guilty of errors that caused irreparable harm to my claim. He failed to win for me even two nights a month in an application for visitation in the vital time shortly after separation. I switched to a top-flight City firm, (FOS) using a family lawyer to take up the appeal and a property lawyer to pursue the fiduciary claim against Krasnopovich. Roland Chambers read my file (for £30,000) and was very optimistic that a 'horrible decision' would be reversed on appeal. During this time I travelled 19 times from California to the UK. I was resident in the US because Mr. Krasnopovich had gone to extraordinary lengths to ensure that my home was not repaired by the insurance. The only place I had 'credit' accommodation was in the US. The cost of travel and hotel to see my son and to attend legal meetings was considerable. (I would say it exceeds $100,000 to date.) I missed my son terribly as did he me. I would write to him and skype him and send gifts. Books. Toys. A bicycle. Amazon deliveries. It became clear the gifts were not reaching him. Even that small comfort of sending him gifts was denied to my son. Mr. Krasnopovich's standard reply to my concerns over withholding deliveries for my son was *'so sue me.'*

It became clear that Mr. Krasnopovich, and on occasions his new girlfriend, also a family lawyer, were grooming Sam during our skype talks, making him visibly uncomfortable, and then using short extracts from those private Skype talks as evidence in court to show me as 'unfit'. The Skype conversations stopped for this reason. I could not watch my son being groomed with replies during our only means of communication, via Skype. He was aware of what was happening. It was a painful sight of my own child being abused by two members of family-law. I kept on contact by writing letters through post. Photos with stories written on the back. And then in April 2016, my letters started arriving back. *"Return to sender. Address unknown."* I wrote directly by email to Mr. Krasnopovich's work address requesting the address where my son was. He did not provide me with the address. His reply was *'Talk to my lawyer.'* I wrote to Tim Clock. He knew that would annoy me as he had won costs for Tim Clock against me. At 8% interest. So, I would on the face of it be generating another bill with Tim Clock which I would have to pay for. Just to find out where my son was. It is a fact that I received the address of where my son was 9 months after I first requested it from Mr. Krasnopovich. I was upset that my son must have wondered why he had no contact with me for 9 months. This blocking of contact extended to all my family and friends. It was depressing. I reported this to family law. Nothing was done. Evidently because I had by now run out of funds with which to pay a lawyer. A fact exploited mercilessly by Krasnopovich and Clock.

Members of family law withheld my sons address from me despite my repeated requests, for a period of Nine Months. As the President of family-law, I wonder if you would care to comment on this?

I wonder if I would recognize Sam now if I saw him in the street. We last saw each other on 16 February 2016. He was 4 on fathers-day, when he was taken away. The expensive Permission to Appeal hearing was in the High Court. You were there. I was impressed. It is a grand old building and one forms the firm impression that the scales of justice balance with truth and wisdom. Sure enough, you appeared to grasp the extent to which DDJ Flaherty's judgment was flawed, and agreed the 'Permission to appeal', even offering my barrister some advice on how to present the appeal. (Stick to three or four of the strongest points. Don't confuse the judge.) I travelled back to the US that evening feeling a new confidence in British family law and a new hope that I would see my boy soon. And win costs that were so unfairly awarded against me. I thought then that this (appeal) was money well spent. By now I had spent well over £300,000 on family-law and formed a very poor impression of the honesty in family-court by the members. But I was reassured that the President of family-law was now aware of the conduct of members Flaherty, Krasnopovich and Clock and had found the judgment to be flawed. 'The truth will out.' I thought. I will admit I was impressed with your estimable presentation as a Judge, my confidence in British Justice being restored to what it was prior to my sight of British family-law in Flaherty's court. Months later I travelled back to the UK for an overnight visit to attend the Appeal hearing before Judge Andre Le Clerc. He read the submission, with the big red ring around my name for the contempt for late submission, the David Clam error, and I would say at that moment, the first two minutes of the hearing, it was clear that his mind was made up. It turned out that Richard Castello was correct when he told me "She has made an un appealable judgment." By now, my legal fees, having had Mr. Krasnopovich's legal costs awarded against me (with an 8% interest charge) approached £500,000 and the Insurance matter was coming to the fore. Family law barrister Richard Castello was correct twice in my case. First when he told me *"If we get switch judge Flaherty we will lose"*, because he had a historical grievance with her, and then in his email advice that *"Flaherty's judgment is un appealable."* So quite how you, as President of family law did not know that, is a mystery to me. Why award permission to appeal when a judgment is un appealable? That was another £60,000 I might have put to better use towards my son's education.

In DDJ Flaherty's court, I was suspicious when Flaherty tried to bully me into agreeing to indemnify Mr. Krasnopovich from any claim relating to the Insurance on the house. I believed this was at odds with her authority being beyond DDJ Flaherty's remit. Why would a judge seek to indemnify a deficient freeholder who has breached freehold fiduciary responsibility from any liability in family court? In the mafia atmosphere of these proceedings, I can confirm this appeared indistinguishable from a protection racket. On one hand, Mr. Krasnopovich had claimed to be the freeholder saying "I am the legal freeholder". Perjury as it turns out. In writing, in the course of these proceedings, he had offered to sell me the Freehold for £17,000. And on the other hand, when the judgment was written, DDJ Flaherty said the title should be returned to me, clearly accepting it was held in trust by Mr. Krasnopovich, and yet, writing in her judgment that he is exonerated from any liability for his actions while the title was in his name. In any interpretation, I have not received one penny from the Insurance and Flaherty's judgment has awarded Mr. Krasnopovich 100% benefit from the costs I paid to make the property habitable, reflecting in the sale price. This is plainly wrong. Allowed to stand, it will validate my mafia comparisons. These two findings, cannot mutually co-exist absent of complete dishonesty legitimizing larceny. Either Flaherty accepted he was the freeholder and based her award on this fact. (Which she did.) Or Flaherty accepted he was a trustee all along who breached the trust by claiming to be freeholder simply to cause malicious harm to me, and attempted to smudge over it by simply making it an order of court that the freehold be returned to me. (Which she did.) Awarding the advantage of being freeholder in her judgment. And then averting the fiduciary responsibility contained in that award by simply ordering I take back my freehold and the fiduciary faults are overlooked. Indemnifying Krasnopovich in this process. It is blatantly dishonest abuse of the Judges authority, to ignore legal fact.

12. Post forced sale accounting

You may appreciate by this stage that an enormous residue of acrimony accompanies the forced sale of my home and rental property business. Which will inevitably meet the hopelessly inadequate consideration DDJ Flaherty has given to the matter, bereft of financial awareness as Richard Castello so accurately explained. This means, Mr. Krasnopovich is incentivized to not sell. He has 'Sole conduct of sale' on my property, as well as accruing interest of 8% on his costs award. The judgment incentivizes him to not sell. DDJ Flaherty's accounting calculation for the forced sale is based on ignoring my input and accepting his. It is plainly wrong. It means there is no real chance of selling at close to the actual value of my property. All Krasnopovich has to do to continue his approach of causing me maximal financial harm is nothing. And I have to keep on paying the mortgage and costs of maintaining an empty property. It provides for Mr. Krasnopovich walking away with 100% of everything after I go in default with the lender, as is inevitable because the judgment ended my income stream, as well as leaving me a massive crippling debt. DDJ Flaherty has ignored my notice, as the owner of the property, regarding the flood damage and the consequence of Insurance blight affecting the value of the property. Instead she has accepted his valuation, and set a target price for sale based on that, and then for good measure, awarded him 'sole conduct of sale'. I say it is wrong and the properties will not sell at the price the court has set. The judgment simply leaves me paying mortgage and maintenance and 8% interest on the costs award, while having no place to live, no income from my rental properties, which I was forced to make vacant for the forced sale and refused permission to enter my home? The amounts and dates that Judge Flaherty has allocated to the sale will not work. Because, as I have pointed out, Krasnopovich and Clock have lied about the AXA flood claim. Affecting the valuation. If I am wrong, then the properties will sell at fair market price. If they do not, that I suggest is the evidence of precisely the fraud I accuse them off. Which, in its full measure, is child abuse. In its effect on my son. Perhaps, in good conscience, you will keep a copy of my letter for future reference to use this foolproof indicator as confirmation that, "I put it to you Judge Flaherty based her deviant judgment on a series of lies." Causing real, lasting harm to my child. Causing me financial losses measured in multiple millions. Making it impossible for me to even remain in the UK.

Only your silence can indemnify her, and more holistically, the reputation of British family-law as an unimpeachable, appeal free arbiter of one individual's unchallengeable opinion, whether it harms children or not. Whether their actions are reported to the president, or not. If this case does not warrant intervention and redress, then I suggest, family-court is no more than a member's club for personal enrichment at the expense of children's lives. At the rate of 10,000 a year according to CAFCASS. I have a solicitor looking at the forced house sale and Insurance accounting arising from Flaherty's judgment but as I mention, because I have run out of funds to pay him in advance, his firm is not motivated to pursue proper accounting to include the fiduciary failures and the Insurance deficit. The non-payment of money legally due to me and the failure to factor in the costs I incurred to make the properties habitable and therefore sellable. Mr. Krasnopovich's approach to proper accounting is 'so sue me'. Unless Roland Court agrees to progress this on credit, which so far he has not done, it seems likely that Nico Krasnopovich and his family law accomplices will have succeeded in a multi-million-pound fraud that is at the same time awful, life changing abuse of a young child. And I will have no redress other than to write to the President in the hope that this is clearly unjust and represents transparent abuse of the system, warranting action by the head of this organization to protect its reputation with children's rights from parity with that of Jimmy Saville.

Conclusion

Here we are then. Almost five years since my child was stolen from my life on fathers-day in a contrived 'fathers-day mafia hit' which enabled the father to remove the child from my home while I was in a state of shock. Family law supported that rainbow theft in a judgment whose consequences include me not even able to live in the UK anymore, with a debt in court fees and insurance shortfall that exceeds a million pounds. The three solicitors I have referenced have serially abused the SRA code of ethics in achieving their six figure paydays. The judge I have referenced is by her own hand as deviant as shown in her judgment and in her social media profile. Guilty of child abuse and still allowed to carry on unchecked, free from any accountability in a system where judgments can be made un appealable. Where naming and shaming is prevented by the secrecy laws protecting flawed judgments, leaving miscreants free to continue abusing children in the same way as mine.

I do apologise for the length of my letter. I am aware of your imminent retirement and imagine you have a full diary. Unfortunately I simply lack the skills with brevity to have presented sufficient factual detail to enable you to make an informed decision in any shorter version, absent of repetition which I notice may be less than ideal towards presenting you with a decision. However I do expect you to acknowledge my matter. You are the President and this happened on your watch. In fact, partly adjudicated by yourself, in the one stage that was honest. As President of family law I retain the hope that you will take a personal interest in my son Sam's misfortune as a victim of family-court corruption. You have already heard my matter in the Permission to Appeal which you judged and your awareness that, by the most modest of measures; something stinks in this family court judgment which has abused a child's rights. I conclude mindful of managed expectation with one request. That if you are unable to assist directly, investigating and prosecuting the miscreants, with appropriate damages awarded to my son and myself, you will at least consider this proposal. I intend publishing a book on my experience of family-law. I approach this literary challenge entirely with the intention of assisting the implementation of an effective decision-making child-centric process that puts an end to the kind of child abuse my son has experienced in your family court. A reform that will help build public confidence including the principle that the law must be seen to be transparent. I would very much like to assist identifying meaningful reforms to end the awful statistic of 10,000 children abused by family court judgments every year in 'disputed' cases. At the same time I am mindful that the miscreants in my story are presently working in family law and have every reason to continue defending their right to place financial benefit above a child's best interests without regard for truthfulness or ethical standards. For this reason, a brief forward from yourself, confirming, at least, that my matter did reach a Permission to Appeal hearing in which you found the judgment by Judge Flaherty flawed, will help dissuade efforts to prevent me disclosing the material facts of what happened in family-court in my sons' case. Your name attached to my story would show willingness to acknowledge mistakes happen and measures exist to address court sponsored child abuse. Imagine, if that is possible in these circumstances, how much I miss my son every day. Imagine how much he misses me. Our horrific experience in family-court speaks to a cruel, irregular and unjust abuse of the very office that exists to protect children, for nothing more than personal gain by members bereft of the very ethical qualities their role should require. Whilst deviating significantly from the ethical code published on the Solicitors regulation Authority website. All if which you are personally aware of, having looked me in the eye and made a judgment that Flaherty's judgement was flawed.

I will be grateful if you will acknowledge receipt of my letter and even if you are unable to assist directly at this time of imminent retirement, please bear in mind the names of the miscreants in my matter. I am sure I am not alone in seeing how they represent family-law. Perhaps the next author writing to your office with a similar complaint about these names will flag a revisit to this letter?

      Nico Krasnopovich
      Tim Clock
      David Clam
      Cecelia Flaherty

Yours sincerely,

Andrea Leandros

I sent that letter by post as well as email. After two weeks I had no reply, and followed up with an email request to which I received a reply by return. It read *"Sir President has read your letter and has no comment."*

Shortly after he retired and a new President of Family-law took office, who included the word 'depressing' in his early summation of conditions in family-court. There has been no change in the fabric of family law since.

39 The last legal letter
Clock and Krasnopovich cover tracks, but do not allow unfettered visitation

2018 saw me try again for summer holiday visitation. As ever, with the same outcome. And then, again, I tried to arrange visitation for winter holidays. And this time it looked like something was going to happen. I imagined that Sam had been badgering Krasnopovich constantly and worn him down. There was at least a reply though Tim Clocks office indicating that a December visit was possible. By this stage I was extremely cautious in any negotiation in which Krasnopovich and Clock could impose conditions. The totality of the learning experience in this regard is just two words.

Unfettered visitation.

Visitation would be based on Sam being allowed to travel to California, spend the December holiday with me, and then return to London at the end of the holiday. It was that simple. I was not going to enter into lengthy expensive discussions with known liars looking to misrepresent my words to whatever benefit they chose while running up more legal bills for me. (Still accruing 8% interest charge following Flaherty's award of costs.) I wanted to see that Krasnopovich agreed to support Sam's visitation as a parent acting responsibly and to avoid any doubt in this regard the default position was those two words. Unfettered visitation. In practical terms that understanding required no more than a date of arrival and a date of departure. I was not prepared to walk the same path of back and forth emails inviting conditions, replicating events over the past 5 years that had brought about this entirely one-sided negotiation with the same outcome every time. For the avoidance of doubt I offered a specific detail that would demonstrate to me that Krasnopovich was supporting the visit; made in full awareness that allowing them to dictate the conditions for visitation would produce the identical outcome to every effort over the past 5 years. Been there. Done that. Either you let the child see his parent. Or you do not. It is not the opportunity to present a new set of terms and conditions for visitation, which 5 years of experience show, always ends the same way.

Philips view was *"Don't get your hopes up. Most likely they are just offering it to show they are not obstructing visitation, but they will not actually allow Sam to travel. You know that."*

I did know that that was the perceived and actual wisdom behind this proposed visit. I had laid out the visitation offer clearly, (As I had done twice annually) and received a reply that, on this occasion, was at least presenting a possibility until the stumbling block was introduced. That stumbling block was Sam flying (at age 9) as an unaccompanied minor. I had investigated airlines offering this service from LHR to LAX and had no doubt it was well within Sam's means to have his parent put him on a plane in LHR and have me collect him directly from the plane at LAX, while an appointed steward monitors him during the flight. I had myself travelled unaccompanied minor at age ten from Johannesburg to Athens on a Boeing 707. I remember it well. It was an exciting adventure. I felt certain Sam would love to travel to be with me. He had been flying long distance since age 6 months.

But none the less, I agreed to compromise. Krasnopovich would pay Sam's travel to and from LAX. And I would pay a companion flight for someone to accompany Sam on the aircraft for the 10-hour flight. Knowing that team-Krasnopovich modus in all visitation was to seize on one small element and present that as a plausible reason to cancel the visit, making it look as if I was the unreasonable person in cancelling the visit, I offered this companion element unreservedly. His first position was then to say I had to collect and return him personally from Heathrow. That was a flag to me. Why were the so determined to make me fly to LHR? Considering they had previously used awareness of my whereabouts to hire a goon process server to attack me, I have never strayed from the sensibility that it is best they do not know where I am at any time. Because they have this history. It is reasonable to consider that he wanted to me to appear at a set time in LHR in order to confront me personally for some sinister purpose. I was not able to fly 12,000 miles in 24 hours myself, both because it was unnecessary, when any number of friends and family would jump at travelling free to LA, and also because I was physically unable to undertake this journey. I was injured in a motor accident. In June 2018 I was in a vehicle that was hit from behind by a loaded Peterbilt dump truck. Knocked unconscious by the impact, which cause real damage to my lumbar vertebra. (L3.) This compressed disc in my lower back affected my mobility to the extent that making a 12,000-mile trip in the economy seat of a plane was "asking for trouble" in the words of my GP. I would not be able to collect and return my son. But I was able to pay for his adult brother to do that. Of course, my adult son Evan was first in line to be asked to accompany Sam as I would have loved to see him too. I speculated in advance of writing on this subject that the only reason they would not accept this companion offer is if they had a sinister motive in wanting me to present myself in England for whatever purposes they might have, that would be consistent with their aggressive and hostile approach over a six-year period of ever-increasing animosity.

Summarized. Sam could have spent December 2018 with me. Three weeks. Evan would have collected and returned him from Heathrow at the agreed dates. Unfettered visitation was a realistic proposition. There were no doubts about his 'safety' or the possibility of his non return.

Here is my letter for the December 2018 visit, accepting the compromise of paying for a companion flight.

To: N Krasnopovich
28 October, 2018.

Re: Sam's visit, December 2018.

I confirm that Sam is expected for the duration of the December school holiday with myself. I am aware that you have agreed this visitation subject to the condition that I collect him from LHR for the outgoing leg as you have determined that he is not able to travel as an unaccompanied minor.

While I do not agree that he is unable to travel as an unaccompanied minor and it is a fact that for reasons of health I am unable to travel 12,000 miles for the collection, and the same for the return, I am prepared to work around your condition by booking a companion flight for a responsible adult escort to travel with Sam for collection and return. (Probably Evan.)

In order for the practicalities of flight booking to succeed I will need the flight details for Sam, the dates fro departure and return, with Flight numbers, following which I will book the two flights for the adult accompanying Sam. Once I have Sam's flight details I will book the companion flight immediately and rely on you to ensure the passenger will be seated next to Sam when you do the check in. (24 hours pre departure.) I will provide these passenger details in good time for this purpose.

I will ensure Sam is at LAX for the return leg at the specified time with his travelling companion. Philip has agreed to WhatsApp connect to you to provide confirmation at each stage of the departure process. You will also have the number of the companion to coordinate his arrival and collection from LHR.

I propose that you maximize Sam's time with me by agreeing a few days off school as you will struggle to find tickets on the exact days you prefer. Weekends are always harder to find and more expensive, especially at this late notice with Christmas being a peak demand time. Rather than cutting into his time with me to suit flight availability, err on the side of longer than shorter for this visit. I know his school master will agree to supporting Sam seeing his parent at the expense of some time off school. Why not arrange for Sam take a week off school to make it a proper visit? Three weeks with me would be a good start.

Sam will require an ESTA visa. Easy to do online. Please do not let this opportunity fail. Sam needs to see me.

Andrea Leandros

Krasnopovich did not send the flight details. Of course as events make plain, he never intended to book any ticket for Sam. The condition they locked into was, unless I flew to collect and return him myself, then he could not travel. (Knowing I was unable to fly.) Even if I overlooked the reasons why I should not fly 12,000 miles in 24 hours, twice in 3 weeks, I could not fly to collect him due to my back injury. But even if I had been able to fly, my distrust of Krasnopovich and his City lawyer, based on first-hand experience is such that I would put nothing past them using specific knowledge of my whereabouts to cause me harm. Including another violent attack. Perhaps he remembered that one time I promised to give him one of my kidneys if one of his relatives ever needed it. A matter for a claim in family-court. His beneficial entitlement to it would lead to a claim for detriment if I did not give him 50% of my kidney assets. I was not prepared to place myself in any position where these unprincipled liars with a history of lying and bringing dishonest litigation against me knowing they would face no accountability in family-court could continue to act as they have done. Given the extent of how they have used knowledge of my whereabouts to pay for an assault on my person, I was suspicious as to why they made it a defining condition of my visit with Sam that I present myself at a time and place of their choosing. Clearly, any responsible adult, from his brother onward would have been perfectly acceptable to remove concerns over him being 'unaccompanied' for this direct flight.

The practicalities of the flight were not complicated. He had done it before. It's a journey lasting under 11 hours. From LHR to LAX. Introduced to a flight steward at LHR who would show him to his seat. He could watch a few movies. Enjoy some food. Have a snooze and presto, less than 11 hours later I would be there to collect him at the plane door. A provision many airlines cater for. But, accepting that Krasnopovich would use this as his objection I agreed to pay for a companion to accompany Sam. But as expected, Krasnopovich and Clock sidestepped any possibility with the usual obfuscating legalese and the visit was off. Either I collect and return him. Or he cannot come. Of course, changing the subject quickly as they so commonly did, I could accept their very fair alternative suggestion that I go to London for my visit with Sam. With no mention that if I did I would have nowhere to live because their court order prevented me staying in my home, (which was vacant and which I was forbidden to enter by Court order of Flaherty) and over which they had sole conduct of sale. Of course, their success in costing me over £500,000 in legal fees and ending my property income meant I had limited means by way of budget. Simply put. I had no means to book a nice hotel even if I had been physically able to make that long journey. And overlooked the warning signs about any inappropriate confrontation during my visit. My time for that December visit with Sam was to be in my home. The same unfettered visitation Sam had every right to expect.

The proof I required that Krasnopovich was no longer obstructing Sam's right to see me was simple. Unfettered visitation. Just agree to let the child spend the December holiday with the parent he has been prevented from seeing for so many years. Once again, for the umpteenth time in a row, visitation was mooted, and then cancelled with nonsense reasons given which in no way concealed the reality. That Krasnopovich and his lawyer Clock simply found specious reasons to cancel any visitation for my son while writing shoddy legal letters showing how they had made every effort to encourage visitation. As they had done from the outset. Even despite the fact they had so vigorously opposed my application for twice monthly overnight visits at the outset (July 2013) and then written confirming how hard they had tried to encourage visitation. Now, five years later, after seeing this exact sequence play out twice annually by these child abusing members of family-law, this really was the last straw. As expected Tim Clock worded the cancelation letter appropriately. Sending it at 5.25 PM on a Friday. The peak time for sleazy lawyers to ruin parents' weekends. As I remembered was a popular tactic used by Krasnopovich in his line of family law. Clocks late-Friday letter disregards the facts of previous correspondence entirely, presenting his standard obfuscating legalese to demonstrate his client was encouraging the visit. How it was entirely my fault there would be no visit, yet they would '*happily consider some future possibility*'. It also ended my willingness to correspond again with the Office of Tim Clock. Any prospects of seeing my son again would have to happen without the involvement of this man so committed to maintaining his perfect record in winning minimal visitation at every opportunity. While trying for maximal animosity. Al the while celebrating his 8% interest win on the costs award he had from a judge who felt that was best for Sam's interests.

From: Tim Clock
Date: Friday, November 2, 2018 at 05:25
To: Andrea Lee

Subject: Sam's December visit

Dear Ms. Lee,

Thank you for your email which I received on the 29ᵗʰ October.

It is an odd concept that a nine-year-old boy should have to travel across the world to see his mother rather than the other way round, but my client was prepared in principle to consider this. He is not happy, however, with the practical arrangements. There is no way he will agree to Sam travelling as an unaccompanied minor or with a stranger and you have not put forward a proposal that gets round this. You have indicated that you are not willing/able to travel to collect Sam yourself.

If you wish to travel to London to see Sam then my client will accommodate this and please let me know what arrangements you would propose. If this Christmas is too soon this could happen for example over easter or in the summer next year.

If you are prepared to come to London for the purpose of collecting Sam and taking him back to California for a stay with you, then my client will happily consider this, it may be that this could be organised for the summer next year. Next Christmas would not work for this because of Sam's 11 plus exams.

Your sincerely,

Tim

Chronologically the end of this book comes with the end of my prospects for seeing Krasnopovich support any relationship between my son and myself. His position has not changed since he so strenuously defended my application for visitation in the early months post separation. At the same time, some three years after being made to vacate my properties and still keep paying mortgage costs while he fails to sell, I cannot keep hoping my property lawyer will somehow act now when he has not in the four years he has had every opportunity to be proactive. At some point I have to accept that Flaherty's judgment was badly flawed with consequences including that her judgment has no prospect of being workable. The basic numbers in this forced sale by this incompetent judge remain as wrong now as they were when she was told by myself, in 2015. Although I had representation by one of London's top law firms, a property law partner, Roland Court, at FOS, with whom I spent many hours in preparing the case against Krasnopovich for fiduciary failures, to progress the accounting for the remedial costs I incurred on the properties since 2014, to be repaid before any award to Krasnopovich as per the Flaherty Court Order, no demand for payment ever flowed through Roland's office. He had invoices and supporting documentation to show losses, in the fiduciary failures and in the Insurance matter, far north of £3 million. But not one demand for payment ever indicated that Krasnopovich's advice 'so sue me' was coming.

Roland almost brought proceedings against Krasnopovich to make him accountable for his fiduciary failures but these efforts floundered on my inability to front the £60,000 (+VAT) request for FOS costs to underwrite the action. After more than three years of seeing no actual progress towards the accounting liability, I simply could not keep on paying the mortgage in the hope that Roland would win anything on my behalf. I could only get the £60,000 once the properties sold, and it was clear the properties were not going to sell. That was the catch 22. My lawyer would not act without payment. Krasnopovich had sole conduct of sale. I could not pay my solicitor to act until the property sold. The property was not going to sell. And I was still paying the mortgage 3 years after I could more effectively have saved £100,000 of expenses by defaulting from the moment of the judgment. The facts were glaring. Krasnopovich had 'sole conduct of sale'. And the property was the longest running stale listing on Rightmove. Years passed with the same original listing unchanged. Generating no market interest. The valuations Krasnopovich had used to convince Flaherty were as wrong as I had said they were at the time. I had been called a liar and a ruling followed based on a Judge believing him and calling me a liar. I grew weary of pointing out how corrupt this process was, facing an indeterminate wait until what? The fact is, as the facts show abundantly, judge Flaherty made a ruling based on a lie. Borne out by the fact that the properties had not sold. For the exact reasons I had explained and been labelled a liar for. There is no less wordy way of saying it.

With no end in sight, by February of 2019 I saw that my mortgage/maintenance repayment costs since the October 2015 court order forcing the sale exceeded £85,000. And I recognized that it was beyond three years since I last spoke to Sam. Nothing had worked. There was no visible prospect of any upside in maintaining the status quo of the deficient court order by the switch judge. Not only had Krasnopovich failed to sell, but all of the reasons I had given as to why he was lying in court were borne out by the sale reality. He had perjured himself and the judge had made numerous dishonest assessments and prejudicial errors in the process of awarding him whatever he chose to write into the judgment. That these events were substantiated by a very clear paper trail that was consistently and roundly ignored in my efforts to disclose the extent of their fraud aggravated my sense of injustice to a point that I lost all confidence in the British Court system. My words have fallen on deaf ears. Once I ran out of money to pay members of family-law, my prospects of seeing my son again reduced still further.

After some six years of dispute with a member of family law over my son, it was time to say goodbye to hope that my sons' case in family-court would resolve differently to the other 10,000 children every year who are victims of this flawed child abusing process called Britain's family-court. I decided to end all hope of seeing any return on the forced sale of my home and rental business rather than continue throwing good money after bad, by ending my mortgage payments. I would write to the bank (also my mortgage lender) and disclose my intention to default, after 40 years as a faultless customer. It took a great deal before I could bring myself to default on my mortgage. (I have a perfect credit history. Now I stood to lose that as well.) I took advice from the smartest people and the outcome was. Fold the tent. There is no possibility that this court judgment will ever lead to a sale that generates as much as you have spent on the property. Ironically this was legal advice from the same law society that pays Cecelia Flaherty, the author of the judgment.

Before I wrote to the bank to foreclose, I wrote one last letter to my property lawyer Roland Court, the purpose of which was to see if there was any intention of pursuing accounting for the errors in my case, and especially the fiduciary failures by Krasnopovich claiming to be the freeholder and his decisions while his name was on that title, obligating him to a specified course of action in which he was so clearly in breach on multiple instances measured monetarily in damages totaling millions. I also wanted to remind him of one of many examples in which the paper trail of dishonesty in the entire Flaherty case as glaring. Referring to the costs award, where the barrister bases his calculation for costs on numbers that are;

1.) simply wrong and
2.) refer to an unexplained withdrawal of all proposals for settlement.

This after he himself agreed and confirmed a settlement that was later withdrawn by Krasnopovich. So. Clearly not 'unexplained' at all. Why wouldn't a litigious lawyer as Mr. Court claimed to be, make hay out of this point alone? I knew the answer was 'because you can't pay him the £60,000 he needs to file for you' but none the less, I did want to have it in writing, just in case his reassurances about how strongly he felt about my case might be sincere. I had invested a great deal in time and hope that Roland Court was the lawyer able to win damages for the offences committed in this case. To return me to the position I was in before the actions of Krasnopovich, Clock and Flaherty changed my life. Or to paraphrase, win a fair and just outcome to a damages claim.

From: Andrea Lee
To: Roland Court

Dear Roland,

I am setting out to compose a letter to the bank, explaining why my mortgage payment will end from March 2019, and in the course of that process, thought I would write for your awareness on two points. 1.) Prospects of any sale in line with Flaherty's court judgment. And 2.) In so far as you may have interest in addressing legal errors in my matter, including the costs hearing which you attended on my behalf.
My two quotes come from court documents copied below.

First, Flaherty's judgment sets a value for the sale of my home. And a date for the sale.

> *The properties shall be sold at the best price reasonably obtainable on
> the open market and as is agreed between the parties SAVE that it
> is directed that the applicant shall be entitled to accept any offer and
> consequently that a sale may proceed for 28a Thameside at £705,000
> or above for 28b Thameside at £540,000 or above.*

*28a Thameside at £705,000 or above for 28b Thameside at £540,000 or above. The
properties shall be marketed for sale by no later than 15 October 2015.*

At this time we are three and a half years down the line. That is to say. Krasnopovich
has failed to sell, despite winning sole conduct of sale. Of course, I cannot argue with
a court order. It is based on two set valuation amounts that were put forward by
Krasnopovich and accepted by Flaherty. And the costs award follows those amounts.
I have no influence on whether the court ordered sale trigger amount is accepted or
not. Plainly it would be a breach of Flaherty's direction to sell below the amounts
specified in her judgment. Even though you are aware those trigger amounts are
significantly below the valuation done for the April 2015 hearing. Flaherty's ruling
prevented me selling my property in full, freehold and three leaseholds for a sum that
would have produced double the amounts she set as a trigger for 28A and 28B. I told
you that her figures were wrong. And her judgment would cause me unnecessary
financial losses, entirely manageable by an efficient accountability process. They lied.
They got away with it. I have lost my home.

Second, you will see in Hazelwood's costs application (attached) that he claims:

> *It is notable that under the valuations of the properties used at the final
> hearing the equity totals £706,000, 50% of which is £353,000. Father's
> offer made clear that under CPR 36.14 he would seek her costs on an
> indemnity basis if he obtained a judgment which was more advantageous
> than the offer. He plainly has.*

I said at the time, the valuation Krasnopovich presented did not reflect his fiduciary
failures with the insurance. Plainly the values Hazelwood applied in the cost's
calculation are wrong. Exactly as I said at the time.

The fathers cost win is 50% of 28A, sale price less mortgage, and 28B. Sale price in
total.

I say on 28a that will likely be a net loss of, say, £200,000. (The bank will likely
auction it and at auction I don't expect more than £300K) 50% being -£100,000. And
I say 28b will be lucky to get £400K after the lender's surveyor has done due diligence
and found Krasnopovich's fiduciary failures. (Almost half of what I could have got
for 28B in a sale as a going concern when Krasnopovich got Flaherty to hear the case,
and was awarded *sole conduct of sale*.) Say that 50% is £200,000. However, I have
paid on average £25,000 each year since October 2015 in mortgage and associated
sale costs alone. That is a sum approaching £100,000. Then there is the £250K I spent
making up 'Insurance shortfall' that is still by any measure due to be paid in any
calculation of what must be repaid before the 50% share can be calculated. Then there
is the council tax. They will need to be paid from the proceeds of sale. I say, in all
probability, his costs award, as by Hazelwood's calculation is below zero. Not

£353,000. The costs award itself is plainly wrong. He has been claiming 8% interest on a costs amount that is plainly wrong. I have laid out all this money, hundreds of thousands of pounds, to enable the sale of these properties despite his fiduciary negligence, and am not only being ignored in terms of repayment accounting, forcing me to engage your services which has built up another significant cost, but have I no interest calculation reflecting the fact this sum has been out of pocket for over 3 years. It is simply madness to expect this fraudulent miscalculation to work out any differently to every other aspect of this child abusing judgment which has ruined a child's life with his parent. My observation is this. The court has awarded him costs based on a valuation that is plainly wrong. Presented by Hazelwood in a way that is deceitful. I confirm. Hazelwood knew that he was representing dishonest claims by his friend Krasnopovich. Secondly, why is the valuation wrong? Did I not disclose that the property flooded? Was he not the freeholder and insured party, bound by fiduciary obligation to 'restore the property to its pre-incident condition and make up any shortfall in Insurance?' Did Krasnopovich not know that there was a fiduciary breach leading to a non- payment by the AXA in the flood of 2014?

You will see in Hazelwood's costs breakdown that;
14.   On 25/2/15 Father made a proposal. He sought:
a.   A payment from Father of £17,000 in return for transfer of the freehold;

Clearly on *25/2/15* they are offering to sell me the freehold in their valuation calculation. Here in his own hand is the claim that he owns the freehold. And they owned the freehold at the time of the flood. And at the time when he called Fairtimes brokers to cancel the policy I had in place for buildings and contents for 2013/2014. Was cancelling a policy on my home acting in my fiduciary interests, or was it, as I suggest, clear malice. For which there must be accountability. Because that malicious act had clear and direct cost consequences. There is no doubt that he did it. Notice that in the same document – they claim £17K for the freehold. Which Flaherty saw because it was presented in evidence. Yet Flaherty's judgment simply awards the freehold to me. (And attempts to have me indemnify Krasnopovich from any consequences of claiming he owned the freehold.) Which is it then? One of those two contradicts the other. Both cannot mutually co-exist.

The fact is, as freeholder, Krasnopovich breached his fiduciary responsibility to restore the property to its pre-incident condition and make up any shortfall out of his own resources. Using the freehold to bring this TOLATA claim was itself a fiduciary breach. Krasnopovich is by any measure of justice liable for all costs relating to that (2015) claim.

I have read through Hazelwood's costs document. (Below) It is wrong. In fact it is a fraudulent deceit by a family law barrister. It does not disclose the settlement detail correctly. It deliberately misleads the reader by omission. A settlement was reached. Between Hazelwood and Castello. I have it in writing. It was Krasnopovich who agreed the settlement and then reneged, refusing to settle when I did not agree to indemnify him from any liability as freeholder in the flood claim. I have the mail in Hazelwood's own hand confirming that a settlement had been reached. This was weeks ahead of the Burkes hearing in April 2015. Castello represented me in a conference call negotiation (With Clam and Clock) leading to a settlement which

Hazelwood then confirmed by email back to Castello. It is therefore a deceit to present the costs document as he has done. But there you go. Nothing was done about it. I disclosed details of this email confirmation of Hazelwood accepting the settlement to you on more than one occasion. That document exists.

11.   On 24/7/14 Father made an open proposal. He sought £100,000 in settlement of his TOLATA claim. He sought a further payment of £150,000 under the Children Act which would revert to mother on Sam's maturity. He also sought child maintenance of £500 per month from Mother. Father was very keen to bring the proceedings to an end.

12.   On 10/9/14 Mother withdrew all proposals; with no explanation.

The omission occurs between point 11 and point 12. Point 12 is a lie. The author knew that a negotiation occurred, he was the negotiator and he knew all too well why the settlement of the TOLATA claim was ended by his client.

The £100,000 part is correct. He did claim £100,000 from me before he would allow Sam visitation. Before he instructed Clock he wrote to me demanding that sum in exchange for letting me see Sam. Unmistakably blackmail using a child as leverage. A claim made to witnesses (who were available to give evidence at the court hearing) where he disclosed that, unless he received this payment (£10,000 for each year I spent with him) "*she will not see Sam again until she pays*". Recorded in his conversation with Sam's godfather, when attempting to mediate.

"*This is what I do*" he told Chris Andiotis when he asked why he thought he should get £100,000 before letting Sam see his mother. Hardly surprising Krasnopovich tried so hard to have Chris' evidence excluded by claiming his statement included comments made '*Without Prejudice*'. Ask yourself, is it coincidence that Flaherty cancelled all the witnesses after switching with Burkes to take that case which had provided for 'multiple witnesses' from both sides. Where even the barrister Richard Castello told me "*If we get Flaherty we will lose*" because it was that obviously a fix. That judge switch on the morning replacing Burkes with Flaherty and immediately cancelling the witnesses.

There you have it. I put it to you, family Court barrister Simon Hazelwood has lied. Family court judge Flaherty has accepted his lie. And made a lying judgment perfected by family court members Krasnopovich and Clock. The consequence of which is child abuse. Far more serious than simple fraudulent theft of my home and business.

I have disclosed to you the extent of my financial losses arising from the fiduciary failures of Nico Krasnopovich, and that after paying over £75,000+ towards my mortgage liability since the date of the court award to him, I can no longer continue paying the mortgage. My sole reason for paying this long (Which was done by borrowing money at interest generating cost) was in order that you would be able to ensure accounting for the matters we have discussed so exhaustively and with so little effect. I had asked you for input on how best to approach the lender to end my payment obligation, and I note here that you have not replied to that request. It remains the case that I cannot continue paying the mortgage in this situation where, plainly, I am a victim of fraudulent activity that has made it impossible for me to pay on an indefinite basis with no end in sight and with no confidence that I will see any accounting process providing me with one penny of what is owing.

There is no prospect of either flat selling at the court order valuation. Three and a half years have passed. And all that has happened is:

1.) I pay the monthly costs and

2.) He accumulates 8% interest (or is it 10% - who knows) on a ridiculous costs award based on figures that are plainly wrong.

At this time I cannot continue with this hopeful inertia. I cannot point to one action you have taken on my behalf that has produced one positive outcome. If you are not able to proactively represent me, confirming that you will commit to pursuing the accounting as you indicated you would at the outset, (*They will know we are coming*), my request is that you inform me in writing so that I can either find effective representation to take my claim forward or simply default on the loan and start again with a new life far away from this shameful chapter of British family-law.

I can assure you it is as painfully tiresome for me writing the same thing over and over as it is for you reading. And evidently, as pointless.

With kind regards,
Andrea

That letter received no reply, as was often the case with Roland Court. Lawyers seldom offer their best when not paid in advance. Although of course, I remain grateful that at least one member of the law society made the effort to tell me how sorry they felt about what happened. And Roland did talk a good fight on the occasions when I needed convincing. One week later I wrote to the bank providing them with the detail of why I was unable to continue paying the mortgage. I mentioned that the fiduciary responsibility to name both the Lender and the Lessee in the Policy cover was one further breach by a freeholder who was 100% liable for the down value of the asset in which they had a vested interest as mortgage lender. I copied my IFA and my bank manager in. They were in any event witnesses to the Krasnopovich theft by deceit and perjury and both offered their support as character references. And when that letter went, being the end of any hope I had of getting any money from the sale of my home, I was reminded of that same unexpected sense of relief as when my home burned down. (In 2001.)

Owning nothing is at least a clean slate from which to start again. The end of the daily disappointment of hoping against hope felt very much like the best decision after so many years of seeing British law serving its members above any pursuit of justice. A hopefulness that tied me to constant health sapping disappointment was now over. Once the worst has happened the only way is up. And that is where I am looking. West – towards new beginnings. I cannot even imagine calculating damages on losses arising from family-court judgments and the lost years with my son. Possibly a trillion plays of one of my songs on Spotify? Or sales of 10 million copies of this book? Hopes that have a firmer grasp on realistic probability than that of British family-law members being held accountable for perjury, fraud, larceny, deceit, breaches of their own regulators ethical code, grand theft, parental alienation and child abuse. The President of family law who I dealt with has changed. The new President appears to be just as indifferent to the flaws in family-law. And my interest in fighting for that change which would save some 10,000 British children's lives every year from the blight of a legal system that could so easily be repaired, has waned under the roaring silence my efforts have met to date.

Nico Krasnopovich achieved his dream of marriage, with multiple children, with Carol, a divorcee with three kids. Both continue to work in family-law.

Tim Clock continues to work in the same London firm and may or may not still be married to the long-suffering Debs. If it's a litigious adversarial obnoxious win-at-all costs fighter without regard for traditional parental values that you want to pay to win your family matter in the high court, his reputation precedes him.

Michele Flaherty continues to work as a Deputy District judge. Still promoting herself socially as "*Lawyer; Juvenile delinquent; lover of champagne and fun.*"

David Clam no longer works at the same firm, Spoons LLP, but continues to charge separating parents for advice in family-law.

Richard Castello is still family law junior counsel for hire.

Simon Hazelwood is still family law junior counsel for hire.

At this time of writing, 2019, I have not received one penny from the AXA insurance following the flood of February 2014.

Sam has not been able to be with me since 16 February 2016. Every holiday I plan on having him here. Every holiday passes with the same outcome.

When Sam was moved in 2016, it took 9 Months between my request to his parent and the date of when I received his new address. If he has moved in the past 3 years, I would have no way of knowing. Sam is now ten. I still write every week, posted in an online blog, "Letters to Sam', hoping that he reads these letters, and knowing if not now, one day he will. As recently as July 2019, his godfather Chris Andiotis, made numerous attempts to visit him, travelling to London for this express purpose on July 11th and 12th. He was not able to see Sam. No one I know has been able to see Sam. Philip has written to Krasnopovich again, within the last 6 months, requesting visitation. No reply. My current hope, as has been the case at this time of year annually since 2013, is that I will have Sam with me for December Holidays.

I remain hopeful that Sam will find me and especially, while he is young enough to enjoy the educational opportunities being with me in California represent.

41 Letter to Harriet

Just sell it at half price. He will never notice. And then let the bank foreclose on the flooded one and he will be left with the debt

In August of 2019 I received an e mail from a Wimbledon firm of Conveyancing solicitors appointed by Flaherty's court order, confirming the sale of 28B Thameside. It was in the £400's, exactly as I had predicted when I read Flaherty's court order where I also read her trigger price was £560,000. So, here was Krasnopovich trying to sneak through a sale in breach of the Court order. While at the same time making no mention of the sale of 28A, the flood damaged apartment still not resolved with the AXA Insurance. If I had tried to sell it at below the court mandated price, I would likely have been arrested and jailed.

But if you're a member of family-law? No problem. You have sole conduct of sale and who cares about the court ordered trigger price.

Here is the letter I sent to the Conveyancing solicitors, to one 'Harriet' who I have never met, and is probably the first person to receive a letter of this length in reply to her request that I sign the title deed to my property for the sale. I did pause before sending it to this poor unwitting recipient who may well have had no forewarning of the conditions attached to this sale. Who was simply expecting to see a signed page returned to complet ethe sale and pocket her commission. Unaware that this property that was valued at £710,000 in 2016 by the courts own appointed surveyor. With a fire-sale trigger price of £540,000 put in by Flaherty to be sure of selling it, come what may.I admit I was annoyed to think they simply go ahead and sell my property, the one I have owned since 1986, withought even consulting with me. At a price that is in breach of what was agreed in court as well as what was used to calculate the costs award. Base don this new give away price, the entire valuation of the costs award changes. To the point that his 50% becomes a negative and in fact he would owe me money on the loss the cumulative award of both properties represents. Flaherty has fucked up royally. Apart from the money, the harm her gross negligence has caused my son is, in my view, criminal. Her fellow family-law conspirators have really raised the bar for what is acceptable in Britains family court. Sir Andrew McFarlane can't do anything about it. There is nothing to see here. Except my letter to Harriet, which I wrote in one hour, sent, and then put the whole mess out of my mind, as is the only way forward for wellness, pausing only to wonder whether Harriet might feel even the slightest bit guilty for her part in the child abuse this process represents, even though her roe is peripheral. A peripherally involved child abuser.

12 August, 2019.

Dear Harriet,

Thank you for your letter, which I have received since you used the correct e mail address, detailing your proposed sale of my property 28B Riverbank. I am grateful for this news.

As you may recall when I agreed your firm as conveyancers for my two proprties, 28B Thameside is subject to a forced sale by a court order which I say is a fraud. I am concerned that you appear not to know the specifics by which I agreed to the choice of your firm for the sale of the two court awarded properties. I was very clear at the time and that is in writing. So imagine my surprise to hear you have proceeded with the sale of my property below the court ordered minimum price. In breach of the curt order by switch Judge Flaherty.

The words in the judgment relating to this forced sale, in which I am excluded from any conduct of the sale, are copied here:

The properties shall be soldat the best price reasonably obtainable on the open market and as is agreed between the parties SAVE that it isdirected that the applicant shall be entitled to accept any offer and consequently that a sale may proceed for 28A Thameside at £705,000 or abovefor 28b Thameside at £540,000 or above.

Once there is an offer at £540,000 or above, I will be obliged to proceed as per the courts order. Untll then, it would breach the Order by (the fun-loving, champagne guzzling) family-court deputy-district switch judge Cecilia Flaherty who made this order, being in full awareness that her judgment was based on disputed valuation numbers.

My property flooded. (in 2014). Repair estimates following the Insurers own surveyor's statement were in excess of £500,000. (The AXA Insurance. In writing by the surveyor they sent post flood.) The fraudulent trustee freeholder (Nico Krasnopovich, also the winner in my family court application to see my son on weekends which resulted in me not seeing my son, until I paid her a ransom demand) ensured the Insurance did not repair my property after the particularly heavy flood. When the Thames burst its banks in February 2014. This was intended specifically to cause maximum financial hardship for me while she prosecuted her wholly unsubstantiated, dishonest 'Beneficial entitlement' claim that I had 'promised her' half of my wealth. In the course of which she ran me up a legal bill in excess of half a million pounds.

The un-repaired property remains a significant flood risk. There is an outstanding Insurance liability This is particularly relevant to the honest disclosure necessary for the sale of my properties.

28B is tied to 28A Riverbank, in a ceiling and floor relationship, both form a part of the award to family law member Nico Krasnopovich by family law member, switch-judge for the day, Cecilia O'Leary. All costs in repairing the damage to 28A become shared by

28B. As is common in freehold leasehold arrangements.

In other words, any buyer of 28B must be aware that their share of freehold and obligations under the freehold make them liable for the costs of 28A Riverbank. I would expect that as a conveyancer you know this and have made them aware. In the wider context of the forced sale, 28A Thameside needs to achieve a sales trigger price of £705,000 in accordance with Flaherty's judgment. I say, this is as unlikely now as it was when I disclosed the realistic condition and valuation of my properties to Flaherty in 2015. 28A already owes the mortgage company £500K and myself £300K. And the blown tanking will cost more than £500,000 to restore it to its pre-incident condition as it was insured for, and as I had paid the AXA premiums for 27 years to provide policy cover for.

I suggest you verify my disclosure by calling the AXA Insurance and check the validity of my claim, and particularly, the Insurance fraud by family-law member Nico Krasnopovich, who was investigated for fraud in the course of these proceedings.

You may also check that I had a valid policy cover (with the AXA) paid for and in place that would have covered the flood, in my name, had Krasnopovich not phoned and dishonestly forced the broker to cancel it. Had she not caused my policy to be cancelled, I would have had policy cover in my name, and the property would have been restored to its pre-incident condition. This is conduct unbecoming of a member of family law. In fact it is simply criminal. Your client is for this reason liable for cancelling the policy in my name, and ensuring, quite deliberately, that the property was not restored to its pre-incident condition. At the same time she was bound by a fiduciary responsibility to act in my best interests, whilst trustee freeholder of my property.

The difference between the sale price of 28A Thameside and the amounts it owes (£800,00+) must come from the sale of 28B Riverbank, which is mortgage free. I bought it in 1986. When Krasnopovich was 14. It is that property which has the highest value. The Trustee Freeholder (Nico Krasnopovich) defrauded the Lessee (myself) by cancelling my policy, and then, following an investigation by the AXA for fraud, coming to an agreement with them to not claim for the restoration of the property as per policy. The property was not restored to its pre-incident condition. It was left uninhabitable post flood, while I received not one penny from Insurers and while Krasnopovich continued serial failures in the fiduciary responsibilities attached to being the freeholder. Which includes bringing proceedings against me in the first place for this so called 'beneficial entitlement' which reads like an amateur B movie reject plot with more holes than a Gorgonzola. Even our mutual friend, Suki Johal, a DDJ and family law Barrister, weighed in to confirm Adler's claim that Suki was the only person who ever heard mention of this nefarious claim to an invented promise, was untrue. Flaherty knew that a DDJ and family law barrister had not supported Adler's lie and still she persisted with this bogus case.

The non-payment of insurance following the flood meant I had to pay many hundreds of thousands to make the property habitable and presentable for sale, albeit without repaired tanking. All of which is a matter of record and accounting procedure that is available for any litigation that may follow. Over £300,000 shortfall in insurance, that as per the freehold wording, is to be made up 'out of the freeholders' own resources.'

That money outlaid to make 28A saleable, along with the mortgage payments, (another £100,000) must be repaid to me before any further disbursements. The simple math's at the price you propose selling for will not work. The judgment values the trigger price for sale based on the judge's certainty of property valuations. It was also the valuation used in the costs-award that followed a costs hearing using these exact figures we now know are as incorrect as I said they were at the time of the hearing.

For the judgment to be credible in any way, 28A must sell at no less than **£705K** and 28B at no less than **£540K.** Any shortfall must be attached to liability. As Flaherty made this judgment who else could be more liable? Cecilia did have the correct information available to her, but chose instead to go with the request of her family law colleague, Nico Krasnopovich, who is known as a liar even within her profession, where she was at one time (2012) expelled as an equity partner from her then firm TWM for dishonesty. Not that easy to do. Getting expelled by your partners for dishonesty. Clear your desk right now and get escorted off the property never to be spoken to again.

The valuation numbers for 28A and 28B that Flaherty used in awarding costs against me in that hearing, in favor of her family-law colleague, Nico Krasnopovich, the fraudulent freeholder and lying claimant, were transparently wrong. There is a clear paper trail of the deceits used in the award of costs where even her barrister friend, Simon Webster has plainly and deliberately made an untrue claim in his cost's application in writing, not-with-standing that the claim itself is based on valuation amounts that events have proven wrong, precisely as I made clear would be the case.

Roland Court, of PHB LLP, who represented me in the property aspect of this claim in family court is familiar with the facts I am repeating here. Although we have not spoken for some time following his inability to proceed in my matter without advance payment, I am copying Mathew in this correspondence, as well as the SRA, in the event that the names in this letter ring any bells there. I am available to disclose any of 17 serious breaches that occurred in the matter of Krasnopovich vs Leandros, heard by switch judge Cecilia O Leary in April 2015, leading to the judgment that the President of family-law declared was flawed. At no charge. Just in the hope that they will not be able to continue ruining children's lives and getting paid for doing it.

Unfortunately, after losing £500,000 in legal costs to family-law in the hope of seeing my son again, I cannot afford litigation to progress accountability of the miscreants in this corrupt court hearing by a family-court judge who knowingly and deliberately ended my relationship with the child I raised for four years.

My son Sam, whom I love dearly, miss daily, and have not seen or spoken to since 2016, February 16th, because of this disgraceful 'judge' who went on to allow Krasnopovich to get away with a 9-month period in 2016 during which time, as one of many examples of ethical breach by a member of family-law, despite repeated requests, I was not even provided with my sons address for correspondence, as their own family-law requires.

Imagine if you will how cruel and inhumane this is for a 7-year-old boy to suddenly stop seeing the weekly letters from his father assuring him of ongoing love and hope for a future together, left only with the consolation that in some future therapy he will be a poster boy for Dr. Ira Turkats 'Malicious Mother syndrome' and not just another statistic of British family courts parental alienation and child abuse by several of its own members. A family court service where CAFCASS CEO Anthony Douglas reports is batting at 100% in judgments leading to parental alienation and child abuse whenever children cases are disputed in family court. Who would have guessed a member of family law would have been unaware of this when she elected blackmail litigation with her son's future as the carrot.

This is a special breed of deviant family-law friends, who are never found accountable for anything despite a career lifetime of lying professionally. Krasnopovich can even win sole conduct of sale on a property she has no financial interest in at all, beyond having been invited to stay rent free as a guest, happy to borrow many thousands in unpaid loans, and then, after having lied again to win sole conduct of sale, fail to sell for 3 years, (Picking up the 8% interest on costs awarded to her by O'Leary) causing me to keep paying the £500,000 mortgage on 28A, before selling it well below the already ridiculously low price set by the court. Without even notifying me.

Secure knowing the financial harm they have visited on me – above three million pounds and rising – means I cannot afford legal representation to even secure proper accounting in the proceeds of sale. I can't even afford to remain in my home country after having my home force sold and receiving not one penny from this process.

The outcome of this judgment by Cecilia Flaherty has been:

1) I get nothing (£O) for my £2.5 million valued home. After 30 years of hard work. Because someone lied saying I promised it to them in some unspecified place and some unclear time without one single email or witness to confirm one single shred of supporting evidence to a claim that followed a blackmail demand. And despite writing a will in which she declares all her assets with no mention of any interest in my properties, all in my sole name.

2.) I get nothing for loss of my income generating business, averaging £6k pm until the flood. No income and no home to live in. No compensation for the loss of earning this fraudulent claim has caused.

3.) I get nothing for the £300,000+ I spent on making my property habitable. Because I cannot afford to pay a lawyer to go to court, or bring proceedings against the miscreants for any number of offenses that would, in any fair and equitable judiciary, lead to prison time.

4.) I lose my credit because the mortgage is not properly discharged, as it would be by the proceeds of 28B. Meaning, even if I could raise the deposit for a new home, I cannot get a mortgage.

5.) 	I have not seen or spoken to my son since Feb 16th, 2016. Every effort to arrange unfettered visitation is obstructed. Even his godfathers recent attempt to see him, flying to London for this purpose, was obstructed.

6.) The AXA insurance claim owes some £800,000 on the flood claim arising from Krasnopovich cancelling the policy in my name. And then deliberately fouling the claim leaving the property, 28A Riverbank, unsaleable in over 3 years of trying. While I remain liable for all the costs. Having only recently ended mortgage payments when those costs post judgment reached another £100,000 of money I was required to pay by court order while sole conduct of sale was awarded to Adler, who was incentivized not to sell by a very generous 8% interest on the costs Cecilia awarded her in court.

7.) I am afraid to even enter the UK after the historical aggression by Krasnopovich and

Clock which includes hiring a goon to attack me outside my home. In the guise of being a process server. Effecting service on me personally, and causing physical harm, instead of delivering the summons to my family law solicitor, as any member of family law not looking to create maximal animosity would know is the appropriate procedure.

8.) Selling 28B as you propose, without accounting for the proceeds of sale or linking it to 28A, means Clock/Krasnopovich and Flaherty have succeeded fully in ensuring I get not one penny to pursue legal redress. Not one penny to contest visitation with my son. And I lose my credit when 28A goes into foreclosure. And with that, my son's prospects of ever seeing me again take one more step backwards.

I assure you that the Flaherty order that was signed reads; *28B Thameside at £540,000 or above. The properties shall be marketed for sale by no later than 15 October 2015.*

Until that sum is achieved I consider it a breach of a court order should you continue with this sale. While it is true that O'Leary, Krasnopovich and Clock have breached their own court order multiple times in these proceedings without any redress, on this occasion I will insist we all respect the letter of Flaherty's judgment. (Even though The President of family-law, who reviewed her judgment took about three minutes to declare it flawed and award what is called 'Permission to Appeal'.) Funny that the President of family law found Flaherty's judgment flawed and even then, no accountability has followed. It is almost like family-law operates on its own set of exemptions from law.

If you presented a story like this to HBO for a TV drama series, they would likely say it was far too implausible for any audience to believe any judiciary could get away with this conduct. Flaherty was dealing in alternate truth long before Trump. Just not as intelligently. The very act of agreeing a sale price outside of the trigger price in the court order without the courtesy of notifying me, the owner since 1986 of a property Krasnopovich is not named on in any way, until Flaherty declared she was in fact the owner, is itself a breach of an existing court order by members of family law.

Please consider this my notice that I do not agree to vary the Order of Cecilia Flaherty valuing the trigger for **28B Thameside at £540,000. Or 28A for £705,000**.

28B Thameside is a property I have owned since 1986, with no mortgage. Which was valued at £750,000 when I could have sold it but for being denied any involvement in the sale after Flaherty awarded '**sole conduct of sale**' to the lying lawyer Nico Krasnopovich, contender for parent-of-the-decade following his six-year ongoing abuse of our son.

The sale price you are considering for my property is little more than 50% of what I could have sold for, but for Flaherty preventing my selling my own property, as well as below the amount that I am owed in the total award of the two properties in the Flaherty judgment. The value of the judgment is in the figures that were agreed and form the direction from which there can be no variation without the admission that they were wrong in the first instance, as I made plain was the case.

None the less, disregarding my own credible disclosure as the owner of the properties for 27 years, in her court, Flaherty made a very specific award of two properties to family law member and litigant, Nico Krasnopovich. The property sale award for Krasnopovich by switch judge Flaherty is for two apartments; 28A and 28B. But, visibly flood damaged 28A is likely to show a loss on the sale. It may be that Flaherty's trigger valuation of

£705,000 is not achieved. It is possible that in fact, Flaherty was as wrong in her numbers as I pointed out during the hearing. In which case, someone has made a mistake that will cause a loss of many, many hundreds of thousands of pounds. A loss running into seven figures. Money that will never be available for my son's future. It is now, as I said then, an error. Who is accountable? I wonder if there is anyone at the SRA who can answer this question?

The fact that team Krasnopovich lied repeatedly, and were validated by Flaherty writing a series of lies in her so called 'judgment', a typo strewn masterpiece of prejudice and profiling delivered by email 3 months late, declaring she now had time because she was 'on holiday' and 'what else are holidays for.' Michele's folly is self-evident to anyone reading the conduct of these individuals during that hearing. The President of family law read Flaherty's judgment and arrived at the same conclusion. These are not small mistakes at odds with the prevailing truth. This is a clear a fix as you would expect to see in a mafia corruption movie.

That shortfall in the total judgment award is tied to the sale of 28B. After 3 years with no sale, I was unable to continue paying the mortgage, losing a further £100,000 I paid to keep my properties available for sale following Flaherty's fully thought-through judgment left her colleague Krasnopovich with sole conduct of sale. That mortgage amount must be repaid to me in accordance with Flaherty's judgment. Has the sole conduct of sale lawyer, Adler, informed you of this? Or indeed any of the facts pertaining to the responsible sales accounting for the proceeds of 28B Riverbank?

The overall shortfall on the sale of both 28A and 28B must be calculated on the totality of both. For the avoidance of doubt, there is no possibility that 28B can be sold at a give-away price with my consent.

Cecelia Flaherty
@Flatulent666fla

Lawyer; juvenile delinquent; lover of
champagne and fun

Joined September 2016

Tweet to Cecelia Flaherty

By all means call the judge who made this judgment to confirm if you have any doubts. I have attached a picture with her address and public profile for you. It is always interesting to see how people who rule on children's lives present themselves. If you do call her, I propose you congratulate Cecilia on the excellent job she does representing children's lives as a deputy district switch-judge. In my case, a 100% win for members of family law that conformed to all of the SRA guidelines for members of family law apart from the 17 instances that didn't, but be sure not to mention that. Judges should always be allowed some wiggle room when it comes to lying. That is the clear inference for the letter I received from the ministry of justice when it comes to accountability in family court.

I no longer even live in the UK, after Judge Flaherty declared me '*mentally-infirm*' 13 times in a 12-page judgment, made me homeless, took 100% of my income generating business, awarded a ludicrous sum of costs against me based on demonstrably untrue declarations by Krasnopovich and her family-law capo, Tim Clock, ensuring that my son never saw me again.

Sam is the same son I raised as a stay-at-home mom, there for him 100% of the time through his first four years, enabling as close to an ideal upbringing as can be imagined, while his Father worked in family-court charging £500 an hour to separating parents, trained by a system that places monetary gain above children's right to see both parents, building a resentment that her son was so close to his father, while he was out destroying families for money which led to a dark, dishonest, child abusing decision, placing conscienceless greed above all, and especially, respect for the ethical code published on the SRA website.

Cecilia too remains a credit to British family-law and deserves full recognition for her service to children fortunate enough to have their futures determined in her court.

Family law. Nice people to do business with if you're a young child just wanting his mother. North of three million is a real win for these members of family-law. Especially from a musician. Imagine how many 18-hour studio days I had to perform to have a net worth of this amount. Disappeared in the blink of a lie.

It is not necessary to reply to this email, other than to confirm receipt. I confirm you do now have the correct email for contacting me.

With kind regards,

Andrea

cc. Roland Court
cc. Chris Axiotis
cc. Solicitors Regulation Authority (Contact center.)

42 Epilogue
But where is the end, really?

Six years after I began the draft of the 'fathers-day mafia hit' which became 'Who lies wins' I approached the end of this weighty project mindful that every story needs a happy ending and in my efforts to find any light hearted upside to the experience of losing my home, my home country, my business and my son, I was reminded that just as helping and harming may become the same thing, even the darkest of days can have a sunny ending.

My quest for that sunny ending took me back to the start of the book. I read this paragraph in the first chapter.

"I made it to the age of 45 before I learned just how wretched the consequences of helping the wrong person can be. And at that point I had a four-year-old child at the center of my world, the focus of all that I had learned. In terms of the want factor any negotiator identifies in winning an adversarial negotiation, I had one great weakness. I loved my child enormously and would do anything to provide for his best interests. Exactly as you would expect from a loving parent who chose to have a child later in life, twenty years after the first, and raise the child as a stay home parent."

Sam was the center of my world. And those four years we spent together were the most complete experience of joy and expression of meaning in my life. Although what happened next is awful, we did have those four years together. The neural pathways formed in those first four years happened. At least Sam had four years of the opportunity his parents agreed before his conception. That is a beautiful thing and may be sufficient as a platform for his development as a young man, able to find his way to me. In the six years since fathers-day, I have read a great deal and met with many professionals in the subject of separation, parental alienation, deficient family court members, child psychology, PTSD and child abuse. I was reminded all too frequently that the greatest power of legalese is obfuscation, the ability to weave words in such a way that they serve any purpose other than addressing and recalling the simple truth. It is a considerable skill. The deceitful lawyer, unbound by an ethical code, skilled in the dark arts of obfuscation. A skill of ever-increasing value in the current age of false news. And in this regard, much as Trump has demonstrated, a lie told often enough make the truth irrelevant. Yet, the facts in the disputed family-court judgment between Sam's parents stands in the light of one obvious truth, I found in a 2018 published book on parental alienation and child abuse.
"attributing a parent-child problem to both parents, when one parent is clearly more responsible for destructive behavior, is a misguided effort to appear balanced and avoid blame."

Disclosing the sinister purpose in conflating the best interests of a child with the right to secrecy for the offending parent is where the happy ending to this book arrives. The fact is, as I reflect on the conclusion of a literary project and coping mechanism that arrives 6 years to the day after fathers-day 2013, I have recorded the events truthfully and chosen appropriately from the immense volumes of legal correspondence reflecting the £500,000+ of legal charges to family court that I have faced to date. And why have I spent so much time on this project when walking away was the commercial view, literally from the outset? Foremost in my motivation was and remains, my son. Born into a family unit where his arrival was planned and agreed to an unusually well considered detail. I made a deal to have a child and I have not discarded my responsibilities within that arrangement. Whatever happens in the future, this book recalls who did what and why. Means motive and opportunity. The consequences for actions are as evident as the lack of consequences for actions. When I began the book I believed, much as Winston Churchill has described so eloquently, that the power of the written word is timeless and more powerful than any vehicle for change. In the interim, I have come to believe that corruption in institutions empowered by legal process is so complete, no truth stands taller than 'History is written by the victors.' Sam has only the versions of two-family law members to wear down his memory of our love as parent and child. Our communication ended on 16 February 2016. It is my belief that he will receive this book gratefully, and with some relief, knowing through these words on pages exactly how events unfolded since fathers-day when he was four. And tried so hard to find me and stay with me.

I am further mindful that some 10,000 children every year in the UK are victims of disputed judgments in family-court, subject to parental alienation and child abuse. I imagine seeing this story and having the process recorded in black and white will come as some relief to those children, whose circumstances may be quite similar to Sam's. Their experience of family-law as a business model resisting obvious child-centric reforms simply for the financial benefit of its entitled membership. My account of the six years efforts fighting for my sons' rights in the face of bitter malice including physical attack exists for Sam to read; and see the extent to which one parent is clearly responsible for destructive behavior, aided and abetted by fellow members of family-law in a system that cannot continue to operate in the shadows. 'Legal obfuscation and false news' is in reality, only five words. You can't fool children with five words. The heart knows what the heart wants. Intuition is the wisest instruction. I did not disappear because of anything Sam did or any absence of love for my son. I was disappeared by British family-court, empowered by inadequate Government policy, played by dishonest members. But although I am gone from Sam's life, and no longer living in my home which is now no longer my home, the story lives on, in words. And it may be that on some level, eventually, the benefits for the slime layer of family-law membership occupied by the miscreants in Sam's story will be placed below the rights of children to have both parents in their lives without unbalanced constraints. Family law must change. That will be the happy ending. No child should be used as leverage for financial benefit by one parent playing that exposed and ridiculous members club called family-law. No parent should kill themselves because they are hounded as criminals for the inability to pay a court determined child support amount. No parent should execute their ex-spouse and their own children because the court visitation arguments have driven them insane. The list of crimes I have read about in this category, related to family court judgments, is in my view, no less than a crisis.

Millions of lives are affected. This is a matter for national concern in every government in the world.

Unfortunately, as the reply to my letter to the president of Britain's family law shows, the present Government remains unwilling to embrace reform. Below is my reply from the ministry of justice to a 2019 Ministerial petition which requested a commons debate criminalizing Parental alienation. A reply sent, despite the current president of family-law acknowledging parental alienation should be considered on a par with spousal abuse, confirming that the very thing we know is the weakest link in the family court system, that is underqualified deputy district judges empowered to express poorly informed opinions as fact in a court system where 100% of disputed cases include 'parental alienation and child abuse', is the Governments current position.

'Don't worry' is their message, 'we know what's going on and CAFCASS are taking care of it. **Our process is gender neutral.**'

That is the position of the Ministry of Justice in 2019. And here is their gender-neutral reply to the 15,000 signatories to the petition calling for Parental alienation to be made a criminal offense.

FROM: MINISTRY OF JUSTICE.
29 May, 2019.

Ms Lee,

We do not believe that it is necessary to introduce a criminal offence against parents who alienate their child against the other parent as the court can take effective action against such behavior.

The Government is aware of the difficulties that parents can face in continuing a relationship with their child following parental separation or divorce, sometimes because of the obstructive behaviour of the other parent. We recognise that such behaviour causes great harm to children, particularly in situations where children are already distressed by the break-up of their family.

"Parental alienation" describes a situation where a child's resistance or hostility towards one parent is not justified and is the result of psychological manipulation by one of their parents in order to undermine or interfere with the relationship with the other parent.

The Government is confident that the family justice system can robustly address such behaviour when it is alleged in child arrangements cases and we are continuing to strengthen our work in this area.

The legal framework which governs family law cases is gender neutral. There is a statutory presumption that the involvement of either parent in the child's life will further the child's welfare, unless the contrary can be shown. In reaching decisions in cases about the child's upbringing, the court must consider the child's ascertainable wishes and feelings and how capable each of the parents are of meeting the child's needs.

In making decisions about child arrangements, the family court may seek social work analysis and recommendations from the Children and Family Court Advisory and Support Service (Cafcass). CAFCASS practitioners are aware of the potential for children to be influenced by parental views and are alive to this issue when it is raised in child arrangements cases. Any concerns of alienating behaviours by a parent will be reported to the court when assessing the children's best interests, which includes assessing the level of parental influence on a child's wishes and feelings. The focus is on the safety and welfare of the children in each case.

CAFCASS is continuing to develop its work in addressing parental alienation when it arises in child arrangements cases. CAFCASS launched the Child Impact Assessment Framework (CIAF) last year. The framework includes various tools and guidance that further support its practitioners in identifying how individual children are experiencing parental separation and helps assess the impact of different factors on a child, including alienating behaviour by a parent. Further information is available on the CAFCASS website at www.Cafcass.Gov.UK.

Exceptionally, in cases of persistent parental alienation over time, the family court may decide that the child's longer-term welfare is best served by a transfer of the child's residence from one parent to the other. The alienating parent's involvement can then be facilitated by the other parent. Such decisions are, however, profound for the child and are never taken lightly.

Ministry of Justice.

My hopes for reform do not lie in 'change from within'. Current Family law President Sir Andrew McFarlane appears to simply repeat the same bewigged nonsense of his multiply titled predecessors, with titles vacillating as appropriate between political class correctness and ensuring nothing threatens the ongoing rights of the membership to continue enjoying the richly rewarding career for life their position entitles them to. Their remunerative interests must remain above the children's rights, or their entitled system cannot survive.

If there is to be a change it will come from you. Imagine a poster of a pre-drowning Lord Kitchener pointing right here with the caption **"Your children need you."** We, the people, the electorate, the parents, informed and aware that this needs to become an important consideration for any party wishing to win an election. A new child-centric model in which disputed cases involving children are not heard in the same judiciary applying the same legal model designed to process murderers, thieves and rapists. Instead we need skilled decision makers empowered to represent children's rights to be with both parents as close to fifty-fifty percent of the time as practicable. We need to set an example for the world to follow in how children are represented when parents separate. The specifics in this model for family-law do not represent an enormous challenge. The starting point is easy. Place children's best interests above the rewards for members of family-court, operating their mafia-like cartel in the dispensation of child protection services.

Closing I am reminded of Churchill. Perhaps because the past 6 years have felt much like a Blitzkrieg and just as Churchill had words as his most powerful weapon, I imagine how he would have presented this story in the place that matters; the House of Parliament. Where laws are made. Where many great orators presented news of wrongs that need to be righted; like Emily Hobhouse protesting Britain's concentration camp genocidal killing of Boer woman and children in 1902 remarked, as I paraphrase; *"The worst sound I have heard is the silence arising from this house."* In the hearts and minds of those members of that house is where the problem starts and ends. The law indemnifying members of family law from child abuse must be debated and replaced with legislation that supports children's best interests. As determined by the finest minds we have interpreting this matter.

My paraphrase of Churchills remarks to the house.

"There is nothing new in this story. Britain's failure to reform family law is as old as King James' unmentionable love even as he rewrote the Bible for its condemnation. It falls into that long dismal catalogue of the fruitlessness of experience and the confirmed unteachability of a governing elite. Even in the face of overwhelming notice from the most impeccable sources and the most detailed statistics. Black and white bundles of facts from participants living their own truth. Want of foresight, unwillingness to act when action would be simple and effective, lack of clear thinking, confusion of counsel until it is too late, inappropriately skilled amateurs occupying positions of influence, like deputy district judges, ruling absent of any checks or boundaries until, finally, self-preservation strikes its jarring gong. These are the features which constitute the endless repetition of our British parliamentary history."

And if no reform follows from this current Government, here is a quote about British family-law that will be trending round about twenty years from now. When another million children's lives will lie ruined.

"This is a shameful past, in which a prevailing culture of secrecy, reward and self-protection for an entitled elite led to unnecessary suffering for many victims and their families."

The End

End credit music

I know that my experience of family-law is not unique or exceptional. Millions of parents around the world miss their children, because of family-law. The system is what it is. No one is immune. But none the less, I was struck by the numbers affected, and the many forums that exist representing the iniquitous failures arising from family-law legislation, none more so than this song I heard being performed in a famous venue in Los Angeles. *By permission from the author I include the lyric here.*

Family Law by Hugo Fernandes

Four years old on fathers-day, when my mum took me away.
Another love called her to play. Told my dad she couldn't stay.
Daddy was a music man. He found it hard to understand.
The honesty of her demands, ending a lifetime worth of plans.

She moved me to a new address, she called the break up a success,
she spoke about her happiness. She lied and never would confess.
Daddy bet on family law. To win back his child of four.
Our love and bond as father son was what we lost and what she won.
Family Law who is it good for. Family law

This judge saw what she chose to see. Never thought what's best for me.
Ruled it prejudicially. Abused me with dishonesty.
Avarice was the lawyers name. He played the law like it's a game.
My life will never be the same. That's family-law I hold to blame.

Mummy is a lawyer too. She lied to win and saw it through.
Married now to someone new. He calls me son but that's not true.
I think about him every day; feelings just don't go away.
The music and the laughter too I miss my dad, you know I do.
Family Law who is it good for family law

With time I understand, one day I'll be a grown man.
One who looks back with regret. Missing the dad he can't forget.
I know the court faces a choice, the money or the children's voice.
Us children left to court abuse. The ones the judge decides will lose.

I'll thank my mum one day she says. Maybe in my night-mares.
What I think about each day. Is why my daddy went away.
I miss him so you know I do I miss the time we spent as two.
We loved each other from the heart 'Till family-law tore us apart.
Family Law who is it good for. Family law

I miss my daddy yes I do.
I know he misses me too

GLOSSARY

Adam Surman MD   My NHS GP for 15 years. The first doctor I saw following the trauma of fathers-day. Who wrote to the court for the April 2015 hearing. Discarded by switch Judge Flaherty.

Allan Galton   My dear friend and pub-companion for 20 years. Who advised on matters post separation, including a reference to a private investigator, because as he told me *"No one breaks up happy home unless….."*

Andrea Leandros   Me. Author. Mother. Defendant in claim for beneficial entitlement. Parent who has not seen her son since February 2016 despite legal bill of £500,000+ attracting ongoing interest at 8% for costs award by DDJ Flaherty at April 2015 hearing.

Andrew le Clerc   Appeal Court judge who did not allow the appeal to Flaherty's judgment proposed by the President of Family law in his 'Permission to Appeal'. Because 'Ms. Lee was late on her filing when David Clam was her solicitor.'

Bob Marley   Most famous Jamaican musician. Whose remains lie in his birth village of 9 Mile.

CAFCASS   The government funded agency responsible for representing children rights. Whose own CEO says *"100% of disputed cases heard in family court feature parental alienation and child abuse"*. CAFCASS is widely reported as widely incompetent in the personal experience of many, many parents, despite improvements under most recent CEO.

Carol Adrian   Family law solicitor. Married Krasnopovich. Left cigarettes in Sam's backpack during one of his visits with me. Heard on Skype chats grooming Sam off screen with replies leading to end of skype chats for Sam.

Cecelia Flaherty   *"Lawyer; juvenile delinquent; lover of champagne and fun."* In her own words. In reality, the barrister and deputy district court judge, who appointed herself as switch judge in the April 2015 hearing, who ruled an end to Sam's relationship with one parent, awarding 100% of all assets of one parent to the other. Generating child harming animosity between the separating parents in a judgment that was made un appealable.

Christies   Auctioneers of the Onassis jewelry from where I purchased a £16,000 diamond ring as a gift for Krasnopovich.

Chris Andiotis   South African Greek businessman, godfather of Sam. Was a witness set down for April 2015 hearing, ready to fly on the Monday night to attend Tuesday's witness day. Was a frequent visitor to my home throughout the ten years Krasnopovich lived there. Was the negotiator for his godsons' rights before litigation. Knew the specifics of the £100,000 for visitation demand. And the origins of the claim "*I want £10,000 for every year.*" Had a first-hand account and supporting emails of Krasnopovichs assurances relating to the deceit. Had to be stopped for Krasnopovichs case to succeed. Was stopped by the switch judge. Even his statement was excluded.

Christa Small   Family law solicitor. Former head of family law at MWT and first employer of Krasnopovich when he began in family-law. The dinosaur of family-law in his words.

Cliff Murray   Property developer in Thameside area and good friend, who taught me a great deal about property development and was the builder for the refurbishment works to my property in 2005. And aware of where 100% of the payment and direction for the works came from.

David Clam   Family law solicitor. Billed £189,000 for his firm Spoon LLP for losing the application for visitation (2 nights pm) and for losing Beneficial entitlement hearing through multiple errors and gross malpractice. Received payment of £160,000 which he refused to refund when his errors and the consequences were spelled out, choosing instead to blackmail me to not refer his conduct to the Ombudsman office by withholding release of my files to the new law firm appointed for the permission to appeal. Responsible for leaving my name on a court contempt fine for his late filing.

David Essex   Singer and writer of 'Rock On', discovered and managed by my tenant in 28A Thameside. Regular visitor to my former home.

Derek Bowfield   Owner of the lease for 28A Thameside since 1985. Former manager of David Essex. For five years I was the 'first responder' by arrangement with the council as his health failed. (Because he lived alone and had no close family.) I was able to check on him almost every day for the last 18 months, usually taking food.

Dia Mirza   A family-law barrister and Deputy District judge and for 9 years a close friend of mine and regular dinner guest. Who confirmed that Krasnopovich's claim for 'multiple witnesses' to his "entitlement" claim could not be substantiated.

Delia Silver   Close friend of both Krasnopovich and myself. Was intermediary for visitation after Jo. For ten weeks attempted to arrange weekend visitation for Sam. Witnessing the toxic correspondence from Krasnopovich and his lawyer, Tim Clock that resulted in not one single weekend agreed despite every reasonable effort being made to enable Sam's visitation with me.

DDJ Beddy   Judge in the 2013 Visitation hearing who denied my application for 2 nights a month with Sam. Ending the possibility for regular visitation in that early, crucial, period post separation. A judge too lazy to do his job. Allowing a CAFCASS officer to decide.

DDJ Berry Judge in the Preliminary Financial Directions hearing. Who fined me £2,600 for contempt in a late filing by David Clam. Who was responsible for the late filing, paid the fine, but allowed my name to appear on the court judgment for this offense. Leading to issues in both the April 2015 hearing as well as the Appeal. The judge who set down three days for the April 2015 hearing to allow for multiple witnesses on both sides.

DDJ Burkes Judge set down for April 2015 hearing. Recused without explanation despite my barrister Richard Castello, checking in advance that he had not worked for either law firm previously.

Dr. Henry Ling. My Primary care Physician in the USA. Who wrote on several occasions to the court. An actual, real doctor, whose credentials were disregarded for the Judges convenience, despite the availability of phone or web site to confirm. Still exists even to this day as an actual real, credible medical doctor. Despite the opinion of Judge Flaherty.

Eric Jarvis My live-in partner for 2 years who bought William the schnauzer and was, but for my hesitance in having a child and marriage, my likely partner for life. Whose departure modelled for me how intelligent mindful people who love each other can separate without burning down the house.

Evan Leandros My octogenarian widower Greek dad in Johannesburg. Born 1935 in Piraeus. Greece. Parent to three. Grandparent to my two boys.

Evan John Leandros My first son. Born 1989. Sam's half-brother.

Fairtime Insurance Brokers In October 2013, they provided Buildings and contents cover for me for my property, 28 Thameside. Three weeks after which Krasnopovich phoned them and had my policy cancelled. In breach of his fiduciary responsibility. Acting in bad faith. Causing me to receive no cover for flood damage. Making himself responsible for losses measured in the millions.

Gab Robbins Loss adjustors in my flood claim of 2008. Who paid to restore property to previous condition and all my rehousing costs. The same Loss adjustors in 2014, who failed to pay one penny for the identical claim, this time managed by Krasnopovich, who contradicted the AXA surveyors report of 'breached tanking' by saying '*Jeff the plumber dun it.*' Causing me losses measured in 7 figures.

Hugo Fernandes Californian musical artist and writer of the song 'Family law.'

John Milos Greek friend for 35 years who knew Krasnopovich well. A leading gemologist and auctioneer who provided a £16,000 ring for me to gift Krasnopovich. And attended many dinners in my Thameside home, being familiar with the balance in the relationship between the partners and the financial arrangements. Was a witness set down for the April 2015 hearing. Was on the calendar to give evidence on the Tuesday.

John B   Handyman at my property since 1987. Cancer survivor after my fundraiser in 2001 provided £10,00 for his successful treatment. Worked as a part of the building team during the refurbishment at 28A Thameside in 2005 and able to give a first-hand account at odds with Krasnopovichs claim regarding the refurbishment. John was a Witness in the April 2015 hearing. Was on the calendar to give evidence on the Tuesday.

Jo Parker   Sam's secular godmother. My neighbor for 27 years. And close friend who was the intermediary in attempting to arrange visitation with Sam during the first 6 months. Without success. Acted as drop off and collection for Sam on the subsequent 19 visits I made to the UK.

Ken Quinton   My Insurance broker since 1986. Firndowne Insurance. Witness to freehold details and fiduciary failures by Krasnopovich. And the Insurance matters relating to my home.

Leo Sayer   Friend, fabulous singer, writer and performer, who donated his time to enable the £10,000 fundraiser concert for John B's cancer treatment which led to a lifechanging recovery. John B still in remission at time of writing, after 18 years.

Larry Chester   My Independent Financial advisor since 1986 and also a key witness at the April 2015 hearing with specific documentation relating to the claim of beneficial entitlement and the fiduciary failures by Krasnopovich in relation to the freehold of my property. Krasnopovich knew his claim could not succeed if Larry had given evidence on the Tuesday when he was set by calendar to give evidence.

Lansbury Club   My local sports club for some 20 years. Where Sam went to pre-school. Where I once held the league tennis title. Where Krasnopovich called to tell the nursery manager not to allow Sam to leave with me.

Manfred Mann   Manny Liebowitz from Yeoville. South African Keyboard player who had many number one pop hits in the sixties and was very helpful to me as well as many other musicians arriving in London from South Africa.

Maria Andiotis   Wife of Chris, Sam's godfather. Sam's first crush on a beautiful woman. (When he was 3.) Died at 32 of cancer leaving a 2-year-old daughter. Maria was disappointed Krasnopovich prevented Sam visiting her as was arranged for his summer holidays in 2015 when he knew it was a final opportunity for her and Sam to say goodbye.

Malicious Mother syndrome   This syndrome was first theorized by the psychologist Ira Turkat to describe a pattern of abnormal behavior during separation where one parent seeks to punish the other parent, sometimes harming or depriving their children in order to make the other parent look bad.

Marie Curie Charity   For ten years I was the local fundraiser for this important charity, raising over £20,000 from the Thameside community.

Mark Zetin. MD   Psychiatrist in Orange County. Author of 'Overcoming Depression'. Lecturer at Chapman University and my doctor for three years. Completed the 'Capacity to Instruct' demand in the Flaherty 'Three Psychiatrists' sketch. One of my most informed advisors on child psychology and how best to advocate for Sam's interests.

Nico Krasnopovich   Successful member of family law. My money borrowing live-in boyfriend and trustee freeholder for ten years. 2003 to 2013. Who won my 'application for visitation', preventing any regular weekend visitation with my son in the crucial 6-month post separation period. Who brought a claim for beneficial entitlement against me, cost me upwards of £500,000 in legal fees and £3 million in losses. Who continues to obstruct unfettered visitation for his son and myself.

Nine Mile   Village in the mountains of Jamaica near Ocho Rios, where Bob Marley was born and raised until age ten. And where he is buried.

Paul Smith   My first husband. (m;1986 to d;1992). Father of my son Evan.

Petrus Smith   Paul's father. My disapproving former father-in law, a rampant South African Catholic who once threatened me with a loaded gun.

Patrick Ruert   Managing Partner at MWT in 2012 who chaired the expulsion meeting where Krasnopovich was summarily expelled as an equity partner in the Firm for 'dishonesty.'

Peter Knightly   My next-door neighbor for 27 years. Dedicated to her Majesty Queen Lisbet, whom he served with devotion for forty years. Peter asked me to be primary responder when he became mobility impaired in his 90's and elected to stay in his own home. My second period as primary responder for elderly. (On 24-hour call.) Shared with me his joy at the Queen sending her car for him to join her for tea at the palace. And his annual gifts from her. I travelled from the US to see him shortly before he passed. *"Take care"* he said. *"There's not many of us left."*

Philip Voula Parker   Former friend of Krasnopovich from California who persuaded him to agree the first post separation visitation with Sam. Who provided me with accommodation after my home flooded and became uninhabitable. Who shares a close loving relationship with Sam who asked Philip to be his parent during the efforts to have Sam schooled in California. A supremely kind person whom Sam recognized and misses.

President of Family law   Who sat as the judge in the "Permission to Appeal Hearing' in 2015 and found that DDJ Flaherty's judgment was flawed, awarding Permission to Appeal.

Richard Castello   Barrister in family-court representing and misrepresenting me at both the April 2015 hearing and the Appeal.

Richard Nastase   Manager of the Lansbury, Sam's nursery school and my tennis club. And the guest in my garden annex for 18 months after his house fire left him homeless. Who knew Sam well and called me when Krasnopovich called the Nursery to instruct them to not allow Sam to leave with me.

Roland Chambers   Partner in family-law department at FOS. Represented me for Permission to Appeal and Appeal.

Roland Spring   Partner in property law at FOS. Represented me in the property matter, the pursuit of the multi-million accountability claim, until I ran out of funds to pay.

Sam Leandros   Born 2009. My son, the child in a disputed hearing in family court brought by his father, Nico Krasnopovich, judged by DDJ Cecelia Flaherty. Sam has not seen me, his former stay home parent, since February 2016. Sam receives no assistance from family-law in being with me even though he has every opportunity to be nurtured and educated in California with the parent who raised him until fathers-day 2013 along with his choice of parental partner for me.

Serena Denning   Equity partner at MWT, made partner in same meeting as Krasnopovich. Who voted for his expulsion for dishonesty in 2012. Who assisted in providing me with the transcripts of the 'Will attendance notes' from my 2010 Will signing at MWT. Confirming my 'beneficial entitlement' intentions in 2010. Years after Krasnopovich claimed he had been gifted my estate in a promise. Written evidence presented in the April 2015 hearing.

Simon Patterson   The name on the process servers' card that was left by the individual hired by Krasnopovich and Clock to attack me in the street outside my home in October 2013. In the guise of serving their claim, which should in conventional procedure have gone to my solicitor. That I was injured and traumatized in a confrontation with an individual hired for this specific purpose by members of family law breaching their own ethical code without any censure remains one more offense they have gotten away with.

Section 12 of the Administration of Justice Act 1960.   Google it. The contempt law that enables any family-court judge to get away with whatever they choose.

Simon Hazelwood   Hare Court Barrister in Family law. Advertised for Krasnopovich's Family Law web firm on his website. Represented Krasnopovich in both the April 2015 hearing and the Appeal. Repeated claims he knew to be untrue in Court.

Suzy DuWee   Psychiatrist in California. The only Psychiatrist in California in 2015 according to DDJ Flaherty's 'Three Psychiatrist ruling'. I was told 3 psychiatrists would be named for me to choose one. (Although I already had a perfectly good one.) Instead, I was given this name and told unless I saw her I would be penalized for contempt. Based on the fact that Suzy DuWee is the only Psychiatrist in California able to sign a 'capacity to instruct' document.

Thameside 450-year-old historical village in Surrey, with good rail access to Waterloo and a community of interesting locals, including a healthy balance of creative liberals and right-wing racists. One of the more attractive Thameside villages. Where I enjoyed living for 29 years until family-court stole my home.

The AXA Insurance Insurer with whom I had policy cover for some 27 years. Who did not pay me one penny for the flood damage to my home in 2014. One consequence of which was foreclosure on my home that was then down valued at a forced sale price because of the failure to provide the Policy cover I had paid for and expected. To date I still have not been paid for the cover the AXA Policy for my home provided. Not one penny from an event that has caused me a loss exceeding £3 million.

Tim Clock Solicitor in family-law working in the City with a reputation for adversarial litigation. Represented Krasnopovich and won the visitation hearing preventing Sam having overnight visitation with his parent. The solicitor who represented another family solicitor in making up a patently untrue claim that cost the child involved his future with one parent.

William Black and silver schnauzer. Born 1998. Died 2013. Aged 15. Named after Braveheart – William Wallace. Was known as William of Thameside, a magnificent example of his breed. Loyal, inquisitive, courageous, perceptive and unconditionally loving. Obsessed by right and wrong and making wrong right. Was kidnapped and ransomed back in 2008 after a national press campaign. Raised my two sons in their early years. Loved and missed by many, none more than me.

ABOUT THE AUTHOR

Andrea Leandros was born in 1965 on the Greek island of Crete. She grew up in Johannesburg, South Africa. After completing high school at 16 she went on to study at Wits University, a liberal School in a repressive, autocratic time where she became politically aware, finding South Africa's cruel apartheid ways incompatible with her ethical ambitions.

Andrea emigrated to London in 1985, working initially as a performing musician, before becoming an accomplished composer, educator and music producer for thirty years. Andrea is a lifelong active advocate for animal protection, especially criminalizing and ending all so called 'Trophy Hunting' and a variety of Environmental education initiatives She is an active contributor in age-concern, supporting vulnerable older adults. And has been supporting cancer research since her first meaningful fundraiser in 2001. Andrea has married and divorced once. She has two sons, born 20 years apart. The older, Evan Leandros, born in 1989, is an academic. The younger, Sam Leandros, born in 2009 is the subject of her 2019 book *'Who Lies Wins.'*

Oh Andrea. That is so sad. What can I do to help Sam see you?

You can write two letters. One to the current President of British family law. Sir Andrew McFarlane. By post. The more letters he receives and the more publicity the book attracts, like Amazon reviews, the greater the likelihood that real action will follow. Sir Andrew is aware of the necessity for legislation to introduce child-centric change that will save lives. And the economic benefits to the Country from countless millions in lost productivity and psychological harm done to children by family-court that allows parental alienation, malicious mother syndrome and the child-abuse any combination of this special separating-parents-hatred opportunes for those ethically unworthy parents. The second letter is to your Member of Parliament. Copy your MP on the letter to Sir Andrew and request their confirmation.

Sir Andrew McFarlane
President of the Family Courts
Royal Courts of Justice Strand
WC2 A2LL

Dear Sir Andrew,

I have read Andrea Lee's book "Who Lies Wins". That is my reason for writing to you today.

The case for reform to family law legislation has never been more pressing. The lives of countless children depend on you doing something now. You are the master of the misery factory that is family-law and have yourself accepted the service you control is depressing. I am convinced the proposals in the book "Who Lies Wins" represent a positive way forward that should be reviewed, presented as a reform bill, and implemented as a matter of urgency.

While you investigate the legal points raised, which must inevitably lead to criminal charges, damages and disbarments, I would like to see an order of court that the child in this story, Sam Leandros, be able to enjoy unfettered access and visitation with his parent without further delay and without any interference by the Father. The solicitor member of family-law, who has proven to be a classic example of Dr. Ira Turkats so called 'Malicious Parent syndrome'.

Please confirm receipt of my request.

Yours sincerely,
(*Your name*)
CC: (*Your Member of Parliament*)

Who Lies Wins
by
Andrea Lee

Made in the USA
Middletown, DE
05 September 2019